An Introduction to the Foundations of Education

An Introduction to the Foundations of Education

Third Edition

Allan C. Ornstein
Loyoia University
of Chicago

Daniel U. Levine
University of Missouri,
Kansas City

Houghton Mifflin Company Boston
Dallas Geneva, Illinois Lawrenceville, New Jersey Palo Alto

Cover photograph by Gabrielle Keller. ©1984 Keller and Peete Associates.

Special thanks to Boston Latin, established in 1635, generally considered to be the oldest existing public school in the United States.

Part-opening photo credits: Part 1, p. xx, Victoria Arlak; Part 2, p. 70, Freelance Photographers Guild; Part 3, p. 214, Sandra Johnson/The Picture Cube; Part 4, p. 320, Elizabeth Hamlin/Stock, Boston; Part 5, p. 442, Bohdan Hrynewych/Southern Light.

Printed in the U.S.A.
Library of Congress Catalog Card Number: 84-82411
ISBN: 0-395-35804-3

BCDEFGHIJ-M-898765

Contents

Pioneers in Education 109

Historical Development of American Education 143

Philosophical Ideas in Education 184

Preface

Audience and Purpose

An Introduction to the Foundations of Education, Third Edition, is a broad-based overview of the foundations of education in the United States. It is meant to interest students who are preparing for a teaching career as well as those who are concerned about educational issues and policies in this country. The text is designed for use both in introductory courses in the foundations of education and in a variety of upper-level and graduate foundations courses. For beginning students in education, it provides a foundation on which to build their later professional curriculum and fosters students' interest in educational issues and the profession of teaching. This volume is appropriate also for upper-level students enrolled in foundations courses because of its systematic attention to providing up-to-date research references and documentation and its interdisciplinary perspectives on education. In addition, the text gives both education and noneducation majors a broad frame of reference for understanding the important problems and issues affecting the past, present, and future in the field of education.

The purpose of the book remains the same as in the previous two editions: to offer a comprehensive body of information on the various foundations of education and significant educational issues from a broad, interdisciplinary viewpoint. The scope of topics has been organized to give students ready access to important ideas and issues and influential thinkers and theories that have had or will have an impact on education. We have summarized and synthesized the important concepts and research findings in a practical way, provided balanced treatment of many controversial issues, and documented a multitude of research references without making the text overly complicated for students.

Coverage in the New Edition

The third edition consists of fifteen chapters divided into five parts. Content throughout the book has undergone major revision. Most notably, three new chapters on political, economic, and legal foundations of education have been added to provide more extensive and substantive coverage of these important foundational subjects. A fourth new chapter—on the nature of effective schools and school reform—examines one of the most critical issues in education today. In addition, the entire text has been thoroughly updated to give attention to the many changes that have taken place in education in the past decade and to reflect current issues and the recent national reports on education and their implications for teaching in American schools.

Part 1, "Understanding the Teaching Profession," considers the climate in which teachers work today and its impact on teaching as well as on the status of the profession. Topics previously covered in separate chapters have been streamlined and combined as part of the opening chapter on motivation, status, and preparation of teachers, and new topics such as the issue of merit pay have been included.

Part 2, "Historical and Philosophical Foundations," provides a context for understanding current educational practices and trends by examining the events and ideas that have influenced the development of American education. Chapters in this part reflect a systematic effort to relate historical and philosophical analysis to current concerns. Among the noteworthy changes in this part is expanded coverage of the education of minorities and women, which is intended to serve as an introduction to the in-depth discussion of these topics later in the text.

Part 3, "Political, Economic, and Legal Foundations," is a significant new addition to this textbook. Its three separate chapters provide an overview of the organization, governance, and administration of elementary and secondary education; the financing of public education; and the legal aspects of education. We added this material in response to the many instructors who told us that these topics were important elements of the courses they taught and that, from their perspective, our book would be even more useful to them if we included these three foundational areas.

Part 4, "Social Foundations," examines society's influence on the educational system—specifically, the relationship between society and the schools that society has established to serve its needs. Coverage of topics related to culture, socialization, and education has been reorganized and is now presented in Chapter 10. Material has been organized to highlight major socializing institutions—family, peer group and youth culture, the school, and the mass media. Chapter 11, "Social Class, Race, and School Achievement," has been revised to improve the logic and impact of the discussion. Major emphasis is placed on analyzing the situation with reference to controversies involving the traditional and the revisionist interpretation of U.S. schools and society. A new chapter devoted to equal opportunity in education pulls together and expands coverage of desegregation, compensatory education, multicultural education, and education of handicapped students.

Part 5, "Schools in a Changing Society," focuses on how the educational system is influenced by social changes, research findings, and the development of new instructional techniques. Coverage specifically addresses the ways in which educational aims and curriculum are directly affected by changes in society. An entirely new chapter on school effectiveness and reform has been added, reflecting much recent knowledge and interest regarding improvement of instruction in the schools.

Special Pedagogic Features

The third edition of *An Introduction to the Foundations of Education* includes a number of useful features to enhance students' understanding and learning. Following is a list of the features incorporated in the text to facilitate its use by both instructors and their students:

Topic overview charts, set off in screened boxes throughout the text, have been added to this edition to summarize and compare key developments and topics.

Chapter-opening focus questions highlight the major topics discussed in each chapter.

Marginal notations reinforce central points throughout the text.

New annotated lists of selected readings that may be of special interest to readers appear at the end of each chapter.

End-of-chapter features also include *summary lists* that facilitate understanding and recall of content and *discussion questions* to stimulate class discussion of text material.

A glossary has been added to this edition to define key terms and concepts that are highlighted in boldface type in the text.

The design of the third edition has been substantially improved to enhance readability. For the first time, *color* has been used to highlight various elements, thereby increasing students' ease in locating specific material. Photographs illustrating concepts discussed in the text appear more frequently throughout the book.

Acknowledgments

The third edition represents an ambitious undertaking which would not have been possible without the help of many individuals. We especially wish to acknowledge Gerald Gutek, Dean of the School of Education at Loyola University of Chicago, who wrote the four chapters in Part 2, "Historical and

Philosophical Foundations," and brought them up to date for this new edition. We would also like to thank Rayna Levine for her collaboration on Chapter 9, "Legal Aspects of Education." Our editors at Houghton Mifflin provided varied and continuous assistance at every step from planning to completion. Lovie Blackwell and Linda Tan offered indispensable help in preparing the manuscript.

A number of reviewers made useful suggestions and provided thoughtful reactions at various stages in the development of this manuscript. We wish to thank the following individuals for their conscientiousness and for their contributions to the organization and content of this edition:

Floyd M. Adams
Cleveland State University

J. Harold Anderson
Western Carolina University

Leon O. Beasley
University of Southwestern Louisiana

Grace M. Burton
University of North Carolina

Alden Carlson
State University of New York, Cortland

William Chance
Arkansas State University

Vernon B. Chapman
Mars Hill College

Charles H. Clark
Harrisburg Area Community College

James Cottingham
South Georgia College

Samuel M. Craver
Virginia Commonwealth University

Kenneth Creel
Presbyterian College

Joseph W. Davis
Lander College

Alan H. Eder
Northern Arizona University

Charles S. Evans
William Woods College

Harry Hadley
Fairmont State College

Dorothy Lee Hawkins
Jackson State University

William H. Howick
Memphis State University

W. Thomas Jamison
Appalachian State University

John H. Jensen
Boise State University

John McClure
University of Iowa

Max McCulloch
Central Missouri State University

Richard A. McEwing
Idaho State University

Robert B. McLaren
California State University, Fullerton

Milton A. Messinger
California University of Pennsylvania

Vincent P. Mikkelsen
East Carolina University

Joseph W. Newman
University of South Alabama

Morgan G. Otis
California State University, Sacramento

Kenneth R. Parsons
Western State College of Colorado

Alma E. Shufflebarger
Oakland City College

Peter H. Smith
Ocean County College

Floyd V. Souter
Georgia College

Ralph E. Stout
Northern Arizona University

Warren Strandberg
Virginia Commonwealth University

Charles E. Tressler
Hood College

Herbert B. Wilson
University of Arizona

A recurring focus in the third edition of *An Introduction to the Foundations of Education* is our deep belief that education and educators must help provide a productive future for our children and youth. With this in mind, we dedicate this edition to our own children: Bruce, Jason, Jennifer, Joel, and Stacey.

Allan C. Ornstein　　*Daniel U. Levine*

An Introduction to the Foundations of Education

Part 1 Understanding the Teaching Profession

Those who intend to teach should be aware of the trends that affect the work of classroom teachers, the issues that involve their status as professionals, and how these concerns change over time. In Part 1, we look at the climate in which teachers operate today, observe how this climate affects both the act of teaching and the status of the teaching profession, and examine what teachers are doing to shape their future.

The first part of Chapter 1 examines why people choose to become teachers, the economic position and prestige of teachers, and the demand for teachers. We consider the basic decision to teach, we analyze salary trends, and we review the current and prospective job market for teachers.

In the second part of the chapter, the focus shifts to teacher preparation. Several questions arise: What is the appropriate mix of general or liberal education, specialization, and professional education courses for preparing effective teachers? How are teachers certified? What are the trends in teacher preparation programs? The chapter then describes recent concern with the quality of the teacher workforce and concludes by describing current efforts to improve the situation and quality of teachers.

Chapter 2 inquires whether teaching is fully a profession. After considering developments and problems regarding the professional status of teachers, we describe recent trends and issues involving greater professionalism. Chapter 2 also describes a variety of teacher organizations and associations, among them the American Federation of Teachers and the National Education Association.

Our portrayal of the teaching profession in the middle of the 1980s may be viewed as generally encouraging. On the one hand, teachers' salaries and prestige are not as high as those of some other professions, and problems and pressures in the schools can make teaching a stressful job. Teacher salaries have improved over the past two decades, but inflation has eliminated much of this gain in recent years. In addition, there has been a general oversupply of teachers, which constricts the job market for many prospective teachers.

On the other hand, during the next decade there probably will be a shortage of teachers, and salaries are likely to increase substantially. In addition, teachers are much better organized than they were in the past, and teaching has become more of a profession. As in previous eras, teachers enter the field because it provides an opportunity to help children learn and grow. Teaching should continue to be a rewarding field for persons interested in making this important contribution to society.

1

Motivation, Status, and Preparation of the Teacher

Focusing Questions

What are the advantages and disadvantages of becoming a teacher?

What is satisfying and dissatisfying in the job of teaching?

How does teachers' prestige compare to that of other occupations?

What do teachers earn? How does this compare with other occupations?

What are the employment trends for teachers?

How are teachers prepared? How are they certified?

What are the trends in teacher education?

What developments are likely to take place regarding quality of the teacher workforce and the conditions of teaching?

ANYONE WHO IS CONSIDERING BECOMING A TEACHER SHOULD understand something about the situation of the teacher. Why do people become teachers? If given a chance to do it all over again, would they still choose teaching? To what degree do teachers enjoy the respect of the American public? What level and range of salaries do they earn? Are teachers still underpaid? What are the supply-demand trends for the profession? How are teachers prepared for elementary and secondary education? These are some of the important concerns that will be explored in this chapter.

Natural partnership between teachers and citizens

The American people and the teachers of the country are natural partners; the people depend on teachers to educate their children and the teachers are paid by the citizenry through taxes. The public must recognize the impact of the teaching profession on their lives; at the same time, teachers must be aware of their professional responsibilities. Together, the public and the teaching profession can work to improve education and, through education, to enhance the general welfare of the country.

Why Teach?

The teaching profession should attract the keenest minds, the finest personalities, and the most humane people. This, of course, does not always happen. Generally, those who enter the profession are average people with average abilities. Women tend to decide earlier in life than men to go into teaching. One reason, perhaps, is that until very recently, a narrower range of professional choices was open to women. Another reason is that women seem to achieve more status in teaching than do men. Parents often encourage their daughters to become teachers but less frequently express similar hopes for their sons. In addition, many women perceive teachers' work schedules as providing unusual opportunity for combining career goals and family responsibilities. As a result, females made up 68 percent of the public school teachers in 1981. More than 80 percent of the elementary teachers and 45 percent of the secondary teachers were female.[1]

Motives for Becoming a Teacher

Reasons for entering the profession

There are many motives, both idealistic and practical, for choosing a career in teaching. Those who are thinking of entering the teaching profession—and even those who are already teaching—should ask themselves why they are making this choice. Their motives may include (1) a love of children, (2) a desire to impart knowledge, (3) an interest in and excitement about teaching, and (4) a desire to perform a valuable service to society. Other reasons may include (1) job security and pension benefits, (2) relatively short working days and long vacations, (3) the relative ease of preparing for teaching,

1 Bernard Bartholomew, *Nationwide Teacher Opinion Poll—1981* (Washington, D.C.: National Education Association, 1981).

There are many motives for becoming a teacher, but perhaps the most powerful is the desire to work with young people.
(Eric Neurath/Lightwave)

compared with other professions, and (4) the ability to earn a reasonable income while preparing for another profession.[2] Also, for people who have not yet decided which profession to enter, teaching may seem to be at least a viable possibility.

As a prospective teacher, an awareness of the importance of the decision to enter the teaching field is essential. Your reasons for choosing teaching as a career will undoubtedly affect your attitude and behavior with your students when you eventually become a teacher. Whatever your reasons for wanting to teach, it might be helpful for you to consider what motivated others to become teachers.

A nationwide stratified sample of 1,533 teachers contacted in 1971 by the National Education Association (NEA) listed the major reasons they decided to enter the profession. The main reason is a *desire to work with young people*. Almost 72 percent of the respondents gave this choice as one

2 Allan C. Ornstein and Harry L. Miller, *Looking into Teaching* (Chicago: Rand McNally, 1980).

Emphasis on helping young people and society

of their three major reasons; it was the *only* reason on the list of a majority of teachers. Next highest response was the *value of education to society* with 37 percent. Predictably, a much larger percentage of secondary than elementary school teachers were drawn to teaching because of their *interest in a subject-matter field.* It was mentioned by 57 percent of the secondary teachers, compared to 14 percent of the elementary teachers.[3] A similar study conducted by the NEA in 1976 yielded almost identical results.[4] A 1980 study of high school seniors also found that the main reason for selecting teaching as a career is the desire to help children and youth.[5]

Satisfaction with Teaching as a Career

Once people become teachers, are they generally satisfied that they made the right decision? Table 1.1 shows the responses of a nationally representative sample of 1,265 elementary and secondary teachers to a 1981 NEA poll. Data in the table show the percentages of respondents who indicated they were more satisfied than dissatisfied with selected job conditions assessed in the study. As indicated in the table, teachers tend to be satisfied with those aspects of their jobs that involve teaching activities. Conversely, a majority of teachers were dissatisfied with nonteaching job characteristics such as the amount of time spent on record keeping and clerical duties, salary, amount of stress associated with the job, and time spent on schoolwork after hours. Nearly half the teachers were also dissatisfied with fringe benefits, support from parents, and respect received as a professional.

Satisfaction with teaching aspects

Table 1.1 indicates that male and female teachers generally do not differ much in job satisfaction, except that men are less satisfied than women with respect to salary, personal fulfillment derived from teaching, and respect received as a professional. Women are less satisfied than men with respect to time spent on schoolwork after school hours, amount of stress associated with the job, and amount of time spent on record keeping and clerical duties.

Older teachers were more satisfied than younger teachers: on every item in Table 1.1 except flexibility in deciding how to teach, more respondents over forty than under forty were satisfied. Age differences probably reflect a variety of phenomena such as a tendency for dissatisfied teachers to leave the profession at a relatively early age, gains by experienced teachers in learning to cope with the demands of the classroom, and efforts made by experienced teachers to improve their working conditions. As regards teaching level, elementary teachers generally appear more satisfied than secondary teachers, but on several items, such as flexibility in deciding how to teach and support from the principal, the pattern is reversed.

Age differences

Another measure of satisfaction with teaching involves the question of

3 National Education Association, *Status of American Public School Teachers, 1970–71* (Washington, D.C.: NEA, 1972), Appendix C, p. 159.

4 National Education Association, *Status of the American Public Teacher, 1975–76* (Washington, D.C.: NEA, 1976).

5 Sandra D. Roberson, Timothy Z. Keith, and Ellis B. Page, "Now Who Aspires to Teach?" *Educational Researcher* (June–July 1983), p. 20.

Table 1.1
Satisfaction with Selected Aspects of Teaching in a National Sample of 1,265 Teachers (Percentage Satisfied)

		Sex		**Age**		**Teaching Level**		
Selected Aspects of Teaching	**Total**	*Men*	*Women*	*Less Than 40*	*40 or Over*	*Elementary*	*Jr. High*	*Sr. High*
Flexibility in deciding how to teach	91	93	90	91	93	88	94	94
Personal fulfill-ment derived from teaching	80	77	82	79	83	83	74	77
Present teaching situation	75	75	75	72	81	76	71	74
Support from principal	73	75	72	68	78	70	71	74
Quantity of instructional material available	72	75	71	67	80	74	71	68
Number of students taught	66	67	66	64	71	62	65	71
Support from parents	59	58	59	55	66	61	57	55
Fringe benefits	55	54	56	51	56	58	53	55
Respect received as a professional	53	45	57	51	62	57	50	48
Time on school-work after school hours	45	56	40	42	49	41	50	49
Salary	43	38	46	36	54	45	38	44
Amount of stress associated with job	41	44	39	38	46	41	39	39
Amount of time on record keeping and clerical duties	40	46	37	36	46	39	45	40

Source: Bartholomew, Bernard. *Nationwide Teacher Opinion Poll—1981.* National Education Association (Washington, D.C.: The Association, 1981). Pages 15–18.

whether teachers would choose teaching as their career if they could decide again. Respondents in the NEA sample were asked the question "Suppose you could go back to your college days and start over again. In view of your present knowledge, would you become a teacher?" As shown in Table 1.2, 46 percent of the respondents said they probably or certainly would not choose to enter teaching. The data in Table 1.2 also show that teachers who are male, under forty years of age, and teaching at the secondary level are less

Willingness to teach again

Table 1.2
Willingness to Teach Again in a National Sample of 1,265 Teachers (Percentages)

		Sex		**Age**		**Teaching Level**		
	Total	*Men*	*Women*	*Less Than 40*	*40 or Over*	*Elementary*	*Jr. High*	*Sr. High*
Certainly would teach	22	15	25	18	27	26	18	17
Probably would teach	33	31	33	35	30	34	34	32
Probably would not teach	32	37	30	34	29	29	34	36
Certainly would not teach	14	18	12	13	14	11	14	16

Note: Totals differ from 100 percent due to rounding.

Source: Bartholomew, Bernard. *Nationwide Teacher Opinion Poll—1981.* National Education Association (Washington, D.C.: The Association, 1981). Pages 15–18.

likely to say they would choose teaching again than are older, female, elementary teachers. This pattern may reflect a long-term trend that leads male teachers to leave the profession in disproportionate numbers at a relatively young age, due in part, perhaps, to dissatisfaction with salary. In any case, it seems clear that the apparently high level of dissatisfaction with career choice shown in Table 1.2 must be associated to some extent with the greatest "dissatisfactions" (amount of time on record keeping and other duties, amount of stress associated with the job, salary, and time on schoolwork after school hours) shown in Table 1.1.

Change over time

It should be noted that the responses to the question on teaching as a career appear to be substantially different from those reported in earlier surveys. For example, an NEA survey of teachers in 1971 found that 75 percent of the respondents said they certainly or probably would begin teaching if they had to decide again,[6] as compared with 55 percent of the 1981 respondents. This difference probably reflects the retirement of an older generation of teachers that may have had relatively lower expectations than teachers in 1981 for salary and other benefits and that was relatively more satisfied with teaching. Nevertheless, the difference probably is due, at least in part, to the decline during the 1970s in both the status and relative income of teachers. Trends regarding teachers' status and salary are discussed later in this chapter.

6 National Education Association, *Status of the American Public School Teacher, 1970–71,* Appendix C, p. 159.

Table 1.3
Selected Data from the 1977 Quality of Employment Survey and the 1978 Quality of American Life Survey

	Teachers	College-Educated Nonteachers
Percentage reporting that family income is inadequate to meet monthly expenses	18	17
Percentage reporting that hours worked interfere with family life or personal life, or family life interferes with work	21	17
Percentage reporting physical or nervous condition caused or made severe by the job	7	5
Percentage reporting that they are "not too happy these days"	6	7
Percentage who describe their job as "very interesting"	80	70
Percentage who describe their pay as "not very good" or "not at all good"	35	26
Percentage who describe "physical surroundings" at work as not pleasant	11	15
Percentage who describe their job security as good	88	82
Percentage who describe "promotion chances" as not good	52	40

Source: Malcolm A. Lowther et al., "The Quality of Teachers' Work and Life: A Multisurvey, Comparative Study" (Paper presented at the annual meeting of the American Educational Research Association, Montreal, April 1983).

Data involving job satisfaction among elementary and secondary teachers also are available from several national studies on the quality of life in the United States. Collected periodically by the University of Michigan Institute of Social Research, these data allow comparisons between the responses of teachers and college-educated nonteachers. Although the small sample size requires caution in interpretation, these studies consistently indicate that the majority of teachers are approximately as satisfied as other college-educated workers with their jobs.

Teachers relatively satisfied

For example, data in Table 1.3 show that only 18 percent of teachers reported that their family income is inadequate, only 7 percent said that they have job-related physical or nervous problems, only 6 percent said that they are "not too happy these days," and barely a fifth reported much interference between personal life and work.[7] None of these responses are very much different from those of college-educated nonteachers. However, teachers appeared less satisfied with their pay and promotion chances than were non-

7 Malcolm A. Lowther et al., "The Quality of Teachers' Work and Life: A Multisurvey, Comparative Study" (Paper presented at the annual meeting of the American Educational Research Association, Montreal, April 1983).

Teachers have the desire to help young people and to perform a service of value to society.

(Joe DiDio/National Education Association)

teachers, and these grievances probably have increased in the 1980s as a result of inflation, declining enrollment in the schools, and budget cuts. On the other hand, 80 percent of the teachers reported that their work was "very interesting," compared with 70 percent of the college-educated nonteachers.

The preceding analysis indicates that most teachers have been motivated by a desire to work with young people and to make a positive contribution to society. The data indicate that a large majority of teachers are satisfied with most aspects of their jobs, but many are dissatisfied with salary and other "nonteaching" considerations. As we shall see later in this chapter, significant efforts are underway to improve salary and other conditions of teaching.

Stress and Coping

Like other occupations, teaching has its difficult and stressful moments. This conclusion was underscored in a 1979 study conducted for the American Academy of Family Physicians. The Academy surveyed six different groups as part of a study on lifestyle and health care in differing occupations: business executives, physicians, farmers, garment workers, secretaries, and teachers. Included in the study were 501 teachers.

Teaching can be stressful

One of the questions asked was, "How stressful is your work environment?" Sixty-three percent of the teachers answered "usually" or "always," as compared with 81 percent of the executives, 65 percent of the physicians, 38 percent of the farmers, 44 percent of the garment workers, and 61 percent of the secretaries. It should not be inferred, however, that stress is necessarily a negative job characteristic. Challenging jobs are bound to involve a significant amount of stress, and many people feel that challenge is desirable as long as stress is manageable. Thus, although 81 percent of executives said their jobs were usually or always stressful, 93 percent said they liked their work. Conversely, although only 44 percent of the garment workers said their jobs usually or always involved stress, only 75 percent said they liked their jobs.[8]

Burnout

Evidence that accumulated in the latter part of the 1970s indicated that elementary and secondary teaching has become more stressful than it was in earlier periods and that greater stress is causing burnout among some teachers. One definition of *burnout* makes it simply synonymous with "physical, emotional, and attitudinal exhaustion."[9] Authorities on burnout believe that it disproportionately strikes persons in the "helping" professions such as counselors, social workers, parole officers, and teachers.

Counteracting burnout

Assistance and counseling

The emphasis in recent years has been to encourage professionals who experience stress to develop a variety of coping techniques. Counselors point out that exercise, rest, hobbies, good nutrition, meditation or other relaxation techniques, efficient scheduling of personal affairs, and vacations can help individuals cope with high-stress jobs.[10] Recommendations for avoiding burnout also advise teachers to participate in professional renewal activities, separate their jobs from home life, and try to maintain flexibility and an open-minded attitude toward change.[11] Activities or projects undertaken by professional organizations and school districts to help teachers avoid burnout include an effort in Chicago to train volunteers to conduct rap sessions for teachers, a program of counseling and possible leaves of absence for teachers experiencing stress sponsored by the Tucson Education Association, and Prevention and Management of Educational Stress workshops conducted by the Northwest Staff Development Center in Wayne County, Michigan.

Status of Teachers

Prestige, salaries, and supply of teachers are all interrelated factors. Their relative positions are major concerns for future and present teachers. Generally,

8 Research and Forecasts, *A Report on Lifestyles/Personal Health Care in Different Occupations* (Kansas City, Mo.: The American Academy of Family Physicians, 1979).

9 Robert Scrivens, "The Big Click," *Today's Education* (November–December 1979), pp. 34–36.

10 "What Can You Do About Teacher Stress?" *NEA Reporter* (October 1979), p. 10.

11 Jim Sweeney, "Responsibility and Fulfillment of Needs—Burnout Remedies?" *Phi Delta Kappan* (May 1981), p. 676.

when the supply of members of a given profession is scarce, demand and salaries increase; when the salaries of a profession are high, professional status is high; conversely, when salaries are low, so is professional status.

The Prestige Factor

Occupational rating

Prestige refers to the estimation an individual or group occupies in the eyes of others in a social system; it connotes that individual's or group's status within the society. A few studies of social status and occupational ratings are available that shed some light on the social status of teachers. Perhaps the best-known studies of occupational prestige are those conducted by the National Opinion Research Center (NORC), affiliated with the University of Chicago. In 1947 NORC asked 2,290 persons throughout the country to rank eighty-eight occupations.[12] The study showed that school teachers ranked thirty-seventh in prestige, and college professors outranked others in the teaching profession. A related study of ninety occupations with similar populations was conducted by NORC in 1964.[13] In the later study, teachers ranked 29.5, moving up 7.5 places. Since most other professional occupations also tended to show gains in prestige, however, the new status of teachers must be qualified on a comparative basis. In a 1970 survey of 650 people who provided prestige ratings of more than 500 overlapping occupational titles, the highest average score was 81.5 for physicians and surgeons and the lowest was 9.3 for a shoe shiner.[14] Elementary school teachers were rated 60.1 and secondary school teachers were rated 63.1—both above the 90th percentile. About the same level of prestige for teachers was reported in a 1977 summary of research on occupational status.[15]

Teaching ranked well above average

Although a combination of factors determines prestige, in our society income is closely related to prestige. As teacher salaries increased, the occupational rating of teaching also rose. It is still evident, however, that teachers do not receive salaries in keeping with the ratings they receive on occupational status scales. In addition, there is evidence that the occupational prestige of elementary and secondary teachers declined somewhat between 1964 and 1980 as teacher salaries failed to keep pace with inflation.[16]

Pay Scales and Trends

In 1930 the average teacher salary was $1,420; in 1950 it was $3,126; in 1980, $16,001. By 1984 this figure had risen to $22,019. The most rapid

12 C. C. North and Paul K. Hatt, "Jobs and Occupation: A Popular Evaluation," *Opinion News* (September 1, 1947), pp. 3–13; Richard Centers, "Social Class, Occupation, and Imputed Values," *American Journal of Sociology* (May 1953), pp. 543–555.

13 Robert W. Hodge, Paul M. Siegel, and Peter H. Rossi, "Occupational Prestige in the United States, 1925–63," *American Journal of Sociology* (November 1964), pp. 286–302.

14 Paul M. Siegel, "Prestige in the American Occupational Structure" (Ph.D. diss., Department of Sociology, University of Chicago, 1971).

15 Donald J. Trieman, *Occupational Prestige in Comparative Perspective* (New York: Academic Press, 1977).

16 Gary Sykes, "Contradictions, Ironies, and Promises Unfulfilled: A Contemporary Account of the Status of Teaching," *Phi Delta Kappan* (October 1983), pp. 87–93.

Increase in teacher salary

growth came between 1960 and 1970, a period of rising teacher militancy. During this period, teacher salaries rose faster than the rate of inflation.[17] Today, it is not uncommon for some experienced teachers to earn $40,000 to $45,000. In addition, there are opportunities to work in after-school programs and summers for supplementary income and to advance to administrative positions with annual salaries well over $50,000.

Decline relative to prices in 1970s

Decline in Purchasing Power However, there is another side to the picture. While the average salaries of teachers more than doubled between 1968 and 1984, prices increased at an even faster pace. Between 1972 and 1982 annual salaries for teachers increased from $10,342 to $20,536, but in terms of the purchasing power of 1972 dollars, the 1982 average salary amounted to only $9,015.[18] Teacher salaries declined in purchasing power at a rate of nearly 1.5 percent a year between 1972 and 1982. (Of course, similar trends were experienced in virtually all occupations; the average worker lost ground during this ten-year period.)

Differences between states

Salary Levels and Differentials Teaching pay varies considerably among and within states. Table 1.4 shows 1983–84 average salaries paid to teachers among states. The range for that year was more than $20,000, from $15,895 in Mississippi to $36,564 in Alaska. Average yearly salaries in the three highest-paying states (Alaska, Michigan, and New York) were nearly twice as high as those in the three lowest-paying states (Mississippi, Arkansas, and South Dakota). Of course, comparative living costs must be taken into account. It is much more expensive to live in Alaska, for example, than to live in the Southeast.

Local variation

Salary differences within states are wide, especially in states where average state pay scales are high. For example, in Niles, Illinois, the average teacher salary in 1983 was approximately $10,000 more than the average for other Illinois teachers. In southern states where average salaries are low the range is narrower, but there are still considerable differences. In Georgia, for example, if you put down your roots in Cobb County your maximum salary in 1980 was more than $5,000 lower than the salary maximum for Atlanta teachers.

Differences within districts

The greatest variation in salaries is based on years of experience and education. Teachers with more years of experience and more education earn more than those with less of either. Thus teacher salaries in Chicago in 1983 ranged from $13,770 for new teachers with a bachelor's degree to $29,268 for experienced teachers with a year of graduate credit beyond the M.A. degree. Equivalent figures for Detroit were $15,027 and $36,315, respectively.[19] Table 1.5 shows how salary increases with years of experience and additional education in a typical salary schedule—that of the Cincinnati Public Schools.

17 Allan C. Ornstein, "Teacher Salaries: Past, Present, Future," *Phi Delta Kappan* (June 1980), pp. 677–678.

18 *Salary Trends for Teachers* (Washington, D.C.: American Federation of Teachers, 1983).

19 Ibid.

Table 1.4
Average Salary of Public Classroom Teachers, 1984

State	Salary	State	Salary
50 states and D.C.	*$22,019*	*Great Lakes (cont.)*	
New England	*21,456*	Michigan	$28,877
Connecticut	22,264	Ohio	21,421
Maine	17,328	Wisconsin	23,000
Massachusetts	22,500	*Plains*	*20,506*
New Hampshire	17,376	Iowa	20,140
Rhode Island	24,641	Kansas	19,598
Vermont	17,931	Minnesota	24,480
Mideast	*24,685*	Missouri	19,300
Delaware	20,925	Nebraska	18,785
Maryland	24,095	North Dakota	20,363
New Jersey	23,044	South Dakota	16,480
New York	26,750	*Southwest*	*20,065*
Pennsylvania	22,800	Arizona	21,605
Southeast	*18,506*	New Mexico	20,760
Alabama	18,000	Oklahoma	18,490
Arkansas	16,929	Texas	20,100
Florida	19,545	*Rocky Mountains*	*21,596*
Georgia	18,505	Colorado	22,895
Kentucky	19,780	Idaho	18,640
Louisiana	19,100	Montana	20,657
Mississippi	15,895	Utah	20,256
North Carolina	18,014	Wyoming	24,500
South Carolina	17,500	*Far West*	*25,934*
Tennessee	17,900	Alaska	36,564
Virginia	19,867	California	26,403
West Virginia	17,482	Hawaii	24,357
Great Lakes	*23,680*	Nevada	23,000
Illinois	23,345	Oregon	22,833
Indiana	21,587	Washington	24,780

Source: National Education Association, Research. Estimates of School Statistics, 1984. Copyright © 1984. Washington, D.C.: The Association. April 1984. Regional average is based on a weighted number of elementary and secondary teachers by state.

As shown, the salary schedule negotiated for 1981 through 1984 provided $13,226 for a first-year teacher with a B.A. and $27,056 for a teacher at the highest level of experience and education.

Low beginning salary

Although a teacher at the top of the salary schedule (based on experience and graduate degrees or certificates) can earn an attractive salary considering that the academic year is only about ten months long, starting salaries still tend to be low. As a matter of fact, it is difficult to see how beginning teachers in many school districts can support a family adequately or finance graduate education on a basic salary of $14,000 or $15,000 a year. Recogniz-

Table 1.5
Steps in the Salary Schedule for the Cincinnati Public Schools, 1984

	B.A.	M.A.	M.A. + 30 Hours	Maximum
First year (Step 1)	$13,226	$14,707	$15,214	$16,637
Fifth year (Step 5)	16,821	18,347	18,856	20,278
Tenth year (Step 10)	20,418	21,987	22,495	23,919
Maximum (Step 15)	23,129	25,202	25,635	27,056

ing this problem, many political and educational leaders are working to increase initial salaries as well as those for experienced teachers in order to attract and retain high-quality teachers. In particular, some states are providing additional funds so that all school districts can raise beginning salaries to a state-determined minimum.

Prospects for improvement

Comparison with Other Fields A good way to measure the economic position of an occupational group is to compare its salaries with those of other groups of workers having similar years of education. While Figure 1.1 shows that beginning teacher salaries have increased greatly between 1965 and 1983, it also presents data on beginning salaries for four other occupational groups (usually entered, like teaching, at the bachelor's degree level). These four groups have consistently started at an annual average salary higher than teachers; moreover, the gap between these four groups and teachers has widened since 1965.

Salary relative to other fields

In addition, the price of goods and services increased faster than teacher salaries between 1967 and 1983. Prices rose by over 300 percent during this period, but teacher salaries increased by less than 250 percent. We also should note that while the median family income in the United States for 1982 was $23,895, the average teacher salary was only $20,536. Average teacher salary as a percentage of median family income declined from 93 percent in 1972 to 82 percent in 1978.[20] However, this trend reversed in 1980, and average teacher salary increased to 86 percent of median family income in 1982. Furthermore, of some 2.1 million persons employed as elementary and secondary school teachers in 1983, almost 1.4 million are women. Note, however, that where the teacher is a married woman (about two-thirds of the female teachers *are* married), we can assume that their spouses generally earn similar or higher salaries. Thus their combined incomes are likely to put a great many teachers in the top five percentiles in the country, having family incomes of $50,000 or more.

It also should be kept in mind that teachers have many opportunities to increase their salaries by taking on additional responsibilities. For example, many teachers receive significant payments for coaching athletic teams or supervising other extracurricular activities, and teachers also gain in both sal-

Opportunities for more pay

20 Ibid.

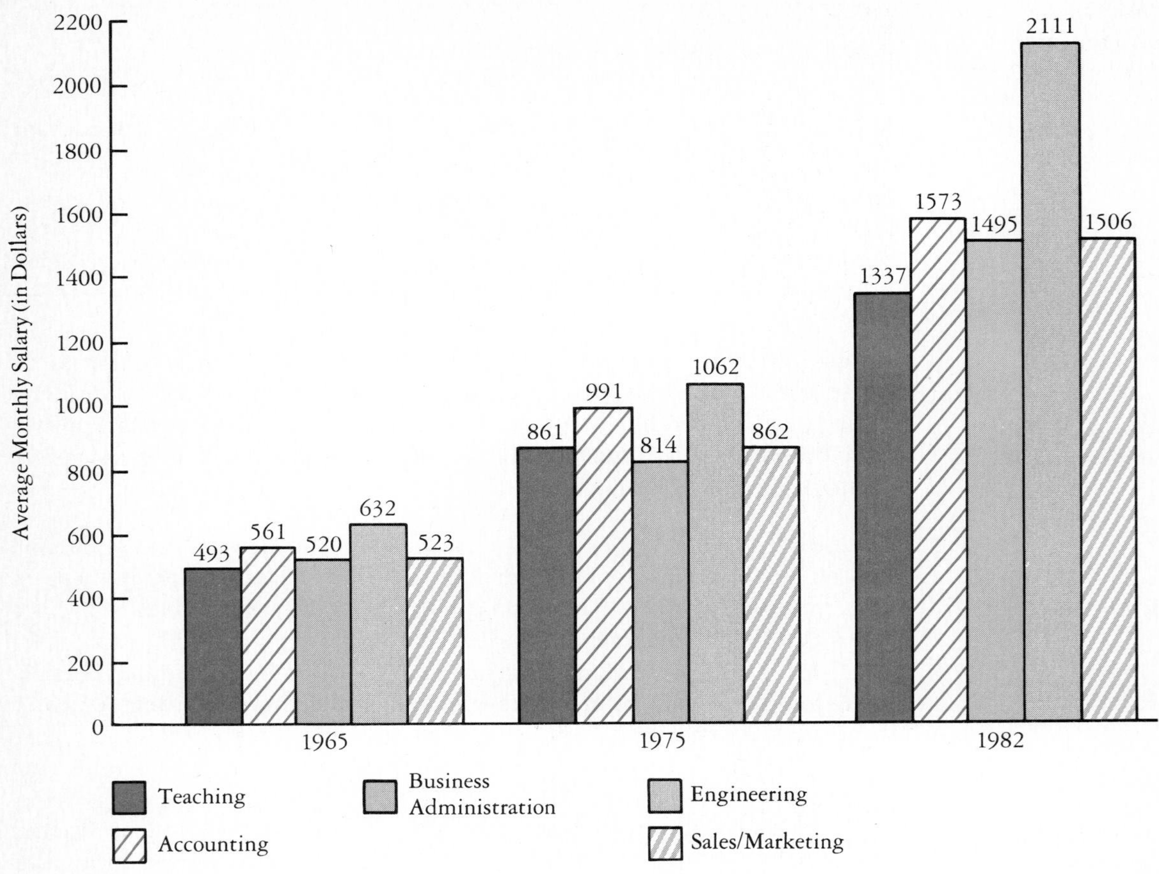

Figure 1.1
Average Monthly Salaries of Beginning Teachers and Graduates with Bachelor's Degrees in Four Other Occupations, 1965 to 1982

Note: Teacher salaries are based on a ten-month year; other salaries are based on a twelve-month year

Source: Frank S. Endicott, *Trends in Employment of College and University Graduates in Business and Industry,* Annual Reports (Evanston, Ill.: Northwestern University, 1966, 1976); National Education Association, *Economic Status of the Teaching Profession, 1972–73* (Washington, D.C.: NEA, 1973); National Education Association, *Prices, Budgets, Salaries, and Income* (Washington, D.C.: NEA, 1980); Victor R. Lindquist, *Northwestern Endicott Report 1983* (Evanston, Ill.: Northwestern University, 1982); American Federation of Teachers, *Salary Trends for Teachers: Survey and Analysis 1983* (Washington, D.C.: AFT, 1983).

ary and prestige when they are appointed to serve as administrators, curriculum developers, staff development specialists, master teachers, or in other specialized positions. In the past few years there has been some movement toward developing both career ladders, which enable outstanding teachers to take on additional responsibility, and merit pay plans, which provide higher salaries for superior classroom teachers. (We will discuss these possibilities at greater length in Chapter 2.)

Teachers have many opportunities to supplement their salaries by taking on additional responsibilities such as, for example, supervising extracurricular activities.
(Bob Daemmrich/ TexaStock©)

Salary improvements probable

As we will illustrate in the concluding section of this chapter, the quality of education and the situation of teachers have become important national concerns in recent years. In many states, governors and other political leaders have made improvement of public education a top priority. Several states, such as Arkansas, Mississippi, and Tennessee, have developed plans for substantial statewide increases in teacher salaries. As a result of these developments, teacher salaries probably will increase significantly faster than inflation during the next few years.

Supply and Demand

From 1950 until the mid-1960s the schools were bursting at the seams with record enrollments that had their beginning in the post–World War II baby boom. These high birthrate groups had to rely on teachers born during the low birthrate years of the Great Depression—a trickle of teachers for a flood of students. Thus a widespread shortage of teachers developed in the 1950s and early 1960s.

However, the pattern was reversed in the late 1960s, and a general oversupply of teachers was available in the 1970s and early 1980s. This surplus of teachers reflected two major interrelated factors.

First, the U.S. birthrate fell steadily from 1955 to 1973 and then remained low, leading to a decline in school enrollment in the elementary and then the secondary schools. Second, the college-age population increased as the baby boom generation grew up, and many of this generation entered teaching, partly because there had been a shortage of teachers. By 1969

Excess of teachers in 1970s

there was an "excess" of 16,000 beginning teachers, and by 1974 the number of surplus beginning teachers was more than 60,000, with several additional thousands no longer even applying for jobs.[21]

It should be noted that in certain subject areas the teacher shortage has persisted through much of the past fifteen years. These fields include special education, bilingual education, and early childhood education—which were expanding rapidly despite general enrollment decline—and science, mathematics, and industrial arts—in which financial rewards were far better in business and industry than in teaching.

Declining enrollment in teacher education

As college students, teacher educators, and state government officials realized that there was a substantial oversupply of teachers, enrollment in teacher education programs decreased in the 1970s. The number of education degrees awarded to new teachers fell from 176,614 in 1971 to 108,309 in 1981. Reflecting the same trend, the percentage of college freshmen intending to become teachers declined from 22 percent in 1966 to 5 percent in 1982. If recent trends continue, this number will decline to 77,270 in 1988—44 percent of the 1971 figure.[22] However, some colleges and universities reported an increase in teacher education enrollment in 1984, for the first time in ten or twelve years.

As of 1985, however, it appears that the overall trend is again being reversed: there is likely to be a significant shortage of teachers by the late 1980s. Reasons for predicting an improvement in the market for new teachers during the next ten years include the following:[23]

1. The number of students graduating annually from teacher-preparation institutions has been drastically reduced.

2. A "mini" baby boom is beginning to develop as the original baby boom generation grows up and produces its own children. As a result, school enrollment will increase after 1985 (see Table 1.6). This will substantially increase opportunities for elementary teachers beginning in 1985, and for secondary teachers beginning in 1992.

Many teachers approaching retirement

3. In many communities a significant proportion of the current teaching force will be reaching or approaching retirement within the next ten years.[24] Some observers perceive this as a "window of opportunity," during which time well-trained new teachers can be prepared to function in the schools.

4. The recent rise in national and local concern with the quality of education (discussed elsewhere in this book) may lead to reductions in class

21 "Trends in Teacher Supply and Demand in Public Schools, 1973–76." *NEA Research Memo* (June 1973), pp. 2–3; Stanley M. Elam, "A Somber Economic Picture for Teachers, *Phi Delta Kappan* (November 1974), p. 170.

22 Susan W. Masland and Robert T. Williams, "Teacher Surplus and Shortage: Getting Ready to Accept Responsibilities," *Journal of Teacher Education* (July–August 1983), p. 6.

23 Allan C. Ornstein, "The Urban Setting: Frostbelt/Sunbelt Differences," *Phi Delta Kappan* (October 1982), pp. 102–107.

24 Gary Sykes, "Teacher Preparation and the Teacher Workforce: Problems and Prospects for the 80s," *American Education* (March 1983), pp. 23–31.

Table 1.6
Public and Private School Enrollments, 1960–2000

	Total Enrollment	Public K–12		Private K–12	
		Students	*Percent*	*Students*	*Percent*
1960	42,181,000	36,281,000	86.0	5,900,000	14.0
1965	48,473,000	42,173,000	87.0	6,300,000	13.0
1970	51,309,000	45,909,000	89.5	5,400,000	10.5
1975	49,991,000	44,791,000	89.6	5,200,000	10.4
1980	46,094,000	41,094,000	89.1	5,000,000	10.9
Projections					
1985	44,794,000	39,794,000	88.8	5,000,000	11.2
1990	46,667,000	41,267,000	88.4	5,400,000	11.6
2000	47,707,000	41,744,000	87.5	5,963,000	12.5

Source: *Projections of Education Statistics to 1990–91* (Washington, D.C.: National Center for Education Statistics, 1983), table 6, p. 34; *U.S. Catholic Elementary and Secondary Schools, 1982–83* (Washington, D.C.: National Catholic Education Association, 1983), table 3, p. 5; figures for the year 2000 are the authors' estimates based on Census Bureau projections.

size, expansion of preschool education, greater emphasis on science and mathematics, and other changes that require an increased number of teachers.

5. Population in the United States has shifted from the Frostbelt states of the North and East to the Sunbelt states of the South and West. In addition, immigration from Mexico and elsewhere also has increased the population of the Sunbelt. Both these phenomena have created teaching opportunities, particularly in the Southwest.

Combining liberal arts and education

Alternate career possibilities

6. Among the more positive responses to the supply-demand gap in teaching has been a movement to help teacher education students prepare for careers other than those in schools or classrooms. In conjunction with programs leading directly to a teaching certificate, many colleges and universities are offering interdisciplinary majors that blend the liberal arts with an educational-studies major to prepare students for a broad range of careers.[25] These new career programs frequently reduce or eliminate teaching-methods requirements and substitute courses of study that can lead to one of several fields or career options, such as adult education, consulting and research, state or federal agencies, community organization and development, vocational guidance, youth-serving organizations (for example, Boy Scouts), and private-sector training.

However, it is very difficult to predict exactly the market for new teachers in the future. In addition to uncertainties regarding enrollment and pro-

25 Beverly T. Watkins, "Education Schools Worry about Expansion into 'Human Services,'" *The Chronicle of Higher Education,* March 3, 1982, p. 9.

gramming in the schools, market opportunities on the demand side will depend on whether developments affecting salary and other teaching conditions encourage or discourage retirement and resignation. On the supply side, several factors may increase the number of new teachers: improvements in teacher salary vis-à-vis other jobs; efforts to recruit and provide financial support for students in teacher education; the extent to which certified teachers who left teaching or never obtained a job may return to teaching; a decline in opportunities in law, business, and other fields; and related developments. Despite these uncertainties, it is likely that opportunities for teachers will improve over the next decade. The most recent estimates prepared by the National Center for Education Statistics indicate that by 1990 the supply of new teachers will be only about 75 percent of the demand.[26]

Market uncertainties

Probable teacher shortage

Preparation of Teachers

During the colonial period and well into the early nineteenth century, an individual who wanted to become a teacher usually obtained approval from a local minister or a board of trustees associated with a religious institution. A high school or college diploma was not considered a necessary prerequisite. If you could read, write, and spell and were of good moral character, you could teach school. By the 1820s future teachers began attending **normal schools** to prepare for teaching, although formal certification procedures still were not required. These teaching institutions did not grant a degree; rather, they offered a number of courses that prepared the candidate for teaching. Eventually, the normal schools became teachers colleges, and most of the latter have now become diversified colleges and universities. Today, except for emergency or temporary certification, all states require a bachelor's degree or five years of college work for entrance into teaching.

Evolution of training arrangements

Preservice Teacher Education

The preparation of teachers now consists of three components: (1) liberal (or general) education, (2) specialized subject-field education, and (3) professional education. In general, the purpose of a *liberal* education is to liberate the mind, to provide knowledge of self and culture worthy of a citizen in a free society. A liberal program combines the arts and sciences and seeks to give the student a broad cultural background. The *specialized subject* field comprises a cluster of courses in a specific subject area and provides the prospective teacher with in-depth preparation for his or her chosen teaching field. In most colleges and universities this part of the program is described as the student's "major" or "minor." Whereas secondary teachers are typically certified in one subject field, and for this reason usually take a greater amount of work in one or two areas, most elementary teachers are

Major components of preservice preparation

26 National Center for Education Statistics, *Projections of Education Statistics to 1992–93* (Washington, D.C.: Government Printing Office, 1984).

responsible for all subject fields. Elementary teachers may specialize, however, in areas such as music, art, physical education, and foreign language. *Professional education* refers to educational courses designed to provide professional orientation and training in the art and science of teaching. Typical liberal and specialized subject courses enroll students with diverse interests and occupational goals; professional courses enroll those who are interested in the career goal of teaching.[27]

Almost all educators agree that the preparation of good teachers rests on these three components. The relative emphasis that each area should receive, however, provokes strong arguments. That is to say: How much time should the education student devote to liberal or general education, to specialization or subject-matter field, and to professional or education courses? One leading authority on teacher education recently offered the following observation on the need for additional attention to clinical training of professionals in education:

Need for clinical emphasis

> Emphasis upon academic studies has been retained with only a slight increase in emphasis on the role of clinical work. The tendency in recent years to bring into pedagogical schools professors from the disciplines of history, sociology, and the like from liberal arts colleges is witness to that fact. This hankering for academic respectability is understandable historically but makes little sense in a professional school where clinical work has been so long neglected.[28]

Credit distribution

Today most colleges of education require approximately 31 semester hours of professional studies for elementary school teacher candidates, and an average of 19 hours for secondary teacher candidates. For both groups, an average of 10 additional semester credit hours is devoted to student teaching. For future elementary teachers, about 45 percent of the professional studies curriculum is devoted to theoretical analysis of education, and the remaining 55 percent concentrates on methods of teaching. For secondary school candidates, the pattern is reversed.[29]

Fifth-year programs

Of course there are some colleges of education that encourage or require more than this number of credits or specify courses beyond state certification requirements. Most colleges and universities distribute these courses throughout the four-year program, but some cluster them during the last year. Others either have implemented a fifth-year component consisting of subject-field and professional courses or have initiated a five-year program providing for field work in schools beginning the second or third year and culminating in a graduate-credit internship in schools during the fifth year. Approximately 5 percent of colleges of education now offer a five-year pro-

27 See B. J. Chandler, Daniel Powell, and William R. Hazard, *Education and the New Teacher* (New York: Dodd, Mead, 1971); Allan C. Ornstein and Harry L. Miller, *Looking Into Teaching* (Chicago: Rand McNally, 1980).

28 B. Othaniel Smith, "Teacher Education in Transition," in D. Smith, ed., *Essential Knowledge for Beginning Educators* (Washington, D.C.: The American Association of Colleges for Teacher Education and the ERIC Clearinghouse on Teacher Education, 1983), p. 141.

29 Douglas Wright, "Survey of Teacher Education: Perceptions of Methods for Improvement," *National Center for Education Statistics Bulletin* (October 1983), p. 5.

gram (leading to a teaching certificate) on either an optional or required basis.[30]

Certification

In order to teach in a public school in the United States, prospective teachers are required to be certificated by the state in the subject areas or grade levels they wish to teach. Until recently, most states granted **certification** based on documentation that the candidate possessed sufficient appropriate professional preparation and good moral character. In some states preparation is assessed through evaluation of transcripts and credits; in others certification is automatic if the candidate has completed an approved program at an accredited college or university.

Focus on competence

One consequence of the recent national debate about education has been a focus on teacher competence. Demands for and passage of legislation mandating competency testing for new teachers are attributable largely to this debate. Nearly every state either has passed some type of competency requirement for teachers seeking initial certification or is discussing it seriously in legislative committees.

Renewing certificates

In past years teaching certificates were issued for life. Some states have revised these laws and now issue certificates valid for only three to five years. Teachers currently holding life certificates are not affected, but those possessing renewable certificates usually have to furnish proof of university coursework or continuing education units for renewal.

Certification Requirements

Part of the problem concerning the preparation of teachers is that the certification requirements vary so much from state to state. Each state has its own procedures. The situation can be summarized as follows: from state to state the power to determine requirements for teacher certification is divided among legislatures, state departments of education, superintendents of public instruction, and boards of education. Whatever these requirements, the programs of teacher education must respect them in preparing prospective teachers. Content, sequence, and the number of educational courses vary even within states, because some colleges and universities establish supplementary requirements or course work beyond minimum requirements.

Variation in requirements

There is tremendous variation in the extent to which the requirements are spelled out by state authorities. For example, the range of semester hours in general education (that is, arts and sciences) required for a secondary certificate ranges from 22 hours at the low end to 60 at the high end. Within the general education requirement, fifteen states prescribe credit hours in specific disciplines such as history or natural science, but the majority do not specify amounts of credit in particular subjects.[31] The number of semester or

30 Wright, "Survey of Teacher Education."

31 Tom Weible and Wayne Dumas, "Secondary Teacher Certification Standards in Fifty States," *Journal of Teacher Education* (July–August 1982), pp. 22–23.

quarter hours needed to teach an academic subject also varies with the field as well as the state. Some states require that the teacher have a "major" in the subject field of an "approved curriculum"; the hours required in that field are left to the training institutions. Across the country it is usually the responsibility of the teacher preparation institution to decide what courses in the subject field will be used to meet the semester requirements.

The requirements for professional education also vary. For example, Michigan's minimum requirements are 20 semester hours for elementary teachers, whereas Mississippi's minimum requirements are 33 semester hours. New York requires a minimum of 12 semester hours for secondary teachers, while Tennessee requires 24.[32]

Decisions by training institution

Despite the state regulation mandating a certain number of professional semester requirements, the training institution usually decides which courses will in fact be used to meet requirements and whether additional course work will be prescribed at the given institution. Even when course titles are similar, there are often wide differences in the content, the intellectual level of instruction, and the competencies mandated. This is true for both academic and professional courses. The result is that state requirements and teacher training institutions do not guarantee that teachers have mastered a uniform or universal set of skills and understandings.

How do we end this confusion? One of the characteristics of a profession is that its practitioners control entry to its practice. Perhaps teachers will soon exercise a greater role in shaping programs for their own training and certification. Teacher training institutions could maintain their autonomy and have considerable freedom to develop their own programs, but they would still have to guarantee a minimum level of competency for their students—and work out these levels with teacher organizations or state departments of education. Or, perhaps more likely, state departments of education may agree on a common set of requirements for training and testing teachers. This already has happened to a significant degree; more than half the states follow broad general requirements endorsed by the National Association of State Directors of Teacher Education Certification (NASDTEC).

Movement toward common requirements

Reciprocity of Teacher Certificates Differences in the certification requirements of the individual states have traditionally stifled the free movement of teachers throughout the country. For example, a teacher certified to teach in New York might not meet the requirements for teaching in Oregon. Even where reciprocity exists, differences in supply and demand, salaries, and tenure provisions hamper interstate movement.

Some organizations, such as the National Council for Accreditation of Teacher Education (NCATE), have concerned themselves with this problem. The advantages of free interstate movement for teachers have been enumerated by these organizations and include (1) a means of nationally balancing teacher supply and demand, (2) improved opportunities and mobility for

Advantages of interstate movement

32 Roger E. Goddard, ed., *1984 Teacher Certification Requirements* (Grover Hill, Ohio: Teacher Certification Publications, 1984).

teachers, (3) less inbreeding and provincialism in local school systems, (4) increasd professionalism and higher morale among teachers, and (5) a means of balancing minimum preparation standards among states.[33] With varying degrees of success, reciprocity compacts were established between some states as early as 1900. More recently there was a trend toward granting reciprocity in certification on the basis either of NASDTEC guidelines or of program approval by NCATE. Where formal reciprocity agreements exist, persons graduating from approved programs leading to certification in one state are automatically eligible for similar certification in other states participating in the agreement. As of 1983, thirty states had adopted reciprocity of basic teaching credentials.[34]

Reciprocity agreements in 30 states

Trends in Preservice Education

Over the past two decades, teacher education programs generally placed greater stress on competency-based preparation, on utilization of school-based field centers, and on earlier field experience. Competency-based teacher education was particularly prominent in the 1970s, and at many colleges and universities it is still a central aspect of teacher education.

Testing of performance

Competency-based Teacher Education

Competency-based teacher education (CBTE), an alternative approach to teacher education, requires prospective teachers to demonstrate minimum levels of performance. The important question is, What can the prospective teacher *do* in a simulated or actual teaching situation? Rather than describing what a teacher might or should do, the candidate must perform a specific task. For example, rather than identifying an appropriate teaching strategy by writing a short essay or selecting from among multiple-choice alternatives, a candidate may be required to teach a simulated class and then discuss the reasons for his or her teaching behaviors. Skills and understandings tested are based on research concerning the characteristics of effective teachers.

Data collected in the 1970s indicated that about half the teacher training institutions in the United States utilized some degree of CBTE in their preservice programs.[35] However, this figure declined as colleges and universities experienced financial problems—CBTE is expensive if done well—and as questions were raised about its utility and feasibility. A few of the most important questions are listed below.[36]

33 *Standards for the Accreditation of Teacher Education* (Washington, D.C.: National Council for Accreditation of Teacher Education, 1977).

34 *Educational Governance in the States* (Washington, D.C.: U.S. Department of Education, 1983).

35 Kenneth Howey, Sam Yarger, and Bruce Joyce, "Reflections on Preservice Preparation: Impressions from the National Survey. Part III: Institutions and Programs," *Journal of Teacher Education* (January–February 1978), pp. 38–40.

36 Robert O. Brinkerhoff, "Competency Assessment: A Perspective and an Approach," *Journal of Teacher Education* (March–April 1978), pp. 21–24: Sam J. Yarger and Bruce R. Joyce, "Going Beyond the Data: Reconstructing Teacher Education," *Journal of Teacher Education* (November–December 1977), pp. 21–25.

Problems in CBTE

1. CBTE may further fragment teacher education. Although it deliberately breaks down the acts of teaching and training, there is a point at which this becomes excessive. For example, at one time the Michigan State University elementary education model identified as many as 2,700 modules. Are all of these components necessary or appropriate?
2. Reliability and validity of competency tests are not well established.
3. How shall the information regarding a prospective teacher's competency be translated into certification units and communicated to licensing authorities? Questions of how to match student credits with degree requirements and faculty credits and work-load definitions have not been answered adequately. What makes CBTE exercises 1–10, or any number of exercises, equivalent to the content tested under the traditional college methods course?

Translating competencies into credits

To make CBTE programs operational, it is necessary to identify appropriate competencies, assess those competencies accurately, define good teaching while accommodating different teaching styles and roles, develop and prepare instructional materials, switch to an analytical and research focus in teacher education, and train educators to manage these programs. Can all these things be accomplished? No one knows. It remains to be seen whether effective CBTE will be further developed and maintained in the future.

Moving from college classrooms to school centers

School-based Field Centers One of the ways in which teacher trainers have attempted to make teacher preparation more realistic and practical is by conducting a significant part of the training at cooperating elementary or secondary schools specifically designated to provide preservice preparation. Much of the training that previously was provided at the college or university campus is now provided at school-based teacher education centers, which generally have office space for college faculty, special equipment for use in teacher training, and outstanding teachers to serve as supervisors and models for future teachers.

The growth of school-based teacher education centers has been documented in the National Survey of the Preservice Preparation of Teachers. Whereas in 1968 only 22 percent of higher education teacher training institutions had established centers for this purpose either on or off campus, 36 percent of such institutions had done so by 1975. The vast majority of these centers were at elementary or secondary schools in local school districts. The trend toward establishment of such centers was particularly evident among public colleges and universities: 64 percent of the public higher education institutions had established a teacher education center of some kind, and about half of these centers were located in local school districts.[37]

Early assignments in schools

Early Field Experience Another way in which teacher education programs have become more practical is by requiring or encouraging future teachers to spend a significant amount of time in elementary or secondary

37 *The State of Teacher Education, 1977* (Washington, D.C.: Government Printing Office, 1978).

Today's teachers in training are being given more and earlier opportunities for practical classroom teaching experiences.
(Victoria Arlak)

schools shortly after they enter the preparation program. This trend was identified in a 1977 study of teacher training programs, which found that students in about one-fourth of the programs have classroom experience as early as the freshman year.[38] In many cases professional courses in subjects like introduction to education, educational psychology, or teaching methods are closely coordinated with classroom observation, teacher aide assignments, or other field experiences in local schools. In general, institutions that require early and continuous field experience have constructed a sequence of assignments such that students move from observation to service as a teacher's aide to relatively full-scale teaching responsibility similar to the traditional "practice teaching" semester.[39]

In-service Education and Staff Development

Growing stress on in-service education

As positions for new teachers largely dried up in the 1970s and the teaching workforce became older and more experienced, in-service education grew in importance relative to preservice preparation of new teachers. In-service education, it was hoped, would transmit the findings of research on effective teaching and effective schools and respond to demands for improving stu-

38 Howey, Yarger, and Joyce, "Reflections on Preservice Preparation: Impressions from the National Survey."

39 *The State of Teacher Education, 1977.*

dent achievement. Today in-service education has become a large national enterprise. Some districts spend $1,000 to $2,000 per teacher per year for this purpose.[40]

Historically, **in-service education** consisted largely of occasional workshops and training sessions at which teachers from a number of schools gathered to obtain information about promising practices and techniques for improving the quality of instruction. In addition, continuing education in the form of attendance at college and university courses, work on advanced degrees in education or specific teaching fields, and enrollment in summer training sessions frequently has been considered to be part of in-service education for teachers.

In-service education more concentrated and ongoing

In recent years in-service education has become much more concentrated and ongoing. It has frequently focused on building-level efforts to improve the effectiveness of individual schools or groups of schools. Today's emphasis has shifted toward collaborative planning in which teachers work together to plan and implement instructional improvement. This type of ongoing training is generally called **staff development**. Two well-known experts in staff development view the shift toward collaborative, school-based, instructionally relevant staff development as a rejection of "band-aid" efforts, which are increasingly viewed "as unacceptable when compared with the magnitude of the challenges" to improve education.[41]

It also should be noted that contemporary staff development is based on research and theory related to how adults learn. Its design and implementation typically reflect such principles as the following: (1) growth should be toward more complex levels of cognitive development; (2) learning should be based on experience; (3) emphasis should be on continuous, guided reflection; and (4) instruction should provide for both personal support and challenge.[42]

Efforts to Improve the Quality of Teachers

In recent years there has been much discussion about possibilities for improving the quality of the teaching workforce. Many political and educational leaders have expressed alarm about a perceived decline in the average scholastic ability of teachers and about school conditions that make it difficult to teach effectively. Much of the effort to improve the quality of teachers and teaching in U.S. elementary and secondary schools has centered on testing of teachers and on a variety of recommendations publicized and supported in influential national reports on the problems of our educational system.

40 Kenneth R. Howey and Joseph C. Vaughan, "Current Patterns of Staff Development," in G. A. Griffin, ed., *Staff Development* (Chicago: University of Chicago Press, 1983), pp. 92–117.

41 Ibid., p. 96.

42 Norman A. Sprinthall and Lois Thies-Sprinthall, "The Teacher as an Adult Learner: A Cognitive Developmental View," in G. A. Griffin, ed., *Staff Development* (Chicago: University of Chicago Press, 1983), pp. 13–35.

Ability of the Teaching Workforce

Discussions and data on the "quality" of the teaching workforce generally are misleading because they almost always focus entirely or largely on "ability" scores derived from standardized tests such as the Scholastic Aptitude Test (SAT). In most cases there is an implied assumption that the aptitudes and ability measured by such tests are synonymous with "quality" of the workforce.

Standardized tests imperfect

Many variables are at least as important as academic ability. In many cases, stress on academic ability, as measured by widely used standardized tests, may lead to the selection of teachers who are misfits because they are intellectually superior but have relatively little understanding of or commitment to teaching and to students. Nevertheless, it is important that teachers possess sufficient intellectual ability to master the subject matter they teach and to function successfully in a difficult job. Although one should be careful about explicitly or implicitly equating such terms as "quality," "academic ability," and "effective teachers," the average ability level of teachers is a legitimate concern.

Decline in SAT scores

Data on the academic ability of teachers and potential teachers indicate a decline in this particular measure of workforce quality. For example, between 1973 and 1982, the average SAT verbal score of college students intending to teach fell from 418 to 394, and the average math score fell from 449 to 419. These declines were five points greater in verbal score and sixteen points greater in math score than the comparable declines for the college test-taking population as a whole.[43] (Other data indicate that decline in the ability scores of prospective teachers is accounted for largely by falling scores among white females and minority students, probably because individuals in these categories have had expanding opportunities outside education in the 1970s and 1980s.[44]) Even before this decline was evident, education majors ranked very low in average ability compared with students majoring in most other fields.[45]

Loss of high-ability teachers

In addition, the available data indicate that declines in the ability of the teaching workforce occur at several steps in recruitment, selection, and retention of teachers. For example, a comparison of education students who did and did not find teaching jobs indicated that the latter group has higher ability scores than the former, and several studies suggest that those who leave teaching have higher average ability than those who stay.[46] Gary Sykes, head of the Teaching-Policy Studies Team at the National Institute of Education, has summarized the results of these studies as follows:

43 Gary Sykes, *The Schools, the Teachers, and Excellence in Education* (Washington, D.C.: National Institute of Education, 1982).

44 Roberson, Keith, and Page, "Now Who Aspires to Teach?"

45 Nancy B. Borkow and K. Forbis Jordan, "The Teacher Workforce: Analysis of Issues and Options for Federal Action" (Paper prepared for the Library of Congress Congressional Research Service, November 7, 1983).

46 Ibid.

> In teaching, the processes of recruitment and retention systematically result in selection by academic ability, but not in the way we would prefer. Rather, at every point of choice, from initial selection of a college major through the decision to remain in teaching, the academically able opt out. To a disproportionate degree the teaching ranks are filled by those below the median on distributions of academic ability.[47]

Attracting capable candidates

Discussions of quality in the teacher workforce by Sykes and other observers necessarily address a set of interrelated issues: How can the most capable students be attracted into teaching? To what degree must teacher salaries improve to attract and retain top candidates? What can be done to demonstrate to the public that higher salaries are justified? What preparation approaches are necessary or desirable in ensuring that capable candidates receive superior training so that they will function successfully and justify higher salaries? Can expensive improvement in teacher education programs provide more effective clinical experience comparable to the training of interns and residents in medicine and other health sciences?

Low expenditures on teacher education

In considering this latter point, Sykes observes that the "basic scheme [of teacher education] in most states still involves a fraction of time for education courses during pursuit of an undergraduate liberal arts degree, plus several weeks of inadequately supervised practice teaching." In part, he asserts, the problem is due to the fact that the average annual per student expenditure on training future teachers is far below the average annual expenditure on educating elementary and secondary students.[48] Based in part on this type of analysis and consideration, teacher education and quality of the teacher workforce became central topics of widespread national concern when a number of well-publicized reports on problems in education were released in 1983 and 1984. We will review these reports' implications for teachers and teaching in the concluding section of this chapter.

Testing of Teachers

Some of the efforts being made to improve the quality of the teaching force in elementary and secondary education involve **basic skills testing** of future teachers, new teachers, and—sometimes—experienced teachers. Based on the argument that teachers who are very low in reading, mathematics, communications, and/or professional knowledge probably are ineffective in their teaching, some educators and many laypersons have advocated that qualifying examinations be introduced to test teachers' basic skills and knowledge. These efforts have led to developments such as the following:

Approximately thirty states now require that prospective teachers pass some form of minimum skills tests in reading and language, math, sub-

47 Sykes, "Teacher Preparation and the Teacher Workforce."

48 Ibid.

ject-area specialty, and/or professional knowledge, and at least twelve others are planning to introduce such tests.[49] In particular, several of the southern states now use the National Teacher Examination for this purpose.

Between 1977 and 1982, approximately three-quarters of the nation's colleges of education raised entrance criteria for their teacher education programs.[50] This trend intensified in 1983 and 1984 as national reports critical of elementary and secondary education drew public attention to problems in the schools.

In 1982, the State of California began to administer a test in reading, writing, and math to new candidates for teaching positions. Slightly more than 6,000 applicants took the first test, and 27 percent failed, even though state government officials described the test as "relatively easy."

In July 1983 the Florida Department of Education decertified thirty-eight teacher training programs because less than 80 percent of their graduates passed the statewide teacher certification exam.

The Arkansas legislature enacted a law in 1983 specifying that all teachers in the state must pass an academic skills test in addition to passing a second test or earning 6 hours of graduate credit in their area of specialization. This law makes Arkansas the first state to require experienced teachers to pass a basic skills test.

Dallas and several other school districts now require that all teachers pass a basic skills test.

Testing of teachers likely to increase

Testing of prospective and current teachers has become a controversial topic that is not likely to go away soon, because many political leaders see it as one of the few feasible steps they can take to quickly improve the quality of the teacher workforce. Supporters also argue that the best time to introduce basic skills testing of teachers and to take other steps aimed at raising professional entry standards is during the current period of teacher surplus, when qualified candidates are available to replace weak candidates or practicing teachers who fail to meet minimum standards.

Criticism of testing

Opponents argue that the tests unjustifiably exclude persons who do poorly on paper-and-pencil instruments of the kind heretofore used almost universally for basic skills testing of teachers. Opponents also assert that many teachers who graduated from college ten or more years ago are capable professionals even though they may have forgotten subject matter that is tested but irrelevant to their teaching situation. Most oponents also believe that we do not have sufficient knowledge about effective teaching to allow for construction of valid tests—particularly of the paper-and-pencil variety—and that existing tests are biased against minority candidates whose background and experience do not provide equal or adequate preparation.

49 Ibid.; Wright, "Survey of Teacher Education," p. 5.

50 "Teacher Competency Assessment Expected in More States," *Teacher Education Reports* (March 15, 1984), pp. 4–6.

Proponents of basic skills testing generally counter that all or nearly all teachers must be able to demonstrate that they can function at least at the seventh- or eighth-grade level in reading, writing, and math—the minimum level currently specified on some of the tests—if they are to perform effectively in their jobs. Most proponents also argue that recent research has provided sufficient information about effective teaching to justify minimum standards in testing the professional knowledge of experienced as well as prospective teachers.

Argument for minimum test scores

As testing of teachers has become more frequent in the 1980s, issues involving equity for minority candidates who do not perform well on paper-and-pencil tests have risen to prominence. In Florida, only 37 of the black students completing teacher education programs passed that state's teacher candidacy exam in 1982 (compared to 84 percent of the candidate population as a whole), resulting in appointment of only about 200 black teachers among more than 5,000 new teachers employed in Florida that year.[51] In Louisiana, only 398 (29 percent) black teacher-certification candidates graduating from public institutions passed the National Teacher Examination between 1978 and 1982.[52] These kinds of data have led the executive director of the American Association of Colleges for Teacher Education to declare that "we deserve a teaching force that reflects the ethnic and racial composition of this country. . . . today we stand in danger of creating significant majority-minority imbalances ... [and] are on the verge of a major policy problem."[53]

Loss of minority candidates

Recommendations of National Reports

The mid-1980s saw a rash of reports and publications dealing with problems of education in the United States. These reports were prepared by various national commissions as well as individuals supported by philanthropic or government grants. Frequently referred to collectively as the "national reports," they are discussed in detail in Chapter 13.

A Nation at Risk, the best known and most influential of the national reports, was prepared by The National Commission on Excellence in Education sponsored by the U.S. Department of Education. Arguing that the U.S. is "at risk" in the sense that our "once unchallenged preeminence in commerce, industry, service, and technological innovation is being overtaken by competitors throughout the world," the commission concluded that one major cause of decline has been in a "rising tide of mediocrity" in the schools.[54] The commission pointed to a variety of risk indicators, such as a twenty-six-

National Commission on Excellence

51 Lucia Solorzano, "What's Wrong with Our Teachers," *U.S. News and World Report,* March 14, 1983, pp. 37–40.

52 Donald Kauchak, "Testing Teachers in Louisiana: A Closer Look," *Phi Delta Kappan* (May 1984), pp. 626–629.

53 David G. Imig, "Ferment and Momentum: Teacher Education and School Reform" (Paper delivered at Central Washington University, May 10, 1984), p. 12.

54 The National Commission on Excellence in Education, *A Nation At Risk: The Imperative for Educational Reform* (Washington, D.C.: U.S. Department of Education, 1983), p. 5.

year fall in SAT scores of students graduating from high school, a functional illiteracy rate as high as 40 percent among minority youth, and recent declines in science and math achievement—particularly among high achievers. Its recommendations centered on the following themes:[55]

***Recommendations in* A Nation at Risk**

Content of education. Increase high school graduation requirements in "Five New Basics": English, mathematics, science, social studies, and computer science.

Standards and expectations. Adopt higher expectations for student performance and conduct at the elementary, secondary, and postsecondary levels, and raise admission requirements at four-year colleges and universities.

Time. Devote more time to the new basics. Make more effective use of the existing school day, extend the school day, and/or lengthen the school year.

Teaching. Make teaching a more rewarding and respected profession. Set higher standards for entry into the profession; increase salaries so that they are "professionally competitive, market-sensitive, and performance-based," making them part of a system that gives greater rewards to superior teachers (in other words, institute merit pay); add an additional month of employment with pay for teachers; institute a "career ladder" that distinguishes between beginning, experienced, and master teachers; use incentives such as grants and loans to attract outstanding candidates into teaching, particularly into shortage areas such as science and mathematics; and involve master teachers in preparing and supervising probationary teachers.

Many educators believe that the *A Nation At Risk* and similar reports were generally too simplistic in their diagnoses and solutions.[56] Although some educators saw more a "rising tide of national reports" than a "rising tide of mediocrity," there is no doubt that these reports helped focus attention on and stimulate interest in the problems of education. Responding to growing public interest and support, virtually every governor proposed legislation based in part on the recommendations of the various national reports.

Major improvement efforts

One of the most publicized and comprehensive sets of proposals was in Tennessee, where Governor Lamar Alexander and the state legislature's committee on education had been working for several years to improve the quality of education. By January 1984, Governor Alexander and the committee had prepared a series of reforms, to be supported through a $351 million tax increase that included an across-the-board pay increase for all teachers, intensive staff development for new teachers, a probationary year before licensing,

55 Ibid., pp. 24–31. For documentation of achievement declines, see Archie E. LaPointe, "The Good News About American Education," *Phi Delta Kappan* (June 1984), pp. 663–668.

56 For examples, see the October 1983 issue of *Educational Leadership*. Also see Lawrence C. Stedman and Marshall S. Smith, "Recent Reform Proposals for American Education," *Contemporary Education Review* (Fall 1983), pp. 85–104.

a possible reduction in class size in elementary and secondary schools, and establishment of "centers of excellence" at selected colleges and universities. The plan also included career ladder arrangements to designate and offer greater rewards as teachers move through the ranks of "apprentice," "professional," "senior," and, finally, "master" teacher.[57]

Similarly, Governor Mark White took the lead in formulating legislation for statewide improvement in public schools in Texas. Signed into law on July 13, 1984, this legislation provided for an increase of $809 million over three years in state funding for public education and included provisions such as the limitation of elementary school class size to twenty-two students, the establishment of required prekindergarten classes for disadvantaged students, an increase in beginning teachers salaries, and the allocation of up to $6,000 each year for additional pay for experienced teachers.[58]

Need for some caution

No one set of recommendations in any of the national reports will be put fully into practice throughout the United States. Problems vary too much within states and from one state to another, views of influential individuals and organizations are too frequently at odds, and too many contradictory recommendations have been put forward to expect or allow for a single nationwide response. In some cases, recommendations from prestigious commissions probably should not be followed, or should be adopted only partially and with great caution. For example, the National Commission on Excellence apparently recommended that persons not certified as teachers should be hired and trained to fill positions in science, mathematics, or other shortage areas. It stated: "Qualified individuals, including recent graduates with mathematics and science degrees . . . and retired scientists could, with appropriate preparation, immediately begin teaching in these fields.[59] Several other national groups have offered similar but stronger statements. Although California, New Jersey, and several other states have moved to ease certification requirements in this way, many educators will work hard to resist such policies because they believe that short-cut licensing approaches of this kind nearly always are unwise.[60]

Merit pay and differential salaries

Several of the national reports have proposed that teachers be paid according to their students' achievement and that teachers in shortage areas such as science be paid more than other teachers. Although these proposals would attract candidates from business and industry, these types of merit pay and differential salary proposals probably will not be widely adopted—teacher organizations oppose them and they are difficult to design and implement equitably and productively. This topic is discussed at greater length in the next chapter.

Much of the content and many of the recommendations of recent na-

57 "Tennessee Teachers Agree to Gov. Alexander's Master Teacher Plan, with Modifications," *Education Times,* February 6, 1984, p. 1.

58 Georganne O'Conner, "Texas Governor Signs Sweeping Education Reforms Passed in Special Session of State Legislature," *Education Times,* July 16, 1984, pp. 1, 5.

59 National Commission on Excellence in Education, *A Nation At Risk,* p. 31.

60 Masland and Williams, "Teacher Surplus and Shortage," pp. 6–9.

tional reports on the quality of education focus on the problems and status of elementary and secondary teachers. Many of the reports address issues and trends described in this chapter: decline in commitment to teaching; dissatisfaction with job conditions, particularly as regards pay and promotion opportunities; decline in salary and occupational prestige; and the need to strengthen preparation programs in order to improve the skills of entering teachers. Delineating the implications of these reports, the Forum of Educational Organization Leaders summarized the most important changes that its member organizations will work to bring about:[61]

Recommendations to improve conditions for teachers

1. Enact a substantially higher base pay schedule for all teachers.
2. Establish a career ladder with differing roles and responsibilities for the beginning teacher, the experienced teacher, and the master teacher.
3. Through a variety of recruitment efforts, forgivable student loans, and year-round employment, attract future teachers from the highest-achieving 25 percent of college graduates.
4. Guarantee safe schools, with defined codes of discipline and orderly classrooms.
5. Provide financial incentives, such as quicker advancement on salary scales, to retain career teachers in the classroom and profession.

More specific recommendations were offered in 1984 by the National Education Association's Blue Ribbon Task Force on Educational Excellence. Addressing needs for improvement in teaching conditions, the task force recommended that teacher salaries increase to an average of $24,000, teacher training be improved, and new teachers not be hired unless they have satisfactorily completed a training program. The task force also argued strongly that average class size should be reduced and that teachers should be given more time to prepare for classes.[62]

Outlook for Teaching

Brighter prospects for teachers

In the 1970s, college students majoring in education were confronted with a buyer's market for teachers, and many wondered whether it was wise to enter a field that seemed to be declining in real salary, status, and general attractiveness. Now national attention has focused on education, and there is good news regarding teachers' prospects for the future. The pattern of teacher oversupply is likely to be reversed in the next ten years, and governments at all levels are initiating action to improve salary and other teaching conditions as well as teacher recruitment and preparation. Individuals dedi-

61 "Education Group Produces First Collective Response, *AACTE Briefs* (December 1983), pp. 5–9. The Forum of Educational Organization Leaders represents fourteen important national organizations, including the American Association of Colleges for Teacher Education, the American Association of School Administrators, the American Federation of Teachers, the Education Commission of the States, the National Education Association, the National Association of School Boards, and the Council of Chief State School Officers.

62 Blue Ribbon Task Force on Educational Excellence, *Letter to America on Schools, Students, and Schools* (Washington, D.C.: NEA, 1984).

cated to the task of helping children and young people learn and grow in the schools probably will face much brighter professional opportunities than has been true in the past decade.

Summing Up

1. Although there are many reasons for entering the teaching profession, research indicates that most people enter the profession to help young children and to provide a service to society.
2. Most teachers are satisfied with most aspects of their jobs, but there is significant dissatisfaction with salaries and other nonteaching considerations.
3. Although the prestige of the profession is well above average, the occupational status of teachers has probably declined over the past two decades.
4. Salary increases for teachers did not keep pace with rising prices during the 1970s, but teachers can probably anticipate an improved salary situation in the future.
5. There was a sharp drop in demand relative to supply of teachers in the 1970s. This situation has reversed, and there probably will be a shortage of teachers in the future.
6. The preservice preparation of teachers rests upon a threefold set of components: general education, specialized subject-matter education, and professional studies. Each of these interrelated areas is important for the proper education of teachers.
7. Requirements for teacher certification vary among states and institutions of higher learning.
8. In general, teacher education is becoming more practical and reality oriented. Trends in this direction include the establishment of school-based centers for preparing future teachers and provision of early field experience in elementary and secondary classrooms.
9. There is widespread national concern with the quality of the teaching workforce. Efforts to improve the quality of teachers include an emphasis on testing new and future teachers. The major national reports on education have expressed concern with teacher quality, and efforts are underway to improve salaries and other conditions of teaching.

Discussion Questions

1. Why are you thinking of becoming a teacher? Give some of your reasons. How do your reasons compare with those in the chapter?
2. What jobs other than teaching in elementary or secondary schools may be open to persons with a teaching certificate? What additional preparation would be needed to obtain such jobs?
3. What kinds of education courses should be required for teacher preparation?
4. Do you believe the trends in teacher education identified in this chapter are desirable? Why or why not?
5. What steps can be taken to improve teacher salaries?

Suggested Readings

Boyer, Ernest L. *High School.* New York: Harper & Row, 1983.

Much of the discussion involves the situation of teachers and the steps that should be taken to improve the quality and conditions of teaching.

Griffin, Gary A., ed. *Staff Development.* Chicago: University of Chicago Press, 1984.

Includes chapters describing and discussing the components and characteristics of effective staff development.

Herndon, Joseph. *The Way It Spozed to Be.* New York: Bantam, 1968.

This classic describes the satisfactions and difficulties of teaching in the inner city.

Journal of Teacher Education.

Regularly provides information and analysis regarding important issues in preservice and in-service education.

Joyce, Bruce R., Richard H. Hersh, and Michael McKibbin. *The Structure of School Improvement.* New York: Longman, 1983.

This book describes what staff development may become in the future, within the context of efforts to improve the quality of education.

2

The Teaching Profession

Focusing Questions

In what ways is teaching not fully a profession?

What trends show that teaching is becoming more of a full-fledged profession?

How does merit pay help (hinder) the teaching profession?

What are the essential differences between the NEA and the AFT? Can these differences be reconciled?

What are some other important professional organizations for teachers?

UNTIL THE TWENTIETH CENTURY, TEACHERS HAD RELATIVELY little preparation for their job and relatively little voice in determining the conditions of their employment. Teacher training consisted of one or two years and sometimes less at a normal school or teachers college, and teachers had to follow strict rules and regulations concerning their behavior outside the school. Unorganized and isolated from one another in small schools and school districts, teachers could be summarily dismissed by a board of education. Many were told they could not teach any material that someone in the community might find objectionable.

Times have changed. Today, teachers aspire to be professionals with expert knowledge concerning the content and methods of instruction in their particular fields. In addition, teachers are well organized as a group and have gained greater rights to be judged mainly on the basis of their performance rather than on the basis of their behavior outside the school and to participate in making decisions about the conditions in which they work. The first part of this chapter describes the ways in which teachers are striving for full professional status; the second discusses how teacher organizations have grown in power and prominence.

Is Teaching a Profession?

Characteristics of a profession

Whether teaching can be considered a profession in the fullest sense has been an issue of great concern to educators for many decades. A number of educators have tried to identify the ideal characteristics of professions and, by rating teachers on these, to determine whether teaching is a profession. Here is a list of the characteristics of a full **profession,** based on the works of noted authorities in the field.[1]

1. A sense of public service; a lifetime commitment to career
2. A defined body of knowledge and skills beyond that grasped by laypersons
3. Application of research and theory to practice (to human problems)
4. A lengthy period of specialized training
5. Control over licensing standards and/or entry requirements
6. Autonomy in making decisions about selected spheres of work
7. An acceptance of responsibility for judgments made and acts performed related to services rendered; a set of standards of performance
8. A commitment to work and client; an emphasis on service to be rendered

1 Ronald G. Corwin, *Sociology of Education* (New York: Appleton-Century-Crofts, 1965); Robert Havighurst and Daniel Levine, *Society and Education,* 5th ed., (Boston: Allyn and Bacon, 1979); and Robert B. Howsam et al., *Educating a Profession* (Washington, D.C.: American Association of Colleges for Teacher Education, 1976).

9. Use of administrators to facilitate work of professionals; relative freedom from detailed on-the-job supervision
10. A self-governing organization comprised of members of the profession
11. Professional associations and/or elite groups to provide recognition for individual achievements
12. A code of ethics to help clarify ambiguous matters or doubtful points related to services rendered
13. A high level of public trust and confidence in individual practitioners
14. High prestige and economic standing

The general consensus is that teaching is not a profession in the fullest sense: it does not possess some of the characteristics professions are supposed to possess. In some ways it may be viewed as a "semiprofession" or an "emerging profession" in the process of achieving these characteristics.

Viewed as a semiprofession

Teaching is a semiprofession, according to Amitai Etzioni, because "the training [of teachers] is shorter, their status less legitimated [low or moderate], their right to privileged communication less established; theirs is less of a specialized knowledge, and they have less autonomy from supervision or societal control than 'the professions.' . . ."[2] (Several sociologists contend that nursing and social work are also semiprofessions.)

Viewed as an emerging profession

Teaching should be viewed as an emerging profession, according to Robert Howsam, and thus is higher in status than a semiprofession, near the periphery of full professional status. In this connection, both emerging and full professionals are recognized in courts of law as competent to give expert professional testimony.[3] Considering that teaching is as old as ancient civilizations, however, and goes back to the colonial period in American history, it is hard to imagine that teaching is an *emerging* profession.

If readers are asked whether teaching is marked by the characteristics of a profession, some would probably answer yes, some no, and others would be ambivalent. The general conclusion would follow that at present teaching is partially but not entirely a full profession, although it is moving in the direction of becoming one. More important, probably *no* profession is marked by all the characteristics listed above.

Knowledge, control, autonomy, and prestige

Of the fourteen characteristics of a profession listed, perhaps the four most important are (1) a defined body of knowledge and skills beyond that grasped by laypersons, (2) control over licensing standards and/or entry requirements, (3) autonomy in making decisions about selected spheres of work, and (4) high prestige and economic standing. The following discussion of these characteristics clearly indicates that the teaching profession does not possess them all. Although no profession has achieved the ideal state, teaching seems to lag behind some others, such as law and medicine.

2 Amitai Etzioni, *The Semiprofessions and Their Organizations: Teachers, Nurses, and Social Workers* (New York: Free Press, 1969), p. v.

3 Howsam et al., *Educating a Profession.*

A Defined Body of Knowledge

All professions have a monopoly on certain knowledge that separates their members from the general public and allows them to exercise control over the vocation. Members of a profession have mastered a body of knowledge that establishes their expertise and protects the public from quacks, untrained amateurs, and special-interest groups. There is, however, no agreed-upon specialized body of knowledge that is "education" or "teaching." Whereas the behavioral sciences, physical sciences, and health fields can be guided by extensive rules of procedure and established methodologies, education lacks a well-defined body of knowledge that is applicable to the real world of teaching[4] and that has been validated and agreed upon by most authorities.[5]

No agreed-upon knowledge

As a result, too many people, especially the lay public, talk about education as if they were experts—resulting in a great deal of conflicting and sometimes negative conversation. Another result of this ill-defined body of knowledge is that the content of teacher education courses varies from state to state and among teacher training institutions within states.

Moreover, it is estimated that many teachers working in the secondary schools are teaching out of license; in other words, teachers of English did not major in English in college, nor are they certified to teach English. This problem is especially acute in the areas of science and mathematics although it has declined with the recent surplus of teachers.

Teaching out of license

Whether teachers possess a defined body of knowledge is also determined by training standards. Despite state regulations requiring a certain number of education courses, minimum requirements and content vary among states. As late as 1946 only fifteen states required a bachelor's degree for elementary teachers; in 1976 only three states required that its teachers hold a master's degree.[6] In 1984 as many as 40 percent of the 1,200 colleges involved in training teachers were not accredited by the national accrediting agency.[7]

Nonaccredited training institutions

To develop and gain acknowledgment of a specialized body of knowledge and to upgrade weak teacher training institutions, teachers must acquire decision-making influence. Teacher organizations have the potential power and leadership to work with interested parties, such as teacher training colleges and school districts, to develop exemplary models. Teacher training institutions that do not cooperate might not be allowed to send their student teachers to work in nearby school systems, and their graduates might not be licensed to teach in the schools.

4 Dan C. Lortie, *Schoolteacher: A Sociological Study* (Chicago: University of Chicago Press, 1975); B. O. Smith, *A Design for a School Pedagogy* (Washington, D.C.: Government Printing Office, 1980).

5 Henrick D. Gideonse, "The Necessary Revolution in Teacher Education," *Phi Delta Kappan* (September 1982), pp. 15–18; Paul Woodring, *The Persistent Problems of Education* (Bloomington, Ind.: Phi Delta Kappa, 1983).

6 Corwin, *Sociology of Education;* Allan C. Ornstein, "Characteristics of a Profession," *Illinois School Journal* (Winter 1976–77), pp. 12–21.

7 *30th Annual List of Accredited Programs, 1983–84* (National Council for Accreditation of Teacher Education, 1984); Telephone conversation with Gloria Cheray, Assistant Director of the National Council for Accreditation of Teacher Evaluation, April 6, 1984.

Control over Requirements for Entry and Licensing

No minimum competencies

Whereas most professions have uniform standards and requirements to ensure minimum competencies, this is not the case in the teaching profession. The problem concerns both the types of individuals who enter teacher education programs and the skills held by those who emerge from the programs and are certified to teach.

As mentioned in Chapter 1, students who enter teacher training programs have lower aptitude scores than students in most other fields and there are no widely accepted tests used to determine whether the graduate of a teacher training program is adequately prepared to be a teacher. Not only is there wide variation in the certification requirements for teaching in various states; in several states new standards, which were intended to eliminate teacher shortages in selected subject areas or to upgrade the quality of new teachers, have replaced long-established certification procedures. California, New Jersey, and Virginia, for example, are assigning instructional duties on an experimental basis to people who have earned college degrees in subjects but have not taken the education courses prerequisite for a teaching license. New teachers who have not taken education courses can receive on-the-job pedagogical training, which will eventually qualify them for certification. Other states, such as Michigan and West Virginia, are exploring ways to utilize retirees or industrial personnel as part-time teachers to alleviate shortages in mathematics, science, and computer instruction.[8]

Noncertified teachers

Whatever they may think about these differing requirements, teachers do not have much say on these matters. The outcome is that teacher mobility is limited from state to state by the different licensing procedures. Most people, including teachers themselves, reject teacher regulation of licensing requirements because teachers are publicly employed. From an educator's point of view, however, professional autonomy would be enhanced if teachers could establish licensing laws or if certification standards were functionally recognized by states. It is in the public interest to place some control of professional standards and requirements in the hands of educators rather than to continue to leave such decisions entirely to laypersons who know little about teaching.

Different licensing procedures

Autonomy in Deciding About Spheres of Work

In a profession every member of the group, but not outsiders, is assumed to be qualified to make professional judgments on the nature of the work involved. Professionals usually establish laws of exclusive jurisdiction in a given area of competence; custom and tradition are relied on to maintain effective control over matters relating to work and dealing with clients. Indeed, lay control is considered the natural enemy of professions; it limits the power of the professional and opens the door to outside interference.

Lay control vs. professional control

8 Jim Gallagher, "On the Job Teacher Training Makes Grade," *Chicago Tribune,* December 25, 1983, Sect. 1, p. 4.

Teachers accept the assumption that local and state officials have the right to decide on the subjects, instructional materials, and books to be used. While they sometimes doubt the wisdom of the community in exercising such rights, the legitimacy of these rights is rarely questioned. At best, teachers are permitted minimal input in curriculum decisions, and they are vulnerable when they seek to introduce textbooks or discuss topics considered controversial by pressure groups. Taxpayers are said to "reasonably" claim a share in decision making, since they foot the bill and provide the clients.

Guarding against client interference

The physician and lawyer also provide services that their clients pay for, yet no one expects the client or the public to prescribe drugs or write the clauses in a contract. When the client interferes with the decisions of the practicing physician or lawyer, the professional-client relationship ends. This protects clients from being victimized by their own lack of knowledge, while it safeguards the professional from the unreasonable judgments of the lay public. Peter Blau and W. Richard Scott observe that "professional service . . . requires that the [professional] maintain independence of judgment and not permit the clients' *wishes* as distinguished from their *interests* to influence his decisions." The professional has the knowledge and expertise to make judgments, "and the client is not qualified to evaluate the services he needs." Professionals who permit their clients to tell them what to do "fail to provide optimum service."[9]

Teacher accountability

Teachers, on the other hand, can be told what to do by parents and other citizens, principals, superintendents, and school board members, even in opposition to the teachers' professional judgments. Although collective bargaining has resulted in new arrangements between teachers and administrators, most people still believe that teachers are public servants and are therefore accountable to the people and to the school officials who are hired, elected, or appointed by the people. While it is true teachers must not lose sight of the welfare of their clients or ignore those who are in the position to make decisions for the public, they should not completely surrender the power to determine the nature of the service they render.

State governing boards

Professional autonomy does not imply the total absence of any control over professionals. On the contrary, it means that controls requiring technical competencies are exercised by people who possess such competencies; it calls for the development of controls related to the work of members of the profession. This can be enhanced by initiating collective negotiations that define areas in which teachers can make use of their experiences and competencies, by increasing teacher representation on school boards at the local level and teaching licensing and governing boards at the state level, and by helping to elect political candidates who are pro-teacher and pro-education.[10]

9 Peter Blau and W. Richard Scott, *Formal Organizations* (San Francisco: Chandler, 1965), pp. 51–52.

10 James Browne, "Power Politics for Teachers, Modern Style," *Phi Delta Kappan* (October 1980), pp. 158–64; Leonard L. Gregory, "Unintended Consequences of Public School Negotiations, *School Business Affairs* (January 1979), pp. 26–27; and Susan M. Johnson, "Teacher Unions in Schools," *Harvard Educational Review* (August 1983), pp. 309–326.

High Prestige and Economic Standing

As pointed out in Chapter 1, teachers have registered major gains in salary and status during the past fifty-five years. Although teachers' salaries since 1930 have increased more than those of the average worker in industry, teacher pay remains lower than that of the average college graduate.[11] In addition, teachers still earn far less than lawyers, business executives, and some other professionals with similar levels of formal education. Of course, there is no realistic salary comparison between teachers with a master's or doctor's degree and physicians, lawyers, dentists, or top business executives. Although levels of formal education are nearly similar, earnings of the latter group approach $100,000 per year, with some earning as much as $500,000; these groups also have traditionally high occupational ratings.

Lower salaries than other college graduates

The fact is that while the prestige and income standards of teachers have risen relative to their past station, they have risen only slightly more than those of the average worker and have declined in comparison to other professions and groups that have similar levels of education. The ***status-consistency hypothesis*** holds that a group tends to compare its achievements (prestige and salary) with other groups and strives to bring its rewards up to a level with people who have similar jobs, even similar years of education.[12] If this is true, we can expect teachers to make comparisons with other professional groups, to remain dissatisfied, and to express this dissatisfaction through militancy; in fact, this has been one of the major reasons for teacher militancy since the mid-1960s.

Dissatisfaction among teachers

Overall, one can conclude that while the status of the teacher has improved, teachers' income and prestige still lag far behind those of many professions. Teaching is still not fully a profession in terms of its economic standing and occupational prestige.

Trends Toward Professionalism

Although teaching probably should not be considered a fully professionalized occupation, its status has been improving. Collective bargaining can enhance teachers' capacity to make decisions about their work in the classroom. In addition, several other major aspects of a long-range trend toward the professionalization of teaching are apparent.

The Scope of Collective Bargaining

By 1980, teachers had won the right to have their representatives formally bargain with their employers in most of the United States. The extent and nature of **collective bargaining** varied from negotiations conducted in the

11 Victor R. Lindquist and Frank S. Endicott, *Employment Trends for College Graduates,* Thirty-Eighth Annual Survey (Evanston, Ill.: Northwestern University, 1984).

12 Ronald G. Corwin, *Militant Professionalism: A Study of Militant Conflict in High Schools* (New York: Appleton-Century-Crofts, 1970).

absence of a law allowing or forbidding it to full-scale contract bargaining backed by the right to strike. Knowledgeable observers feel that further development of teachers' collective bargaining power will depend partly on congressional action to extend bargaining rights to all public employees. There is considerable uncertainty, however, regarding the position of teacher organizations on specific proposals for federal legislation, the willingness of Congress to pass additional legislation, and constitutional limitations concerning its power to extend bargaining rights to state employees.[13]

Congressional action to extend bargaining rights

In some ways collective bargaining may be considered a nonprofessional or even an antiprofessional activity. In the law, medicine, or the ministry, for example, few professionals work in organizations in which terms of employment are determined by collective bargaining. From another point of view, however, collective bargaining can significantly enhance professionalization of teaching by giving teachers greater authority to determine the conditions of their work and their effectiveness as teachers. The trend in collective bargaining has been to include a growing number of concerns other than the fundamental salary issue. Collective bargaining in the 1980s is often concerned with educational problems and issues, such as class size, grouping of students in classes, instructional materials, testing, classroom discipline and management, teacher-supervisory relations, and community relations.[14]

Collective bargaining as a movement in education now seems to be an integral part of teacher unionism and teacher militancy. Educators on both sides of the negotiating table have gained maturity and experience during this new era in school board–administration–teacher relationships. It is believed that when key players participate intelligently and with legal and professional skill, collective bargaining can resolve conflicts between school boards and teachers; enhance the role, status, and working conditions of teachers; and establish new, positive, and more equitable relationships among various education groups—thereby improving the teaching profession.

Resolving conflicts

Professional Practice Commissions

It is not likely that educators will be given complete autonomy in setting standards for professional practice, but teachers have been gaining a greater role in setting professional standards than they formerly had. Thirty-four states have developed teacher standards and practice commissions, among them Alaska, South Dakota, and Utah, in which teachers compose a majority of the commission members and set standards for the preparation of teachers and maintenance of minimal competence in professional practice. These commissions have even placed a few teachers on probation, suspended certificates, and reprimanded teachers for unprofessional or illegal behavior.

Setting professional standards

13 Richard Wynn, *Collective Bargaining* (Bloomington, Ind.: Phi Delta Kappa, 1983); Telephone conversation with Donald Walker, Collective Bargaining Department, NEA, February 13, 1984.

14 Marc Gaswirth and Garry Whalen, *Collective Negotiations* (Trenton: New Jersey School Boards Association, 1983); Stephen J. Knezevich, *Administration of Public Education,* 4th ed. (New York: Harper & Row, 1984).

These powers will probably be used more frequently in the future, and educators will thus begin doing what they long have said they wanted to do: clean their own house and weed out those who do not meet minimal professional standards—and secure governance of the profession.[15]

Teacher Centers

Another way in which teachers are achieving greater professional status by exercising more control over their own affairs involves the important area of staff development. To stay up to date in their preparation and to acquire new classroom skills, teachers have traditionally participated in various kinds of in-service training. Most of this training has been provided on college campuses, frequently to meet school district requirements for additional college credit for continuing certification. Many observers have viewed this kind of in-service training as a "cafeteria of courses and workshops" with no relationship "to job roles and student needs."[16]

Partially governed by teachers

In the past few years, however, a growing percentage of teachers' in-service training opportunities have been provided by **teacher centers** that are governed partly by teachers themselves. They are intended to make staff development more relevant to teachers' actual training needs and more useful in terms of applicability in the classroom. As used here, the teacher center refers to an in-service training center; it does not focus on preservice training. This movement to establish teacher centers may represent a significant advance toward teachers' participation in making decisions that have important implications for their professional performance.

Teacher centers have existed for years in the form of exchange centers where teachers can obtain ideas about new instructional practices and talk with colleagues about how to apply appropriate methods in their classrooms. Centers of this kind have provided valuable services to teachers but have been dependent on unstable financing and generally have not been able to undertake systematic efforts aimed at improving instructional practice in the schools. Partly for this reason, and partly because many teachers and administrators have felt that colleges and universities have not provided preservice and in-service training adequate to cope with the challenge in contemporary classrooms, teacher centers have spread to many parts of the country—totaling more than two hundred different centers.[17]

Both the National Education Association (NEA) and the American Federation of Teachers (AFT) support the establishment and expansion of the teacher center program, with teachers having a major and sometimes predominant voice in their operation. Once established, a teacher center is sup-

15 *Standards and Certification Bodies in the Teaching Profession* (Washington, D.C.: NEA, 1983).

16 Arnold M. Gallegos, "Politics and Realities of Staff Development," *Educational Leadership* (January–February 1980), p. 21; Bruce Joyce, "The Ecology of Staff Development" (Paper presented at the Annual Meeting of the American Educational Research Association, Boston, April 1980).

17 Roy A. Edelfelt, "Critical Issues in Developing Teacher Centers," *Phi Delta Kappan* (February 1982), pp. 390–394; Sally Mertens, "Teacher Centers: Support for Professional Practice," *Journal of Teacher Education* (March–April 1982), pp. 7–12.

In-service training centers like the one at which these elementary school teachers are conducting a scientific experiment are an important aspect of the growing professionalism of teachers.
(Bob Kalman/The Image Works, Inc.)

Local in-service needs

posed to function and evolve in accordance with local in-service needs. Some of the centers serve a single school district, others serve a region or an entire state.

For example, the Kohl Teacher Center in Wilmette, Illinois, has been in operation for more than ten years, is privately funded, annually serves nearly 50 school districts, 800 schools, and 15,000 to 20,000 teachers in Illinois, Wisconsin, and Indiana. It offers a wide variety of services, including recertification courses, graduate level courses for college credit, educational conferences and workshops; it sponsors summer trips for educators, small grants for instructional projects, and awards for excellence in teaching. The New York City Teacher Center, by way of contrast, not only includes the entire city, but in so doing serves teachers who work with approximately 950,000 public school students and a third of a million private school students. Governed by a twenty-five-member policy board that represents the teachers' union, board of education members, the supervisors' council, the United Parents Association and other community groups, and the deans of education from the City University, the New York City Teacher Center coordinates the work of nearly thirty higher education institutions in attempting to provide practical in-service training for area teachers.[18]

Funding teacher centers

Although most of the funds for teacher centers came from the federal government in the 1970s, we can expect the bulk, if not all, of the funding to be based on state and local monies for the remainder of the 1980s. Most of this funding will be derived from staff development funds, a common term now used by school administrators and teacher educators promoting in-service needs of teachers.

Mediated Entry

Supervised stages of assistance

Mediated entry refers to the practice of inducting persons into a profession through carefully supervised stages that help them learn how to apply professional knowledge successfully in a concrete situation. One good example is in the profession of medicine, in which aspiring physicians serve one or more years as an intern and then as a resident before being considered a full-fledged professional.

Trial and error in the classroom

Dan Lortie has studied the teacher's job from a sociological perspective and concluded that in terms of sequenced professional entry, teaching ranks in between occupations characterized by "casual" entry and those that place protracted and difficult demands on would-be members.[19] The lack of more carefully mediated entry has profound consequences, because it means that there is relatively little chance to include empirically derived and rigorously grounded principles and practices of pedagogy. Teachers too frequently report that their main teacher has been experience, and that they learned to teach through trial and error in the classroom. They also report that the beginning years of teaching can be "a period of anxiety and fear, even of trauma."[20] But, then, the beginning period of almost any occupation or profession has its problems and anxieties.

Although efforts have been made to provide for more effective induction of new teachers into the profession, in general past efforts have not been

18 Telephone conversation with Myra Cooper, Director of the New York City Teacher Center, January 9, 1984; Leon Intrater, Associate Director of the Kohl Teacher Center, Wilmette, Illinois, January 9, 1984.

19 Lortie, *Schoolteacher.*

20 Frederick J. McDonald and Patricia Elias, "The Transition into Teaching: The Problems of Beginning Teachers and Programs to Solve Them" (Paper prepared for the Educational Testing Service, Berkeley, Calif., 1983), pp. 4–5.

either widespread or systematic enough to ensure their success in practice. Most school districts, for example, now require a probationary period for new teachers, but in too many cases relatively little concrete assistance is provided to help those teachers develop and refine the skills needed for effective performance. Many school districts and a few states require a fifth year of preparation beyond the traditional bachelor's degree and initial certificate, but too often this requirement is implemented in a way that allows new teachers to take a few more courses that may or may not help them improve professionally.[21] As a rule, most new teachers are still largely on their own in their first professional position.

Induction period

The teaching profession now recognizes the need to develop a period of induction and transition into teaching. The concept of mediated entry is supported by many school district officials, who no longer feel they must immediately accept and put new teachers to work as was done during the teacher shortage of the 1960s and early 1970s. With many applicants vying for a limited number of teaching jobs, school officials can make probationary requirements stronger and more meaningful than they were in the recent past.

The trend toward more carefully mediated entry will probably continue—at least as long as the current oversupply of teachers continues; moreover, mediated entry is supported by the NEA and AFT and several teacher education groups. Most important, the notion of mediated entry would focus on the school as the workplace as well as the training place for beginning teachers; like teacher centers, it would address the practical nature of teaching, involve experienced teachers in training beginning teachers, establish closer ties between teacher educators and school people, and insure greater control by the profession over teacher training.

Closer ties between professors and teachers

Merit Pay

Salaries tied to performance

Real changes in teacher remuneration are in the offing. Many recent task force reports on education—including *A Nation At Risk,* the report by the Commission on Excellence in Education—are calling for higher teacher salaries based on performance. President Reagan, borrowing from the principles of productivity of free enterprise, has proposed on several occasions that we identify "master teachers" and pay them higher salaries. A growing number of school boards have taken the position that **merit pay** (a supplement to a teacher's base salary to reward superior performance) is a cost-effective method of motivating teachers and encouraging excellence in teaching.

Both the NEA and AFT have reservations about merit pay plans, although the AFT is willing to entertain incentive proposals as long as there are sufficient safeguards in the evaluation procedures and so long as monetary

21 G. Thomas Fox, "Challenging How Teachers Are Educated: A Source for Dialogue and Action" (Paper published by the ERIC Clearinghouse on Teacher Education, February 1983).

awards do not compete with salaries or pay hikes for all teachers.[22] Where master teachers or merit plans have been tried, both organizations contend that teachers did not agree with administrators on the teachers selected for preferential pay. The NEA and AFT question whether objective performance standards can be implemented, and both fear that merit pay will lead to politics and patronage rather than improved pedagogy.[23]

Politics, patronage, and pedagogy

The concern is that the process will further the aims of the school administration rather than the educational aims of the school. Both organizations feel that "good" teachers who submit required paperwork a little late or who criticize or have different views than the administration or school board will be penalized; "average" or "poor" teachers who comply with bureaucratic mandates, or who consider themselves discriminated against and threaten to litigate, will be rewarded. Finally, both organizations are afraid the effort to reward a few teachers will take place at the expense of the remaining teachers and that merit pay will threaten the unity of teachers and the collegiality among educators. They maintain that the effort should be to increase all teachers' salaries—not just a few and not to pit teachers against each other.[24]

Conflict among teachers

Milton Friedman, the well-known economist who believes in a competitive market, interestingly rejects the idea of merit pay for teachers.[25] He argues that merit pay would work only in a truly competitive marketplace, one in which consumers had a variety of genuine choices. There is little competition and diversity among public schools today. Consumers have little to say about where they can send their children. If there were more private schools or alternative schools, there would be more incentive to meet the needs of customers and merit pay would be a realistic proposal. Productive teachers would be in demand, and schools would vie for them.

Consumer input

Regardless of all these practical and theoretical reservations, the *idea* of merit pay—and its various derivatives—is spreading to many school districts and even entire states. The states of Illinois, New York, and Ohio are considering state-funded pay incentives. Tennessee, North Carolina, and Virginia have introduced the career ladder as a means of rewarding teachers and increasing their responsibilities. It is viewed by some as an alternative to (and by others as an extension of) merit pay. The **career ladder** combines rewards for good teaching with improved in-service education for all teachers.[26] Both the AFT and NEA support career ladders for teachers, and it is

Merit plans spread

Career ladders

22 "The Teaching Profession: Taking A New Look," *Annual Report of the American Federation of Teachers, 1982–83* (Washington, D.C.: AFT, 1983), p. 22.

23 "Merit Pay for Teachers: Worth Another Try," *American School Board Journal* (May 1983), pp. 8, 13; Nancey R. Needham, "Descheduling Teacher Salaries," *Today's Education* (1982–83), pp. 103–107.

24 Ibid. Also see Robert S. Soar and Ruth M. Soar, "Teacher Merit Pay: Can Research Help?" *Journal of Human Behavior and Learning* (no. 1, 1984), pp. 3–13.

25 Milton Friedman, "Busting the Monopoly," *Newsweek,* December 5, 1983, p. 96.

26 Chris Pipho, "An End to the State Revolt—Maybe," *Phi Delta Kappan* (January 1984), pp. 309–310.

likely that other states will move in this direction, also. Meanwhile, in Alaska, the idea of merit pay is being considered for schools, not teachers. Entire schools could be rewarded for outstanding team efforts, and the morale of the teaching staff would not be damaged as it might be if a few teachers in each building were singled out for extra pay.

Incentive plan

Then, there is the Houston school district incentive plan, begun in 1979 and well known because of the district's size and visibility. Six categories qualify for incentive pay: (1) service in a high-priority school; (2) teaching a special subject where staff shortages exist; (3) teacher attendance that exceeds minimum requirements; (4) professional growth or in-service training appropriate to one's current teaching assignment or in an area where critical shortages exist; (5) service in a school where the average academic gain of students, as measured by standardized tests, is greater than statistical predictions; and (6) service at a unique or experimental school site.[27]

It is important to note that the categories for merit are for the most part based on objective criteria, not subjective evaluations. During the first year, two-thirds of all Houston teachers collected stipends totaling some $11 million. The average stipend was $936; the range was $300 to $3,500. School officials claim that (1) standardized test scores in the district have improved for three consecutive years, since the plan began; (2) teacher absenteeism (a costly item for most big-city school districts) and teacher turnover have dropped, especially in inner-city schools; (3) teacher shortages in areas like science, mathematics, special education, and bilingual education have been reduced sharply; and (4) teacher morale has increased.[28]

Increased teacher morale

The teaching profession can benefit from merit pay in terms of money and prestige so long as certain guidelines or principles are followed: (1) teachers must be evaluated objectively on clear and agreed-upon standards; (2) teacher raters, those who evaluate teachers, must receive training in the use of objective measures; (3) teachers must be afforded appeal procedures, but those procedures cannot be time consuming; (4) teachers should receive assistance to meet the standards for merit; (5) public disclosure of merit awards should be minimized, since it often humiliates nonrecipients before students, parents, and colleagues; and (6) the expense of incentive pay should not be offset by lowered annual salaries.[29]

Right to appeal

In general, the administration, school board, public, and teachers must be willing to accept the fact that teaching is a position of professional importance. To accept this assumption means to believe that school administrators (and teachers themselves) can make competent judgments about the worth of teaching and the individual performance of teachers; it means that if we replace traditional pay scales, based on experience and education, with some

27 John Dahl, "America's New Bonus Babies: Teachers," *New York Times,* Educational Survey, sect. 12, January 8, 1984, p. 23; Elaine Say and Leslie Miller, "The Second Mile Plan: Incentive Pay for Houston Teachers," *Phi Delta Kappan* (December 1982), pp. 270–271.

28 Ibid.

29 Larry W. Barber and Karen Klein, "Merit Pay and Teacher Evaluation," *Phi Delta Kappan* (December 1983), pp. 247–251; Brian Burke, "Merit Pay for Teachers," *Phi Delta Kappan* (December 1982), pp. 265–266; and Soar and Soar, "Teacher Merit Pay: Can Research Help?"

$50,000 teacher salaries

form of merit plan, master teachers might have the opportunity to earn $50,000 or more by the late 1980s.

The fact that teacher salaries have been capped historically at a low figure, and that we have avoided making distinctions based on performance, has hurt the profession. Granted there are risks in merit pay plans, but there are risks in any endeavor. By raising the lid on teaching salaries and by making distinctions based on merit, we will improve the teaching profession; subsequently, we will raise the prestige of teachers, attract brighter students into the profession, and keep good teachers from leaving classrooms for more competitive salaries in other fields.

Teacher Organizations

Restrictions on teachers

A critical factor in the development of teaching as a profession has been the growth of professional organizations for teachers. Although today's working conditions still need to be improved, they sharply contrast with the restrictions teachers once endured. Here are the details of what is reputed to be a Wisconsin teacher's contract for 1922, calling for a salary of $75 a month.

> Miss ______ agrees:
> 1. Not to get married. This contract becomes null and void immediately if the teacher marries.
> 2. Not to keep company with men.
> 3. To be home between the hours of 8 P.M. and 6 A.M. unless in attendance at a school function.
> 4. Not to loiter downtown in ice-cream parlors.
> 5. Not to leave town at any time without the permission of the chairman of the Trustees.
> 6. Not to smoke cigarettes.
> 7. Not to drink beer, wine, or whiskey.
> 8. Not to ride in a carriage or automobile with any man except her brother or father.
> 9. Not to dress in bright colors.
> 10. Not to dye her hair.
> 11. Not to wear less than two petticoats.
> 12. Not to wear dresses shorter than two inches above the ankles.
> 13. To keep the schoolroom clean:
>   a. To sweep the classroom floor at least once daily.
>   b. To scrub the classroom floor at least once weekly.
>   c. To clean the blackboard at least once daily.
>   d. To start the fire at 7 A.M. so that the room will be warm at 8 A.M. when the children arrive.
> 14. Not to wear face powder, mascara or to paint the lips.[30]

Consider these requirements in the context of the times: the status of women, the image of teachers, and what Small Town, U.S.A. was like. Those

30 *Chicago Tribune*, September 28, 1975, sect. 1, p. 3.

were the days of the Model T Ford, the protest marches of suffragettes, the growing pains of labor, the "muckrakers," and Sinclair Lewis's *Main Street* and *Babbitt.*

NEA and AFT are rivals

Obviously, the conditions described above no longer exist, and to a large extent the growth of teacher organizations and teacher militancy have played a role in improving the conditions of teaching. In this endeavor, the National Education Association and the American Federation of Teachers are the two most important organizations. These two organizations usually are considered rivals, competing for members, recognition, and power. Although some educators believe that perpetuation of this division is a healthy form of professional competition, others view it as detrimental to the teaching profession—a splitting of power and a waste of resources.

National Education Association (NEA)

1.7 million members

The National Education Association, which was founded in 1857 by forty-three educators, is a complex, multifaceted organization involved in many areas of education on local, state, and national levels. The NEA, unlike the AFT, includes both teachers and administrators. As shown in Table 2.1, membership grew tenfold from 1900 to 1920 and another tenfold by 1940. Membership totaled 450,000 in 1950 and nearly 1.7 million in 1984.[31]

Since 1980 membership has leveled off, primarily because of the minimal change in the total supply of teachers. Among the members in 1984 approximately 25,000 were students, 40,000 were retired members, 50,000 were auxiliary staff (school secretaries, teacher aides, cafeteria workers, bus drivers, and custodians), 55,000 were college professors, 200,000 were professional support staff (guidance counselors, librarians, and administrators), and nearly 1.3 million were classroom teachers.[32] This figure comprises more than half of the nation's 2.4 million teachers. By 1990, membership is expected to increase slightly because there should be a small rise in the supply of teachers.

Suburban and rural members

4,000 members in every congressional district

Disproportionately suburban and rural, the membership is served by a large network of affiliates in every state, Puerto Rico, and the District of Columbia and by an Overseas Educational Association. There are more than 7,000 local affiliate groups. In sheer numbers, the NEA represents the second largest lobbying force in the country, outnumbering all other public employee organizations. Among unions it trails only the Teamsters. Its combined annual budget is over $350 million, and it averages about 4,000 members in every congressional district. The state affiliates are usually among the most influential education lobbies at the state level.[33]

31 *NEA Handbook, 1983–84* (Washington, D.C.: National Education Association, 1984), table 1, p. 134; Telephone conversation with Simeon Taylor, Department of Membership, NEA, April 12, 1984.

32 Ibid.

33 Anthony M. Cresswell and Michael J. Murphy, *Teachers, Unions, and Collective Bargaining* (Berkeley, Calif.: McCutchan, 1980); Allan C. Ornstein and Harry L. Miller, *Looking into Teaching* (Chicago: Rand McNally, 1980); "Your NEA," *Today's Education* (1983–84), pp. 78–79.

Table 2.1
Membership of the NEA and AFT by Decades

Year	NEA Membership	AFT Membership
1857[a]	43	
1870	170	
1880	354	
1890	5,474	
1900	2,322	
1910	6,909	
1916[a]		1,500
1920	22,850	10,000
1930	216,188	7,000
1940	203,429	30,000
1950	453,797	41,000
1960	713,994	59,000
1970	1,100,000	205,000
1980	1,650,000	550,000
1985[b]	1,700,000	600,000
1990[b]	1,800,000	700,000

[a]Year organization was founded.
[b]Estimated membership.

Source: "AFT Membership Growing Again," *Annual Report of the American Federation of Teachers, 1982–83* (Washington, D.C.: AFT, 1983), p. 43; Allan C. Ornstein, *Education and Social Inquiry* (Itasca, Ill.: Peacock, 1978), pp. 311, 329; and "Your NEA," *Today's Education* (1983–84), pp. 78–79.

The Representative Assembly, consisting of some 7,240 delegates who are elected by members in state and local affiliates, meets annually to set NEA policy. The board of directors, consisting of 116 directors, and the executive committee (consisting of the NEA president, vice president, secretary-treasurer, and six other members), are both elected by the Representative Assembly and act for the NEA between assembly meetings.[34]

Today's Education

A wide range of professional services is offered by the NEA. The Research Division, organized in 1922, conducts annual research studies on the status of the profession; it also publishes the *NEA Research Bulletin* and several research memos and opinion surveys on an annual basis. The major publication of the NEA is *Today's Education,* now an annual publication, with a supplementary monthly newspaper. In addition, the national councils for the various subjects—mathematics, science, social studies, modern language, speech, home economics, business education, art, and so on—also publish professional journals. (These councils are loosely affiliated with the NEA.) Most of the fifty state affiliates publish a monthly magazine as well.

34 *NEA Handbook, 1983–84.*

American Federation of Teachers (AFT)

The AFT was formed in 1916. It is affiliated with the AFL-CIO and is open to classroom teachers only. Membership in 1984 was 590,000, organized in some 2,200 locals in large and medium-sized cities. As shown in Table 2.1, membership limped along in the 1920s and 1930s as a result of antilabor sentiments and a feeling in some quarters that labor organizations were led by radicals. Most of the AFT membership increase has taken place within the last twenty-five years. Among its 590,000 members in 1984 were some 25,000 paraprofessionals, 60,000 municipal workers and nurses who are not teachers, 75,000 college professors, and 430,000 teachers.[35] By 1990, the AFT membership is expected to reach 700,000, with most of the increase coming from the ranks of classroom teachers, college professors, and municipal workers.

590,000 members

The national governing body of the AFT is the Annual Convention, representing local affiliates according to a proportional formula. The Executive Council (consisting of the AFT president and thirty-four vice presidents) assumes the leadership between the annual conventions. Unlike the NEA affiliates, the AFT locals tend to be militant in philosophy and more eager to bargain collectively over economic matters and working conditions, although the NEA state affiliates have become more aggressive since 1968.

The AFT has not, in the past, been involved with research and publication to the extent of the NEA, but the union does publish a professional magazine, *Changing Education,* a *Consortium Yearbook,* and a monthly newspaper, *American Teacher.* In addition, the local affiliates put out a monthly newsletter. Unlike the NEA, the AFT members have always been required to join the local, state (twenty-two in all), and national organizations simultaneously. Only recently has the NEA encouraged unitary membership. The NEA dues policy emphasizes local support, whereas the AFT channels a large portion of local funds to the national level. Most contracts negotiated with schools by an AFT local affiliate require an automatic dues deduction and agency fee (whether or not the teachers belong to the union). Only a few local NEA contracts insist on this provision, although one might expect a move in this direction because of the obvious advantages to the organization.

American Teacher

Automatic dues deduction

The AFT remained quite small until criticism of the schools mounted at the end of the 1950s. The membership breakthrough came when AFT leaders decided to concentrate on the New York City school system. In 1961 the union group defeated the organization supporting the NEA, and the United Federation of Teachers (UFT) was chosen to represent New York City teachers. Following its victory, the UFT engaged in a number of strikes in New York City over the next decade—for improved working conditions, salary increases, health benefits, pensions, and teacher rights. Success in New York

35 *Annual Report of the American Federation of Teachers, 1983–84* (Washington, D.C.: AFT, 1984; telephone conversation with Robert Porter, Secretary-Treasurer, American Federation of Teachers, April 16, 1984.

City led to a series of victories over the NEA in several other large cities for the right to represent teachers. The AFT became the dominant teacher organization in many large urban centers where unions have traditionally flourished, where militant tactics such as collective bargaining and strikes have been common, and where teachers in general perceived a need for a powerful organization to represent them. In rural and suburban areas, where union tactics have typically received less support, the NEA remains dominant.

Strength in urban areas

Past Differences Between the NEA and AFT

Without question there has been intense organizational rivalry between the NEA and the AFT for years. These two organizations have competed for members and for exclusive local rights to represent teachers. The NEA has historically viewed itself as a professional association, not a union. It shunned collective bargaining, strikes, and other militant tactics. It vehemently criticized the AFT for its labor affiliation and maintained that this relationship was detrimental to the professional image. For its part, the AFT criticized the NEA's more conciliatory tactics as unrealistic and argued that union affiliation provided political and economic clout; it also criticized the NEA for permitting administrators in the organization.

Professionalism vs. unionism

Teacher Strikes Until the mid-1960s, the NEA relied on sanctions as the most aggressive measure against a school board. It condemned the AFT for its strike tactics, which the NEA considered illegal and unprofessional. In 1968 the NEA did an about-face, largely for two reasons: the AFT's successful use of strikes and the growing demand by its own members that it assume greater responsibility for improving their occupational status.

Becoming more militant

For the last two decades, then, the NEA has viewed the strike as a legitimate option. Along with mediation, fact finding, binding arbitration, and political action, the strike is considered a viable process for obtaining better salaries, smaller classes, and other bread-and-butter concerns.[36] Indeed, the strategies or options the NEA now advocates coincide with the tactics of organized labor, and there is little difference with the AFT on these strategies. Now both are considered to be aggressive unions that strike freely and negotiate with roughly equal success for the benefit of teachers. Today the NEA is quick to point out that there are more NEA-related strikes than AFT-related strikes. (This is due to the fact that there are more than three times as many local affiliates—7,000 versus 2,000—and three times the number of members—1.7 million versus 590,000—in the NEA than the AFT.)

Increased NEA strikes

The AFT has always taken a strong position on the right and need to strike in order to improve salaries, benefits, and working conditions of teachers. Albert Shanker, the president of the AFT, has also viewed the strike as a

36 National Education Association Annual Meeting. Philadelphia, July 1983, Resolution E-17; "NEA Resolutions," *Today's Education* (1983–84), p. 145.

Vestiges of paternalism

tactic "to eliminate all vestiges of paternalism" that school boards have "in their dealings with teachers."[37]

Prior to 1966, teachers' strikes were sporadic and infrequent. From 1940 to 1966, a total of 108 such stoppages occurred (or about 4 per year). These early strikes were spearheaded by the AFT, especially the local affiliates in New York, Michigan, Minneapolis, and Rhode Island.

Early teacher strikes

The year 1966 saw a dramatic upswing in the number of teachers' strikes. Thirty stoppages were recorded during that year alone, followed by 76 in 1967 and 88 in 1968. Whereas the major issues prior to 1966 involved salaries and working conditions, this new period also involved the right to organize collectively.

From 1969 (after the NEA had sanctioned the strike tactic) through 1980, the number of strikes increased significantly. During this twelve-year period, the number of strikes exceeded 100 almost every year and snowballed to over 200 in 1975 and 1980. During this new period, a fourth issue involving strikes surfaced—job security.

More than 200 annual strikes

The 1980s is seeing a noticeable decline in the number of teacher strikes; there have been fewer than 100 annual strikes between 1981 and 1983.[38] The AFT has toned down its original militant position and is now encouraging fact finding, mediation, and binding arbitration—much like the NEA, which sees a strike as only one of several options available when an impasse is reached. Both the NEA and AFT are developing other organizing strategies, among them forming coalitions with business and civic groups, participating in public hearings regarding school budgets, and enhancing their political clout at the state and local levels.

Decline in teacher strikes

Why the decline in strikes? Today unions of all kinds are losing many strikes, and government is more rigid and less willing to listen to union demands. President Reagan's confrontation with striking air traffic controllers in 1981, and their subsequent loss of jobs, gave antilabor sentiment a big boost. The taxpayer revolt of recent years has made it financially necessary—and in some cases politically popular—to confront public employees at state, county, and local levels.

Across the country, government officials are now willing to have a show down with striking employees, to curtail and cut back contract provisions won by unions in the past, to suspend and dismiss striking employees, to refuse to budge on many issues, and to say no to pay increases. Indeed, government workers (including teachers) are finding that government work isn't necessarily permanent—a hard pill to swallow since it was assumed prior to

Dismissing striking employees

37 Albert Shanker, "Why Teachers Are Angry," *American School Board Journal* (January 1975), p. 23.

38 *Work Stoppages Involving Teachers, 1940–62* (Washington, D.C.: U.S. Department of Labor, 1963), table 1, p. 2; *Work Stoppages in Government, 1958–68* (Washington, D.C.: U.S. Department of Labor, 1970), table 9, p. 13; *Government Work Stoppages, 1960, 1969 and 1970* (Washington, D.C.: U.S. Department of Labor, 1971), table 9, p. 6. From 1971 to 1980, annual reports from the U.S. Department of Labor, *Work Stoppages in Government,* are used as sources. For 1981 to 1983, Robert Porter, Secretary-Treasurer of the AFT, and Will Meyer of the Collective Bargaining Department of the NEA supplied the appropriate information for their respective organizations, April 16, 1984; Pat Strongin of the Bureau of National Affairs supplied information for all teachers, April 23, 1984.

The number of teacher strikes has declined in recent years; nevertheless, teacher organizations still consider the strike—and the threat to strike—to be an important tactic for improving teachers' salaries and working conditions. *(Bruce Kliewe/ Jeroboam, Inc.)*

the 1980s that working for the government (or working as a teacher) assured lifelong job security.[39]

The mood of taxpayers, who fund our schools, is vividly illustrated by California's Proposition 13 and Massachusetts' Proposition 2½, which impose property tax limitations that reduce monies available to municipalities and school districts. It is further demonstrated by the increasing number of teacher layoffs, some 100,000 per year since 1980, and by the fact that there are often hundreds of unemployed teachers willing to fill vacancies (just as there are hundreds of people willing to fill vacancies for air traffic controllers, police officers, firefighters, and transit workers).

Unemployed teachers

As municipal officials get tougher in bargaining with public workers and tax-cut fervor increases, the NEA and AFT will be forced to once more reassess the goals and tactics of striking. As school districts demand that teachers agree to contract concessions, the two unions will be fighting to protect members' jobs and previous benefits.

Administrative Membership In the past, the AFT criticized the NEA for encouraging administrators to join. It argued that the NEA was "management oriented." So long as administrators were in the organization and wielded power, the NEA could not make adequate progress toward securing a professional level of income and status for teachers. The NEA countered that the organization was concerned with the interests of teachers, and that it was good professional practice to include both teachers and administrators. At-

39 See William M. Bulkeley, "Getting the Ax: Government Workers Find That Job Security Can Suddenly Vanish," *Wall Street Journal,* July 29, 1981, pp. 1, 17; Martin Feldstein, "The Job of Controlling Public Sector Pay," *Wall Street Journal,* October 1, 1981, p. 13; and Barbara Mahany and Patricia Tennison, "Suburban School Districts Face Teacher Strike Peril," *Chicago Tribune,* August 21, 1983, Sect. 2, pp. 1, 3.

The issue of administrators

tacks and counterattacks at both organizations are found in the literature of the 1950s and 1960s. A number of teacher negotiation statutes and state administrative agency decisions have settled the issue over administrative membership basically along the lines advocated by the AFT. In many cases, state legislation permits and even mandates the inclusion of administrative personnel in a teacher bargaining unit. But the NEA local affiliates have come to realize that this creates too many practical problems for all parties concerned.

School principals and superintendents in many parts of the country have pulled out of the local and/or state NEA affiliates. The issue of administrative membership is seen as a conflict of interest during grievances or lawsuits, contract negotiations, arbitration, work stoppages, and strikes. In some school districts, the issue is seen as pertaining to local affiliates; it is argued that administrators can retain membership in the state and national NEA on an individual basis. In other places, it is accepted that administrative personnel should not be regular members of the local and state units, but that they should continue as members of the national NEA.

Administrators organize

Compounding the problem today is the fact that school administrators, mostly in the big cities, have organized into separate unions and bargaining associations with more than 70 local units and 11,000 school administrators and supervisors as of 1984. Most of these people are middle-ranked administrators who engage in collective bargaining with their own bosses (the school board and superintendent). Although the AFT has refused to become affiliated with them, its parent organization, the AFL-CIO, has granted these administrative units a charter, referred to as the American Federation of School Administrators.[40]

Current Differences Between the NEA and AFT

A number of important differences in philosophy and strategy still exist between the two organizations; these differences have contributed to continued tension and conflict and prevent a potential merger of the two organizations.

AFL-CIO affiliation

1. *Conflict over labor affiliation.* The AFT's affiliation with the AFL-CIO remains an important difference. The NEA has always considered itself a professional organization as opposed to any kind of labor affiliation; this stance coincides with its predominantly conservative and suburban-rural membership, a group that is traditionally antilabor and identifies city strikes and job dislocations with the politics and tactics of labor.[41]

40 *American Federation of School Administrators Affiliated Locals* (New York: AFSA, 1984); *American Federation of School Administrators: Who Are We?* (New York: AFSA, 1984). Also see Bruce S. Cooper and Kent F. Murmann, "Managerial Identification and Unionization of School Administrators," *Administrator's Notebook* (January 1982), pp. 1–4.

41 Marshall O. Donley, *The Future of Teacher Power in America* (Bloomington, Ind.: Phi Delta Kappa, 1977)

Membership of professors

2. *The battle for professors.* Recent rivalry between the NEA and AFT has intensified over enrolling professors into their organizations. The desire among professors to organize is linked to financial stringencies and hiring and tenure problems plaguing the colleges and universities; henceforth, we can expect large membership gains within the NEA and AFT—and also greater rivalry.

College and university teachers have been somewhat slow to seek organized labor's support, but the picture seems to be changing. A survey found that in 1978 three-fourths of all professors, a majority at every type of institution of higher learning, said that they would vote for collective bargaining and a prounion agent if an election were held at their institution. As many as 76 percent of the respondents credited collective bargaining with bringing higher salaries and improved benefits to professors.[42]

Despite the higher percentage of professors who now endorse collective bargaining and unionization, a considerably smaller percentage have actually voted to be represented by such agents. Perhaps the reasons for the gap are that the professors cannot agree on what organizations should represent them and that there is rivalry not only among the organizations but also among professors themselves. In addition, inertia must be overcome if college professors are to join militant organizations.

Still another problem is that the National Labor Relations Board ruled in two separate rulings in 1984 that professors at Boston University and Polytechnic Institute of New York are "managers" and "supervisors" (with authority over the hiring process) and thus do not have the right to bargain collectively under federal labor law. This ruling followed the Supreme Court's decision in 1980 involving Yeshiva University that restricted efforts to organize faculty members at *private* institutions of higher learning. Although we can expect the board's ruling to be appealed, we can also assume that NEA-AFT attempts to organize professors in the future will be focused on *public* higher education institutions.

Municipal workers and nurses

3. *Organizing noneducational workers.* The AFT has announced a major campaign to broaden its membership to include state and county white-collar municipal employees, school custodians, health-care workers, and nurses. On the whole, rank-and-file members support the idea and are willing to funnel a substantial amount of money into organizing these workers.

The biggest organizational attempt has occurred within the health-care field, affecting a potential 4.2 million workers including 750,000 registered nurses. The AFT has developed a new division called the Federation of Nurses and Health Professionals to unionize these people.[43] The AFT has also been successful in its efforts to improve the salaries, working conditions, and job security of state and county social, recreational, and clerical workers.[44]

42 Everett Ladd and Seymour M. Lipset, "Faculty Support for Unionization," *Education Digest* (May 1978), pp. 56–58.

43 "Health Care: Looking Ahead," *Annual Report of the American Federation of Teachers, 1982–83,* pp. 28–30.

44 "Public Employees: Preparing for Change," *Annual Report of the American Federation of Teachers, 1982–83,* pp. 26–27.

Organizing noneducators

The NEA dismisses the idea of unionizing noneducational workers as a further dilution of the AFT's interest in teachers, an attempt to shore up sagging membership that cannot compete with the NEA's, and an illustration that the AFT is willing to organize any group that is willing to join. The AFT, on the other hand, sees much potential political and economic advantage in broadening its membership.

Raiding members

4. *The fight over existing members.* Declining student enrollments, the recent recession, and school budget cuts fan the animosity between the unions. Neither one of these organizations faces a growth market, so they are beginning to raid each other's ranks more often. The two unions have been fighting over members for the last twenty-five years, but now the rivalry is more intense, the quarreling is more costly, and the stakes involve existing turf. The fight has changed its focus because about 85 percent of public school teachers now belong to one of the two organizations. Also, it is increasingly difficult to win big contract concessions from schools so that teachers are more willing to listen to the other side and to switch unions.

5. *Different styles of leadership.* Deep differences in organizational make-up and style still divide the two groups. It shows up in differences in the way the local and national offices in Washington, D.C., are run. The AFT offices are staffed by a handful of informally dressed people (70 in Washington) and the workplace is buzzing with noise and activity. The NEA offices are dominated by staff (500 in Washington) who tend to be formally dressed and more deliberative and quiet.[45]

Different attire and atmosphere

Shanker's visibility

Then there is Albert Shanker, president of the AFT, who has a distinctive leadership philosophy and style. The AFT tends to be Shanker's one-man show. As AFT president for more than ten years, he has traveled extensively (both nationally and internationally) for purposes of organizing and building stronger ties with political and labor groups. He is frequently the main speaker at conventions; he gives testimony and advice to government agencies, Congress, and the presidents; and he writes a regular column in the *New York Times*. Without doubt, he is a very controversial, outspoken, and visible person.

In contrast, the NEA leadership is diffuse and lacks well-known leaders who can deliver votes on controversial issues. The president is elected for two years and is eligible for only one additional term. This creates a somewhat weak presiding officer and makes it difficult for a strong, well-known NEA leader to emerge. Few people in education, much less the public, know the NEA president by name.

Low-profile NEA president

6. *Divided over bread-and-butter issues.* Besides differences in philosophy and style, the two groups split on many current, hotly contested educational issues. The two organizations have locked horns on (1) merit pay

45 Joann S. Lublin, "Two Rival Teachers' Unions Quarrel Even More," *Wall Street Journal,* November 22, 1983, p. 58.

Competency tests

(the AFT is willing to consider this plan, the NEA is more reluctant to do so); (2) competency tests for students and teachers (the AFT wants the tests to count, the NEA is unwilling to accept the results as a standard or criterion for achievement or entrance); (3) block grants and formulas for urban and rural school districts (the AFT is opposed to block grants and favors urban schools, the NEA is more neutral on this issue); (4) public employee bargaining laws (the AFT favors collective bargaining for municipal workers, the NEA feels the issue is not a matter for teachers; (5) student rights and the handling of disruptive students (the AFT emphasizes student responsibilities, the NEA wishes to expand student rights); (6) multicultural education (the AFT sees potential danger in emphasizing ethnic and racial differences, the NEA feels that cultural differences should be encouraged); and (7) school equality and academic standards (the AFT wants tough academic requirements, the NEA stresses school equality).[46]

Quality vs. equality

All these differences leave scars and intensify the two unions' rivalry. For these reasons, both groups will continue to spend big dollars fighting each other, pressuring legislators, and developing their own political base of parent, business, and other interest groups.

Areas of Agreement

Political activism

Both the NEA and AFT recognize the need to elect proteacher and proeducation political representatives at the local, state, and federal levels. Both organizations now spend millions of dollars annually and encourage their teachers to volunteer time in election contests. They have been successful in this approach, and most of the candidates whom they have supported in recent years have won election.[47] Behind these successes lies the fact that in states where the NEA and AFT decide to support selected candidates, they usually throw their muscle behind the same candidates—illustrating that their political views are compatible.

The combined political strength of the NEA and AFT is considerable. The organizations drew wide attention in 1982 and 1983 by adopting a joint resolution, their first, assailing proposed tax credits for private school tuition. Their coordinated lobbying helped stall the bill in Congress. And the AFT, laying aside its past opposition to the creation of the Department of Education, joined the NEA to thwart President Reagan's plan to abolish the agency.

Guaranteeing collective negotiation

Both the NEA and AFT advocate a federal law guaranteeing collective bargaining. As of 1984, as many as thirty-five states had laws providing some form of collective bargaining, although they varied considerably.[48] No doubt

46 *The Annual Report of the American Federation of Teachers, 1982–83,* pp. 32–42; "The NEA Legislative Program for the 98th Congress," *Today's Education* (1983–84). Also see Lublin, "Two Rival Teachers' Unions Quarrel Even More."

47 Stanley E. Elam, "The NEA Political Powerhouse or Paper Tiger?" *Phi Delta Kappan* (November 1981), pp. 169–174.

48 *Government Employee Relations Report* (Washington, D.C.: Bureau of National Affairs, 1984).

more states will adopt collective negotiation laws, but the NEA and AFT would prefer a uniform federal law to safeguard their right to strike and, more important, to guarantee their benefits on retirement, sick leave, seniority and tenure, holidays, work days and work year, leave benefits (personal, military, maternity, and the like), and other protections and benefits now provided to public sector employees by statute.

In an era of teacher retrenchment, the NEA and AFT are also in basic agreement on securing unemployment benefits for teachers (only eight states currently provide them), enlarging the demand for teachers by extending free public education to all children and youth from prekindergarten to grade 14, convincing the public of the proved value of smaller classes, increasing tax-free fringe benefits, raising teacher pay and implementing cost-of-living adjustments, increasing teacher retirement benefits, and stepping up teacher militancy to resist possible cutbacks.

Questions concerning tenure laws, accountability, school budget cutbacks, as well as teacher unemployment, may force teachers to conclude that the best way to combat the dangers facing them is to end the organizational rivalry and move toward greater unity—and ultimately toward merger. To be sure, there are immense political and economic advantages to be gained by such a merger. As many as 2.3 million teachers, paraprofessionals, professors, and miscellaneous educators from state and federal departments and non-profit and foundation organizations would provide enormous potential power unavailable to the two separate organizations. Many of the nearly 1 million teachers and professors who presently belong to neither organization would probably join the united "super" teacher organization.

General Professional Organizations for Teachers

In addition to the NEA and AFT, there are more than three hundred other national teacher organizations.[49]

Specialized Professional Organizations

Subject-related teacher organizations

At the working level of the classroom, the professional organization of greatest benefit to a teacher (and education student) is usually one that focuses on his or her major field. Each such subject-centered professional association provides a meeting ground for teachers of similar interests. The activities of these professional organizations customarily consist of regional and national meetings and publication of a professional journal, usually monthly or quarterly, that provides current teaching tips and describes accepted curriculum practices. Below are fifteen major teaching organizations that focus on specific subject matter.

49 See *Directory of Education Associations: 1980–81* (Washington, D.C.: U.S. Department of Education, 1981).

1. American Alliance for Health, Physical Education, Recreation and Dance
2. American Council on the Teaching of Foreign Languages
3. American Industrial Arts Association
4. American School Health Association
5. American Vocational Association
6. Association for Education in Journalism
7. International Reading Association
8. Modern Language Association
9. Music Teachers National Association
10. National Art Education Association
11. National Business Education Association
12. National Council for the Social Studies
13. National Council of Teachers of English
14. National Council of Teachers of Mathematics
15. National Science Teachers Association

Student-related teacher organizations

For those readers who identify with a particular type of student—say by age or grade level, or by cognitive, physical, or ethnic characteristic—the teaching organizations listed below should be of interest. These professional organizations, also national in scope, focus on the needs and rights of special students and are organized to ensure that these children and youth are served by well-prepared school personnel. These associations attempt to advance the teaching profession by improving teaching techniques for specialized groups of students. The associations also hold regional and national meetings and publish monthly or quarterly journals.

1. American Association for Gifted Children
2. American Association of Workers for the Blind
3. American Association for Asian Studies
4. American Montessori Society
5. American Speech-Language-Hearing Association
6. Association for Childhood Education International
7. Association for Children with Learning Disabilities
8. Convention of American Instructors of the Deaf
9. Council for Exceptional Children
10. National Association for Bilingual Children
11. National Association for Creative Children and Adults
12. National Association for the Education of Young Children
13. National Rehabilitation Association
14. National Scholarship Service and Fund for Negro Students
15. Rural Education Association

Still another type of organization that merits comment is the professional organization whose members cut across various subjects and student types. These organizations tend to highlight innovative teaching practices in general, describe new trends and policies impacting on the entire field of education, comprise a wide range of membership, and work for the advancement of the teaching profession in general.

Religious Education Organizations

As of 1984, there were approximately 280,000 nonpublic school teachers in grades K–12, of which 75,000 belonged to one of eighty religious education associations. The largest of these religious teacher organizations is the National Association of Catholic School Teachers (NACST), founded in 1978 and comprising in 1984 over 3,000 teachers—mainly from large cities. The organization is expected to grow in membership, since the great majority of Catholic teachers are not organized on a national or local level.[50] The largest and oldest Catholic education organization is the National Catholic Education Association, founded in 1904 and comprising 15,000 institutions. Most administrators, as principals or superintendents of their respective schools, join the organization. It is estimated that no more than one thousand teachers are members.[51]

Catholic teacher organizations

In the meantime, the 9,500 Catholic schools, which constitute approximately 46 percent of all private schools and two-thirds of all private teachers, now permit their teachers to bargain in matters dealing with salary, job security, advancement, and grievances. Furthermore, they have established procedural recommendations for collective bargaining. Although concern has been expressed about Catholic teachers belonging to the NEA or AFT, no more than a few thousand belong to either organization.[52]

Parent-Teacher Associations (PTAs)

A forum for parents and teachers to work together to plan and to resolve educational problems on the local, state, and national levels is provided by **parent-teacher associations**. Teachers usually take an active part in these associations and work with parents on curriculum and instructional programs, student policy, and school-community relations.

50 *Projections of Education Statistics to 1990–91* (Washington, D.C.: National Center for Education Statistics, 1982), table 20, p. 84; telephone conversation with Rita Schwartz, Secretary-Treasurer, National Association of Catholic School Teachers, April 13, 1984.

51 *United States Catholic Elementary and Secondary Schools, 1983–84* (Washington, D.C.: National Catholic Education Association, 1984); telephone conversation with Bruno Manno, Director of Research and Statistics, National Catholic Education Association, April 13, 1984.

52 *Digest of Education Statistics, 1982* (Washington, D.C.: National Center for Education Statistics, 1983), figure 5, p. 48; table 40, p. 49; telephone conversation with Rita Schwartz, Secretary-Treasurer, National Association of Catholic School Teachers, April 13, 1984; and telephone conversation with Simeon Taylor, Department of Membership, NEA, April 12, 1984.

5.2 million members

Founded in 1897, the PTA—the most prominent of the groups—is a loose confederation of fifty branches and 25,000 local units, with over 5.2 million members (mostly mothers) in 1984. Its branches include all fifty states, the District of Columbia, and the European Congress of American Parents, Teachers, and Students. No local unit is exactly like any other, although all local PTA members belong to the national PTA. Every PTA unit devises its own pattern of organization and service to fit its school and neighborhood. Membership in the PTA is open to anyone interested in promoting the welfare of children and youth, working with teachers and schools, and willing to support the goals of the PTA.[53]

The *PTA Today* and *What's Happening in Washington* are the official monthly magazines of the association. Many teacher and administrative associations, including the NEA and AFT, maintain a working relationship with the PTA on important issues; in fact,the NEA is loosely affiliated with the PTA.

In some school districts, however, parents and teachers have preferred not to affiliate with the state or national PTA organization because of political differences and because they want to keep local monies in the community. The Parent-Teacher Organization (PTO) and Parent-Teacher Student Organization (PTSO) have replaced the PTA in some communities.[54]

Local school influence

Although the PTA claims to wield considerable power in shaping local school–community relations and local school policy, its actual influence at the local level is often determined by the philosophy and attitudes of the superintendent, principal, and teachers. Actually the PTA tends to have more influence on the national, than on the local, level. As the nation's largest child-advocacy organization, the national PTA is constantly assessing children's welfare so that it can respond to changes in our society and in the needs of children. For a number of years, the national PTA has lobbied to reduce violence on television and to improve the quality of children's television programing. The national PTA is also very active in programs related to reading, urban education, special education, sex education, child nutrition and health education, and drug abuse prevention as well as in improving school discipline and combating censorship of school and library materials.

National impact

Organizations for Prospective Teachers

Students who are thinking of or are committed to a career as a teacher may join a number of professional organizations. These organizations help answer many questions; develop an understanding of the profession; stimulate ideals of professional ethics, standards, and training; provide an opportunity to meet other education students and educators at local and national meetings; and publish materials that help members keep up with current trends in the

53 *Partners in Education: Teachers in the PTA* (Chicago: The National PTA, 1983).

54 *The National PTA Handbook, 1983–1985* (Chicago: The National PTA, 1983).

profession. Education-related organizations open to students include the following:

1. *Student National Education Association.* Founded in 1937, the Student NEA was originally called Future Teachers of America and admitted high school and college students. Currently there are about 25,000 Student NEA members (a drop of 50,000 between 1975 and 1984) in about thirty-five college chapters. Members receive *Today's Education* and the annual *NEA Handbook* and are entitled to request free research reports. They also obtain automatically free liability protection when they student teach.

Free insurance for students

The Student NEA strives to develop an understanding of the education profession; its major purpose is to encourage young men and women to enter teaching and join the NEA. The AFT has not established student organizations for prospective teachers, although local chapters are exerting pressures to organize them. The AFT takes the position that with the current oversupply of teaches, there is no pressing need to move in this direction.

2. *Honorary Eductional Associations.* Professional and honorary groups in education include Phi Lambda Theta, Phi Delta Kappa, and Kappa Delta Pi. Phi Lambda Theta has initiated more than 100,000 individuals since its inception in 1910 and has grown from seven chapters to more than a hundred chapters (mostly campus based) in thirty-one states. Originally open to undergraduate and graduate female students and faculty members who met the necessary qualifications, it began to admit men in 1974. Current membership is 16,000. General qualifications include superior scholastic achievement (B+ or higher), evidence of high professional standards, and leadership potential. Phi Lambda Theta publishes a quarterly entitled *Educational Horizons,* as well as a newsletter.

Educational Horizons

Phi Delta Kappa, founded in 1906, now includes 585 local and 7 regional chapters in the United States and Canada, as well as 8 international chapters. About half are campus based. As of 1984, there were approximately 140,000 members, with no distinctions made among graduate students, teachers, and administrators. Originally open only to men, it opened its membership to women in 1974. Membership requirements include high scholastic achievement, completion of a minimum of fifteen semester hours of graduate work in education, commitment to a life career of educational services, and residence status in an approved institution at the time of election. The purpose of the organization is to promote quality education, with particular emphasis on publicly supported education. Members receive *Phi Delta Kappan,* a highly respected professional journal published ten times a year, and the fraternity newsletter. Other publications are available at reduced rates.

Phi Delta Kappan

Kappa Delta Pi, founded in 1911, has always been open to men and women. Total membership is 430,000, of which 60,000 are considered active. Approximately 20,000 members are students. The purpose of the association is to recognize outstanding contributions to education. To this end, it invites to membership persons who exhibit worthy educational ideals, sound scholarship, and commendable personal qualities. The association is international in scope and comprises several hundred alumni and active chapters. Kappa Delta Pi publishes two well-known journals, *Educational Forum,* a quarterly, and *Kappa Delta Pi,* a monthly, as well as a limited number of books on education as part of the Kappa Delta Pi Research Publications series.

Educational Forum

3. *American Educational Research Association.* The American Educational Research Association (AERA), founded in 1915, is a national organization of educators and social scientists who have a vital interest in research in education and the application of research to education practice. It is considered by many to be the most prestigious research organization in education. AERA is constituted in ten divisions and more than seventy special interest groups. Membership in 1984 totaled 14,000, of which 2,500 were students. Members are entitled to three periodicals: the *Educational Researcher,* a monthly news and feature magazine, and *American Educational Research Journal* and *Review of Educational Research,* both quarterlies. Members also receive discounts for AERA-sponsored publications and research training sessions at the annual meeting. The annual meeting is held in a different city each year and attracts a wide array of researchers and educators from across the country; several thousand original papers on a broad spectrum of topics are presented at these meetings.

Review of Educational Research

Students interested in joining any of these organizations can ask their professors for appropriate information, since many of them are members. If you visit your college library, you can track down the respective journals for each organization. The first or second page of each issue will list the membership address and membership dues; some journals will also indicate lower membership rates for students.

Summing Up

1. It is generally agreed that teaching is not as yet a full profession, although it is moving towards becoming one.
2. Many trends in education are increasing the status of teacher professionalism. Professional practice commissions, for example, enable teachers to participate in setting criteria for entering the profession. Teacher centers and mediated entry enable them to play a major role in professional training and development. Merit pay provides an opportunity for increased salaries and professional responsibilities.
3. During the past few decades teachers have become more militant and have gained increased status as professionals. Teacher organizations have played a crucial role in this quest for greater power and professionalism.
4. The NEA and AFT now represent the large majority of classroom teachers; these organizations have improved teachers' salaries and working

conditions and have gained them a greater voice in decisions that involve teaching and learning in the schools.

5. There are other professional organizations that teachers can join that work to improve education. Some of these, like Phi Delta Kappa and the American Educational Research Association, are open to students of education.

Discussion Questions

1. Is teaching a profession? Defend your answer.
2. Does a teacher surplus tend to make teaching more or less a full-fledged profession? Why or why not?
3. What trends are giving teaching more status as a full-fledged profession than it has had in the past?
4. What are some similarities and differences between the NEA and the AFT? Is a merger desirable? Defend your answer.
5. What professional organizations other than the NEA or AFT might you join? Why?

Suggested Readings

Hosford, Philip L., ed. *Using What We Know About Teaching,* 1984 ASCD Yearbook. Alexandria, Va.: Association for Supervision and Curriculum Development, 1984.

The book examines how knowledge is utilized and applied in the teaching profession and compares the diffusion of knowledge in the teaching profession with what goes on in other professions.

Howsam, Robert B., et al. *Educating a Profession.* Washington D.C.: American Association of Colleges for Teacher Education, 1976.

A recent overview concerning the problems and prospects of enhancing the profession of teachers as well as future policies of the profession.

Lortie, Dan C. *Schoolteacher: A Sociological Study.* Chicago: University of Chicago Press, 1975.

An interesting book with observations on and interpretations of the nature of teaching and the social dynamics of the classroom and school.

Ornstein, Allan C., and Harry L. Miller. *Looking into Teaching.* Boston: Houghton Mifflin, 1980.

An examination of crucial issues and ideas related to the teaching profession, including what is taught, who teaches, how teachers are prepared, what constitutes the work of teachers, and what organizations teachers join.

Smith, B. O. *A Design for a School of Pedagogy.* Washington, D.C.: Government Printing Office, 1980.

An examination of various strategies for improving teacher education and teacher professionalism.

Woodring, Paul. *The Persistent Problems of Education.* Bloomington, Ind: Phi Delta Kappa, 1983.

The author describes why certain problems in education persist from generation to generation, including what should be taught in schools, how teachers should be educated, and how teachers can improve their professional status.

Part 2 Historical and Philosophical Foundations

Insight into the present and future rests on the ability to understand the past and raise intelligent questions. An appreciation of historical trends and philosophical thought reveals the folly of attempting simple answers to complex problems. Schools do not exist in a vacuum; they are influenced by a changing society rooted in historical and philosophical foundations. The four chapters in Part 2 examine the history and philosophy of education in this context.

In each chapter we learn that certain trends and lines of thought seem to have had a marked influence in shaping the character of American education. In Chapter 3, an analysis of its origins will help us understand that our education is rooted mainly in European movements and people and that it has been shaped by certain important periods—ancient Greek and Roman, Arabic, medieval, the Renaissance, and the Reformation.

Next, in Chapter 4, we examine some of the ideas that have been advanced by philosophers and other scholars concerned with education. Twelve major pioneers in education are discussed—Comenius, Locke, Rousseau, Pestalozzi, Froebel, Herbart, Spencer, Montessori, Dewey, Counts, Hutchins, and Piaget. Emphasis is placed on these scholars' ideas about learning and schooling and their influence on educational practice.

In Chapter 5 we look at the development of education in America, starting with the colonial period and ending with a discussion of contemporary events. We see the complex interaction of schools and society as we learn how changing institutions and ideas of the nation influenced the development of American education. Particular emphasis is placed on the development of universal education through the establishment of the common school and the extension of educational opportunity to the secondary level.

Chapter 6 shifts the discussion to some philosophical questions. First of all, what is philosophy? How does it relate to our view of schools? What philosophies have been most influential in education? The following major philosophic approaches are described and discussed: idealism, realism, perennialism, essentialism, pragmatism, progressivism, social reconstructionism, existentialism, and philosophical analysis. The educational philosophies that teachers and other educators adopt interact with historical events—and it is this relationship that affects our schools and classrooms today.

3

Origins of Our Educational Heritage

Focusing Questions

Why should teachers study the history of education?

How did the leading educators of the past define knowledge, education, schooling, teaching, and learning?

What concepts of the educated person were dominant during each period of Western history discussed in this chapter?

How have educational ideas changed over the course of time?

How have the educational theories of the leading educators of the Western world contributed to modern education?

AS A PROSPECTIVE TEACHER, YOU MAY SERIOUSLY QUESTION THE need to study the history of education. Why, you may ask, should I be concerned with the past when my main concern is what I will be doing in the classroom tomorrow? Is it not more worthwhile to spend my time trying to solve current educational problems? The next three chapters will attempt to answer these questions. Some new ones that may challenge you also will be raised.

The ideas of John Dewey, one of the world's leading educational philosophers, suggest a rationale for studying and using history. As he emphasized in his momentous book, *Democracy and Education,*

> The past just as past is no longer our affair. If it were wholly gone and done with, there would be only one reasonable attitude toward it. Let the dead bury their dead. But knowledge of the past is the key to understanding the present. History deals with the past, but this past is the history of the present.[1]

Dewey is saying that you are who you are right now *because of* your past experience. Your personal hopes and problems are the product of your personal history. Similarly, the social, political, and educational achievements, controversies, and problems of today's schools are a result of twenty-five centuries of historical development.

Dewey's perspective on human experience suggests that the history of education is valuable for the following reasons:

1. Educational issues and problems are often rooted in the past; the study of educational history can help us to understand and solve today's problems.
2. Realistic efforts to reform education begin with present conditions, which are a product of our past; by using our past, we can shape the future.
3. The study of education's past provides a perspective that explains and illuminates our present activities as teachers.

In approaching the study of educational history from the perspective of your present concerns, it might be helpful to look to the experience of past educators for answers to questions that you will have to face as a teacher. The questions that will be put to these educators will be broad ones, dealing with the very nature of teaching and learning. For example: What is knowledge? What is education? What is the purpose of the school? Who should attend school? How should teaching and learning be carried on?

1 John Dewey, *Democracy and Education: An Introduction to the Philosophy of Education* (New York: Macmillan, 1916), pp. 250–251.

Education in Primitive Societies

In its long march to the present, humankind developed skills of creating, sustaining, and transmitting culture. These cultural survival skills, which have persisted from prehistoric times to the present, became the basis of formal schooling. Preliterate persons faced the problem of survival in an environment that pitted them against natural forces, animals, and other hostile human beings. To survive, human beings needed food, shelter, warmth, and clothing. In order to transform a frequently hostile environment into a life-sustaining one, humankind developed life skills that eventually became cultural patterns.[2]

Cultural transmission

For the culture of a particular group to continue, that culture must be transmitted from the group's adults to its children. As the children learn the language, skills, knowledge, and values of their society, they inherit the culture. The earliest patterns of education involved (1) tool or instrument making, (2) the mores of group life, (3) and language learning.

As toolmakers, humans created instruments for their protection and for food gathering. Clubs, spears, bows and arrows, pottery, sleds and other instruments were means of gaining control over the environment. Whenever and wherever parents taught their offspring to make and use spears to catch fish or kill animals, informal educational forces were operating.

Primitive humans found security in group life, based on kinship and tribal patterns. Group life provided greater efficiency in gathering or growing food, in building shelters, and in protecting group members against enemies. Life in the human group was educational as children observed and learned from the older members of the group. Children were deliberately instructed in specialized tasks and roles by their parents, tribal storytellers, and priests. Over time, many of the patterns of group life became moral behavioral codes that were ritualized ways of dealing with the environment.

Important among the human being's powers was the ability to use abstract thought. As toolmakers, human beings could fashion and manipulate instruments; as abstract thinkers, they could create, use, and manipulate symbols. Through gestures, sounds, and words, they could communicate with each other. When these symbols were expressed in signs, pictographs, and letters, human beings created a written language and made the great leap to literacy.[3] Humanity's powers to abstract, conceptualize, and communicate in oral and written language had tremendous educational consequences. Education involved an emphasis on language learning as children participated, in the songs, stories, and rituals that formed the group's cultural inheritance.

2 R. F. Butts, *A Cultural History of Western Education* (New York: McGraw-Hill, 1955), pp. vii–x, 1–18.

3 Bernard Mehl, *Classic Educational Ideas: From Sumeria to America* (Columbus, Ohio: Merrill, 1972), pp. 10–22.

Overview 3.1

Key Periods in Educational History, to A.D. 1600

Historical Group or Period	Educational Goals	Curriculum	Agents	Influences on Western Education
Primitive societies 7000 B.C.–5000 B.C.	To teach group survival skills; to cultivate group cohesiveness	Practical skills of hunting, fishing, food gathering; stories, myths, songs, poems, dances	Parents, tribal elders, and priests	Emphasis on the role of informal education in transmission of skills and values
Greek 1600 B.C.–300 B.C.	To cultivate civic responsibility and identity with city-state; Athenian: to develop well-rounded person Spartan: to develop soldiers and military leaders	Athenian: reading, writing, arithmetic, drama, music, physical education, literature, poetry Spartan: drill, military songs and tactics	Athens: private teachers and schools; Sophists; philosophers Sparta: military teachers, drill sergeants	Athens: The concept of the well-rounded, liberally educated person Sparta: The concept of the military state
Roman 750 B.C.–A.D. 450	To develop sense of civic responsibility for republic and then empire; to develop administrative and military skills	Reading, writing, arithmetic, Laws of Twelve Tables, law, philosophy	Private schools and teachers; schools of rhetoric	Emphasis on ability to use education for practical administrative skills; relating education to civic responsibility
Arabic A.D.700–A.D. 1350	To cultivate religious commitment to Islamic beliefs; to develop expertise in mathematics, medicine, and science	Reading, writing, mathematics, religious literature; scientific studies	Mosques; court schools	Arabic numerals and computation; re-entry of classical materials on science and medicine

Education in Ancient Greece

Historians of Western civilization and education often look to ancient Greece as an originating source of Western culture. The study of classical Greek culture illuminates many problems that today's educators face. What are worthy models for children to imitate? How does education help to shape good citizens? How does education reflect changing social, economic, and political conditions? How does education serve humankind's search for truth?

Overview 3.1 (*cont.*)

Key Periods in Educational History, to A.D. 1600

Historical Group or Period	Educational Goals	Curriculum	Agents	Influences on Western Education
Medieval A.D. 500–A.D. 1400	To develop religious commitment, knowledge, and ritual; to reestablish social order; to prepare persons for appropriate roles	Reading, writing, arithmetic, liberal arts; philosophy, theology; crafts; military tactics and chivalry	Parish, chantry, and cathedral schools; universities; apprenticeship; knighthood	Establishing the structure, content, and organization of the university as a major institution of higher education; the institutionalization and preservation of knowledge
Renaissance A.D. 1350–A.D. 1500	To cultivate a humanist who was expert in the classics—Greek and Latin; to prepare courtiers for service to dynastic leaders	Latin, Greek, classical literature, poetry, art	Classical humanist educators and schools such as lycée, gymnasium, Latin grammar school	An emphasis on literary knowledge, excellence, and style as expressed in classical literature; a two-track system of schools
Reformation A.D. 1500–A.D. 1600	To cultivate a sense of commitment to a particular religious denomination; to cultivate general literacy	Reading, writing, arithmetic, catechism, religious concepts and ritual; Latin and Greek; theology	Vernacular elementary schools for the masses; classical schools for the upper classes	A commitment to universal education to provide literacy to the masses; the origins of school systems with supervision to ensure doctrinal conformity

Generations of readers have thrilled to the tension and suspense of Homer's epic poems, the *Iliad* and *Odyssey*. Appearing about 1200 B.C., Homer's epics served educational purposes as they presented Greek children with heroic models that were worthy of imitation. Agamemnon, Ulysses, Achilles, and other characters in the epics vividly personified the heroic dimension of life. By studying the behavior of these heroes, the young Greek learned (1) the characteristics and qualities that made life worth living; (2) the behaviors

Homeric education

that were expected of warrior-knights; (3) the flaws or weaknesses in human character that brought harm to oneself and one's friends.[4]

The study of ancient Greek civilization provides valuable lessons on citizenship and civic education that illuminate the role of education in shaping good citizens. A number of small and often competing city-states such as Athens, Sparta, and Thebes were noteworthy for their well-defined conception of civic duties, responsibilities, and rights. Athens, in particular, emphasized the humane, rational, and democratic form of social and political organization. Sparta, the chief adversary of Athens, was a military dictatorship. As each city-state developed its own form of political organization, it also evolved an appropriate kind of education.

For the Greeks, **enculturation**—immersion and participation in the total culture—was more important than formal schooling. Through enculturation the Greek youth became a citizen of his society. In most of the Greek city-states, formal education was reserved for boys. In Athens, for example, girls generally learned domestic skills at home. In contrast, Spartan girls received more schooling, including strenuous athletic training to prepare them to be healthy mothers of future Spartan soldiers.

More structured education began with the appearance of the Sophists. Following these teachers came Socrates and Plato, the moral philosophers; Aristotle, who attempted to formulate rational and systematic explanations of natural phenomena; and Isocrates, the educator and rhetorician.

The Sophists

In the middle of the fifth century B.C., altered economic conditions generated social and educational change in Greece, especially in Athens. The older landed aristocracy was slowly being displaced by commercial classes, who had profited from Athenian expansion and colonization. This social change created the condition for a new type of educator—a Sophist.

Wandering teachers

The first professional educators were the Sophists, a group of wandering teachers who developed a variety of methods for instructing the rising commercial class of Athens and other Greek city-states in needed intellectual and rhetorical skills. By cultivating rhetoric—the art of persuasion—the students of the Sophists came to control the legal agencies of the city-state. The Sophists claimed that they could teach any subject or skill to anyone who wished to learn it. While their pedagogical expertise was often exaggerated, they brought educational opportunities to more people than had previously enjoyed them and contributed to socioeconomic mobility.

Grammar, logic, and rhetoric

The Sophists specialized in teaching grammar, logic, and rhetoric; these subjects later developed into the liberal arts. Logic, the rules of argument, aided students in clarifying their own thinking; grammar helped them express ideas clearly; rhetoric—the power of persuading others through speech—was considered most important. Essentially, the Sophists were con-

4 H. I. Marrou, *A History of Education in Antiquity* (New York: New American Library, 1956), pp. 21–34.

cerned with developing the communication skills of their students so that they might become successful advocates and legislators. Skill in communication was the means to power.

> In the middle of the fifth century B.C. there was a verbal explosion of unprecedented magnitude. . . . Men argued, debated, soliloquized, declaimed, contradicted, orated. In trade, in politics, in litigation, in estate management, in war, in courtship, in international relations, he who had the gift of words was victor.[5]

Protagoras's method

Some of the Sophists were excellent teachers who were well prepared to teach their subjects and skills. Unfortunately, others were fakes who offered instant success through tricks and gimmicks. Protagoras (485–415 B.C.) was one of the most effective teachers among the Sophists. His method involved (1) the presentation of a simple lecture or declamation to his students to provide them with an excellent model of speech; (2) an examination of great orations that could be used as models of speech; (3) the study of rhetoric, grammar, and logic; (4) practice orations by the young orator, which were criticized by the teacher; and, finally, (5) a public oration delivered by the student. Protagoras believed it was possible for one to argue for or against any proposition and to win any kind of argument.

Information for persuasion

The Sophists were not particularly concerned with knowledge as a search for truth. Rather, they promised to provide their students with techniques needed to acquire wealth, political power, and social prestige. In ancient Athens, the key to power in the assembly and courts was the ability to attract people and to persuade them to follow you. For the Sophists, knowledge was not speculation about abstract concepts of truth, beauty, and goodness. It was the ability to use information in such a way as to motivate and persuade people to accept your point of view. It was not what you said but how you expressed yourself that won the argument or the case of law.

Opportunistic attitude

As itinerant or traveling teachers the Sophists did not establish schools in an institutional sense. They instructed anyone who could afford to pay them. Their students were ambitious young men who sought instant success. The teachers tried to give their students the image or appearance of confidence, skill, and talent. In one sense, the Sophists were democratic educators who did not restrict their teaching to an upper class or a hereditary aristocracy. In another sense, they contributed to the opportunistic attitude that stressed appearance and technique rather than truth and honesty. In some respects, the Sophists resembled the modern image makers, who try to "package" political candidates as if they are products to be sold to voters. In fact, the word *sophistry,* which means misleading but clever and subtle argument, is derived from the methods used by the ancient Greek Sophists.

5 James L. Jarrett, *The Educational Theories of the Sophists* (New York: Teachers College Press, Columbia University, 1969), p. 3.

Socrates: Education by Self-Examination

Unlike the Sophists, the Athenian philosopher Socrates (469–399 B.C.) sought to discover the universal principles of truth, beauty, and goodness, which he believed should govern human conduct. Socrates is important in Western educational history because he firmly defended the freedom to think, to question, and to teach.[6] He was also significant as the teacher of Plato, who later systematized many of Socrates' ideas. In fact, what we know about Socrates is known through the writings of Plato. Socrates also developed the **Socratic method**—the methodology of searching questions and answers, or dialogue, that bears his name.

Principles of truth, beauty, and goodness

Socrates' philosophy was a simple ethic; it stated that a person ought to seek to live a life of moral excellence. Such an individual would live wisely and act rationally. A true education was one that aimed to cultivate morally excellent people. Socrates held moral excellence to be superior to technical or vocational training. Unlike the Sophists, Socrates did not believe that knowledge or wisdom could be transmitted from a teacher to a learner. He asserted that true knowledge existed within everyone and needed to be brought to consciousness. A liberating education would stimulate learners to discover ideas by bringing to consciousness the truth that was latently present in their minds.

Socrates' basic educational aim was that individuals should define themselves through self-examination and self-analysis. By self-examination each person should seek the truth that is universally present in all people. As a teacher Socrates used the method of asking probing questions that stimulated his students to investigate the perennial human concerns about the meaning of life, truth, and justice. As a result of the dialogue with the teacher, the student constructed, criticized, and reconstructed his basic conceptions.

Probing questions

Socrates frequented the Athenian marketplace, raising political, aesthetic, moral, and philosophical issues. As a social critic, he made powerful enemies. In 399 B.C. he was brought to trial on the charge of impiety to the gods and of corrupting Athenian youth and was sentenced to death by his fellow Athenians.

Plato: Eternal Truths and Values

Socrates' educational efforts were continued by his pupil, Plato (429–347 B.C.). A speculative philosopher, Plato founded the Academy in 387 B.C. and wrote *Protagoras,* a discourse on virtue, and the *Republic* and the *Laws,* treatises on political, legal, and educational theory. In general, Plato was a conservative social and educational philosopher who disliked the changes encouraged by the Sophists and held that reality consisted of an unchanging world of perfect ideas—universal concepts such as truth, goodness, justice, and beauty. As these images appear to our senses, however, individual ex-

6 J. Kelley Sowards, *Makers of the Western Tradition: Portraits from History* (New York: St. Martin's, 1983), pp. 41–66.

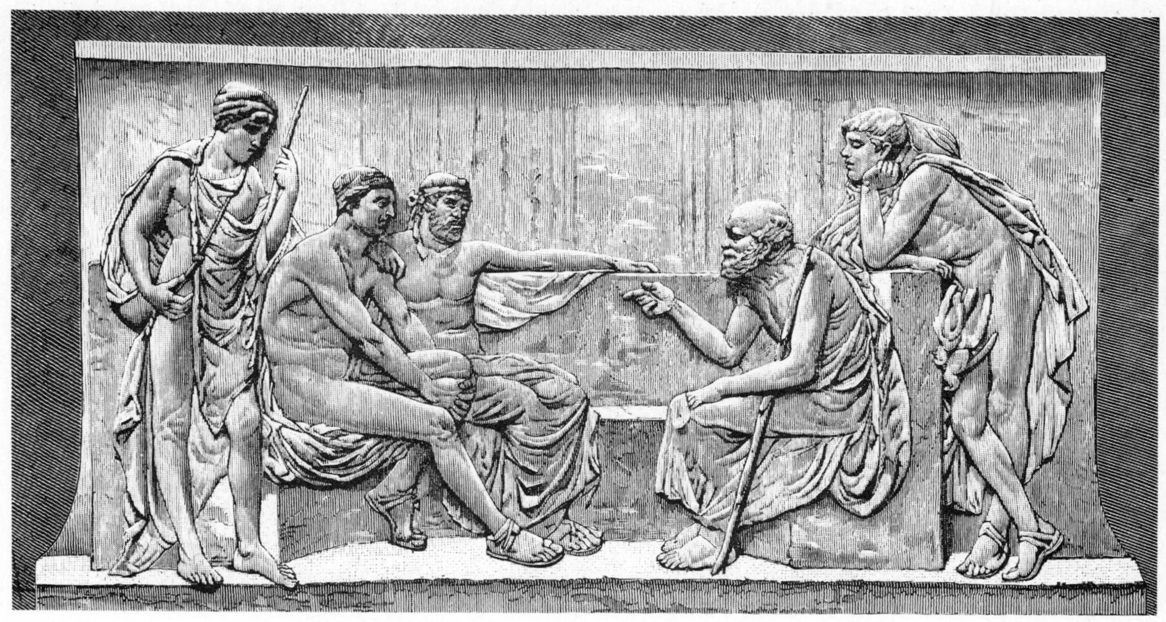

Socrates asked probing questions of his students to help them reach a clearer understanding through self-examination of the meaning of life, truth, and justice. (Historical Pictures Service, Chicago)

amples are imperfect representations of these universal and eternal ideas. In structuring an unchanging order of reality, Plato challenged the Sophists' methodology of sense experience. In contrast, he asserted that human beings are good and honorable only when their behavior agrees with the ideal concepts of justice and goodness.[7]

Universal and unchanging education

Plato's theory of knowledge is based on the theory of "reminiscence," by which individuals recall the truths or ideas that are present in latent form in their minds. Reminiscence implies that the human soul, before birth, has lived in a spiritual world of ideas, which is the source of all truth and knowledge. At birth, this knowledge of truth is represented within one's subconscious mind. For Plato, learning was the rediscovery or recollection of this latent knowledge of perfect forms by bringing it to consciousness.[8] Since sense impressions, according to Plato, are distortions of reality, genuine knowledge is intellectual, not sensory. True knowledge, as contrasted with sensation, is changeless and eternal. There is but one idea of perfection that is common to all human beings regardless of their time and circumstances. Since truth is universal, education should also be universal and unchanging.

7 Adolphe E. Meyer, *Grandmasters of Educational Thought* (New York: McGraw-Hill, 1975).

8 Robert S. Brumbaugh, "Plato's Philosophy of Education: The Meno Experiment and the Republic Curriculum," *Educational Theory* (Summer 1970), pp. 207–228.

Since reality can be apprehended only intellectually, education also should be intellectual.

Plato's Ideal Society In the *Republic,* his most famous work, Plato fashioned a plan for a perfect state ruled by an intellectual elite of philosopher-kings. Plato's Republic, existing to cultivate truth and virtue in its inhabitants, rested on assumptions that only knowledgeable men should rule and that all inhabitants should contribute to the general welfare according to their particular aptitude. Inhabitants were divided into three major classes: the intellectual rulers or philosopher-kings; the auxiliaries and military defenders; and the workers who produced goods and services. A person's intellectual capacity, defined primarily in cognitive terms, determined the class to which he or she belonged.

Intellectual elite

The educational system rated individual intellectual competencies and sorted people into categories. Once assigned to a class, individuals received the education appropriate to their assigned social role. Plato gave the philosopher-kings the task of selecting those who were intellectually able. Because of their intellectual expertise, the philosopher-kings were judged to be virtuous and intelligent men who possessed the capacity for leadership. The second class—auxiliaries (warriors)—were subordinate to the philosopher-kings. Strong of will, rather than intellectual, they were to defend the Republic. The lowest class, the workers, provided the needed economic products. For each class, there was an appropriate educational track to prepare them for their functions. Plato believed that each class would fulfill a necessary socioeconomic function as it contributed to the community. Such a society, he believed, would be harmonious.

Contrary to the prevailing Athenian opinion that held women to be inferior, Plato believed that women should enjoy many of the intellectual and educational privileges and responsibilities accorded men.[9] Like their male counterparts, women, too, fell within the three basic categories to which Plato assigned human beings. Some women, possessing a high degree of intellectual powers could become members of the ruling philosophical elite; others of lesser cognitive abilities were assigned to the ranks of defenders or workers. Like men, women received the education appropriate to their abilities and their destined occupation in the Republic.

Plato on women's education

Plato's Educational Curriculum Since Plato believed that parents often passed on their prejudices and ignorance to their children, children were separated from their parents and reared in state nurseries in the Republic. The nurseries constituted a prepared environment, from which ideas and practices regarded as injurious to the child's proper development had been excised. From ages six to eighteen, music and gymnastics were studied. Music included letters, reading, writing, choral singing, and dancing. After mas-

State-run schools

9 James Mulhern, *A History of Education: A Social Interpretation* (New York: Ronald Press, 1959), p. 159.

tering reading and writing, the students read the classics, which had been carefully censored. Plato, who regarded literature as a powerful force in character formation, believed that children should read only poems and stories that epitomized truthfulness, obedience to authorities, courage, and control of emotions. After mastering basic arithmetic, the students applied themselves to geometry and astronomy. Gymnastics consisted of functional exercises useful for military training, such as fencing, archery, javelin throwing, and horseback riding. Gymnastic exercises were considered essential for character building and for physical development. Plato also included the rules of diet and hygiene in his curriculum.

Athletics for building character

From ages eighteen to twenty, the students pursued intensive physical and military training. At twenty, the future philosopher-kings were selected for ten years of additional higher education in mathematics, geometry, astronomy, music, and science. At age thirty, the less intellectually capable became civil servants; the most intellectually capable continued the higher studies of metaphysics and dialectic. In Platonic terms, intellectual capacity was related to a person's ability to reason in metaphysical terms. Since metaphysics dealt with questions of the nature of ultimate reality, those who were to continue their education had to penetrate beyond the effects of immediate sense perception and grasp intellectually the ultimate cause of existence. The search for the ultimate cause of existence involved the process of **dialectic**—the process by which all truth is derived from the single principle of the Form of the Good, according to Plato. When their studies were completed, the philosopher-kings began to direct the military and political affairs of the Republic. At age fifty, the philosopher-kings became the Republic's elder statesmen.

Metaphysic and dialectic studies

Concerned with questions of universal truth and virtue, Plato opposed the Sophists' stress on technique and method. For Plato, truth, learning, and education were intellectual, not technical. Hence, those who showed a propensity toward abstract thought were to be selected by teachers for studies that developed their reasoning powers. Individuals who were not suited to philosophical inquiry were given vocational training. Students admitted to a Platonic school were a carefully selected intellectual elite. Educational opportunity was reserved for those competent to master highly intellectual and abstract studies.

Focus on intellectual learning

Aristotle: Cultivation of Rationality

Plato's student Aristotle (384–322 B.C.) was the tutor of Alexander the Great. Aristotle founded the Lyceum, an Athenian philosophical school, and wrote extensively on such subjects as physics, astronomy, zoology, botany, logic, ethics, and metaphysics. Aristotle's *Nicomachean Ethics* and *Politics* examine education in relation to society and government.[10]

As a philosophical realist, Aristotle held that reality was posited in an objective order. Objects, composed of form and matter, exist independently of

10 John H. Randall, *Aristotle* (New York: Columbia University Press, 1960).

our knowledge of them. Human beings are rational; therefore they have the ability to know and observe the natural laws that govern them. Aristotle also saw a basic duality in human nature. Human beings possess souls or minds and material bodies. Like the animals, people have appetites or physical needs, which must be satisfied for them to survive. Unlike the lower animals, men and women have intellect, which gives them the power to think. The good person has activated and fully uses this rational power. The truly educated person exercises reason in judging ethical and political behavior. Humankind's goal is happiness, and the good life is one of moderation—an avoidance of extremes.[11]

Moderation

For Aristotle, thinking and knowing begin with one's sensation of objects in the environment. From this sensory experience, concepts are formed by extracting the forms or patterns of these objects from matter that appears to the senses. The Aristotelian emphasis on sensory experience as the beginning of knowing and of instruction later was stressed by eighteenth- and nineteenth-century educators, such as Locke and Pestalozzi. Aristotle's philosophical position was the historical predecessor of realism, which is discussed in Chapter 6.

Aristotle on Education In *Politics* Aristotle set forth an educational theory that states that the good community is based on the cultivation of rationality. If education is neglected, then the community suffers. Aristotle gave education a major role in cultivating human and civic excellence or perfection. Like most of the Greek theorists, Aristotle made a distinction between liberal education and vocational training. Aristotle saw the liberal arts as a liberating factor, enlarging and expanding one's choices. Occupational and vocational training in trade, commerce, and farming were servile pursuits that interfered with intellectual pursuits. (Contemporary debates between liberal educators and career educators often reflect the same basic issues that were examined by Aristotle and the other Greek theorists.)

Cultivation of rationality

Aristotle, who saw that education cultivated both the rational person and the rational society, recommended compulsory public schools. Infant schooling consisted of play, physical activity, and appropriate stories. Children from ages seven to fourteen were to develop proper habits by moral and physical education. They were to have gymnastic training or physical education. Music cultivated proper emotional dispositions. The basic skills needed for liberal education—reading and writing—were to be taught. From age fifteen through twenty-one, youths were to study mathematics, geometry, astronomy, grammar, literature, poetry, rhetoric, ethics, and politics. At age twenty-one, the students followed more theoretical subjects such as physics, cosmology, biology, psychology, logic, and metaphysics. Like many of the Greek theorists, Aristotle was concerned exclusively with the education of boys. Following the conventional mores of Athens, he believed women to be intel-

Compulsory schooling

11 Eva T. H. Brann, *Paradoxes of Education in a Republic* (Chicago: University of Chicago Press, 1979); Paul Nash, *Models of Man: Explorations in the Western Educational Tradition* (New York: Wiley, 1968).

lectually inferior to men. He had a limited view of female education; girls were to be trained only to perform household and child-rearing duties necessary for their roles as future wives and mothers.

Aristotle's Theory of Knowledge For Aristotle, knowledge is always about an object. While cognition begins with sensory data about an object, knowledge is conceptual—it is based on the form of the object. Concepts are the generalized classes of objects. For example, if you walk through a forest, you might see such trees as pines, oaks, elms, and maples. While these trees vary in some aspects of their appearance, they are all similar in that they are members of a class. As trees, they share or participate in the form of "treeness." If a teacher of botany uses the Aristotelian method, he or she can teach about trees as a class or as a general category in botanical reality and can also teach about the particular trees that are members of the class. Since knowledge is always about an object, education and teaching are always about an object and should have a content. In the Aristotelian teaching act, the teacher instructs a learner about some object, some body of knowledge, or some discipline. Teaching and learning never represent merely an interpersonal relationship or the expression of feelings. They are always about disciplined inquiry into some aspect of reality.

The Aristotelian school was an institution for teaching and learning about knowledge. Instruction was both theoretical and practical. In fact, Aristotelians assert that theory is the best guide to conduct. Their theory of reality is based on careful observation of objects as they occur in nature. The teacher can be called a demonstrator of theory. Since Aristotle defined human beings as rational, the school should cultivate and develop each person's rationality. A school, in Aristotle's view, should be a highly academic institution.[12] It should offer a prescribed subject-matter curriculum based on scholarly and scientific discipline. Within such a school, teachers would have expert knowledge of their subject and would be skilled in transmitting that knowledge to students who are motivated to learn it. Aristotle's philosophy became the foundation of medieval Scholastic education and is the basis of the educational philosophies of such modern humanist educators as Robert Hutchins and Mortimer Adler.

Focus on scholarship and science

Isocrates: Oratory and Rhetoric

The Greek rhetorician Isocrates (436–388 B.C.) is significant in Western educational history because he developed a well-constructed educational theory based on rhetorical skills and knowledge.

Isocrates wrote *Against the Sophists* as a prospectus for his own school and method of instruction.[13] He denounced the Sophists for their superficiality, their stress on tricks and gimmicks, and their often exaggerated promises.

12 Kenneth J. Freeman, *Schools of Hellas* (New York: Teachers College Press, Columbia University, 1969), p. 203.

13 Edward J. Power, *Main Currents in the History of Education* (New York: McGraw-Hill, 1970), pp. 105–112.

In a more positive sense, Isocrates indicated that his major educational objective was to prepare rational men who would be rational speakers of the truth. Civic reform, he believed, could be secured only by educating virtuous leaders who could capably administer the state. Of the liberal studies, Isocrates held that rhetoric, the rational expression of thought, was most important in cultivating morality and political leadership.

Rhetorical education as humanistic

Isocrates opposed those Sophists who taught rhetoric as a set of isolated persuasive routines or public relations techniques. Rather, he believed that rhetorical education should be completely humanistic and cultural, including the tools and techniques of speech. The worthy orator should recognize and should serve those honorable causes that advance the public good. As a man above reproach, the orator would persuade men to follow good programs.[14] In this connection, Isocrates' students, who enrolled in his school for a term of three to four years, studied rhetoric, examined model orations, and practiced public speaking. To develop humanely educated men, Isocrates also taught politics, ethics, and history. The teacher was important in Isocrates' method of rhetorical education, since he had to be capable of influencing his students through his own demonstration of knowledge, skill, and ethical conduct.

Although Isocrates opposed the crass opportunism of the Sophists, he also rejected the Platonic perspective that education was to lead to the purely speculative and the abstract. For Isocrates, education had objectives that led to public service because informed action was based on and guided by knowledge.

Influence on Roman education

An effective and methodological educator, Isocrates contributed to the rhetorical tradition in education. He had a direct influence on the Roman theorists Cicero and Quintilian. By recognizing the humanistic dimension of rhetorical study, Isocrates contributed to the ideal of the liberally educated man.

The Greek Contribution to Western Education

Western culture and education inherited a rich legacy from ancient Greece. It included the following:

1. A profound conviction of the possibility of achieving human excellence.
2. The idea that education had civic purposes that were related to the political well-being of the community.
3. A distinction between liberal education and vocational training, which has led to curricular controversies throughout Western educational history.
4. The legacy of the Socratic method, by which skilled teachers might use dialectical processes to ask universal questions relating to truth, goodness, and beauty.

14 George Kennedy, *The Art of Persuasion in Greece* (Princeton, N.J.: Princeton University Press, 1963).

Education in Ancient Rome

While the Greeks were developing their concepts of culture and education in the eastern Mediterranean, the Romans were consolidating their political position on the Italian peninsula and throughout the western Mediterranean. In their drive from small republic to great empire, the Romans first were preoccupied with war and politics. After they had created their empire, they concentrated on the administration, law, and diplomacy needed to maintain it. The Greeks were concerned with speculative philosophy; the Romans were most interested in educating the practical politician and able administrator.

War and politics

The Roman educational ideal was exemplified by a conception of oratory similar to that held by Isocrates. The Roman orator was the broadly and liberally educated man of public life—the senator, lawyer, teacher, civil servant, and politician. Cicero and Quintilian are important examples.

Cicero: Master Orator

Practical and liberal education

The distinguished Roman senator Cicero (106–43 B.C.) had himself studied both Greek and Latin grammar and literature, history, and rhetoric. He appreciated both the old Roman stress on practicality and utility and the Greek emphasis on humanistic and liberal culture. His work *de Oratore* combined the Roman and Greek conceptions of the educated man.[15] In the Roman context, the practical results of oratory were winning debates and arguments in the Forum. Cicero added the Greek perspective of rhetorical education, which stressed broad and liberal culture, or *humanitas*. Cicero recommended that the orator, as a rational man, should be educated in the liberal arts and should use his education in the public interest. Commenting on the education that was preparatory to rhetoric, Cicero also prescribed the role of the *grammaticus,* the secondary school teacher. The *grammaticus* was to comment on the poets, teach history, correct diction and delivery, and explain the meaning of language. Although Greek was the medium of instruction, the young Roman boy was also to be adept in using his own language, Latin.[16]

Importance of history

After the prospective orator had been prepared adequately in grammar, he went on to the higher studies. Like Isocrates, Cicero believed that the humanistically educated orator should be prepared thoroughly in the liberal arts—ethics, psychology, military science, medicine, natural science, geography, astronomy, history, law, and philosophy. In particular, Cicero believed that the great orator needed a knowledge of history. History would provide the young Roman with perspective into his own past and tradition. It would provide him with rhetorical illustrations and examples by examining the biographies of great Greeks and Romans. Students were to study the speeches

15 Aubrey Gwynn, *Roman Education from Cicero to Quintilian,* rev. ed. (New York: Teachers College Press, Columbia University, 1966).

16 A. S. Wilkins, *Roman Education* (London: Cambridge University Press, 1931).

Overview 3.2

Major Educational Theorists, to A.D. 1600

Theorist	Philosophical Orientation	View of Human Nature	Views on Education and Curriculum	Contribution and Influence
Plato 420–348 B.C. (Greek)	Philosophical idealist; sociopolitical conservative	Human beings can be classified on the basis of their intellectual capabilities	Music, gymnastics, geometry, astronomy, basic literary skills; philosophy for ruling elite of philosopher kings	Use of schools for testing and sorting students according to intellectual abilities; education closely tied to civic (political) purposes; basis of "Great Books" curriculum
Aristotle 384–322 B.C. (Greek)	Philosophical realist; view of society, politics, and education based on classical realism	Human beings have the power of rationality, which should guide their conduct	Objective and scientific emphasis; basic literary skills, mathematics, natural and physical sciences, philosophy	Emphasis on the liberally educated, well-rounded person; importance of reason; basis of "Great Books" curriculum and "the Paideia Proposal"
Isocrates 436–388 B.C. (Greek)	Rhetorician; oratorical education in service of self and society	Human beings have the power of using their speech (discourse) for social and political improvement	Rhetorical studies; basic literary skills; politics, history, rhetoric, declamation, public speaking	Use of knowledge in pursuit of public affairs and as a means of exercising political leadership; teacher education having both a content and a practice dimension
Quintilian A.D. 35–A.D. 95 (Roman)	Rhetorician; oratory for personal gain and public service	Certain individuals have the capacity for leadership, based on	Basic literary skills; grammar, history, literature, drama, philoso-	Role of motivation in learning; recognition of individual

of great statesmen and the ancient Roman Laws of the Twelve Tables. Cicero's emphasis in the Laws of the Twelve Tables revealed his desire to preserve the ethical principles of Republican Rome as the basis of moral educa-

Overview 3.2 (cont.)

Major Educational Theorists, to A.D. 1600

Theorist	Philosophical Orientation	View of Human Nature	Views on Education and Curriculum	Contribution and Influence
		humane disposition, liberal knowledge, and oratorical skill	phy, public speaking, law	differences
Aquinas A.D. 1225–A.D. 1274 (Italian Medieval theologian)	Christian theology and Aristotelian (realist) philosophy	Human beings possess both a spiritual nature (soul) and a physical nature (body)	Education should be based on human nature, with appropriate studies for both spiritual and physical dimensions	Teacher as moral agent; education related to universal theological goals; synthesis of the theological and philosophical; basis of philosophy used in today's Roman Catholic schools
Erasmus A.D. 1465–A.D. 1536 (Dutch Renaissance humanist)	Christian orientation; the educator as social and intellectual critic	Human beings are capable of great achievements but also of profound stupidity	Education for a literary elite that stressed criticism and analysis	Concept of the role of secondary and higher education in literary and social criticism; emphasis on critical thinking as an educational goal
Luther A.D. 1483–A.D. 1546 (German Protestant)	Reformed theology stressing salvation by faith and individual conscience	Human beings are saved by faith; individual conscience shaped by Scripture and Reformed theology	Elementary schools to teach reading, writing, arithmetic, religion; secondary schools to prepare leaders by offering classics, Latin, Greek, and religion; vocational training	Emphasis on universal literacy; schools to stress religious values, vocational skills, knowledge; close relationship of religion, schooling, and the state.

tion. These laws covered one's duties to honor parents, to respect property, and to serve the state. Effective speakers also needed to be versed in philosophy, which included psychology, ethics, politics, and logic.

Emphasis on rhetoric

Upon the broad framework of the liberal arts, the orator then studied rhetoric. As a public speaker, the orator had to select his words with care so that he could structure his arguments persuasively. He needed to use psychology to excite the emotions of his audience and to influence public affairs. The orator needed to be quick intellectually; he needed to be versatile in using a number of speaking styles and types of argument. Cicero also believed that oratory was a functional study that could actively influence public opinion and shape state policy. The word *humanitas,* which signifies all that is worthy in an individual as a humane and intelligent being, best expresses his ideal of the educated man.[17]

Quintilian: Teacher of Rhetoric

Marcus Fabius Quintilianus, or Quintilian (A.D. 35–95), worked in Rome as a legal assistant. It was as a teacher of rhetoric, however, that he gained the fame that led to his appointment to the first chair of Latin rhetoric. As the foremost Roman rhetorician, Quintilian served emperors. Cicero had written when Rome was a republic; Quintilian's program of oratorical education reflected the political realities of imperial Rome, which was ruled by decree rather than by group decisions shaped by oratorical argument.[18] Unlike Cicero, who served in Rome's Senate, Quintilian was primarily a teacher, whose chief involvement was with education. Nevertheless, both Quintilian and Cicero believed that the orator should be a man of *humanitas,* of liberal disposition and culture.

Quintilian's *Institutio Oratoria,* appearing in A.D. 94, was a systematic educational work that dealt with education preparatory to the study of rhetoric, rhetorical theories and studies, and the practice of public speaking or declamation. Quintilian recognized that instruction should be based on the stages of human growth and development. In the first stage, from birth until age seven, the child was impulsive and concerned with immediately satisfying its needs and desires. Since the early childhood years established later attitudes and values, parents were to select well-trained nurses, pedagogues, and companions for their children. It was very important that the future orator should have a Greek nurse and pedagogue who used correct speech and pronunciation patterns so that good language usage became habitual to the student.

Stages of growth

In Quintilian's second stage of education, from seven to fourteen, the child learned from sense experiences, formed clear ideas, and exercised his memory. Now he wrote the languages that he already spoke. The reading and writing instructor, the *litterator,* was to be of good character *and* a competent teacher. Instruction in reading and writing was to be slow but thorough. The school should include games and recreation. A set of ivory letters was to aid in learning the alphabet. By tracing the outline of the letters, the child learned writing.

17 *Cicero on the Good Life,* trans. Michael Grant (New York: Penguin, 1979).

18 George Kennedy, *Quintilian,* (New York: Twayne, 1969).

Study of liberal arts

In the third stage of education, Quintilian stressed the study of the liberal arts with the *grammaticus* in the secondary school. Both Greek and Latin grammars were to be studied concurrently. Grammar involved Greek and Roman literature, history, and mythology. Music, geometry, astronomy, and gymnastics also were studied. After grammar and the liberal arts, the prospective orator began rhetorical studies, which Quintilian identified as drama, poetry, history, law, philosophy, and rhetoric.[19]

Declamations—systematic speaking exercises—were of great importance for the orator. The themes of the declamations were to be factual rather than fictitious. If students proved incapable of oratory they were dismissed, so as not to waste the teacher's time and energy. As soon as possible, the novice orator spoke in the Forum before an audience and then returned to the master rhetorician for expert criticism. The teacher was to correct the student's mistakes with a sense of authority but also with patience, tact, and consideration.

Instruction appropriate to the learner's abilities

For Quintilian, oratorical perfection depended on the speaker's own moral excellence.[20] To persuade, the orator had to be trustworthy. Quintilian's significance in Western educational history lies in his attention to the theory and practice of teaching and learning. In anticipating the modern teacher's concern for the learner's individual differences, he recommended that instruction be made appropriate to the learner's abilities and readiness. He also recommended that the teacher motivate students by making learning interesting and attractive.

The Roman Contribution to Western Education

Many of the cultural and educational structures that shaped Western civilization emerged and developed in the Roman republic and empire. Among them were the following:

1. An emphasis on training administrators and civil servants who could maintain the political infrastructure of a vast and diverse empire.
2. A pragmatic propensity to translate theories into practices.
3. An institutionalization of informal educational practices into more formal school arrangements.
4. The practice of cultural and educational borrowing and readaptation, which reached a high point in Rome's selective use of Greek philosophy and education.

Influence of Arabic Learning on Western Education

In the tenth and eleventh centuries, Arabic learning had a pronounced influence on Western educational development, particularly on the evolution of medieval scholasticism (the philosophy underlying medieval thought and

19 E. Brandenburg, "Quintilian and the Good Orator," *Quarterly Journal of Speech* (February 1948), pp. 23–29.

20 William M. Smail, *Quintilian on Education,* rev. ed. (New York: Teachers College Press, Columbia University, 1966).

higher learning). From contact with Arab scholars (the Moors) in North Africa and Spain, Western educators learned new ways of thinking about mathematics, natural science, medicine, and philosophy. For example, Arab scholars had discovered and translated the philosophical and scientific treatises of Aristotle. It was through the Arabic conduit that early medieval Scholastics, such as Abelard and Aquinas, received some of Aristotle's works. Arabic medical theories and practices also were introduced to the medieval university of Salerno in Italy.

Arabic learning

Arabic scholarship and science stemmed from the earlier religious movement led by Mohammed (569–632) who developed the Islamic theological framework. United by a missionary zeal to spread the Islamic religion, Arabic culture and education were diffused throughout North Africa, as far east as India, and as far west as Spain. Because of their extensive conquests, the Arabs came into contact with a wide variety of peoples and cultures—Hindus, Egyptians, Syrians, and others. Although religious purists, they incorporated elements from these cultures into their own civilization. Along with the Islamic faith and the Arabic language, Arab culture also embraced literature, science, philosophy, and architecture. Of great practical significance to Western education was the Arabic number system, which is the basis of arithmetic.[21] Under the influence of their religious leaders, Arabic higher schools were established at Baghdad, Cairo, Córdoba, Grenada, Toledo, and Seville.

In time, a division developed among the Arabs. While some were fundamentalist believers, others were more inclined to philosophy. Scholars such as Avicenna (980–1037) and Averroes (1126–1198) had an impact on Western European education. Of particular importance to Western education were the translation and preservation of such important Greek scholars as Aristotle, Euclid, Galen, and Ptolemy.

Arab scholars—Avicenna and Averroes

Avicenna, who believed that philosophy could illuminate and enrich religious experience, encountered many of the texts of Aristotle and translated them into Arabic. While Western European educators were familiar with Aristotle's logic, his philosophical texts were presumed to be lost. When European Scholastic educators encountered Avicenna's translations of Aristotle, they in turn translated them into Latin. The rediscovery of Aristotle's philosophy was to have a profound impact on Western education, especially on higher education.

Averroes, a physician in Córdoba, was also a translator of and a commentator on Aristotle. An original thinker, he wrote treatises on medicine, astronomy, and philosophy. Keenly interested in education, Averroes believed that teachers should seek to find the truth and transmit it to their students.

The Arabic scholars contributed to education in their own culture and also to Western European culture. Among their contributions were (1) the translation of Greek classical works into Arabic and (2) the development of important advances in mathematics and science.[22] The entry of ideas from

Arab contribution to education

21 Power, *Main Currents in the History of Education*, pp. 271–273.

22 For a recent commentary on Islamic culture, see Daniel G. Bates and Amal Rassam, *Peoples and Cultures of the Middle East*. (Englewood Cliffs, N.J.: Prentice-Hall, 1983), pp. 29–57.

the Arabic world into Western culture and education typifies cross-cultural transference of educational ideas.

Medieval Culture and Education

Decline, then revival, in learning

The years between the fall of Rome and the Renaissance (c. 500–1400) have been labeled by historians as the Middle Ages, or the medieval period. This era of Western culture and education began at the end of the ancient classical period of Greece and Rome and came to an end at the beginning of the modern era. The medieval period was characterized first by a decline in learning and then a revival by the Scholastic educators. In the absence of strong, centralized political authorities, the medieval order of life, society, and education was brought to a synthesis and unified by the Latin Catholic church, headed by the pope in Rome.[23]

During this period the tradition of learning was carried on at elementary parish, chantry, and monastic schools conducted under church auspices. At the secondary level, both monastic and cathedral schools offered a curriculum of general studies. Schools that provided basic education as well as training for a trade were also maintained by the merchant and craft guilds. Knights received their training in military tactics and the chivalric code in the palaces. In the development of educational institutions, the rise of the medieval university merits the most attention because together with the flowering of Scholastic education it was the major contribution to education during this period.[24]

Education of medieval women

The condition of women in medieval society was mixed in terms of their status and educational opportunities. While medieval Christianity stressed the spiritual equality of women and the sacramental nature of marriage, women were consigned to prescribed roles. For the vast serf and peasant classes of agricultural poor, women's roles were the traditional ones of household chores and child rearing. Girls of the peasant classes learned their future roles by imitating their mothers. Women of the noble classes also followed the prescriptions of their class and learned the roles accorded them by the code of chivalry, which often meant managing the domestic life of the castle or manor.

As was true for men, the medieval church provided an institutional opportunity for the education of women through religious communities or convents. Convents, like the monasteries, had libraries and schools to prepare nuns to follow the religious rules of their communities.

Aquinas: Scholastic Education

A method of inquiry and teaching

By the eleventh century, medieval educators had developed **scholasticism**—a method of inquiry, scholarship, and teaching. The Scholastics, as the teaching clerics were called, relied on faith and reason as complementary sources

23 Edward Peters, *Europe and the Middle Ages* (Englewood Cliffs, N.J.: Prentice-Hall, 1983).

24 Donna R. Barnes, *For Court, Manor, and Church: Education in Medieval Europe* (Minneapolis: Burgess, 1971).

of truth. They accepted the sacred Scriptures and the writings of the church fathers as sources of God's revealed word and also trusted in human reason. The Scholastics believed that the human mind could deduce first principles that, when illuminated by scriptural authority, were a source of truth. When the Scholastics encountered the works of Aristotle and other Greek philosophers that came to them from Arabic scholars, they faced the problem of reconciling philosophical and theological principles.

Scholastic philosophy and education reached its zenith in the *Summa Theologica* of Saint Thomas Aquinas (1225–1274), a Dominican theologian who taught at the University of Paris.[25] Aquinas was primarily concerned with reconciling the authority of faith as represented by the Scriptures with the authority of Greek rationalism as represented by Aristotle. He used both faith and reason to answer basic questions dealing with the Christian conception of God, the nature of humankind and the universe, and the relationship between God and human beings. As a philosopher and theologian, Aquinas knew both Christian doctrine and Aristotelian philosophy and sought to integrate these two important sources of the Western intellectual and educational tradition into a coherent world view. In the Thomistic context, human beings possess a physical body and a spiritual soul. While living temporarily on earth, their ultimate purpose is to experience eternity with God. Like Aristotle, Aquinas asserted that human knowledge of the world originates in sensation and is completed by abstraction or concept formation.

Relationship between God and human beings

In *De Magistro (Concerning the Teacher),* Aquinas discussed the teacher's vocation as one that combines faith, love, and learning.[26] The teacher needs to be a contemplative scholar, an active agent of learning, a master of his discipline, and a lover of humanity. The teacher needs to know subject matter thoroughly and also to be expert in the method of teaching it. Aquinas and the other Scholastic educators saw no conflict between research and teaching. The good teacher needs to do both and do them well so that teaching and scholarship are carefully blended.

Informal vs. formal education

Aquinas also recognized that informal education had to be related carefully to the discipline of formal schooling. Informal education involved *all* the agencies, such as family, friends, and environment, that developed a person's virtue or excellence. Schooling was learning that was stimulated by formal teaching. Schooling was about bodies of knowledge and subject-matter disciplines, based on first principles and containing demonstrated conclusions. Such subject-matter disciplines formed the basis of formal instruction in schools. Scholastic teachers used the syllogism—a form of deductive reasoning—to accumulate an ordered body of demonstrated knowledge. The teacher aided the students in recognizing basic principles and in developing the implications of these principles. Aquinas held that the teacher had to select the language that effectively communicated the subject to the students. In curricular matters Aquinas followed the liberal arts tradition: logic, math-

25 Frank P. Cassidy, *Molders of the Medieval Mind: The Influence of the Fathers of the Church on the Medieval Schoolmen* (Port Washington, N.Y.: Kennikat Press, 1966).

26 John W. Donohue, *St. Thomas Aquinas and Education* (New York: Random House, 1968).

ematics, natural and moral philosophy, metaphysics, and theology were the organized subject matters of the curriculum of higher education.[27]

Aquinas and the other Scholastics had definite ideas about the nature of knowledge, the meaning of education, and the purpose of schooling.[28] For the Scholastic, knowledge came from two complementary and mutually supporting sources: faith and reason. The Scholastic's faith, or belief system, assumed that God's truth came to the world through revelation. Certain divinely inspired men had recorded God's revealed word in the sacred Scripture of the books of the Bible. The medieval church believed that it had a mission to teach God's revealed truth to people of all nations, and the church fathers and the church councils interpreted and explained the meaning of sacred Scriptures. For the medieval Scholastic, then, faith in the authority of the Scriptures and in church teaching was one component of knowledge; hence, the most important subjects in the medieval university were theological.

Scholasticism

The medieval Scholastics also believed it was possible for people to use their rational potentiality, or power, to find truth. The Scholastic school was an institution that taught the principles of the Christian religion and of rational philosophy. Generally, it was governed and protected by the church. Its teachers were clerics under religious protection and governance. During the medieval period, schooling functioned to prepare priests, monks, court officials, scribes, and administrators. The serfs, the farmers bound to the soil, generally had no formal schooling.

The work of Aquinas and other Scholastic educators centered about the medieval university, the institution of higher education. An examination of the origins, development, and organization of the medieval university is useful to students of contemporary education, since the basic patterns of higher education were established in the medieval period.

Medieval Universities

Intellectual revival

Such famous medieval seats of learning as the universities of Paris, Salerno, Bologna, Oxford, Cambridge, and Padua grew out of the intellectual revival of the twelfth and thirteenth centuries.[29] It is generally believed that the major universities evolved from the expanding enrollments of the cathedral schools, which by the twelfth century were unable to accommodate the growing number of students. The universities evolved from associations, called *universitas,* which the students and teachers organized for their own protection and security. Enrollment had increased because of the improved

27 Ibid., pp. 76–89.

28 For medieval thought, see Philippe Wolff, *The Awakening of Europe* (Baltimore: Penguin, 1968); Alexander Murray, *Reason and Society in the Middle Ages* (Oxford: Clarendon Press, 1978).

29 For the medieval universities, the classic study is Hastings Rashdall, *The Universities of Europe in the Middle Ages,* 3 vols., ed. R. M. Powicke and A.B. Emden (Oxford: Oxford University Press, 1936). Also see Anders Piltz, *The World of Medieval Learning* (Totowa, N.J.: Barnes & Noble, 1981); Lynn Thorndike, *University Records and Life in the Middle Ages* (New York: Norton, 1975); Gordon Leff, *Paris and Oxford Universities in the Thirteenth and Fourteenth Centuries* (New York: Wiley, 1968).

economic conditions stimulated by the Crusades. Crusaders had also come into contact with Byzantine Greek and Arabic scholarship, which was then brought back to western Europe. As mentioned earlier, the medieval educators discovered the works of Aristotle, Euclid, Ptolemy, Galen, and Hippocrates through the Byzantine and Arab scholars.[30] Theological interpretation and investigation of these newly discovered works were of major interest to the Scholastics, especially at the University of Paris, where Thomas Aquinas attempted to reconcile Aristotle's rationalism with the Scriptures and doctrines of Christianity.

Professional schools

A high level of scholarship resulted from the rise and development of the medieval universities. The medieval universities established specialized professional schools of law, medicine, and theology in addition to the liberal arts curriculum. The University of Bologna in Italy and the University of Paris in France represented two distinctive patterns of institutional organization in higher education; the former was shaped by students; the latter, by faculty.[31]

Other universities were established throughout Europe between the twelfth and fifteenth centuries: in Italy, the University of Padua and the University of Naples; in France, the universities of Montpellier, Orleans, and Toulouse; in England, Oxford University, and Cambridge University a hundred years later. By the fourteenth century Europe had the Scottish universities of St. Andrew and Aberdeen, the Spanish university of Salamanca, and the German universities of Erfurt, Heidelberg, and Cologne. There were also universities in Vienna and Prague.

The Medieval Contribution to Western Education

The medieval contribution to Western education primarily resulted from the institutionalization and preservation of knowledge. While parish, monastic, and cathedral schools were places of learning in which knowledge was transmitted in an organized, formal, and institutionalized framework, the epitome of such institutionalization was the medieval university. The medieval conception of higher education took its institutional form in the university, which served as the model for the modern university. In addition to institutionalizing knowledge, medieval centers of learning preserved it by recording and codifying it.

Renaissance Classical Humanism

Revival in humanism and classics

The Renaissance, beginning in the fourteenth century and reaching its height in the fifteenth century, witnessed a marked revival of interest in the humanistic aspects of the Greek and Latin classics. It was also a period of transition

30 Byzantine culture is examined in Peter Arnott, *The Byzantines and Their World* (New York: St. Martin's, 1973); Dean A. Miller *The Byzantine Tradition* (New York: Harper & Row, 1966).

31 Pearl Kibre, *The Nations in the Medieval Universities* (Cambridge, Mass: Medieval Academy of America, 1948).

Renaissance schools emphasized classical humanist education and especially the study of Latin, Greek, and classical literature.
(Culver Pictures, Inc.)

between the medieval and modern ages. The Renaissance classical humanist, like the medieval Scholastic, found his authorities in the past and stressed classical manuscripts. Unlike the Scholastics, the humanist educators were interested more in the earthly experience of human beings than in a God-centered world view.[32]

The effects of the Renaissance were particularly noticeable in Italy, where the revival of commerce had produced a financial surplus that fostered art, literature, and architecture. Wealth, flowing into the prosperous Italian cities, supported humanist educators and schools. The Italian classical humanists, considering themselves an aristocratic literary elite, were self-proclaimed "custodians of knowledge." Coinciding with the spirit of the age, rulers in the Italian city-states established court schools to prepare their children in the new learning.

The literary birth of the Italian Renaissance came with the works of Dante, Petrarch, and Boccaccio. Rejecting Scholastic techniques, the classical humanist writers and educators rediscovered Cicero and Quintilian. In the ancient classics of Greek and Rome, the humanist educators found models of

32 Robert Schwoebel, *Renaissance Men and Ideas* (New York: St. Martin's, 1971).

literary excellence and style, the ideal of the educated person, and a view of life based on the wisdom of antiquity.

Challenge to scholasticism

Classical humanist education challenged the older Scholastic model. The cleric, trained in Scholastic logic, was no longer the preferred model of the educated man. In the Renaissance, the courtier became the model. The courtier was a man of style and elegance; he was liberally educated in classical literature; he was a capable diplomat and could serve his ruler well in the affairs of state. Baldesar Castiglione (1478–1529) described the courtier and his education in a famous work, *The Book of the Courtier*.[33]

In northern Europe, also, classical humanist scholars began to critically examine the Scriptures and theological writing. They considered Scholastic education to be in a state of decay. Educators now sought to develop teaching methods and materials designed to produce the well-rounded, liberally educated courtier. The most suitable curriculum was classical Greek and Latin literature. The imitation of Cicero's style of writing would cultivate the elegance of style and expression needed by the cultured gentleman. An examination of the teaching style of Erasmus of Rotterdam provides an example of the northern Renaissance humanist educator.

Educated courtier

Erasmus: Critic and Reformer

Desiderius Erasmus (1465–1536), who was born in the city of Rotterdam in the Netherlands, was educated in the schools of the Brethren of the Common Life and had studied scholastic philosophy at the University of Paris. *The Praise of Folly* is his best-known book of a general nature.[34] Erasmus's writings reveal his interest in literary criticism and social reform. His contribution to Western education was that of a critic of contemporary institutions, a humanist educator, and an advocate of cosmopolitan humanism.

The Praise of Folly shows Erasmus to be a biting and satirical commentator on the professions and institutions of his day. He criticized the teachers of grammar for stressing trivial and obscure facts, and for ignoring the important aspects of learning while emphasizing unimportant matters that only confused students. Philosophers, Erasmus charged, were concerned only with the most abstract sort of speculations. Theologians, too, felt the jab of Erasmus's pen. Instead of examining the basic relationship of human beings with God, the doctors of theology were busily spinning subtle corollaries to demonstrate their own erudition. In some ways, Erasmus was like Socrates, who delighted in deflating the puffed-up egos of those who considered themselves to be exalted men of wisdom.

Erasmus was the leading classical scholar of the late Renaissance. Concerning the teaching of classical languages, he advised that the teacher

33 Baldesar Castiglione, *The Book of the Courtier,* trans. C. S. Singleton (New York: Doubleday, 1959).

34 William H. Woodward, *Desiderius Erasmus Concerning the Aim and Method of Education,* rev. ed. (New York: Teachers College Press, Columbia University, 1964).

should be well acquainted with archeology, astronomy, etymology, history, and Scripture since these areas were related to the study of classical literature. Recognizing the importance of early childhood, Erasmus recommended that the child's education begin as early as possible. Parents were to take their educational responsibilities seriously. Children should receive gentle instruction in good manners and hear stories that had a beneficial effect on the development of their character.

Early childhood education

Erasmus believed that understanding content was more important than mastering style and grammar. Students should understand the content thoroughly; conversation in the language would make learning interesting. Games and contests were also to be encouraged. Erasmus's concern for content and not just for style is clearly seen in his discussion of teaching methods. The teacher of language, he recommended, should: (1) present the author's biography, (2) examine the type of work under study, (3) discuss the basic plot, (4) analyze the author's style, (5) consider the moral implications of the work, and (6) explain the broader philosophical issues raised by the work.

Teaching methods

The Renaissance's Contribution to Western Education

The Renaissance established some basic trends that influenced the future development of Western education. Most significant was the emphasis on the study of Latin as the hallmark of the educated person. (Until the end of the nineteenth century, knowledge of Latin was required for admission to many colleges and universities in both Europe and the United States.) Also significant was the class basis of secondary schooling; the humanist schools were primarily intended for the children of the nobility and the upper classes, whereas vernacular elementary schools attended to the needs of the commercial class and those of the lower classes who received little, if any, formal schooling. The aim of secondary education was to produce people skilled in languages. Learning at this level was seen as the mastery of bodies of knowledge. The later pedagogical revolt and reforms of Rousseau, Comenius, Pestalozzi, and Dewey (discussed in Chapter 4) were directed against schools that gave exclusive emphasis to the study and mastery of literature, while neglecting experience.

Study of Latin

The classical humanists' conceptions of knowledge, education, and schooling established the outlines of secondary education that have persisted in many Western countries. Erasmus and other Renaissance humanist educators were moving slowly to a humanistic or human-centered conception of knowledge.[35] However, they did not approach their human subject as an object of scientific inquiry. Rather than facing the human experience directly in biological or sociological terms, the humanist educators preferred to deal

Absence of scientific inquiry

35 Charles D. Marler, *Philosophy and Schooling* (Boston: Allyn and Bacon, 1975); Meyer, *Grandmasters of Educational Thought*, pp. 66–81.

with it indirectly through literature. Although they created their own literature about humanity, they went about their task of human rediscovery by returning to the ancient literatures of classical Greece and Rome.

The Renaissance humanist educators were literary figures—writers, poets, and translators—as well as teachers. In many respects they were artist-teachers who approached learning through the medium of literature. To be educated meant to have read and mastered books and to have learned classical languages. For centuries these classical humanist preferences would both shape and confine secondary and higher education. The educated person would be defined as one who knew the classical languages and who had acquired that knowledge from books.

As artist-teachers the Renaissance humanists viewed their human subject with a sense of detachment and distance. They did not get close to their living and breathing human subject but kept a safe distance between themselves and the mass of humanity. Their conception of human nature was distilled from a carefully aged literature. As a vintage wine is used to grace a carefully prepared dinner, the humanist education was reserved for the connoisseur. Humanist education was not given to everyone but was reserved for an elite who could appreciate and savor it.

Elitist education

As an artist-teacher, the humanist educator was a critic of literature, of taste, and of society. Such a person brought a witty and penetrating mind and pen to his work as a critic. In broad terms the education advocated by the humanist produced a critical person who challenged existing customs and mediocrity in literature and in life.

During the Renaissance, educational opportunities for women improved slightly, especially for the daughters of the upper classes and the aristocracy. Girls of wealthy families might attend the humanist court school or receive private lessons. The curriculum pursued by young ladies of the upper classes still reflected the notion that certain studies were appropriate for their gender, such as art, music, needlework, dancing, and poetry. Convents and convent schools continued to educate a small minority of young women as they had in the medieval period. For the daughters of the working classes, especially the rural peasantry, education still consisted almost entirely of training in household duties.

Women's education during Renaissance

Religious Reformation and Education

The religious reformations of the sixteenth and seventeenth centuries were related to the northern European humanist criticism of institutional life and to the search for new authorities. The rise of the commercial middle classes and the concurrent rise of national states were also important factors. Primarily, however, the various Protestant religious reformers—such as John Calvin, Martin Luther, Philip Melanchthon, and Ulrich Zwingli—sought to free themselves and their followers from papal authority and to reconstruct religious doctrine and forms. These reformers, who were conversant with

Rise of middle class

classical humanism, sought to develop educational philosophies and institutions that would support their religious reformations.[36]

The Protestant reformers significantly shaped the development of educational philosophies and institutions. The various religious sects developed their own educational theories, established their own schools, structured their own curricula, and sought to convince their children of the rightness of the reformed gospels that were preached to them. The general impact of the Protestant Reformation on education was a push toward a general extension of literacy among the masses of the population. Most of the reformers insisted that the faithful should read the Bible in their mother tongue. To do so, the members of the various churches had to be made literate.

Extension of mass literacy

The commitment to defend the faith also led to the use of the catechetical method of religious instruction. The catechism was an elementary book that summarized the principles of the Christian religion, as interpreted by the various denominations, into systematic questions and answers. It was believed that as a result of memorizing the lessons in the catechism, the student would internalize the principles of his or her religious faith. **Vernacular schools** (primary or elementary institutions that offered a basic curriculum of reading, writing, arithmetic, and religion) were used to make the lower classes literate. The language of instruction was that of the community. Vernacular schools in England, for example, used English as the language of instruction. A variety of secondary schools were maintained to educate the upper classes in Latin and Greek. The gymnasium in Germany, the Latin grammar school in England, and the lycée in France were college preparatory schools that trained the leadership elite, particularly those who were to be clergymen, in the classical languages.

Although there were many strong personalities at work in the Protestant Reformation and Roman Catholic Counter Reformation, special attention to the educational ideas of Martin Luther will exemplify the work of a major leader in the religious Reformation.

Luther: Advocate of Reform

Of all the religious leaders of the era, Martin Luther (1483–1546) stands out as perhaps the most influential in shaping the history of Western civilization. Born and educated in Germany, Luther was awarded the Master of Arts in 1505 and then became an Augustinian monk. His intellectual brilliance brought him to the attention of the head of his religious order, and Luther was sent to Wittenberg to lecture on theology. In 1517 Luther nailed his famous "Ninety-five Theses" to the door of the castle church at Wittenberg. From this time on Luther was involved in a series of challenges to the Roman Catholic Church and the pope on matters dealing with indulgences, the sacraments, papal authority, and freedom of individual conscience. Luther's chal-

36 Kenneth O. Gangel and Warren S. Benson, *Christian Education: Its History and Philosophy* (Chicago: Moody Press, 1983), pp. 135–151.

lenges stimulated great religious ferment and caused many others to preach religious reform. The culmination of this ferment was the Protestant Reformation, which spread through western and northern Europe.

Educational and religious reformation

Luther, who had been a university professor, recognized that educational reform was a potent ally of religious reformation. The church, state, family, and school were to be agents of reformation. The family, in particular, was an important agency in forming the character of children and in shaping values that were compatible with Christian life. He admonished parents to teach their children reading and religion. Each family should pray together, read the Bible, study the catechism, and practice a useful trade. Once children had acquired the right values they were ready to benefit from a cognitive program of formal schooling. Luther believed that public officials needed to be made conscious of their educational responsibilities. His "Letter to the Mayors and Aldermen of All Cities of Germany in Behalf of Christian Schools" stressed the spiritual, material, and political benefits that come from schooling.[37] Schools were to produce literate citizens and members of the church. They would prepare trained ministers to lead their flocks in the Reformed religion.

Luther on women's education

Luther's views of the social, religious, and educational status of women did not differ substantially from the medieval perspective. He believed that the husband, as the head of the household, had authority over his wife. Domestic duties and child rearing remained, in his view, the appropriate role for women. However, because of his emphasis on reading the Bible in one's own language, women, too, were afforded opportunities for elementary schooling. In turn, they had a shared, but subordinate, role in educating their children.

In implementing his educational reforms, Luther was assisted by Philip Melanchthon (1497–1560). Both men wanted to end the monopoly of the Roman Catholic Church over formal schools. They looked to the state to supervise schools and to license teachers. In 1559 Melanchthon drafted the School Code of Würtemberg, which became a model for other German states. Vernacular schools were to be founded in every village to teach religion, reading, writing, arithmetic, and music. The classical secondary school, the gymnasium, was to provide instruction in the higher studies and the classical languages.

Vernacular schools

Even though Luther and Melanchthon argued for the establishment of elementary vernacular schools to teach reading, writing, and religion to the common people, they strongly believed that the Latin and Greek language curriculum patterned in the Renaissance was most appropriate to prepare the leaders of the church and state. Thus, the German gymnasium followed the basic pattern of humanist education, with the addition of Lutheran theology. It is especially important to note that the general effect of the Protestant Reformation on educational institutions was to fix firmly the dual track

37 W. Baskin, ed., *Classics in Education* (New York: Philosophical Library, 1966).

system of schools: there was one set of schools for the common people and a second set of schools for the upper classes.

Reformation Views on Knowledge

Luther, Melanchthon, Calvin, and the other Protestant reformers had to concern themselves with questions of knowledge, education, and schooling because they wanted to use these powerful tools to advance the cause of the Reformed theology.[38] While they differed in particular theological perspectives, these religious reformers shared a number of educational ideas. On the question of the nature of knowledge, they emphasized the authority of the Christian Bible. For them, individuals were to read the sacred Scriptures for themselves. Because they regarded Bible reading as necessary to gain salvation, the religious reformers emphasized literacy in the European vernacular languages. They favored universal schooling, not only to enable people to read the Bible, but also to make them useful citizens of the nation-state.

Authority of the Bible

Since the reformers were deeply religious men, they emphasized religious education and values. Schooling was a means of indoctrinating the masses of the population with religious tenets and values. The sixteenth and seventeenth centuries were times of fierce religious rivalries and contentions as the various Christian churches competed against each other for adherents to their particular creeds. To achieve doctrinal conformity through schooling, teachers used the official catechisms prepared for that purpose. Through a question-and-answer approach, the teachers hoped to fix religious principles in the student's mind.

The Protestant reformers also were concerned with preparing an educated elite who would become the ministers of the church and the officials of the state. To prepare the elite, they retained the classical humanist secondary school with its Latin and Greek language studies. While this elite would share the Reformed religion with the masses of people, their higher education would be based on those classical studies that had identified the educated man in earlier periods of western European educational history.

The Reformation's Contribution to Western Education

The educational consequences of the Protestant Reformation reconfirmed many of the institutional developments from the Renaissance, especially the dual track system of schools. Vernacular schools, which provided primary level instruction, were designed for the lower socioeconomic classes; the various types of classical humanist and Latin grammar schools were preparatory for higher education. The colonists who settled in North America were transplanted Europeans who brought the dual structure of schools with them to the New World.

Dual school system

38 Frederick Mayer, *A History of Educational Thought* (Columbus, Ohio: Merrill, 1966); Elmer L. Towns, ed., *A History of Religious Educators* (Grand Rapids, Mich.: Baker Book House, 1975).

Overview 3.3

Significant Events in the History of Western Education, to A.D. 1600

Period	Political and Social Events		Significant Educational Events	
Greek	1200 B.C.	Trojan War	c. 1200 B.C.	Homer's *Iliad* and *Odyssey*
	594 B.C.	Athenian constitutional reforms		
	479–338 B.C.	Golden Age of Greek (Athenian) culture		
	445–431 B.C.	Age of Pericles		
	431–404 B.C.	Peloponnesian War between Athens and Sparta	399 B.C.	Trial of Socrates
			395 B.C.	Plato's *Republic*
			392 B.C.	School established by Isocrates in Athens
			386 B.C.	Academy founded by Plato
	336–323 B.C.	Alexander the Great	330 B.C.	Aristotle's *Politics*
	146 B.C.	Rome conquers Greece		
Roman	753 B.C.	Traditional date of Rome's founding		
	510 B.C.	Roman Republic established	449 B.C.	References appear to the existence of Latin schools, or *ludi.*
	272 B.C.	Rome dominates Italian peninsula		
	146 B.C.	Greece becomes Roman province	167 B.C.	Greek grammar school opened in Rome
	49–44 B.C.	Dictatorship of Julius Caesar	55 B.C.	Cicero's *de Oratore*
	31 B.C.	Roman Empire begins	A.D. 96	Quintilian's *de Oratoria*
	A.D. 476	Fall of Rome in the West		
Medieval	713	Arab conquest of Spain		
	800	Charlemagne crowned Holy Roman Emperor		
	1096–1291	Crusades to the Holy Land	1079–1142	Abelard, author of *Sic et Non*
	1182–1226	St. Francis of Assissi	1180	University of Paris granted papal charter and recognition

In addition to their adherence to the dual track system of schools, the Protestant reformers bequeathed to Western education an emphasis on literacy. Luther, Calvin, and others related literacy to salvation. For many Protestants, Bible-reading was a necessary feature of reformed Christianity. It was this emphasis on literacy that contributed ultimately to universal schooling.

Overview 3.3 (cont.)

Significant Events in the History of Western Education, to A.D. 1600

Period		Political and Social Events		Significant Educational Events
			1209	University of Cambridge founded
			1225–1274	Thomas Aquinas, author of *Summa Theologica*
	1295	Explorations of Marco Polo		
Renaissance	1304–1374	Petrarch, author of *Divine Comedy*		
	1313–1375	Boccaccio, founder of Italian vernacular literature		
	1384	Founding of Brethren of the Common Life		
	1393–1464	Cosimo de Medici encourages revival of art and learning in Florence	1428	Da Feltre, classical humanist educator, established court school at Mantua
	1423	Invention of printing	1507–1589	Sturm, creator of gymnasiums in Germany
	1456	First book printed		
	1492	Columbus arrives in America	1509	Erasmus's *The Praise of Folly*
Reformation	1517	Luther posts Ninety-five Theses calling for church reform	1524	Luther's letter *On Behalf of Christian schools*
	1509–1564	John Calvin, Protestant Reformer, founder of Calvinism.	1524	Melanchthon, an associate of Luther, organizes Lutheran schools in German states
	1509–1547	King Henry VIII of England, founder of the church of England		
	1540	Jesuit order founded by Loyola		
	1545	Council of Trent launches Roman Catholic Counter-Reformation	1630–1650	Calvinist schools organized in Scotland by John Knox

Influence of the Enlightenment on Western Education

As we examine the eighteenth-century Age of Enlightenment (also called the Age of Reason), we should keep in mind that our own governmental institutions as a republic are products of that era. The ideas of the Enlightenment influenced such major educational reformers as Rousseau, Pestalozzi, and Froebel. Although most of these reformers were European, their ideas were transplanted to the New World. To the extent that American schools cultivated the scientific method, they reflected the general influence of the Enlightenment.

Transplanted to the New World

Foremost among the ideas of the Enlightenment was the supremacy of reason. The philosophers, scientists, and scholars of the Enlightenment clearly believed that it was possible for human beings to improve their lives, their institutions, and their condition by using their minds to solve problems.[39] Using the scientific method, scientists of the day formulated "natural laws," which construed the universe as operating according to orderly processes. Philosophers and social reformers developed social theories as hypotheses for the investigation of society. The ideas underlying the American and French revolutions were designed to reconstruct the political order according to the dictates of reason. Clearly, these ideas implied that schools should seek to cultivate the reasoning powers of their students.

Reason and the scientific method

The learned men of the Enlightenment, such as Diderot, Rousseau, Franklin, and Jefferson, were committed to the view that humankind was progressing toward a new and a better world. No longer was it necessary to look backward to the "golden age" of Greece or Rome. If humankind followed reason and used the scientific method, it would be possible to have continual progress on this planet. Once again the work of the schools would be to cultivate a questioning attitude, which meant a willingness to use scientific and empirical methods. Further, these methods were to be applied to the problems of human society.

So it was the Enlightenment concepts of the scientific method, of reason, and of progress that formed the basis for the theories and practices that came from the educational reformers. As they sought to reform society, they tried to create a new kind of education and a new pattern of schooling based on equality, individualism, civic responsibility, and intellectual reasoning.[40] These efforts were to have a lasting influence on American education.

Reforming society

The ideas of the Enlightenment had their greatest impact on American education in the period after the American Revolution. In particular, Benjamin Franklin's emphasis on utilitarian and scientific education and Thomas Jefferson's stress on civic education were influenced by Enlightenment theories. In the twentieth century, the concept of "progress" that originated in the Enlightenment contributed to the progressive educational philosophy, which saw schooling as an instrument of social reform and improvement.

In the next chapter we turn to an examination of the educational contributions of the major pioneers of education—beginning with those from the Enlightenment era.

39 Robert Anchor, *The Enlightenment Tradition* (New York: Harper & Row, 1967).

40 J. J. Chambliss, ed., *Enlightenment and Social Progress: Education in the Nineteenth Century* (Minneapolis: Burgess, 1971).

Summing Up

1. We have examined in historical context the questions dealing with the nature of teaching and learning that were formulated at the beginning of this chapter. What is knowledge? What is education? What is schooling? Who should attend school? How should teaching and learning be carried on? Clearly, some of the answers given by past educators have influenced our own responses in the present. Often the historical responses to these questions were incomplete and ambiguous. Moreover, these answers varied from time to time and place to place. In many respects, contemporary educators are still attempting to answer these important but difficult questions.
2. The origins of American education are to be found in the European educational experience. Although the relationship between education in primitive societies and American society is remote, schooling—throughout the centuries of human history—has involved to some degree the transmission of the cultural heritage from one generation to the next. This feature was found in both primitive and modern education. In ancient Greece the concepts of the educated man, of rational inquiry, and of freedom of thought were enunciated by Socrates, Plato, and Aristotle. The idea of rhetorical education was developed by the Sophists, refined by Isocrates, and further elaborated by the Roman rhetoricians, Cicero and Quintilian.
3. During the medieval period the foundations of the modern university were established at Bologna and Paris. Medieval education was influenced to a degree by mathematical and scientific contributions that entered the Western world by way of the Arabs. The concept of the well-rounded, liberally educated man was developed by the classical humanist educators of the Renaissance. With its emphasis on literacy and vernacular education, the Protestant Reformation had a direct impact on the schools that were established in colonial America. The ideas of the Enlightenment were especially influential in America after the Revolutionary War, but they continue to influence American education even today.

Discussion Questions

1. What is your definition of education? How does your definition agree with or differ from that of the educational theorists discussed in this chapter?
2. Discuss five educators treated in this chapter on the basis of their contribution to modern educational theory.
3. How has the concept of the teacher changed through history? Use evidence from the chapter to support your argument.
4. What educational idea treated in this chapter is most relevant to your preparation for teaching? What educational idea is most irrelevant?
5. Describe a problem that you have experienced in your own education. Choose two educational theorists treated in this chapter and indicate how they would go about solving your problem.

Suggested Readings

Butts, R. Freeman. *The Education of the West: A Formative Chapter in the History of Civilization.* New York: McGraw-Hill, 1973.

The author, the leading educational historian in the United States, examines Western education as a process of civilization building and of modernization. It is a highly recommended book.

Gangel, Kenneth O., and Warren S. Benson. *Christian Education: Its History and Philosophy.* Chicago: Moody Press, 1983.

This book examines the leading thinkers, educators, and movements that have shaped the course of Western culture. It is a solid and well-written work that is generous in its coverage of educational topics.

Lucas, Christopher J. *Our Western Educational Heritage.* New York: Macmillan, 1972.

The book is a clearly written and carefully researched rendition of the historical development of education in Western civilization.

Mehl, Bernard. *Classic Educational Ideas: From Sumeria to America.* Columbus, Ohio: Merrill, 1972.

The author presents a panoramic and readable treatment of the evolution of the major theories and ideas that have shaped our thinking on education, schooling, teaching, and learning.

Silver, Harold. *Education as History.* New York and London: Methuen, 1983.

This book is a historical analysis of policy issues in education that have emerged in the recent past. The author, a distinguished British historian and educator, examines ideology, social science, and vocationalism in their historical context.

4

Pioneers in Education

Focusing Questions

What constitutes an educational pioneer?

How did the pioneers modify the traditional concepts of the child and the curriculum? What major innovations in teaching and learning did they bring about?

How have the pioneers expanded the definitions of knowledge, education, schooling, instruction, and learning?

What aspects of the pioneers' ideas or practices can be found in current educational practices or in modern thought about schools and the educational process?

MANY DISTINGUISHED INDIVIDUALS HAVE CONTRIBUTED TO educational theory and practice, but it is not possible to treat them all here. Therefore, judgment must be made on the basis of two criteria: Was the person a pioneer in education? Is the educator's work significant for you as a future teacher? Educational history provides the means for identifying those pioneers who were the first or earliest to work in the field of educational theory and practice and who succeeded in opening that area to further development by others.

But how significant are such pioneers for today's teachers? You can best answer that question by considering how these educational pioneers might have answered the global questions raised in Chapter 3: What is knowledge? What is education? What is the purpose of the school? Who should attend school? How should teaching and learning be carried on? By examining the contributions of these educational pioneers, one can gain further insights into such issues.

European influence on our schools

Before turning directly to the study of these educational pioneers, it is important to remember that education in the United States has been influenced by pedagogical developments that took place in other nations. Although certain aspects of the American common school and high school movements are unique to historical, social, economic, and political developments in the United States, other aspects of the development of American education reveal a trans-Atlantic influence. By examining the educational contributions of such pedagogical pioneers as Comenius, Locke, Rousseau, Pestalozzi, Froebel, Herbart, Spencer, Montessori, and Piaget, it is possible to appreciate the significance of this influx of educational theories and practices.

Despite differences in the educational methods developed by these major European educational theorists, parallel patterns can be identified. The work of such naturalistic educators as Comenius, Rousseau, Pestalozzi, and Spencer challenged the older view of child depravity and passive learning that had long dominated schooling. The theory of child depravity held the child to be evil at birth, and it stressed that corruptive weakness could be corrected by a strong teacher who used authoritarian teaching methods.

Child depravity theory

Innate goodness theory

In contrast, the naturalistic educators believed that the child was innately good. Concerned with examining the child's nature, they believed that the stages of human growth and development provided clues for the development of educational method. These pioneering educators came to be called *naturalistic* because they believed that children learn by working with and by examining the objects in their immediate natural environment. The stress on the educative impact of the environment was a theme that would be carried forward by such later American progressive educators as Dewey and Counts. Froebel's kindergarten and Montessori's prepared environment represent deliberate attempts to create learning situations that respect and utilize the child's own rate and pace of development.

Social and political context

Educational pioneers such as Locke, Spencer, Dewey, and Counts examined education's social and political context. Hutchins turned to enduring philosophical themes to provide a frame of reference for his educational proposals. Piaget, a pioneer in studying children, explored the psychological dimensions of learning and originated a concept of the developmental stages of cognitive growth that influenced many educators.

Comenius: The Search for a New Method

Jan Komensky (1592–1670), known as Comenius, was born in the Moravian town of Nivnitz. His family were members of the Moravian Brethren, a small, frequently persecuted sect of Protestants. Young Comenius attended the Brethren's vernacular school, where he studied the conventional elementary curriculum of reading, writing, singing, arithmetic, and catechism. He attended a Latin preparatory school and then went on to the University of Heidelberg in Germany. Upon completing his education, Comenius returned to his native province to pursue a career as a teacher and administrator first in the Moravian schools and later in Poland and the Netherlands. His educational theory contained pioneering ideas that stressed the establishment of a permissive school environment based on the natural principles of child growth and development.

Permissive school environment

As an educational reformer Comenius occupied a middle position between the humanist educators and the naturalistic reformers. While he still emphasized the teaching of Latin, he wanted it to be learned by natural means. Since language, especially Latin, was necessary to acquire universal knowledge, Comenius wanted to make language instruction both interesting and efficient. In his book *Gate of Tongues Unlocked,* he approached the study of Latin through the learner's own vernacular.[1] Beginning with short, simple phrases, the student gradually progressed toward more complicated sentences. He also prepared a picture book for the teaching of Latin, *The Visible World in Pictures,* consisting of pictures that designated objects in both their Latin and vernacular names.[2] The picture of the object combined language learning with sense perception. Note that Comenius was beginning to emphasize sensory experience in learning. This tendency toward sensory learning would receive further emphasis in the work of Locke, Rousseau, and Pestalozzi.

Language and sensory learning

Principles of Learning and Instruction Comenius sought to develop an efficient method of instruction based on the principles of child growth.[3] He believed that nature revealed certain patterns of growth and development that should be followed in educational methodology. Teachers, he argued, should recognize that children have stages of readiness for specific kinds of

1 See Jean Piaget, ed., *John Amos Comenius on Education* (New York: Teachers College Press, Columbia University, 1967); John Sadler, ed., *Comenius* (New York: Macmillan, 1969).

2 Adolphe E. Meyer, *Grandmasters of Educational Thought* (New York: McGraw-Hill, 1975), p. 117–120.

3 M. W. Keatinge, ed. and trans., *Comenius* (New York: McGraw-Hill, 1931); Keatinge, *The Great Didactic of John Amos Comenius* (London: Adam Black, 1896).

learning. Materials and instruction should be based on these developmental stages. Since nature was orderly and gradual, instruction should be organized carefully into easily assimilated steps so that learning might be gradual, cumulative, and pleasant.

Stages of growth and development

One of Comenius's most important methodological principles was his belief that instruction should parallel the appropriate stage of human development. Instruction should be arranged according to four 6-year periods: (1) infancy, when education is informal and centered primarily in the home; (2) childhood, when learning takes place in the formal school; (3) adolescence, when the student is exposed to the learning of Latin; and (4) youth, when the student attends to the higher studies of the university.

Principles of teaching

Among his pioneering contributions to education was his effort to develop teaching methods that paralleled inductive reasoning and the general pattern of human growth and development. His nine principles of teaching reflect his concern for the inductive method and for logical relationships: (1) teaching should involve presenting the object or idea in a concrete and direct way, not merely through symbols or concepts; (2) teaching should involve practical application to everyday life; (3) whatever is taught should be presented in a straightforward and uncomplicated way; (4) whatever is taught should be related to its true nature and origin; (5) general principles should be taught first; then details may be considered; (6) all things should be learned with reference to the whole and to how the parts are connected; (7) things should be taught in succession, and one thing should be taught at a time; (8) the teacher should not leave a specific subject until it is completely understood; and (9) differences among things should be taught so that the knowledge that is acquired may be clear.[4]

Rejection of corporal punishment

Although many people believed children were inherently bad and that strict corporal punishment was the best discipline to be used in managing schools, Comenius sought to enlist gentle and loving persons as teachers. He also argued that schools should be joyful and pleasant places.

Education and School For Comenius, education was to be carried on according to natural principles. Like other creatures in nature, human beings follow patterns of natural growth and development. Since natural development is slow and cumulative, education should be a slow and gradual process. Comenius did not believe that the child should be hurried, coerced, or forced to learn before he or she was ready to do so.

Influence on Educational Practices Today Comenius, a well-known and respected educator in his own lifetime, developed many of the ideas associated with modern and especially progressive education. For example, he believed strongly in the concept of universal education, which argues that every human being should have the opportunity for education. To make universal education a reality, Comenius developed plans for organizing and ad-

4 Edward J. Power, "Comenius: The Champion of Realism," in *Evolution of Educational Doctrine: Major Educational Theorists of the Western World* (New York: Appleton-Century-Crofts, 1969), pp. 238–241.

Child's interest and senses

ministering schools. He believed that teaching methods should build on the child's interests and should actively involve the senses; in fact, he emphasized sensation as a basis of learning. The teacher should be a patient and permissive person who gently leads children to use and to understand the world in which they live. Such later educational theorists as Rousseau and Pestalozzi would follow Comenius's pioneering work in the field of naturalistic education.

Locke: Empiricist Educator

John Locke (1632–1704) was an English scholar, physician, scientist, and philosopher.[5] As a member of the Whig political party, Locke opposed the efforts of King James II to impose an absolute monarchy in England. After the Glorious Revolution of 1688, which exiled King James II, Locke gained prominence as the foremost philosophical champion of religious toleration and political liberalism.[6] This section examines his ideas on knowledge, politics, and education.

Blank slate

Principles of Learning and Instruction Locke's major philosophical contribution, *An Essay Concerning Human Understanding,* published in 1690, examined the question of how we acquire ideas.[7] Locke held that at birth the human mind is a blank slate, a *tabula rasa,* empty of ideas. We acquire knowledge, he argued, from the information about the world that our senses bring to us. Through sensation, we learn about the objects in the environment. Simple ideas become more complex through comparison, reflection, and generalization. Locke was a pioneer of the inductive, or scientific, method. His empirical theory of knowledge had tremendous educational implications.

Inductive or scientific method

Locke questioned the long-standing traditional view that knowledge came exclusively from literary sources, particularly the Greek and Latin classics. He argued that learning was an active process that used the senses to investigate and acquire data about the world. Locke's stress on studying objects present in the environment was shared and developed further by Rousseau, Pestalozzi, and Dewey. Later educators would use Locke's pioneering ideas as they came to advocate the scientific method as the best approach for teaching and learning.

Locke's interests extended into political questions. His outstanding work on political philosophy was *Two Treatises of Government,* which appeared in 1689.[8] In it, he opposed the "divine right of kings" theory, which held that the monarch had the right to be an unquestioned and absolute ruler over his

5 Robert Rusk and James Scotland, *Doctrines of the Great Educators* (New York: St. Martin's, 1979).

6 James L. Wiser, *Political Philosophy: A History of the Search for Order* (Englewood Cliffs, N.J.: Prentice-Hall, 1983), pp. 209–228.

7 John Locke, *An Essay Concerning Human Understanding,* ed. Alexander Fraser (New York: Dover, 1959).

8 John Locke, *Two Treatises of Government,* ed. Peter Laslett (New York: New American Library, 1965).

subjects. Locke argued that political order should be based on a contract between the people and the government, which ruled by the consent of those who had established it. He asserted that all human beings possessed inalienable rights of life, liberty, and property. Locke's political philosophy contributed to the concept of representative government and to the system of checks and balances between the legislative, executive, and judicial branches of government that would later characterize the American political system. His theories inspired Thomas Jefferson and the other founders of the American republic.

Inalienable rights

Locke's political theory implied that the people were to establish their own government and select their own political leaders. No longer were aristocrats destined by birth to be rulers—the people were to elect their own leaders from among themselves. Locke's concept meant that the people should be educated to govern themselves intelligently and responsibly. This idea became a major theme of the nineteenth-century American common school movement and remains a major responsibility of American public schools.

Utilitarian and practical learning

Education and School In *Some Thoughts Concerning Education,* written in 1697, Locke recommended utilitarian and practical learning.[9] Since it was a powerful force in shaping the course of a person's life, a good education, he reasoned, should cultivate the ability to manage social, economic, and political affairs in a practical manner.

Specifically, Locke believed that a sound education began very early in a child's life. Stressing the maxim of a sound mind in a strong and healthy body, Locke directed attention to a child's physical environment, diet, and activities. Children should breathe fresh air, have plenty of sleep, eat light and plain food, bathe frequently, exercise regularly, and have time for play and recreation.

Slow and cumulative learning

Learning, Locke insisted, should be a gradual process. The child's instruction in reading, writing, and arithmetic should be slow, gradual, and cumulative. Beyond the basics, Locke's curricular recommendations included conversational learning of foreign languages, especially French; mathematics; and the study of civil government through history. Physical education, games, and athletics were to be continued. Locke's educational goal was to cultivate the person who was ethical, who would manage economic affairs prudently, and who would participate in government effectively.

Influence on Educational Practices Today John Locke has exerted a significant influence on present-day educational practices. His emphasis on learning by sensory experience and on civic education helped to shape the practical and vocational aspects of Benjamin Franklin's plan for an English grammar school in Philadelphia in 1741. Franklin's proposal, in turn, was a forerunner of the modern high school. Locke's stress on empirical learning

9 Peter Gay, *John Locke on Education* (New York: Teachers College Press, Columbia University, 1964).

helped to shape the more pragmatic and experimental views of modern education, which emphasizes "learning by doing" and interaction with the environment. Like Comenius, Locke challenged inherited educational traditions and moved educators to a more modern conception of learning.

Rousseau: The Natural Person

Jean Jacques Rousseau (1712–1778), a Swiss-born French theorist, profoundly influenced social, political, and educational ideas. Rousseau studied for a variety of careers but achieved fame as a social and educational philosopher. His works *On the Origin of the Inequality of Mankind* and *The Social Contract* state that the distinctions based on wealth, property, and prestige that give rise to social inequalities are artificial.[10] In the original state of nature, humankind, portrayed as a noble savage, had been free and uncorrupted; it was the artificialities of society that corrupted people. Property had produced inequalities, and government and other institutions had legitimized these artificial distinctions.

Rousseau's most famous educational treatise is *Emile,* a novel written in 1762, which tells the story of the education of a boy from infancy to adulthood.[11] Rousseau's novel attacks the doctrine of child depravity and an exclusively verbal and literary education. Such doctrines and practices, he felt, ignored the child's natural interests and inclinations. Society has imprisoned us in a set of institutions. The child needs to be freed from one of the most coercive of these institutions—the school.

The child's natural interests

Principles of Learning and Instruction Like Comenius, Rousseau recognized stages of human growth and development. For Rousseau, there are five stages of growth: infancy, childhood, boyhood, adolescence, and youth. Each stage requires an appropriate kind of education to stimulate further development and growth. Most important, the early and formative stages of growth are to be free from the corruption of society. Emile, the subject of Rousseau's novel, was to be educated by a tutor on a country estate away from the blandishments and temptations of a ruinous society.

Stages of growth

Rousseau's first stage, infancy (from birth to five), sees the human being as essentially helpless and dependent on others. The infant needs freedom to move and to exercise his body. He needs to make his first contacts with the objects of the environment. The infant's diet should be simple but nourishing.

During childhood (from five to twelve) the child is growing physically stronger. He is beginning to develop his own personality as he becomes aware that his actions have either painful or pleasurable consequences. Dur-

Pain and pleasure

10 Jean Jacques Rousseau, *The First and Second Discourses,* ed. R. D. Masters (New York: St. Martin's, 1964): idem., *The Social Contract,* rev. ed. (Baltimore: Penguin, 1969).

11 William Boyd, *The Emile of Jean Jacques Rousseau* (New York: Teachers College Press, Columbia University, 1962); Allan Bloom, *Emile or On Education* (New York: Basic Books, 1979).

ing this stage the child is egotistical but also curious. He explores the environment and learns about the world through his senses. Rousseau calls the person's eyes, ears, hands, and feet the first teachers. These natural teachers are far better and more efficient than the school-master who teaches words that the learner does not comprehend; they are better than the silence of the schoolroom and the rod of the master. Emile's tutor did not attempt to introduce books at this stage. Reading was not substituted for the child's own direct experience with nature.

Nature as the best teacher

During boyhood, ages twelve to fifteen, the boy's bodily strength is still increasing. Nature, still the best teacher, gives instruction in science and geography. By watching the cycles of growth and development of plants and animals, Emile learned natural science. By exploring his surroundings, he learned geography far more realistically than he could have from the study of maps. Emile now read *Robinson Crusoe,* the story of a man marooned on an island who had to meet nature on its own terms. He also learned a manual trade so that he could understand the relationship between mental and physical work.

Interacting with society

Next, in Rousseau's developmental schema, come the years of adolescence, fifteen to eighteen. During these years Emile returned to society. Becoming aware of and interested in sex, he asked his tutor questions about human sexuality. His questions were to be answered honestly, directly, and sincerely by the tutor. Now that Emile had experienced a natural education, he was ready to cope with the outside world. He needed to be aware of society, government, economics, and business. His aesthetic tastes, too, were cultivated by visiting museums, art galleries, and libraries and by attending the theater. During the last stage of education, from eighteen to twenty, Emile traveled to Paris and to foreign countries to see different peoples and societies.

Education and School For Rousseau, knowledge was based on sensations and feelings. Preferring the natural to the social, Rousseau stressed the human instincts as the means to knowledge. He was definitely opposed to relying on books as the pathway to truth. It was far better, he believed, to rely on direct and immediate experience with nature than to seek wisdom through the indirect source of the printed page. Rousseau was a true pioneer; he challenged existing conventions and sought to destroy those that he felt impeded human freedom and progress. Rousseau was decidedly romantic and preferred the spontaneous, primitive, and emotional person to the rational and scientific individual. His personal bent was to demolish restrictive and coercive social institutions and customs.

Schools impede learning

Unlike the classical humanists, who equated education and schooling, Rousseau carefully separated the two. Like the contemporary advocates of deschooling, Rousseau believed that the school as an institution often interferes with and impedes learning. As a social institution the school puts the child into a straightjacket that confines him to socially accepted customs, manners, and ideas. Rousseau wanted to liberate the child and adult from artificial social restrictions. His Emile was a child of nature who followed his impulses and acted on them. If pleasure was the result, then Emile earned his own reward. If his actions brought pain, then Emile brought these consequences upon himself.

Influence on Educational Practices Today Rousseau influenced such innovative educators as Pestalozzi and contributed to broad movements in education, such as the child study movement and child-centered progressive education. One of Rousseau's major contributions was the idea that curriculum should be based on the child's interests and needs rather than the child being forced to conform to a prescribed program of learning. In some respects, Rousseau anticipated the "romantic" view of child development, according to which children create their own reality rather than learning to deal with information given to them in a final form by adults.

Rousseau's *Emile* exerted a strong influence on the development of Western education. Johann Pestalozzi put Rousseau's ideas into a more methodological and group-centered context. In the United States, such child-centered progressive educators as Francis Parker and Marietta Johnson elaborated a pedagogy based on the child's interests, needs, and inclinations.

Influential, progressive educators

Pestalozzi: Theoretician and Experimenter

The Swiss educator Johann Heinrich Pestalozzi (1746–1827) had been an attentive reader of Rousseau's *Emile*. He agreed with Rousseau's basic contentions that human beings are naturally good but are spoiled by the contagion of a corrupt society, that traditional schooling was a dull mess of deadening memorization and recitation, and that a pedagogical reform could lead to social reform. A natural society could arise based on the foundation created by a natural education.[12]

Natural education

Pestalozzi established an educational institute at Burgdorf to educate children and prepare teachers. Here he worked to devise a more efficient method of group instruction. He taught spelling by having the children begin with the shortest words and then proceed to longer ones by gradual and cumulative steps. Concrete objects, such as pebbles and beans, were used to teach counting. After becoming familiar with the basic mathematical processes, the children were introduced to the numbers that represented the quantities of the objects they had counted earlier. The first writing exercises consisted of drawing lessons in which the children made a series of rising and falling strokes and open and closed curves. These exercises were intended to exercise the hand muscles and thus prepare the child for writing. The school's atmosphere was generally permissive and there were physical exercises, play activities, and nature study walks.[13]

Permissive school atmosphere

12 Robert B. Downs, *Heinrich Pestalozzi: Father of Modern Pedagogy* (Boston: Twayne, 1975); Gerald L. Gutek, *Pestalozzi and Education* (New York: Random House, 1968).

13 Johann Pestalozzi, *How Gertrude Teaches Her Children*, trans. L. E. Holland and F. C. Turner (Syracuse, N.Y.: Bardeen, 1900).

Johann Pestalozzi believed that teachers should encourage the development of the whole child in a secure, loving, and homelike school environment. (Culver Pictures, Inc.)

Principles of Learning and Instruction Pestalozzi's method of instruction can be divided into the "general" and the "special" methods. The general method is of great importance since it was used prior to the special method. In working with orphans, with the victims of poverty and ignorance, and with those who might be called the "disadvantaged" of the nineteenth century, Pestalozzi felt that—to be effective—schools needed to be like secure and loving homes. The general method called for educators who were loving persons, who were emotionally secure, and who could contribute to the emotional health of students by winning their trust and affection.

Warm and emotionally secure teachers

Once the general method had brought about the right emotional predispositions, then Pestalozzi used the special method. Since he believed that all learning comes through the senses, all teaching should likewise be sensory. To this end, Pestalozzi devised the *object lesson*. Children would study the common objects found in their environment. They would study the plants, rocks, artifacts, and objects that they saw and lived with in their daily experience. The object lesson of the special method consisted of three basic sorts of learnings: form, number, and sound. The children would determine the form of the object and would draw and trace the form or shape. They would count the objects and then name them.

Sensory learning

From the lessons in form, number, and sound came the more formal exercises in drawing, writing, counting, adding, subtracting, multiplying, dividing, and reading. The basic methodological innovation was that Pestalozzi insisted that learning begin with the senses rather than with words. Actually, he was following Rousseau's rule that mere verbal learning or abstract lessons are futile. Like Rousseau, Pestalozzi urged that lessons be based on sense experience originating in the learner's home and family life. This basic innovation became an important part of progressive school reform in the twentieth century. It is also an obvious part of the current school reforms based on the work of the British primary schools.

From concrete to abstract

Pestalozzi was concerned that instruction should follow the ways of nature. He developed a set of instructional strategies that are usually identified with Pestalozzian pedagogy. Instruction, he urged, should (1) begin with the concrete object before introducing abstract concepts; (2) begin with the learner's immediate environment before dealing with that which is distant and remote; (3) begin with easy exercises before introducing complex ones; and (4) always proceed gradually, cumulatively, and slowly.[14]

Education and School As an educational pioneer, Rousseau had attacked schools as social institutions that chained humankind to conventional thinking. Like Rousseau, Pestalozzi wanted to base learning on natural principles and stressed the importance of the human emotions. Unlike Rousseau, however, Pestalozzi did not abandon the school; he tried to reform it.

Empirical learning

Rousseau and Pestalozzi were both naturalistic educators who believed that nature was the source of knowledge. To know, for Pestalozzi, meant to be involved with and to understand nature, its patterns, and its laws. Pestalozzi also had much in common with John Locke. Both stressed the empirical method of learning, through which human beings come to know their environment by actively using their senses in carefully observing natural phenomena.

Pestalozzi is significant to teachers because he stressed methodology. Learning could be efficient and enjoyable if it were based on nature's own method. Like Comenius, Pestalozzi felt that the child should learn in a slow and precise manner, understanding thoroughly whatever he or she was studying. Since nature appears to human perception in the form of objects, Pestalozzi reasoned that the object lesson is the correct way to teach children about reality.

Devoted to disadvantaged learners

While Pestalozzi believed that all children should attend school, he was especially dedicated to those who were poor, hungry, and socially or psychologically maladjusted. If children were hungry, Pestalozzi fed them before he attempted to teach them. If they were frightened, Pestalozzi comforted and loved them. For him a teacher was not only a person who was skilled in instructional methodology but also someone who was capable of loving all children. In fact, Pestalozzi believed that love of mankind was necessary for successful teaching.

14 Dieter Jedan, *Johann Heinrich Pestalozzi and the Pestalozzian Method of Language Teaching* (Bern, Switzerland: Peter Lang, 1981), pp. 45–67.

Influence on Educational Practices Today Pestalozzi's ideas and methods had a great impact on the course of western European and American education. William Maclure and Joseph Neef, in the early nineteenth century, and Henry Barnard, U.S. commissioner of education in the late nineteenth century, worked to introduce Pestalozzian ideas into the United States. Barnard's *Pestalozzi and Pestalozzianism* introduced American educators to the basic principles of the new method of instruction.[15] Edward Sheldon was another major figure in introducing Pestalozzi's object lesson.[16] Horace Mann and William Woodward, leaders of the American common school movement, were familiar with Pestalozzianism and sought to incorporate its tenets into school practice. The impact of Pestalozzi has been a continuing one. Many of the educational reforms associated with the progressive movement in American education exhibit the Pestalozzian imprint. For example, the stress on the environment, the use of concrete objects, and the cultivation of sensory experience were all progressive emphases that had been anticipated by the Swiss pedagogue. When the focus of American educators came to center on the education of disadvantaged children, Pestalozzi's ideas took on a special relevance. His emphasis on emotional security as a precondition of skill learning bore a strong resemblance to the need for the close school-home relationships that many urban educators advocate.

Impact on American progressive education

Froebel: The Kindergarten Movement

Friedrich Froebel (1782–1852), a German educator, is known for his introduction of a school for early childhood education—the kindergarten, or child's garden.[17] Froebel, the son of a Lutheran minister, was born in the German state of Thuringia. His mother died when he was only nine months old. As a mature person, Froebel frequently reflected on his childhood and youth. He believed that those who were to be teachers should continually think back to the days of their own childhood to find insights that could be applied to their teaching. Like Pestalozzi, with whom he studied, Froebel was very shy as a child and highly introspective as an adult.

Student of Pestalozzi

He worked as a forester, a chemist's assistant, and a museum curator before turning to education. His attraction to teaching led him to Pestalozzi's Institute at Yverdon, where he interned from 1808 to 1810. He accepted certain aspects of Pestalozzi's method: the reliance on nature as the chief educator, the permissive school atmosphere, and the object lesson. Froebel believed, however, that Pestalozzi had not established an adequate philosophical underpinning for his theory. Froebel gave the object lesson a more symbolic

15 Thomas A. Barlow, *Pestalozzi and American Education* (Boulder, Colo.: Este Es Press, University of Colorado Libraries, 1977), pp. 35–48, 74–88.

16 Ned H. Dearborn, *The Oswego Movement in American Education* (New York: Teachers College Press, Columbia University, 1925).

17 Irene M. Lilley, *Friedrich Froebel: A Selection from His Writings* (Cambridge, Mass.: Harvard University Press, 1967).

meaning in that the concrete object was to stimulate recall of a corresponding idea in the child's mind.

Principles of Learning and Instruction Like Pestalozzi, Froebel was determined to improve the educational methods of teaching. Both protested vigorously against teaching children ideas that they did not understand. They believed that the teacher must become an active instructor instead of a taskmaster and hearer of individual recitations.

Active teachers

The kindergarten

In 1837 Froebel founded the kindergarten in the city of Blankenburg. It emphasized games, play, songs, and crafts and subsequently attracted a number of visitors. Froebel's kindergarten was to be a prepared environment in which the first formal learning of the child would be based on self-activity. The kindergarten teacher was to be a moral and cultural model or exemplar who was worthy of the child's love and trust. Froebel readily accepted the Pestalozzian concept of the general method of emotional security for the child, but he raised it to a spiritual and highly symbolic level.[18]

Prepared environment

The kindergarten curriculum had as its objective the cultivation of the child's self-development, self-activity, and socialization. It included songs, stories, games, "gifts," and "occupations." The songs, stories, and games, generally a part of early childhood education, were to stimulate the child's imagination and to introduce the child to the customs, heroes, and ideas of the cultural heritage. Games provided the cooperative activities that socialized children and developed their physical and motor skills. As the boys and girls played with other children, they became part of the group and were prepared for further group learning activities. As they played the various games, they also developed coordination and physical dexterity. Froebel's "gifts" consisted of objects whose form was fixed, such as spheres, cubes, and cylinders. The gifts were designed to stimulate children to bring to full consciousness the underlying concept that was implied in the object. The kindergarten "occupations" consisted of materials that could be shaped by the children and used in designs and construction activity. For example, clay, sand, cardboard, and mud could be manipulated and shaped into castles, cities, and mountains.[19] Together these activities were to serve as the learning environment; they were to be the garden in which children could grow naturally and correctly in a prepared environment.

Gifts and occupations

Education and School For most of us, kindergarten was our first introduction to school. First impressions of schools and of teachers were acquired there. We noted earlier that Froebel encouraged teachers to reflect on their early childhood experiences. Through this kind of introspection they would come to understand their own childhood, and thus could gain insights and perspectives that would help them to understand young children. According to Froebel, the personality of the kindergarten teacher is paramount. The

18 Robert B. Downs, *Friedrich Froebel* (Boston: Twayne, 1978).

19 Friedrich Froebel, *The Education of Man*, trans. W. Hailmann (New York: Appleton, 1889).

Dignity of the child

teacher should be a person who respects the dignity of human personality and who embodies the highest cultural values, so that children can imitate the values that they see represented in the teacher's own personality. Above all, the kindergarten teacher should be an approachable and open person.[20]

Influence on Educational Practices Today The kindergarten is now an established part of American education. Immigrants who fled from Germany after the Revolution of 1848 brought the concept of the kindergarten with them. The wife of the German-American patriot Carl Schurz established a kindergarten in Watertown, Wisconsin, in 1855. Elizabeth Peabody founded the first English-language kindergarten and a training school for kindergarten teachers in Boston in 1860. The kindergarten was given great encouragement by William Harris, superintendent of schools in St. Louis, Missouri, and later U.S. commissioner of education. Harris believed that the kindergarten was an important first stage of the school system because it prepared the child for the order and routine of the elementary school.[21]

Influence on American educators

Herbart: Moral and Intellectual Development

Johann Herbart (1776–1841) was a German philosopher known for his contributions to moral development in education and for his creation of a methodology of instruction designed to establish a highly structured mode of teaching. Herbart attended the conventional German schools and then went on to study philosophy at the University of Jena, where he worked with the famous professor Gottlieb Fichte. Early in Herbart's career, while he was a tutor in Switzerland, he became interested in the educational theory of Pestalozzi. In 1809 Herbart was appointed to the chair of philosophy at the University of Konigsberg. He now turned to serious scholarship and conducted a seminar in the psychological and philosophical aspects of education.[22]

Moral development

Education and School For Herbart the chief aim of education was moral development; it was basic and necessary to all other educational goals or purposes. The chief objective of Herbartian education was to produce the good person who had many interests. Herbart argued that virtue is founded on knowledge and that human beings do not deliberately choose evil. Misconduct is the product of inadequate knowledge or of inferior education. Thus, he gave education a vital role in shaping moral character. For Herbart moral education involved the presentation of ethical ideas to the child's mind. In elaborating his work on moral education, Herbart specified five major kinds

20 Evelyn Lawrence, *Froebel and English Education: Perspectives on the Founder of the Kindergarten* (New York: Schocken Books, 1969), pp. 95–124.

21 Daniel Tanner and Laurel N. Tanner, *Curriculum Development,* 2nd ed. (New York: Macmillan, 1980); Evelyn Weber, *The Kindergarten: Its Encounter with Educational Thought in America* (New York: Teachers College Press, Columbia University, 1969).

22 Harold B. Dunkel, *Herbart and Education* (New York: Random House, 1969).

Convictions, harmony, social welfare, justice, retribution

of ideas as the foundations of moral character: (1) the idea of inner freedom, which referred to action based on one's personal convictions; (2) the idea of perfection, which referred to the harmony and integration of behavior; (3) the idea of benevolence, by which a person was to be concerned with the social welfare of others; (4) the idea of justice, by which a person reconciled his or her individual behavior with that of the social group; and (5) the idea of retribution, which indicates that reward or punishment accrues to certain kinds of behavior.

Knowledge and ethics

Drawing from his ideas on moral education, Herbart also specified two major bodies of interests that should be included in education: knowledge interests and ethical interests. Knowledge interests involve empirical data, factual information, and also speculative ideas. Knowledge interests were broadly conceived to include logic, mathematics, literature, music, and art. Ethical interests included sympathy for others, social relationships, and religious sentiments. Herbart's aim was to produce an educated individual of good character and high morals. He believed that if your cognitive powers are properly exercised and if your mind is stocked with ideas, then you will use that knowledge to guide your behavior. The person who lives and acts according to knowledge will be a moral person.

Integrating ideas

Principles of Learning and Instruction In terms of organizing instruction, Herbart developed the concepts of curriculum correlation. These were to have a decided impact on education in the United States. According to the doctrine of correlation, each subject should be taught in such a way that it refers to and relates to other subjects. Knowledge would then appear to the learner as an integrated system of ideas that forms an apperceptive mass—the whole of a person's previous experience—to which new ideas could be related. Herbart believed that the subjects of history, geography, and literature were ideally suited as core subjects.

In the United States Herbartian pedagogical principles were accepted enthusiastically. The American Herbartians were especially interested in Herbart's formal steps of instruction: (1) clearness, or the careful analysis and comprehension of each single fact or element of the lessons; (2) association, the relating of the facts with each other and with previously acquired information; (3) system, the ordering of ideas into a coherent system; and (4) method, the development of projects by the student that would involve the learning acquired in the earlier steps.[23]

Herbartian method

Formal steps of instruction

Herbart's followers revised the four original steps and developed the well-known five phases of the Herbartian method that came to be popular in the United States. These five steps are (1) preparation, by which the teacher stimulates the readiness of the learner for the new lesson by referring to materials that were learned earlier; (2) presentation, in which the teacher presents the new lesson to the students; (3) association, in which the new lesson is deliberately related to ideas or materials that were studied earlier; (4)

23 Johann F. Herbart, *Textbook of Psychology* (New York: Appleton, 1894).

Overview 4.1

Educational Pioneers

Pioneer	Purpose of Education	Role of the Teacher	Significance	Influence on Today's Schools
Comenius 1592–1670 (Czech)	To relate instruction to children's natural growth and development; to contribute to peace and human understanding	To be a permissive facilitator of learning; to base instruction on child's stages of development	Helped to develop a more humane view of the child; devised an educational method	Schools organized according to children's stages of development
Locke 1632–1704 (English)	To develop ideas in the mind based on sense perception; to educate individuals capable of self-government	To encourage sense experience; to base instruction on empirical method	Developed a theory of knowledge based on sensation	Schooling that emphasizes sensory observation
Rousseau 1712–1778 (Swiss-French)	To create a learning environment that allows the child's innate, natural goodness to flourish	To assist nature; not to impose social conventions on the child	Led a romantic revolt against the doctrine of child depravity; a forerunner of child-centered progressivism	Permissive schooling based on child freedom
Pestalozzi 1746–1827 (Swiss)	To develop the human being's moral, mental, and physical powers harmoniously; use of sense perception in forming clear ideas	To act as a loving facilitator of learning by creating a homelike school environment; skilled in using the special method	Devised an educational method of simultaneous instruction that changed elementary education	Schooling based on simultaneous instruction, emotional security, and object learning
Froebel 1782–1852 (German)	To bring out and to develop the latent spiritual essence of the child in a prepared environment	To facilitate children's growth through gifts, occupations, songs, and stories	Created the kindergarten, a special early childhood learning environment	Preschools designed to liberate the child's creativity
Herbart 1776–1841	To contribute to the human being's moral	To stimulate the learner's intellectual	Devised a formal method of instruction	Schooling that stresses literary and

systematization, which involves the use of examples to illustrate the principles or generalizations to be mastered by the student; and (5) application, which involves the testing of the new ideas or the materials of the new lesson to determine if the students have understood and mastered them.

Herbart's formal steps of instruction were also applied to teacher training. In theory, the teacher would prepare by thinking of the five steps, asking: What do my students know? What questions should I ask? What events should I relate? What conclusions should be reached? How can students apply what they have learned?

Influence on Educational Practices Today To some extent, Herbart's principles have influenced today's instructional program, especially to the degree that lessons are classified into subjects or skills such as drill, content area, or motor-activity. Lesson planning, based on units of instruction, resem-

Overview 4.1 (cont.)

Educational Pioneers

Pioneer	Purpose of Education	Role of the Teacher	Significance	Influence on Today's Schools
(German)	development through knowledge and ethics	and moral development by formal stages of instruction	based on the planned and sequenced lesson	historical materials designed to enlarge the learner's interest
Spencer 1820–1903 (English)	To enable human beings to live effectively, economically, and scientifically	To organize instruction in terms of basic life activities	A leading curriculum theorist who stressed scientific knowledge	Schooling that stresses scientific knowledge and competitive values
Montessori 1870–1952 (Italian)	To assist children's sensory, muscular, and intellectual development in a prepared environment	To act as a facilitator or director of learning by using didactic materials in a prepared environment	Developed a widely used method and philosophy of early childhood education	Early childhood schooling that is intellectually and developmentally stimulating
Dewey 1859–1952 (American)	To contribute to the individual's personal, social, and intellectual growth	To create a learning environment based on the shared experience of the community of learners	Developed the pragmatic experimentalist philosophy of education	Schooling that uses the scientific method of problem solving
Counts 1889–1974 (American)	To create a new society that encompasses science, technology, and democracy	To become an educational statesperson who serves as a leader in reconstructing society	Originated the social reconstructionist view of the school	Schools designed to stimulate social planning and reconstruction
Hutchins 1899–1977 (American)	To educate human beings to search for truth, which is found in the wisdom of the human race	To ask leading and challenging questions that stimulate students to pursue truth	A leading spokesman for the perennialist perspective in education	Schooling that emphasizes the liberal arts curriculum
Piaget 1896–1980 (Swiss)	To organize education in terms of stages of cognitive development	To organize instruction according to stages of cognitive development	Formulated a theory of cognitive development	Schooling organized around cognitive developmental stages

bles the Herbartian stages of teaching. Educators who follow a prearranged order of presenting lessons adhere to some extent to Herbart's instructional designs. It was the reliance on prearranged lessons that caused John Dewey and more progressive educators to rebel against the Herbartian approach to education in the early years of the twentieth century.

Spencer: Utilitarian Education

Herbert Spencer (1820–1903) was an English social theorist who sought to fit Charles Darwin's theory of biological evolution into a comprehensive sociological and educational theory.

According to Darwin's theory, species evolved naturally and gradually over long periods of time. Members of certain species survived and reproduced themselves by means of selective adaptation to changes in the environment. As their offspring inherited these characteristics, they survived and reproduced themselves and thus continued the life of the species. Those who were unable to adapt perished.

Social Darwinism

The concept of "survival of the fittest," which was expressed as a biological theory, was translated by Spencer and other Social Darwinists into the area of social relationships. Spencer believed that human development had gone through an evolutionary series of stages from the simple to the complex and from the uniform to the more specialized kind of activity.[24] Social development had also taken place according to an evolutionary process by which simple, homogeneous societies had evolved to more complex societal systems, characterized by an increasing variety of specialized tasks. Spencer's theory of Social Darwinism was developed in the last half of the nineteenth century, when industrialization was indeed transforming American and western European societies into more complicated social systems characterized by specialized professions and occupations. Industrialized society required vocational and professional education based on scientific and practical (utilitarian) objectives rather than on the very general educational goals associated with humanistic and classical education.

Evolutionary stages of human development

Survival of the fittest

In arguing for social ethics based on competitive principles, Spencer asserted that the fittest individuals of each generation would survive because of their skill, intelligence, and propensity to adapt to environmental requirements. Because of this competition, the fittest would inherit the earth and populate it with their intelligent and productive offspring. Those individuals who were lazy, stupid, or weak would slowly disappear. Thus, the doctrine of the survival of the fittest postulated that individual competition would bring about socioeconomic progress.

Principles of Learning and Instruction According to Spencer, human life exhibited a series of basic activities that fostered the survival of the human race; the curriculum should emphasize the practical, utilitarian, and scientific subjects that allowed humankind to perpetuate itself and to master the environment. Of all the human areas of knowledge, Spencer gave the highest priority to science.

In many respects, Spencer resembled Pestalozzi. He argued that learning should be based on sensory experience that involved the learner with the environment. Instruction, too, was to be gradual, cumulative and unhurried. Disinclined to memorization and rote learning, Spencer related schooling to life and to the activities needed to earn a living. Spencer believed that scientific knowledge should be applied to industry, commerce, government, and society.

24 Richard Hofstadter, *Social Darwinism in American Thought* (Boston: Beacon Press, 1955).

Education and School Spencer's Social Darwinism and his advocacy of industrial society influenced his educational theory.[25] Like such naturalistic educational theorists as Rousseau, Pestalozzi, and Herbart, Spencer opposed the excessively verbal, literary, and classical education associated with traditional schooling. He believed that the traditional schools of England were impractical and ornamental; they failed to meet the needs of a modern industrial society.

Stress on the sciences

Spencer dealt with the social and political bases of modern education and featured a curriculum based on science and utility.[26] The most valuable education, in Spencer's view, was based on the physical, biological, and social sciences. Spencer influenced curriculum construction by classifying and arranging human activities according to their priorities for advancing human survival and progress. According to Spencer's curriculum rationale: (1) educational priorities should be based on those human activities that sustain life; (2) education that is valuable should prepare men and women to perform these activities efficiently; and (3) science should have curricular priority since it aids in the effective performance of life activities.

Self-preservation as a priority

Spencer gave highest priority to the activities that contributed to self-preservation, since those were basic to all other activities. Since physical health was needed to perform all the other human activities, a scientific education should include knowledge of human physiology and health in order to combat disease. Indirectly supporting self-preservation are the activities connected to a person's economic occupation or profession. The basic skills of reading, writing, and arithmetic have immediate utility. The populace of an industrial society requires an education that contributes to technological, industrial, and scientific efficiency. Expertise in the physical and biological sciences, the social sciences, and the applied and technological sciences is needed.

To prepare students for social and political participation, Spencer recommended the study of sociology. He was a pioneer in developing the sociological foundations of educational theory and practice. The educated members of modern societies needed knowledge of the science of society, of how social progress occurs, and of sociopolitical structures. They needed to be able to formulate scientific generalizations from masses of sociological data. Spencer relegated aesthetic and literary cultivation to the least important area of the curriculum. Such activities, he felt, were for leisure and did not directly relate to sustaining life or to earning a living. The defenders of the classical and literary curriculum attacked Spencer for neglecting the knowledge that developed one's artistic and literary nature.

Consideration of Herbert Spencer's educational theory provides a number of insights into questions about knowledge, education, and schooling. In replying to his own question, "What knowledge is of most worth?" Spencer

25 Andreas Kazamias, *Herbert Spencer on Education* (New York: Teachers College Press, Columbia University, 1966).

26 Herbert Spencer, *Education: Intellectual, Moral and Physical* (New York: Appleton, 1881).

argued that scientific knowledge was most useful in dealing with practical economic, social, and political problems. His educational ideas, which were readily accepted in the United States, influenced the NEA committee that published the seven Cardinal Principles of Education in 1918.

Influence on Educational Practices Today Spencer's theories of society and education continue to exert an influence on contemporary thought and practice. The Social Darwinist conception of survival of the fittest often takes the form of competition in which individuals compete for grades, honors, distinctions, rank, and eventually social, economic, and political power. For the Spencerian educator, individual competition leads to social progress.

In education, Spencer's greatest impact was on curriculum formulation and implementation. Rather than structuring curriculum on traditional or inherited bodies of knowledge, such as the classical languages, Spencer argued that it should be based on the most important human activities—those that sustained human life and prosperity. Modern curriculum designers have continued to use the analysis of human activities as a basis for instruction.

Montessori: Preplanned Experiences

Early childhood education

Maria Montessori (1870–1952), an Italian educator, devised a method of early childhood education that enjoys international popularity. Montessori schools can be found in Europe, the United States, and India. Since the 1950s there has been a revival of interest in the principles of Montessorian education in the United States. Montessori left the conventional schooling that was considered appropriate for girls of the Italian upper-middle class to attend a technical school. She then became the first woman in Italy to earn the degree of doctor of medicine.[27]

Work with handicapped and brain-damaged children

As a physician, Montessori's work brought her into contact with children who were regarded as mentally handicapped and brain damaged. Her work was so effective with these children that Montessori concluded that it had merits for the education of the normal child.

Teaching and learning methods

Principles of Learning and Instruction In 1908 Montessori established a children's school, the *Casa dei Bambini*. The children who attended this school came from the slums of Rome and generally were described as disadvantaged. Montessori devised a set of teaching materials and learning exercises that has become associated with her special formula for early childhood education. The "specially prepared environment" of her school was based on a number of pedagogical insights that she developed from school practice. Children, she found, were capable of sustained concentration and work. Furthermore, children enjoyed order and preferred work to play. They enjoyed repeating actions until they had mastered a given activity.

27 E. M. Standing, *Maria Montessori: Her Life and Work* (New York: New American Library, 1962).

Maria Montessori developed an educational method that emphasized a structured and orderly prepared environment.
(Historical Pictures Service, Chicago)

Based on these insights gained from observation, Montessori developed several concepts that have come to characterize her method of education. "Spontaneous discipline" and "spontaneous activity" meant that children have within them an inner need to work at that which interests them without the prodding of teachers or without the use of external rewards and punishments. This spontaneity of learning leads the child to begin and pursue writing and reading.[28]

Education and School Montessori's curriculum includes three major types of activities and experiences: practical, sensory, and formal skills and studies. It was designed to introduce the child to such practical activities as setting the table, serving a meal, washing dishes, tying and buttoning clothing, and practicing basic manners and social etiquette. Repetitive exercises developed sensory and muscular coordination. The formal skills and subjects included reading, writing, and arithmetic. Children were introduced to the

Sensory and muscular coordination

28 Maria Montessori, *The Discovery of the Child* (New York: Ballantine Books, 1972).

alphabet through the use of unmounted, movable sandpaper letters. Reading was taught after writing. Colored rods of various sizes were used to teach measuring and counting.

The preplanned materials designed to develop the practical, sensory, and formal skills included lacing and buttoning frames, weights, and packets to be identified by their sound or smell. The use of these didactic materials was to follow a prescribed method so that the child would obtain the desired skill mastery, sensory experience, or intellectual outcome. The Montessori teacher served as a director of activities, rather than a teacher in the conventional sense. He or she was to be a trained observer of children. Since the child in the Montessori school is primarily involved in individualized activity, the activities of the director are geared to each child rather than to group-centered teaching and learning.

Didactic materials

Influence on Educational Practices Today Montessori education has experienced two periods of interest in the United States. The first round of enthusiasm occurred just before World War I. Montessori visited the United States in 1913 and lectured on her method. However, the criticisms of William Kilpatrick and other progressive educators weakened the movement, and it declined after an initial burst of popularity.[29] The progressive critics charged that the Montessori method was overly structured and provided insufficiently for children's socialization. Kilpatrick, a progressive disciple of Dewey's experimentalist philosophy, believed that children should define their problems and carry through in solving them by projects. Kilpatrick believed that children learned and developed social skills as they worked together on group projects. According to Kilpatrick, the Montessori method concentrated too much on doing things correctly and in isolation and thereby restricted the opportunities for creative and experimental problem solving.

Decline and then revival of interest

Kilpatrick's critique

Since the 1950s there has been a marked revival of Montessorian pedagogy and Montessori schools in the United States, coinciding with the rise of preprimary and early childhood education. In addition, interest in Head Start stimulated a renewed interest in the methods of the Italian educator. The Montessori revival that began in the 1950s has gained momentum. By the mid-1980s, private Montessori schools enroll preschool children throughout the country. Many parents send their children to Montessori schools in order to enhance their children's intellectual development and to give them a head start in academic studies. It is difficult to assess the long-range significance of Montessorianism in American education. While it has stimulated the rise of numerous private schools and current public and governmental early childhood programs, the Montessori method has not yet made a pervasive impact on teacher education in the United States.

Maria Montessori was an early childhood educator who concentrated her efforts on improving learning opportunities for children. Like Pestalozzi, she

29 William H. Kilpatrick, *The Montessori System Examined* (Boston: Houghton Mifflin, 1914).

was concerned initially with educating the disadvantaged child. Her methods proved so successful that they were applied to all children. Like Froebel, she created a special setting for the child's first learning experiences. She believed that she had discovered the laws of learning through her careful observation of children's work and play activities. Her method of instruction was a carefully organized one that followed her discovery of the patterns of human growth and development.[30]

Dewey: Learning Through Experience

An examination of leading educational pioneers would be incomplete without some comments on John Dewey (1859–1952), the American philosopher and educator. Dewey's synthesis of Darwinian evolutionary theory, the philosophy of pragmatism, and the scientific method formed the basis for his work as an educational reformer. Viewing education as a process of social activity, Dewey recognized that the school was intimately related to the society that it served.

Dewey was born in Vermont. After receiving his doctoral degree in philosophy from Johns Hopkins University in 1884, he taught philosophy at several universities. Dewey's years at the University of Chicago, where he headed the combined departments of philosophy, psychology, and pedagogy, were important for the development of his educational theory. As the director of the University of Chicago's Laboratory School from 1896 until 1904, he tested his pragmatic educational philosophy by using it as the basis of learning activities.[31]

Laboratory school

Principles of Learning and Instruction Dewey's well-known work, *The Child and the Curriculum,* provides a guide to the ideas that he used at the laboratory school.[32] Viewing children as socially active human beings, Dewey believed that learners want to explore their environment and gain control over it. In exploring their world, learners encounter both personal and social problems. It is the problematic encounter that leads children to use their intelligence to solve the difficulty—to use the collected knowledge of the human race in an active and instrumental manner.

Dewey outlined three levels of activity that would be used at the school. The first level, for preschool children, involved exercise of the sensory organs and development of physical coordination. The second stage involved use of the materials and instruments found in the environment. The school was to be rich in the raw materials that excited children's interests and caused them to build, to experiment, and to create. Children in the third

Learning through activity

30 Paula P. Lillard, *Montessori: A Modern Approach* (New York: Schocken Books, 1972), pp. 50–90.

31 R. S. Peters, ed., *John Dewey Reconsidered* (Boston: Routledge & Kegan Paul, 1977); Arthur G. Wirth, *John Dewey as Educator: His Design for Work in Education 1894–1904* (New York: Wiley, 1966).

32 John Dewey, *The Child and the Curriculum* (Chicago: University of Chicago Press, 1902).

stage discovered new ideas, examined them, and used them. Now learning moved from simple impulse to careful observation, planning, and thinking about the consequences of action.

Education and School Dewey conceived of education as the social process by which the immature members of the group, especially the children, are brought to participate in the society. The school is a special environment, established by the members of society, for the purpose of simplifying, purifying, and integrating the social experience of the group so that it can be understood, examined, and used by its children.

Personal and social growth

For Dewey, education's sole purpose is to contribute to the personal and social growth of individuals. According to Dewey, education "is that reconstruction or reorganization of experience which adds to the meaning of experience, and which increases ability to direct the course of subsequent experience."[33]

Scientific method

Solving problems according to the scientific method is the process by which the learner comes to direct and control his or her experience. It is the process by which human beings think reflectively and publicly, and it is also the method of intelligent teaching and learning. The following steps of the scientific or reflective method are extremely important in Dewey's educational theory:

1. The learner has a "genuine situation of experience"—involvement in an activity in which he or she is interested.
2. Within this experience the learner has a "genuine problem" that stimulates thinking.
3. The learner possesses the information or does research to acquire the information needed to solve the problem.
4. The learner develops possible and tentative solutions that may solve the problem.
5. The learner tests the solutions by applying them to the problem. In this way one discovers their validity for oneself.[34]

For Dewey knowledge was not an inert body of information. It was, rather, an instrument to solve problems. The fund of knowledge of the human race—past ideas, discoveries, and inventions—was to be used as the material for dealing with problems. This accumulated wisdom of the cultural heritage was to be tested. If it served human purposes, it became part of a reconstructed experience.

Schools translate the cultural heritage

Education was the process by which immature human beings were introduced to the cultural heritage and used this heritage to deal with their problems. Since human beings and the environment were constantly changing, knowledge was also continually being reconstructed or repatterned in the

33 John Dewey, *Democracy and Education* (New York: Macmillan, 1916), pp. 89–90.

34 Ibid., p. 192.

light of present needs. Each time a person solved a problem as an individual and as a member of the human group, he or she added to the store of experience that could be used in the future.

Reconstruction of experience

Dewey's concept of the school was social, scientific, and democratic. The school introduced children to society and their heritage based on each child's own interests, needs, and problems. The school as a miniature society was the means of bringing children into social participation. The school was scientific in the sense that it was a social laboratory in which children and youth could test their ideas and values. It was also scientific in a methodological sense; the learner was to acquire the disposition and procedures associated with scientific, or reflective, thinking and acting.

School as a miniature society

Dewey was an advocate of democratic education and schooling. A democratic criterion of education meant that the learner must be free to test all ideas, beliefs, and values. Cultural heritage, customs, and institutions are all subject to critical inquiry, investigation, and reconstruction. As a democratic institution the school should be open to and used by all. He opposed barriers of custom or prejudice that segregate people from each other. People ought to live, share, and work together to solve common problems. He opposed the authoritarian or coercive style of administration and teaching that blocked genuine inquiry; his ideal school was a place where children and teachers together planned the curriculum and activities that they would pursue and where there was enjoyment in teaching and learning.

Children and teachers plan together

Influence on Educational Practices Today John Dewey exercised an enormous influence on American education. He developed and applied the open-ended philosophy of pragmatism to education and as a result helped to open the process of schooling to change and innovation. For him, education was a social activity and the school was a social agency that helped shape human character and behavior. Today, educators who relate schooling to social purposes are following Dewey's pioneering educational concepts.

Dewey's educational ideas contributed to certain phases and aspects of progressive education. While many educators associated with progressivism were "Deweyean" in their thinking, others followed their own version of progressivism. Although he rejected a romantic version of freedom that gave license to children to follow their whims and impulses, Dewey did encourage learners to experiment and to learn from the reflective reconstruction of their experience. For Dewey, the genuinely progressive school was a learning laboratory in which educational theories were tested in practice. Truly experimental schools that recognize the importance of shared human experience are continuing to practice Dewey's version of progressive education.

Dewey, whose writing is frequently complex and difficult to interpret, has often been misunderstood. Although he advocated freedom to learn through inquiry, Dewey did not encourage aimless educational anarchy. Although Dewey emphasized the testing of ideas by their consequences in the present, he did recognize that present experience is based on past experience. While Dewey favored relative values, his educational philosophy was not value free. For him, sharing, cooperation, community, and democracy were significant human values that should be encouraged by schools.

Education as a social activity

There is no doubt that Dewey's ideas influenced the course of educational development in the United States and throughout the world. His concepts of learning by experience and by solving problems were particularly influential in American teacher education. Viewing education as a process of social activity, Dewey recognized that the school was intimately related to the society that it served.

Counts: Building a New Social Order

Reconstructing society

George Counts (1889–1974) believed that education was not based on eternal truths but was relative to a particular society living at a given time and place. Counts asked the profound but still unanswered question: "Dare the school build a new social order?"[35] A professor of education at Columbia University Teachers College, Counts asked this question in 1932, when the United States was gripped by a severe economic depression. He believed that the American schools needed to identify with such progressive forces as the labor unions, the farmers' organizations, and disadvantaged minority groups. By allying themselves with groups that wanted to change or reconstruct society, the schools would become an instrument for social improvement rather than an agency for preserving the status quo.

Education for social reform

Principles of Learning and Instruction Counts, who was associated with the experimentalist philosophy and the socially oriented wing of progressive education, believed that learning and instruction should incorporate content of a socially useful nature and a problem-solving methodology. The subject matter most appropriate for social reform was based on history and the various social sciences. Historical knowledge, in Counts's view, was a product of the "new history," based on the interpretations of Charles A. Beard, the noted American historian. The new history did not pretend to be completely objective or neutral in terms of the great social conflicts of the day. It was written from a point of view that saw America on the road to becoming a more cooperative and technological society. Although Counts did not neglect the sciences and mathematics, he favored sociology and economics. The new history and the emergent social sciences were expressly emphasized, as was a commitment to democratic ethics and values.

Problem solving, following the experimentalist methodology, was an appropriate mode of instruction for Counts. Students would be encouraged to work on problems that had a significant social importance. As a cultural relativist, Counts—while believing that all education was value-oriented—as-

35 George S. Counts, *Dare the School Build a New Social Order?* (New York: John Day, 1932); a recent edition is Counts, *Dare the School Build a New Social Order?* (Carbondale: Southern Illinois University Press, 1978).

serted that more comprehensive values would emerge from uniting the viable elements of existing values with emergent social values.

Education and School Counts believed that education is always conditioned by the particular culture of a given society. American education, as a whole, reflected the American historical experience and needed to be reconstructed to meet the social, economic, political, and ethical needs of the people of the United States.[36] The Industrial Revolution, by uniting science and industry, had created a technological society.[37] Counts concluded that the democratic and equalitarian ethic of the American heritage needed to be reconstructed so that it had meaning in this modern technological society. The schools, Counts said, should emphasize the dynamic forces of democracy and technology in their curriculum and methods of instruction.

Democracy and equalitarian ideas

Lag between materialism and ethics

Counts was concerned that a cultural lag had developed between our material progress and our social institutions and ethical values. Material inventions and discoveries were dynamic and had pronounced effects on many other areas of life. Unfortunately, organized education had not developed a method for planning the course of social change. Counts wanted the schools to stress an attitude of planning and an engineering mentality so that students could begin to understand and cope with the problems of social change that arose from technology.[38]

Teachers as agents of change

Counts urged teachers to lead society rather than follow it. As leaders they were to be policy makers who would have to choose between conflicting goals and values. In the broadest sense of the term, educational statesmanship would not only be concerned with school matters but would also make important choices in the controversial areas of economics, politics, and morality. According to Counts each generation of educators would be called on to make these choices. If they failed to do so, then others would make these decisions for them.

For Counts, the school was an agency that was involved in society's politics, economics, art, religion, and ethics. Involvement meant that the school could either reflect the knowledge, beliefs, and values of the society, or it could seek to change them. When schools reflected society, they were simply acting like a mirror that reflected an image. If schools were to be socially reconstructive, their involvement must express itself as an active attempt to solve problems and not merely to reflect the status quo. If schoolteachers were to act as statesmen, then the solving of major social issues would result in a new social order.

Counts saw the democratic ethic as an enduring value of the American heritage. For him it was based on the social equality of the American people.

36 Gerald L. Gutek, *The Educational Theory of George S. Counts* (Columbus: Ohio State University Press, 1970).

37 George S. Counts, *Secondary Education and Industrialism* (Cambridge, Mass.: Harvard University Press, 1929).

38 Gerald L. Gutek, *George S. Counts and American Civilization* (Macon, Ga.: Mercer University Press, 1984).

Equal opportunity

Therefore, everyone had the right to attend school. Further, schools ought to provide an education that afforded equal learning opportunities to all students.[39]

Influence on Educational Practices Today Counts has influenced American education in several ways. For him, the educator was an educational statesperson who was responsible for shaping humankind's future as well as transmitting its past. He urged educators to exercise their role in determining the future.

Count's advocacy of a broadened and more socially relevant curriculum has influenced the development of the social sciences in today's elementary and secondary schools. To the degree that teachers and students are engaged in identifying and seeking to solve society's problems, they are engaged, as Counts urged, in making a "new social order."

Hutchins: Liberal Educator

Robert Maynard Hutchins (1899–1977) was a leading voice for educational reform in the United States. Although many of his curricular criticisms were directed toward higher education, his educational ideas were relevant to elementary and secondary schools as well. A graduate of Yale University and its law school, Hutchins became dean of the Yale Law School in 1928. He became a leader in legal education by advocating that law schools prepare generally educated persons as lawyers who knew the philosophic roots of jurisprudence and the social responsibilities of law. He did not believe that lawyers should know merely the rules and how to manipulate them.

Hutchins's success as a reformer of legal education brought him national recognition. In 1929, at age thirty, he became president of the University of Chicago. As a university president, Hutchins was committed to major curricular changes and not merely to administration. Hutchins earned a national reputation as a storm center of educational criticism, change, and reform. Often called a radical reformer, Hutchins's pioneering role in education was, nevertheless, very different from that of the other educators treated in this chapter. While Rousseau, Pestalozzi, and even Dewey sought to devise an educational method for dealing with socioeconomic and political change, Hutchins—like Aristotle and Aquinas—was more concerned with cultivating the human person's rational powers.[40]

Emphasis on rationality

Principles of Learning and Instruction Hutchins believed that principles of learning flowed from the rational nature of human beings. Genuine learning had to do with identifying, examining, and reflecting on intellectual

39 Lawrence J. Dennis and William E. Eaton, eds., *George S. Counts: Educator for a New Age* (Carbondale: Southern Illinois University Press, 1980).

40 Gerald L. Gutek, *Philosophical Alternatives in Education* (Columbus, Ohio: Merrill, 1974), pp. 70–74.

issues. In Hutchins's search for intellectual excellence, learning related to general education—the general cultivation of mind—rather than to vocational training. Learning was an intellectual effort to come to know the truth about reality.

Instruction, from Hutchins's perspective, occurred when teachers challenged students to think and to question—when teachers introduced the great ideas that were developed in the history of civilization, not as an end in themselves, but as a means to future ideas. Instructors were well advised to follow the Socratic method of searching for truth by asking significant and challenging questions.

Education and School Hutchins argued that the perennial role of education was to cultivate human intellect. For him, educational institutions should develop human intellect by examining, reflecting on, and analyzing the great ideas of humankind. As a pioneer in American education, Hutchins's efforts were focused on restoring educational premises, which had surfaced in ancient Athens, that he regarded as timeless.

Based on a perennialist philosophical commitment to rational and intellectual education, Hutchins worked directly to reform higher education. Among his educational beliefs were the following:[41]

Perennialist educational ideas

1. Education is based on humankind's perennial and constant search for truth; since what is true is always true and is everywhere true, the truth is universal and timeless. Therefore, education should also be universal and timeless.
2. Since the life of the mind is intellectual and consists of ideas, education should also be about ideas; education's primary function is to cultivate human rationality.
3. The true purpose of education is to stimulate and encourage students to think carefully about important ideas. Correct and critical thinking is the only defensible method that should be used in education.

Anti-materialism

Hutchins knew what he stood for in education; he also knew what he opposed. He rejected the tendency of American education to devote its resources to materialistic ends, to premature specialization and vocationalism, and to gimmicks and panaceas. Hutchins believed that the search for financial profit often distorted true educational purposes. The lure of money-making turned students to search for careers that promised wealth rather than cultivated the mind. Instead of providing a general and liberal education based on the sciences, arts, and humanities, many colleges and secondary schools had introduced specialized vocational and career programs. These specialized programs often came too early in the individual's life and quickly became obsolete. Hutchins also opposed the tendency of some educators to reduce

41. Robert M. Hutchins, *A Conversation on Education* (Santa Barbara, Calif.: The Fund for the Republic, 1963).

learning to the mastery of procedures and techniques rather than of thinking and ideas.

Influence on Educational Practices Today Through his leadership role in the Encyclopaedia Britannica, the Great Books of the Western World Foundation, and the Center for the Study of Democratic Institutions, Hutchins kept his educational philosophy and proposals before the American people. His influence continues to have an impact on contemporary American education. It is expressed in secondary schools and colleges that are committed to intellectual disciplines and to the liberal arts and sciences as the basic curriculum pattern. Such institutions emphasize general education based on the arts and sciences for all students rather than vocational training or specific career preparation.

Hutchins's recommendation for an intellectually-based curriculum has been the basis for Mortimer Adler's *Paideia Proposal,* which is treated in Chapter 6. Essentially, Hutchins, as well as Adler, advocated an intellectually based curriculum for all students.

Piaget: Developmental Psychologist

Jean Piaget (1896–1980), a Swiss psychologist and early childhood educator, made a significant contribution to research in educational psychology and early childhood education. From 1921 on, Piaget was a member of the Rousseau Institute in Geneva, Switzerland, becoming codirector in 1932. He also founded the International Center of Genetic Epistemology in Geneva.

Piaget's contributions to early childhood education and developmental psychology, especially in the areas of the development of children's thought, cognition, and language are notable. His research and writing examine children's conceptions of moral judgment, number, space, logic, geometry, and physical reality.

Principles of Learning and Instruction Piaget saw children as the primary agents in their own education and development in that they fashion their conception of reality.[42] In identifying the major developments in cognitive growth, Piaget discerned that mental development takes place through complex and continuous interaction between the child and the environment. Human behavior results from the adaptation of the child to the environment. Adaptation is a process in which the person (1) assimilates the factors of the environment and (2) adjusts to the requirements of the environment. Cognitive development is a process by which children arrive at a balance between assimilation and accommodation. As a result of this interactive process, children acquire the ability to generalize, differentiate, and coordinate

Child as primary agent

Cognitive development

42 Jean Piaget, *The Origins of Intelligence in Children,* trans. Margaret Cook (New York: Norton, 1952), pp. 23–42.

their concepts of reality. Children form mental constructs or images that correspond to their experience of the external world and continually modify these constructs in light of new experiences.

Piaget articulated the theory that human intelligence develops in sequential stages. Because of their mental structures and organization of experience, children are ready to learn appropriate items at specific times. Children proceed from one stage of development to the next through their own activity. Learning is a continuous process in which the learner assimilates the external facts of experience and integrates them into his or her own internal mental constructs. Each stage, based on a particular organization of cognitive structures, depends on the preceding stage and leads to the next stage. Piaget has identified four major stages in the development of human intelligence:

Sequential steps

1. Sensorimotor, from age eighteen months to two years
2. Preoperational, from two to seven years
3. Concrete operations, from seven to eleven years
4. Formal operations, from eleven to fifteen years

Programs of instruction that follow Piaget's developmental psychology rely heavily on these four stages of human development.

Education and School Although complete curricula and schools based on Piaget's psychology of learning are rare, it is possible to extrapolate certain guidelines for education and schooling by examining Piaget's stages. In the **sensorimotor stage,** Piaget found that infants first carry out isolated explorations of their environment by using their mouths, eyes, and hands. Later, they coordinate their senses for more environmental exploration. Through this exploratory activity, children construct an organized view of the world. The **preoperational stage** occurs between ages two and seven as children continue to organize their perception of the environment. Objects are classified into related groups and named. The child's organization and classification approximates that of adults. During the preoperational stage, children continue to build on the concepts developed in the preceding sensorimotor stage. Although their thinking differs from that of adults in many respects, children are now beginning to develop logical relationships.

Sensorimotor stage

Preoperational stage

Concrete operations stage

Piaget's third stage, **concrete operations,** occurs between ages seven and eleven as children isolate the general characteristics of objects—size, duration, length, and so on—and use them in more complex mental operations. While the child's cognitive operations are still based on concrete objects, they are becoming more and more abstract. Children can comprehend number signs, processes, and relationships. Although outwardly appearing to accept adult authority, they question it in their own minds.

Formal operations stage

The stage of **formal operations,** which begins sometime between ages eleven and fifteen, is characterized by the individual's ability to formulate abstract conclusions. The person, at this stage, functions at a high level of abstraction. Since individuals at this stage understand causal relationships, they can use the scientific method to explain reality. They are capable of learning complex mathematical, linguistic, mechanical, and scientific processes.

Piaget's cognitive theory has important educational implications: (1) human growth and development occur in sequential stages; (2) there are stages of readiness and activities appropriate to each stage. Since learning is sequential and cumulative, instruction should begin at an early age.

For Piaget, the teacher's function is to assist children in their learning processes.[43] Learning cannot be forced before the individual child is ready to learn. The question is, should it be delayed when the child is ready to learn? Teaching should create situations where children can actually discover structures. In the Piagetian school environment the following things should occur:

1. Teachers should encourage children to explore and experiment.
2. Instruction should be individualized so that children can learn in accordance with their own readiness.
3. Children should be provided with concrete materials to touch, manipulate, and use.

Influence on Educational Practices Today Piaget's influence on contemporary education is based on his developmental psychology, which has had its greatest impact on early childhood education and preschool education; however, it also has implications for elementary and secondary schooling. The most important of these implications are the concepts of readiness and appropriate learning experiences for each developmental stage. Piaget's general influence has contributed to a reorganization of our thinking about the development of thinking in children.

Summing Up

1. The pioneers in education who are treated in this chapter made distinctive contributions to the development of education in their own countries and throughout the world.
2. In challenging the dogma of child depravity, Comenius, Locke, and Rousseau developed a method of education more closely based on the learner's natural growth and on the child's natural goodness.
3. The work of Pestalozzi led to instructional methods based on the use of the immediate environment and the objects in it. Throughout the nineteenth and early twentieth centuries, the Pestalozzian educational method was the basic strategy used in teacher education institutions and schools throughout the United States. Froebel's theory was the basis of the kindergarten movement in the United States. Both Pestalozzi's and Froebel's methods liberalized the American conception of early child-

43 Hans G. Furth, *Piaget for Teachers* (Englewood Cliffs, N.J.: Prentice-Hall, 1970).

hood education by making teachers more sensitive to the interests and needs of children. Herbart's principles of instruction and moral development have strongly influenced classroom teachers.

4. The concept of the sociological foundations of education developed by Spencer was a pioneering effort to relate the school to the broad currents of society. His theory of identifying social activities contributed to curriculum development based on social use and efficiency.
5. The impact of Maria Montessori is currently felt in early childhood education. John Dewey's pioneering work at the University of Chicago Laboratory School pointed the way to progressive educational reform in the first half of the twentieth century.
6. George Counts was a frontier thinker who saw education as a means of creating a new social order. He challenged educators to become statesmen.
7. Robert Hutchins, a perennialist thinker, used old truths to point the way to new educational reforms.
8. Jean Piaget's developmental psychology illuminated our thinking on children's cognitive operations.

Discussion Questions

1. What are your conceptions of knowledge, education, and schooling? How do your conceptions agree or differ with those of the educators treated in this chapter?
2. Identify the various educational methods that were devised by the pioneer educators treated in this chapter. What are the strengths and weaknesses of each method?
3. Of the pioneer educators discussed in this chapter, whose ideas are most relevant to you as a prospective teacher? Whose are least relevant?
4. Can you find any evidence of the influence of the pioneer educators mentioned here on your own education?
5. Identify a current educational controversy. How would the educators discussed in this chapter react to it?

Suggested Readings

Beard, Ruth M. *An Outline of Piaget's Developmental Psychology for Students and Teachers.* New York: Basic Books, 1969

This book is a useful examination of Piaget's psychological principles and their implications for instruction.

Bloom, Allan. *Emile or On Education.* New York: Basic Books, 1979.

Bloom's annotated edition of Rousseau's Emile *is well translated and includes an introductory essay.*

Downs, Robert B. *Heinrich Pestalozzi: Father of Modern Pedagogy.* Boston: Twayne, 1979.

This book is a very readable commentary on the life and educational theory and practices of Pestalozzi, the pioneering Swiss educator.

Froebel, Frederick. *The Education of Man.* Translated by W. N. Hailman. New York: Appleton, 1896.

Hailman's translation of Froebel's classic work remains the most useful version of the kindergarten founder's philosophy.

Gutek, Gerald L. *George S. Counts and American Civilization.* Macon, Ga.: Mercer University Press, 1984.

Gutek's book places Counts's education theory in the context of American culture.

Lillard, Paula. *Montessori: A Modern Approach.* New York: Schocken Books, 1973.

Lillard presents a contemporary appraisal of Montessori and her educational method.

Piaget, Jean. *The Origins of Intelligence in Children.* New York: Norton, 1952.

This book is Piaget's own statement of his ideas on children's intelligence.

Wirth, Arthur G. *John Dewey as Educator.* New York: Wiley, 1965.

Wirth examines John Dewey's work at the University of Chicago Laboratory School.

5

Historical Development of American Education

Focusing Questions

How were European educational ideas and institutions modified in the American environment?

How did American democratic ideas contribute to the rise of public schooling in the United States?

How does the American educational ladder differ from the European dual system?

How was American education shaped by major historical forces?

What uniquely American problems of education have persisted over the course of time?

How has American education become more inclusive over time?

CHAPTER 5 PROVIDES A HISTORICAL OVERVIEW OF THE ORIGINS and development of American education. It traces the evolution of educational institutions and identifies the contributions of leading individuals whose decisions shaped American education. The chapter examines: (1) the colonial period, when European educational ideas and institutions were transported to America; (2) the creation of a uniquely American educational system during the revolutionary and early national eras; (3) the spread of universal education; (4) the development of secondary education from the Latin grammar school, through the academy, to today's comprehensive high school; (5) the development of institutions of higher learning; and (6) the education of minorities throughout American history.

The Colonial Period

Influence of European schools

The historical foundations of education in the United States were laid by colonists from England seeking to re-create in North America the patterns of British schools. The colonists were familiar with European institutional arrangements based on the dual track system of schools in which the lower socioeconomic classes attended elementary schools and the upper classes attended separate preparatory schools and colleges. The curriculum of the lower schools included the basic skills of reading, writing, arithmetic, and religious indoctrination. The chief preparatory school was the Latin grammar school, which stressed the Latin and Greek classics as the means to higher education. Education of the colonial upper classes was still heavily influenced by the Renaissance humanists, who believed that the classics contained the main body of wisdom needed by an educated man. The two kinds of schools—the elementary school and the Latin grammar school (precollege)—were separate systems. Neither the inherited European arrangements nor the social ideas of the British colonists in North America questioned the idea of class distinctions in education. The colonists also imported their Old World conceptions about the kind of education that was appropriate to males and females. Formal education, especially at the secondary and higher levels, was reserved for males. Although girls attended the elementary schools and the dame schools (private schools taught by women in their homes), they rarely attended Latin grammar schools and colleges during the colonial period of American history.

Different education for boys and girls

To the American colonist, a "public school" was not the institution with which we are familiar. In many cases the school was privately financed; the term *public* distinguished it from a school catering exclusively to a special group—usually a religious group. The modern idea of public education—a local system of schools supported by taxes and administered by public officials certified by license, which compels attendance of all children up to a certain age (usually sixteen years), and which is separated from private interests—did not exist in the colonies. Granted, the colony sometimes orga-

Limited role of government

The New England town school was often a single room in which students sat on benches until called before the schoolmaster to recite.
(Historical Pictures Service, Chicago)

nized the schools, but its role (outside of New England) was limited. Instead, several other agencies assumed the major responsibility of education—the family, the apprenticeship system, and private schools of various sorts. Of these agencies, the family carried the greatest burden; frequently, children had no formal learning or picked up only a little vocational training.

Regional differences on educational matters

The various colonies handled education matters differently. In New England the governing bodies exerted general authority over education and directly supported their schools. In the Middle Atlantic colonies, a tolerant policy toward religion fostered several different sects, each group wanting its own religious principles taught in its schools. Consequently, various schools with various policies emerged. The southern colonies did not pass laws requiring communities to establish schools. Individual parents educated their own children by making arrangements with private tutors or by sending them to private schools.[1]

New England Colonies

The New England colonies of Massachusetts Bay, Connecticut, and New Hampshire were very important in the development of American educational

1 R. Freeman Butts, "Search for Freedom: the Story of American Education," *NEA Journal* (March 1960), pp. 33–48; idem., *Public Education in the United States* (New York: Holt, 1978).

First education laws in Massachusetts

ideas and institutions. The colony of Massachusetts, in particular, enacted the first laws that governed formal education in the British colonies of North America. Much of the history of education in early America can be generalized from the educational experiences of colonial Massachusetts.[2]

Massachusetts Bay Colony was settled mainly by the Puritans, a Protestant group that adhered to the theology of the Swiss religious reformer John Calvin. Unlike the contemporary situation in the United States, in which a strict separation between church and public school exists, the first schools established in New England were closely related to the Puritan church. As practiced by the Puritans, Calvinist theology had several significant implications for education. First, the doctrine of predestination held that those souls who were elected (predestined) by God for salvation (others were damned to Hell) were to exhibit outward signs of correct and religiously defined behavior. Second, the good person respected the sanctity of property and would prosper. As a steward of wealth, the good man would use his income wisely and for the enlightenment of his fellows. Third, educated persons who knew God's commandments, as revealed by Calvin and preached by the Puritan ministers, were likely to resist the temptations of the world, especially the flesh and the devil. The school was seen as handmaiden of the church. Schooling was intended to cultivate a respect for the laws of the theocratic state and for the sanctity of property. In Puritan New England education encouraged social conformity and religious commitment.

Schooling for economic and social usefulness

There was also an economic rationale for schooling in New England, which was reinforced by Puritan outlook. The good citizen of the Puritan commonwealth was to be an economically productive individual who would produce wealth by hard work in farming, manufacturing, and trade. It was further assumed that schooling would contribute to a person's economic and social usefulness by cultivating literacy, resourcefulness, enterprise, punctuality, and thrift.

Child Depravity The Puritan conception of the child was another important element in New England colonial education. The child was regarded as being naturally depraved—conceived in sin and born in corruption. Childish play was regarded as idleness, and child's talk was considered gibberish. In order to civilize the child, the Puritan teacher applied constant discipline.

Harsh discipline

Over time childish ways would yield to the disciplined behavior that was regarded as the outward sign of the Elect. The good child appeared to be a miniature adult. A study of the Puritan child notes that the children of New England had always before them the vision of their own evil and of the punishment that they would receive in the hellfires of eternity. The stories that they heard and the books that they read were designed to impress on them the constant need for prayer and repentance. In their schools the New Eng-

2 Sheldon S. Cohen, *A History of Colonial Education,* 1607–1776 (New York: Wiley, 1974).

Religious rhymes

land children began to learn the alphabet with the rhyme: "In Adam's fall/we sinned all."[3]

"Old Deluder Satan" The Puritans of New England were a literate people. Their political ideas and the Congregational form of church governance made it necessary for them to train an educated leadership and a literate and disciplined followership. Even in the first years of their settlement of Massachusetts, the Puritans sought to establish schools. In 1642, legislation of the Massachusetts General Court required parents and guardians of children to make certain that their charges could read and understand the principles of religion and the laws of the Commonwealth. In 1647 the General Court enacted the "Old Deluder Satan" Act, which required every town of fifty or more families to appoint a reading and writing teacher. Towns of 100 or more families were to employ a teacher of Latin so that students could be prepared for entry to Harvard College.[4] The other New England colonies, except for Rhode Island, followed Massachusetts' example. These early laws indicated how important education was to the Puritan colonists of Massachusetts. Some historians have regarded these laws as the beginnings of American school law. It is clear that the Puritans did not want to see the growth of an illiterate class in North America. Such a class might be the beginning of a group of dependent poor as had existed in England. They also wanted to ensure that the children of the commonwealth would grow up as adults who were committed to Puritan theology.

A literate and committed citizenry

The Town School The New England **town school** was a locally controlled institution attended by both boys and girls. They might range in age from five or six to thirteen or fourteen. Attendance was not always regular; it depended on weather conditions and the need for children to work on the farms.[5] The school's curriculum included reading, writing, arithmetic, catechism, and the singing of religious hymns. The child learned the alphabet, the syllables, words, and sentences by memorizing the **hornbook,** a single sheet of parchment covered by a transparent material made by flattening the horns of cattle. The older children read the *New England Primer,* which included more detailed materials of a religious nature, such as the Westminster catechism. Religion and reading were carefully integrated. Children combined memorization of the Ten Commandments, the Lord's Prayer, and the

The three Rs

3 Stanford Fleming, *Children and Puritanism: The Place of Children in the Life and Thought of the New England Churches* (New Haven, Conn.: Yale University Press, 1933); Ross W. Beales, "In Search of the Historical Child: Miniature Adulthood and Youth in Colonial New England," *American Quarterly* (October 1975), pp. 379–398.

4 Nathaniel Shurtleff, ed., *Records of The Governor and Company of the Massachusetts Bay in New England,* II (Boston: Order of the Legislature, 1853).

5 George H. Martin, *The Evolution of the Massachusetts Public School System* (New York: Appleton, 1894); S. Alexander Rippa, *Education in a Free Society: An American History* (New York: McKay, 1976).

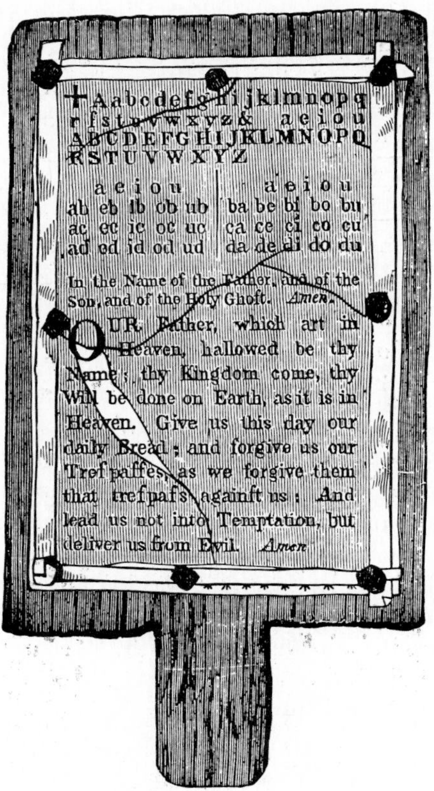

The hornbook was the colonial New England child's first "textbook" and consisted of the alphabet, vowels, and Lord's Prayer printed on a single sheet of parchment. (Brown Brothers)

Creed with instruction in reading. Arithmetic was primarily a matter of counting, adding, and subtracting.

The New England town school was often a crude structure, dominated by the teacher's pulpit, located at the front of the single room. The students sat on benches. They studied their assignments until called before the schoolmaster to recite. The teachers were males. Some earned their living as teachers while preparing for the ministry. Others took the job to repay the passage money that had brought them to North America. Many, unfortunately, were incompetents who governed their charges by the use of the rod. Although there were undoubtedly some variations, the New England elementary school was characterized by rote learning, memorized responses, and corporal punishment. It should be remembered that the children who attended town schools were often of the lower classes.

Rote learning and corporal punishment

The Latin Grammar School The sons of the upper classes attended the **Latin grammar school,** which prepared them for entry to the colleges of Harvard or Yale. These children generally had learned to read and write English from private tutors. A boy would enter the Latin grammar school at the

Classics

age of eight and remain there for eight years.[6] His lessons were based on such Latin authors as Cicero, Terence, Caesar, Livy, Vergil, and Horace. The Greek authors, such as Isocrates, Hesiod, and Homer, were read by the advanced students who had already mastered Latin grammar and composition. Little or no attention was given to mathematics, science, history, or modern languages. The masters who taught in the Latin grammar schools possessed college degrees and were generally held in high esteem. The regimen of study in the Latin grammar school was exhausting and unexciting. As historian Samuel Morison points out, the Latin grammar school was one of colonial America's closest links to the European educational experience, resembling the classical humanist schools of the Renaissance.[7]

After completing the Latin grammar school, the student applied for admission to Harvard College, established in 1636. Harvard was based on the Puritan conception that those called to the ministry and other positions of leadership needed to be soundly educated in the classics and the Scriptures. The student had to demonstrate his competency in Latin and Greek to be admitted to Harvard, where the curriculum consisted of grammar, logic, rhetoric, arithmetic, geometry, astronomy, ethics, metaphysics, and natural sciences. In addition, Hebrew, Greek, and ancient history were offered for their usefulness in scriptural study.

Middle Atlantic Colonies

The Middle Atlantic colonies of New York, New Jersey, Delaware, and Pennsylvania differed markedly from the New England group. In contrast to New England, where a common language, religion, and value structure existed, the Middle Atlantic colonies were characterized by linguistic, religious, and cultural pluralism. Although English-speaking people were in the majority, there were the Dutch in New York, Swedes in Delaware, and Germans in Pennsylvania. In addition to linguistic pluralism, there was also religious diversity. The Dutch were members of the Dutch Reformed Church; the Quakers dominated Pennsylvania; the Germans might be Lutherans or members of small pietistic denominations; and there were also Baptists, Roman Catholics, and a small Jewish population.

Linguistic, religious, and cultural pluralism

In such a situation, where there were divergent ideas and values, no single system of schools could be established. While New England created the town school, the Middle Atlantic colonies used parochial and independent schools that were closely related to the different churches.

New York The colony of New York, which had first been under Dutch control, continued to operate the schools of the Dutch Reformed Church when it became a royal colony under English domination. The Dutch parochial

6 Robert Middlekauff, *Ancients and Axioms: Secondary Education in Eighteenth-Century New England* (New Haven: Yale University Press, 1963).

7 Samuel E. Morison, *The Intellectual Life of Colonial New England* (New York: New York University Press, 1956).

schools taught reading, writing, and religion.[8] After the coming of English rule, a number of charity schools were established by a missionary society of the Church of England.

Since New York was a commercial colony, a number of private schools were established there to teach specific trades or skills. These private schools taught such subjects and skills as navigation, surveying, bookkeeping, Spanish, French, and geography. Some of them came to be known as "academies."

School for middle-class children

These schools made education available to middle-class children whose parents could afford tuition. The idea soon spread to other colonies. One of the most famous of these private schools was the Philadelphia Academy, founded in 1751 by Benjamin Franklin. Others were the Newark Academy in Delaware and the Washington Academy in New Jersey.

Pennsylvania The colony of Pennsylvania became a haven for Quakers under the leadership of William Penn. The Society of Friends, sometimes called Quakers, was a religious sect that rejected violence. The Friends refused to support war efforts or to serve in the military forces. They maintained a number of schools in Pennsylvania that were open to all children, including blacks and Native Americans.[9] Their teachers, unlike those in New England, rejected corporal punishment. They respected the individual dignity of the child and opposed the view of child depravity that was common at that time. Like the other elementary schools of the colonial period, the Quaker schools taught reading, writing, arithmetic, and religion. In addition to these basic skills, a small amount of vocational training was given in the form of handicrafts, domestic science, and agriculture.[10]

Schools for all children

Southern Colonies

The southern colonies of Maryland, Virginia, the Carolinas, and Georgia represented still another pattern of colonial education. Unlike the New England and the Middle Atlantic colonies, where concentrations of population had developed in cities and towns, the population of the southern colonies was dispersed over a large land area. This made it difficult to bring groups of children together in school classes. Those who could afford to do so resorted to tutorial education. Wealthy families engaged private teachers to educate their children; a few families sent their children to private schools.

Tutorial and private education

Effects of the Plantation System A second important characteristic of life and education in the South resulted from the unique agricultural econ-

8 William H. Kilpatrick, *The Dutch Schools of New Netherlands and Colonial New York* (Washington, D.C.: Government Printing Office, 1912).

9 James D. Hendricks, "Be Still and Know!: Quaker Silence and Dissenting Educational Ideals, 1740–1812," *Journal of the Midwest History of Education Society* (Annual Proceedings, 1975), pp. 14–40.

10 Thomas Woody, *Early Quaker Education in Pennsylvania* (New York: Teachers College Press, Columbia University, 1920).

omy that developed in that region. The plantations often produced a single, staple crop such as tobacco, cotton, or rice. This type of agriculture became the mainstay of the economy. In an era when mechanization was minimal or nonexistent, a large and cheap labor force was needed to maintain this plantation economy. The African slave trade provided large numbers of black men and women, seized in their native land and brought to the New World to work as unpaid labor.

The slave system of labor and the plantation system of land holding and ownership contributed to a development of education in the South that differed from that of both New England and the Middle Atlantic colonies.[11] The children of the privileged class of white plantation owners had the benefit of private tutors, who often lived in the plantation manor. Occasionally, the Anglican missionary society established a school for these children. In the late colonial period boarding schools were established, usually in towns such as Williamsburg or Charleston. As for the black slaves, they were trained to be agricultural workers, field hands, craftsmen, or domestic servants, but generally were forbidden to learn to read or to write. For the poor whites, who tilled the infertile soils of the back country or the mountainous areas, formal education was nonexistent. The white children of the poor usually grew up to be subsistence farmers like their parents before them. The unique situation of the southern colonies tended to retard the development of a large-scale system of schools. This educational retardation was felt long after the Civil War period.

No schooling for blacks and poor whites

Colonial Education: A Summary View

Despite these regional variations between the schools of New England, the Middle Atlantic colonies, and the South, certain parallels also must be considered. All three sections were dominated largely by British political rule. Moreover, despite the linguistic and religious variations present, all three sections were heirs to the western European educational tradition. There was similarity in the basic ideas and values that governed individuals and groups.[12] Religion held a high priority in the value structure, and the dual track system of education represented the social-class structure. Among informal sources of education, the family played a strong formative role as it shaped ideas, values, and skills.[13]

In all three regions, educational opportunities were limited by sex and by socioeconomic class. Both girls and boys attended the town or district

11 James C. Klotter, "The Black South and White Appalachia," *Journal of American History* (March 1980), pp. 832–849.

12 Lawrence A. Cremin, *American Education: The Colonial Experience, 1607–1783* (New York: Harper & Row, 1970).

13 Bernard Bailyn, *Education in the Forming of American Society* (New York: Random House, 1960).

schools; Latin grammar schools and colleges were restricted to males. There were several reasons for such discriminatory practices:

1. The role of women was specifically defined as that of wives and mothers. Girls needed to learn to read and write so that they could carry out their religious and family responsibilities. Since women in the colonial period did not have career choices, their schooling was limited to the basics.
2. There was a general opinion, mainly held by males who controlled educational institutions, that women were incapable of exacting higher studies. Such a prejudiced opinion was based on traditional sex biases rather than on scientific research. In the late nineteenth century, this sexist myth was challenged; it was largely discredited in the twentieth century.
3. The curriculum of the Latin grammar school and college stressed Latin and Greek classics, theology, and philosophy. These studies were designed to prepare future ministers and lawyers. During the eighteenth and nineteenth centuries, these professions were closed to women.

In addition to sex or gender discrimination, colonial schools followed the social and economic class biases of Europe, according to which schooling was divided into two tracks. The elementary town or district schools were designed for the lower classes. Although they provided basic literacy, they generally did not provide for upward social mobility. While there were some exceptions, most pupils who completed their schooling in elementary town and district schools did not continue for further study in the Latin grammar schools and colonial colleges. The sons of the upper classes attended the preparatory Latin grammar schools and, if successful, entered college.

The dual track system was a European importation to North America. Throughout the nineteenth century, the forces of frontier egalitarianism, political democratization, and economic change worked to erode these educational structures and to create the American system of universal, public education.

The Early Period of Nationhood

The American Revolution of 1776 ended British rule in the thirteen colonies. A new government based on a system of checks and balances distributed political power among the executive, legislative, and judicial branches. Although the inherited vernacular and denominational elementary schools and Latin grammar schools continued for some time, the leaders of the new republic sought to create new patterns of education that would be suited to the self-governing citizens of the United States.[14]

14 Rush Welter, *Popular Education and Democratic Thought in America* (New York: Teachers College Press, Columbia University, 1962); David Madsen, *Early National Education: 1776–1830* (New York: Wiley, 1974).

Under the Articles of Confederation, Congress sought to administer the lands of the Northwest Territory. The first national educational legislation, included in the Northwest Ordinance of 1785, called for the surveying and division of the Northwest Territory into townships of 36 square miles. Each township was further divided into thirty-six sections, the sixteenth section of which was to be used for education. While the provisions of the Northwest Ordinance are no longer in effect, they established the pattern of the land grant, often used to finance education in the early nineteenth century.

Northwest Ordinance

The U.S. Constitution made no mention of education, but the "reserved powers" clause of the Tenth Amendment (which reserved to the states all powers not specifically delegated to the federal government or prohibited to the states by the Constitution) served as the basis for leaving responsibility for education with the individual states. The colonial tradition of local school control and the opposition to centralized political power contributed to a state rather than a national school system in the United States.

Education reserved to the states

Until the establishment of the common school system, leaders in the new republic grappled with the problem of designing an educational system that would serve the needs of a new political system and contribute to nation building. Numerous plans were put forth by such people as George Washington, Benjamin Rush, Robert Coram, Samuel Smith, and Noah Webster. These plans shared certain aims: (1) education should meet the needs of a self-governing polity; (2) education should reflect the needs of a developing nation that included vast expanses of frontier land and abundant supplies of natural resources; (3) education should be useful rather than classical or ornamental; and (4) education should be American rather than European.[15] To indicate the nature of the educational plans in the early days of the republic, special attention will be given to the educational proposals of Benjamin Franklin, Thomas Jefferson, and Noah Webster.

Rejection of European ideas

Franklin: The Academy

Benjamin Franklin (1706–1790) represented the rising American business class. His own formal education was brief, consisting of one year at the Boston grammar school, some writing and arithmetic lessons by private teachers, and experience as a printer's apprentice. He was a self-educated man who studied the major political and social tracts of his day. Franklin inaugurated several major scientific and educational organizations in Philadelphia, such as the Library Subscription Society, the Junto, and the American Philosophical Society. The proverbial folk wisdom of his *Poor Richard's Almanack* was very popular among the American middle classes, who readily accepted his emphasis on the virtues of frugality, diligence, thrift, hard work, and inventiveness.

Virtues of thrift and hard work

15 David Nasaw, *Schooled to Order* (New York: Oxford University Press, 1979); Frederick Rudolph, *Essays on Education in the Early Republic* (Cambridge, Mass.: Harvard University Press, 1965).

In 1749, Franklin wrote "Proposals Relating to the Education of Youth in Pennsylvania." This treatise served as a basis for the academy that he founded. The **academy** was a private secondary school, which offered a practical curriculum that included a variety of subjects and useful skills.[16] English grammar, classics, composition, rhetoric, and public speaking were to be the chief language studies rather than Latin and Greek. Students could also choose a second language based on their vocational interests. For example, prospective clergymen might study Latin and Greek; physicians could choose Latin, Greek, and French; businessmen might elect French, German, and Spanish. Mathematics was to be taught for its practical application to bookkeeping rather than as an abstract intellectual exercise. History would be the chief ethical study. By studying biographies of great men, students were to learn moral and ethical principles. Franklin's curricular proposal was especially noteworthy because it brought many practical skills into the formal school that hitherto had been ignored. They included carpentry, shipbuilding, engraving, printing, painting, cabinetmaking, farming, and carving. With a prophetic insight into the course of civilization and education, Franklin suggested that special attention be given to science, invention, and technology.

Practical curriculum

By the mid-nineteenth century, there were many academies functioning throughout the nation, especially at the secondary level. These academies offered a wide variety of curricula and courses, ranging from traditional Latin and Greek to very practical and utilitarian studies. The late nineteenth and twentieth centuries saw the emergence of high schools and the junior high or middle school, which incorporated utilitarianism, vocationalism, and commercialism, much as Franklin had recommended in his proposals of the mid-eighteenth century.

Jefferson: Education for Citizenship

Thomas Jefferson (1743–1826), a leading statesman of the revolutionary and early republican periods, attended the local English vernacular school and Latin grammar school near his home in Virginia. He also attended William and Mary College. Jefferson was a man of wide-ranging interests, embracing politics, philosophy, architecture, agriculture, and science. His political career was distinguished by his service as a member of the Virginia legislature and the Continental Congress, governor of Virginia, secretary of state, vice-president, and president of the United States. As the principal author of the Declaration of Independence, Jefferson stated his political belief that everyone is endowed with inalienable rights of "life, liberty, and the pursuit of happiness." Deeply involved in intellectual and educational affairs, he was a

16 John H. Best, *Benjamin Franklin on Education* (New York: Teachers College Press, Columbia University, 1962); Henry J. Perkinson, *Two Hundred Years of American Educational Thought* (New York: Longman, 1976).

member of the American Academy of Arts and Sciences and was president of the American Philosophical Society.[17]

Jefferson's Philosophy of Education Jefferson's "Bill for the More General Diffusion of Knowledge" was introduced in the Virginia legislature in 1779. This legislation, expressing Jefferson's philosophy of republican education, assumed that the state had the responsibility to cultivate an educated and literate citizenry. The major purpose of education was to serve the general welfare of a democratic society by seeing to it that the knowledge and understanding necessary to exercise the responsibility of citizenship were made available to all. "If," said Jefferson, "a nation expects to be ignorant and free, in a state of civilization, it expects what never was and will never be." Hence, it was proper for the state to play an educational role and to provide the opportunities for the education of both the common people and the leaders of society "at the common expense of all."[18] To Jefferson, formal education was largely a state or civic concern, rather than a matter reserved to religious denominations. Schools should be financed through public taxes.

State responsibility for education

Education as a civic concern

Jefferson's plan would have subdivided the counties of Virginia into wards, each of which would have had an elementary school to teach reading, writing, arithmetic, and history. All white children in Virginia were to attend the ward school for three years of elementary education supported by taxes. After the first three years the children would have been able to continue in the ward schools if their parents paid their tuitions. Jefferson's proposal also provided for the establishment in Virginia of twenty grammar schools at the secondary level. In each ward school the most academically gifted student who could not afford to pay tuition would have been awarded a scholarship to continue his education for three additional years in the grammar school. There he would have studied Latin, Greek, English, geography, and higher mathematics. Upon completing grammar school, half of the scholarship students would have been assigned positions as elementary or ward schoolteachers. The ten scholarship students of highest academic achievement would have attended William and Mary College. Jefferson's plan used the school as an agency to identify and provide the most competent students with continuing education.

Scholarships based on merit

Although Jefferson's proposal was not enacted by the Virginia legislature, the bill reveals the educational theorizing in the early republic. It clearly demonstrates that a primary purpose of education was to promote good citizenship. It also shows that the earlier influence of the religious denominations was beginning to decline. Jefferson was concerned with the general education of the population and also with identifying individuals of superior

Education to promote citizenship

17 Roy J. Honeywell, *The Educational Work of Thomas Jefferson* (Cambridge, Mass.: Harvard University Press, 1931); Robert D. Heslep, *Thomas Jefferson and Education* (New York: Random House, 1969).

18 Thomas Jefferson, "A Bill for the More General Diffusion of Knowledge," in P. L. Ford, ed., *The Writings of Thomas Jefferson*, II (New York: Putnam, 1893), p. 221.

ability who would exercise political leadership. The educational ideas of the leaders of the Revolutionary generation, such as Franklin and Jefferson, were to be defined and expressed by the proponents of the American common school in the nineteenth century.

Webster: Schoolmaster of the Republic

One of the leading cultural nationalists of the early republic was Noah Webster (1758–1843). A native of Connecticut and a Yale graduate, Webster was a lawyer, schoolmaster, politician, and writer.[19] His prominence in American intellectual and educational history rests on his writing of the *American Spelling Book* and the *American Dictionary.* Webster articulated a concept of cultural nationalism according to which nationality was based on and reflected the unique intellectual identity of a nation's citizens. For Webster, the major challenge was to create a sense of American cultural identity and unity.

In 1789 when the Constitution went into effect, Webster argued that the United States should have its own system of "language as well as government." The language of Great Britain, he reasoned, "should no longer be our standard; for the taste of her writers is already completed, and her language on the decline."[20] By the act of revolution, the American people had declared their political independence of England; now they needed to declare their cultural independence as well. Realizing that a sense of national identity was conveyed through a distinctive national language and literature, Webster set out to reshape the English language used in the United States. He believed that a uniquely American language would (1) eliminate the remains of European usage; (2) create a uniform American speech that would be free of localism and provincialism; and (3) promote self-conscious American cultural nationalism. The creation of an American language would become the linguistic mortar of national union.

Cultural independence from England

Webster directly related the learning of language to organized education. As they learned the American language, children also would learn to think and act as Americans. The American language that Webster proposed would have to be taught deliberately and systematically to the young in the nation's schools. Since the curriculum of these Americanized schools would be shaped by the books that the students read, Webster spent much of his life writing spelling and reading books. His *Grammatical Institute of the English Language* was published in 1783. The first part of the *Institute* was later printed as *The American Spelling Book,* which was widely used throughout the United States in the first half of the nineteenth century.[21] Webster's *Spell-*

Specific American language

Spelling books and dictionaries

19 For biographies of Webster, see Harry R. Warfel, *Noah Webster: Schoolmaster to America* (New York: Octagon, 1936); Ervin C. Shoemaker, *Noah Webster: Pioneer of Learning* (New York: Columbia University Press, 1936).

20 Noah Webster, *Dissertations on the English Language* (Boston: Isaiah Thomas, 1789).

21 Henry Steele Commager, ed., *Noah Webster's American Spelling Book* (New York: Teachers College Press, Columbia University, 1962).

ing Book went through many editions; it is estimated that 15 million copies had been sold by 1837. Webster's great work was *The American Dictionary,* which was completed in 1825 after twenty-five years of laborious research.[22] Often called the "schoolmaster of the republic," Noah Webster was an educational statesman of the early national period whose work helped to create a sense of American language, identity, and nationality.

The Rise of Universal Education

Education designed for frontier society

In the first two decades of the nineteenth century individuals and groups were seeking a new form of education, an institution of learning suited to the republican needs of a frontier society. Although they rejected the highly class-centered European model, proponents of a new form of American education borrowed selectively from European educators. For example, Robert Owen's infant school, developed in the factory community of New Lanark, Scotland, gained some support.[23]

In the infant school, young children from three to six were given both play activity and intellectual experiences. Although some infant schools were established, they were not widely instituted in the United States.

Like western Europe, early nineteenth-century America was undergoing the first phase of industrialization. Women and children worked in the factories of the industrial Northeast. To give the child factory workers some minimal learning, Sunday schools were opened in some of the larger cities such as New York and Philadelphia. The Sunday school concept was developed by Robert Raikes, an English religious leader and publicist, who wanted to take children off the streets on the Lord's Day and give them some basic literary and religious instruction. In the United States, classes were conducted on the one day of the week when the factories were closed. Writing, reading, arithmetic, and religion were taught to those who attended.

Monitorial method utilized student teachers

The European method of instruction that received the most attention in the early nineteenth century was the monitorial method, promoted by two rival English educators, Andrew Bell, an Anglican churchman, and Joseph Lancaster, a Quaker teacher. The **monitorial method,** as the name implies, relied heavily on the use of student teachers, or monitors, who were trained by a master teacher in the rudiments of a subject.[24] It sought to cultivate basic literacy and arithmetic by having a master teacher train a number of student teachers, who then trained other students to act as monitors. The monitorial method attracted those who believed it possible to have a large system of education at very little cost.

22 Robert K. Leavitt, *Noah's Ark, New England Yankees and the Endless Quest* (Springfield, Mass.: Merriam, 1947); Richard M. Rollins, "Words as Social Control: Noah Webster and the Creation of *The American Dictionary," American Quarterly* (Fall 1976), pp. 415–430.

23 Harold Silver, ed., *Robert Owen on Education* (Cambridge, Mass.: Harvard University Press, 1969); Gerald L. Gutek, "New Harmony: An Example of Communitarian Education," *Educational Theory* (Winter 1972), pp. 34–46.

24 David Salmon, *Joseph Lancaster* (London: Longman, Green, 1904).

At first, monitorial schools were very popular in the United States. In New York, Philadelphia, and elsewhere they were supported by private funds and by some state and city appropriations. When the New York Free School Society turned its property over to the public school system in 1853, over 600,000 children had been served in monitorial schools.[25] By the early 1840s, however, interest faded when people realized that the monitorial approach provided only the barest minimum of learning. The following contributions of monitorial schools should be noted, however:

1. They made educational opportunities more easily available.
2. They acquainted parents with the concept of formal education for their children.
3. They demonstrated the possibility of mass education for most children.
4. They demonstrated both the need for and possibility of systematic teacher preparation.

Early industrialism

As the frontier was expanding, the northern states were experiencing the early stages of industrialization. The cities were growing into large urban centers with increasing populations of immigrants and needed a system of schools that would provide systematic elementary education in reading, writing, arithmetic, and citizenship. Both industrialization and the frontier movement produced a spirit of practicality that encouraged schools to cultivate basic skills as opposed to the traditional and classic subjects.

The need for basic skill learning was one of the early nineteenth-century arguments advocating schooling for all the people. There was also a strong conviction that the character and destiny of the United States required the participation of all citizens in the institutions of government. The advocates of popular education in both the West and North argued that in a democratic, self-governing society citizens needed to be able to intelligently elect competent officials to conduct the affairs of state. Thus a mixture of political, social, and economic motivations characterized the demand for universal schooling that culminated in the common school movement.

The Common School

While the major thrust of the American common school movement of the first half of the nineteenth century was to win popular support in publicly financed elementary education, it also had broad social, political, intellectual, and economic ramifications. The **common school** may be defined as an institution devoted to elementary education in the basic tools of reading, writing, and arithmetic. It was common in that it was open to the children of all

25 John Reigart, *The Lancasterian System of Instruction in the Schools of New York City* (New York: Teachers College Press, Columbia University, 1916).

26 H. Warren Button and Eugene F. Provenzo, Jr., *History of Education and Culture in America* (Englewood Cliffs, N.J.: Prentice-Hall, 1983), pp. 67–70.

Melting pot theme

social and economic classes. Through a common or a shared program of civic education, it was to cultivate a sense of American identity and loyalty.[27] Its major social purpose was to integrate children of various social, economic, and ethnic backgrounds into the broad American community. The political objective of common schooling had been enunciated earlier by such leaders as Jefferson. It was to educate the future citizens of a country with self-governing political institutions.

Practical education

Intellectually, the common school curriculum was to cultivate the basic tools of literacy that could be used in everyday life and for ongoing practical education. It was not intended to teach the traditional classical curriculum. Economically, the common school was seen as a place to learn the skills and the attitudes that made one into a competent shopkeeper, merchant, artisan, and worker. It was an agency to develop the practical economic competencies that facilitated upward mobility and occupational choice.

State and local variations among school districts

Because the Tenth Amendment of the U.S. Constitution reserved powers over education to each state, the patterns of common school establishment varied considerably from state to state. As noted earlier, the American educational system really was a decentralized system. Even within a given state, especially in the frontier areas where a number of small school districts emerged, there might be significant variations in school support and organization from one local district to another.

The basic roots of the common school movement were established prior to the Civil War—actually between 1820 and 1850. Common schools generally were established first in the New England states, where first Massachusetts and then Connecticut provided the leading examples.[28] The northern states generally followed the common school model of New England. As the frontier expanded and new states entered the Union, they too adopted the model and enacted the necessary provisions for setting up a common or public elementary system of schools. In the South the establishment of common schools was generally delayed until after the Civil War.

Three stages of legislation

Although the pattern for establishing a common school varied from state to state, a general set of procedures occurred in the process of establishing elementary public education systems. Three legislative stages have been identified: *permissive, encouraging,* and *compulsory.* In the permissive stage the state legislature gave permission for the organization of each local school district subject to the approval of the majority of voters in the given school district. In the second stage the state legislature deliberately encouraged the establishment of school districts, the election of school boards, and the raising of tax revenues for school support. In this second stage, however, the state did not compel or require the establishment of common schools;

27 Frederick M. Binder, *The Age of the Common School, 1830–1865* (New York: Wiley, 1974).

28 In 1826 Massachusetts passed a law that required every town to choose a school committee that would be responsible for all the schools in the local area. Thus began the policy of organizing public schools into a school system under a single authority. Eleven years later the Massachusetts legislature established the first state board of education. Connecticut quickly followed the example of its neighbor. See Lawrence A. Cremin, *The American Common School, A Historical Conception* (New York: Teachers College Press, Columbia University, 1951).

rather, the states encouraged such institutions by providing funds. In the third stage the state compelled the establishment of school districts, the election of school boards, and the tax support of common schools by the setting of a minimum tax rate. The state also might specify in the common school code the minimum curriculum and specification requirements governing school construction, lighting, and maintenance.

Tax support of common schools

Since the amount of taxation varied considerably from school district to school district, the quantity and quality of the education provided were uneven. For a considerable period of time, many districts also charged a tuition payment per child, called a rate bill. The coming of the common school laid the foundation of the American public school system. Later in the nineteenth century the public high school would be fashioned to complete the educational ladder that led to the state college and university. Perhaps the most prominent American educator who worked in establishing the foundation of the common school system was Horace Mann.

Foundation of the American public school

Mann: The Fight for Free Schools

Horace Mann (1796–1859) was born in Massachusetts, attended Brown University, and prepared for a legal career. He was elected to the Massachusetts legislature in 1827, where he became a proponent of the common school cause. When the legislature created a state board of education in 1837, Mann was appointed secretary. His *Annual Reports* contain his philosophy of education and his surveys of the condition of common schooling in Massachusetts. As editor of the *Common School Journal,* Mann gained a nationwide audience for his arguments advocating popular elementary education. When he retired from the Massachusetts Board of Education in 1849, Mann was elected to Congress. Later, he served as president of Antioch College.[29]

Horace Mann skillfully executed a consensus style of leadership and administration to gain support for the common school cause. He had to convince several major segments of the Massachusetts population. First, taxpayers had to be shown that it was in their interest to support public schools. To enlist the support of the business community, Mann developed the stewardship theory. He argued that wealthy people have a special responsibility in providing public education. Those who have prospered, Mann asserted, are the guardians or stewards of wealth. Their support of public education actually would create an industrious class of men and women who would obey the law, be diligent in their work, and add to the state's economic well-being. Tax support of education was really an investment that would yield high dividends of public safety, progress, and prosperity. To the workers and farmers of Massachusetts, Mann argued that the common school would be a great social equalizer. It would be the means by which the children of a lower socioeconomic class could gain the necessary skills and knowledge to

Enlisting support for the common schools

A social equalizer

29 Jonathan Messerli, *Horace Mann: A Biography* (New York: Knopf, 1972).

achieve a higher status. Common schooling would be the instrument of social and economic mobility; it would open the doors to greater opportunities.

As an administrator Mann realized that he had to have the support of the common school teachers. He sought to improve teacher preparation by encouraging normal schools to professionalize teaching and to secure higher salaries for teachers. His efforts generally were supported although some teachers opposed his liberal views on discipline and classroom management.

A unifying bond of common culture

In addition to being a wise and effective administrator, Mann was an educational statesman. He clearly recognized the relationship between the common school and the political climate of a democratic society. Citizens in our society needed to be prepared to study the issues of the day and to vote intelligently. The United States differed from the more homogeneous nations of western Europe; it was composed of people of different religious beliefs and of varying ethnic origins and languages, crosscut by special and often conflicting interests. If the United States was to develop the unifying bond of a common culture, there needed to be a common basic education that developed a sense of national identity and purpose. Mann was convinced that common schooling was a national necessity. His quest was for a new public philosophy and a sense of community to be shared by Americans of all backgrounds—and the instrument for reaching that goal would be the common school.[30]

The school would be part of the birthright of every child, financed by the state and local community. It would be for rich and poor alike; it would not only be free, but also as good in quality as any private school; it would be nonsectarian, receiving children of all religions and classes. Through state legislatures and local boards, popularly elected officials rather than professional educators would exercise ultimate control and authority. Mann reasoned that the public, which must support the schools, should govern them. Thus he set in motion the built-in dynamism that characterizes today's public schools and the underlying ideals of universal education.[31]

In addition to providing publicly supported elementary education for the majority of American children, the common school movement had two important complementary consequences: (1) it firmly established the normal school as a teacher preparation institution, and (2) it established elementary school teaching as an important career choice for women.

Normal schools

By the mid-nineteenth century, the normal school became widely accepted as an institution for preparing teachers. It was modeled after the French *école normale,* from which its name was derived. **Normal schools,** first established in New England in 1823, were two-year institutions providing courses in history and philosophy of education, instructional principles, methodology, and practice or demonstration teaching for prospective teach-

30 Lawrence A. Cremin, ed., *The Republic and the School: Horace Mann on the Education of Free Man* (New York: Teachers College Press, Columbia University, 1957).

31 Horace Mann, *Lectures and Annual Reports on Education* (Cambridge, Mass.: Cornhill Press, 1867).

ers. At first normal schools were somewhat like academies. By the end of the nineteenth century, however, many normal schools were converted into four-year teacher education colleges.

The development of common schools created a demand for trained teachers, and many women were attracted to teaching careers in the expanding system of elementary schools. The normal schools provided women with opportunities for higher education. While it is true that salaries were low, teaching careers gave women a chance to begin to develop other career opportunities.

The One-Room School

A homely building

An especially distinctive type of common school was the one-room school, often referred to as the district school. In rural areas it was usually small and plain, housing children of many different ages. Rural schools were governed by an elected board of trustees, who set the tax rate and employed the teacher. The interior of one of these small country schools was described at the turn of the twentieth century as follows:

> A door on the left admits us to the school-room. Here is a space about twenty feet long and ten wide, the reading and spelling parade. At the south end of it, at the left as you enter, was one seat and writing bench, making a right angle with the rest of the seats. This was occupied in the winter by two of the oldest males in the school. At the opposite end was the magisterial desk, raised upon a platform a foot from the floor. The fire-place was on the right, halfway between the door of entrance and another door leading into a dark closet, where the girls put their outside garments and their dinner baskets. This also served as a fearful dungeon for the immuring of offenders. Directly opposite the fire-place was an aisle, two feet and a half wide, running up an inclined floor to the opposite side of the room. On each side of this were five or six long seats and writing benches, for the accommodation of the students at their studies.[32]

The "little red schoolhouse"

The simplicity of the "little red schoolhouse," which was established in almost every rural community, especially throughout the West, eventually formed one of the nation's most lasting, sentimental pictures. The schoolhouse not only symbolized the local commitment to schooling—meager in outlook and facilities though it was—it coincided with the conditions and spirit of the age. In the classroom the basic skills of reading, writing, arithmetic, spelling, geography, and history were taught.[33] An important element was the cultivation of the virtues of punctuality, honesty, and hard work.

The one-room rural school helped to shape American culture in many ways. It was governed by an elected school board that levied taxes, created the budget, and set the governing policies for the institution. Its direct, grass roots approach to school government was a form of direct democracy. The

32 Warren Burton, *The District School as It Was* (Boston: Lee & Shepard, 1897), p. 4.

33 Ruth S. Freeman, *Yesterday's Schools* (Watkins Glen, N.Y.: Century House, 1962).

The one-room schoolhouse was common in nineteenth-century rural America and can be found in some communities of the United States even in the 1980s. *(Ron Engh/Freelance Photographers Guild)*

board hired, certificated, and supervised the teacher. The local rural school was not only an educational institution, it was also a cultural center for the community. Spelling bees, patriotic celebrations, and graduation exercises often drew the members of the community to the local district school.[34]

The McGuffey Readers

The simple ideals of literacy, hard work, diligence, and virtuous living that characterized nineteenth-century American public schools were epitomized by McGuffey and his readers. William Holmes McGuffey (1800–1873), clergyman, professor, and college president, is best known for the series of readers that bears his name. It is estimated that over 120 million copies of McGuffey's readers were sold between 1836 and 1920. McGuffey himself was nurtured in the theology and values of Scotch Presbyterianism, and his readers emphasized the importance of individual virtue and goodness.[35]

120 million copies sold

Stressing the basic moral outlook of white Anglo-Saxon Protestant rural America, the McGuffey readers also emphasized patriotism and heroism. Among the selections included as representative of American literature were the orations of Patrick Henry, Daniel Webster, and George Washington.

Morality, patriotism, and heroism

34 Wayne E. Fuller, *The Old Country School: The Story of Rural Education in the Middle West* (Chicago: University of Chicago Press, 1982).

35 John H. Westerhoff, *McGuffey and His Readers: Piety, Morality, and Education in Nineteenth-Century America* (Nashville: Abingdon, 1978).

Through his readers, McGuffey, in many ways, was a teacher to several generations of Americans. McGuffey also provided the first graded readers for our school systems and paved the way for a totally graded system, which had its beginnings in the 1840s.

The Secondary School Movement

The establishment of the common school created the framework for a tax-supported and locally controlled public elementary school education in the United States. It was upon this base that the public high school would be created—the institution that linked the elementary school with the state colleges and universities. With the creation of public secondary schooling, the institutional links of the American educational ladder were forged.

Increasing enrollments

As the common school movement expanded, the ideal was to provide as much education as possible for all children and youth. The keynote to the late nineteenth century became "more education for more people." While there were setbacks and criticism, the surge toward greater educational opportunity for more and more students continued. By 1900 the majority of children aged six to thirteen were enrolled in elementary schools. By 1980, the percentage had climbed to 99 percent. More remarkable was the expansion of secondary enrollments. At the turn of the century about 10 percent of the youth aged fourteen to seventeen were in school; in 1930 the figure was 50 percent; by 1980 as many as 93 percent were attending and 75 percent were graduating. The concept of universal education had been achieved—something of which few countries could boast. (See Table 5.1 for specific enrollment figures.)[36]

The Academy: Forerunner of the High School

Decline of Latin grammar school

In the early nineteenth century the Latin grammar school of the colonial period was replaced by the academy. The academy was the dominant institution of secondary education during the first half of the nineteenth century. Serving the educational needs of the middle classes, it offered a wide range of curricula and subject matter.[37] By 1855 there were more than 6,000 academies in the United States, with an enrollment of 263,000 students. These academies served the needs of both college preparatory and terminal students.

The academy was characterized by loose organization and ill-defined programs of instruction. The quality and the quantity of these programs varied considerably from academy to academy. Despite the wide range of curricula,

36 *Digest of Educational Statistics, 1980* (Washington, D.C.: Government Printing Office, 1980), table 29, pp. 36–37; *Statistics of Public Elementary and Secondary Day School: 1977–1978 School Year* (Washington, D.C.: Government Printing Office, 1978), table 11, p. 32. Also see Allan C. Ornstein and Harry L. Miller, *Looking into Teaching* (Chicago: Rand McNally, 1980), table 12.3, p. 403.

37 Theodore R. Sizer, *The Age of Academies* (New York: Teachers College Press, Columbia University, 1964).

Table 5.1
Public Elementary and Secondary School Enrollment, 1880–1980

Year	Total Enrollment	Elementary (K–8)	Secondary (9–12)
1880	9,867,000	9,757,000	110,000
1890	12,722,000	12,519,000	202,000
1900	15,503,000	14,983,000	519,000
1910	17,813,000	16,898,000	915,000
1920	21,578,000	19,377,000	2,206,000
1930	25,678,000	21,278,000	4,399,000
1940	25,433,000	18,832,000	6,601,000
1950	25,111,000	19,386,000	5,724,000
1960	36,281,000	27,692,000	8,589,000
1970	45,909,000	32,577,000	13,332,000
1980	41,094,000	24,002,000	17,092,000

Source: This chart has been prepared by the author and is based on the *Standard Education Almanac,* 1981–82 (Chicago: Marquis Academic Media, 1981), pp. 98–99 and *Historical Statistics of the United States* (Washington, D.C.: U.S. Bureau of the Census, 1960), p. 207.

three basic patterns were discernible: (1) the traditional college preparatory curriculum; (2) the English language course, which was the general curriculum for those who were completing their formal education; and (3) the normal course, which was intended for prospective common school teachers. There were, in addition, some specialized military academies.

Variations in quality

The range of curriculum alternatives, however, was not a sure guide to the quality of instruction. There were great variations in the degree of competency of the instructors and a wide range in the aptitude of the students. Uniformity in accreditation was lacking. The length of the courses also varied considerably. Some courses might be the so-called short courses, which were taught for a few weeks or months; others might require a semester or a year of study.

The academies were generally under the control of private boards of trustees or governing bodies. Occasionally, they might be semipublic and receive some support from cities or states. The era of the academies extended to the 1870s, when they declined in numbers and in popularity and were replaced by the public high school. A few private academies still exist in the United States and continue to provide secondary education for a small percentage of the population.

The academies and the normal schools of the nineteenth century extended the opportunities available to young women for a formal education. While some academies were founded expressly for young women, others were coeducational. Among the academies founded for women was the Troy Female Seminary, established in 1821 in New York, by Emma Willard, a leader in the women's rights movement of the nineteenth century. Mary

Lyon founded Mount Holyoke Female Seminary in Massachusetts in 1837. Along with the conventional domestic science program, female seminaries and academies offered classical and modern languages, science, mathematics, art, and music. The teacher preparation, or normal curriculum, was also popular as a course of study.

The High School

Although a small number of high schools had existed in the United States since the founding of the English Classical School of Boston in 1821, the high school did not become the major institution of American secondary education until the second half of the nineteenth century, when it gradually replaced the academy. In the 1870s the courts ruled in a series of cases (especially the *Kalamazoo,* Michigan, case in 1874) that the people of the states could establish and support public high schools with tax funds if they desired. After that, the public high school movement spread rapidly. By 1890 the 2,526 public high schools in the United States were enrolling more than 200,000 students. This can be contrasted to the 1,600 private secondary schools and academies that enrolled at that time fewer than 95,000 students.[38]

Taxes for public high school

Eventually, the states passed compulsory school laws. Provision of public secondary schools thereafter became an obligation of the states, rather than a voluntary matter for parents of the local district to decide. Children were permitted to attend approved nonpublic schools, but the states had the right to supervise and set minimum standards for *all* schools.

Urbanization and the High School The rise of the high school as the dominant institution of secondary education in the United States was the result of a variety of socioeconomic forces. The United States in the mid-nineteenth century experienced a great transition from an agricultural and rural society to an industrial and urban nation. For example, New York City's population grew from 1,174,779 in 1860 to 4,766,833 in 1910. By 1930 more than 25 percent of all Americans lived in seven great urban areas: New York, Chicago, Philadelphia, Boston, Detroit, Los Angeles, and Cleveland. This rapid urbanization also brought with it a growing need for specialization of occupations, professions, and services, and the high school was seen as the major institution for meeting this need.[39]

As an educational agency of an urban and industrialized society, the high school provided a more intensive and specialized education for more and more people who were continuing their formal education beyond the eight years of elementary schooling. It served the needs of the so-called terminal students who would complete their formal schooling in the high school, and

38 Edward A. Krug, *The Shaping of the American High School, 1880–1920,* I (New York: Harper & Row, 1964).

39 Edward A. Krug, *The Shaping of the American High School: 1920–1941,* II (Madison, Wis.: University of Wisconsin Press, 1972).

it continued to provide college preparatory schooling for those who were bound for institutions of higher education.[40] In the late nineteenth and early twentieth centuries, it began to include career or vocational courses such as home economics, manual training, industrial and shop training, and clerical-commercial preparation. In these ways the high school was an institutional response to the socioeconomic needs of a society that was becoming increasingly industrialized, urbanized, and specialized.

Academic and vocational courses

The Popularization of Secondary Schools As a school for students from varying social, economic, racial, religious, and ethnic backgrounds, the high school represented a new kind of secondary institution. In contrast to the European track system of secondary education, which rigidly separated the academic students from the terminal students, the American high school evolved into a democratic and comprehensive institution, which aimed at social integration while providing simultaneously some degree of curricular differentiation. As a school for adolescents, the American high school was a product of a society that was becoming increasingly affluent. It was a society that could afford the financial costs of educating large numbers of fourteen- to eighteen-year-olds. In contrast, poorer nations are unable to provide large systems of secondary education for the general adolescent population. In such countries, where the economy is underdeveloped, people usually go immediately from childhood to adulthood without the benefit of an education designed for the middle years of adolescence.

Social integration

The American high school may be viewed as an institutional response to the pronounced social, economic, and educational changes in a nation that was becoming a modernized world power. When the high school became the dominant institution of American secondary education, it was possible for a student to attend an articulated sequence of publicly supported and controlled institutions that began with the kindergarten, extended to the elementary school, continued through high school, and reached the college and university. It was the high school that linked elementary and higher institutions of education and completed the American educational ladder. The creation of the high school also did away with the possibility that a dual system of educational institutions, similar to the European model, might be established in the United States.

Response to needs of society

Link between elementary and higher education

The Committee of Ten The early years of the American high school witnessed some of the same confusion that had beset its institutional predecessor, the academy. Educators of the more traditional view defined the school as a college preparatory institution. Those who took a broader perspective saw the high school as a "people's school,'" which would offer a wide range of practical courses. In order to standardize the curricula of the high school, the National Education Association in 1892 established the Committee of

Efforts to standardize curricula

40 George S. Counts, *Secondary Education and Industrialism* (Cambridge, Mass.: Harvard University Press, 1929).

Ten. This committee was chaired by Charles Eliot, president of Harvard University and a major leader in higher education who had extended his interests to both elementary and secondary education. Eliot, a forceful chairman, guided the committee to two major recommendations: earlier entry of several subjects, and uniform treatment in the teaching of subjects for both college and terminal students.[41]

The committee recommended eight years of elementary and four years of secondary education. Four separate curricula were recommended as appropriate for the high school: classical, Latin-scientific, modern language, and English. Each curriculum included foreign languages, mathematics, sciences, English, and history—what we now call the basic academic courses. The first two options were more traditional in nature, and the latter two were considered more contemporary.

Subjects prescribed for the high school curriculum were Latin, Greek, English, German, French, and Spanish; algebra, geometry, and trigonometry; astronomy, meteorology, botany, zoology, physiology, geology, and physical geography; and physics and chemistry. History was to be studied by concentrating on well-defined historical periods.

Emphasis on college preparation

The Committee of Ten structured the high school curriculum along the lines of the traditional college preparatory program. But its recommendations served to liberalize the school program by identifying alternatives to the prevalent Latin and Greek classical curriculum. The committee was influenced by the popular educational psychology of the time, which stressed mental discipline. For example, the committee concluded that the same subjects would be equally useful to both terminal and college preparatory students, since these subjects trained the mind in observation, memory, reasoning, and expression.

Broadened view of high school

Still, the Committee of Ten had established a basically college preparatory orientation for the high school's program and curriculum; this view was soon challenged by a number of educators who believed that a truly comprehensive secondary institution had to provide a broader program and a larger number of educational alternatives. During the period from 1910 through 1930, several educators argued that the principle of social efficiency should be applied to high school education.[42] Social efficiency simply meant that each person should be prepared to contribute to his or her own personal well-being and the society's good. It represented a departure from the exclusively college preparatory point of view. Education was perceived as a rational and efficient mechanism that could cultivate an individual's capacities as a producer, as a citizen, and as a parent. While the social efficiency educators sought to broaden the context of the high school, they sometimes narrowly defined "useful" and "efficient" in challenging the humanistic aesthetic aspects of secondary education.

41 National Education Association, *Report of the Committee on Secondary School Studies* (Washington, D.C.: Government Printing Office, 1893).

42 Walter H. Drost, *David Snedden and Education for Social Efficiency* (Madison: University of Wisconsin Press, 1967).

In the early twentieth century, the number of high school students was rising. These students were no longer only the children of the professional and business classes. The population of the high school was coming from the adolescent population at large. The school, for some, was being viewed as the upward extension of the elementary school. This was clearly revealed by the enactment of compulsory school attendance laws in a majority of the states. By 1918 thirty states had laws that specified full-time attendance until age sixteen.[43]

Compulsory school attendance

The Commission on the Reorganization of Secondary Education The basic change in the high school from a college preparatory institution to a comprehensive institution was revealed clearly in the *Cardinal Principles of Secondary Education,* stated in 1918 by the National Education Association's Commission on the Reorganization of Secondary Education. In its statement of the need for reorganization the commission was clearly aware of the pervasive social changes that had occurred in the United States:

> Secondary education should be determined by the needs of the society to be served, the character of the individuals to be educated, and the knowledge of educational theory and practice available. These factors are by no means static. . . . The evidence is strong that such a comprehensive reorganization of secondary education is imperative at the present time.[44]

The commission noted that:

Shift to comprehensive orientation

1. The high school ought to be a truly comprehensive institution based on the various social groups that make up the population of the United States.
2. The high school curriculum could be differentiated to meet agricultural, business, commercial, industrial, and domestic as well as college preparatory needs without losing its integrative and comprehensive social character.
3. The results of educational theory, psychology of education, measurement, and evaluation should be applied to the programs and instruction of the high school.
4. American education comprises a set of articulated institutions that should function together rather than in isolation.

Secondary School Organization

Different programs for various students

As the high school assumed its institutional form, four basic curricular patterns could be identified: (1) the college preparatory or academic program, which included courses in English language and literature, foreign languages,

43 Krug, *The Shaping of the American High School, 1920–1941,* p. 7.

44 Commission on the Reorganization of Secondary Education, *Cardinal Principles of Secondary Education,* Bulletin No. 35 (Washington, D.C.: Government Printing Office, 1918), p. 1.

mathematics, natural and physical sciences, and history and social sciences; (2) the commercial or business program, which offered courses in bookkeeping, shorthand, and typing; (3) industrial, vocational, home economics, and agricultural programs; and (4) a modified academic program for terminal students who planned to complete their formal education upon high school graduation.

Despite some regional variations, the usual high school pattern followed a four-year attendance sequence that encompassed grades nine, ten, eleven, and twelve and was generally attended by the age group from fourteen to eighteen. There were exceptions, however, in that some reorganized six-year institutions could be found in which students attended a combined junior-senior high school after completing a six-year elementary school. The junior high school of three years, seventh, eighth, and ninth grades, combined with the senior school of tenth, eleventh, and twelfth grades, also began to appear in some large school districts in the 1920s.

The rise of junior high schools

The junior high school concept grew out of the Committee of Ten's suggestion that secondary education begin two years earlier to reduce the elementary school from eight years to six years.[45] In many instances, the junior high school was initially the first three years of a six-year school. As it developed in the 1920s and 1930s, the **junior high school** often became a separate facility housing grades seven, eight, and nine. Today, the junior high school has become part of the pattern of school organization for many districts; it represents 31 percent of all secondary schools, compared with 27 percent traditional high school (four years), 23 percent junior-senior school, and 19 percent senior school (three years).[46]

Emergence of middle schools

During the 1960s, the middle school appeared. The **middle school** generally includes students who are ordinarily enrolled in grades six, seven, and eight. The middle school concept was designed to meet the needs of preadolescents, usually ages eleven through thirteen, in an institution that is transitional between elementary and high school. It is intended to permit a gradual transition from childhood to adolescence by emphasizing special programs uniquely designed for preadolescents. Some educators classify the school as part of the elementary grade sequence.

The American high school today is a multipurpose institution: it provides a general education for all students; college preparation for those who wish to continue their formal schooling; and vocational and career preparation in agriculture, industry, and trade. It is comprehensive in the social sense, bringing together students of varying religions, social and economic classes, and ethnic and racial groups. Any institution that performs such varied social and educational services will necessarily be the scene of controversy and conflict. Despite disagreements about purposes, goals, and programs, the high

45 Nelson Bossing and Roscoe Cramer, *The Junior High School* (Boston: Houghton Mifflin, 1965).

46 *Digest of Educational Statistics, 1977–78* (Washington, D.C.: Government Printing Office, 1978), table 60, p. 60.

school as an institution is a crucial component in the American educational ladder; in the 1980s, it will continue to serve as the main institution for achieving the notion of "equalization of opportunity" for most children and youth in our country.

The American College and University

The British model

The colleges of the colonial period followed the British pattern of Oxford and Cambridge. In addition to preparing the scholar and theologian, the colleges in England sought to educate the well-rounded gentleman of the upper socioeconomic classes. The essential curriculum comprised grammar, rhetoric, logic, music, astronomy, geometry, and mathematics.

Religious roots of colonial colleges

The early colonial colleges were established under religious auspices. Believing that an educated ministry was needed to establish Christianity in the New World, the Massachusetts General Court created Harvard College in 1636. Yale was founded in 1701 as an alternative to Harvard, which some regarded as too liberal in theological matters. In 1693 Virginia's William and Mary College was granted a royal charter. Princeton, in New Jersey, was chartered in 1746 as a Presbyterian college, and King's College (later Columbia University) was chartered in 1754 to serve New York's Anglicans. Other colonial colleges were the University of Pennsylvania, Dartmouth in New Hampshire, Brown in Rhode Island, and Rutgers in New Jersey. Although there were curricular variations among these institutions, the general colonial college curriculum included: (1) Latin, Greek, Hebrew, rhetoric, and logic during the first year; (2) Greek, Hebrew, logic, and natural philosophy during the second year; (3) natural philosophy, metaphysics, and ethics during the third year; and (4) mathematics and a review in Greek, Latin, logic, and natural philosophy during the fourth year.[47]

Land-Grant Colleges

During the first half of the nineteenth century, the liberal federal land-grant policy encouraged the establishment of many of our state colleges and universities. In addition to state colleges, many religious denominations also founded their own private colleges as a wave of religious revivalism swept the country. These colleges offered liberal arts and frequently included seminaries for the training of ministers.

Agricultural and technical colleges

By the early 1850s critics of traditional liberal arts education were arguing that colleges for agricultural and mechanical science should be established with support from federal land grants.[48] Such institutions were deemed

47 Frederick Rudolph, *The American College and University: A History* (New York: Knopf, 1962).

48 Allan Nevins, *The State Universities and Democracy* (Urbana: University of Illinois Press, 1962).

essential to further agricultural and industrial progress. Justin Morrill, a United States congressman from Vermont, sponsored a bill to use federal land grants for the support of agricultural and industrial education. The Morrill Act of 1862 granted each state 30,000 acres of public land for each senator and representative in Congress, based on the apportionment of 1860.[49] The income from this grant was to be used to support at least one state college for agricultural and mechanical instruction.

Higher education for more individuals

The effect of the Morrill Act was to bring higher education within reach of the masses. The general impact of land-grant colleges was to further agricultural education, engineering, and other applied sciences, as well as the more traditional liberal arts and professional education. It is interesting to note that many of today's leading state universities originated as land-grant colleges. Among them are the University of Illinois, Iowa State University, Michigan State University, Pennsylvania State University, and the University of Wisconsin.

German University Model

American higher education was influenced in the late nineteenth century by the importation of the German research model of scholarship to the United States. Many American professors went to Germany in the late nineteenth century to complete their doctoral studies. While at the German universities, they were engaged in research seminars with learned professors who investigated limited topics in the sciences and the humanities. When they returned to the United States, they brought with them the German concepts of the seminar and the scholarly dissertation.

Growth of Higher Education

Rising student enrollments

After World War II, American higher education experienced its greatest growth. From 1950 to 1965, college enrollments doubled from 2.4 million to 4.9 million students. By 1975, the number had almost doubled again to 9 million. By 1980, 12 million students were enrolled in institutions of higher education.[50] Whereas in 1910 about 5 percent of all youth age 18–21 were attending college in a degree program, by 1960 the percentage was 36; by 1970 it was 52; by 1980, it was close to 60 percent.[51] Millions more were attending adult education classes offered by business, labor, the armed services, and social agencies. Educational television and adult continuing edu-

49 Benjamin F. Andrews, *The Land Grant of 1862 and the Land-Grant College* (Washington, D.C.: Government Printing Office, 1918).

50 *Digest of Educational Statistics, 1980,* table 94, p. 102; *Projections of Educational Statistics, 1986–87* (Washington, D.C.: Government Printing Office, 1978), table 2, p. 14; table 5, p. 20.

51 *Projections of Educational Statistics to 1983–84* (Washington, D.C.: Government Printing Office, 1974), figure 6, p. 7; table 2, pp. 17–18; *Projections of Educational Statistics to 1986–87*, table B-2, p. 158.

cation programs enrolled thousands of others. The concept of "equality of educational opportunity" had reached the institutions of higher learning.

In the 1970s, enrollment patterns in higher education began to change. Although the number of college students had grown slightly, the massive increases in student enrollments of the 1950s and 1960s had apparently leveled off. While it is difficult to estimate future enrollment patterns, three implications of this trend can be considered: the enrollment or population of college age students, the planning of colleges and universities, and the degree of socioeconomic change.

Leveling-off period

1. *Enrollments.* The number of students who attend college depends on the size of the population in the eighteen-to-twenty-one age group. Although this population remained constant until the early 1980s, it is anticipated that in the late 1980s and into the 1990s, the number of college age persons in the total U.S. population will decline dramatically, especially in the northern and eastern states. At the same time, in-state migration and slight population increases due to a higher birthrate may increase the college age population in the southern and western Sunbelt states. Colleges and universities in the regions that will experience the greatest population decline will need to take extraordinary measures to recruit and retain students. Although larger numbers of older adults are expected to enter college for the first time or return to study, the competition among colleges for students will become more intense as the smaller institutions struggle to survive. Rising costs and smaller enrollments will probably force smaller and weaker institutions to close.

2. *Planning.* During the 1950s and 1960s, colleges and universities expanded physical facilities, faculties, and supportive staff. The increasing costs of higher education placed tremendous financial burdens on lower- and middle-income students and their families. These costs may affect future student enrollments, especially at private colleges where tuition fees are higher than at public institutions.

Increasing financial burdens on students

3. *Socioeconomic change.* The future of higher education in the United States is correlated to basic socioeconomic trends. The attraction of higher education to many college age students depends on the national economy and the job outlook.

The Education of Minorities

A major historical tendency in American education has been to bring increasing numbers of children and youth into the educational mainstream. Unfortunately, some groups in the American population have not shared fully in the opportunities presented by public education until relatively recent times. Blacks, Native Americans, and Hispanic Americans, for example, have had to struggle to gain admittance to the institutions that make up the American educational ladder. For them, it has been a slow and painful struggle.

From Colonial Times to the Twentieth Century

Native Americans In the colonial era, efforts to educate the American Indians were undertaken by religious groups and societies. It should be pointed out, however, that such educational efforts by Europeans involved a certain degree of Europeanization or Westernization. In their indigenous tribal societies, the various Indian tribes immersed young people in the culture and traditions of their own society. Depending on the ways in which the tribe sustained itself, tribal education involved a degree of vocational training as young men learned to hunt, fish, or trap. Young women learned their duties from their mothers. Through the inculcation of the tribal religious rituals and folkways, young people were brought into participation in tribal life. Essentially, tribal modes of education were conservative. They were designed to perpetuate and transmit the cultural heritage of the particular tribe. When education assumes such a traditional stance, the chief educational agents of the tribe are elders and priests.

Indigenous education

In the Mississippi Valley, French missionaries, especially Jesuits, accompanied the explorers, fur traders, and soldiers attempting to create "New France" in the North American continent. The missionaries sought to convert the Indians living in the region to Catholicism. They also brought with them the French language and culture. In conjunction with their missionary efforts, the French attempted some rudimentary educational activities.

Missionary educational efforts

In the Southwest, which was controlled by Spain, Franciscan missionary priests and monks attempted to alleviate the exploitation of the Indians by the Spanish landlords, who sometimes sought to impose servitude on the Indians living on land granted to them by the king. The Franciscans established missions to protect the Indians who lived on them. Some of the Indian children learned religion, reading, and writing in mission schools.

In the English colonies, some schools were established by Anglican, or Church of England, missionaries under the auspices of the Society for the Propagation of the Gospel in Foreign Parts. English missionary and educational activities among the Indians were sporadic, however, and never took place on a large scale. Noteworthy educational efforts were also made by Moravians, a German religious group who were followers of the Bohemian bishop and educational reformer John Amos Comenius, the author of the *Great Didactic* and the *Orbis Pictus.* Comenius and the Moravians, who regarded education as an instrument for bringing peace to the world, went out to teach the Indian tribes. The Moravians translated the Bible and religious tracts into the Indian languages spoken in Pennsylvania, North Carolina, and Ohio.

After the United States gained its independence, the Indian tribes were pushed westward. Eventually, the majority of Indians were resettled on reservations, usually against their will, in areas of the Great Plains and the Southwest. In the late nineteenth century, the federal government, assisted by well-intentioned reformers, pursued a policy designed to assimilate Indians into the larger white society. This policy attempted to erode tribal traditions by inculcating individualistic values into what was traditionally a cooperative society.

Assimilationist education

An important agency for assimilationist education was the boarding school. In these schools, Indian children were separated from their parents and taught industrial skills. The language of instruction was English. Efforts were made to eradicate tribal loyalties and customs in these schools.

Hispanic Americans As a result of expansionist efforts in the Southwest, Texas was annexed to the United States in 1844. Three years later Mexico was defeated by the United States. As a result California, Utah, New Mexico, and other western territories were added to the national territory. These regions contained a large Mexican population that for some time lived as a conquered people.

For much of the nineteenth century, Mexican-American children attended Roman Catholic parochial schools when they were available. As public schools were established in the western states, Spanish-speaking children in many of the school districts received instruction only in English. It was not until the mid-twentieth century that concerted efforts were made to establish bilingual and bicultural educational programs to meet the needs of Spanish-speaking youngsters.

Black Americans The Civil War, Reconstruction, and the Thirteenth Amendment ended slavery in the United States. Although free blacks had attended school in some northern states long before the Civil War, southern states had prohibited the teaching of black children, whether slave or free. Emancipation brought with it the challenge of providing educational opportunities for the freedmen and women and their children, particularly in the former Confederate states.

Freedmen's Bureau

In 1865, Congress created the Freedmen's Bureau to help former slaves adjust to freedom. The Bureau continued to function until 1872. Under the leadership of General O. O. Howard, the Freedmen's Bureau established schools throughout the South. At their peak in 1869, these schools enrolled some 114,000 students. The schools followed a "New England" common school curriculum of reading, writing, grammar, geography, arithmetic, and music, especially singing. As their northern counterparts did, the Freedmen's Bureau schools relied on the standard textbooks—including Webster's spell-

The Tuskegee Normal School was established in 1881 by Booker T. Washington. This history class met at Tuskegee in 1902. (Library of Congress)

ers and the McGuffey readers. The schools were usually staffed by northern school teachers, who brought with them their values, their educational ideas, and their methods. A small number of black teachers were trained in these schools.

Washington: From Slavery to Freedom Booker T. Washington (1856–1915) was the leading educational spokesman for black Americans in the half century after the Civil War. As he recounts in his autobiography, *Up From Slavery,* Washington was a transitional figure who was born a slave, experienced the hectic decades of Reconstruction, and painfully articulated the outlines of a compromise with the white power establishment.[52] Today, Washington is a controversial figure. Some say he made the best of a bad situation. Although he compromised on racial issues, they say, he can be viewed as one who preserved and slowly advanced the educational opportunities of black Americans. Critics see Washington as an opportunist whose compromises restricted the progress of black Americans. In any event, Booker T. Washington should be judged in terms of the realities in which he lived.

Advanced opportunities of blacks

As a student at Hampton Institute, Washington had studied the educational ideas of General S. Armstrong, who had established the Institute to prepare black youth for teaching, agriculture, and industry. Armstrong argued that industrial education was an important force in building character and

52 Booker T. Washington, *Up From Slavery* (New York: Doubleday, 1938).

"Uplift" through work

economic competence for blacks. Washington subscribed generally to Armstrong's philosophy of moral and economic "uplift" through work.

In 1881, Washington was named to head the institute that the Alabama legislature had established in Tuskegee. Washington shaped the Tuskegee curriculum according to his perceptions of the living and working conditions of southern blacks. Basically, he felt that southern blacks faced the problem of being a landless agricultural class. The remedy, he believed, consisted of creating an economic base—primarily in farming but also in occupational trades—that would provide southern blacks with some degree of economic security. His curriculum stressed basic academic, agricultural, and occupational skills. The essential values emphasized were those of hard work and the dignity of labor. Although he encouraged his students to become elementary school teachers, farmers, and artisans, he discouraged them from careers in medicine, law, and politics. The pursuit of these fields, he believed, was premature and would result in strife with the dominant white power structure in the South.

Academic, agricultural, and vocational skills

Washington, a popular platform speaker, developed a theory of racial relations that argued that blacks and whites were mutually dependent economically but could remain separate socially. In 1885, Washington summed up his philosophy in an address at the Cotton Exposition in Atlanta, Georgia, when he said, "In all things that are purely social, we can be as separate as the fingers, yet one as the hand in all things essential to mutual progress."[53]

Du Bois: Challenger to the System W.E.B. Du Bois (1869–1963) was a sociological and educational pioneer who challenged the established system of education that tended to restrict rather than to advance the progress of black Americans.[54] Du Bois challenged what was often called the "Tuskegee machine" of Booker T. Washington. A sociologist and historian, Du Bois called for a more determined and activist leadership than Washington provided.

Unlike Washington, whose roots were in southern black agriculture, Du Bois's career spanned both sides of the Mason-Dixon Line. He was a native of Massachusetts, received his undergraduate education from Fisk University in Nashville, did his graduate study at Harvard University, and directed the Atlanta University Studies of Black American life in the South. Du Bois approached the problem of racial relations in the United States from two dimensions: as a scholarly researcher and as an activist for civil rights. Among his works was the famous empirical sociological study, *The Philadelphia Negro: A Social Study,* in which he examined that city's black population and made recommendations for the school system.[55] Du Bois's Philadelphia study was the pioneer work on urban blacks in America.

Scholar and activist

53 Booker T. Washington, *Selected Speeches of Booker T. Washington* (New York: Doubleday, 1932), p. 34.

54 Virginia Hamilton, *W.E.B. Du Bois: A Biography* (New York: Crowell, 1972).

55 W.E.B. Du Bois, *The Philadelphia Negro: A Social Study* (Philadelphia: University of Pennsylvania Press, 1899).

Du Bois had a long and active career as a leader in the civil rights movement. He helped to organize the Niagara Movement in 1905, which led to the National Association for the Advancement of Colored People (NAACP), established in 1909. From 1910 until 1934, Du Bois edited *The Crisis,* the major journal of the NAACP. In terms of its educational policy, the NAACP position was that *all* American children and youth should have genuine equality of educational opportunity. This policy, which Du Bois helped to formulate, stressed the following themes: (1) public schooling should be free and compulsory for all American children; (2) secondary schooling should be provided for all youth; (3) higher education should not be monopolized by any special class or race.[56]

Helped organize the NAACP

Du Bois and the NAACP were persistent adversaries of racial segregation in the schools. Their continuous efforts led to the series of court cases that culminated in the momentous 1954 decision by the U.S. Supreme Court in *Brown et al. v. Board of Education of Topeka,* which outlawed racial segregation in the U.S. public schools.

As a leader in education, Du Bois challenged not only the tradition of racial segregation in the schools but also the accommodationist ideology of Booker T. Washington. The major difference between the two men was that Washington sought change that was evolutionary in nature and did not upset the social order, whereas Du Bois demanded immediate change no matter what the consequences. Both, however, believed in an educated leadership for blacks, developing a concept referred to as the "Talented Tenth," according to which 10 percent of the black population would receive a traditional college education in preparation for leadership. The difference between Washington and Du Bois was one of leadership style and power rather than of strong ideological disagreement. Both believed strongly in the dignity of work, but Du Bois was especially adamant that a person's vocational calling should be dictated by ability and choice, not by race.

Desegregation and equality

Du Bois, an advocate of equality of educational opportunity, believed that no one who possessed the necessary intellectual ability should be denied the opportunity for higher education. He was not afraid to challenge the traditional view of both blacks and whites on social and educational issues. He did not hesitate to take the unpopular position. In many respects, the career of W.E.B. Du Bois set the stage for the changes in American race relations that have taken place since the mid-1950s.

Challenged the system

Since 1950

Since the 1950s, American society has experienced concerted social, legal, political, and educational efforts to expand the opportunities of minority groups such as blacks, Native Americans and Hispanic Americans. The effort

56 W.E.B. Du Bois, *Dusk of Dawn: An Essay Toward an Autobiography of a Race Concept* (New York: Harcourt, Brace & World, 1940).

to end racial discrimination gained impetus after World War II when the Commission on Civil Rights, appointed by President Harry S Truman, recommended in its 1947 report, *To Secure These Rights,* that legislation be enacted to prohibit segregation in schooling on the basis of race, religion, or national origin.

The NAACP, through a series of court cases, sought to overturn the "separate but equal" doctrine that permitted de jure segregation of schools, based on race, in seventeen border and southern states. In 1954, the United States Supreme Court held that racially segregated schools generated "a feeling of inferiority" and that "separate educational facilities are inherently unequal."

After the mid-1950s, the movement for civil and educational equality accelerated. Martin Luther King, Jr., emerged as the leader of a national nonviolent civil rights movement, which worked to increase educational opportunities for blacks and members of other minority groups. At the same time that civil rights advocates were mobilizing throughout the nation, recalcitrant segregationists sought to evade compliance with the *Brown* decision. In 1957, President Eisenhower ordered federal troops to Little Rock, Arkansas, to enforce the Supreme Court's antisegregation decision.

The enactment of the Civil Rights Act of 1964 further involved the federal government in efforts to end practices of racial discrimination. The act authorized federally initiated law suits to compel compliance with desegregation in schools. It also authorized the withholding of federal funds from school districts that continued to discriminate. In the early 1970s, efforts were made to end de facto segregation policies, which were based on residence patterns. Some school districts embarked on busing programs, transporting students from one attendance area to another to achieve racial balance and integration.

Along with the movement to improve educational opportunities for blacks, the 1960s saw greater attention devoted to the education of Native Americans. Whereas the assimilationist educational policies of the past had neglected the native tribal heritages, education in the 1960s and 1970s gave greater attention to tribal integrity and traditions. At the same time, Native Americans showed a marked increase in attendance and completion of secondary schooling.

In the 1960s and 1970s, Hispanic Americans organized to achieve greater social, economic, and educational opportunities. While the southwestern states had traditionally had a large Hispanic population, the large cities of many northern states experienced a marked inflow of Spanish-speaking residents from Puerto Rico, Cuba, and Central America. The development of bilingual and bicultural educational programs was a response to the educational needs of Hispanic Americans.

While Chapter 5 has provided the historical perspective on some of the major issues relating to the education of minority groups, Chapter 12 will deal with the topics of integration and bilingual and multicultural education in greater detail.

Overview 5.1

Significant Events in the History of American Education

Major Political Events		Significant Educational Events	
1620	Arrival of Pilgrims in America	1635	Boston Latin grammar school established
1630	Settlement of Massachusetts Bay Colony	1636	Harvard College founded, first English-speaking college in Western Hemisphere
		1642	First education law enacted in Massachusetts
		1647	Old Deluder Satan Act enacted in Massachusetts, requiring establishment of schools
		1751	Benjamin Franklin's Academy established in Philadelphia
1775–1783	American Revolution	1783	Noah Webster's *American Spelling Book* published
1788	U.S. Constitution ratified	1785	Northwest Ordinance, first national education law, enacted
		1821	First public high school in the United States opened in Boston
			Emma Willard's Female Seminary, first school of higher education for women, established in Troy, New York
		1823	First private normal school in the United States opened in Concord, Vermont
		1825	Webster's *The American Dictionary* completed
		1827	Massachusetts law requiring public high schools passed
		1837	Horace Mann appointed secretary of Massachusetts state board of education
		1839	First public normal school opened in Lexington, Massachusetts
		1855	First German-language kindergarten in the United States established
		1860	First English-language kindergarten in the United States established
1861–1865	Civil War	1862	Morrill Land Grant College Act passed, establishing in each state a college for agricultural and mechanical instruction
		1865	Freedmen's Bureau established
		1872	*Kalamazoo* decision upheld public taxation for high schools
		1881	Tuskegee Normal School established by Booker T. Washington

Overview 5.1 (cont.)

Significant Events in the History of American Education

Major Political Events		Significant Educational Events	
		1892	Committee of Ten established by NEA
		1896	*Plessy* v. *Ferguson* decision used to uphold constitutionality of "separate but equal" schools for white and black students
		1909	First junior high school established in Berkeley, California
		1910	First junior college established in Fresno, California
1914–1918	World War I	1917	Smith-Hughes Act passed, providing money grants for vocational education, home economics, and agricultural subjects.
		1918	*Cardinal Principles of Secondary Education* published
		1919	Progressive Education Association organized
1929	Start of the Great Depression	1930s	New Deal programs during the Great Depression provided federal funds for education of unemployed and school construction
1939–1945	World War II	1944	G.I. Bill passed, providing federal funds for continued education of veterans
		1954	*Brown* v. *Board of Education of Topeka* decision required eventual racial integration of public schools
		1957	Soviet Union launched Sputnik, leading to criticism and re-evaluation of American public education
		1958	National Defense Education Act passed, providing federal funds to improve science, math, and modern foreign language instruction, and guidance services
		1965	Elementary and Secondary Education Act passed, providing federal funds to public schools, especially for compensatory education
		1972	Title IX Education Amendment passed, outlawing sex discrimination in schools receiving federal financial assistance
		1975	Education for All Handicapped Children (Public Law 94-142) passed
		1980	Department of Education established in federal government with cabinet status

Summing Up

1. The origins of schooling in America began in the colonial era and were based on elitist and religiously oriented European antecedents. When the English colonists settled in North America, they brought with them the conventional European structures of educational institutions based on a rigid social-class pattern. Primary or vernacular schools for the lower socioeconomic layers of society offered a basic curriculum of reading, writing, arithmetic, and religion. Preparatory schools, such as the Latin grammar school, and the colonial colleges were reserved for the upper classes. Offering a classical curriculum, Latin grammar schools and colleges were elitist and prepared the sons of favored families for leadership roles in church, state, and society. Although girls might attend the elementary vernacular schools, their formal educational opportunities were limited to the basic skills offered by the primary schools.
2. After the United States won its independence, the forces of democracy, social mobility, and frontier egalitarianism worked to erode the elitism of the educational structures that were imported from Europe. The American common school arose as the educational institution designed to supply basic civic and skill competencies. The common or public school movement led to the establishment of elementary schools that were open to all white children, both boys and girls.
3. The emergence of the public high school in the nineteenth century contributed to the growing inclusiveness of public schooling in the United States. The rise of state colleges and universities and the enactment of the Morrill Act in 1982 created the final step of an educational ladder that replaced the vestiges of the exclusive European dual-track system.
4. At the beginning of the twentieth century the American public school system embraced elementary, secondary, and higher institutions. By the mid-twentieth century concerted efforts were being made to bring equality of educational opportunity to the children of minority groups, especially blacks, Native Americans, and Hispanic Americans. The major educational problem of the present and the future lies in devising ways for these educational institutions to serve all Americans equally well, regardless of race, sex, or socioeconomic class.

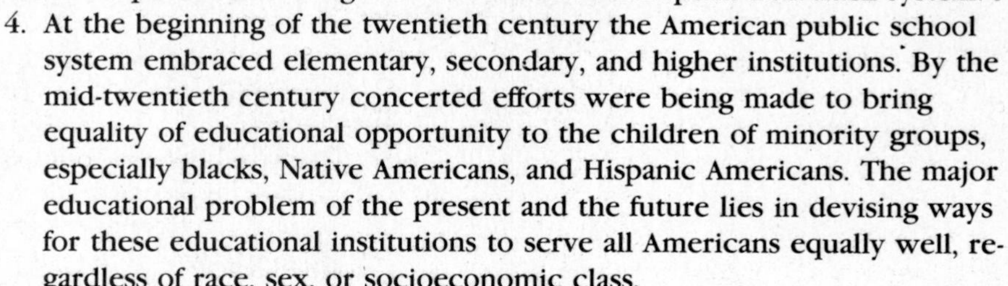

Discussion Questions

1. How has American education become more inclusive over time?
2. What has been the influence of the Puritan ethic on American culture and education?
3. Is Jefferson's concept of political education adequate for the needs of contemporary American society?
4. In terms of the history of American secondary education, why is the purpose of the high school so frequently a subject of controversy?
5. In terms of the history of American education, what seems to be the American public school philosophy?

Suggested Readings

Button, H. Warren, and Eugene Provenzo. *History of Education & Culture in America.* Englewood Cliffs, N.J.: Prentice-Hall, 1983.

This book provides an excellent overall perspective on the history of education in relation to American culture.

Johannigmeier, Erwin. *Americans and Their Schools.* Chicago: Rand McNally, 1980.

This text is a well-written and judicious treatment of the historical development of American education.

Nasaw, David. *Schooled to Order: A Social History of Public Schooling in the United States.* New York: Oxford University Press, 1979.

Nasaw's book provides a good interpretation of the development of public schools in the United States.

Perkinson, Henry. *Two Hundred Years of American Political Thought.* New York: McKay, 1976.

Perkinson describes the contributions of leading figures in American education.

Pulliam, John D. *History of Education in America.* Columbus, Ohio: Merrill, 1976.

This book is a clearly written treatment of major events in the history of American education.

Warren, Donald R., ed. *History, Education, and Public Policy.* Berkeley, Calif.: McCutchan, 1978.

Warren's book is an articulate examination of the role that the history of education has on the development and implementation of educational policy.

6

Philosophical Ideas in Education

Focusing Questions

How do general philosophy and philosophy of education relate to one another?

How do philosophers' conceptions of human nature influence their views of education?

How do philosophers of education treat the ethical or value dimension of education?

How does educational philosophy affect everyday school practice?

Is there a dominant American philosophy of education at this time?

TODAY AMERICAN EDUCATORS FACE COMPELLING AND PROfound questions about the condition of American education and the future of our nation's schools. Many of the questions have a philosophical dimension. For example, the following questions of quality, equity, and standards are essentially philosophical:

1. What is the meaning of a quality education? Should all students—in a democratic society—have an education that is of the same quality? When schools offer different curricula to different populations, are they diluting or enhancing the quality of the individual's educational experience?
2. What is the meaning of equity in education? Does it mean an equal education or does it mean equal access to education? Is it possible to have both quality and equity?
3. What standards should be met by American schools and their students? How do these standards relate to personal, social, and national goals for education?

The issues of quality, equity, and standards are related to the basic questions discussed in historical context in Chapter 3. What is knowledge? What is education? What is schooling? Who should attend school? How should teaching be carried on? As a future teacher, you will be called upon to answer such questions. This chapter explores them at the most basic, general level. If an answer to a question is stated in its most abstract and general terms, it will transfer to a wide variety of human situations.

When you teach, you will be caught up in many immediate concerns—the day-to-day problems of preparing lessons and classroom management. These immediate concerns will be specific to a given day, time, or event, but how you choose to deal with them will reveal your educational philosophy. Of necessity, as you examine yourself as a teacher you will be thinking about the purposes of education. You will be faced with the challenge of establishing your own meaning and significance in teaching. In essence, each of you will be creating your own philosophy of education. An examination of the systems of philosophy of education that have already been elaborated can help in your personal search for your own philosophy of education.

In this chapter we shall be examining five educational philosophies and four educational theories. Although there are similarities between philosophies and theories of education, some distinctions can be made. Traditional philosophies, such as idealism and realism, refer to complete bodies of thought that present a world view of which education is a part. (Other, newer philosophies such as philosophical analysis are primarily methodological. They seek to establish meaning for human experience.) Theories of education such as progressivism and social reconstructionism are often derived from parent philosophies, but they concern themselves primarily with education and learning and do not necessarily present a fully developed world view.

The educational philosophies we shall examine have helped to shape American education. Idealism and realism have long guided educational the-

ory and practice in Western culture. From Chapter 3, for example, you will recall that Plato espoused an idealist philosophy; Aristotle was a realist. Closely related to these important traditional philosophies are the educational theories of perennialism and essentialism. In contrast to these more traditional philosophies, pragmatism emphasizes the *process* of education. John Dewey, whose work as a pioneer in education was discussed in Chapter 4, stressed the processes of experience and problem solving in his work at the University of Chicago Laboratory School. The educational theories of progressivism and social reconstructionism are closely related to pragmatism and were derived from it. Existentialism and philosophical analysis are newer contributions to the philosophy of education.

We need to explore these often conflicting approaches to education so that the goals, purposes, curricula, and methodologies of teaching and learning can be viewed in philosophical perspective. Before we do so, however, certain terms and areas of philosophy need to be defined.

Special Terminology

Practitioners in every field of disciplined inquiry develop a special terminology. In the philosophy of education the basic terms used are *metaphysics, epistemology, axiology,* and *logic.* Most succinctly, these terms have the following meanings: Metaphysics deals with the nature of reality. Epistemology deals with the nature of knowledge. Axiology deals with the nature of values. Logic deals with the nature of reasoning.

Reality and existence

Metaphysics examines the nature of ultimate reality. In speculating about the nature of reality and existence, metaphysicians have not developed a single agreed-upon conclusion. Idealists see reality in nonmaterial, or spiritual, terms. Realists see it as an objective order that exists independently of humankind. For pragmatists reality is a result of human experiences with the social and physical environment. In educational philosophy, metaphysics relates to the particular conception of reality reflected in the subjects, experiences, and skills of the curriculum. Much school learning represents the efforts of curriculum makers, teachers, and textbook writers to describe reality to students. Such subject areas as the social and natural sciences attempt to describe certain dimensions of reality to the learner.

Knowledge and knowing

Epistemology, which deals with knowledge and knowing, is closely related to methods of teaching and learning. Again, different philosophies hold different epistemological conceptions. Idealists see knowing, or cognition, as the recall of ideas that are latent in the mind. For them the Socratic dialogue is the most appropriate teaching method. In the **Socratic method** the teacher stimulates the student's consciousness by asking leading questions, which bring forth the ideas hidden in the learner's mind. For realists knowledge begins with our sensations of objects. Through abstracting these sensory materials, we form concepts that correspond to the objects in reality. A teacher who uses the realist formula of sensation and abstraction would develop classroom activities that utilize sensory stimuli. Pragmatists contend that we create knowledge by interacting with our environment; hence problem solving is the appropriate method of teaching and learning.

What is of value?

Axiology seeks to specify what is of value. Axiology is divided into *ethics* and *aesthetics.* **Ethics** examines moral values and the rules of right conduct; **aesthetics** deals with values in beauty and art. Teachers, concerned with forming values in students, encourage certain preferred behaviors. Parents, teachers, and society reward or punish behavior as it conforms to or deviates from their conceptions of what is right, good, and beautiful. Idealists and realists subscribe to the objective theory of value, which asserts that the good, true, and beautiful are universally valid in all places and at all times. Pragmatists hold that values are culturally or ethically relative and depend on group or personal preferences that vary with the situation, time, and place.

Deductive and inductive thinking

Logic, which is concerned with the requirements of correct and valid thinking, examines the rules of inference that enable us to frame correctly our propositions and arguments. Deductive logic, associated with idealism and realism, moves from general statements to particular instances and applications. Inductive logic, associated with pragmatism, moves from the particular instance to tentative generalizations that are subject to further verification.

In this chapter we discuss nine different philosophical orientations. After describing each, we answer the basic questions raised at the beginning of the chapter from the perspective of its adherents.

Idealism

From Hegel to Butler

Idealism is among the oldest of the traditional philosophies. Plato developed the classic formulation of idealist philosophical principles. The German philosopher Hegel created a comprehensive philosophical and historical world view based on idealism. In the United States, the transcendentalist philosophers Ralph Waldo Emerson and Henry David Thoreau elaborated on the idealist conception of reality. The founder of the kindergarten, Friedrich Froebel, was an exponent of idealist pedagogy. William Harris, a historically significant American educational leader, used idealism as a rationale for his administration as a U.S. commissioner of education at the end of the nineteenth century. The leading contemporary proponent of idealist education is J. Donald Butler.[1]

Key Concepts

Metaphysics To the idealists, only the mental or the spiritual is ultimately real. For them the universe is an expression of a highly generalized intelli-

1 J. Donald Butler, *Idealism in Education* (New York: Harper & Row, 1966); John P. Strain, "Idealism: A Clarification of an Educational Philosophy," *Educational Theory* (Summer 1975), pp. 263–271.

Overview 6.1

Philosophies of Education

Philosophy	Metaphysics	Epistemology	Axiology	Proponents
Idealism	Reality is spiritual or mental and unchanging	Knowing is the rethinking of latent ideas	Values are absolute and eternal	Berkeley Butler Froebel Hegel Plato
Realism	Reality is objective and is composed of matter and form; it is fixed, based on natural law	Knowing consists of sensation and abstraction	Values are absolute and eternal, based on nature's laws	Aquinas Aristotle Broudy Martin Pestalozzi
Pragmatism (experimentalism)	Reality is the interaction of an individual with environment or experience; it is always changing	Knowing results from experiencing use of scientific method	Values are situational or relative	Childs Dewey James Peirce
Existentialism	Reality is subjective, with existence proceding essence	Knowing for personal choice	Values should be freely chosen	Sartre Marcel Morris Soderquist
Philosophical analysis	Reality is verifiable	Knowing involves empirical verification or logical analysis of language	Values are regarded as emotional feelings	Soltis Russell Moore

gence and will—a universal mind. The individual's spiritual essence, or soul, is durable and permanent. One's mind, or life force, gives one vitality and dynamism. This world of mind and ideas is eternal, permanent, regular, and orderly. Representing a perfect order, the eternal ideas are unalterable. Truth and values are absolute and universal.

Idealists, such as the transcendentalists, have used the concepts of the macrocosm and the microcosm to explain their version of reality. **Macrocosm** refers to the universal mind, the first cause, creator, or God. Regardless of the particular name used, the macrocosmic mind is the whole of existence. It is the one, all-inclusive, and complete self of which the lesser selves are parts. The universal, macrocosmic mind is continually thinking and valuing. The **microcosm** is a limited part of the whole—an individual and lesser self. But the microcosm is of the same spiritual substance as the macrocosm.

Overview 6.2

Theories of Education

Theory	Goal	Curriculum	Proponents
Perennialism (rooted in realism)	To educate the rational person	Subject matter that is hierarchically arranged to cultivate the intellect (Great Books, etc.)	Adler Hutchins Maritain
Essentialism (rooted in idealism and realism)	To educate the useful and competent person	Basic education: reading, writing, arithmetic, history, English, science, foreign languages	Bagley Bestor Conant Morrison
Progressivism (rooted in pragmatism)	To educate the individual according to his or her interests and needs	Activities and projects	Dewey Johnson Kilpatrick Parker Washburne
Reconstructionism (rooted in pragmatism)	To reconstruct society	Social sciences used as reconstructive tools	Brameld Counts Stanley

In educational terms the student can be conceived of as a spiritual entity that is also a part of the larger spiritual universe. Although there are metaphysical differences among idealists, all agree that the universe is made up of spiritual realities that are personal and that the individual or microcosmic selves are part of the one comprehensive and universal whole.

Epistemology Idealist knowledge is based on the recognition or reminiscence of latent ideas that are already present in the mind. Such ideas are **a priori;** that is, they concern knowledge or concepts that exist prior to and independent of human experience about them. Through introspection the individual examines his or her own mind and finds a copy of the macrocosmic mind. What is to be known is already present in the mind. The teacher's task is to bring this latent knowledge to consciousness. Through learning, the student comes into a gradually larger apprehension of mental awareness. As a primarily intellectual process, learning involves recalling and working with ideas. Since reality is mental, education is properly concerned with conceptual matters. The learner seeks a broad and general perspective of his or her universe.[2]

Latent knowledge

The idealist educator prefers the order and pattern of a subject-matter curriculum that relates ideas and concepts to each other. The synthesis of

2 Morris L. Bigge, *Educational Philosophies for Teachers* (Columbus, Ohio: Merrill, 1982), pp. 25–36.

conceptual systems such as those of language, mathematics, and aesthetics represents the varying dimensions of the absolute. For example, the liberal arts embrace many conceptual systems, or learned disciplines, such as language, history, mathematics, science, and philosophy. The highest level of knowledge recognizes the relationships between and integrates these subject matters.

The hierarchy of subjects

The idealist curriculum, constituting the cultural heritage of humankind, is hierarchical. At the top are the most general disciplines, philosophy and theology. These more general subjects are abstract; they transcend the limitations of time, place, and circumstance, and they transfer to a wide range of situations. Mathematics is especially valuable because it cultivates the power to deal with abstractions. History and literature also rank high since they are sources of moral and cultural models, exemplars, and heroes. Somewhat lower in curricular priority are the natural and physical sciences, which deal with particular cause-and-effect relationships. Since it is necessary for communication, language is an essential tool at all levels of learning.

Absolute, eternal, and universal values

Axiology To the idealist, values reflect the good inherent in the universe. They are absolute, eternal, and universal. Ethical conduct grows out of the permanent aspects of our cultural heritage. Since the ethical core is contained within and transmitted by this heritage, philosophy, theology, history, literature, and art are rich value sources. Value education requires that the student be exposed to worthy models, especially the classics—the great works of the human race that have endured over time.

The Basic Questions

If you were to ask an idealist teacher, "What is knowledge?" he or she would reply that knowledge concerns the spiritual principles that are the base of reality. This knowledge of reality takes the form of ideas. If knowledge is about transcendent and universal ideas, then education is the intellectual process of bringing ideas to the learner's consciousness.

Intellectual pursuit of truth

In answering the question, "What is schooling?" the idealist educator would say that the school is a social agency where students seek to discover and pursue truth. It is an intellectual institution where teachers and students deal with the basic ideas that provide answers to the questions Socrates and Plato first asked: What is truth? What is beauty? What is the good life? These answers, though hidden, are present in our minds, and we need to reflect deeply to bring them forth. Nothing should be allowed to distract us from the intellectual pursuit of truth.

Who should attend school? To this question the idealist would say everyone. Not all students will demonstrate the same intellectual aptitude, but all of them need to cultivate their minds to the limits of their capacities. The brightest students will need the greatest intellectual challenges that the teacher can provide. The goal of learning is the creative person.

Socratic dialogue

How should teaching be carried on? The idealist would say that thinking and learning are names for the process of bringing ideas to consciousness. The Socratic dialogue, a process by which the teacher stimulates the learner's awareness of ideas, is appropriate to idealist teaching and learning. The use of this method requires skillful questioning on the part of the teacher. Another important aspect of idealist methodology is the role of imitation. The teacher should have wide knowledge of the cultural heritage, lead a well-ordered life, and serve as a model worthy of imitation by the students.

In examining the issues of quality and equity, idealists would assert that the quality of education is safeguarded by maintaining high intellectual standards for all students. While students reach the truth at their own pace, truth itself is universal. Teachers should insist on high academic standards. In Plato's *Republic,* for example, the intellectual and academic standards were so high that only a gifted minority entered the ruling elite of philosopher-kings.

While many teaching-learning situations can be examined in terms of idealism, the study of literature provides an appropriate illustration. Consider the situation in which a high school teacher is leading a discussion based on the reading of Henry David Thoreau's *Walden.* Through skillful Socratic questioning, the teacher can stimulate her students to put themselves into Thoreau's frame of mind as he pondered the meaning and the purpose of human life. From such questioning, the students can probe their own conceptions of freedom, choice, duty, and responsibility.

Realism

Realism, like idealism, stresses objective knowledge and values, but the realist view of metaphysics and epistemology is different. A basic definition describes the essential doctrines of realism as follows: (1) there is a world of real existence that human beings have not made or constructed, (2) this real existence can be known by the human mind, and (3) such knowledge is the only reliable guide to human conduct, individual and social.[3] This definition provides a convenient starting point for considering the educational implications of realist metaphysics, epistemology, and axiology.

Key Concepts

Metaphysics and Epistemology For the realist a material world exists that is independent of and external to the mind of the knower. The basis for understanding reality is found in a world of objects and in the perceptions of these objects. All objects are composed of matter. Matter must be encased in a form and has to assume the structure of a particular object.

Human beings can *know* these objects through their senses and their reason. Knowing is a process that involves two stages: sensation and abstraction. First, the knower sees an object and records the sensory data about it such as color, size, weight, smell, or sound. These sensory data are sorted out in the mind into those qualities that are always present in the object and

Knowing involves sensation and abstraction

3 P. H. Hirst and R. S. Peters, *Education and the Development of Reason* (Boston: Routledge & Kegan Paul, 1975); John Wild, *Introduction to Realist Philosophy* (New York: Harper & Row, 1948).

those qualities that are sometimes present in the object. Upon the abstraction of the necessary qualities of an object (those that are always present), the learner comes to a concept of the object. Conceptualization results when the mind has abstracted the form of an object and has recognized the object as belonging to a class. Objects are classified when they are recognized as having qualities that they share with other members of the same class but not with objects that belong to a different class.[4]

The realist theory of knowledge has also been referred to as a "spectator theory." This simply means that people are spectators or onlookers in the world. In their experience people see many objects. Some of them are two-legged creatures like themselves, others are four-legged or other forms of the animal kingdom, and still other objects are plants or minerals. As spectators of reality, men and women engage in a process of sorting out these objects according to their form or structure. They sort objects that are alike into related classifications. Their conception of an object is accurate when it corresponds to the structure of an object in reality.[5]

Sorting and classifying objects

Like the idealist, the realist believes that a curriculum consisting of organized, separate subject matters is the most effective and efficient way of learning about the reality of the objective order. Organizing subject matter, as scientists and scholars do, is simply a sophisticated method of classifying objects. For example, the past experiences of humankind can be organized into history. Plants can be studied in a systematic way according to their classifications in the subject matter of botany. The study of animals can be organized into the subject of zoology. Units of political organization such as nations, governments, legislatures, and judicial systems can be organized into the study of political science. For the realist the way to gain knowledge of reality is to pursue ordered and disciplined inquiry through these compartmentalized bodies of knowledge or subject matters.

Axiology Based on the realist's conception of knowledge, certain identified prescriptions govern intelligent behavior. For example, human beings ought to behave in a rational way; behavior is rational when it conforms to the way in which objects behave in reality. From their study of the subjects that explain reality, men and women can arrive at theories that are based on natural, physical, and social laws. The rational person governs his or her behavior in the light of such tested theory.

Rational behavior

The Basic Questions

To begin our philosophical cross-examination, we again ask, What is knowledge? Realists would reply that knowledge concerns the physical world in which we live. According to the realists' metaphysics, an objective order of reality exists. When we know something, our knowledge is always about an

4 Harry S. Broudy, *Building a Philosophy of Education* (Englewood Cliffs, N.J.: Prentice-Hall, 1961).

5 Edward J. Power, *Philosophy of Education: Studies in Philosophies, Schooling, and Educational Policies* (Englewood Cliffs, N.J.: Prentice-Hall, 1982), pp. 89–106.

object. The concepts that we have in our minds are true when they correspond to those objects as they really exist in the world.

Organized bodies of knowledge

Education, the realists would say, is the study of the subject-matter disciplines into which knowledge has been sorted and classified. History, language, science, mathematics—these are organized bodies of knowledge. If we know them, we will know something about the world in which we live. This knowledge is our best guide in conducting our daily affairs.

The school is the institution that has been established to teach students about the objective world. The instruction that takes place in school should impart a body of knowledge. Students should learn subjects that will help them understand their world so that they can live full and satisfying lives. The realist teacher needs to be able to recognize the basic concepts in the subject and the generalizations that explain their interactions, and to render these into a teachable and learnable order that meets the needs of the learner. The teacher should be an authority both in knowledge of the subject and in the methods of teaching it.[6]

Realist educators welcome standards that require students and teachers to demonstrate mastery of academic subject matter. They would argue that genuine quality of education requires teachers who are competent in the subjects that they teach. To maintain academic standards, teachers, administrators, and school boards should resist social promotion policies.

How would a high school physics teacher with a realist philosophical orientation plan a unit on Isaac Newton's laws of motion? First, the teacher would present a short discussion of Newton's scientific research and contributions; second, he would illustrate the laws of motion in a laboratory demonstration; third, the students would discuss the demonstration and frame the basic scientific generalization that the demonstration illustrated; finally, students would take a test to demonstrate their understanding of Newton's laws of motion.[7]

Perennialism

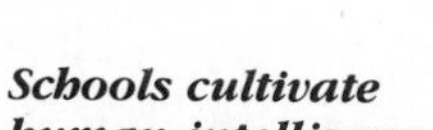

Schools cultivate human intelligence

Perennialism is an educational theory that draws heavily on the principles of realism. It presents a conservative or traditional view of human nature and education. Agreeing with Aristotle's statement that human beings are rational, perennialists see the school as an institution designed to cultivate human intelligence.[8]

The perennialists see the universal aim of education as the search for and the dissemination of truth. Since truth is universal and unchanging, a genuine education is also universal and constant. The school's curriculum should emphasize the recurrent themes of human life. It should contain cognitive sub-

6 William O. Martin, *Realism in Education* (New York: Harper & Row, 1969); Bigge, *Educational Philosophies for Teachers,* pp. 37–60.

7 Philip H. Phenix, *Philosophies of Education* (New York: Wiley, 1961), pp. 22–24.

8 Eva T. Brann, *Paradoxes of Education in a Republic* (Chicago: University of Chicago Press, 1979); John Stoops, *Philosophy and Education in Western Civilization* (Danville, Ill.: Interstate, 1971).

jects that cultivate rationality and the study of moral, aesthetic, and religious principles to cultivate the attitudinal dimension. Like idealists and realists, perennialists prefer a subject-matter curriculum. The perennialist curriculum includes history, language, mathematics, logic, literature, the humanities, and science. The content of these subjects should come from the classical works of literature and art. Mastering the subject matter of these learned disciplines is regarded as essential for training the intellect.

Great books of western civilization

One of the most articulate perennialist spokespersons was Robert Hutchins, president of the University of Chicago, whose influence as an educational pioneer was examined in Chapter 4. Hutchins argued that education ought to cultivate the intellect as well as the harmonious development of all human faculties.[9] The central aim of education should be to develop the power of thought. Whereas most educators justify the emphasis on thought because it organizes and enriches life experiences, Hutchins derived it from a definition of the fixed and essential nature of human beings. Hutchins described the ideal education as

> one that develops intellectual power. I arrive at this conclusion by a process of elimination. Educational institutions are the only institutions that can develop intellectual power. The ideal education is not an *ad hoc* education, not an education directed to immediate needs; it is not a specialized education, or a pre-professional education; it is not a utilitarian education. It is an education calculated to develop the mind.[10]

Hutchins based his educational philosophy on two major premises: human nature is rational and knowledge resides in unchanging, absolute, and universal truths. Since the rationality of human nature is universal, Hutchins stressed that education must also be universal.[11] Since reason is our highest power, the development of the intellect should be education's highest priority. Hutchins advocated a curriculum that consists of permanent, or perennial, studies. He particularly recommended the study of the classics, or the great works of Western civilization. Reading and discussing great books cultivates the intellect and prepares students to think carefully and critically. In addition to these classics, he urged the study of grammar, rhetoric, logic, mathematics, and philosophy.

In general, perennialism represents a conservative theoretical position centered on the authority of tradition and the classics. Among its major educational principles are the following: (1) truth is universal and does not depend on the circumstances of places, time, or persons; (2) a good education involves a search for and an understanding of the truth; (3) truth can be found in the great works of civilization; and (4) education is a liberal exercise that develops the intellect.

Education for truth

9 Robert M. Hutchins, *The Learning Society* (New York: Praeger, 1968).

10 Robert M. Hutchins, *A Conversation on Education* (Santa Barbara, Calif.: The Fund for the Republic, 1963), p. 1.

11 Robert M. Hutchins, *The Higher Learning in America* (New Haven: Yale University Press, 1962).

The Paideia Proposal

In the early 1980s, a revival of perennialism appeared with the publication of Mortimer J. Adler's *Paideia Proposal: An Educational Manifesto.*[12] In it Adler argued that there exists a general learning that all human beings should possess. Although based on a sophisticated philosophical rationale, the essence of the *Paideia Proposal* was as follows:

1. Since American society is a democracy based on political and ethical equality, the same quality of schooling should be provided for all students.
2. Schooling—as an important component of education—should aid "human beings" to "become educated persons."

Adler and his Paideia associates advocated a general curriculum for all students. They identified the following organized subject matters as indispensable for all students: language, literature, fine arts, mathematics, natural sciences, history, geography, and social studies. While emphasizing fundamental subjects, the Paideia group did not see subject matter as an end in itself but rather as the context for developing a repertoire of intellectual skills. Among the sought-after intellectual skills were reading, writing, speaking, listening, calculating, observing, measuring, estimating, and problem solving.[13] Together, the fundamental subjects and intellectual skills lead to a still higher level of learning, reflection, and awareness. Through the Socratic dialogue, students can be challenged to enlarge their understanding of ideas and values. For Adler, like Hutchins, the purpose of education is to cultivate an awareness and understanding of significant ideas.

The Basic Questions

Progressive educational critics of perennialism have charged that it fosters educational elitism. In denying this charge, Hutchins and Adler have asserted that their educational proposals are truly democratic. They argue that all persons should have the right to the same education and that this education should be of the highest quality. Students, they contend, should not be grouped or streamed into tracks that would prevent some from acquiring the general education to which they are entitled by their common humanity.

For Hutchins, Adler, and other perennialists, genuine equality of educational opportunity is maintained by providing a learning experience of high intellectual quality for all. To track some students into an academic curriculum and others into a vocational curriculum is to deny the latter genuine equality of educational opportunity. In other words, true equity can be satisfied only by access to a quality education.

12 Mortimer J. Adler, *The Paideia Proposal: An Educational Manifesto* (New York: Macmillan, 1982); also see, Mortimer J. Adler, *Paideia Problems and Possibilities* (New York: Macmillan, 1983).

13 Ibid., pp. 22–23.

Essentialism

Essentialism is a conservative educational theory that arose in response to progressive education. It is rooted in both idealism and realism. Essentialism basically emphasizes the authority of the teacher and the value of the subject-matter curriculum. For the essentialists, education involves the learning of the basic skills, arts, and sciences that have been developed in the past. These essential skills—reading, writing, and arithmetic—are to be found in every sound elementary school curriculum.[14] At the secondary level the basic curriculum consists of academic subjects in the arts and sciences. Mastering these skills and subjects prepares the student to function as a member of a civilized society. In addition, the student also should acquire the behavior needed for successful living. The learning of the essential curriculum requires discipline and hard work. Those who aspire to be teachers should be skilled professionals both in subject matter and in teaching.

Basic skills and academic subjects

Discipline and hard work

Arthur Bestor, an advocate of contemporary essentialism, sees the liberal arts and sciences as the core of a general education that will enable all men and women to function intelligently. Bestor and the members of the Council on Basic Education have argued that the intellectual quality of American education has been weakened by those professional educators who have stressed life adjustment and other nonessentials. Bestor's book *The Restoration of Learning* argues that a good education should provide "sound training in the fundamental ways of thinking represented by history, science, mathematics, literature, language, art and other disciplines evolved in the course of mankind's long quest for usable knowledge, cultural understanding, and intellectual power."[15]

Essentialists hold that these intellectual disciplines are the necessary foundations of modern life. In the elementary school curriculum, reading, writing, arithmetic, and research skills are the indispensable studies. The high school curriculum should consist of science, mathematics, history, English, and foreign languages. These are the tools of a liberal education and the most reliable aids in meeting the requirements of both personal and social life. It is the task of the school to channel the accumulated experience of humankind into organized, coherent, and differentiated disciplines. Only after mastering these basic disciplines can the student be expected to use them to solve personal, social, and civic problems.

Liberal education

Certain common themes can be found in the essentialist position. Among them are (1) the elementary school curriculum should aim to cultivate basic tool skills that contribute to literacy and mastery of arithmetical computation; (2) the secondary curriculum should cultivate competencies in history, mathematics, science, English, and foreign languages; (3) schooling requires

14 Gerald L. Gutek, *Basic Education: A Historical Perspective* (Bloomington, Ind.: Phi Delta Kappa Educational Foundation, 1981); Christopher J. Lucas, *Foundations of Education: Schooling and the Social Order* (Englewood Cliffs, N.J.: Prentice-Hall, 1984), pp. 25–70.

15 Arthur E. Bestor, *The Restoration of Learning* (New York: Knopf, 1955), p. 7.

Essentialists believe that learning requires disciplined attention, regular homework assignments, and a respect for legitimate authority. (David S. Strickler/Atoz Images)

discipline and a respect for legitimate authority; and (4) learning requires hard work and disciplined attention.

Basic Education

Revival of essentialism

Since the 1970s, the United States has experienced a revival of essentialism with the "back-to-basics" movement. Since the movement has been a grass roots rather than professional one, it does not yet have a coherent philosophical rationale.[16]

Back-to-basics proponents contend that social experimentation and untested innovations have lowered academic standards. They charge that many

16 Ben Brodinsky, "Back to the Basics: The Movement and Its Meaning," *Phi Delta Kappan* (March 1977), pp. 523–527; William G. Huitt and Eui-Do Rim, "A Basic Skills Instructional Improvement Program: Utilization of Research to Improve Classroom Practice" (Paper presented at the annual meeting of the American Educational Research Association, Boston, April 1980).

children have not mastered basic literary and computational skills. Also contributing to the academic weaknesses of American education at the secondary level has been a rejection of prescribed courses in favor of electives and minicourses. The back-to-basics position is that schools should concentrate on the essential skills and subjects that contribute to literacy and to social and intellectual efficiency.

In this view teachers should be restored to instructional authority. They must be well-prepared and held accountable for children's failure to learn. Instruction should be geared to organized learning, often in the form of textbooks. The method of instruction should center on regular assignments, homework, recitations, and frequent testing and evaluation. Chapter 14 discusses other aspects of the back-to-basics movement.

Homework and testing

The Basic Questions

Traditional-conservative view of education

Since the perennialists and essentialists share many ideas about knowledge, education, schooling, and instruction, their views can be examined as a defense of educational conservatism in a cultural sense. They see historical experience as the surest guide to questions about educational issues. For them, the school is concerned with ideas, knowledge, the cultivation of human intellectuality, and the cultural heritage. The school's task, then, is to civilize human beings.

Perennialists and essentialists are suspicious of the argument that the school should be an agency of socialization, of life adjustment, or of vocationalism. They claim that such nonintellectual activities detract from and will ultimately destroy the school's intellectual and civilizing roles. Perennialists and essentialists are also suspicious of educational change for the sake of change. They see the teaching-learning relationship as centered on the transmission and mastering of academic subject matter.

Both the essentialists of the past and current back-to-basics proponents believe that the school is an institution designed to teach basic skills and subjects. To ensure a skilled, civil, and literate society, schools need to maintain standards that require the mastery of such skills and subjects. Social promotion policies or compensatory programs that weaken academic mastery of skills and subjects have no place in the school. Genuine equity, essentialists argue, is based on rigorously maintained standards and on examinations or requirements that demonstrate competency on the part of students. The recently adopted requirements in many states that tie promotion to the demonstration of academic competency through testing is an example of modern-day essentialism.

Pragmatism

In contrast to the traditional views of education discussed thus far, John Dewey's pragmatism (or experimentalism) represents a philosophy of education that is based on change, process, relativity, and the reconstruction of experience.[17] Dewey's work as an educational pioneer was examined in Chapter 4. In this chapter the focus will be directed to his pragmatic philosophy.

Dewey was a commanding figure in the field of education and wrote extensively on his educational philosophy.[18] Charles Darwin's theory of evolution had a marked impact on Dewey's work. He applied the terms *organism* and *environment* to education. The human being is a biological and sociological organism possessing drives or impulses that function to sustain life and to further growth and development. Every organism lives in a habitat or environment. In the process of living the human organism experiences problematic situations that threaten his or her continued existence or that interfere with ongoing activities. The successful human being can solve these problems and add the details of the particular problem-solving episode to his or her general stock of experiences. In Dewey's philosophy of education, *experience* is the key word. Experience can be defined as the interaction of the human organism with its environment. Since living depends on the ability to solve problems, then education becomes that which cultivates problem-solving skills and methods.[19]

Cultivating problem-solving skills

Dewey's concept of experience was a key component of his experimentalist philosophy. Rejecting the a priori foundation of the older idealist, realist, and perennialist philosophical perspectives, Dewey's test of experience meant that human purposes and plans could be validated only by acting on them and judging them by their consequences. To judge by consequences also applied to educational programs. Did a particular educational program, curricular design, or methodological strategy achieve its anticipated goals and objectives? For Dewey, the only valid test was to try out the proposal and judge the results.

While idealism, realism, perennialism, and essentialism all emphasized bodies of substantive knowledge or subject-matter disciplines, Dewey stressed the methodology or the process of problem solving. According to Dewey, learning occurs as the person engages in problem solving. In Dewey's experimental epistemology, the learner, as an individual or as a member of a group, utilizes the scientific method to solve both personal and social problems. For Dewey the problem-solving method can be developed into a habit that is transferable to a wide variety of situations.[20]

17 R. S. Peter, *John Dewey Reconsidered* (Boston: Routledge & Kegan Paul, 1977); Arthur G. Wirth, *John Dewey as Educator: His Design for Work in Education 1894–1904* (New York: Wiley, 1966).

18 John Dewey, *The Child and the Curriculum* (Chicago: University of Chicago Press, 1902); idem., *Democracy and Education* (New York: Macmillan, 1906); idem, *The School and Society* (Chicago: University of Chicago Press, 1923); idem., *Experience and Education* (New York: Macmillan, 1938).

19 George R. Knight, *Issues & Alternatives in Educational Philosophy* (Berrien Springs, Mich.: Andrews University Press, 1982), pp. 60–68.

20 Henry W. Hodysh, "Historical Theory and Social Change in John Dewey's Philosophy," *Educational Theory* (Summer 1970), pp. 245–252.

Key Concepts

Metaphysics and Epistemology Where the more traditional philosophies of idealism and realism had a carefully separated metaphysics and epistemology, pragmatism or experimentalism construed epistemology as a process in which reality is constantly changing.

The epistemological or knowing situation involves a person, an organism, and an environment. The person interacts with the environment in order to live, grow, and develop. This interaction may alter or change the environment, and it may also alter or change the person. Knowing is thus a *transaction* between the learner and the environment. Basic to this interaction is the concept of change. Each interaction may have some generalizable aspects or features that can be carried to the next interaction, but each episode is somewhat different. Thus, the person is constantly changing, the environment is constantly changing, and the experiences or transactions are also changing.

Environmental interaction and change

If reality is continually changing, then a curriculum based on permanent realities such as that of the perennialists or the essentialists, cannot be acceptable for the pragmatists. What is needed is a method for dealing with change in an intelligent manner. Since reality is a process of transformation or reconstruction of both the person and the environment, how can the course of change be directed toward desired outcomes? The Deweyites stress problem solving as the most effective and efficient method for dealing with the direction or course of change. Concepts of unchanging or universal truth, such as the realists and idealists suggest, become untenable. The only guides that human beings have in their interaction with the environment are established generalizations or tentative assertions that are subject to further research and verification. Each time that a human experience is reconstructed to solve a problem, a new contribution is added to humanity's fund of experience.

Dealing with change

Axiology and Logic Pragmatic conceptions of axiology are highly situational. Values are relative to time, place, and circumstances. That which contributes to human and social growth and development is regarded as valuable; that which restricts or contracts experience is unworthy. It is necessary to test and reexamine value assumptions in the same way that scientific claims are subjected to verification. Knowledge and values are subject to further experimentation and reconstruction.

The logic used in experimentalist education is inductive and based on the scientific method. Tentative assertions are based on empirical experience and must be tested. Experimentalist logic is suspicious of a priori truths and deductions based on them.

Scientific method

The Basic Questions

The pragmatist answers to questions about knowledge, education, schooling, and instruction are very different from those of the more traditional schools of educational philosophy. For the pragmatists, knowledge is tentative and subject to revision. They are more concerned with the process of using knowledge than with truth as a body of knowledge. In contrast, the traditional philosophers tend to emphasize truth as a permanent body of knowledge.

For the pragmatist, education is an experimental process; it is a method of dealing with and solving problems that arise as people interact with their world. Dewey argued that human beings experience the greatest personal and social growth when they interact with the environment in an intelligent and reflective manner. The most intelligent way of solving problems is to use the scientific method.[21] When you face a problem, the information needed to solve the problem comes from many sources. It is interdisciplinary, rather than located within a single discipline or academic subject. For example, the information needed to define the problem of pollution of the physical environment and to suggest ways of solving it comes from many different sources. The factors that must be considered are historical, political, sociological, scientific, technological, and international. An educated person, in the pragmatic sense, knows how to take information from various sources and disciplines and use that knowledge in an instrumental manner. The more traditional philosophical perspectives represented by idealism, realism, perennialism, and essentialism are suspicious of the interdisciplinary approach in education because they believe that a student must first master organized subject matter before attempting to solve problems.

School as an agency of society

Pragmatists such as Dewey see the school as a specialized environment that is an extension of the more general social environment. For them, no separation exists between school and society. The school is society's agency for selecting and simplifying the cultural elements that an individual needs to participate in social life. As a specialized environment, the school deliberately brings the young into cultural participation. As a selective agency, it transmits part of the cultural heritage and seeks to reconstruct other aspects of the culture. The school's threefold functions are simplifying, purifying, and balancing the cultural heritage. To simplify, the school selects elements of the heritage and reduces their complexity into appropriate units for learning. To purify, the school selects worthy elements of the cultural heritage and eliminates unworthy ones that limit human interaction and growth. To balance, the school integrates the selected and purified experiences into a harmony. Since many different groups participate in society, the school assists the children of one group in understanding members of other social groups. As a genuinely integrated and democratic learning community, the school should be open to all.

Transmitting the cultural heritage

Pragmatists consider teaching and learning to be processes of reconstructing experience according to the scientific method. Learning takes place in an active way as the learners, either individually or in groups, solve problems. These problems will vary in response to changing circumstances and

21 Alan Lawson, "John Dewey and the Hope for Reform," *History of Education Quarterly* (Spring 1975), pp. 31–66.

environments. The important objective is that the learner will acquire the method or process of solving problems in an intelligent manner. Most significant, the teacher does not attempt to dominate learning but seeks to guide it by acting as a director or facilitator of the student's research.

Dewey, in particular, was an advocate of an open and sharing society. For him, quality and equity were not mutually exclusive. A society and its educational system reach their zenith when they provide for the widest possible sharing of resources among all people in the society. Sharing does not diminish quality but enriches it. In Dewey's terms, quality and equity are reciprocal and related social and educational "goods" to be shared by all.

Progressivism

Although progressive education, or the educational theory of progressivism, is often associated with John Dewey's pragmatism or experimentalism, the progressive education movement wove together a number of diverse strands. In its origins the progressive education movement was part of the larger sociopolitical movement of general reform that characterized American life in the late nineteenth and early twentieth centuries. Political progressives such as Robert La Follette and Woodrow Wilson wanted to curb powerful trusts and monopolies and to make the system of political democracy truly operative.[22] Jane Addams and other progressives worked in the settlement house movement to improve social welfare in Chicago and in other urban areas. Progressive education was part of this general movement to reform American life and institutions.[23]

Part of a larger reform movement

By the 1920s the general reform currents had ebbed, but progressive education continued to flourish. Although there was no central dogma, progressive educators stressed the view that all learning should center on the child's interests and needs. One described the principles of organic education as follows:

Child's interests and needs

> We believe the educational program should aim to meet the needs of the growing child. We believe that childhood is for itself and not a preparation for adult life. Therefore, the school program must answer the following questions: What does the child of any particular age need to minister to the health of his body, to preserve the integrity of the intellect, and to keep him sincere and unself-conscious of spirit?
>
> The answers to these questions will constitute the curriculum of the school, and as we grow in understanding of the nature and needs of childhood, the curriculum will change.[24]

22 For the contrasting leadership styles of two progressive presidents, see John M. Cooper, Jr., *The Warrior and the Priest: Woodrow Wilson and Theodore Roosevelt* (Cambridge, Mass.: Belknap Press of Harvard University Press, 1983).

23 For the history of the general progressive movement in American life, see J. Leonard Bates, *The United States 1898–1928: Progressivism and a Society in Transition* (New York: McGraw-Hill, 1976). The progressive movement in education has been given an excellent treatment in Lawrence A. Cremin, *The Transformation of the School* (New York: Random House, 1961).

24 Marietta Johnson, "The Educational Principles of the School of Organic Education, Fairhope, Alabama," in H. Rugg, ed., *The Foundations and Technique for the Study of Education,* National Society for the Study of Education, Part I (Bloomington, Ind.: Public School Publishing Co., 1926), p. 349.

School as a pleasant place

Others stressed as well the need to make school a pleasant place for learning.

> Every child has the right to live naturally, happily, and fully as a child. . . . Childhood in itself is a beautiful section of life, and children should be given a chance for free, full living.
>
> We try to make the schools happy, attractive places for children to be in. . . . We believe in colorfulness, coziness, hominess in our classrooms; in an opportunity for spontaneity. We want children to *want* to come to school.[25]

Progressive Principles

Criticized traditional school practices

The loosely structured Progressive Education Association, organized in 1919, was not united by a single comprehensive philosophy of education. The progressives differed in many of their theories and practices, but they were united in their opposition to certain traditional school practices. They generally condemned the following: (1) the authoritarian teacher, (2) exclusive reliance on bookish methods of instruction or on the textbook, (3) passive learning by memorization of factual data, (4) the four-walls philosophy of education that attempted to isolate education from social reality, and (5) the use of fear or physical punishment as a form of discipline.

The Progressive Education Association refused to proclaim a philosophy of education but did announce certain unifying principles. Among them were the following: (1) the child should be free to develop naturally; (2) interest, stimulated by direct experience, is the best stimulus for learning; (3) the teacher should be a resource person and a guide to learning activities; (4) there should be close cooperation between the school and the home; and (5) the progressive school should be a laboratory for pedagogical reform and experimentation.[26]

Focus on learner, not the subject

Progressive education was both a movement within the broad framework of American education and a theory that urged the liberation of the child from the traditional emphasis on rote learning, lesson recitations, and textbook authority. In opposition to the conventional subject matter of the traditional curriculum, progressives experimented with alternative modes of curricular organization—utilizing activities, experiences, problem solving, and the project method. Progressive education focused on the child as the learner rather than on the subject; emphasized activities and experiences rather than verbal and literary skills; and encouraged cooperative group learning activities rather than competitive individualized lesson learning. The use of democratic school procedures was seen as a prelude to community and social reform. Progressivism also cultivated a cultural relativism that critically appraised and often rejected traditional value commitments.

Although the major thrust of progressive education waned in the 1940s and came to an end in the 1950s, it did leave its imprint on education and

25 Carleton Washburne, "The Philosophy of the Winnetka Curriculum," in Rugg, *The Foundations and Technique for the study of Education,* pp. 222–223.

26 Patricia A. Graham, *Progressive Education: From Arcady to Academe* (New York: Teachers College Press, Columbia University, 1967).

Progressive educators encourage cooperative group learning activities and view the teacher as a facilitator and resource person rather than as a director of learning.

(Rick Friedman/The Picture Cube)

the schools of today. Contemporary child-centered progressivism is expressed in humanistic education and in the open educational arrangements based on the British primary school.

The Basic Questions

Since the progressives were not of a single mind, they gave a variety of responses to questions about the nature of education, the school, teaching, and learning. However, they were able to agree on their opposition to traditionalism and authoritarianism. While some progressives believed that education was a process intended to liberate children, others were more concerned with social reform.

Liberating children and social reform

Child-centered progressives saw the school as a place where children would be free to experiment, to play, and to express themselves. Those inclined to a more societal perspective saw the school as a community center or as an agency of social reform.

Progressives generally were not interested in using the curriculum to transmit subjects to students. Rather, the curriculum was to come from the child. Learning could take a variety of forms such as problem solving, field trips, creative artistic expression, and projects. Above all, progressives saw the teaching-learning process as active, exciting, and everchanging.

Progressive teachers who follow an experimentalist philosophical orientation generally seek to incorporate problem solving, projects, group work, and activities into their instructional methodology and classroom style. For example, a junior high or middle school teacher might engage her students in a social studies unit on the black contribution to American life. Students might work in groups, each group having the mission of contributing to the total project. Among the group projects, there might be the following:

Group A would investigate the origins of American blacks in Africa and their coming to North America as slaves. Such an investigation would involve research and reading of a geographical, economic, anthropological, and historic nature. Each student in Group A would investigate a particular phase of the problem that would then be integrated into the whole project.

Group B might identify the leading blacks who contributed to American culture and prepare biographical sketches to present to the class. They could also arrange an exhibit that included photographs and evidence of each black leader's contribution.

Group C might research current achievements, problems, and issues facing black Americans. They could consult current newspapers and magazines and prepare a scrapbook of clippings to illustrate the contemporary condition of black Americans.

As the various groups work on their projects, the teacher serves as a resource facilitator. Working with each group individually he or she suggests sources and helps students discover other ways of pursuing the project.

Progressive educators reject barriers of class, race, or creed that tend to keep people apart from each other. They believe that as students work together on projects based on their common shared experience, they break down the isolation that diminishes the quality of the human experience.

Social Reconstructionism

Creation of a new society

While the Deweyite practitioner and the project-method, child-centered, and creative-oriented progressive educators emphasized the individuality of the child, other progressives were vitally concerned with social change. These progressives, called social reconstructionists, argued that progressive education should do more than reform the social and educational status quo; it should seek to create a new society. Social reconstructionism will be examined here as a separate educational theory; its origins, however, were originally part of the progressive movement in education.

Social reconstructionism postulates that humankind is in a state of profound cultural crisis. If schools reflect the dominant social values, as the traditional educational theorists suggest, then, according to the reconstructionists, organized education will merely transmit the social ills that are symptoms of the pervasive problems and afflictions that beset humankind. The reconstructionists generally assert that the only legitimate goal of a truly humane education is to create a world order in which people are in control of their own destiny. In an era of nuclear weapons, they see an urgent need for society to reconstruct itself before it destroys itself.[27]

Lag in cultural adaptation

In analyzing the cultural crisis, the reconstructionists contend that while humankind has moved from an agricultural and rural society to an urban and technological society at the level of invention and scientific discovery, there is a serious lag in cultural adaptation to the realities of a technological society. Humankind has yet to reconstruct its values in order to catch up with the changes in the technological order, and organized education has a major role to play in reducing the gap between the values of the culture and technology.[28]

Reconstructionist Thinking

Social and economic problems

The reconstructionists recommend that teachers and schools embark on a critical examination of the culture in which they live. They should seek to identify the major areas of controversy, conflict, and inconsistency and seek to explore and to resolve them. For example, certain nations enjoy plenty while other peoples face the constant threat of starvation. While a few people enjoy luxury, many are victims of disease and poverty. Although the social and economic gap is not as wide in the United States as in some other countries, it is still evident and causes many of our present problems. Education should expose these social inconsistencies and seek to resolve them in such a way that the common people can determine the distribution and control of the resources of the planet.

The reconstructionists believe, further, that the technological era is one of tremendous interdependence. Events in one area of the globe will have an impact on other areas. Pollution, for example, is not restricted to a single place or to a single people. In such an interdependent world the old forms of education that stressed either isolationism or nationalism are obsolete. The new education for the reconstructed society must recognize the reality of an interdependent world that is international in scope. In an era when nuclear weapons are proliferating, a war or conflict in any area of the globe poses a potential threat to all of humankind. Therefore, the reconstructionist generally would seek to internationalize the curriculum so that men and women would learn that they live in a global village.

The social reconstructionists share a common concern that human sur-

27 Gerald L. Gutek, *George S. Counts and American Civilization: The Educator as Social Theorist* (Macon, Ga.: Mercer University Press, 1984).

28 Theodore Brameld, *Toward a Reconstructed Philosophy of Education* (New York: Dryden, 1965).

Human survival depends on education

vival and education are reciprocally related. To ensure the continuation of our species on this planet, we must become social engineers, plotting our course of change and then using our scientific and technological expertise to arrive at the defined goal. A reconstructionist program of education will be one that (1) critically examines the cultural heritage; (2) does not fear to examine the most controversial of social issues; (3) is deliberately committed to bringing about constructive social change; (4) cultivates a planning attitude; and (5) enlists students and teachers in definite programs of social, educational, political, and economic change as a means of total cultural renewal.

Concern with social issues has led reconstructionist theorists to propose educational policies that are related to important national and world problems. They have encouraged policies designed to alleviate racial discrimination and poverty. A reconstructionist orientation is compatible with programs of compensatory education, school integration, and bilingual and bicultural education. Reconstructionists have encouraged international education as a means of reducing world conflict. Since they are interested in policy formulation, reconstructionists are interested in examining the ideas of the great utopian thinkers and in conducting futuristic studies that serve to predict the course of things to come.

Futuristic studies

The Basic Questions

The social reconstructionists are convinced that a new social order will come about only as educators challenge obsolete conceptions of knowledge, education, schooling, and instruction and initiate carefully planned and directed educational change that will lead to social change. Like the progressives, social reconstructionists see knowledge in instrumental terms. The knowledge areas that are particularly useful are the social sciences such as anthropology, economics, sociology, political science, and psychology. These social sciences provide insights, information, and methods that can be used in devising strategies for planned social change in contemporary society.[29]

Active problem solving

Education, for the social reconstructionists, is designed to awaken the students' consciousness about social problems and to engage them actively in the solving of problems. To awaken social consciousness, students are encouraged to question the status quo and to investigate controversial issues in religion, economics, politics, and education. It is by examining controversial issues that the student will develop alternatives to the conventional wisdom.

The school, as a social agency, is an institution where new suggestions for changing society are to be emphasized and encouraged, but not as a purely intellectual exercise. The school is rather an instrument for creating alternative political, social, and economic forms, institutions, and processes. Since it is on the cutting edge of change, the school will be in the center of controversy.

29 William O. Stanley, *Education and Social Integration* (New York: Teachers College Press, Columbia University, 1952).

Social reconstructionists are firmly committed to equality or equity in both society and education. For them, barriers of socioeconomic class and racial discrimination need to be identified, examined, and eradicated. In the American context, social reconstructionists have often been political and educational activists who believe that the school should contribute to a greater sharing of the intellectual, social, and material resources of American life. Social reconstructionists also are proponents of an education that emphasizes the international dimension of life. In an interdependent world, the quality of human life needs to be considered and enhanced on a global basis.

Existentialism

Rather than constituting a systematic philosophy, existentialism is a way of examining life in a very personal manner. It became popular in the post–World War II period.[30] In some ways existentialism represents a feeling of desperation, but it also contains a spirit of hope. An education that follows the existentialist orientation will emphasize deep personal reflection on one's commitments and choices.

Self-examination

Key Concepts

The existentialist author Jean-Paul Sartre stated, "Existence precedes Essence." This sentence means that human beings are born and enter the world scene without their being consulted. They simply are here in a world that they did not make or shape. However, they are born possessing volition, or will, which gives them the freedom to make choices and to create their own purposes for existence. As people live, they are thrust into a number of choice-making situations. Some choices are minute and trivial. Other choices, however, deal with the purpose of life. These are decisions that lead to personal self-definition. A person creates his or her own definition and makes his or her own essence. You are what you choose to be.

The existentialist conception of a human being as the creator of his or her own essence differs substantially from that of the idealists and realists, who see the person as a universal category. While the idealist or realist sees the individual as an inhabitant of a meaningful and explainable world, the existentialist believes that the universe is indifferent to human wishes, desires, and plans. Human freedom is total, say the existentialists, who also hold that one's responsibility for choice is total.

Total responsibility for choices

Another important concept in existentialism is that of the sense of *Angst*, or dread. Each person knows that his or her destiny is death and ultimate disappearance and that his or her presence in the world is only temporary. As a conscious being, the individual must carry the knowledge of ultimate demise every day of his or her life. It is with this sense of philosophical dread that each person must make choices about freedom and slavery, love and

30 George F. Kneller, *Existentialism and Education* (New York: Wiley, 1958).

hate, and peace and war. As one makes these choices, the question is always present—What difference does it make that I am here and that I have chosen to be what I am?

Desperation and hope

As was stated earlier, existentialism carries feelings of both desperation and hope. Human beings are indeed desperate creatures who realize that life is temporary. They live in a world where others—persons, institutions, and agencies—are constantly seeking to impinge upon and violate their choice-making freedom. One's response to life has to be based on an answer to the question—Do I choose to be a self-determined person or do I choose to be defined by others? At the same time that men and women are desperate, they also have the possibilities of loving, creating, and being. One has the possibility of being an inner-directed and authentic person. An authentic person is one who is free and aware of his or her freedom.[31] Such a person knows that every choice is really an act of personal value creation. The authentic person is his or her own definer and is aware that self-definition is a personal responsibility.

Essence and values

Since existentialists have deliberately avoided systematization of their philosophy, it is difficult to categorize its metaphysial, epistemological, axiological, and logical positions. However, some comments on these areas will serve to illustrate the existentialist point of view. The person creates his or her own metaphysical position, which is the being or essence created by individual choice. Epistemologically, the individual chooses the knowledge that he or she wishes to possess. It is axiology that is most important for existentialists, since human beings create their own values through the choices that they make. Finally, the logic to which a person subscribes is a matter of individual preference.

The Basic Questions

The educational implications of existentialism are many. The existentialist realizes that we live in a world of physical realities and that we have developed a useful and scientific knowledge about these realities. However, the most significant aspects of our lives are personal and nonscientific. So to the questions we have asked about knowledge and education, existentialists would say that the most important kind of knowledge is about the human condition and the choices that each person has to make, and that education is a process of developing consciousness about the freedom to choose and about the meaning of and responsibility for one's choice.[32] It is designed to create in us a sense of self-awareness and to contribute to our authenticity as human beings.

Meaning of life, love, and death

An existentialist educator would encourage students to engage in philosophizing about the meaning of the human experiences of life, love, and death. An existentialist teacher would also raise these questions and put

31 Maxine Greene, *Landscapes of Learning* (New York: Teachers College Press, Columbia University, 1978); Van Cleve Morris, *Existentialism in Education* (New York: Harper & Row, 1966).

32 Harold Soderquist, *The Person and Education* (Columbus, Ohio: Merrill, 1966).

them before the students. The questioning process would grow into a dialogue between the members of the learning groups. It should be remembered that the answers to these questions would be personal and subjective for each individual. They would not be items to be measured on standardized tests.

An existentialist curriculum would consist of the experiences and subjects that lend themselves to philosophic dialogue. They would be subjects that vividly portray individual men and women in the act of choice making. Since existentialist choice making is so personal and subjective, those subjects that are emotional, aesthetic, and poetic are appropriate to an existentialist curriculum.[33] Literature and biography are important sources for revealing choice-making conditions.[34] Drama and films that vividly portray the human condition and human decision making ought to be seen and discussed by students. In addition to the literacy, dramatic, and biographical subjects, students also need to find modes of self-expression. They should be free to experiment with artistic media, to dramatize or make concrete their emotions, feelings, and insights. The existentialist classroom should be rich in the materials that lend themselves to self-expression.

Modes of self-expression

The school, for the existentialist educator, is a place where individuals can meet to pursue dialogue and discussion about their own lives and choices. It is a place where subjects can be pursued that will illuminate choice making by examining the human condition as it is presented in literary, dramatic, and other aesthetic forms. Since every person is in the same predicament and has the same possibilities, every individual should have opportunities for schooling. In the school both teachers and students should have the opportunity to ask questions, to suggest answers, and to engage in dialogue.

Philosophical Analysis

Philosophical analysis, or language analysis, is one of the newer approaches to issues in educational philosophy. Basically, it is a method of examining the language used in making statements about knowledge, education, and schooling, and of seeking to clarify it by establishing its meaning. Philosophical analysis has gained prominence among educational philosophers who believe that our communications about educational matters have grown increasingly confused and obscure.[35] To establish meaning, the philosophical analysts seek to reduce statements about education to empirical terms.

Language analyses

Empirical analyses

33 Maxine Greene, *Existential Encounters for Teachers* (New York: Random House, 1967).

34 An example of the examination of values in literature is Susan Resneck Parr, *The Moral of the Story: Literature, Values, and American Education* (New York: Teachers College Press, Columbia University, 1982); For history, see Carl Ubbelohde and Jack R. Fraenkel, eds., *Values of the American Heritage: Challenges, Cases Studies, and Teaching Strategies* (Arlington, Va.: National Council for the Social Studies, 1976).

35 Richard Pratte, "Analytic Philosophy of Education: A Historical Perspective," in Jonas F. Soltis, ed., *Philosophy of Education Since Mid-Century* (New York: Teachers College Press, Columbia University, 1981), pp. 17–37.

Philosophical analysis does not pretend to establish a school of educational philosophy. To understand more clearly the analytical view of the philosophy of education, it can be examined in reference to the educational philosophies already treated in this chapter. The idealists, realists, and perennialists describe their philosophies in terms of a world view or a total philosophical system. For these more traditional educational philosophies, humankind is part of this universal system. The philosophical analysts reject cosmic system building as a purely speculative exercise that has no real meaning for educators. The analysts assert that the metaphysical basis of cosmic philosophies cannot be verified in human experience. In addition, they find the expressions of the existentialists to be primarily poetic and emotional. While the existentialists may be expressing personal feelings, the analysts find them sorely deficient in supplying empirical data that could be used to establish meaning in educational issues. Since the pragmatists rely on the use of the scientific method in education, they are agreeable to the analytical view. But even the pragmatists have failed to use language with precise meaning. For example, Dewey's use of terms such as "democracy," "growth," "interests," and "experience" has caused much debate among philosophers of education.[36]

Establishing precise meaning

It was this dissatisfaction with the schools of philosophy that led a number of philosophers to develop a new way of working with ideas and their expression in language. Two major philosophers who led the movement of language analysis were G. E. Moore and Bertrand Russell.[37] Russell in particular sought to identify the logical structure that underlies language usage. For him philosophy's function is to formulate the logical rules that are the basis of language.

Key Concepts

Although operational differences exist among analysts, a few generalizations can be made to illustrate their contributions to education philosophy. For example, we express ourselves in terms of sentences that attempt to convey propositions about reality. According to the analysts, only some of these sentences are meaningful communications between persons. Meaningful sentences are either analytically true or empirically true.[38] If we say that $2+2=4$, we have expressed a mathematical statement that is analytically true because the 4 is analyzed out of and means the same as $2+2$. The statement can be reversed and can be stated as $4=2+2$. Other statements are true in that they can be verified in empirical terms. For example, the statement that water boils at 212° Fahrenheit can be tested and verified empirically. If meaningful statements are those that are either analytically or empirically true, then many other statements are meaningless in scientific communication since they cannot be examined by these two methods. For example, the

Verifiable propositions

36 George F. Kneller, *Movements of Thought in Modern Education.* (New York: Wiley, 1984).

37 Barry Gross, *Analytical Philosophy: An Historical Introduction* (New York: Western, 1970); Jonas F. Soltis, *An Introduction to the Analysis of Education Concepts* (Reading, Mass.: Addison-Wesley, 1966).

38 Albert J. Taylor, *An Introduction to the Philosophy of Education* (Dubuque, Iowa: Kendall/Hunt, 1978).

idealist proposition that "World is Mind" cannot be tested. Neither can the existentialist statement that "Existence precedes Essence" be verified empirically. However, it is possible to examine and find meaning in the experimentalist proposition that "Experience is the interaction of the human organism with the environment." To verify this statement, it would be necessary to render the words,"experience," "human organism," "interaction," and "environment" in terms that can be measured and verified empirically or analyzed logically.

Growing specialization

In many respects philosophical analysis is a response to the condition of knowledge in the twentieth century. The lives of men and women, their occupations, and their areas of knowledge competency have grown increasingly complicated and specialized as technology advanced and institutions were modernized. Each area of specialization has developed its own highly specialized language, which is used by and is particular to the experts who work within it. The growing use of highly specialized terminologies has made it difficult even for those in the same field to communicate with each other across their specialties. By explaining the language used in a complex technological society, the philosophical analyst can contribute to more meaningful communication.

In addition to specialization, modern society is now characterized by the mass media of communications. More people than ever before in human history are receiving the same message via the press, radio, and television. We are beset by all sorts of communications that range greatly in their truthfulness, reliability, and validity. By analyzing the language used in these messages, philosophical analysts can help us to distinguish myth from truth and perhaps find meaning in an inceasingly strident environment.

The Basic Questions

Concern with educational issues

Philosophical analysts have not attempted to provide broad answers to questions about knowledge, education, schooling, and instruction. Quite the contrary, they have tried to narrow these questions to specifics concerned with our speaking and writing about educational issues. In dealing with problems of knowledge, they have focused their interest on those knowledge claims and propositions that can be verified empirically. The philosophical analysts have not created new curricular proposals but have instead examined educational theories, programs, and practices in terms that can be evaluated empirically. They certainly have deflated many grandiose educational claims that cannot be put to the test of experience. In matters that concern teaching and learning, the philosophical analysts have given their careful attention to the language transactions that take place between the teacher and the learner in the classroom.

Analytical philosophers would also apply the same strategies in examining such questions as, What is the meaning of a quality education? How can schooling promote equality or socioeconomic opportunity? What standards should be applied for entrance to educational institutions? Their basic approach would be to establish definitions that make the key concepts in such questions meaningful.

Summing Up

1. Chapter 6 has attempted to put into perspective traditional philosophies of education, such as idealism and realism, and traditional theories of education, such as perennialism and essentialism. The more contemporary, process-oriented philosophy of pragmatism, or experimentalism, and the theories of progressivism and social reconstructionism have been discussed, too. The chapter concluded with a treatment of two newer schools or approaches to contemporary philosophy of education: existentialism and philosophical analysis.
2. The major concepts of these philosophies and theories are summarized in overview charts 6.1 and 6.2, which appear on pages 188 and 189. The study of these philosophies and theories of education reveals how varied are the goals and objectives of education.
3. By studying these philosophical approaches to education, you can appreciate the rich complexity of educational theorizing and can work toward formulating your own philosophy of education.

Discussion Questions

1. How would you answer the basic philosophical questions about knowledge, education, and schooling? How does your philosophy of education reflect or differ from the philosophies of education treated in this chapter?
2. Suppose you are a realist. How would you assess pragmatism and progressivism?
3. Which of the philosophies of education treated in this chapter has had the greatest impact on American education? Why?
4. Suppose you are a social reconstructionist. Identify the major problems facing American society, construct an educational agenda, and devise a teaching strategy designed to promote the solution of these problems.
5. Which of the philosophies treated in this chapter is most relevant to contemporary education and which is most irrelevant? Why?

Suggested Readings

Bigge, Morris L. *Educational Philosophies for Teachers.* Columbus, Ohio: Merrill, 1982.

This book presents a useful discussion of the major philosophies of education.

Kneller, George F. *Movements of Thought in Modern Education.* New York: Wiley, 1984.

Kneller's book treats recent developments in educational philosophy such as romanticism, structuralism, and analysis.

Knight, George R. *Issues & Alternatives in Educational Philosophy.* Berrien Springs, Mich.: Andrews University Press, 1982.

Knight presents a succinct and clearly written description of leading philosophies of education.

Power, Edward J. *Philosophy of Education: Studies in Philosophies, Schooling and Educational Policies.* Englewood Cliffs, N.J.: Prentice-Hall, 1982.

In this well-written textbook, Power provides an analysis of educational philosophies in relation to the development of educational policy.

SAVE OUR SCHO
2½ CRACKS IN THE LIBERTY BELL
PUBLIC EDUCATION WAS BORN IN MASSACHUSETTS
REST IN PEACE 1981
COURSE REQUESTS
STUDENT 2½
ENG. HONORS
A.P. SCIENCE
MUSIC
ART
DRAMA
CANCELLED
GIFTED STUDENT!
WHAT a LAUGH! 2½

Part 3 Political, Economic, and Legal Foundations

The three chapters in Part 3 deal with governance and administration of public education, school finance, and legal aspects of education. These chapters provide an overview of political, economic, and legal issues—considerations that are most relevant for classroom teachers.

Chapter 7, on governing and administering public education, begins by describing the organization and characteristics of schools and school districts. After delineating local and state roles and responsibilities, the chapter discusses the role of the federal government and of non-governmental forces and agencies that impact significantly on public education.

In Chapter 8 we focus on arrangements for financing schools. After describing local, state, and federal contributions to and responsibilities for the finance of public education, we consider a variety of recent trends in school finance.

Chapter 9 is devoted to legal aspects of education. Larger themes involve the functioning of the court system, teachers' and students' rights and responsibilities, religion and the schools, and affirmative action. Teachers obviously must know what their rights and obligations are in order to discharge their responsibilities effectively, and they also must understand the rights and responsibilities of the students with whom they interact. Lack of knowledge regarding important legal issues such as employment contracts, freedom of expression, suspension of students, and religion in the schools not only can place the teacher's job in jeopardy but can generate or reinforce serious problems in the operation of the educational system.

7

Governing and Administrating Public Education

Focusing Questions

How do governments—local, state, and federal—influence education?

How does the local school board work with the district superintendent in formulating school policy?

Why have schools consolidated, decentralized, and retrenched in recent years?

What are the different roles and responsibilities of the governor, state legislature, state board of education, state department of education, and chief state school officer in determining school policy?

How has the federal role in education changed in recent years?

What are some of the nongovernmental influences on school administration?

EDUCATION IN THE UNITED STATES IS ORGANIZED ON VARIOUS governmental levels—local, intermediate, state, and federal. Knowing about the formal organization of schools and how they are governed is important to people who work in schools. Teachers—or prospective teachers—who know how schools are organized and how they are influenced at different levels of government will be in a better position to make wise choices and realistic decisions about schools and to take political action. In this chapter we will examine the various governmental levels and how they impact on education. We will also explore a number of other important influences on the administration of schools.

No national system of education

A national system of education does not exist in this country in the same sense that it does in Great Britain, France, or the Soviet Union. Education here is considered a state and/or local function; we have fifty different state systems and many differences among local school systems even within the same state.

State responsibility for public education

The U.S. Constitution makes no mention of public education, but the Tenth Amendment to the Constitution reserves to the states all powers not specifically delegated to the federal government or prohibited to the states by the Constitution. This amendment is the basis for allocating to the states primary legal responsibility for public education in the United States. However, responsibility for the practical day-to-day operation of school systems has been delegated by the states to local districts. So we begin our discussion of how schools are governed and administered at the local level.

Local Responsibilities and Activities

Limited corporation

Every public school in the United States is part of a local school district. The district is created by the state. Subject to the restrictions of the state constitution, the state legislature can modify a local district's jurisdiction, change its boundaries and powers, or even eliminate it altogether. The local district encompasses a relatively small geographical area and operates the schools for children within a specific community. It is the avenue through which local citizens act in establishing districtwide policies in education. However, because a school district operates to carry out a state function—not a local function—local policies must be consistent with policies set forth in the state school code. The local district can be compared to a limited corporation whose powers are granted by state laws: it has only those powers expressly granted to it and those discretionary powers essential to its operation.

Local School Boards

Delegated powers from the state

The local boards of education have been delegated powers and duties by the state for the purpose of assuring that their schools are operated properly. The school boards have limited power and can exercise only those prerogatives specifically delegated to them by the state legislatures. Nevertheless, by law and custom, school boards have assumed significant decision-making responsibility. School boards have the power for the most part to raise money through taxes with a debt limitation. They exercise power over personnel and school property. Some states leave curriculum and student policy pretty much in the hands of the school board, but others, by law, impose specific requirements. In general, the school board must conform to state guidelines to qualify for state aid, as well as conform to federal guidelines where U.S. government monies are involved.

Most school boards elected

Methods of selecting board members are prescribed by state law. The two basic methods are election and appointment. Election is thought to make for greater accountability to the public, but some people argue that appointment leads to greater competence and less politics. Election is the most common practice. In 1981, 86 percent of school board members nationwide were elected in nonpartisan elections, 10 percent were elected in partisan elections, and 4 percent were appointed. Appointment is more common in large urban districts than in suburban or small-town districts: 11 percent of urban board members in 1981 were appointed.[1] A few states specify a standard number of board members, still others specify a permissible range, and a few have no requirements. Most school boards fall within a three-to-nine-member range, with the largest known school board having nineteen members.

Characteristics of board members

Based on a recent nationwide survey of school board members, a significant trend in recent years is the increase in the number of women on school boards, from 28 percent in 1982 to 37 percent in 1983. Minority representation has remained stable at 6 percent. (Most interesting, southern states show a higher minority representation on school boards: 14 percent black and 5 percent Hispanic.)[2] School board members tend to be older than the general population (73 percent are over forty); more educated (65 percent have had four or more years of college); wealthier (53 percent have family incomes of $40,000 or more, 4 percent earn more than $100,000 annually); and more likely to be professionals or managers (55 percent).[3]

The largest school systems (those enrolling 50,000 or more students) tend to have more heterogeneous boards. A 1981 survey indicates that minority members constitute 29 percent of the school board composition; women make up 36 percent.[4]

Types of board meetings

There are three general types of board meetings: regular, special, and executive. The first two are usually open meetings and the public is invited. Open board meetings obviously enhance school-community relations and allow parents to understand the problems of education as well as to air their

1 "Statistics on Elected vs. Appointed Boards" (Paper prepared by the National School Boards Association, Washington, D.C., 1981).

2 "Sixth Annual Survey of School Board Members," *American School Board Journal* (January 1984), pp. 24–27, 40.

3 Ibid.

4 Allan G. Ornstein, "Composition of Boards of Education of Public School Systems Enrolling 50,000 or More Students," *Urban Education* (July 1981), pp. 232–234.

The success of public education in the United States is dependent upon the selection of able men and women to serve on local school boards.
(Jerry Howard/Positive Images)

concerns. The use of closed board meetings to reach major policy is generally disdained but is occasionally used by central school boards in some large cities if conflict and tension arise.[5] Many school districts, however, have mandated open meetings except under certain specified, and rather limited conditions.

The School Superintendent and Central Office Staff

Executive officer of school system

Subject to board approval

One of the most important responsibilities a school board has is to appoint a competent superintendent of schools. The superintendent is the executive officer of the school system, whereas the board is the legislative policy-making body. Since the school board consists of laypeople who are not experts in school affairs, it is their responsibility to see that the work of the school is properly performed by professional personnel. The board of education often delegates many of their own legal powers to the superintendent and staff. The superintendent's policies, of course, are subject to board approval.

5 Jay Scribner and David O'Shea, "Political Developments in the Urban School Districts," in C. W. Gordon, ed., *Uses of the Sociology of Education,* 73rd Yearbook of the National Society for the Study of Education, Part II (Chicago: University of Chicago Press, 1974), pp. 380–408.

One of the major functions of the school superintendent is to gather and present data so that school board members can make intelligent policy decisions. Increasing reliance on the superintendent and staff is evident as school systems grow in size. The superintendent advises the school board and keeps members abreast of problems; generally, the school board will refuse to enact legislation or make policy without the recommendation of the school superintendent. However, it is common knowledge that when there is continuous disagreement or a major conflict over policy between the school board and the superintendent, the latter is usually replaced. The average time in office of superintendents is only approximately three to four years.[6]

The superintendent's powers are broad and his or her duties are many and varied. Besides being an adviser to the board of education, he or she is usually responsible for certain functions.[7] They include the following:

Duties of the superintendent

1. Serves as supervisor and organizer of professional and nonteaching (for example, janitors and engineers) personnel
2. Makes recommendations regarding the employment, promotion, and dismissal of personnel
3. Ensures compliance with directives of higher authority
4. Prepares the school budget for board review and administers the adopted budget
5. Serves as leader of long-range planning
6. Develops and evaluates curriculum and instructional program
7. Determines internal organization of the school district
8. Makes recommendations regarding school building needs and maintenance

In addition, the superintendent is responsible for the day-to-day operation of the schools within the district and serves as the major public spokesperson for the schools.

To fulfill these responsibilities the superintendent is assisted by a central office staff, as well as by support personnel, consultants, and citizen groups. The larger the school district, the greater the number of central administrators and professional staff needed to assist the superintendent (see Figure 7.1).

The Principal and the School

Small vs. large schools

Usually, each school has a single administrative officer—a principal—who is responsible for the operation of the school. In small schools this person may teach part-time as well. In a large school, in addition to the principal, there

6 Ralph B. Kimbrough and Michael Y. Nunnery, *Educational Administration,* 2nd ed. (New York: Macmillan, 1983).

7 Edgar L. Morphet, Roe L. Johns, and Theodore L. Reller, *Educational Organization and Administration,* 4th ed. (Englewood Cliffs, N.J.: Prentice-Hall, 1982); Allan C. Ornstein, *Education and Social Inquiry* (Itasca, Ill.: Peacock, 1978).

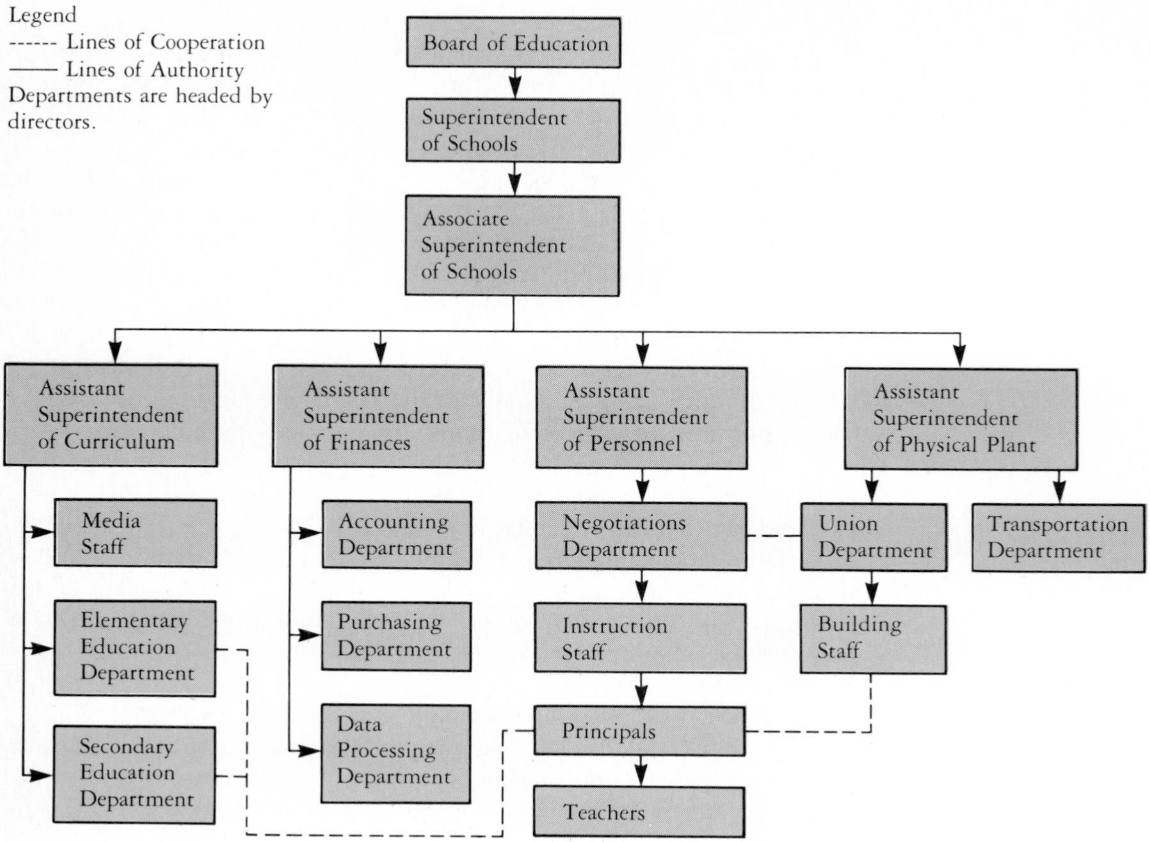

Legend
------ Lines of Cooperation
—— Lines of Authority
Departments are headed by directors.

Board of Education
Superintendent of Schools
Associate Superintendent of Schools
Assistant Superintendent of Curriculum
Assistant Superintendent of Finances
Assistant Superintendent of Personnel
Assistant Superintendent of Physical Plant
Media Staff
Elementary Education Department
Secondary Education Department
Accounting Department
Purchasing Department
Data Processing Department
Negotiations Department
Instruction Staff
Principals
Teachers
Union Department
Building Staff
Transportation Department

Figure 7.1
Typical Medium-sized School District (10,000–25,000 Students)

may be one or more assistant or vice principals. The administrative hierarchy may also consist of a number of department chairpersons, a discipline officer (for example, dean of boys, dean of girls), a director of guidance, and so on.

Although functions vary by locality and size, the principal is primarily responsible for administering all aspects of a school's operations. It is common practice for the principal to work with some type of community group for the improvement of the school. In the past, this function was often performed by a parent-teacher association and various advisory school-community committees that had little influence or real power. Since the 1960s, however, many people have demanded greater input into the operation of the schools, particularly in the cities. As teachers have become more militant, principals are being more careful to follow contract provisions and to include teacher representatives in policy-making decisions for the school unit.

Although principals juggle many different roles, there is overwhelming agreement that their major task is to provide instructional leadership (improving teacher techniques, developing appropriate curricula, and affording optimal learning situations for students). Authorities also recommend that principals spend from 50 to 75 percent of their time on improving instruction.[8] The trouble is, as principals point out, their numerous organizational and managerial tasks take up an inordinate amount of time, and in many cases prevent them from exerting instructional leadership.

Instructional leader

Nevertheless, the principal is at his or her best in the role of instructional leader when (1) teachers can openly share concerns with the principal, (2) there is open communication among teachers and between teachers and the principal, (3) teachers feel they can count on the support and expertise of the principal, (4) the principal values and encourages the professional growth of teachers, and (5) teachers are recognized or rewarded for competent performance by the principal.

Size of School Districts

What is the ideal size for a school district? In terms of minimum size, how many students must be enrolled to justify offering the diversified programs, services, and personnel needed to meet modern educational requirements? A 1934 study of city and county school systems concluded that a minimum of 10,000 to 12,000 students was needed to justify specialized and adequate staff size, as well as a varied program, in relation to reasonable costs of the educational program.[9] At the time, those numbers were criticized severely by many educators who believed that a district of that size was unattainable and impractical for most parts of the country.

Ideal school district size

Regarding maximum size, a research team headed by Paul Mort and Francis Cornell developed a method for measuring the effectiveness of a school system based on an adaptability index.[10] The index was correlated with school characteristics such as financial policies, curriculum innovation, community and staff participation, location, and size. These studies considered the maximally effective school district to comprise 100,000 students. This estimate was supported by other researchers, but later was disputed by advocates of decentralization who put the figure between 12,000 and 40,000.[11] Another study has concluded that the optimal size for a school district is between 10,000 and 50,000 pupils.[12]

8 William H. Roe and Thelbert L. Drake, *The Principalship,* 2nd ed., (New York: Macmillan, 1980); J. Lloyd Trump, *A School for Everyone* (Reston, Va.: National Association of Secondary School Principals, 1977).

9 Howard A. Dawson, *Satisfactory Local School Units,* Field Study No. 7 (Nashville, Tenn.: George Peabody College for Teachers, 1934).

10 Paul R. Mort and Francis G. Cornell, *American Schools in Transition* (New York: Teachers College Press, Columbia University, 1941); Paul R. Mort, William S. Vincent, and Clarence Newell, *The Growing Edge, An Instrument for Measuring the Adaptability of School Systems,* 2 vols. (New York: Teachers College Press, Columbia University, 1955).

11 Mario D. Fantini, Marilyn Gittell, and Richard Magat, *Community Control and the Urban School* (New York: Praeger, 1970); A. Harry Passow, *Toward Creating a Model Urban School System* (New York: Teachers College Press, Columbia University, 1967).

12 *Summary of Research on Size of Schools and School Districts* (Arlington, Va.: Educational Research Service, 1974).

Table 7.1
Distribution of Public School Systems by Size of District, 1980–1981

Size of District (Number of Pupils)	Public School Districts		Public School Students	
	Number	*Percentage*	*Number*	*Percentage*
Total operating districts	15,625	100.0	42,851,396	100.0
25,000 or more	183	1.2	11,907,985	27.8
10,000–24,999	511	3.3	7,434,630	17.3
5,000–9,999	1,106	7.1	7,705,372	18.0
2,500–4,999	2,065	13.2	7,181,460	16.8
1,000–2,499	3,457	22.1	5,665,386	13.2
600–999	1,820	11.7	1,437,725	3.4
300–599	2,316	14.8	1,014,640	2.4
Less than 300	4,161	26.6	504,198	1.2

Source: *Digest of Education Statistics, 1983–84* (Washington, D.C: National Center for Education Statistics, 1984), table 50, p. 62.

Small rural school districts

Historically, 10,000 students is a large number for a school district. Our schools, we must remember, are an outgrowth of one-room school houses and school districts in rural America. With the exception of a few urban areas, even as late as the turn of the twentieth century, most school districts consisted of three, four, or five schools and a few hundred students. As late as 1930, nearly 50 percent of American school districts had fewer than 300 students.[13]

Large school districts

By 1980, nearly half of public school students were in school districts containing 10,000 or more students. There were only 183 school districts with 25,000 or more students, but they accounted for 11.9 million students or 28 percent of the nation's public school enrollment. Table 7.1 shows how school systems are distributed according to enrollment size.

Most of the largest school systems (50,000 or more students) are located in California, Florida, Texas, Ohio, and Maryland. In most cases, the larger school systems are located in or near cities, the largest being the New York City system with approximately 960,000 students as of 1980, followed by Los Angeles with 545,000 students and Chicago with 475,000 students. (Two other large school systems, Puerto Rico and Hawaii, span an entire territory and state, respectively.) The medium-sized and smaller school systems have followed metropolitan sprawl and tend to be located in the outer ring of the suburbs or in rural areas.[14]

13 Newton Edwards and Herman C. Richey, *The School in American Social Order* (Boston: Houghton Mifflin, 1947).

14 A list of the largest 120 school systems, enrolling 30,000 or more students, can be found in the *Digest of Education Statistics, 1983–84,* table 49, pp. 58–61.

Consolidation Trends The number of school districts in the United States continues to decline. In 1930, there were more than 130,000 school districts. By 1950 the number had shrunk to 83,718; by 1980 to 15,625. Figure 7.2 illustrates the declining number of school districts in ten-year intervals from 1930 to 1980, with projections for 1990.

Declining number of school districts

The reduced number of school districts is a result of **consolidation,** the combination of a number of smaller school districts into one or two larger ones. Consolidation is thought to bring about more effective schools by increasing the tax base, quality of professional personnel, breadth of educational program, special services, and transportation facilities and by reducing overall educational costs per student.

Benefits of consolidation

A great many of the reorganized school districts are still too small to provide a comprehensive educational program and adequate specialized personnel to meet the needs of all the students. While the trend toward consolidation continues in the rural and small school districts (although at a slower pace today than in the past), there is a recent countertrend in large urban school districts to decentralize and divide into smaller school districts.

Decentralization Changes in the urban population after 1950 became noticeable as more and more low-income and minority residents pushed middle-class and white populations to the suburbs. The white flight movement became apparent in the 1950s and 1960s and to a lesser extent in the 1970s. As a result, schools in the cities became multiethnic and many schools in the suburbs became more homogeneous in terms of income and race. By the 1960s, the frustration of diverse ethnic groups, especially blacks, found a common "solution" in the call for decentralization, accompanied by greater community involvement in the schools. By definition, **decentralization** divides the school system into smaller units, but the focus of power and authority in a single central administration and board of education remains intact. There is usually little controversy over decentralization, so long as jobs are not consolidated or expanded on the basis of racial or ethnic patterns; even professional educators today see a need to reduce school bureaucracy and accept decentralization because it allows the professional educators to retain power. At the same time, school critics and minority spokespersons see decentralization as a first step toward increasing community involvement in the schools; they believe that decentralization will give the people greater access to the schools.

White flight

Smaller units

A nationwide survey on decentralization of school systems with 50,000 or more students was conducted in 1980.[15] Of the sixty-nine school systems in this category, 64 percent reported that they were decentralized.

Seventeen reasons were given for decentralization in a recent study. The top eight reasons, in order of priority and representing 79 percent of the re-

15 Allan C. Ornstein, "Decentralization and Community Participation Policy of Big School Systems," *Phi Delta Kappan* (December 1980), pp. 225–257.

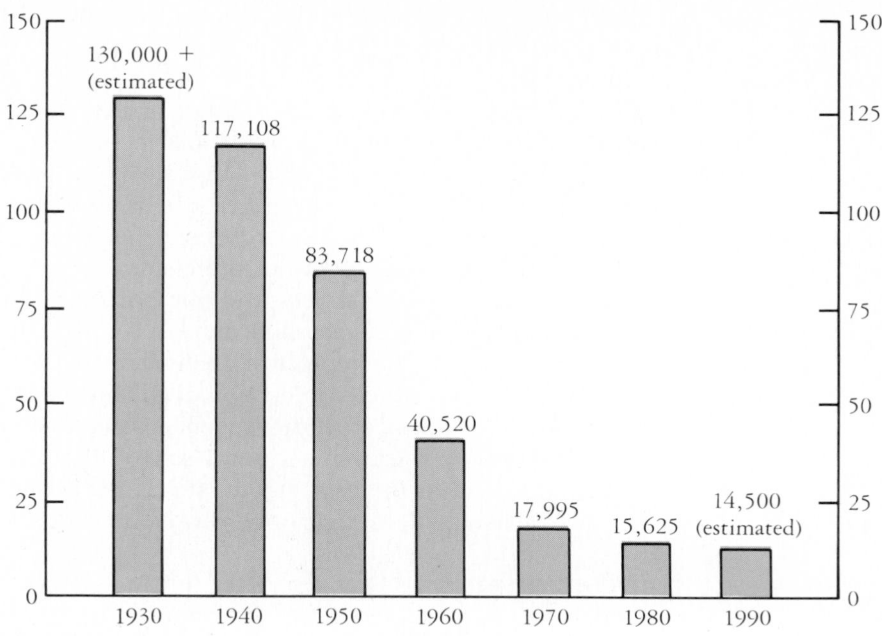

Figure 7.2
Declining Number of Public School Districts, 1930–1990

Source: *Digest of Education Statistics, 1979* (Washington, D.C.: National Center for Educational Statistics, 1979), figure 5, p. 62; table 58, p. 61; *Educational Directory: Public School Systems, 1980–81,* (Washington, D.C.: U.S. Government Printing Office, 1980), table 2; 1990 estimate is based on authors' projections after speaking with Dr. Vance Grant, director of the National Center for Educational Statistics, May 29, 1984.

Reasons for decentralization

sponses, were (1) to enhance school-community relations, (2) to provide greater community input at the local level, (3) to provide local schools with more field and resource personnel, (4) to provide efficient maintenance and support for local schools, (5) to reduce administrative span of control, (6) to provide greater linkages between local schools and the central school board, (7) to redirect spending for local school needs, and (8) to provide greater curriculum continuity, from kindergarten through grade twelve. These results closely correspond with the findings of other studies.[16]

Oddly enough, little evidence has been found to support these generalizations about decentralization. Very few of the school systems have conducted evaluations of their new organizational models or tested the assumptions, goals, and recommendations related to decentralization. There is little hard evidence that school decentralization improves education.

16 Mario D. Fantini and Marilyn Gittell, *Decentralization: Achieving Reform* (New York: Praeger, 1973); Passow, *Toward Creating a Model Urban School System;* Daniel U. Levine and Robert J. Havighurst, *Society and Education,* 5th ed. (Boston: Allyn and Bacon, 1979); and Don Davies, *Communities and Their Schools* (New York: McGraw-Hill, 1981).

Community Involvement

Increasing pressure from minority groups, accompanied by growing pressure for reform from educators, has played a part in forcing school authorities in many large school systems to seek additional ways to increase community involvement in the schools. What has emerged are the following, not mutually exclusive, community alternatives for governing metropolitan schools: community participation, community control, and community education.

Advisory committees

Community participation connotes the formation of advisory committees or groups beyond the usual parent-teacher associations. These committees may operate at various levels within the system—the local school or central level. The main function of these groups is to make recommendations (not policy) and to serve as a liaison between the schools and community. **Community control** connotes a legal provision for an elected community school board functioning under specific guidelines and in conjunction with the central school board. It means a sharing of decision-making authority and power between the local and central school boards; it also means that the powers of the professionals and central school board members are abridged and transferred to community groups. **Community education** changes the focus of school-community relations from the schools to a broader perspective (that is, education) and includes several cooperative educational extensions of the community. The idea envisions the schools as only one of many educational agencies within the community, and the notion of education is extended in both directions: from prekindergarten to the retired and elderly. School people, under this arrangement, share educational responsibilities with various community institutions.

Sharing of decision-making authority

Broadened view of education

Community Participation and Control

In New York City and Detroit a form of community control has evolved in which elected local school boards function in conjunction with the central school board. A far more frequent school-community arrangement has been some form of increased community participation with the appointment of advisory committees at either the neighborhood school or central board level. These committees are usually appointed by school officials; only in a few cases are the advisory groups elected by the community. Nevertheless, the committees are advisory, as their names suggest, and whenever guidelines are established, the school boards usually reaffirm their own authority and expectations that the advisory committees abide by the rules and regulations of the system.

Support for community participation

For the most part, school officials have encouraged community participation but have resisted any movement toward community control of schools. A survey of the 399 school systems that enrolled more than 15,000 students in 1975 showed that superintendents were much more positive about community participation (defined as input that involved giving advice on school policy) than about community control (defined as determining school policy).[17] They envisioned that community control entailed the for-

17 Harriet Talmage and Allan C. Ornstein, "School Superintendents' Attitudes Toward Community Participation and Control," *Educational Research Quarterly* (Summer 1976), pp. 37–45.

feiture of their perceived or actual decision-making power; furthermore, they perceived community participation as beneficial and in line with traditional school-community relations and community control as disruptive. They felt it carried the potential for overt hostility between different school-community factions. Researchers at the Institute for Responsive Education surveyed hundreds of examples of community participation and found nine general areas in which many citizen groups were providing advice and assistance to educators: (1) identification of goals, priorities, and needs; (2) budget analysis; (3 and 4) selection and evaluation of teachers and principals; (5) development of curricula; (6) extracurricular programs; (7 and 8) community support and financing for schools; and (9) recruitment of volunteers.[18]

Areas of community involvement

In another study of 1,270 parents and 3,700 teachers, it was found that the great majority of parents do not have time, or the inclination, to participate in school matters. Their involvement is limited to helping their children with homework or reading to their children (at the lower grades). More than 70 percent never helped teachers in the classroom or never participated in school functions. Only 4 percent of the parents surveyed were active, that is spending more than twenty-five days per year at the school or on school business.[19] In short, community participation and community control are not relevant issues to the vast majority of parents—suggesting that school-community problems or policies may be confined to a few educators and a few community activists.

Limited parental input

Controversies involving community control, and even community participation, have lain more or less dormant for the past few years, but they may come to prominence again if a serious community effort is made to reform or change public schools. When school officials are forced to confront the problem of making classrooms and schools more effective, they may look for ways to locate more authority and responsibility for solving instructional problems at the local level where the problems are manifested. Considering this prospect, David Selden has pointed out that for urban schools "any successful scheme of parent or community participation ... must take into account [that] most American cities are ... becoming mainly black, Hispanic, and Oriental," and this shift has implications for the political structure of schools (as well as the country). It seems that both schools and society "can best be served by forming a new coalition, based on mutual respect, between teachers and leaders of the new urban power structures."[20]

New coalition

Community Education Important trends suggest that we are entering a new stage of school-community relations. In the 1980s the school has come to be seen as one, but only one, of the educational agencies within the community. Museums, libraries, parks, businesses, private foundations, labor

Many educational agencies

18 Mary E. Stanwick, *Patterns of Participation* (Boston: Institute for Responsive Education, 1975).

19 Joyce L. Epstein, *Study of Teacher Practices of Parent Involvement* (Baltimore, Md.: Center for Social Organization of Schools, Johns Hopkins University, 1983).

20 David Selden, "The Future of Community Participation in Educational Policy Making," in C. A. Grant, ed., *Community Participation in Education* (Boston: Allyn and Bacon, 1979), p. 68.

unions, religious institutions, health care centers, and self-help groups, among others, perform important educational functions. The school serves as a partner—or possibly as a coordinating institution—in developing various community educational, social, recreational, and cultural activities.[21]

Because the school is part of a community educational system, it avoids fragmenting and duplicating services provided by other community agencies. The delivery system is open to all consumers: students, parents, childless adults, and aging populations.[22] The notion of lifelong education, and the education of diverse learners of various age groups, is an integral part of the notion of community education. In Flint, Michigan, for example, there are some fifty schools offering a host of educational, recreational, family, and community services to local citizens—including a wide range of preschool programs for three- and four-year-olds and their parents, as well as adult sports and drama, exercise, recreational, and vocational programs.[23]

Lifelong education

As part of the community education plan, schools share their personnel (such as teachers, counselors, and specialists) and facilities (such as portions of the building, yard, or stadium, and buses) with other community agencies; open their physical plant to a larger segment of the community; and offer programs and services to meet the growing needs of diverse population groups (such as working mothers, business people, and retirees). This sharing process takes place not only after school hours, on weekends or holidays, but also during school hours and school days—wherever underutilized space (say a conference room, auditorium, or pool), equipment, or personnel may be shared for a portion of the day. In return, the schools may expect to share in the facilities, equipment, and personnel of other community agencies—and may expect increased private and public support for their programs and people. This is especially important in a period of retrenchment and school budget cutbacks.

Needs of diverse groups

Each of the three community-involvement models has its proponents. Most educators advocate community participation because it allows them to retain power; moreover, they envision it as a method for encouraging parental support and participation in school matters. An increasing number of liberal and minority leaders, however, favor community control as a vehicle for transferring power to the community, or at least to people who claim to represent the community. The third option—community education—is relatively new, and only a few reform-minded educators speak of or write about this as an alternative form of community involvement.

A new option

In reality, there is little controversy over the first alternative, because most people, both defenders and critics of the schools, accept this community model. Many professional educators see a need for it because it increases community involvement while leaving their decision-making power intact;

21 Mario D. Fantini, Elizabeth L. Loughren, and Horace B. Reed, "Toward a Definition of Community Education," *Community Education Journal* (April 1980), pp. 11–33.

22 Allan C. Ornstein, "Redefining Parent and Community Involvement," *Journal of Research and Development in Education* (Summer 1983), pp. 37–45.

23 Ibid.

many critics accept it because they view it as a first step toward community control. The controversy concerns control: which group—elected public officials and professional educators, or community groups—will have the power and authority to run the schools. The issues are highly political and are related to issues of self-interest, group ideology, and the power of the purse strings. The third option, community education, arouses little concern or conflict since so few people have crystallized the concept, but it is likely to gain increasing support in the next few years as community groups seek to use underutilized schools for their own needs and interests and as educators seek new allies in their attempt to increase sources of school funding.

Intermediate Units

The term **intermediate unit** or **educational service agency (ESA)** refers to an office or agency in a middle position between the state department of education and local school districts. The intermediate unit is usually a legal and political extension of the state department of education, generally created by the state legislature. (A few intermediate units, those sponsored by local school districts, can only be viewed as an extension of the school districts.) As many as thirty-nine states had some form of intermediate units as of 1984. The average intermediate unit comprised twenty to thirty school districts and covered about fifty square miles. The number of intermediate units in a state ranged from two in Alaska, Idaho, and Missouri to fifty-eight in California and Michigan.[24]

Provision of support services

The intermediate unit or educational service agency provides coordination and supplementary services to local school districts and serves as a link between local and state educational authorities in most states. This pattern creates a legally constituted government relationship involving limited regulatory powers and providing support services to school districts. In a few states, however, the intermediate school district is formed by local school districts (not by the state) in a given area or region to provide common services; such districts lack legal, political, and financial support from the state.[25]

Intermediate units are being called on more frequently to regulate and enforce state mandates. In recent years, the intermediate unit has also provided school districts with a wide range of consulting services and resource personnel in such general areas of education as curriculum, instruction, evaluation, and in-service training. Intermediate units have also provided services in more specialized areas, such as education of the handicapped, gifted, and

24 Telephone conversation with William A. Firestone, Director of Research and Evaluation, Research for Better Schools, Philadelphia, February 28, 1984, and Robert Stephens, Professor of Educational Administration, University of Maryland, February 28, 1984. Also see William A. Firestone, Gretchen B. Rossman, and Bruce L. Wilson, *The Study of Regional Educational Service Agencies* (Philadelphia: Research for Better Schools, 1983).

25 Firestone, Rossman, and Wilson. *The Study of Regional Educational Service Agencies;* E. Robert Stephens, *Education Service Agencies: Status and Trends* (Burtonsville, Md.: Stephens Associates, 1979).

talented; bilingual education; prekindergarten education; vocational education; and data processing and computer education.[26] In 1980, 25 million students in 12,000 local school districts were receiving some kind of service from established intermediate units or educational service agencies. That year these agencies spent $1.7 billion for the purpose of improving public education.[27]

Reliance on grant money

Especially during the 1970s, many intermediate agencies actively sought outside funding as a way of expanding their services. In some cases, local educators became jealous of their growth, especially when district budgets were shrinking. Local educators felt that resources going to the intermediate units could have gone directly to their schools. Also, heavy reliance on short-term grants not only reduced the continuity in services and programs, it put these agencies in a difficult bind when cutbacks in educational funding became widespread.[28]

Many of these problems can be reduced, even eliminated by state action that defines more clearly the scope and functions of these intermediate units. Careful attention to the divergent expectations of all the parties who are interested in the work of intermediate units can ensure a constructive state-intermediate-local relationship. It is important that these intermediate units receive their money from the state and that it be allocated by the state legislature, not from other sources. Such funding will reduce tensions between them and local school districts. It is also important that the intermediate agencies serve the needs of the school districts and that local educators perceive those services as useful.

Another bureaucratic layer?

A number of other questions also arise. Since some states seem to get along without intermediate units, why can't the other states do the same? Are we not just creating another bureaucratic layer in the educational enterprise of the states? Is it possible that the functions of the intermediate units are not truly needed, that they are more relevant in rural America or where school districts are more diffuse?

On the other hand, we can argue that many small or financially strapped school districts today need the services of intermediate units; moreover, these services can be provided economically by serving several districts. To those who would have us consolidate these small or poor school districts, the supporters of intermediate units might reply that such arrangements diminish local control of schools and local identification of communities; inter-

26 Carolyn Moran and Larry Hutchins, "Intermediate Service Agencies and School Improvement," in S. McKibbin and M. Malkas, eds., *Dissemination and School Improvement in Education Organizations* (Berkeley, Calif.: Far West Laboratory, 1982), pp. 57–80; Stephens, *Education Service Agencies: Status and Trends;* and Robert K. Yin and Margaret K. Gwaltney, *Organizations Collaborating to Improve Educational Practice* (Cambridge, Mass.: Abt Associates, 1981).

27 *Educational Governance in the States: A Report Prepared by the Council of Chief State School Offices* (Washington, D.C.: U.S. Department of Education, 1983); Rae M. Levis, *The Education Service Agency* (Arlington, Va.: American Association of School Administrators, 1983).

28 Firestone, Rossman, and Wilson, *The Study of Regional Educational Service Agencies;* William A. Firestone, *The Politics of Technical Assistance: Regional Educational Service Agencies in their State Context* (Philadelphia: Research for Better Schools, 1983).

mediate agencies can provide support services to these school districts without any loss of local power.

One might argue that if school districts wish to remain independent they could develop a plan of cooperation without the intermediate unit. Actually a number of school districts have formed cooperative agencies without state regulations or mandates. One wonders, however, how many of these cooperative arrangements are properly staffed or financed or can continue without an outside party (state agency) ensuring financial support and a network of communication, research, and evaluation.

School cooperation

Finally, we cannot ignore the growth of metropolitan areas and their implications for educational organization. Many of the large city school districts are declining in student population, are growing more racially segregated, and are financially strapped. Although suburban communities are no longer the exclusive domain of white, middle-class people, they have grown in size. Many are still experiencing moderate increases in student populations; moreover, these school districts tend to be predominantly white and financially more stable than their adjacent city school districts. Reformers emphasize the need for a city-suburban or metropolitan relationship in education. In the future, the intermediate unit may become a more common metropolitan arrangement, imposed by the courts or state legislatures for purposes of school desegregation or fiscal prudence and to provide many functions and services. In fact, metropolitan arrangements are being organized in St. Louis and Milwaukee for purposes of desegregation, and the intermediate unit is expected to play a role with this new city-suburban school plan.

New metropolitan relationship

State Responsibilities and Activities

Every state, by constitution, statute, and practice, assumes that education is a function of the state, and federal and state court decisions have supported this interpretation. Each state has legal responsibility for the support and maintenance of the public schools within its borders. Local school boards, as we have seen, are considered creatures of the state that have been devised for the purpose of running a system of schools. Being responsible for the schools, the state enacts legislation; determines school taxes and financial aid to local school districts; sets minimum standards for the training, recruitment, and salaries of personnel; decides on the curriculum (some states establish "approved" textbook lists, too); makes provisions for accrediting schools; and provides special services (such as student transportation and free textbooks).

Legal responsibility for education

State school codes are a collection of laws that establish ways and means of operating schools and conducting education in the state. The state, of course, cannot enact legislation that is contrary to, or conflicts with, the federal Constitution. State statutes can be divided into two groups: *mandatory laws* that establish the minimum program of education and *permissive laws*

Mandatory and permissive laws

that define the functions that are delegated to the school district under appropriate conditions.

Although state constitutions and statutes may simply direct state legislators to provide for the establishment and maintenance of a uniform system of schools, provisions in many states are quite detailed concerning methods of operation. The typical state and local organization and relationship of education, and their respective hierarchy of responsibilities, are shown in Figure 7.3.

The Governor and State Legislature

Although the powers of governors vary widely, their authority on educational matters is spelled out in law. Usually a governor is charged with making educational budget recommendations to the legislature. In many states the governor has legal access to any accumulated balances in the state treasury, and these monies can be used for school purposes.

Powers of the governor

The governor can appoint or remove school personnel at the state level. These powers often carry restrictions, such as approval by the legislature. In a majority of states the governor can appoint members of the state board of education and, in a few states, the chief state school officer. A governor can kill educational measures through his or her veto powers or threaten to use the veto to discourage the legislature from enacting educational laws he or she opposes.

Powers of the state legislature

In most states, the legislature is primarily responsible for establishing and maintaining the public schools and has broad powers to enact laws pertaining to education. These powers are not unlimited; there are restrictions in the form of federal and state constitutions and court decisions. But within these parameters, the legislature has the full power to decide basic school policy questions in the state.

The state legislature usually determines how the state boards of education will be selected, what will be their responsibilities, how the chief state officer will be selected, what will be the duties of this office, what the functions of the state department of education will be, what types of local and regional school districts there will be, and what will be the methods of selection and powers of local school boards. The legislature usually decides on the nature of state taxes for schools, the level of financial support for education, and the taxing power for schools to be allocated on a local or municipal level. The legislature may determine what may or may not be taught, how many years of compulsory education will be required, the length of the school day and school year, and whether or not there will be community colleges and adult and vocational schools. The legislature may also determine staff and student policies and testing and evaluation procedures, authorize school programs, set standards for building construction, and provide various auxiliary services (for example, student transportation and school lunches). Where the legislature does not enact these policies, they are usually the responsibility of the state board of education.

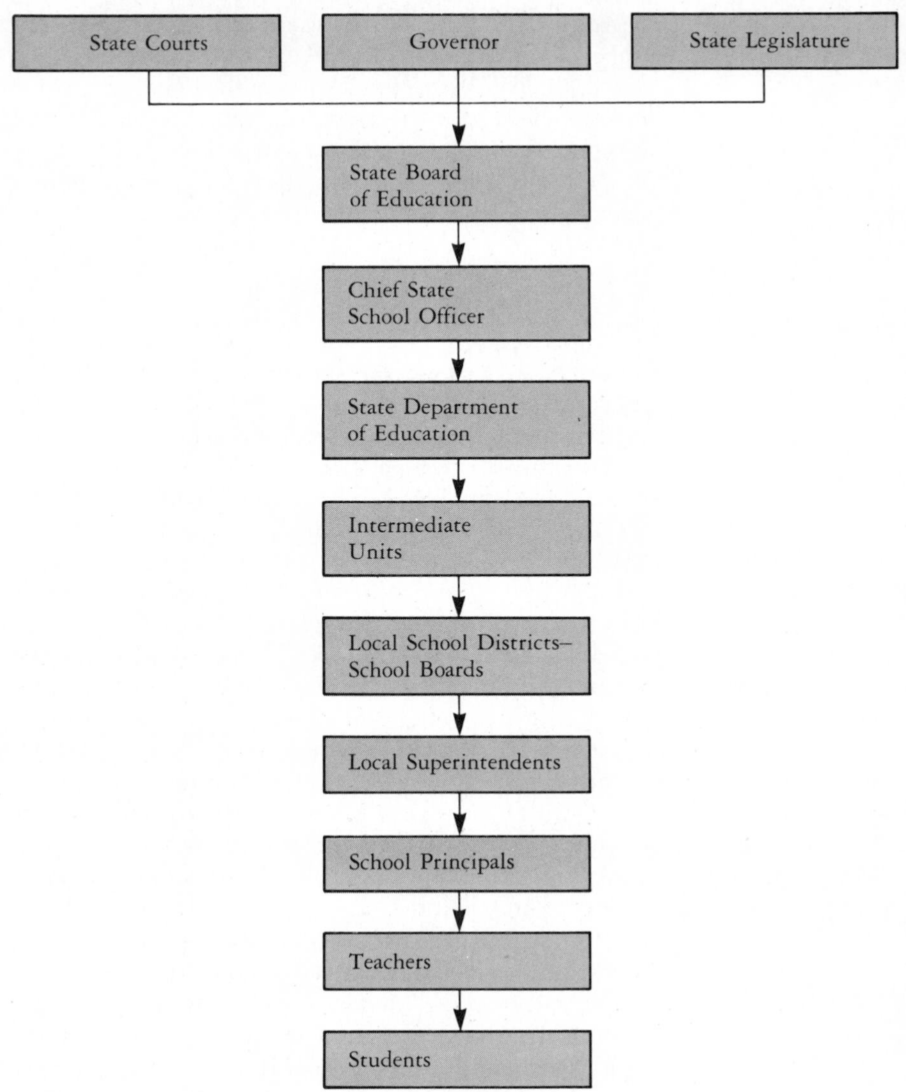

Figure 7.3
Structure of a Typical State School System

The nonpublic or private schools within a state are not exempt from the action of the legislature. General laws apply to private schools, including parochial schools. These laws pertain to health standards, building codes, welfare of children, student codes, and so on. Legislative bodies in many states have passed laws to benefit private schools and, at public expense, provide aid in such areas as student transportation, health services, dual enrollment

Laws affecting nonpublic schools

or shared-time plans, school lunch services, purchasing of books and supplies, student testing services, teacher salary supplements, student tuition, and student loans. Although the courts have generally held that the legislature has the right to pass laws providing for the supervision of nonpublic schools, rarely has a state legislature enacted comprehensive regulatory requirements—and where such laws do exist on the books they are not strictly enforced.

For either the governor or members of the legislature to formulate educational policy without consulting representative educators or the state education agency, and possibly representatives of private industry and pressure groups, seems to many to be an arbitrary and indefensible act. Both the governor and the legislature have available staff members and agencies to help them analyze and interpret data and can obtain additional information on matters of educational concern as needed.

State Board of Education

The state board of education is usually the most influential and important state education agency. Almost all states have some sort of state board of education, which is dependent on the state legislature for appropriations and authority and serves an advisory function for the legislature. (New York's Board of Regents is perhaps the strongest and most respected state board of education.) In addition, most states have a separate governing board for state colleges and universities; thus there are often two separate state boards, one for elementary and secondary education and another for higher education.

Two separate state boards

With the exception of Wisconsin, all states have boards of education. As of 1982, thirty-four were appointed by the governor of the state, thirteen were elected by popular vote (this method has increased during the last twenty years), and two were *ex officio* state boards. The number of members of state boards ranges from three in the state of Mississippi to twenty-seven in Texas, with a nine-member board occurring most frequently.[29] (An odd number of members eliminates tie votes.)

While state boards were originally dominated by white males, their composition has changed dramatically in the past two decades. A survey of board members conducted in 1967 showed that only 18 percent were women and 3 percent were minority.[30] A 1982 survey reveals the growing participation by women and minorities. As many as 34 percent of board members are women, and 16 percent are minorities. This trend toward greater heterogeneity is important, widening the perspectives of board members and insuring that boards reflect a wide range of social and educational concerns. Most board members tend to be older (88 percent are forty or older) and well

29 *Educational Governance in the States.*

30 Gerald Sroufe, *An Examination of the Relationship Between Methods of Selection and the Characteristics and Self-Role Expectations of State School Board Members* (Chicago: University of Chicago, Ph.D. diss., 1970).

Characteristics of state school board members

educated. Currently 99 percent have at least some postsecondary education, compared to 86 percent in 1967; 57 percent have a degree beyond the bachelors. The voluntary nature of service on a state board means, however, the members must have the time and resources to participate. As a result most board members who are in the workforce describe their occupation as "managerial" (25 percent) or "professional" (50 percent); and those not in the paid workforce are either retired (11 percent) or homemakers (12 percent) with a history of voluntary service.[31]

The precise duties and functions of state boards of education vary, but generally the boards are charged with the following functions.[32]

Duties of state boards of education

1. Adopting and enforcing policies, rules, and regulations necessary to implement legislative acts related to education
2. Establishing qualifications and appointing personnel to the state department of education
3. Setting standards for teacher and administrative certificates
4. Establishing standards for accrediting schools
5. Managing state funds earmarked for education
6. Keeping records and collecting data needed for reporting and evaluating
7. Adopting long-range plans for the development and improvement of schools
8. Creating advisory bodies as required by law
9. Acting as a judicial body in hearing disputes arising from state policies
10. Representing the state in determining policies on all matters pertaining to education that involve relationships with other agencies (including the federal government)
11. Advising the governor or legislature on educational matters
12. In some states, appointing the chief state school officer, setting minimum salary schedules for teachers and administrators, and adopting policies for the operation of institutions of higher learning

State Department of Education

Another major state education agency is the state department of education, which usually operates under the direction of the state board of education and is administered by the chief state school officer.

Traditionally, the primary function of state departments of education was to collect and disseminate statistics about the status of education within the state. Since the 1950s, they have enlarged their services and functions to include (1) accrediting schools, (2) certifying teachers, (3) apportioning funds, (4) overseeing student transportation and safety, (5) monitoring state

Functions of state departments of education

31 Dinah Wiley, *State Boards of Education* (Arlington, Va.: National Association of State Boards of Education, 1983), tables 1–2, pp. 15–16.

32 Stephen J. Knezevich, *Administration of Public Education,* 4th ed. (New York: Harper & Row, 1984); Morphet, Johns, and Reller, *Educational Organization and Administration.*

regulations, and (6) conducting research, evaluating programs, and issuing reports.[33] In the 1960s and 1970s, they expanded their functions to include (1) monitoring compliance with federal regulations and (2) identifying and improving programs to meet the needs of special students (in particular, disadvantaged bilingual and handicapped students who were targeted for these programs).

During this twenty-year period, the state departments had to grapple with controversial issues such as desegregation, compensatory education, student rights and unrest, school finance reform and fiscal crisis, aid to minority groups, declining enrollments, collective bargaining, accountability, and competency testing. During the 1960s and 1970s, the federal government, the courts, and active interest groups joined the fray and wrestled with many educational or school issues—forcing governors and legislators to increase the staff budget and functions of state departments of education.

State departments of education, once innocuous and invisible, doubled and tripled in size and assumed major new responsibility in administering complex programs (and policies).[34] By 1982, only six states (Delaware, Idaho, Nevada, South Dakota, North Dakota, and Wyoming) had professional staffs of fewer than 100, and six states (California, Connecticut, Michigan,

Professional staff

New Jersey, New York, and Texas) had staffs of more than 1,000.[35] Although some divisional administrators of these departments change with changes of political party control or with a change in the chief officer, the professional staff—such as the statisticians, secondary administrators, clerks, and secretaries—are usually civil service employees. By and large, staff members of the state departments of education are recruited from public school personnel and from local schools and colleges.

The leadership role of the state departments of education is expected to grow in the 1980s. The 1981 Education Consolidation and Improvement Act (ECIA) presents states with a broad number of options for spending federal monies allocated to the states. Not only did ECIA give the states more responsibility for determining how and where to spend federal money for education, but it also reduced federal funding—and thus put more importance on state funding. This trend is expected to continue into the mid-1980s, a part of the new federalism impacting on education.

Reduced federal funding has put added pressure on state departments to spend educational money wisely, to administer the state programs effectively, and to think about where they are going to get extra money to make up for the deficits created by the federal shortfall.[36] In addition, controversial issues in education will not go away, and public groups are becoming more

33 Knezevich, *Administration of Public Education;* Ornstein, *Education and Social Inquiry.*

34 Martha McCarthy, *A Delicate Balance: Church, State, and Schools* (Bloomington, Ind.: Phi Delta Kappa, 1983); Jerome T. Murphy, ed., *State Leadership in Education: On Being a Chief State Officer* (Washington, D.C.: George Washington University Press, 1980).

35 Knezevich, *Administration of Public Education;* Wiley, *State Boards of Education.*

36 Robert T. Golembiewski and Aaron Wildavsky, *The Costs of Federalism* (New Brunswick, N.J.: Transaction Books, 1984).

and more aggressive and astute in making their demands felt at the state level. In short, state departments of education must now provide real leadership and technical assistance to local school districts as well as to state boards of education, state legislators, and governors.

The Chief State School Officer

Chief executive

The chief state school officer (sometimes known as the state superintendent or commissioner of education) serves as the head of the state department of education and is also the chief executive of the state school board. He or she is usually a professional educator.

The office is filled in one of three ways: in 1982, five states filled the position through appointment by the governor; twenty-seven states through appointment by the state board of education, and eighteen states by popular election.[37] The duties of the chief state school officer and the relationship between that position and the state board and state department vary from state to state. They usually depend on whether the official was appointed or voted into office. Where appointed, greater dependence is likely; where elected, the chief officer tends to have more independence.

Because of differences in method of selection, and in the legal relationship between the state board of education and the chief state officer, the responsibilities of the chief state officer vary widely. However, the major responsibilities associated with the office are likely to include certain functions.[38]

Functions of the chief state school officer

1. Serving as the chief administrator of the state department of education and of the state board of education
2. Selecting personnel for the state department of education
3. Recommending improvements in educational legislation and educational budgets
4. Ensuring compliance with state educational laws and regulations
5. Explaining and interpreting the state's school laws
6. Deciding impartially controversies involving the administration of the schools within the state
7. Arranging for studies, committees, and task forces as deemed necessary to identify problems and recommend solutions
8. Reporting on the status of education within the state to the governor, legislature, state board of education, and the public

37 *Educational Governance in the States;* Morphet, Johns, and Reller, *Educational Organization and Administration.*

38 Ronald F. Campbell et al., *The Organization and Control of American Schools,* 4th ed. (Columbus, Ohio: Merrill, 1980); Jerome T. Murphy and David Crandall, *People, Policies and Practices: Examining the Chain of School Improvement* (Andover, Mass.: The Network, 1983); Ornstein, *Education and Social Inquiry.*

State Courts

State courts are subject to constitutional restrictions and may be overruled by federal district courts or the U.S. Supreme Court. Even though state courts may serve to set a precedent, decisions rendered in one state are not binding in another. Moreover, there are instances (in matters dealing with teacher tenure, teacher strikes, and student rights, for example) in which a decision in one state appears to be in conflict with a decision in another state. In spite of areas of apparent conflict, on major issues relating to control of schools there has been consistency among the state courts.

Education as state function

State courts have repeatedly held that public education is a function of the state and that the ultimate control of school affairs is vested in the lawmaking power of the state. The state courts have also made it clear that the state controls the schools for the fulfillment of the public good, not for the benefit of the individual. The state courts have also taken the position that a local school has no inherent powers of government, and its boundaries may be changed or its district abolished at the will of the state legislature, unless prohibited by the state constitution. State courts have upheld the power of the legislatures to levy taxes for school purposes, to confer upon other governmental units (municipalities, counties, towns, or school districts) such taxing power, and to allocate monies to schools.

The Federal Role in Education

The role of the federal government can be considered in four parts: (1) the federal agencies that promote educational policies and programs, (2) the growing trend that moves most educational decisions from Congress to the President's Office, (3) federal financing of education, and (4) the Supreme Court's decisions concerning education. Here we will focus on the first two parts. Federal spending will be examined in Chapter 8, and court decisions will be discussed in Chapter 9.

Federal Educational Agencies

Although many different federal agencies (about eleven departments and fifteen other agencies or units) are involved in some type of educational program or activity, the U.S. Department of Education is the major agency through which the federal government demonstrates its commitment to education.

The Department of Education When the Department of Education was founded in 1867, its commissioner had a staff of three clerks and a total of $18,600 to spend. From these humble beginnings the department has grown to about 4,800 employees and annual expenditures of more than $15.5 billion in 1984.[39] The department presently administers over 120 separate programs. Its budget has remained fairly constant in recent years, avoiding many of the reductions in federal education expenditures of the early 1980s.[40]

The original purpose of the department was to collect and disseminate statistics and facts and to promote the cause of education throughout the country. Even though it was known as the Department of Education, the commissioner was not a member of the president's cabinet. In fact, the department was attached to the Department of the Interior in 1868 and given the status and name of a bureau.

Department of Health, Education and Welfare

Enlarged responsibilities

In 1929, the title Office of Education was adopted, and ten years later the office was transferred to the Federal Security Agency. Then, in 1953, the Office of Education was transferred again, this time to the newly formed Department of Health, Education and Welfare. The Office of Education continued to perform its original functions, and additional responsibilities and program activities were added by various acts of Congress or by order of the president. In particular, it assumed new responsibilities of (1) administering grant funds and contracting with state departments of education, school districts, and colleges and universities; (2) engaging in educational innovation and research; and (3) providing leadership, consultative, and clearing-house services related to education.

Cabinet-level status

In 1979, after much congressional debate and controversy, a Department of Education was signed into law by President Carter, who declared that education was the "biggest single national investment" and that the creation of the department was the "best move for the quality of life in America for the future." A secretary of education was named, with full cabinet-level status, and the department officially opened in mid-1980.

The establishment of a Department of Education with full cabinet status had long been a goal of a number of professional organizations (especially the NEA). In theory, there now exists a person (the secretary of education) with widespread visibility and influence, who can exert persuasion and pressure in political and educational circles and who is in charge of educational policy and the promotion of programs to carry out those policies.

National Institute for Education (NIE) Established in 1972, its first budget, a modest $142 million for fiscal year 1973, turned out to be its largest. Initially organized within the Department of Health, Education and Welfare, it became part of the Department of Education in 1980. Its primary focus is on research and development in education, but it has had numerous problems getting off the ground. The early years for the NIE were difficult, for many senators and representatives were disappointed by the agency's lack of direction and action and by the general feeling that educational re-

39 Knezevich, *Administration of Public Education; The Fiscal Year 1985 Budget* (Washington, D.C.: U.S. Department of Education, 1984).

40 Ibid.

search has produced little of real value and that it has failed to improve schooling.

Loss of confidence in NIE

Its budgets have been repeatedly slashed below its requests. The NIE has lost the confidence not only of Congress and the Reagan administration but also of many educators and educational organizations. Many of its problems with the educational community involve lack of communication between researchers and practitioners, unfair competition for limited funds, and partisan agreements among favored institutions of higher learning and individuals.[41]

Future directions

It is hoped that the recent national concern over education will spill over to research in education and give an assist to the NIE. Manuel Justiz, the current NIE director, believes that the 1980s will emerge as a new period of stability and opportunity for the NIE to (1) provide leadership in educational research and development, (2) promote excellence and equality in education, and (3) translate research into practical benefits.[42] It is the hope of many educators, especially of the research community, that his visions are on target.

The New Federalism in Education

For most of the last two centuries federal support of education has increased steadily, albeit slowly. For the last two decades, there were dramatic increases in federal commitment to education. For many liberal and egalitarian groups, this increased federal activity was a welcome step.

Shift in federal policy

As we enter the 1980s, there has been a dramatic shift in federal policy. Driven by a belief that the federal government is too intrusive, President Reagan has reduced federal involvement, in terms of money, activities, and regulations—in education as well as in other sectors of society.

The new federalism, according to Jack Schuster, can be viewed in terms of three policy moves by the executive branch of government: (1) deregulation, the reduction of federal bureaucratic rules and regulations; (2) consolidation, the reduction of government proliferation of agencies and programs; and (3) cutbacks, the move to reduce social and educational spending.[43]

Reduced federal role in education

David Clark and his colleagues have analyzed the Reagan administration in terms of five policy shifts—or what they term the "five Ds": (1) diminution, reduction of federal expenditures in education; (2) deregulation, revocation of federal enforcement rules and regulations; (3) decentralization, the belief that the ills of education are related to federal intrusion into what should be a state or local responsibility; (4) disestablishment, limiting the

41 Richard Anderson, Lee Shulman, and William Cooley, "The NIE Centers and Laboratories," *Educational Researcher* (August–September 1983), pp. 13–14; Collen Cordes, "Political Pull Tips NIE Scale," *American Psychological Association Monitor* (January 1984), pp. 1, 14.

42 Manuel J. Justiz, "Emerging Themes and New Partnerships for the 1980s," *Educational Researcher* (August–September 1983), pp. 10–12.

43 Jack H. Schuster, "The Politics of Education in a New Era," *Phi Delta Kappan* (May 1982), pp. 583–591.

powers of the Department of Education and other federal agencies; and (5) deemphasis, the sum of the preceding aspects or the narrowing of the focus and scope of the federal role in education.[44]

What is evolving, then, are three basic and broad trends in federal educational policies for the 1980s. First, there has been a shift in priorities from human and social or educational concerns to business and military interests. It shows up in the Reagan administration's lack of formal policy regarding education and in the belief that the federal government should be involved less, not more, in the education of the nation's children and youth. Second, there is a reduction in federal funds for education; greater monetary and program responsibilities are being shifted to state (and local) agencies. Urban schools will probably suffer more than other schools because many states will distribute funds to local schools on a per child basis rather than on the basis of need. Moreover, nearly 16 percent of big-city school revenues came from Washington, as compared with the national average of 8 percent.[45] Third, there is the growing demise of egalitarianism as a national policy. It is evidenced in a reduction of programs for big-city schools, especially those for minority and low-income groups, and in an increase in federal programs that coincide with national need—say in areas of math and science education. Although the federal government's influence in schools has never been primary, it is expected to become more diffuse and decentralized than it has been in the past.

Reduced federal funding

Diffused and decentralized influence

Nongovernmental Influences on Public Schools

In addition to the agencies and offices that have been established by law to govern and administer public schools, there are also a number of other groups that influence decisions about the administration and operation of schools. Some of the groups seek to influence schools by shaping public opinion and the opinions of national policy makers. Others seek to put more direct pressure on school boards and state legislatures to achieve their goals. All share the belief that in a democracy public schools should be responsive to the views and goals of the community at large.

Pressures on school boards

Here is a brief summary of the important political influences and interest groups that have a significant effect on public education.

Increased interest in schools

1. *Political parties.* Both Republicans and Democrats at the national, state, and local level have exhibited growing interest in schools and have

44 David L. Clark and Mary A. Amiot, "The Reagan Administration and Federal Education Policy," *Phi Delta Kappan* (December 1981), pp. 258–262; David L. Clark, Terry A. Astuto, and Paula M. Rooney, "The Changing Structure of Federal Education Policy in the 1980s," *Phi Delta Kappan* (November 1983), pp. 188–193.

45 *Analysis of the Effect of the FY 82 and FY 83 Reagan Budget Proposals on Urban Schools* (Washington, D.C.: Council of the Great City Schools, 1982); Allan C. Ornstein, "Federal Funding: Frostbelt-Sunbelt Disparities," *High School Journal* (October-November 1983), pp. 46–54.

drawn educational institutions into complex social, political, and economic controversies.

2. *National and state commissions.* Commissions are influential because of their agenda, prominent members, and the publicity they often receive. There are many commissions devoted to various aspects of education, but the most influential ones tend to focus on problems or goals of education. Since the 1980s, these commissions have recommended upgrading schools and curricula, improving teacher quality, and raising student and school productivity.

3. *Pressure and lobbying groups.* Pressure groups in the United States number in the thousands. Many have as their primary interest something other than education, but they are willing to take strong stands on specific educational issues. Pressure groups that represent the extremes of the political spectrum, left or right, for example, are the most controversial. They are often willing to risk engulfing the schools in deep political or social conflict to advance their causes.

Promoting members' interests

4. *Professional groups.* Closely related to pressure groups are hundreds of professional and educational organizations that seek to promote the interests of their members. Among the influential groups are the National Education Association, American Federation of Teachers, Educational Commission of the States, National Association of State Boards of Education, National School Boards Association, National Chief State School Officers, American Association of School Administrators, and National Parent-Teacher Association. These groups exert a major influence on schools and teachers, and on educational policies in general, and they also help to establish professional standards and behavior that impact on education.

Selectivity in funding

5. *Private foundations.* While there are many different private foundations, with different goals and causes, some of the most influential ones in education are the Ford Foundation, Spencer Foundation, Kettering Foundation, Charles Stewart Mott Foundation, Carnegie Corporation, and Rockefeller General Education Board. These foundations, along with many others, tend to be sensitive to changing social and educational issues and selective in their funding patterns. Because of their large endowments and selectivity in funding, they are quite influential. Many fund programs are innovative and promote change, while others generally support social justice and equality of opportunity. In many cases, they assist in the funding of special task forces and committees, as well as research and publications, which have considerable impact on schools. During the Reagan administration, private foundations have been asked to make up for some of the federal cutbacks in educational funding; their response has been mixed and has reflected their own fiscal health and investment portfolios.

Impact on secondary schools

6. *Colleges and universities.* These institutions have a direct impact on the secondary schools in terms of program requirements, curriculum con-

tent, and college admissions—and an indirect effect on the elementary schools. The colleges' greatest influence has obviously been on that segment of the secondary school program to which high status has been attached, namely the college preparatory program (sometimes called the academic track).

Major curriculum source

7. *Textbook publishers and authors.* The influence of textbook companies remains strong—they are the major curriculum source for schools. To a lesser degree, individual authors influence schools and teachers; however, the content and tone of the narrative, the type of exercises and activities, even the pictures (if any) are primarily based on the criteria and decisions of the publishing companies.

8. *Testing companies and services.* Although many large textbook companies have a testing department and publish tests, the most noted testing companies are the nonprofit Educational Testing Service and the College Entrance Examination Board. The latter two organizations are national in scope and exert considerable influence on the curriculum throughout the country.

National Center for Education Statistics

9. *Opinion poll agencies.* Some opinion poll groups are independent organizations. Others are affiliated with colleges or universities, political organizations, or professional organizations. For many years, the NEA's research department, which surveyed teachers and schools about various professional issues, was very influential. Prior to the formation of the National Center for Education Statistics, it was the most important source of research on the status of the teaching profession. Today, the Center, which is now part of the U.S. Department of Education, collects and disseminates much more statistical information than does the NEA Research Division, but it does not, by itself, engage in opinion polls.

The Gallup organization is another source of public opinion about education, although it collects and reports results of attitudes about other issues and institutions as well. Since 1969 *Phi Delta Kappan* has published a nationwide survey conducted by the Gallup organization. The primary focus of the poll is public attitude, but beginning in 1973 a sample of professional educators was included among the respondents. The survey has been established as a major source of information on opinion in education matters, representing a nationwide sample based on approximately 2,000 adults each year and a cross-section of local school opinion. The survey is read by education leaders and administrators throughout the nation and by policy makers at all levels of government.

10. *Educational consultants.* These consultants work on a private for-profit basis; they serve as resource personnel, develop or evaluate programs, speak at professional or public meetings, and/or give testimony in court trials and legislative hearings. While they may work at various levels—local, state, regional, and national—those with the greatest influence provide knowledge and service to people who make legislative policy or judicial decisions.

11. *Research community.* Most researchers in education are members of the American Educational Research Association. Related to but often different from consultants, researchers have gained recent influence among policy makers and even media people who are concerned with important questions regarding education. An essential difference between a consultant and researcher is that the former may serve appropriately in the role of advocate, but the researcher—at least in the traditional sense—should be objective and present information without regard to political consequences. When the researcher limits or slants information, presents a point of view on paper or in public, promotes a position in some political or social debate, or gives advocacy testimony, that person is surrendering his or her role as researcher and has become a consultant (or advocate). That individual's research is value-laden, and the researcher is no longer impartial.

Objectivity vs. advocacy

12. *Citizen groups.* There are many different citizen groups, literally thousands, acting at various national, state, and local levels, whose policies and goals are as divergent as the groups themselves. While some citizen groups are independent and well-established organizations, the great majority come and go. Most are sponsored by an organization—some existing legislative committee, pressure group, or foundation. Most citizen groups in education make the public aware of its rights to participate in school affairs and its obligations to participate constructively; other groups are motivated by strong political and social convictions. Among the independent and influential citizen groups are the Council for Basic Education, Common Cause, and the now defunct National Citizen Council for Better Schools (founded by Omar Bradley, Harry S Truman, and James B. Conant among others). Most groups, however, don't last long enough to have major impact for an extended period. They are frequently issue oriented or organized around a political or social crisis that passes in time. Perhaps the most controversial citizen groups today are affiliated with censorship organizations, taxpayer organizations, and minority organizations. In the 1960s, community and antipoverty groups were particularly active, having evolved as part of the War on Poverty. Although most of these particular community groups no longer exist, many states and cities have encourged local community groups to convene over controversial issues such as school finance, accountability, desegregation, student discipline, and competency tests for teachers.

Summing Up

1. The enterprise of education is organized on various government levels—local, intermediate (in most states), state, and federal. Knowing about the formal organization of schools and the government relationship in which they operate is important to people who work in schools or who are studying to become teachers.
2. Schools are organized into school districts, and there are today approximately 15,000 public school systems—operating under a widely accepted system of laws, regulations, and customs.
3. While most small and rural school districts have consolidated their

schools since 1930, decentralization has been underway in large urban areas since the 1960s.
4. Three forms of community involvement are impacting on schools: community control, community participation, and community education. The first is the most controversial of the three alternatives.
5. Most states have an intermediate agency, which supports and has limited regulatory powers over local school districts.
6. With the exception of Wisconsin, all states have state boards of education. State departments of education operate under the direction of the state boards and are headed by the chief state school officer.
7. The federal role in education has dramatically increased for most of the past two centuries. The 1980s, however, witnessed reduced federal involvement in education.

Discussion Questions

1. How can teachers effect changes at the federal, state, and local levels of education?
2. What are the advantages and disadvantages of an elected or appointed state board of education? A local board of education?
3. Why have school districts consolidated? Why have they decentralized? What are the advantages and disadvantages of each trend?
4. Enumerate the ways in which community control, community participation, and community education differ. Which trend do you prefer? Why?
5. What are the arguments for and against the new federalism as it applies to education?

Suggested Readings

Davies, Don. *Communities and Their Schools.* New York: McGraw-Hill, 1981.
A fresh look into the current movement toward greater community participation and control of local schools.

Golembiewski, Robert T., and Aaron Wildavsky. *The Costs of Federalism.* New Brunswick, N.J.: Transaction Books, 1984.
An analysis of the new role of federal and state governments in various sectors of society, including education.

Kimbrough, Ralph B., and Michael Y. Nunnery. *Educational Administration,* 2nd ed. New York: Macmillan, 1983.
A broad overview of educational administration and the administrative hierarchy in American schools with emphasis on the role of the superintendent of schools and the local board of education.

Knezevich, Stephen J. *Administration of Public Education,* 4th ed. New York: Harper & Row, 1984.
A well-documented examination of past and current trends dealing with public school administration.

Morphet, Edgar L., Roe L. Johns, and Theodore L. Reller. *Educational Organization and Administration,* 4th ed. Englewood Cliffs, N.J.: Prentice-Hall, 1982.
An important work on the organization of American schools, which includes a detailed discussion of the role of federal, state, and local governments in the administration of public education.

8

Financing Public Education

Focusing Questions

What proportion of school revenues do the local, state, and federal governments contribute?

What is wrong with relying on property taxes as revenue sources for schools?

What fiscal problems characterize urban schools?

Why are there significant differences among and within states in spending for education?

How would you view the court's role in school finance reform?

How do block grants help (or hinder) school finance reform?

Will the taxpayers' revolt abate or snowball in the remaining 1980s?

How does public opinion about schools influence financial support of schools?

EDUCATION IN THE UNITED STATES IS BIG BUSINESS, REPRESENTing annual expenditures of over $100 billion for public elementary and secondary education since 1980 and about 7 percent of the nation's annual gross national product (the value of all goods and services produced in the United States).[1] Because most school-related costs (except salaries) have increased more rapidly than inflation between 1975 and 1982,[2] the business of schooling is in deep financial trouble. Indeed, there is no longer any guarantee that all the nation's schools will be able to open up on time in September and finish the full school year and still pay all their bills.

Number one problem

Since the mid-1970s the people who are closest to the problem of school financing—that is, school board members—have consistently ranked "lack of financial support" as the number one challenge facing them.[3] This ranking should come as no surprise; board members have to watch the bottom line. In an era of increasing inflation, declining enrollments, and taxpayers' resistance to higher price tags for education, the people responsible for financial decisions are very sensitive to expenditures and capital outlays.

Major revenue sources

There are three major sources of revenue or financial support for public schools: the local, state, and federal governments. State and local money remains the basic source of revenue for public education. Table 8.1 shows that although revenues from federal sources steadily increased from 0.4 percent in 1929–30 to a high of 9.8 percent in 1979–80, they are now decreasing. The relative decrease in the federal contribution is expected to continue. In contrast, contributions by the states have rapidly increased from a low of 16.9 percent in 1929–30 to 47.4 percent in 1980–81. Estimates are that these revenue sources will increase to 52.3 by 1985—making up for federal and local shortfalls in revenues. Local revenue sources have steadily decreased from a high of 82.7 percent in 1929–30 to the low of 43.3 percent in 1980–81. It is expected that local revenue contributions will continue slightly downward on a national level, especially in large urban areas that are under financial pressure and in some suburban areas where the aging population contains fewer school-age children.

Tax Sources of School Revenues

The operation of public schools relies primarily on revenues generated from taxes, especially the property tax on the local level and sales and income taxes taxes on the state level. Some kinds of taxes are considered better than oth-

1 *Digest of Education Statistics, 1982* (Washington, D.C.: National Center for Education Statistics, 1982), table 16, p. 23; *Digest of Education Statistics, 1983–84* (Washington, D.C.: National Center for Education Statistics, 1984), tables 62–63, pp. 77–78.

2 *Inflation for Schools and Colleges* (Washington, D.C.: National Institute of Education, 1983).

3 "Sixth Annual Survey of School Board Members," *American School Board Journal* (January 1984), pp. 24–27, 40.

Table 8.1
Revenue Receipts of Public Elementary and Secondary Schools by Government Source, 1929–30 to 1984–85

	Amount in Thousands of Dollars				**Percentage of Total School Revenues**		
School Year	*Total*	*Federal*	*State*	*Local*	*Federal*	*State*	*Local*
1929–30	$ 2,088,557	$ 7,334	$ 353,670	$ 1,727,553	0.4	16.9	82.7
1939–40	2,260,527	39,810	684,354	1,536,363	1.8	30.3	68.0
1949–50	5,437,044	155,848	2,165,689	3,115,507	2.9	39.8	57.3
1959–60	14,746,618	651,639	5,768,047	8,326,932	4.4	39.1	56.5
1969–70	40,266,923	3,219,557	16,062,776	20,984,589	8.0	39.9	52.1
1979–80	96,880,944	9,503,537	45,348,814	42,028,593	9.8	46.8	43.4
1980–81	105,904,908	9,808,007	50,207,192	45,809,709	9.3	47.4	43.3
1984–85[a]	146,500,000	10,841,000	76,619,500	59,039,500	7.4	52.3	40.3

[a]Estimates for 1984–85 are based on last two sources below.

Source: *Digest of Education Statistics, 1982* (Washington, D.C.: National Center for Education Statistics, 1982), table 66, p. 75; *Digest of Education Statistics, 1983–84* (Washington, D.C.: National Center for Education Statistics, 1984), table 62, p. 77; Gregory B. Mills and John L. Palmer, "The Deficit Dilemma," *Urban Policy and Research Report* (Fall 1983), tables 1–2, pp. 5–6; Telephone conversation with Vance Grant, Director of the National Center for Education Statistics, March 20, 1984.

Criteria for evaluating taxes

ers. Most people today accept several criteria for evaluating various types of taxes. Most commonly mentioned are the following four:

1. *A tax should not cause unintended economic distortions.* It should not alter economic behavior, change consumer spending patterns in favor of one good or service for another, negatively affect a taxpayer's willingness to work, or cause the relocation of business, industry, or people.
2. *A tax should be equitable.* It should be based on the taxpayer's ability to pay. Those with greater incomes or with property worth more money should pay more taxes than those with less income or less desirable property. Taxes that are not equitable and that require lower-income groups to pay a higher proportion of their income than higher-income groups are called *regressive* taxes.
3. *A tax should be collected easily.* This requires that the tax be collected with minimum costs to the taxpayer or government; it also means that it should be difficult to evade and without loopholes.
4. *The tax should be responsive to changing economic conditions.* During inflation (when government costs and expenditures rise), the tax revenue should also rise; in a recession, the tax revenue should decrease.[4] Responsive taxes are *elastic;* those that are not responsive are *inelastic.*

4 Donald E. Orlosky et al., *Educational Administration Today* (Columbus, Ohio: Merrill, 1984).

Local Financing of Public Schools

Although education is the responsibility of the states, traditionally they have delegated this to local school districts. As indicated earlier, the local contribution to school financing has decreased over recent years while the state contribution has increased. Nevertheless, local funding remains a crucial part of public school financing.

Property Tax

The property tax is the main source of revenue for the local school district, accounting for more than 90 percent of local revenues. It is the most important tax supporting education. The property tax has a long history in this country, having been used since the colonial period. Although a property tax is difficult to evade, the tax creates economic distortions because it tends to discourage rehabilitation of deteriorating properties, especially in inner cities where property taxes are often too high in relation to the market value of the property. It can also cause economic distortions by affecting business decisions with regard to locating plant or office sites.

Long tradition

The property tax does not rate well on the criterion of equity, either. Because of different assessment practices and lack of uniform valuation, people owning equivalent properties may pay different taxes. This results in unequal treatment of equal property. The property tax does not always distribute the tax burden according to the ability to pay. A retired couple may have a home whose market value has increased substantially, along with their taxes, but because they live on a fixed income they cannot afford the increasing taxes. In this respect, it can be argued that the property tax is regressive.

Regressive

In addition, the property tax is not immediately responsive to changing economic conditions. In some states property taxes are reassessed every one to two years, but in others reassessments occur only every three to four years. Thus, a property's assessed valuation and actual tax are often based on old market conditions. If property values have risen since the last reassessment, then the municipal government is losing potential tax income; if property values have decreased, property taxes may be overburdensome, causing a declining neighborhood to deteriorate further.

Finally, the property tax is not always easy to collect. Collection depends on the efficiency of the local tax collection department. Wealthy individuals and businesses who contest their property taxes often receive abatements.

Local Resources and Disparities

Most states specify the basic minimum property tax rate that local school districts can levy. An increase in the tax rate beyond this minimum is common but usually requires voter approval at the local level. Since the mid-1970s,

Despite state and federal efforts to aid poorer school districts, a school's ability to provide its students with an elaborate extra-curricular program or the latest word in educational technology still depends largely on the wealth of the community that it serves.
(Charles Gupton/ Southern Light)

local school districts have had difficulty getting voter approval for raising property taxes.

Large differentials in resources

Helpful as state and federal aid is to most school districts (see Table 8.1), the differential ability of school districts to support education still persists. A school district located in a wealthy area or an area with a broad tax base can obviously generate more revenue from property taxes than can poor school districts. As a result, in the majority of states today, the difference in the total expenditures per student is frequently two to four times as great in the five wealthiest school districts compared to the five poorest school districts.[5] These variations exist among communities in every state, and they tend to be growing wider between cities and the suburban areas adjacent to them. This trend is more apparent in the Northeast and Midwest, due to the flight of urban populations and businesses to the suburbs and Sunbelt states.

Alarmingly high taxes

Fiscal Problems of City Schools Most city property taxes are alarmingly high, about 30 percent higher per capita than taxes in adjacent suburbs. In order to stay competitive (in order to hold onto or attract middle-class residents or businesses), the cities are unable to raise property taxes for schools and other public services. The situation is worse in Frostbelt cities. Local

5 See John Coons, "A Decade After Rodriguez," *Phi Delta Kappan* (March 1983), pp. 479–480; Susan G. Foster, "School Funds Matter," *Education Week*, March 21, 1984, p. 7; David C. Long, "Rodriguez: The State Courts Respond," *Phi Delta Kappan* (March 1983), pp. 481–484.

taxes there are 70 percent higher on average than in Sunbelt cities (with the exception of a few high-need cities such as Miami, Atlanta, and Oakland).[6] Without question, high property taxes make it difficult to attract middle-income residents and new jobs to broaden the tax base. As the cities lose their mobile population and businesses, their tax base is further undermined. They are forced to cut city services, including education, to balance their budgets; these cuts drive away more mobile persons and businesses and more tax revenues. The cycle reinforces itself, which is one reason for the decline of urban schools. Midway through the 1980s, financing has become the major problem for city schools, and recommendations for cutting costs and reducing wasteful programs policies have become important issues.[7]

Diminishing tax base

Cities are plagued by what is commonly called municipal overburden, or severe financial demands for public functions due to population density and the high proportion of disadvantaged and low-income groups. The result is that the large cities cannot devote as great a percentage of their total tax revenues to the schools as suburban and rural districts can. For example, in the mid-1970s, New York City, Buffalo, and Rochester spent less than 30 percent of all local tax revenues for school purposes, while the rest of the state was able to spend 45 percent of its local taxes for schools.[8]

Educational overburden

Then there is the issue of educational overburden. A large percentage of the student population in city schools is in technical, vocational, and trade programs, which cost more per student than the regular academic high school program. Similarly, there is a greater proportion of special-need students—namely bilingual, handicapped, and disadvantaged students—in the city schools than in suburban or rural schools. These students require remedial programs and services, which cost 50-100 percent more per student than basic programs.[9] Moreover, the need for additional services tends to increase geometrically with the concentration of poverty.[10] City schools, therefore, have to spend more educational resources per student than a similar-size school district or group of school districts comprising middle-class students.

Finally, city schools tend to have a greater proportion of senior teachers at the top of the pay scale than their suburban counterparts. Many suburban districts have as a matter of policy replaced many experienced teachers to

6 Allan C. Ornstein, "The Urban Setting: Frostbelt/Sunbelt Differences," *Phi Delta Kappan* (October 1982), pp. 102–107; *The President's National Urban Policy Report, 1980* (Washington, D.C.: U.S. Department of Housing and Urban Development, 1980).

7 Allan C. Ornstein, "Urban Education for the 1980s: Trends and Issues," *Phi Delta Kappan* (April 1982), pp. 516–518.

8 "A Defeat for the Finance Reform Movement," *Education Week*, August 18, 1982, p. 17; Joan Scheuer, "Levittown v. Nyquist: A Dual Challenge," *Phi Delta Kappan* (February 1979), pp. 432–436.

9 Roe L. Johns, Kern Alexander, and Edgar L. Morphet, *The Economics and Financing of Education*, 4th ed.(Englewood Cliffs, N.J.: Prentice-Hall, 1983); Ann M. Miline and Jay Moskowitz, "State Experiences with Special Needs Students" (Paper presented at the annual meeting of the American Educational Research Association, Montreal, April 1983).

10 Daniel U. Levine and Robert J. Havighurst, *Society and Education*, 6th ed. (Boston: Allyn and Bacon, 1984); Miline and Moskowitz, "State Experiences with Special Needs Students"; Joseph F. Murphy and Walter E. Hack, "Fiscal Problems of Central-City Schools," *Urban Review*, No. 4 (1983), pp. 229–244.

Higher operating costs

save money. They have also experienced a high turnover of pregnant female teachers who did not return to the teaching profession. Cities have higher vandalism costs per school, lunch costs, desegregation costs, insurance costs, and maintenance costs (their buildings are older than suburban buildings) than other schools within the state. Both city and rural school districts spend more than suburban districts on transportation.[11]

State Financing of Public Schools

As we noted in Chapter 7, the state is primarily responsible for and has jurisdiction over public schools. Over the years the states have delegated many powers and responsibilities to local school districts; nevertheless, each state remains legally responsible for educating its children and youth. Since many local school districts are having trouble financing their schools through property taxes, states will probably assume greater financial responsibility for and control over the schools.

State Revenue Sources

Sales and personal income tax

The sales tax and personal income tax are the two major sources of revenue for states. Since states currently pay over 50 percent of the cost of education, these two taxes are important elements in the overall support of public education.

Sales Tax As of 1982, as many as forty-five states had statewide sales taxes, with such taxes making up approximately 30 percent of state revenues.[12] Measured against the four criteria for evaluating taxes, the sales tax rates fairly high. It may cause some economic distortions, however, where the difference in the tax rates makes it worthwhile to travel to the low-tax state to purchase expensive items.

Despite this distorting effect, the sales tax meets the criterion of equity if food and medical prescriptions are removed from the tax base. If the tax is placed on all goods, however, low-income groups are penalized since they spend a large portion of their incomes on basic goods such as food and drugs.

Easy to administer and collect

The sales tax is easy to administer and collect; it does not require periodic valuations or entail legal appeals (as the property tax does) by owners or corporations who feel their taxes are too high. The burden of collection is put on the retailer according to actual sales figures. A problem does arise

11 Johns, Alexander, and Morphet, *The Economics and Financing of Education;* Murphy and Hack, "Fiscal Problems of Central-City Schools"; Joel D. Sherman, "The Prospects for Funding Schools with Revenues Match Resource Requirements" (Paper presented at the annual meeting of the American Educational Research Association, Montreal, April 1983).

12 Orlosky et al., *Educational Administration Today; Survey of Current Business* (Washington, D.C.: U.S. Department of Commerce, 1983), table 1, p. 48.

with interstate sales, however, because the state cannot levy a tax on sales to be delivered outside the state or easily collect the tax on purchases made by its residents in another state.

Elastic

The sales tax is elastic, since the revenue derived from it tends to parallel the economy. The trouble is, when the state (or nation) is in a recession, sales tax revenues decrease sufficiently to reduce the state's income.

Personal Income Tax The personal income tax is the second largest source of tax revenue for the states, representing more than 25 percent of state revenues in 1982. Only six states do not levy a personal state income tax.[13] Just as the sales tax rate varies among states, from 2 to 8 percent, the state income tax (based on a percentage of personal income) also varies.

A properly designed income tax should cause no economic distortions.

Equitable

Assuming no loopholes, it rates very high in terms of equity. In theory, the personal income tax is supposed to reflect the taxpayer's income and ability to pay. The income tax is also more equitable than other taxes since it considers special circumstances of the taxpayer, such as dependents, illness, moving expenses, and the like, and uses tax deductions or credits to take into account these variations among individuals. It becomes less equitable only if the taxpayer has many properties or other items that can be depreciated so as to minimize his or her income tax.

Easy to collect

The personal income tax is relatively easy to collect. In most cases, the tax is collected through payroll deductions before the taxpayer receives his or her salary. On the other hand, tax evasion is a problem in the United States, although the use of computers has made evasion more difficult.

The personal income tax is very elastic; it allows the state government to vary rates (if it wishes) according to the economy. On the other hand, the elasticity of the income tax makes it vulnerable to recession, since the revenue derived from it declines at a faster rate than revenue from other tax sources.

Other State Taxes Other state taxes contribute limited amounts to education. These taxes include (1) excise taxes on motor fuel, liquor, and tobacco products, (2) motor vehicle license taxes, (3) the estate and gift taxes, (4) and severance taxes (on the output of minerals and oils).

Excise tax

The excise tax on motor fuel is the third largest source (approximately 9 percent) of state tax revenue, but is designated for highway construction and maintenance; it cannot be used to finance education.[14]

State lotteries

There is a growing trend to establish state lotteries to support education in many of the fifteen states where lotteries currently exist. Although this was a major purpose of the early lotteries, funds have been diverted to meet other social priorities, such as geriatric care, social welfare agencies, and

13 Ibid.

14 Donald E. Orlosky, *Educational Administration Today; State Support for Education, 1982–1983* (Denver, Colo.: Augenblick, Van de Water & Associates, 1983).

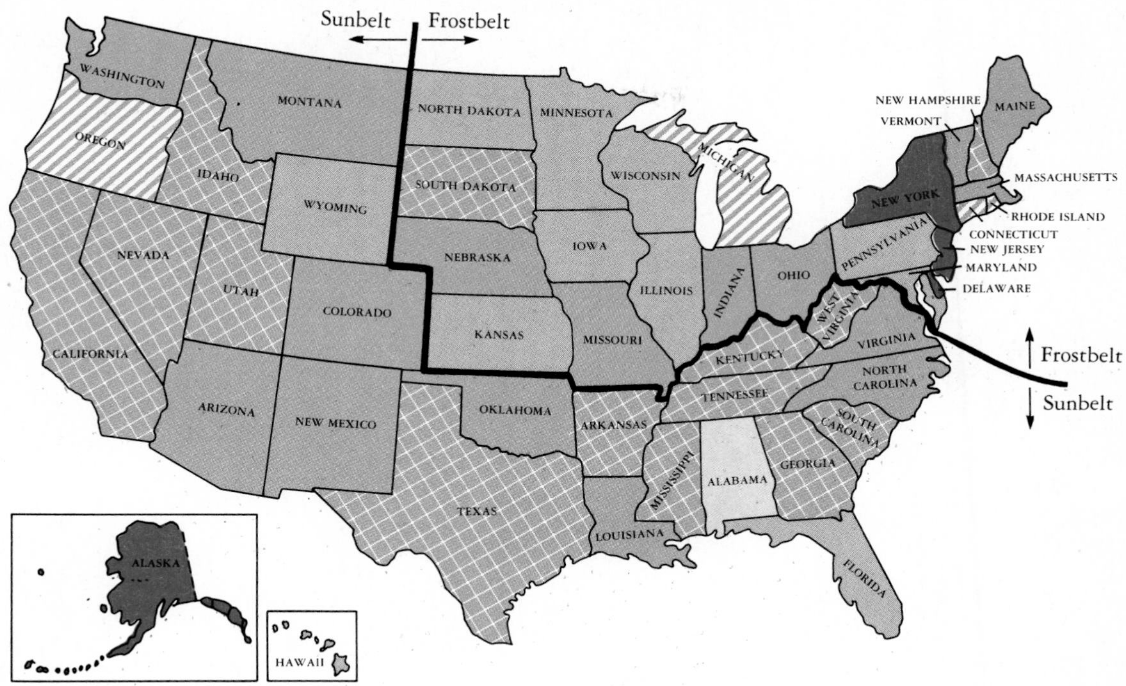

State Expenditure per Student

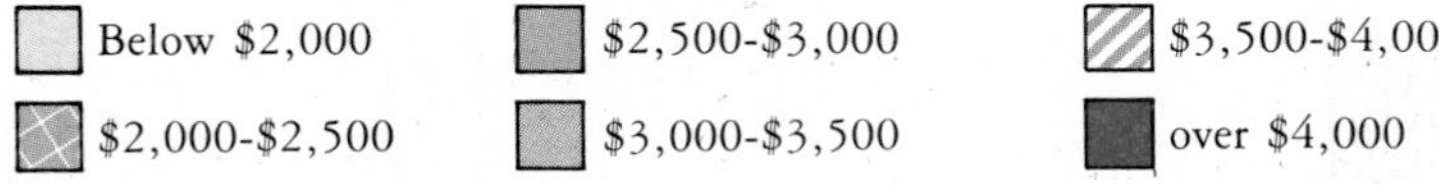

Figure 8.1
State Education Expenditures per Student, 1982–83

Source: *Digest of Education Statistics, 1983–84* (Washington, D.C.: National Center for Education Statistics, 1984), table 63, p. 78. Note: State education expenditures are calculated on the basis of average daily student attendance.

road construction. The result is that in most states, the lottery contributes less than 2 percent of the states' total revenue for education.[15]

The Ability of States to Finance Education

Geographic accident

Some students are more fortunate than others—simply by geographic accident. State residence has a lot to do with the type and quality of education received. In 1982–83, as shown in Figure 8.1 and Table 8.2, Delaware, New

15 *Providing Incentives in the Allocation of State Aid for Schools* (Denver, Colo.: Augenblick, Van de Water & Associates, 1984).

Table 8.2
Revenues and Expenditures of States for Public Education

	Percentage of Revenue Receipts Distributed for Public Education, 1980–81			State Expenditure per Student, 1982–83[a]	State Expenditure as Percentage of Per Capita Personal Income, 1982
	Federal	*State*	*Local*		
50 states and D.C.	9.3	47.4	43.3	$2,917	*2.6*
New England (Northeast)					*2.9*
Connecticut	6.2	29.4	64.4	3,746	2.7
Maine	9.0	47.8	43.2	2,651	2.9
Massachusetts	5.9	36.3	57.8	2,958	3.3
New Hampshire	5.3	6.1	88.6	2,341	1.9
Rhode Island	8.7	32.9	58.4	3,792	3.5
Vermont	7.4	28.4	64.2	2,940	3.1
Mideast (Northeast)					*3.2*
Delaware	11.3	66.3	22.4	4,008	3.4
Maryland	8.2	40.5	51.3	3,486	2.8
New Jersey	6.1	38.8	55.2	4,190	3.2
New York	7.1	39.1	53.8	4,302	3.5
Pennsylvania	8.9	44.0	47.1	3,290	3.0
Great Lakes (Midwest)					*2.9*
Illinois	7.1	38.5	54.4	3,201	2.7
Indiana	6.4	53.0	40.6	2,672	2.7
Michigan	7.0	35.8	57.2	3,648	3.3
Ohio	8.5	42.4	49.1	2,807	2.6
Wisconsin	6.6	37.2	56.2	3,421	3.2
Plains (Midwest)					*2.6*
Iowa	6.1	39.1	54.9	3,147	2.9
Kansas	6.2	43.6	50.2	3,094	2.6
Minnesota	5.7	56.6	37.7	3,157	2.8
Missouri	9.6	40.9	49.5	2,587	2.5
Nebraska	8.7	23.2	68.1	2,605	2.4
North Dakota	11.0	44.3	44.7	3,055	2.8
South Dakota	13.0	27.7	59.3	2,386	2.5
Southeast (South)					*2.5*
Alabama	16.6	60.4	23.0	1,546	1.8
Arkansas	16.6	48.5	34.9	2,093	2.5
Florida	10.3	55.4	34.3	3,009	2.7
Georgia	13.9	55.1	31.0	2,369	2.5
Kentucky	16.0	64.0	20.0	2,193	2.5
Louisiana	12.7	53.1	34.3	2,529	2.5
Mississippi	24.3	56.7	19.0	2,076	2.7
North Carolina	14.0	62.8	23.2	2,680	3.0

Table 8.2 *(cont.)*
Revenues and Expenditures of States for Public Education

	Percentage of Revenue Receipts Distributed for Public Education, 1980–81			State Expenditure per Student, 1982–83[a]	State Expenditure as Percentage of Per Capita Personal Income, 1982
	Federal	*State*	*Local*		
South Carolina	18.0	48.2	33.9	2,016	2.4
Tennessee	15.6	40.6	43.7	2,124	2.4
Virginia	10.3	41.0	48.7	2,740	2.5
West Virginia	9.5	60.0	30.5	2,480	2.8
Southwest (South)					*2.6*
Arizona	12.9	50.2	36.9	2,603	2.6
New Mexico	15.0	65.4	19.7	2,904	3.2
Oklahoma	13.6	56.6	29.8	2,792	2.5
Texas	11.1	48.4	40.5	2,299	2.0
Rocky Mountain (West)					*2.6*
Colorado	5.9	38.7	55.3	2,986	2.4
Idaho	10.3	57.8	31.9	2,110	2.3
Montana	9.8	44.6	45.6	2,981	3.1
Utah	8.1	53.0	38.9	2,128	2.4
Wyoming	5.5	33.2	61.3	3,467	2.8
Far West (West)					*2.8*
Alaska	9.5	73.5	17.0	6,620	4.1
California	10.1	65.8	24.1	2,490	2.0
Hawaii	15.8	84.1	0.1	3,213	2.8
Nevada	7.2	56.0	36.8	2,311	1.9
Oregon	8.4	30.8	60.8	3,643	3.6
Washington	8.9	72.4	18.6	2,887	2.5

[a] Calculated on the basis of average daily attendance.

Source: *Digest of Education Statistics, 1983–84* (Washington, D.C.: National Center for Education Statistics, 1984), table 63, p. 78; *Estimates of School Statistics, 1982–83* (Washington, D.C.: National Education Association, 1983), table 1, p. 8; *Survey of Current Business* (Washington, D.C.: U.S. Department of Commerce, Bureau of Economic Analysis, August 1983), table 1, p. 48.

Jersey, and New York spent more than $4,000 per student (calculated on the basis of average daily attendance) and Alaska spent over $6,000. Arkansas, Idaho, Kentucky, Mississippi, and Tennessee, in contrast, spent barely $2,000 per student. For Alabama, the figure was $1,546.

It is incorrect to assume that the education priorities of some states are twice as high as the priorities of other states. The fact is, we must ask what the states can afford, and this has a lot to do with the personal incomes of the states' inhabitants. For Mississippi, the expenditure represented 2.7 per-

State per capita personal income

cent of state per capita personal income. On the basis of comparative economics, Mississippi spent more on education than twenty-three other states, and it was above the national average of 2.6 percent. For Arkansas and Kentucky, these expenditures represented 2.5 percent of state per capita personal income, and these expenditures represented a greater percentage than eleven other states—including such wealthy states as California and Texas.

Two additional points are worth noting. Table 8.2 shows that the Northeast and Midwest, with the exception of New Hampshire, spend a greater percentage of their state personal income on education than do other regions of the country. Ten years ago, it was not uncommon for the majority of states to spend 5 percent or more of their personal income on education.

Drop in education spending

In 1982–83, the table shows, the best fourteen states could boast 3 to 4 percent. This drop in expenditures represents a real loss and reflects the taxpayers' revolt that started in the mid-1970s.

State Aid to Local School Districts

States use four basic methods to finance public education. Some states combine more than one method.

Oldest, simplest, and most unequal

1. *Flat grant model.* This is the oldest, simplest, and most unequal method of financing schools. State aid to local school districts is based on a fixed amount multiplied by the number of students in attendance. It does not consider the special needs of students (bilingual students are more expensive to educate than native English-speaking students), special programs (vocational programs are more expensive than regular programs), or the wealth of the school districts (wealthy school districts have more money to spend on students or schools than do less wealthy school districts).

In most states the distribution of education funds is based on some type of equalization plan designed to provide extra money for less wealthy school districts. The remaining three methods each seek to bring about greater equality of educational opportunity by allocating more funds to the school districts in greatest need of assistance.

2. *Foundation plan.* This is the most common approach, and its purpose is to guarantee a minimum annual expenditure per student for all school districts in the state, irrespective of local taxable wealth. However, the minimum level is usually considered too low by reformers, and wealthy school districts far exceed the minimum levels.

3. *Power-equalizing plan.* This is a more recent plan, and many of the states have adopted some form of it. Under this scheme, the state pays a percentage of the local school expenditures in inverse ratio to the wealth of the

Inverse ratio to wealth

district. Although the school district has the right to establish its own expenditure levels, wealthier school districts are given fewer matching state dollars. The program is constrained by lower and upper limits, and the matching dollars are insufficient for poor school districts. In the end, the equalization effect is usually insufficient.

Student characteristics and programs

4. *Weighted student plan.* Students are weighted in proportion to their special characteristics (that is, handicapped, disadvantaged, and so forth) or special programs (for example, vocational or bilingual) to determine the cost of instruction per student. For example, a state may provide $2,500 for each student in a basic program, while the state contribution per student may be 1.5 times higher or $3,750 for vocational education and 2 times higher or $5,000 for a handicapped student.

The Courts and School Finance Reform

Efforts to use state funding to equalize educational opportunities among school districts within a state have been spurred by a series of court decisions that have fundamentally changed the financing of public education in most states.

The 1971 landmark decision in *Serrano* v. *Priest* radically altered the way California allocated education funds. California, like nearly all the states, depended on local property taxes to support the schools, and plaintiffs argued that this system of financing resulted in unconstitutional disparities in expenditures between wealthy and poor school districts. The California Supreme Court agreed, stating the following: "We have determined that ... [the California] funding scheme invidiously discriminates against the poor because it makes the quality of a child's education a function of the wealth of his parents and neighbors."

Following the *Serrano* decision, more than thirty similar cases were filed in other states. One of these, *San Antonio Independent School District* v. *Rodriguez,* was taken to the U.S. Supreme Court after a federal court ruled that school finance arrangements in Texas were unconstitutional. By a five-to-four vote, the Supreme Court ruled in 1973 that expenditure disparities based on differences in local property taxes between school districts in a state were not unconstitutional under the federal constitution but might be unconstitutional under state constitutions, depending on the situation and the wording of the laws in a given state. The *Rodriguez* decision placed the issue of inequities in school finance in the hands of the state courts and legislatures.

Since *Rodriguez,* a number of state courts have ruled that financial arrangements that result in large disparities in per pupil expenditures based on wealth differences between school districts are unconstitutional, and state legislatures in these and other states have enacted new laws designed to reduce or eliminate such disparities. In 1976, for example, the California Supreme Court's *Serrano II* decision reaffirmed its earlier finding that large financial disparities between districts are unconstitutional under the equal protection clause of the state constitution. In doing so, the court observed that "there is a distinct relationship between cost and the quality of educational opportunities afforded."

More than twenty states have reformed their school finance laws since *Rodriguez*. The state share of public school revenues has increased in these states from an average of 43 percent in 1973–74 (when *Rodriguez* was decided) to 51 percent in 1982–83 and now provides substantially more money to poorer school districts. Even where the state courts did not directly force a particular reform, the threat of a potential lawsuit altered the political landscape and somewhat narrowed the gap between rich and poor school districts.[16]

Setbacks

The school finance reform movement has also suffered some serious defeats. In 1982 the New York State Court of Appeals ruled in *Levittown* v. *Nyquist* that any attempt to make uniform all local property tax rates would undermine local control of schools and that the system of supporting schools through property taxes had a "rational basis."[17] The court also rejected the notion that the state had a constitutional obligation to take into account the higher noneducational expenditures of urban areas—their municipal overburden and educational overburden.

A 1984 New Hampshire decision was also a serious setback to the school finance reform community. In *Jesseman* v. *State of New Hampshire,* the plaintiffs claimed that the average per student expenditures ranged from $900–$1,000 in poor school districts to $4,000 in wealthy school districts. The state contributed the lowest proportion of state aid to local schools in the nation; only about 6 percent of the schools' total revenue comes from the state, compared with a national average of 47 percent.[18] Consequently, the state was helping to perpetuate inequality of opportunity by permitting wide disparities in student expenditures.

Proving cause and effect

The high court in New Hampshire refused to hear the case on the basis that the plaintiffs did not prove that these expenditure differences had an impact on student achievement. The high court returned the case to the lower superior court and asked it to address the question of whether building conditions, equipment, teachers' salaries, and so on, make a difference in students' academic achievement. The court's order will result in substantial delay. The plaintiffs will probably not be ready to argue their case until the late 1980s because of the massive volume of records and statistical information needed to make their case in the lower court.

Limits to local control

In short, legal challenges to state laws governing school finance have been varied and outcomes have been mixed. In most cases, the courts have not found that the concept of local control justifies discrimination against children in low-wealth school districts. As a matter of law, the courts have viewed education to be a *state* function (unlike other public services such as

16 David L. Kirp, "Education," *New Republic,* March 31, 1982, p. 31; David L. Kirp and Donald N. Jensen, "The New Federalism Goes to Court," *Phi Delta Kappan* (November 1983), pp. 206–210.

17 "A Defeat for the Finance-Reform Movement."

18 Susan G. Foster, "N. H. High Court Refuses School-Aid Case Pending Ruling on Merits," *Education Week,* March 7, 1984, p. 5.

police, fire, and sewer departments, which are considered to be local functions) whereby school districts *assist* the state in carrying out its constitutional obligation to provide a free public education to all children.[19]

Many state courts have ruled that inequalities in educational expenditures are unconstitutional under the equal protection provisions of the state constitution. In other states, however, the courts have decided that education is not a fundamental right under the state constitution; therefore, some inequalities can exist. In addition, some courts have held that local control and local differences in property tax rates are permissible and necessary for purposes of separation of powers. As for municipal and educational overburden, this argument has taken on greater importance as cities lose their financial base (due to the exodus of middle-class residents and businesses) and find themselves hard pressed to raise taxes.

Not a fundamental right

Federal Educational Funding

Until the middle of the twentieth century, the federal government gave very little financial assistance to the states (or local schools) for the education of American students. This attitude was in line with the majority belief that the federal government should have little to do with education and that education is a state responsibility. One might characterize federal programs and activities as passive and uncoordinated during this period. This is not to say that the federal government had no influence on American education. National laws and federal programs had a significant impact on the way education developed in the United States. We will be discussing the most important of these programs in the pages that follow. But what must be kept in mind is that these programs and acts were uncoordinated; they were not part of a broadly conceived national plan for education. After 1957, however, as national policy became more closely linked to education, federal funding dramatically increased and steadily involved specific educational targets. This growth in federal funding came to a halt in the 1980s under President Reagan.

Education a state responsibility

Uncoordinated policies

National policy and education

History of Federal Aid to Education

Grants for Schools The Northwest Ordinances of 1785 and 1787 are the first instances of federal assistance to education. The Northwest Ordinance of 1785 divided the Northwest Territory into townships and each township into thirty-six sections; it reserved the sixteenth section "of every township for the maintenance of public schools within the said township." The Ordinance of 1787 stated that "schools and the means of education shall forever be en-

A school for every town

19 Thomas J. Flygare, "School Finance a Decade After Rodriguez," *Phi Delta Kappan* (March 1983), pp. 477–480.

couraged" by the states. The federal government thus recognized its commitment to education and its willingness to advance its cause, while assuring the autonomy of state and local schools. As a result of these ordinances, thirty-nine states received over 154 million acres of land for schools from the federal government.[20]

Grants for Colleges Seventy-five years were to pass before another major federal educational program was enacted. This program involved institutions of higher learning, not elementary and secondary schools. In the Morrill Act of 1862, federally owned lands totaling 30,000 acres were set aside for each state, with the provision that the income from the sale or rental of these lands be used to establish colleges for the study of agriculture and mechanical arts. A total of 6 million acres of federal lands were given to the states. These "people's colleges" or land-grant institutions were to become the great multipurpose state universities that now enroll students from all segments of society. The Morrill Act demonstrated that the federal government would take action in education for the good and welfare of the nation; it also marks the beginning of any meaningful federal influence on higher education.

Morrill Act

Vocational Education Acts The third phase of federal activity in public education came with the conditional grants for highly specific purposes in public secondary schools. The Smith-Hughes Act of 1917 provided money grants for vocational education, home economics, and agricultural subjects. The original act called for federal appropriations to be matched by state or local educational agencies. It was extended by various acts between 1929 and 1968.

Smith-Hughes Act

The 1917 federal vocational act marked the federal government's first annual appropriations for public secondary education. At one time federal funds accounted for nearly 50 percent of the expenditures for vocational education. Nevertheless, the 1963 federal vocational act appropriated $235 million for vocational training, quadruple the annual appropriations of the original Smith-Hughes Act; by 1970 it exceeded $500 million annually, and by 1980 it was more than $850 million.[21]

Great Depression

Relief Acts The fourth phase of federal activity emerged during the Great Depression. Federal interest in schools at that time was only incidental to the greater concerns for the welfare of unemployed youth, from ages sixteen to twenty-five. The Civilian Conservation Corps (CCC) was organized in 1933 for unemployed males, seventeen to twenty-three. More than half of the youth who joined had never finished grade school, and a substantial number were practically illiterate. The act provided federal appropriations for the education and vocational training of more than 3 million youth until it was

20 Ellwood P. Cubberley, *Public Education in the United States,* rev. ed. (Boston: Houghton Mifflin, 1934).

21 *The Condition of Education, 1983* (Washington, D.C.: National Center for Education Statistics, 1983), table 3.8, p. 152.

abolished in 1943. Almost a generation passed before the CCC idea was brought back as a part of the Job Corps in the mid-1960s.

Other federal programs of the depression era included the National Youth Administration (NYA), 1935, which provided welfare and training programs for unemployed youth ages sixteen to twenty-five, as well as financial aid for needy students attending secondary schools and colleges; Federal Emergency Relief Administration (FERA), 1933, which allocated funds for the employment of unemployed rural teachers; Public Works Administration (PWA), 1933, and Works Progress Administration (WPA), 1935, both of which provided federal money for school plant construction and repairs, amounting to 30 to 45 percent of the national allocation of funding of new schools from 1933 to 1938. All federal relief agencies were terminated by 1940. Although some educators were concerned about possible federal domination of public schooling during the 1930s, these fears subsided and the communities that had participated in these programs were in a better position to meet the classroom shortage that occurred after World War II.[22]

World War II

War Acts The fifth phase of federal activity took place during World War II and the immediate postwar period. Three major bills were passed at this time.

1. The Lanham Act (1941) provided aid for construction and maintenance of local schools in areas where military personnel resided or where there were extensive federal projects.
2. The Occupational Rehabilitation Act (1943) provided educational and occupational assistance to disabled veterans.
3. The Servicemen's Readjustment Act (1944), commonly called the G.I. Bill, provided funds for the education of veterans and enabled hundreds of thousand of Americans to attend institutions of higher learning or special training schools.

G.I. Bill

The benefits of the G.I. Bill were extended to the Korean and Vietnam conflicts. Direct aid, totaling more than $10 billion, has helped more than 500,000 veterans to attend institutions of higher learning or special training schools. The G.I. Bill, along with the baby boom, was a major factor in the growth and expansion of American colleges, including community colleges.[23]

Sputnik

National Defense Education Act The Cold War and the Soviet launching of Sputnik in 1957 increased pressure for better American schools and federal funding. This led to the sixth phase of federal education legislation, particularly the National Defense Education Act (NDEA) of 1958. The act

22 Henry J. Perkinson, *Two Hundred Years of American Educational Thought* (New York: McKay, 1976).

23 Wellford W. Wilms, "Vocational Education and Job Success," *Phi Delta Kappan* (January 1984), pp. 347–350.

spelled out the importance of education to the national defense, and funding was earmarked for educational programs that enhanced "the security of the nation . . . and [developed] the mental resources and technical skills of its young men and women."

The rather broad act emphasized improvement of instruction in science, mathematics, foreign languages, and other critical subjects; provided college and university student loans and scholarships; funded numerous teacher training programs, including those for teaching the disadvantaged; stimulated guidance and counseling programs; and promoted curriculum reform and programs in vocational and technical education. By 1960, the federal government was spending nearly $240 million annually on NDEA programs; in the mid-1960s the act was extended to include history, geography, English, and reading as critical subjects.[24]

Compensatory Education Acts The 1960s and 1970s ushered in two egalitarian movements, the War on Poverty and the civil rights movement. Domestic issues replaced foreign issues as the number one concern for the nation as the seventh phase of federal activity evolved. National policy became linked to education, as the government targeted specific groups, namely minorities and the poor, and specific policies, for improving their educational opportunities. The federal government took on an active and coordinated posture with reference to education, as it substantially increased its contributions to a variety of targeted programs and increased its regulations over specific policies.

Elementary and Secondary Education Act

The most important act of this period was the Elementary and Secondary Education Act (ESEA) of 1965, part of President Lyndon Johnson's "Great Society." It focused on compensatory programs for the disadvantaged student, immediately providing $1 billion for the first year. In 1981, at the height of its funding, monies totaled $3.5 billion or about $300 per disadvantaged child; from 1965 to 1981, $30 billion had been appropriated.[25] (Appropriations for the disadvantaged dropped in the mid-1980s to about $3 billion per year, reflecting general cutbacks in education by the federal government.)

Desegregation and Minority Groups From the mid-1960s through the 1970s, the full force of the federal government came into play to enforce U.S. Supreme Court decisions on school desegregation, first in the South and then in the North and West. The impetus came from the Civil Rights Act of 1964, which provided that all programs supported by federal funds—including those allocated to public education—must be administered and operated without discrimination. If clear evidence of intent to desegregate and to operate in a nondiscriminatory fashion was not provided, all federal funds were

24 Daniel Tanner and Laurel Tanner, *Curriculum Development: Theory into Practice,* 2nd ed. (New York: Macmillan, 1980); Paul Woodring, *The Persistent Problems of Education* (Bloomington, Ind.: Phi Delta Kappa, 1983).

25 *Digest of Education Statistics, 1982,* table 153, p. 171; Allan C. Ornstein, *Education and Social Inquiry* (Itasca, Ill.: Peacock, 1978).

Withholding federal funds

to be withheld. Federal guidelines and enforcement procedures were developed and generated intense activity during the 1970s.

Groups defining themselves as minorities also received considerable attention, federal funding, and preferential treatment in schools and jobs from the mid-1960s to the late 1970s, reflecting political pressure and the egalitarian movement. Groups targeted for special programs and additional funding were bilingual students, Native American students, blacks, low-income (inner-city and migrant) groups, women, and handicapped students. During the 1980s, under the Reagan administration, programs and funding for minority groups received considerably less emphasis.

Federal Aid to Education in the 1980s

In recent years there has been a new conservatism at the federal level. Federal spending for education declined in actual and real dollars (taking inflation into consideration, see Table 8.3) and changed from **categorical grants** (funds for specific groups and designated purposes) to **block grants** (funds for a general purpose without precise categories).

Education Consolidation and Improvement Act

Categorical grants were an important feature of federal involvement in education during the 1970s. But Chapter 2 of the Federal Education Consolidation and Improvement Act (ECIA) of 1981 replaced categorical grants for twenty-eight separate education programs with one block grant that state and local education agencies could use for broadly defined educational purposes.

Table 8.3
Federal Funds for Education, 1960–1984

Year	Amount (billions)	Year	Amount (billions)
1960	$ 1.7	1974	$13.1
1962	2.1	1976	19.6
1964	2.8	1978	21.6
1966	5.8	1980	25.6
1968	7.9	1982	23.1[a]
1970	9.2	1984	20.3[a,b]
1972	11.9		

[a]As a result of the Education Consolidation and Improvement Act in 1981, many programs and funds were shifted among various federal departments; the base of comparison is not exactly the same.

[b]The 1984 estimates are based on the *Fiscal Year 1985 Budget,* and telephone conversations with Esther Tron, Senior Research Specialist, National Center for Education Statistics, March 1, 1984.

Source: *Digest of Education Statistics, 1980* (Washington, D.C.: National Center for Education Statistics, 1980), table 160, pp. 184–186; *Digest of Education Statistics, 1982* (Washington, D.C.: National Center for Education Statistics, 1982), table 153–54, pp. 171–172; *The Fiscal Year 1985 Budget* (Washington, D. C.: U.S. Department of Education, 1984), pp. 6–9.

(Categorical grants for bilingual and handicapped students were saved.) This move must be seen as part of the new federalism, which shifted some forty federal social, education, and public programs from the national to the state governments.

Observers cite a number of advantages of the block grant approach for education programs.

1. Much of the flood of federal regulations and paperwork requirements that have become synonymous with federal aid to education has ceased. In the past, it was necessary to submit multiple applications, consisting of about 20 to 30 pages for a $50,000 program and about 50 to 60 pages for a $100,000 program. The application took a great deal of time and involved several administrative employees. Now, under Chapter 2, the states require only that a single, simple application, usually containing no narrative, be completed once a year.

Simplified procedures

2. School districts no longer have to compete with one another for their shares of federal funds. Instead, the funds are distributed by formula to any school district that submits an application. In the past, some school districts had become very skillful at preparing proposals for categorical funding, while many school districts competed unsuccessfully or chose not to compete. The outcome was that many school districts were unable to gain access to resources afforded by those programs.

3. Prior to consolidation, a school district that was particularly active in competing for federal funds might have received money from several different agencies in the Department of Education and from its own state education agency (SEA). A local school district is now required to interact with only the Chapter 2 office within the SEA.

Lower administrative costs

4. Under the old system, an unnecessary bureaucracy of quasi administrators grew up in many large school districts, which added to the administrative costs of the school district. Much of the busy-work related to formulating objectives, conducting need assessments, and submitting monthly progress reports, quarterly financial reports, semiannual reports, and annual reviews has been eliminated. The system of record keeping—reporting, monitoring and evaluation—has been simplified dramatically, as have the time and costs attendant on those procedures. Now, many administrators can be returned to the classroom or moved to another post to better serve the school district; personnel and money spent on the bureaucracy of federal funding can be eliminated.[26]

A key disadvantage of the block grant approach is that many states may not pick up the programs turned over to them by the federal government.

26 Richard F. Elmore, "Differential Treatment of States in Federal Education Policy," *Peabody Journal of Education* (Fall 1982), pp. 34–52; Anne H. Hastings, "Snipping the Strings: Local and State Administrators Discuss Chapter 2," *Phi Delta Kappan* (November 1983), pp. 194–198.

The states do not have to continue the programs they assume; they can use the money for similar programs or simply eliminate the function and use the funds for other purposes. While this gives the states additional flexibility and enhances local discretion, big-city school districts believe the federal government began providing services and programs in the first place because states did not accept those responsibilities.

In reality, it is likely that urban schools will suffer more than other schools under the block grant approach because many states will distribute funds to local schools on a per child basis rather than on the basis of need. Moreover, nearly 16 percent of big-city revenues came from Washington, as compared with the national average of 8 percent, before the block grants went into effect.[27]

Council of Great City Schools

Members of the Council of Great City Schools (a coalition of the twenty-eight largest urban school districts) reported a shrinkage in federal funds from $1.64 billion in 1980–81 (before block grants went into effect) to $1.27 billion in 1982–83, or 23 percent of the school districts' federal monies. For this two-year period, cities such as Baltimore, Buffalo, Cleveland, Milwaukee, Minneapolis, New York, Philadelphia, Pittsburgh, St. Louis, and Seattle lost 33 to 50 percent of their federal funds for education.[28]

Using recent events as a yardstick, it appears that the amount and form of federal aid for education will change. The Reagan administration has made a concerted move to reduce educational spending and to shift responsibility of schools to the state. While federal aid historically has been categorical, especially from the late 1950s to the 1970s, the block grant concept has changed the format of funding and has provided states with flexibility to make decisions about certain programs that were once funded by the federal government.

New flexibility for the states

It is clear that the federal government, at present, supports the notion of local control and state responsibility for education. Thus, inequalities of school finance are unlikely to be adjusted through federal involvement or aid.

School Finance Trends in the 1980s

The great era of court-mandated school finance reform in the 1970s coincided with a period of apparent national prosperity and economic expansion. The fiscal situation changed markedly during the early 1980s, when most states experienced severe budgetary problems and American consumers lowered their expectations in terms of the houses and cars they bought and their

27 Allan C. Ornstein, "Federal Funding: Frostbelt-Sunbelt Disparities," *High School Journal* (October–November 1983), pp. 46–54.

28 *Analysis of the Effect of the FY 82 and FY 83 Reagan Budget Proposals on Urban Schools* (Washington, D.C.: Council of the Great City Schools, 1982); Ornstein, "Federal Funding; telephone conversations with Michael Cassery, Legislative and Research Associate, Council of Great City Schools, Washington, D.C., October 22, 1982, and March 22, 1984.

Conservative mood

standard of living in general. The public mood grew conservative, and taxpayers were no longer interested in spending more money for schools.

As we examine the trends impacting on school finance and as we try to determine the outlook for financing the schools during the remaining 1980s, we should keep in mind that equal educational opportunity is no longer the key issue that it was in the 1960s and 1970s. Today the key words are *excellence, performance standards, selectivity,* and *economic priorities*. At the very least, educators are being forced to show proof of direct relationships between increased spending and student results.

The Taxpayers' Revolt

A tax revolt swept the country in the late 1970s and early 1980s. It put a damper on the school finance reform movement that was working through the courts. The most important result of the tax revolt nationally was that it induced states to reduce taxes by legislative means between 1978 and 1982. In 1978 and the two years that followed, thirty-two states reduced their personal income or general sales tax by increasing tax exemptions, lowering tax rates, or providing a rebate. Most of these state tax reductions were accompanied by limits on local spending or rates. Twenty-five of these state reductions in taxes were still in effect in 1984.[29] More than half of the states now have limits on property taxes or other revenue sources that are used for school spending.[30]

Limits on property tax

The most dramatic and well-known illustration of the taxpayers' revolt occurred in California in 1978 when Proposition 13 was passed. Proposition 13 limits the amount the state can obtain as a source of revenue for schools; it sets a maximum tax of 1 percent on the fair market value of the property and limits the growth of assessed valuations to 2 percent per year. A similar measure was passed in Idaho in 1978, and in Massachusetts in 1980. (The Massachusetts measure was called Proposition 2½ because it limited property tax levies to 2½ percent of the fair market value.)

Propositions 13 and 2½

Another product of the tax revolt movement was that it inhibited states from raising their taxes; tax increases became politically "unthinkable" in most states. When states were plagued by revenue shortfalls in the early 1980s, their most frequent response was to cut spending rather than to raise taxes. More than forty states chose to reduce spending to avoid budget deficits and/or to balance the budget. As a result, between 1979 and 1982 real revenues (revenues that take inflation into consideration) allocated for education dropped in thirty-five states.[31] As the economy improved in 1983 and

Tax increases become "unthinkable"

29 Stephen D. Gold, *State Tax Increases of 1983: Prelude to Another Tax Revolt?* (Denver, Colo.: National Conference of State Legislatures, 1984).

30 Stephen D. Gold, *State Revenue and Spending Limitations* (Denver, Colo.: National Conference of State Legislatures, 1983).

31 *A Changing Federalism: The Condition of the States* (Denver, Colo.: Education Commission of the States, 1982); Gold, *State Tax Increases of 1983;* Chris Pipho, "Upswing in the Economy and the Public Mood Sets the Stage for the 1984 Legislative Sessions," *Phi Delta Kappan* (December 1983), pp. 237–238; Chris Pipho, "Governors Provide Leadership for Education," *Phi Delta Kappan* (March 1984), pp. 445–446.

1984, there was some additional money for education, but states were and still are faced with some difficult choices among competing interests for state funds.

Still another by-product of the tax revolt movement was the public's demand to cut costs in education by consolidating schools, shortening the school week, increasing classroom size, eliminating teaching and administrative positions, and keeping a lid on teacher salaries. There are many special interest groups today who still wish to cut school spending. This is not only true in deficit-plagued states, but also in states with a high proportion of aging adults and in states that do not have a tradition of spending much money on education.

Deficit-plagued states

Future Predictions Although the deficiencies of the public schools received wide attention in the mid-1980s and the demand for reform in education is real, there is only so much money to go around. A number of states are likely to raise taxes to help the schools, and states showing a surplus will be hard-pressed to resist appeals to increase school spending. But the interests of taxpayers and various special interest groups will influence how and where money is spent. There will always be political pressure to reduce taxes, and some states will certainly opt for this choice.

There are other political and financial considerations to keep in mind as one tries to predict whether taxes and state revenues will increase in the future:

Possible new demands for tax relief

Possibility for tax increases

1. Based on past trends, measures entailing a large tax reduction are more likely to be rejected by voters than measures that limit future tax increases. The public does not favor major service cuts, which would be likely if taxes were sharply reduced.
2. If taxes are perceived as being "out of control," as they were in the late 1970s and early 1980s, the odds for another tax revolt increase. The tax increases of the mid-1980s may precipitate a new clamor for tax relief.
3. When a state surplus exists, voters feel that they can reduce taxes without losing services.
4. Finally, resistance to taxes is greater when the taxpayers' standard of living is declining. This contributed to the tax revolt of the late 1970s and early 1980s, where first inflation and then recession decreased the real income of most Americans. If the economy experiences sustained growth in the late 1980s, the environment for increasing taxes and, also, school spending will be favorable. If stagnation resumes, taxpayer resistance should also resume.[32]

Thus, forecasts in regard to school spending for the remaining 1980s are mixed and largely depend on the economic health of each state and the up-

32 J. Citrin, "Do People Want Something for Nothing? Public Opinion on Taxes and Government Spending," *National Tax Journal* (June 1979), pp. 113–129; Gold, *State Tax Increases of 1983;* Chris Pipho, "An End to the Tax Revolt—Maybe!" *Phi Delta Kappan* (January 1984).

swing or downswing of the nation's economy. Many observers believe the economy will continue to improve (compared to the early 1980s) and state revenues will increase. Hence, state legislatures and governors will be more optimistic, and many states will increase their allocations to education.

Sunbelt states expand

Many Sunbelt states, especially the energy-rich states in the Southwest and West, rank high in the ability to derive revenues from various taxes (including a severance tax on their energy resources) and from expanding business and population. These states will have the ability to spend more money on education if they so choose. Moreover, many Sunbelt states are expecting a considerable increase in student enrollment, which should lead to additional pressure to raise money for educational reform. Educational expenditures may outpace inflation in many Sunbelt states.

Other observers, however, feel that looming federal deficits, high interest rates, unemployment, and high energy costs will persist at uncomfortable levels for the rest of the decade and will limit economic recovery and growth; in turn, these burdens will strain state budgets and adversely affect school spending. Although the nation as a whole has shown signs of recovery from the early 1980 recession, many economists believe that state revenue shortfalls will persist in most states, especially in the Northeast and Midwest. The vast majority of these states are expected to allocate minimal increases for educational spending, no more than 2 to 5 percent per year, far less than the expected rate of inflation.[33]

Shortfalls in the Northeast and Midwest

Wherever the trend of declining state expenditures for education persists, the burden of educational spending and public spending in general will most likely fall on local sources between 1985 and 1990—thus increasing disparities between poor and wealthy school districts and local governments in general.

The Management of Decline

One of the great problems facing the schools during the last fifteen years or so was declining enrollments. This decline in total enrollments hit the grade schools in 1972 and moved to the high schools in 1977. The educational system was ill equipped to manage this drop. For several generations the United States had enjoyed growth in almost all aspects of social and economic life—population, per capita real income, productivity, and gross national product. Almost all its institutions, including its schools, were geared to an age of accelerated growth.

This age came to an end in the 1970s, not only with regard to our schools, but for almost all our social and economic institutions. We entered an age of slowdown and smallness; in fact, the general need to conserve resources gained acceptability. What has been happening in the automobile

33 George B. Mills and John L. Palmer, "The Deficit Dilemma," *Urban Policy and Research Report* (Fall 1983), pp. 4–8; Ornstein, "Federal Funding"; John L. Palmer and Isabel V. Sawhill, *Changing Domestic Priorities* (Washington, D.C.: Urban Institute, 1982); George Peterson, *Fiscal Choices for the Next Decade* (Washington, D.C.: Urban Institute, 1982).

and housing industries—and with our food, natural resources, and energy—now is happening with our schools. We are forced to trim the fat to survive. A demand for thrift has become apparent. School boards are cutting expenses, reducing budgets, and lowering tax rates. Despite the fact that student enrollments are expected first to level off and then to inch up starting in the mid-1980s, we are still in the midst of the management of decline—of downsizing our expectation and of doing more with less money.[34] The management of decline has had a number of significant effects in education.

Trimming the fat

1. *Size.* Classroom size, in the interest of economy, has increased and may continue to increase. The data on classroom size and student achievement are somewhat contradictory, and many studies show no significant differences between achievement in small classes and in large classes. When differences are found, they are about as likely to favor large classes as small. Some recent reviews of the research have shown that class size is only related to pupil achievement when the size of classes is reduced sufficiently (fifteen or fewer students) to result in altered teaching methods.[35] Thus educators should not be too quick to reduce class size without considering whether teachers can adopt appropriate methods for small classes.

Opting for older schools

2. *Modernization.* Instead of building new schools, it is cheaper in many cases to maintain and modernize older schools. Older schools frequently were better constructed than the newer ones, and those not in distress should be saved in an era of declining birthrates. Moreover, older buildings per se are not detrimental to student learning.

Building smaller schools

3. *Smaller schools.* Small schools can be cheaper than large schools, especially if they are well insulated and stress optimal utilization of space. Costs of fuel and light are major expenses today. We no longer need to build big and expensive cafeterias, auditoriums, and gymnasiums. They add to construction costs, are unoccupied for a large portion of the day and year, and cost a great deal for maintenance, heating, and lighting.

4. *Energy economies.* Related to the need for saving fuel, more and more schools will be reducing temperatures during vacation; delaying warming up the school before classes each morning; switching to the night heat cycle earlier in the day; reducing heat in hallways and specialized areas; scheduling custodial care during the day; insulating pipes, walls, and windows; preparing additional cold lunches; reducing lunch periods or activity periods; shortening the school day; and, if things really get rough, rescheduling holidays and even the school year to coincide with warmer seasons.

34 Allan C. Ornstein, "Thinking Small for the Future," *School and Community* (January 1982), pp. 6–7; idem., "Frostbelt-Sunbelt Energy Policies," *High School Journal* (December–January 1984), pp. 92–103.

35 Gene V. Glass and Mary Lee Smith, *Meta-Analysis of Research on the Relationship of Class Size and Achievement* (Boulder, Colo.: University of Colorado Laboratory of Educational Research, 1978). See also Nicola Filby et al., "What Happens in Smaller Classes" (Paper presented at the Annual Conference of the American Educational Research Association, Boston, April 1980).

Between 1973 and 1980 the total bill for heating schools in the United States tripled, despite reduced fuel consumption. School officials have responded by looking for ways to reduce energy outlays and have identified a number of steps that can be taken to cut energy use.[36]

5. *Teacher layoffs.* Teacher layoffs were and still are common in many school districts, as enrollments and public support for schools sag. Most school districts across the country have reduced their teaching force on the basis of seniority or tenure; they rarely get involved in merit or objective evaluations. The reason for avoiding teacher evaluations is that under the rules governing seniority (or tenure), standards for deciding which teachers to lay off are clear and uncertainty is reduced.

Seniority or tenure

Although teachers and administrators do not believe that experienced teachers are always more competent, they support seniority (or tenure) as a criterion for layoffs because it eliminates patronage and provides protection against abuse by vindictive administrators. Administrators argue that such concerns are sometimes warranted.[37]

Because teacher layoffs threatened careers and provoked strikes, many school districts were reluctant to engage in large staff reductions and sometimes preferred to opt for cuts in services and programs—or even for school closings. Nevertheless, some large school systems such as New York and Seattle were forced to reduce their teaching force more than 5 percent per year in the mid-1970s, as were many suburban schools.[38]

School Closings The closing of schools has become the focus of this new era of retrenchment. Some school districts rent their closed schools to tenants which in most cases are service agencies themselves: churches, private schools, and community centers. In other cases, school buildings are sold. For example, in Ithaca, New York, a downtown high school was sold to private investors, who converted it to a shopping mall. In Orlando, Florida, a school became a hotel; in Pittsburgh, a hospital; in Peoria, a bakery.[39] Some one-time school buildings are now condominiums.

Although the closing of schools has resulted in significant savings to school districts, it is an extremely controversial political issue in many communities. Perhaps no institution is more sacred than the neighborhood school. Family life often revolves around local schools, and families often purchase homes on the basis of a school's location and reputation. School clos-

36 John Mulholland, "How to Save 117% in School Fuel," *Phi Delta Kappan* (May 1980), p. 639; Stephen F. Sloan et al., *Energy in Schools Costs Too Much,* A Report on the Impact of Energy Costs on New York State Schools (Albany, N.Y.: New York State Senate Research Service, 1982).

37 Susan Moore-Johnson, "Seniority and Schools," *Phi Delta Kappan* (December 1982), pp. 259–264.

38 William L. Boyd, "Policy Development in Declining Suburban School Districts" (Paper presented at the Conference on Managing Enrollment Decline, Peabody College of Vanderbilt University, February 1982); James G. Cibulka, "Response to Enrollment Loss and Financial Decline in Urban School Systems," *Peabody Journal of Education* (Winter 1983), pp. 64–78.

39 Michael A. Berger, "Retrenchment Policies and Their Organizational Consequences," *Peabody Journal of Education* (Winter 1983), pp. 49–63; Diane Devoky, "Burden of the Seventies: The Management of Decline," *Phi Delta Kappan* (October 1979), pp. 87–91.

ings, especially of elementary schools, raise a community's blood pressure, often create conflict between parents and school officials, and pit one school against another, one neighborhood against the next.

School closings and retrenchment

For these reasons, school closing and retrenchment decisions have been characterized by avoidance and delay. James Cibulka's survey of schools in ten big cities illustrates this point. There were major enrollment declines between 1971 and 1980 for every city surveyed—186,000 students in New York City, 95,000 in Chicago, and 55,000 in Baltimore—but very few schools were closed. Not only does the percentage of enrollment declines exceed the percentage of school closings for every city (and in seven out of ten cases far exceed it), but there is also a lag of about four or five years in responding to the problem. The reluctance of school officials to close schools is especially evident in Los Angeles, which lost 92,000 students during this nine-year period and did not close a single school. Only Boston, Chicago, and Milwaukee came close to closing schools in proportion to their declining enrollments.[40]

Big-city school districts

Why should large urban school districts be prone to such delay? The answer, in part, is documented by a number of case studies, which reveal that urban school districts face more opposition to school closings than do suburban or rural school districts.[41] It seems that every time a superintendent in a big city proposed the closing of a school, a delegation of parents, often led by a local political official and assisted by school employees, would storm the board of education. Because urban neighborhoods are often divided along racial or ethnic lines, attempted school closings often elicit charges of discrimination. Community groups often emphasize claims of equity rather than economy or efficiency, and many coalitions are formed to put pressure on school board members—who are usually elected. In the short run, it is much easier to implement across-the-board budgetary cuts, and minimize conflict, than to focus on concentrated school cuts that tend to galvanize emotional opposition. A situation has been created whereby it is difficult to make painful cutbacks essential for the long-run financial stability of urban schools.[42]

Equity vs. efficiency

Suburban school districts

Although there is also a lag between enrollment loss and retrenchment policies in suburban school districts, these schools take quicker action. Cutting back seems to be less threatening, since a smaller number of employees and constituencies are affected at one time. Suburban and rural schools tend to be more homogeneous and, therefore, do not suffer from the political, racial, and ethnic pressures of cities. Teachers are not as militant as they are in the cities. Finally, school officials and community groups tend to be more sensitive to school expenditures and revenues, since school budgets are

40 James G. Cibulka, "The Politics of School Closings in Ten U.S. Cities" (Paper presented at the annual meeting of the American Educational Research Association, New York, March 1982).

41 William L. Boyd and Dennis R. Wheaton, "Conflict Management in Declining School Districts," *Peabody Journal of Education* (Winter 1983), pp. 25–36; Cibulka, "The Politics of School Closings in Ten U.S. Cities"; James M. Cronin, "Big City School Bankruptcy" (Paper presented at the Institute for Research on Educational Finance and Governance, Stanford University, 1980).

42 Boyd and Wheaton, "Conflict Management in Declining School Districts"; Cronin, "Big City School Bankruptcy."

smaller and most parents in these communities are homeowners who pay property taxes.

School Infrastructure Problems

The nation's educational infrastructure is in a state of critical disrepair. By **infrastructure,** we mean the basic physical facilities that underpin the school plant (plumbing, sewer, heat, electric, roof, masonry, carpentry, and so on). Building experts estimate that our schools are deteriorating at a faster rate than they can be repaired, and faster than most other public facilities. Plumbing, electrical wiring, and heating systems in many schools are dangerously out-of-date; roofing is below code; and exterior materials (brickwork, stone, and wood) are chipped or cracked. The cost of deferred expenditures currently runs to over $100 million in Los Angeles, Detroit, Chicago, Seattle, and Miami's Dade County, with an enormous bill of $680 million for the New York City schools. The accumulated cost to repair the nation's public schools, according to the American Association of School Administrators, "can now be conservatively placed at $25 billion in 1983 dollars."[43]

$25 billion

Schools in cities and in the Frostbelt suffer the greatest infrastructure problems because they are the oldest and the most decayed. Nearly 20 percent of the schools in the older industrial cities of the Northeast and Midwest were built before 1930; a large number were constructed before 1900. For example, nearly half of Chicago's 625 school buildings were built before 1930, and as many as 85 schools still in existence in 1982 were built before 1900.

Several factors other than age contribute to the deterioration of school buildings and the costs for repairs and renovation.

1. *Energy prices.* Like many public facilities, the schools were hit hard in the 1970s by the rapid increase in energy prices. Most schools, particularly in old, Frostbelt communities, continue to be heated by inefficient boilers. Electrical costs are higher because the design does not take advantage of sunlight. The funds devoted to increased energy costs have robbed schools of money for repairs and maintenance.

2. *Expenditure limitations.* During the 1970s and early 1980s most states enacted revenue limitations that resulted in sharp cuts in structural maintenance and capital outlays.

Wide temperature ranges

3. *Weather conditions.* The weather is severe in certain parts of the country, especially in the Frostbelt where the 100- to 120-degree annual temperature range causes considerable contraction and expansion of school buildings and school pavement. The intense cold makes the water and sewer

43 "The Maintenance Gap: Deferred Repair and Renovation in the Nation's Elementary and Secondary Schools" (A Joint Report by the American Association of School Administrators, Council of Great City Schools, and National School Boards Association, Washington, D.C., January 1983).

systems, as well as exterior brick, vulnerable to cracks and leaks. In addition, acid rain, common in heavily industrialized areas, causes deterioration of all structural surfaces.

4. *Density and vandalism.* Big-city schools are usually located in densely populated areas, resulting in concentrated use of and greater demand for facilities. Moreover, many of these schools are located in highly concentrated poverty areas and service youth populations that are more often involved in property destruction and theft than youth from more affluent areas. All this results, not only in higher costs and more frequent repairs, but in higher budgets for security measures, which depletes a system's financial resources and operating funds for repairs and maintenance.

5. *Environmental hazards.* The Environmental Protection Agency's requirements on asbestos removal, safe storage of chemicals and cleaning fluids, and clean air regulations governing boilers and waste are areas where the federal government puts pressure on schools to spend millions of dollars.

Removing asbestos

At an estimated cost of $10 per square foot to remove asbestos, the total cost can run well into the millions for some older school districts.

During the 1970s and early 1980s, the federal government imposed many requirements and regulations on the schools but did not provide funds for compliance. Hence, many school districts were forced to use funds from their school maintenance budgets to comply with federal regulations; even worse, many schools are still in violation or are deficient in remedying these environmental hazards.

6. *Newer buildings.* Many new schools were constructed during the last twenty years, especially in the Sunbelt and suburbs. Many of these schools were constructed with haste to accommodate expanding enrollments.

Poor construction

Quality suffered and the buildings demonstrate minimal survivability, say twenty or thirty years. These buildings are now at the end of their life span. In contrast, the problem with older buildings involves not quality, but their failure to meet health and safety codes, energy inefficiency, and the results of accumulated neglect.[44]

As the 1980s come to an end, more schools may close due to the cost of operation and deferred repairs. The decisions and choices involved in managing decline will eventually shift to these deferred maintenance needs. In comparison with other public sectors, the construction and repair needs for schools rank among the most serious in the nation. Yet it is doubtful if the public is willing to spend sufficient money to meet these needs. For the most part, educators and the public alike are unaware of the time bomb that is ticking in American schools. What catches our attention is the need to improve curriculum and instruction; the safety and operating efficiency of schools, while essential, are not on the minds of the public. Many school of-

44 Allan C. Ornstein, "Infrastructure: Delays and Decay, with Regional Implications," *High School Journal* (April-May 1983), pp. 228–234; "The Maintenance Gap."

ficials are aware of the problem but have left the problem for the next generation of school people. The bill for postponing this maintenance will increase in time; as it does, we can expect infrastructure choices to affect school retrenchment and the management of decline.

The Accountability Movement

Schools in the remaining 1980s will be held accountable for student achievement and for cost effectiveness. Although there are many definitions of the term *accountability,* the idea is rooted in the educational trends of the 1970s. For the present and near future **accountability** will mean that teachers must exhibit some standard of competency or performance and schools must devise methods of relating expenditures to outcomes. For many years the quality of education was measured by the total number of dollars spent per student or the achievement scores of the students. Now results, and a record of the cost of these results, are being compared and educators are being made to answer for them.

Demands for accountability

Demands for accountability have increased over recent years for the following reasons:

1. An increasing number of parents realize that schooling is important for success and that their children are not learning sufficiently well.
2. The public has the impression that school people are accountable to no one but themselves.
3. School costs continue to rise. People feel overtaxed and want to know where their dollars are being spent.
4. Some educators and policy makers claim that we need to develop an information system to identify effectiveness indicators and evaluate schools on the basis of those indicators. Here, the important criterion is not school resources but output or student results.

Modes of proof

5. Some educators assert that modes of proof can be established for assessment purposes. Instead of vague promises to increase student learning, precise objectives can be stated that specify what students are expected to gain from their educational experiences.[45]

In general, many parents' expectations for their children's education have not been met. At the same time the cost of education has increased. The taxpayer, who wants to keep the lid on school spending, wishes to hold educators responsible for the outcomes of instruction and the consequences of any school program.

The majority of states have taken the position that accountability should be mandatory, leaving the specifics to the discretion of local school districts. The legislation ranges in content from very explicit laws to broad and vague guidelines. Some call for assessment of students, some require management goals and methods of evaluation, many require evaluation of teachers, and a

45 Allan C. Ornstein, "Accountability: Prospects for the 1980s," *School and Community* (May 1981), pp. 24–25, 41.

The public increasingly has been holding schools and teachers more strictly accountable for the academic performance of students and their achievement of specific learning objectives. (David S. Strickler/Atoz Images, Inc.)

Statewide assessment plans

few require citizen involvement. Still other states have introduced statewide assessment plans in conjunction with some plan to improve the skills of students as well as the cost-effectiveness of teaching.[46]

Fear of an oversimplified concept

Most people agree that everyone, including teachers and school administrators, should be held accountable for their work. But what many educators fear is an oversimplified concept that determines accountability to be the sole responsibility of the teacher or principal—or that is assessed in dollars only. With an oversupply of teachers, the development of a simple system of accountability may put the total responsibility on the teacher and tie jobs and salaries to student achievement, while ignoring the realities and responsibilities of other groups, including parents, community residents, school board members, taxpayers, and students themselves.

Competency tests for students

In the face of severe difficulties in agreeing on a system for accountability, emphasis has been shifting toward minimum competency testing for students and teachers. In order to ensure that students learn to read, write, and compute at a minimally acceptable level, twenty-seven states have started to administer tests for student promotion or graduation.[47] Many other states, in a move toward excellence and increased productivity, are upgrading the cur-

46 Michael J. Brophy and John L. Davy, "The New Hampshire Accountability Project: A Model for Local Accountability Planning" (Paper presented at the annual meeting of the American Educational Research Association, Boston, April 1980); Rebecca Christian, "Accountability Structures in Statewide Student Assessment Data" (Paper presented at the annual meeting of the American Educational Research Association, Montreal, April 1983).

47 *Educational Governance in the States, Status Report on State Education Agencies* (Washington, D.C.: U.S. Department of Education, 1983).

riculum; putting more emphasis on such core courses as English, science, and math; and implementing stiffer academic requirements for graduation. These trends hold students accountable for their own academic performance.

Testing teachers

In other states the finger of responsibility is being pointed at teachers. The movement to upgrade entry requirements for new teachers draws the most attention. As many as twenty-three states now require beginning teachers to show evidence of minimum competencies in basic skills (spelling, grammar, mathematics), general academic knowledge, and/or pedagogical skills.[48] To the detriment of the profession, the failure rate of new teachers taking such tests is high—approaching 30 to 50 percent in some school districts.[49] Other states are moving to upgrade certification requirements and require either more academic subjects, increased semester hours in teaching specialization or academic major, or a fifth year of college in order to teach. Still other states are calling for competency testing for practicing teachers, modifying the tenure system, or recertifying teachers every five years or so through some form of objective evaluation.[50]

There are numerous career ladder and merit pay plans that use a carrot instead of a stick and also tie into accountability. For example, a number of states are suggesting plans that would remove the cap on dollars available for the higher ranks of a career ladder based on experience and performance. Other states are thinking of awarding pay incentives, ranging from $1,000 to $7,000 a year, for superior classroom performance. Meanwhile, substantial money is being earmarked for in-service training for teachers and principals.

Weeding out incompetent teachers

As tests for weeding out incompetent teachers are developed and validated, as tenure systems are changed, and as career ladders, merit pay, and "master" teachers are introduced, teachers' rights must be protected. The difficulty of equating test scores with performance in the classroom or of distinguishing superior teachers from average or mediocre teachers must be realized. During the 1980s, the public will want to reform education and hold teachers and school officials accountable. There will be trade-offs as financial costs are considered. Knowledgeable legislators and educators must realize that the problems of education and the costs of schooling do not lend themselves to quick fixes.

Tuition Tax Credits

As the 1980s unfold, debate over **tuition tax credits** (tax reductions for tuition payments) has increased, reflecting a barometer of popular dissatisfac-

48 Ibid.

49 B. O. Smith, "Teacher Evaluation in Depth" (Paper presented at the annual meeting of the American Educational Research Association, Montreal, April 1983); Thomas S. Tocco and Jane K. Elligett, "On the Cutting Edge: The Pinellas County Teacher Applicant Screening Program," *The Board* (Winter 1980), p. 5; William J. Webster, "The Validation of a Teacher Selection System" (Paper presented at the annual meeting of the American Educational Research Association, Boston, April 1980).

50 Robert N. Bush, "The Beginning Years of Teaching" (Paper presented at the annual meeting of the American Educational Research Association, Montreal, April 1983); Chris Pipho, "California and Florida Set the Pace for Educational Reform," *Phi Delta Kappan* (October 1983), pp. 85–86; and Smith, "Teacher Evaluation in Depth."

tion and disaffection with the public schools. This is not to deny that tuition tax credits are also a sign of the continuing quest of nonpublic schools for support and for increased choice by the public. But public faith in public institutions, especially the city schools, has wavered.

Supreme Court decisions

Although the Reagan administration's tuition tax credit bill was defeated in Congress, the U.S. Supreme Court gave impetus in 1983 to the movement when it upheld Minnesota's tuition tax-credit law in *Muller* v. *Allen*. The Court upheld the Minnesota plan chiefly because it offers deductions to both public and private school parents, even though only a handful of public school parents receive the law's maximum benefits. (Public education is tuition free; the only tax deductible public school expenses are textbooks, supplies, and possibly transportation in some suburban or rural areas.)

Opponents

Debates over tuition tax credits for nonpublic students have been vigorous and emotional. Opponents have argued that such credits would provide unconstitutional support for church-related schools, would aid the rich, would undermine the public school system by supporting and encouraging the movement of students to nonpublic schools, would result in a large drain on the federal and state treasuries, would reduce the likelihood of obtaining voter support for public school tax increases, and would contribute to additional racial and socioeconomic segregation and isolation of low-status students in the city public schools.[51]

Supporters

Supporters of tuition tax credits argue that such credits are not unconstitutional and would not seriously reduce federal revenues or hamper public school tax levy efforts. They also argue that tax credits would provide wider opportunity for disadvantaged students; thus they would not contribute to, and might even reduce, racial and socioeconomic isolation. In addition, many supporters believe that tax credits not only would provide parents with a choice in selecting schools but would also stimulate reform efforts in the public schools.[52]

Probably the biggest worry is that the quest for tax credits may directly conflict with the desire for students to share in a common educational experience, and only by coincidence might the two coexist. A program of increased aid to nonpublic schools is likely to divert funds from public schools, and any benefits of greater public assistance to private schools must be weighed against the possible loss in benefits to public schools. Since political and financial support for education are interlinked, we need to consider what effect increased financial support for private schools would have on the political support for public schools.

"In the past," points out one educator, "middle-class parents who desired to improve their children's education have worked to improve the public schools; thus improving the schooling of many children," regardless of social

51 Levine and Havighurst, *Society and Education*; Michael W. Kirst, "The Rationale for Public Schools," *Phi Delta Kappan* (November 1981), pp. 164–165.

52 Robert B. Hawkins, "Tuition Tax Credits: Another Voice," *American Education* (August 1982), pp. 9–10; Daniel D. McGarry, "The Advantages and Constitutionality of Tuition Tax Credits," *Educational Freedom* (February 1982), pp. 1–52.

Abandoning public schools

status or religious background. If public aid to private schools is increased, as expected, middle-class parents will have greater incentives to send their children to private schools. This is particularly true if tax breaks or tuition reimbursement is provided. Then, instead of using their resources to improve public schooling in general, "their private interests would be better served if they worked instead to increase the amount of the public subsidy to private schools."[53] This situation would draw more funds away from the public schools, reducing the resources available to those who do not have access to private schools, and further stratify the "haves" and "have nots."

By 1984, proposals for tuition tax credits, tax deductions, or both, were on the agenda in Arizona, Illinois, Iowa, Kansas, Kentucky, Massachusetts, Michigan, Missouri, New Jersey, New York, Ohio, and Pennsylvania. Other states seemed likely to introduce such legislation in the near future. This issue will remain at the forefront of debate through the 1980s.

Educational Vouchers

Use of educational vouchers is another trend associated with school finance reform. Under a voucher system, parents of school-age children are given a voucher or flat grant representing their children's estimated educational cost or portion of school budget. Children then use this voucher to attend any school—public or private—that they and their parents choose.

More choices

Like tuition tax credits, vouchers permit alternatives to the customary public schools—choices among schools, including private options, and thus indirectly threaten public schools. They represent the loss of public confidence in public schools. Here is yet another sign that the public is dissatisfied with the means and ends of public education.

Increased segregation of schools

The NEA, AFT, and other educational organizations take a dim view of vouchers—claiming that the system would lead to increased segregation of low-income, minority, and low-ability students, that many silly and even charlatan experiments would be marketed under the guise of change and innovation, and that most parents lack the knowledge to distinguish a good school from a bad one.[54] They claim that it is wrong to equate the presence of alternatives with either improved quality or the satisfaction of public needs. "Like commercial T.V., the public may be faced with a plethora of 'alternatives' none of which are particularly good or attractive."[55] Critics also point out that vouchers and tax credits will split the public and private schools along socioeconomic lines; reduce financial support for the public schools; and dramatically increase state regulations, paperwork, and bureaucracy.[56]

53 Carol B. Muller, "Perspectives on Tuition Tax Credits," *Education Week*, October 26, 1981, p. 9.

54 Telephone conversation with Robert Porter, Secretary-Treasurer of the AFT, and Bernard McKenna, Department of Instruction and Professional Development of the NEA, July 3, 1984.

55 Arturo Pacheco, *"Educational Vouchers and Their Implications for Equity"* (Paper presented at the Institute for Research on Educational Finance and Governance, Stanford University, January 1980), p. 24.

56 Arthur E. Wise and Linda Darling-Hammond, "Educational Vouchers: Regulating Their Efficiency and Effectiveness," *Educational Researcher* (November 1983), pp. 9–18.

Proponents tell us that vouchers widen the average person's choices for schooling, and they stress the benefits of extending educational choice to those deprived of it. By extending educational choice, a second argument goes, competition and educational quality will increase. Vouchers are expected to force schools to respond to the needs of the consumer. Under the existing system, public schools are considered monopolies. Consumers have few options as to the schools they can attend; poor people, in particular, have fewer choices because they lack mobility and money. Thus, there is little pressure for schools to reform, innovate, or provide greater educational quality. The idea is to leave the elements of quality and competition to the marketplace. Based on consumer demand, if students and parents can choose schools, the effective ones will stay in operation and their enrollments will increase while the less desirable ones either go out of business or improve.[57]

Responding to the consumer

During the 1970s, the federal government funded several voucher experiments in Gary, Indiana; San Jose, California; and Seattle, Washington. The conclusions of the studies were mixed. The experiments did not result in segregation by race or social class; however, academic outcomes were no different between the experimental and control groups. More recently, John Coons and Stephen Sugarman have analyzed the issue of vouchers and conclude that all schools, public and private, should be entitled to receive vouchers so long as they meet state requirements concerning student admissions, teacher personnel, and curriculum and reserve at least 25 percent of their seats for low-income students.[58]

Mixed results

Although support for federally funded vouchers waned in the early 1980s, the idea is alive in the alternative school movement and tuition tax credit movement. So long as dissatisfaction with public schools remains, the voucher concept will not go away. It will remain with us, either as a distinct trend or as part of a larger umbrella of support for competition and choice among schools.

Dissatisfaction with public schools

Summing Up

1. Schools are supported by the federal, state, and local governments, with the greatest share derived from state sources and the smallest share from federal sources. Over recent years, state support has increased dramatically, local support has been reduced, and federal support has leveled off.
2. School finance reform is based on the principle of equality of opportunity; nevertheless, there is wide variation in the financial ability among states and within states (as the local school level) to support education. Not all states or school districts can finance education equally well. Poorer school districts tend to receive more money from their respective states than do wealthier school districts, but the amount rarely makes up for the total difference in expenditures.

57 John E. Coons and Stephen B. Sugarman, *Education by Choice—The Case for Family Control* (Berkeley, Calif.: University of California Press, 1978); Henry M. Levin, "Educational Vouchers and Social Policy" (Paper presented at the Institute for Research on Educational Finance and Governance, Stanford University, July 1979); Patricia M. Lines, "State Regulation of Private Education," *Phi Delta Kappan* (October 1982), pp. 119–123.

58 Coons and Sugarman, *Education by Choice*.

3. Although the courts helped the school finance reform movement in the 1970s, their impact has leveled off in the 1980s. It is not yet clear whether block grants will pick up some of the slack or whether they will hinder the movement toward reform.
4. Since the Sputnik era, federal funding of education has become increasingly linked to national policy. Federal aid generally has been categorical and coordinated to coincide with national policy goals. Under the block grant program of the 1980s, there has been a shift in responsibility for educational funding from the federal government to the individual states.
5. Trends described in this chapter have had a particularly important impact in terms of financing education. The taxpayers' revolt, school closings and declining enrollments, and school infrastructure problems have generated serious problems in the funding of schools. Controversy over accountability, tuition tax credits, and educational vouchers reflects the public attitude toward education and the extent to which most Americans support (or do not support) their schools.

Discussion Questions

1. Why do city schools have more fiscal problems than suburban or rural schools?
2. What are the major reasons for growing state support of education?
3. What are the major reasons for minimal financial support of education at the federal level?
4. What are the primary reasons for the taxpayers' revolt?
5. Why is school infrastructure becoming a serious problem? Given the public attitude toward saving money, how can people be motivated to pay for school repairs and renovation?

Suggested Readings

Burrup, Percey E., and Vern Brimley. *Financing Education in a Climate of Change,* 3rd ed. Boston: Allyn and Bacon, 1982.

The authors examine the economics of education with emphasis on government financing (local, state, and federal), public and nonpublic schools, and methods for administering school budgets.

Johns, Roe L., Kern Alexander, and Edgar Morphet. *The Economics and Financing of Education,* 4th ed. Englewood Cliffs, N.J.: Prentice-Hall, 1983.

A comprehensive text concerning the problems and methods of financing schools.

McCarthy, Martha M., and Paul Diegnan. *What Legally Constitutes an Adequate Public Education.* Bloomington, Ind.: Phi Delta Kappa, 1983.

The book analyzes and synthesizes the legislative, judicial, and political directives that pertain to the issues of school finance.

School Finance Reform in the States, 1983. Denver, Colo.: Education Commission of the States, 1983.

A current report on school finance trends, with emphasis on state and regional differences.

9

Legal Aspects of Education

Focusing Questions

How do state and federal laws affect school district policies and classroom teaching?

What legal rights and responsibilities do teachers have?

What are the legal rights of students?

Can religious activities be conducted in the public schools? Can the government assist nonpublic schools?

How does affirmative action affect education?

DURING THE PAST FORTY YEARS, THE COURTS HAVE FREquently been asked to resolve issues relating to public education. The growing role of the courts in general and the federal courts in particular is evident when one considers the total number of state and federal education-related court cases in the United States between 1789 and 1971. In the 107 years from 1789 to 1896, there were only 3,096 such cases, and only 50 of them were federal. In the 10 years from 1947 to 1956, by way of contrast, there were 7,091 court cases, of which 112 were federal. The growth of the federal role was particularly evident from 1967 to 1971, during which time there were 1,273 federal cases.[1] In the words of one veteran observer, the general increase in educational litigation and the growing role of the federal courts reflect the fact that "Education has assumed an importance in our society that it did not have just a few decades ago."[2]

Many legal decisions have had a significant impact on teachers' and students' behavior, on teachers' employment relationships with their school districts, and on curriculum and instruction. This chapter presents a general overview of the U.S. court system and examines the legal topics and court decisions that have had the most important effect on today's schools and teachers. Among the topics considered are the rights and responsibilities of teachers; the rights and responsibilities of students; religion and the schools; and affirmative action and sex equity.[3]

The Court System

Cases involving education-related issues can be heard either in federal or state courts. The charges or allegations of the **plaintiffs** (the persons who sue) determine where a case is heard. Federal courts decide cases where federal laws and regulations or constitutional issues are raised. State courts are involved when state laws, state constitutional provisions, school board policies, or other nonfederal problems are to be resolved. Most cases dealing with elementary and secondary education are filed in state courts. However, to keep from further overburdening crowded calendars, both federal and state courts usually require that prospective **litigants** (the parties in a lawsuit) exhaust all administrative avenues available for resolution before involving the court system.

Most education cases in state courts

1 Melvin E. Jarvis, "Current Trends in Federal Court Intervention in Public Education" (Paper presented at the annual meeting of the American Educational Research Association, New Orleans, April 1984).

2 Thomas A. Shannon, *Current Trends in School Law* (Topeka, Kans.: National Organization for Legal Problems in Education, 1974), p. 5.

3 Other chapters of this book also discuss selected legal issues in education. For example, court decisions regarding school finance are discussed in Chapter 8 and desegregation law is summarized in Chapter 12.

State Courts

There is no national uniformity in state court organization. The specific details of each state's judicial system are found in its constitution. At the lowest level most states have a court of original jurisdiction (often called a municipal or superior court) where cases are tried. That is, the facts are established, evidence is presented, witnesses testify and are cross-examined, and appropriate legal principles are applied in rendering a verdict. Adverse decisions may be appealed to the next level, usually an intermediate appellate court, by the losing side. This court reviews the trial record from the lower court and additional written materials submitted by both sides. The appellate court has the primary goals of insuring that appropriate laws were properly applied, that they fit with the facts presented, and that there was no deprivation of constitutional rights. (See Figure 9.1 for a diagram of a typical state court organization.)

Appeals process

Should one side still not be satisfied, another appeal may be made to the state's highest court, often called its supreme court. A state supreme court decision is final unless a question involving the U.S. Constitution has been raised. The U.S. Supreme Court can be petitioned to consider such issues.

Federal Courts

Federal courts are organized into a three-tiered system. The jurisdiction and powers of federal courts are set forth in the Constitution and are subject to congressional restrictions. The lowest level, district court, holds trials. For appeals at the federal level, the nation is divided into twelve regions called circuits. Each circuit is numbered and has an appeals court located in a large city within the region. That court handles appeals only from district courts within its geographic area. (See Figure 9.2.)

Federal court appeals

Unsuccessful litigants may request that the U.S. Supreme Court review their case. If four of the nine justices agree, a writ of certiorari (request for the transcripts of a case) is granted. Refusal to grant certiorari means the appellate court ruling stands.[4]

Decisions of courts below the U.S. Supreme Court have force only in the geographic area served by that particular court. For this reason, it is possible to find conflicting rulings in different circuits. Often judges look to previous case law for guidance and precedent in rendering decisions. Frequently, it is possible to find precedent for a variety of legally defensible positions on a single issue.

Conflicting rulings

As noted in Chapter 7, education is not specifically mentioned in the U.S. Constitution, but based on interpretations of the reserved powers clause of the Tenth Amendment, it is a responsibility reserved to the states. Much of the federal litigation concerning educational issues has involved interpreta-

4 Some case citations in this chapter include the term "cert. denied." This means that the losing parties petitioned the U.S. Supreme Court for review, but their request was denied.

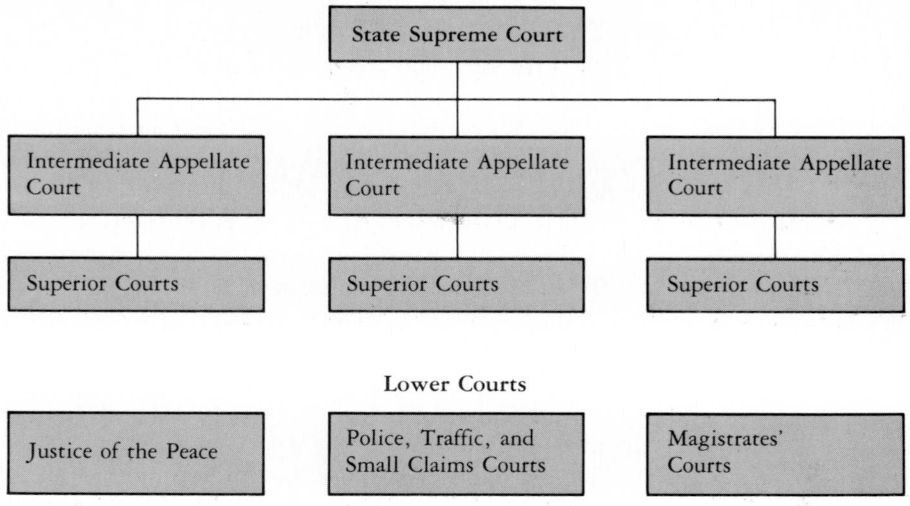

Figure 9.1
A Typical State Court System

First Amendment

tion of the First and Fourteenth Amendments. The First Amendment concerns freedom of religion, speech, press, and assembly, and the right "to petition the government for redress of grievances." First Amendment cases have dealt with the role of religion in public education and with the extent of protection guaranteed to expression by students and teachers. The equal protection clause of the Fourteenth Amendment says that no state shall "deprive any person of life, liberty, or property, without due process of law; nor deny to any person within its jurisdiction the equal protection of the law." Fourteenth Amendment cases have included the issue of school desegregation as well as suspension and expulsion of students.

Until 1868 U.S. citizens had a dual relationship with government—one with their state and another with the national administration. While most state constitutions contained Bill of Rights provisions, these guarantees were not uniformly adopted; thus, citizens' rights varied widely among the states. In many sections of this country residents felt greater allegiance to their state than to the federal government. This changed in 1868 with passage of the Fourteenth Amendment, which, in effect, made U.S. citizenship primary. States were prohibited from depriving persons of rights guaranteed them under the U.S. Constitution. The immediate purpose underlying the Fourteenth Amendment was to extend constitutional rights to blacks following their emancipation from slavery.

Fourteenth Amendment

Liberty and property interests

Litigants citing the Fourteenth Amendment must show that a liberty or property interest is a major element in the case. A liberty interest is involved if "a person's good name, reputation, honor or integrity is at stake"[5] because

5 *Goss* v. *Lopez,* 419 U.S. 565 (1975).

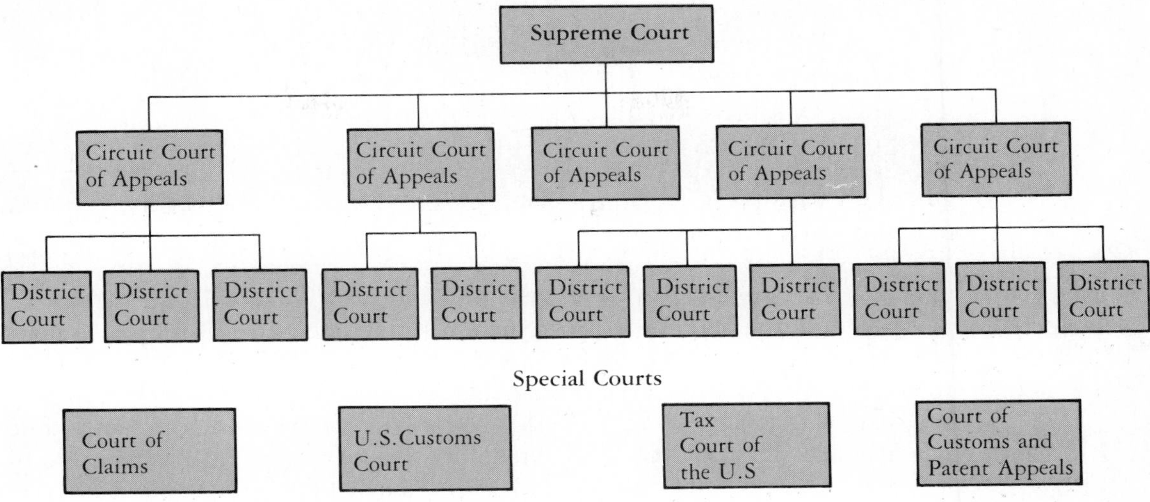

Figure 9.2
The Federal Court System

of action(s) taken by a school district. A property interest arises from legal guarantees granted to tenured employees under the laws, rules, regulations, and contracts of the state.[6] Thus, teachers have a property interest in continued employment beyond the probationary period. Similarly, students have a property interest in their education. If either a liberty or a property interest is claimed, then a school district must provide due process to those whose rights it may attempt to restrict.

Teachers' Rights and Responsibilities

Employment rights

Court decisions have clarified both the rights and the responsibilities of teachers in carrying out their jobs. As pointed out in Chapter 2, until quite recently teachers were vulnerable to dismissal by local boards of education for virtually any reason and without recourse. Collective negotiation statutes, tenure laws, mandatory due process procedures, and the like have been established to curb abuses and to guarantee teachers certain employee rights. Along with rights come responsibilities and many of these, too, have been written into law.

Teachers who are unaware of their rights and responsibilities may suffer because they will be more vulnerable to deprivation of their constitutionally guaranteed freedoms. They are also more likely to make mistakes that could result in their dismissal or in costly litigation. This section provides a brief

6 *Board of Regents of State Colleges* v. *Roth*, 408 U.S. 564 (1972).

introduction to major court decisions involving the rights and responsibilities of elementary and secondary public school teachers.

Employment Contracts

Contract components

Local school boards are empowered to employ teachers and other support personnel; their decisions usually are based on recommendations from the superintendent, who may be assisted by a personnel officer. Employment decisions must comply with laws prohibiting discrimination with respect to age, sex, race, religion, or national origin. Upon appointment, the teacher receives a written contract for signature. The contract describes the relationship between the teacher and the district and establishes the teacher's legal rights. One section of the contract may refer to applicable state laws; another may require adherence to school board policies then in effect, and a third might commit the teacher to abide by rules or regulations promulgated by the board after the contract takes effect. In addition to the conditions stated in the contract, if the school district has recognized and negotiated with a representative teacher group, the provisions of that agreement apply as well.

Tenure, Breach of Contract, and Probation

Terms of tenure

Tenure provides job security for teachers by preventing their dismissal without cause and by requiring that due process be provided in termination cases. What constitutes "cause" is defined by each state; the usual reasons include incompetency, immorality, insubordination, or unprofessional conduct.[7] Tenure is granted to public school teachers by local school districts under terms established by state legislatures. Today nearly every state has enacted some type of tenure law. Tenure often is not transferable between school districts even if they are in the same state, and it is lost after a specified time period if a teacher leaves a district. Granting of tenure in a new district usually requires that the teacher serve another full probationary period.

History of tenure

The concept of tenure was developed about a century ago as part of a general reform movement to eliminate political patronage and replace it with a merit system for making governmental appointments, including those for teaching positions. An 1885 report by a National Education Association committee on tenure concluded, "The public school system should be independent of personal or partisan influence and free from the malignant power of patronage and spoils."[8] Academic freedom (discussed below) is a second important reason for tenure.

7 W. Lance Landauer, John H. Spanger, and Benjamin F. Van Horn, Jr., "Good Cause Basis for Dismissal of Education Employees," in Joseph Beckham and Perry A. Zirkiel, eds., *Legal Issues in Public School Employment* (Bloomington, Ind.: Phi Delta Kappa, 1983), pp. 154–170.

8 Richard D. Gatti and Daniel J. Gatti, *Encyclopedic Dictionary of School Law* (West Nyack, N.Y.: Parker Publishing, 1975).

From its inception there has been uneasiness with the notion of tenure. On the one hand there is the desire to attract, keep, and protect good teachers, but, on the other hand, tenure sometimes provides protection for indifferent, lazy, or ineffective teachers. Tenure laws do contain mechanisms for dismissing the latter group; however, the process is lengthy and laborious.

Continuing contract

Once tenure has been granted, many teachers do not actually sign a contract annually. Instead, they are said to be employed under a **continuing contract**. The term, as generally used, means that reemployment is guaranteed unless school officials give notice, including reasons, by a specific date (often set by state law) that a contract will not be renewed for the next year.

Breach of contract

Contracts are binding on both parties. When one side fails to perform as agreed, the contract is broken. This is referred to as a **breach of contract**. In such instances the party that breached the contract may be sued for damages. In lieu of monetary damages some states permit a teacher's certificate to be revoked in breach of contract cases. When school districts break contracts, teachers may be awarded damages and/or reinstatement to their former positions.

Probationary period

Most states have probationary periods before teachers receive tenure. Three years of consecutive, satisfactory service and the offer of the fourth contract frequently are required for tenured status. Probationary teachers have contracts that, in most states, allow them to be discharged at the end of the contract term for any reason and without explanation. No due process is required. However, if the probationary teacher is able to demonstrate that nonrenewal involved a constitutionally guaranteed liberty or property interest, then procedural due process, as described below for tenured faculty, would be required.

Dismissal of Tenured Teachers and Due Process

Dismissing tenured faculty for such potentially legitimate reasons as incompetence has proven to be a costly, time-consuming, and frequently unsuccessful process involving procedural due process and often court appeals.

Procedural Due Process Due process of law means following those rules and principles that have been established for enforcing and protecting the rights of the accused. In procedural due process, the form used in teacher dismissal cases, specified steps must be followed exactly.

Due process requirements

The core element of procedural due process is "fairness." Most states have laws describing, in detail, a teacher's rights and the applicable time limitations regarding due process proceedings within that state. While due process requirements vary from state to state, certain basic elements generally are recognized:

1. The teacher must be given timely, detailed, written notice of the charges.

2. The teacher must be accorded a hearing and sufficient time to prepare a defense prior to dismissal.
3. The teacher has a right to be represented by legal counsel.
4. The teacher may present written and oral evidence including witnesses.
5. The teacher may cross-examine witnesses and challenge evidence.
6. The hearing is to be conducted before an impartial body. The U.S. Supreme Court has ruled that under the U.S. Constitution a school board may be that impartial body unless bias can be proven.[9]
7. The teacher is entitled to a written transcript of the proceedings.
8. The teacher has the right to appeal an adverse ruling to a higher legal authority, usually the state court system.

Insubordination Firing a teacher for incompetence frequently requires documentation of prior efforts to assist that person in improving. An Arizona teacher was rated unsatisfactory by his principal. A plan was instituted that required him to meet daily with the principal to review his lesson plans as a method of improving his teaching performance. After a number of these meetings the teacher balked at attending more, contending they were unproductive and merely a scheme designed to foster his dismissal. His termination, based on insubordination, was upheld. The court said he showed "willful disregard of a reasonable order."[10]

Example of insubordination

In reviewing state and federal court records of the past forty years, Bridges and Gumport found only eighty-six cases involving teacher incompetence; the dismissals were upheld in two-thirds of the cases.[11] However, administrators sometimes acknowledge use of less formal procedures for separating incompetent teachers from their school districts. Some of the techniques used include counseling incompetent teachers out of the profession, suggesting and financing early retirement, and allowing the teacher to resign. Note, however, that proceedings to dismiss incompetent faculty are increasing, according to Bridges and Gumport. Half the cases they found were heard in the last six years. The increase in these cases may be related to recent national concern with teacher competency.

Few dismissals

Negotiation and Strikes

Teachers have the right to form and belong to unions and other professional organizations. Since the 1960s, teacher groups have lobbied for state legislation to permit school boards to negotiate agreements with them. This effort has been successful in a majority of states; however, a few, such as North Carolina and Virginia, continue to prohibit negotiations between teachers and school boards. The laws enacted vary widely, but they usually allow the

Negotiation allowed in most states

9 *Hortonville District* v. *Hortonville Education Association,* 426 U.S. 482 (1976).

10 *Siglin* v. *Kayenta Unified School District No. 27,* 655 P. 2d 353 (Ariz. Ct. App. 1982).

11 Edwin M. Bridges and Patricia J. Gumport, "The Dismissal of Tenured Teachers for Incompetence" (Palo Alto: Institute for Research on Educational Finance and Governance, Stanford University, 1984).

two sides to bargain collectively or, at least to "meet and confer." Some states specify the procedure that must be followed if the two sides fail to agree (for example, fact-finding in Kansas; binding arbitration in Maryland).

Education is considered to be a vital public service for which the law prohibits strikes by employees. A few states (Hawaii, Minnesota, Oregon, Pennsylvania, Vermont, and Wisconsin) condone withholding of services by teachers under specific conditions written into state law. Teachers do strike despite the legal prohibitions. In such instances, school officials are empowered to seek court injunctions ordering teachers to return to their classrooms. Defiance of a court order can result in penalties imposed in accordance with state law. Florida and Minnesota, for example, prohibit striking teachers from receiving salary increases for one year after a strike, New York law allows striking teachers to be penalized two days' pay for each day on strike, and Michigan permits dismissal of striking teachers.

Penalties for striking

Pregnancy and Employment

Within the last decade the rights of pregnant teachers have been established by the courts, federal and state law, and school district policies. In 1974 the U.S. Supreme Court decided *Cleveland Board of Education* v. *LeFleur.*[12] Jo Carol LeFleur, a junior high teacher, had challenged her board's policy, which required all pregnant teachers to take unpaid leaves of absence beginning five months before the expected birth. Return to work was not permitted until the child was at least three months old. The Court found these rules rigid and concluded there were less arbitrary ways of meeting the board's classroom continuity needs. Boards of education may establish leave policies designed to assure continuity of classroom instruction by requiring teachers to notify the districts early in their pregnancies so that school needs may be anticipated; however, such policies may not contain arbitrary leave and return dates.

Traditional policies overturned

Freedom of Expression

Courts have tended to uphold teachers' rights to express themselves in public or in school; however, in determining whether the expression is "protected" under the First Amendment, a number of factors are pertinent—impact on operation of the school, impact on the teacher's performance, effect on teacher-superior relationships, effect on co-workers, and appropriateness of time, place, and manner of remarks.[13]

Protected freedom of expression

Marvin Pickering was a tenured high school teacher whose letter to the editor, criticizing the board and superintendent about bond proposals and expenditures, was published in a local newspaper. The letter resulted in his

12 *Cleveland Board of Education* v. *LeFleur,* 414 U.S. 632 (1974).

13 Martha M. McCarthy and Nelda H. Cambron, *Public School Law: Teachers' and Students' Rights* (Boston: Allyn and Bacon, 1981).

Examples of court decisions

termination. The U.S. Supreme Court held that publication of the letter did not impede the "proper performance of his daily duties in the classroom or . . . [interfere] with the regular operation of schools generally."[14] For this reason, Pickering's dismissal was found to be improper.

On the other hand, two teachers in Alaska were dismissed for writing a letter that was highly critical of their superintendent and contained many false allegations. The school district was small. Reaction to the letter was immediate and prolonged. As a result the teachers were terminated. The terminations were upheld; the Alaska Supreme Court agreed that the teachers' effectiveness had been impaired by their remarks and that their ability to work closely with colleagues, as appropriate in teaching situations, was diminished.[15]

Behavior itself not at issue

A comparison of these cases indicates that the behavior itself was not the sole basis for the decision. Rather, what happened as a result had a bearing on whether the behavior was judged to have impeded the "proper performance" of a teacher's work or to have disrupted the "regular operation" of the schools.

Teachers in nonpublic schools not necessarily protected

It should be noted that *Pickering* and similar decisions would not be applicable to private or parochial school teachers because those schools are not publicly funded. Private and parochial school teachers do not necessarily have the civil rights protections guaranteed public school teachers (tenure, freedom of expression, due process, and the like). Their rights are dependent primarily on the terms of their individual contracts with the school.[16]

Academic Freedom

In elementary and secondary education much of the curricular content and basic textbook selection is decided by the state, the local school board, or the district's central office staff. The classroom teacher's areas of responsibility commonly include selection of teaching methods, supplemental and enrichment activities and materials, assignment of projects, and the like. Sometimes these choices arouse controversy within the school or the district. The U.S. Supreme Court has made no definitive ruling on academic freedom at the elementary and secondary levels, so judges must rely on lower federal and state court decisions, which are often conflicting. In reaching these decisions, though, an attempt must be made to balance teacher and state or district interests.

Balancing of teacher and district interests

Vulgar language?

In *Keefe* v. *Geanakos,* Robert Keefe, a Massachusetts high school English teacher assigned students an article from the *Atlantic Monthly* that contained a word described by the First Circuit Court of Appeals as "a vulgar term for an incestuous son."[17] A few parents protested; the teacher was re-

14 *Pickering* v. *Board of Education,* 391 U.S. 563 (1968).

15 *Watts* v. *Seward School Board,* 454 P. 2d 732 (Alaska 1969), cert. denied, 397 U.S. 921 (1970).

16 Michael W. LaMorte, *School Law: Cases and Concepts* (Englewood Cliffs, N.J.: Prentice-Hall, 1982).

17 *Keefe* v. *Geanakos,* 418 F. 2d 359 (1st. Cir. 1969).

quired to appear before the board and give assurances the offending word would not be used again. The teacher refused and was suspended. Subsequently, the teacher filed suit alleging board infringement of academic freedom. The appeals court found that the offending term was in common usage and printed in books available in the school library. The decision in favor of the teacher ultimately turned on the board's failure to notify the teacher that use of such material was prohibited.

Kurt Vonnegut's *Welcome to the Monkey House* was assigned as outside reading by an Alabama high school teacher. Several students and parents complained and school administrators threatened dismissal if the teacher persisted in using any portion of the story, which her superiors labeled "literary garbage." The teacher resigned and filed suit.[18] The district court said the assignment was appropriate for the age group (eleventh grade) and presented no disruptive threat at the school.

Considerations affecting decisions

The cases cited above deal with high school English classes. Social studies assignments and sex education classes at both the elementary and secondary levels also have been subjects of heated court cases. Judicial deliberation over all these issues includes consideration of (1) the age and grade level of the students, (2) the relevancy of the questioned material to the curriculum, (3) duration of the material's use, (4) the general acceptance of a disputed teaching method within the profession, and (5) the prior existence of board policy governing selection of materials and teaching techniques.

Censorship

The availability of certain books and magazines in school libraries periodically becomes a controversial issue. In one case, a parent objected to the language in a poem written by a fifteen-year-old student at a New York City high school. The poem was published in an anthology entitled *Male and Female Under 18*. After examining the book's contents, the Chelsea, Massachusetts, School Committee voted to remove the volume from the high school library. The Right to Read Defense Committee brought suit challenging that decision.[19]

Removal of library books

The school committee's defense was that it had statutory authority to oversee curriculum and support services and, consequently, had unconstrained authority to remove books from school library shelves. The district court disagreed, indicating that where First Amendment rights were implicated, a substantial, legitimate governmental interest must be shown before a book could be removed. Further, the judge said, "If this work may be removed by a committee hostile to its language and theme, then the precedent is set for removal of any other work. The prospect of successive school committees 'sanitizing' the school library of views divergent from their own is alarming. . . ."

Restrictions on removal

18 *Parducci* v. *Rutland,* 316 F. Supp. 352 (N. D. Ala. 1970).

19 *Right to Read Defense Committee* v. *School Committee of the City of Chelsea,* 454 F. Supp. 703 (D.C. Mass. 1978).

More recently, the U.S. Supreme Court heard a case where a school board was challenged for removing library books it described as "anti-American, anti-Christian, anti-Semitic and just plain filthy."[20] In a 5-4 decision, the justices sent the case back to the district court for rehearing on the circumstances surrounding the removal: four justices indicated they would have voted to uphold the board's action. Those justices who sought more information indicated, "If the petitioners *intended* by their removal decision to deny respondents access to ideas with which petitioners disagreed, and if this intent was a decisive factor in petitioners' decision, then petitioners have exercised their discretion in violation of the Constitution."

Intention is important

School board powers

School boards can determine which books are placed in a library and even if there is to be a library, but there are limitations on the removal of books. Obsolete, irrelevant, obscene, pervasively vulgar, or educationally unsuitable books may be removed provided the reason for removal can be substantiated if challenged.

Teacher as Exemplar

Chapter 2 quoted a number of rules governing teacher conduct in Wisconsin in 1922. Teachers' lives were regulated because communities believed they should be examples to their students of high moral standards; impeccable character; conservative, neat dress and grooming; and polished manners. While these standards have relaxed somewhat over the last sixty years, in some places teachers remain vulnerable to dismissal under immorality statutes for such activities as living unmarried with members of the opposite sex, professed homosexuality, or sexual involvement with students.

Immorality standards

Although many cities and counties have specifically affirmed the rights of homosexuals in employment and housing, teaching positions are governed by state laws. Only Pennsylvania and California have state laws protecting the rights of homosexual teachers.

Examples of court cases

James Gaylord, a Tacoma, Washington, high school teacher, lost his job because he was adjudged a "known homosexual."[21] The school district demonstrated to the court's satisfaction that knowledge of his lifestyle impaired his teaching effectiveness and that his retention might signal "adult approval of his homosexuality" to students. The U.S. Supreme Court refused to review this case, thereby affirming the lower court decisions dismissing Gaylord.

In New York, a sixth-grade teacher admitted to putting his arm around and kissing some of the girls in his class, giving them a "pat on the behind," and allowing obscene jokes to be told in his classroom as well as the use of profanity. The state commissioner of education found him unfit to teach, and

20 *Board of Education, Island Trees Union Free School District No. 26* v. *Pico,* 50 U.S.L.W. 4831, 102 U.S. 2799 (1982).

21 *Gaylord* v. *Tacoma School District No. 10,* 88 Wash. 2d 286, 559 P. 2d 1340, cert. denied, 434 U.S. 879 (1977).

that decision was upheld by the New York Appellate Court. The court noted the "potentially harmful effect upon the young minds entrusted" to his care.[22]

A tenured Tennessee teacher admitted to driving under the influence of alcohol. The school board dismissed her for conduct unbecoming a teacher even though this was a first offense. The teacher sued and won her case.[23] The court found no relationship between this incident and her teaching performance; and further, the court noted, she was dismissed without adherence to due process requirements.

Lewis Walton, a Florida teacher, pleaded no contest to a possession of marijuana charge. His court record was sealed. Nevertheless, the state's Education Practices Commission suspended his teaching certificate for three years on grounds of moral turpitude and gross immorality. Walton sued and lost.[24] The court agreed with the commission that Walton's conduct reduced his teaching effectiveness. A Little Rock teacher was dismissed for offering to raise the grades of students who bought raffle tickets. The teacher fought the dismissal, but lost.[25]

Dress and grooming cases

Beginning in the late 1960s courts were asked to decide a number of cases where teachers' dress and grooming reflected the styles of the day, which often conflicted with school district policies or traditions concerning these matters. The cases below provide examples of issues that required legal resolution.

A California court ruled that Paul Finot's wearing of a beard was symbolic expression protected by the First Amendment, as well as a liberty right protected under the Fourteenth Amendment.[26] Due process would be necessary, a federal district court determined, before the school district could restrict David Lucia's freedom to wear a beard. The school board had tried to dismiss him.[27]

Beards and sideburns

Max Miller's contract to teach math was not renewed because of his beard and long sideburns. The judges said, if a school board decided a "teacher's style of dress or plumage" adversely affected students, "the interest of the teacher is subordinate to the public interest." Even if personal appearance is declared a protected interest, the court indicated, this still does not mean that every rule concerning appearance is unconstitutional. Miller lost his job.[28]

Neckties

Richard Brimley, a secondary English teacher, was reprimanded for not wearing a necktie. His teachers' association joined with him in challenging

22 *Katz* v. *Ambach,* New York Appellate Division, *Education Law Reporter,* April 5, 1984.

23 *Turk* v. *Franklin Special School District,* 640 S. W. 2d 218 (Tennessee 1982).

24 *Walton* v. *Turlington,* 444 So. 2d 1082 (Fla. App. 1984).

25 *Gatewood* v. *Little Rock Public Schools,* 616 S. W. 2d 784 (Ark. Ct. App. 1981).

26 *Finot* v. *Pasadena City Board of Education,* 58 Cal. Rptr. 520 (1976).

27 *Lucia* v. *Duggan,* 303 F. Supp. 112 (D.C. Mass., 1969).

28 *Miller* v. *School District No. 167 of Cook County, Illinois,* 495 F. 2d 65 (7th Cir. 1974).

the district's dress code in court. Brimley claimed infringement on his rights of free speech and privacy. He lost. The judges stated:

> In view of the uniquely influential role of the public school teacher in the classroom, the board was justified in imposing this regulation. As public servants in a special position of trust, teachers may properly be subjected to many restrictions in their professional lives which would be invalid if generally applied.[29]

Short skirts

Finally, there is the case of a high school French teacher who lost her job because she chose to wear the then-stylish short skirts to school. The appeals court upheld the dismissal of this twenty-five year old teacher, saying her image was "overexposed."[30] Fischer, Schimmel, and Kelly have concluded that the "trend of recent decisions seems to be against granting constitutional protection to teacher grooming."[31]

Role model expectations

In summary, then, restraints on teachers' behavior are not as stringent as in earlier times, but teachers are still expected to be role models for their students and to behave in exemplary ways. When questions about teacher conduct are raised in courts a major concern is whether the behavior in question seriously impairs the teacher's classroom effectiveness.

Tort Liability and Negligence

Student injuries

Torts are civil wrongs. Under tort law individuals who have suffered because of the improper conduct of others may sue for damages. For example, educators may be found guilty of negligence in instances where students are injured during classes, on the playground, or elsewhere, where injury resulted from failure to take appropriate preventive action. This does not mean that a case could be filed every time a child is accidentally injured. It does mean that when injury results from negligent or intentional action, legal remedies could be pursued where state law permits. Tort law is based on "reasonableness" and on determination of fault.

Decline of immunity

Twenty-five years ago nearly every school district was immune from tort liability. This immunity had its origins in English common law where the king, as sovereign, could not be sued. Since 1960 about half the states have eliminated or modified this view of governmental immunity. In states where suits are permitted, the persons sued may include the school district, as well as specifically named school administrators and teachers (or other designated responsible parties) involved in a given situation.

29 *East Hartford Education Association* v. *Board of Education,* 562 F. 2d 838 (1977).

30 *Tardif* v. *Quinn,* 545 F. 2d 761 (1st Cir. 1976).

31 Louis Fischer, David Schimmel, and Cynthia Kelly, *Teachers and the Law* (New York: Longman, 1981), p. 177.

If this child were to fall and be injured, you as teacher might be considered legally responsible—but only if it could be proven in court that you had been negligent.
(Jerry Howard/Positive Images)

Negligence is decided by courts after examining the evidence. A finding of negligence in educational settings usually involves demonstration of each of the following:

Standards for negligence

1. Existence of a legal "standard of care" requiring educators to protect students from harm
2. Demonstrated failure by a statutorily responsible person to discharge that duty
3. Proof that there is a substantial relationship between the educator's conduct and the injury that occurred (in other words, that without the edu-

cator's conduct the injury probably would not have happened), this is known as *proximate cause*

4. Tangible loss or damage from the injury

Proximate cause must be determined on a case-by-case basis. Suppose, for example, that a group of middle school students are given dangerous chemicals to handle while completing a required class experiment, but no instruction is provided in how to properly work with those chemicals. Several students are injured. The teacher's failure to instruct students in the safe handling of these chemicals could be called the "proximate cause" of their injuries.

Reasonable and prudent

Teachers are required by law to protect their students from injury or harm. In all states the standard of care required is that which a reasonable and prudent person would use under similar circumstances. (Illinois is the sole exception. It has statutorily lowered its standard of care so that liability can only be charged for willful or wanton misconduct.) In one case, a kindergarten teacher was charged with negligence when a child fell from the jungle gym while the teacher was attending to other children on the playground. The court ruled that the teacher was not required to have all children in sight at all times. Her presence in the immediate area was sufficient to establish that the teacher was fulfilling her duty.[32]

Foreseeability

An important principle is whether the injury could have been foreseen and, thus, prevented. An overweight student expressed concern to her physical education teacher about a class requirement to perform a back somersault. The teacher insisted the somersault be done; the student's neck snapped in the attempt. The court said the teacher showed utter indifference for the student's safety and the jury awarded $77,000 in damages.[33] In another case, a school band member was injured while picking corn. This happened during a supervised and required fund-raising activity for the band. The parents sued the school district and the two teachers who had supervised the corn-picking, alleging negligence.[34] South Dakota adheres to governmental immunity and the case was dismissed. As another example, a student was struck in the eye by a pencil thrown by another pupil while a Philadelphia teacher stood just outside the classroom door. The injured child's family sued, but lost.[35] The court ruled that momentary absence from the classroom was not negligence.

Negligence cases

Parental consent forms

School districts require parents to sign consent forms when students are involved in activities such as field trips or athletic competition. The form as often written has two purposes: to inform parents of their children's whereabouts and to release school personnel from liability in case of injury. However, parents may not waive a child's right to sue for damages should an

32 *Clark* v. *Furch*, 567 S. W. 2d 457 (Mo. App. 1978).

33 *Landers* v. *School District No. 203, O'Fallon*, 383 N. E. 2d 645 (Ill. App. Ct. 1978).

34 *Guillaume* v. *Tatum*, 328 N. W. 2d 259 (S.D. 1983).

35 *Simonetti* v. *School District of Philadelphia*, 454 A. 2d 1038 (Pa. Super. Ct. 1983).

injury result from negligent supervision, so these forms actually serve the first purpose only. Obtaining a parental waiver *does not* release teachers from their legal obligations to protect the safety and welfare of students in their care.

Duty to supervise

There are numerous places and activities within the school setting where negligence could occur. There is a duty to supervise school grounds during recess as well as before and after school. Transportation of students, either by bus or in cars, requires careful attention to loading and unloading procedures, waiting areas, supervision, and so on. School corridors must be monitored. Physical education instructors, extracurricular activity sponsors, shop, and laboratory teachers must exercise special care. In these situations a clear set of written rules, verbal warnings to students about inherent dangers and how to avoid them, regular inspection of equipment used, adherence to state laws and district policies governing hazardous activities, thoughtful planning, and diligent supervision are prudent safeguards.

Liability insurance

As governmental immunity protection has waned and the number of lawsuits has increased, both school administrator and teacher organizations have begun to offer members liability insurance. In addition, these organizations often provide legal assistance to members in the event that they are sued for an act related to their professional positions.

Reporting Child Abuse

Requirements to report

During the past few years child abuse has become a national issue. Increased media attention has prompted state legislatures to review and stiffen existing abuse laws. A high percentage of abuse is directed at school-age children; thus, schools play an important role in protecting such youngsters. In most states, educators are required by law to report suspected cases of child abuse to authorities or designated social service agencies.

A Wisconsin survey found teachers cognizant of their reporting responsibilities but reluctant to get involved, only vaguely aware of child abuse signs, and unsure of how to properly discharge their reporting responsibilities.[36] Increasing numbers of school districts have written policies describing how teachers should proceed when abuse is suspected. In many locales, community agencies sponsor workshops and distribute literature designed to help school personnel familiarize themselves with legal requirements and with signs of abuse.

Legal penalties

In some communities where school personnel have received training in the identification of child abuse signs, teachers have become the single best source for uncovering abuse cases.[37] Because teachers are important in detecting and reporting suspected abuse, legal penalties exist for failure to discharge this responsibility. Under West Virginia law, for example, failure to

36 S. Barvolek, "The Identification and Reporting of Child Abuse and Neglect Among School Personnel in Wisconsin: An In-Depth Study" (Eau Claire: University of Wisconsin-Eau Claire, October 1981).

37 Alex Molnar and Christine Gliszczinski, "Child Abuse: A Curriculum Issue in Teacher Education," *Journal of Teacher Education* (September–October 1983), pp. 39–41.

report suspected cases of child abuse is a misdemeanor punishable by ten days in jail or a $100 fine.

Educational Malpractice

Malpractice is a concept we tend to associate with medicine or law, not education. Within the last decade, however, suits have been filed against school boards alleging negligence as the root cause for an individual student's failure to achieve in school. Thus far, each case has been dismissed, but these attempts raise interesting issues that educators cannot ignore simply because plaintiffs have been unsuccessful.

Examples of alleged educational negligence

One student filed suit against the San Francisco Unified School District charging negligence because he was graduated from high school despite reading achievement at only the fifth-grade level.[38] In tort law the burden of proof is on the plaintiff. The court, in dismissing this action, noted the difficulty of establishing a link between Peter W.'s low reading achievement and allegedly negligent actions of the school district.

Of the cases filed, *Hoffman* v. *Board of Education of City of New York*[39] appeared to have the best chance to succeed. When young Hoffman was five years old, a school psychologist administered the Stanford-Binet Intelligence Test. A portion of this test requires verbal responses, but Hoffman had a severe speech defect. He scored 74 and was placed in a class for mentally retarded students. Included in the psychologist's report was the recommendation that he be reevaluated within two years. Hoffman spent the next eleven years in special classes and graduated from high school without ever being retested.

Student mistested

When Hoffman turned eighteen, Social Security Administration regulations required an IQ test score from Hoffman to demonstrate his need for continued payments. He scored over 100 and became ineligible for either financial assistance or training programs for the retarded. He sued the school board charging negligence. The jury awarded $750,000; the appellate court reduced the award to $500,000, and New York's highest court reversed the lower courts' decision and dismissed the case. In a 4-3 decision the majority said "courts of this state may not substitute their judgment, or the judgment of the jury, for the professional judgment of educators and government officials actually engaged in the complex and often delicate process of educating the many thousands of children in our schools."

Standards not clear

Four basic points emerge from decisions in the malpractice cases under discussion. First, no standard of care could be determined; second, in the opinion of the judges no clear-cut reasons for failure to learn could be definitively established; third, the monetary value of the harm was indeterminable; and fourth, judges feared that a successful suit would occasion a flood of sim-

38 *Peter W.* v. *San Francisco Unified School District,* 131 Cal. Rptr. 854 (1976).

39 *Hoffman* v. *Board of Education of City of New York,* 424 N.Y.S. 2d 376 (1979).

ilar suits, which would severely strain the resources of both the public school and court systems.[40]

Copyright Laws

A copyright gives authors and artists control over the reproduction and distribution of works they create; consequently, permission for reproduction usually must be obtained from the owner. The widespread use of copying machines has bred serious and regular violations of copyright laws. Congress amended the original 1909 copyright laws in 1976 to include, among other concerns, photocopying and the educational use of copyrighted materials. In addition, "fair use" guidelines were developed by a committee of librarians, publishers, authors and educators. **Fair use** is a legal principle that allows use of copyrighted materials without permission from the author under specific, limited conditions. Restrictions on copying for classroom use or for other educational purposes are summarized below.[41]

Fair use guidelines

Copying of prose is limited to excerpts of no more than 1,000 words.

Distribution of copies from the same author more than once a semester or copying from the same work or anthology more than three times during the semester is prohibited.

Teachers may make one copy per student for class distribution; if charges are made they may not exceed actual copying costs.

It is illegal to create by photocopying anthologies or other compilations as substitutes for purchasing the same or similar materials.

Consumable materials, such as workbooks, may not be copied.

Under the fair use doctrine, single copies of printed material may be made for personal study, lesson planning, research, criticism, comment, and news reporting.

Most magazine and newspaper articles may be copied freely.

Items in weekly newspapers and magazines designed for classroom use by students may not be copied without permission.

Individual teachers must decide, independently, to copy material; they may not be directed to do so by higher authorities.

Plays and musical productions

Plays and musical productions usually are copyrighted by their authors. Therefore, school presentation of such works requires permission from the author or that person's agent. Often payment of a royalty is necessary to secure permission. Whether or not admission is charged can affect the amount of the royalty payments.

40 Delbert Clear, "Malpractice in Teacher Education: The Improbable Becomes Increasingly Possible," *Journal of Teacher Education* (March–April 1983), pp. 19–24.

41 Miriam R. Krasno, "Copyright and You," *Update* (Winter 1983); Thomas J. Flygare, "Photocopying and Videotaping for Educational Purposes: The Doctrine of Fair Use," *Phi Delta Kappan* (April 1984), pp. 568–569.

Videotapes

Videotapes also fall within the fair use guidelines of the copyright laws. These guidelines specify that without a license, educational institutions may not keep tapes of copyrighted television programs for more than forty-five days. During the first ten days, a tape may be used once by an individual teacher and may be repeated once when "instructional reinforcement is necessary." After the forty-five day period expires, the tape must be erased. Videotaping may occur only when a faculty member requests it in advance; thus, it may not be done on a regular basis in anticipation of faculty requests.[42]

Computer Ethics

Legal violations

Computer technology has spawned abuses few dreamed of just a few years ago. Along with teaching of computer literacy, some observers are calling for accompanying instruction covering the ethical use of computers. "Hackers" have cracked codes permitting entry into school record-keeping systems and duplication of copyrighted software; they have used school-owned equipment to enter and tamper with the computerized files of banks and other businesses.

Schools vulnerable

Computing systems used by public schools and universities are particularly vulnerable to unauthorized entry because many of these systems emphasize accessibility to encourage learning. In an attempt to curb abuses, about half the states now have laws covering computer crime. Comprehensive laws to deter hackers and others intent on inflicting serious damage await legislative action.

Students' Rights and Responsibilities

***Decline of* in loco parentis**

During the 1960s, students increasingly began to challenge the authority of school officials to control what they perceived as constitutionally protected aspects of their behavior and activities. Before these challenges, students' rights were considered to be limited by their status as minors and by the concept of *in loco parentis,* under which school authorities assumed the powers of the child's parents during the hours the child was under the school's control and supervision. Beginning in the 1960s, courts affirmed that elementary and secondary students do have some constitutional protection. Consequently, *in loco parentis* may be fading as a basis for school actions. In *Horton* v. *Goose Creek* the appeals court suggested that "unlike parents, administrators do not discipline students with only their best interest in mind but with concern for all students. Moreover, in a compulsory education system, a parent does not voluntarily delegate his authority over his child to the school."[43]

42 Flygare, ibid.

43 David Schimmel, "Horton v. Goose Creek: Reexamining Canine Searches in the Schools," *Education Law Reporter,* 15, No. 4 (April 5, 1984), p. 1038.

Students have constitutional rights, and in recent years these have been clarified and expanded by the courts.
(Clemens Kalischer/ Image Photos)

Student-teacher relationships have changed

As a result of such court cases, students' relationships with teachers and administrators have substantially changed. This section summarizes some of the most important court decisions that influenced these changes.

Freedom of Expression

Tinker

John Tinker, fifteen, his sister Mary Beth, thirteen, and Dennis Eckhardt, sixteen, a friend, were part of a small group planning to wear black armbands to school as a silent, symbolic protest against the war in Vietnam. Hearing of this plan and fearing problems, administrators responded by adopting a policy prohibiting the wearing of armbands; the penalty was suspension until the armbands were removed. The Tinkers and Eckhardt wore armbands as planned, refused to remove them, and were suspended. Their parents filed suit. In finding for the plaintiffs the Court outlined the scope of student rights.[44] *Tinker* has become the standard for examining students' freedom of

44 *Tinker* v. *Des Moines Independent Community School District,* 393 U.S. 503 (1969).

speech guarantees. The lengthy quotation below is from the majority opinion written by Justice Fortas.

> It can hardly be argued that either students or teachers shed their constitutional rights to freedom of speech or expression at the schoolhouse gate. . . . On the other hand, the Court has repeatedly emphasized the need for affirming the comprehensive authority of the States and of school officials, consistent with fundamental constitutional safeguards, to prescribe and control conduct in the schools. . . . Our problem lies in the area where students in the exercise of First Amendment rights collide with the rules of school authorities. . . . School authorities do not possess absolute authority over their students. . . . In order for the State in the person of school officials to justify prohibition of a particular expression of opinion, it must be able to show that its action was caused by something more than a mere desire to avoid the discomfort and unpleasantness that always accompany an unpopular viewpoint. . . . In the absence of a specific showing of constitutionally valid reasons to regulate their speech, students are entitled to freedom of expression of their views. . . . [However] conduct by the student, in class or out of it, which for any reason . . . materially disrupts classwork or involves substantial disorder or invasion of the rights of others is, of course, not immunized by the constitutional guarantee of freedom of speech. . . . The Constitution says that Congress (and the States) may not abridge the right to free speech. This provision means what it says.

Limitation on authority of school officials

Nondisruptive expression protected

Regulation of the content and distribution of student publications has generated considerable controversy between school officials and students. A major area of difficulty has involved district policies requiring administrative review and approval prior to publication or distribution. In these "prior restraint" cases the burden of proof is on the district to show that its actions have been fairly imposed and that regulation is necessary for maintaining order.

Student publications

A tenth-grade Texas student was suspended twice for distributing an underground newspaper in violation of a district policy stating that all written material distributed at school needed prior approval by the principal. In finding for the student, the appeals court stated: "What is lacking in the present regulation . . . [is] any criteria to be followed by the school authorities in determining whether to grant or deny permission, and of any procedural safeguards in the form of 'an expeditious review procedure of the decision of the school authorities'."[45]

Specific criteria required

The Farm News was the school newspaper at Hayfield Secondary School in Fairfax County, Virginia. In the fall of 1976, students submitted an article entitled "Sexually Active Students Fail to Use Contraception" for approval by the principal. The school board had a policy prohibiting courses in sex education. Citing this policy, the principal refused permission to publish the article. Her prohibition was upheld by all review groups within the school system. The students filed suit in federal district court.[46]

Contraception story rejected

45 *Shanley* v. *Northeast Independent School District,* 462 F. 2d 960, (5th Cir. 1972).

46 *Gambino* v. *Fairfax County School Board,* 564 F. 2d 157 (4th Cir. 1977).

School officials claimed the newspaper was supported by tax monies and was part of the school's curriculum. While this case was being decided, the school board approved a sex education program, but specifically excluded birth control as a topic of discussion. As a result, district officials asserted that publication of the article would override the board's decision. The students argued that the First Amendment protected their right to publish the article.

School newspapers not part of required curriculum

The federal district and appellate courts upheld the students. *The Farm News* was found to be protected by the First Amendment. These courts indicated that a school newspaper was not part of the curriculum, but rather was more akin to the school library, where information on birth control was available.

Specific rules required

Adverse court decisions such as those described above have prompted many school boards to develop written regulations likely to withstand judicial scrutiny. Generally, these include specific rules concerning the time, place, and manner of distribution; a method of advertising the rules to students; a prompt review process; and speedy appeal procedures. Students may not distribute literature that is obscene by legal definition, libelous, or likely to cause the substantial disruption specified in *Tinker*.

Suspension and Expulsion

Nine students received ten-day suspensions from their Columbus, Ohio, secondary schools for various alleged acts of misconduct. The suspensions were imposed without hearings, but in accordance with state law. The school board had no written procedure covering suspensions. The students filed suit claiming deprivation of their constitutional rights.[47] In defense, school officials argued that since there is no constitutional right to education at public expense, the due process clause of the Fourteenth Amendment did not apply.

Minimum due process procedures

A majority of the U.S. Supreme Court disagreed, reasoning that students had a legal right to public education. In other words, they had a property interest in their education that could not be "taken away for misconduct without adherence to the minimum procedures" required by the due process clause. Further, the justices said that "students facing suspension [up to ten days] . . . must be given some kind of notice and afforded some kind of hearing. . . . the student first [must] be told what he is accused of doing and what the basis of the accusation is." The student then must be "given an opportunity to explain his version of the facts." Also, "as a general rule notice and hearing should precede removal of the student from school." Finally, the Court commented that longer suspensions or expulsions might require more elaborate due process procedures.

High schoolers expelled for spiking punch

Tenth-graders Peggy Strickland and Virginia Crain spiked the punch at a school-related party. For this they were suspended and then expelled from school for the balance of the semester. The school board took this action without affording the girls any of the due process requirements to which

47 *Goss* v. *Lopez,* 419 U.S. 565 (1975).

they were entitled. The families filed suit.[48] School board members indicated they were not aware of the specific requirements in expulsion cases. The justices ruled that ignorance of the law was no excuse and that school board members could be liable for monetary damages if they know or should have known that actions they took would deprive a student of constitutional rights.

In response to decisions like those cited above, numerous school districts have developed written policies governing short- and long-term suspensions and expulsions. Short-term suspension rights typically include oral or written notice describing the misconduct, the evidence on which the accusation is based, a statement of the planned punishment, and an opportunity for the student to explain his or her version or refute the stated facts before an impartial person. The thrust of these procedures is to provide "rudimentary precautions against unfair or mistaken findings of misconduct and arbitrary expulsion from school."[49] Expulsions require full procedural due process similar to those necessary for teacher terminations.

Current requirements and procedures

Search and Seizure

Freedom from unreasonable search and seizure is guaranteed by the Fourth Amendment. Lawfully issued search warrants commonly are required to conduct searches. The rise of drug use in schools has renewed interest in Fourth Amendment protections. Where courts are involved, the issue usually is whether searches by school authorities were conducted in violation of the Fourth Amendment. Other issues concern whether school officials acted under authority granted them by the state or as private citizens in conducting searches. The Fourth Amendment protects citizens against government action, but not against the acts of private persons. Courts have tended to rule that school officials are private individuals when conducting searches.

Fourth Amendment rights

Searches usually are conducted because administrators have reason to suspect that illegal or dangerous items are on the premises. For legal purposes, suspicion exists in differing degrees. Where searches have been upheld, courts have said "reasonable" cause was sufficient for school officials to act. Police, for example, need "probable" cause, a higher standard, before searching individuals.

Reasonable cause

A fifth-grade boy complained to his teacher that $3.00 was missing from his coat pocket. The class had experienced a problem with things disappearing. Aware that no student had left the room since entering, the teacher, assisted by other teachers and administrators, searched the children's coats and had them empty their pockets. The missing money was not found. The boys

48 *Wood* v. *Strickland,* 420 U.S. 308 (1975).

49 *Goss* v. *Lopez,* 419 U.S. 565 (1975).

and girls then were taken to their respective restrooms and required to strip to their underwear. The money was never recovered. Parents filed suit claiming that the search had been unlawfully conducted.[50]

In ruling against school personnel, the judges noted that there may have been reasonable cause to suspect *someone* in the class had stolen the money, but no facts existed

Particularization required

> to particularize ... which students might possess the money, something which has time and again ... been found necessary to a reasonable search under the Fourth Amendment. ... For this reason, the search must be held invalid ... there being no reasonable suspicion to believe that *each student* searched possessed contraband or evidence of a crime.

For two and one-half hours junior and senior high school students in Highland, Indiana, waited in their seats while six teams using trained dogs searched the 2,780 students. A school official, police officer, dog handler, and German shepard entered the classroom where Diane Doe, thirteen, was a student.

The dog went up and down the aisles sniffing students. The dog reached Diane, sniffed her body, and repeatedly pushed its nose on and between her legs. The officer understood this behavior to be an "alert" signaling the presence of drugs. Diane emptied her pockets as requested but no drugs were found. Still the dog kept sniffing her. Finally, Diane was taken to the nurse's office and strip-searched. No drugs were found. Diane had played with her own dog before school. Her dog was in heat and this smell remaining on her body had alerted the police dog.

Diane Doe vindicated

The Does filed suit. Both the district court and the appeals court concluded that the only thing done improperly that day was the strip-search of Diane. The Court of Appeals said, "It does not require a constitutional scholar to conclude that a nude search of a thirteen-year-old child is an invasion of constitutional rights of some magnitude. More than that: It is a violation of any known principle of human decency."[51] Diane was awarded $7,500 damages. Sniffing of student lockers and cars was not considered a search because these occurred when they were unattended and in public view. The issue of the legality of having dogs sniff students remained.

In sum, when conducting warrantless searches the following guidelines seem appropriate.

Standards for searches

1. Lockers are considered school property and may be searched if reasonable cause exists. Dogs may be used to sniff lockers and cars.

50 *Bellnier* v. *Lund*, 438 F. Supp. 47 (N.Y. 1977).

51 *Doe* v. *Renfrow*, 635 F. 2d 582 (7th Cir. 1980), cert. denied, 101 U.S. 3015 (1981).

2. Students may be sniffed if there is particularized, reasonable suspicion that an individual possesses contraband. If a court case results, school officials may have to prove the dog's reliability for drug alert purposes.
3. Strip-searches are unconstitutional and should never be conducted.

Corporal Punishment

Corporal punishment in American education dates back to the colonial period. This method of discipline, unacceptable to many educational theorists and practitioners, enjoys considerable support within some segments of the community and is administered more frequently than educators like to admit. Four state legislatures have prohibited all corporal punishment in public schools—Hawaii, Maine, Massachusetts, and New Jersey.[52] Where state law is silent on corporal punishment, local boards have wide latitude in implementing disciplinary policies, including banning of physical punishment; however, where state statute explicitly permits corporal punishment local boards may regulate, but not prohibit, its use. Numerous local school boards have elected to develop detailed policies restricting the use of corporal punishment. Violations can lead to dismissal; legal charges are possible for excessive force, punishment based on personal malice toward the student, or unreasonable use of this technique.

Prohibited in some states

Florida law allows corporal punishment. In 1977 the U.S. Supreme Court ruled on the constitutionality of this law from two federal perspectives: one, whether use of corporal punishment was a violation of the Eighth Amendment barring cruel and unusual punishment; two, whether prior notice and some form of due process were required before administering punishment.

James Ingraham and Roosevelt Andrews were junior high school students in Dade County, Florida.[53] Because Ingraham had been slow to respond to the teacher's instructions, he received twenty paddle swats administered in the principal's office. As a consequence, he needed medical treatment and missed a few days of school. Andrews, too, was paddled, but less severely.

Eighth Amendment inapplicable

The justices reviewed the history of the Eighth Amendment and determined that the intent of its inclusion in the U.S. Constitution was to protect those convicted of crimes. For this reason, the Eighth Amendment was deemed inapplicable to corporal punishment of school children. As to due process, the Court said, "We conclude that the Due Process clause does not require notice and a hearing prior to the imposition of corporal punishment in the public schools, as that practice is authorized and limited by common law." Comment was made on the severity of the paddlings in this case; the Justices indicated that in such instances "school authorities ... may be held

52 The Maryland State Board of Education outlawed corporal punishment in that state, and California statutes require prior parental consent. Illinois state regulations permit parents to exempt their children from corporal punishment by notifying the principal annually. In 1982, the West Virginia Supreme Court ordered the State Board of Education to promulgate rules prohibiting the use of a "paddle, whip, stick or other mechanical device" on the state's schoolchildren.

53 *Ingraham* v. *Wright*, 430 U.S. 651 (1977).

liable in damages to the child and, if malice is shown, they may be subject to criminal penalties."

Student Records

Until 1974 most school records were closed to students' and parents' examination. At the same time that inspection of personal files was denied to students and their families; prospective employers, government agencies, credit bureaus, and others encountered no access problems. As might be guessed, abuses occurred. The Family Educational Rights and Privacy Act (also called either FERPA or the Buckley Amendment) was passed by Congress in 1974 to curb abuses in institutions receiving federal funds.

FERPA (the Buckley Amendment)

The Buckley Amendment required public school districts to develop policies allowing parents access to their children's official school records. The act prohibited disclosure of these records to most third parties without prior parental consent (in cases of students under eighteen years of age). Districts adopted procedures to amend records where parents challenged the accuracy or completeness of information contained in them. Hearing and appeal mechanisms regarding disputed information were required as well. Finally, parents who have children in elementary and secondary schools must be notified annually of their rights under the Buckley Amendment and how to exercise them.

Parents' rights

Access to records

Parents retain rights of access to their children's school records until the child reaches the age of eighteen or is enrolled in a postsecondary institution. From that point on the student alone possesses the right to examine his or her school records, to request amendment or a hearing on disputed contents, and to control dissemination to third parties.

Exceptions to general rules

The Buckley Amendment allows several exceptions. Private notes and memoranda of teachers and administrators (including grade books) are exempt from view. Records that are kept separate from official files and maintained for law enforcement purposes (for example, special education records) also are immune under FERPA. Nothing may be disclosed that would jeopardize the privacy rights of other pupils. Lastly, schools may disclose directory-type information without prior consent; however, students or their families may request that even this information be withheld if they choose.[54]

Compulsory Attendance

Every state has a law requiring children to attend a public, private, or parochial school. Penalties for noncompliance are set by each state. Attendance ages vary among the states; generally laws require enrollment beginning at

54 E. Gordon Gee and David J. Sperry, *Education Law and the Public Schools: A Compendium* (Boston: Allyn and Bacon, 1978).

Pierce case

six or seven and continuing until sixteen or seventeen. *Pierce* v. *Society of Sisters* established that compulsory school attendance laws could be satisfied through enrollment in a private or parochial school.[55] The question then arose over how much control a state might exercise with regard to the education offered in nonpublic schools. *Farrington* v. *Tokushige* allowed nonpublic schools "reasonable choice and discretion in respect of teachers, curriculum and textbooks."[56] Since then, states have enacted legislation to regulate nonpublic schools. These laws vary widely—from virtually no intervention to considerable regulation. As examples, some states require the employment of certified teachers only, specify the number of days and/or hours that school must be in session each year, or insist that state accreditation standards be met.

Amish case

Compelling state interest conflicts with religious freedom

Wisconsin requires students to attend school from ages seven to sixteen. The Old Order Amish of that state were in violation of this law and three parents were tried, convicted, and fined for not sending their children to high school. Testimony revealed that the Amish believed such attendance to be contrary to their religion and way of life. In this case the compelling interests of the state in educating its youth came in conflict with the religious freedoms guaranteed all citizens. Both the Wisconsin and U.S. Supreme Courts ruled for the parents.[57] Chief Justice Warren Burger, writing for the majority, emphasized that this decision was to be narrowly applied to the Amish and not to groups "claiming to have recently discovered some 'progressive' or more enlightened process for rearing children for modern life."

Home Schooling

Most states allow home schooling

During the past decade there has been a revival of interest in home schooling. A small number of parents who object to some subject matter taught in public schools, the teaching methods used, or the absence of religious activities have chosen to teach their children at home. Thirty-eight states allow home schooling subject to varying restrictions.[58]

Home schooling must be comparable

Where such parents have been brought before courts as violators of compulsory attendance laws, they usually must demonstrate that the home program is essentially equivalent to that offered in public schools with respect to subject matter covered, adequacy of texts used, and number of hours of daily instruction provided; they also must show through standardized test results that the education provided is comparable to that of school-educated

55 *Pierce* v. *Society of Sisters,* 268 U.S. 510 (1925).

56 *Farrington* v. *Tokushige,* 273 U.S. 284 (1926).

57 *Wisconsin* v. *Yoder,* 406 U.S. 205 (1972).

58 Arkansas, Illinois, Kansas, Kentucky, Minnesota, Nebraska, New Hampshire, North Carolina, North Dakota, Tennessee, Texas, and Wyoming have neither state legislation nor court decisions permitting home schooling.

peers. Parents have tended to prevail in court decisions where state or case law supported their actions and where they demonstrated to judicial satisfaction that the education their children received was at least equal to education in the public schools.

Rights of Nonpublic School Students

Rights limited

As with teachers, students enrolled in nonpublic schools may not enjoy the constitutional guarantees discussed in this chapter. These rights are available to public school pupils because their schools fulfill state constitutional obligations. Private school activity would be considered state action only if a substantial relationship between the school and government could be demonstrated.[59] First Amendment restrictions make this an unlikely possibility for religiously affiliated schools, which enroll approximately 84 percent of all nonpublic school students.

Religion and the Schools

First Amendment

The framers of our Constitution were acutely aware of religious persecution and sought to prevent the United States from experiencing the serious and often bloody conflicts that had occurred in Europe. The First Amendment, adopted in 1791, prohibits the establishment of a nationally sanctioned religion (the establishment clause) and government interference with individuals' rights to hold and freely practice their religious beliefs (the free exercise clause). The position of government toward religion was succinctly stated by Judge Alphonso Taft over one hundred years ago: "The government is neutral, and while protecting all, it prefers none, and it disparages none."[60]

Prayer and Bible Reading

Prayer proposed in New York

The New York State Board of Regents composed the following nondenominational prayer: "Almighty God, we acknowledge our dependence upon thee, and we beg thy blessings upon us, our parents, our teachers and our Country." Students in New Hyde Park were required to recite this prayer daily. Exemption was possible upon written parental request. Ten parents challenged the constitutionality of the prayer requirement and the authority of school officials to impose it.

The U.S. Supreme Court agreed with the plaintiffs and, in 1962, the state-written prayer was declared unconstitutional. The decision created a storm

59 Michael LaMorte, *School Law: Cases and Concepts,* (Englewood Cliffs, N.J.: Prentice-Hall, 1982).

60 Quoted by Justice Tom Clark in *School District of Abington Township* v. *Schempp,* 374 U.S. 203 (1963).

The courts have held that organized prayer in public schools is unconstitutional because it violates the separation of church and state protected by the First Amendment. Such restrictions do not apply to nonpublic schools, however.
(Paul Conklin)

of protest, which has not subsided to this day. The Justices' reasoning in this decision is instructive:

Organized prayer prohibited

> Neither the fact that the prayer may be denominationally neutral nor the fact that its observance on the part of students is voluntary can serve to free it from the limitations of the Establishment Clause. . . . When the power, prestige and financial support of government is placed behind a particular religious belief, the indirect coercive pressure upon religious minorities to conform to the prevailing officially approved religion is plain. . . . The New York laws officially prescribing the Regents' prayer are inconsistent both with the purposes of the Establishment Clause and with the Establishment Clause itself.
>
> It has been argued that . . . to prohibit state laws respecting an establishment of religious services in public schools is to indicate a hostility toward religion or toward prayer. Nothing, of course, could be more wrong. . . . It is neither sacrilegious nor antireligious to say that each separate government in this country should stay out of the business of writing or sanctioning official prayers and leave that purely religious function to the people themselves and to those the people choose to look to for religious guidance.[61]

A year later the Court again decided a case concerning religious exercises in public schools. This time the issue involved oral reading of Bible verses and recitation of the Lord's Prayer at the beginning of each school day.

61 *Engle* v. *Vitale*, 370 U.S. 421 (1962).

Violation of establishment clause

Again, the Court held that these officially imposed practices were unconstitutional under the establishment clause of the First Amendment. Justice Tom Clark wrote:

> These exercises are prescribed as part of the curricular activities of students who are required by law to attend school. They are held in the school buildings under the supervision and with the participation of teachers employed in those schools. . . . The trial court . . . has found that such an opening exercise is a religious ceremony and was intended by the State to be so. We agree with the trial court's finding. . . .[62]

Free exercise clause

Proponents argued that because accommodation was made for those who did not wish to participate, continuation of these exercises should be permissible. Justice Clark responded: "Nor are these required exercises mitigated by the fact that individual students may absent themselves upon parental request, for that fact furnishes no defense to a claim of unconstitutionality under the Establishment Clause. ... The Free Exercise Clause," he wrote, "has never meant that a majority could use the machinery of the state to practice its beliefs."

Individual prayer constitutional

The Court, then, has banned state-organized, obligatory recitation of prayer and Bible reading in public schools. Neither writing of a broadly inclusive nondenominational prayer nor excusing those who prefer not to participate has overcome First Amendment prohibitions. Students, privately and individually, may pray in school whenever they are so moved. Further, public schools lawfully may teach comparative religion, the history of religion, and the Bible as literature, as part of secular curricular offerings.

Over the past twenty years numerous state legislatures have passed laws permitting prayer in some form. Statutes have been worded carefully to withstand possible court challenges. Almost half the states now have legislation allowing silent prayer or meditation. Cases challenging these laws have come before courts at all levels. Where the new law was found to advance religion it was struck down. However, silent meditation and personal reflection statutes have tended to be upheld.

Equal access for student religious groups

Opinion polls show that 80 percent of Americans favor prayer in public schools. A federal law passed in 1984 requires schools receiving federal funds to provide "equal access" to students who wish to meet before or after school to discuss religion or pray. As long as such activities are initiated and conducted by students and do not involve school personnel, schools must allow the use of their facilities on the same basis as they are made available to other groups.

Pledge of Allegiance

Several Jehovah's Witnesses went to court over a West Virginia requirement that their children recite the pledge of allegiance at school each morning.

62 *School District of Abington Township* v. *Schempp* and *Murray* v. *Curlett*, 374 U.S. 203 (1963).

The parents' objection was based on religious doctrine. The court ruled that the children could be exempted from this requirement because it conflicted with their religious beliefs. The court stated that "no official, high or petty, can prescribe what shall be orthodox in politics, nationalism, religion or other matters of opinion or force citizens to confess by word or act their faith therein. If there are any circumstances which permit an exception, they do not now occur to us."[63] Using this ruling as precedent, a federal appeals court decided that a student who refused to stand and recite the pledge, in defiance of a state statute, could not be compelled to do so.[64]

Religious objections

Public Support of Nonpublic Schools

The New Jersey Constitution allowed state aid for transportation of private and parochial students. This provision was challenged by opponents, who charged that such aid expended public funds for a private purpose and provided government support to religion. The U.S. Supreme Court held that where state constitutions permitted such assistance, there was no violation of the U.S. Constitution.[65] The amount and type of support available to nonpublic schools vary among the states and are dependent on the language and interpretation of each state's constitution. The distinction made by courts between permissible and impermissible state aid to nonpublic schools is usually based on the **child benefit theory**. That is, aid that directly benefits the child is permissible, whereas aid that primarily benefits the nonpublic institution is not.

Transportation of nonpublic students acceptable

Wolman v. *Walter* addressed state support for specific educational services to nonpublic schools as permitted by the Ohio Constitution.[66] The U.S. Supreme Court decided each question by applying a three-part test. "In order to pass muster, a statute must have a secular legislative purpose, must have a principal or primary effect that neither advances nor inhibits religion, and must not foster an excessive government entanglement with religion. . . ."

Standards for assistance to nonpublic schools

The Court's decisions regarding the issues involved in *Wolman* v. *Walter* were as follows:

Supreme Court decisions

1. Providing for the purchase or loan of secular textbooks is constitutional.[67]
2. Providing standardized tests covering secular subjects and scoring for them is constitutional.
3. Providing speech, hearing, and psychological diagnostic services at the nonpublic school site to enrolled pupils is constitutional.

63 *West Virginia State Board of Education* v. *Barnette,* 319 U.S. 624 (1943).

64 *Lipp* v. *Morris,* 579 F. 2d 834 (3rd Cir. 1978).

65 *Everson* v. *Board of Education of Erving Township,* 330 U.S. 1 (1947).

66 *Wolman* v. *Walter,* 433 U.S. 229 (1977).

67 In Ohio, the nonpublic school channels its requests through the public school district in which it is located.

4. "Providing therapeutic and remedial services at a neutral site off the premises of the nonpublic schools is permissible." These services are provided by public school employees. "It can hardly be said that ... public employees performing public functions on public property ... creates an excessive entanglement between church and state."
5. Providing for the purchase and loan of other instructional materials and equipment such as projectors, science kits, maps and globes, charts, record players, and so on was ruled unconstitutional because of the "impossibility of separating the secular education function from the sectarian, the state aid inevitably flows in part in support of the religious role of the schools."
6. Providing funds for field trips was unconstitutional because "where the teacher works within and for a sectarian institution, an unacceptable risk of fostering religion is an inevitable byproduct. ... Moreover, the public school authorities will be unable adequately to insure secular use of the field trip funds without close supervision of the non-public teachers. This would create excessive entanglement."

Situation is muddled

The conclusions in ***Wolman*** v. ***Walter*** show clearly why many legal scholars believe that constitutional law regarding religion and the schools is something of a muddle. Why should government purchase of textbooks and tests for nonpublic schools be constitutional but not purchase of maps, globes, charts, and record players? Why can government-supported psychological services be provided at nonpublic schools, when therapeutic and remedial services must be provided at a neutral site? Although the Court provided reasons to support these conclusions, many observers view its overall decision as convoluted and as very difficult, if not impossible, to explain and justify to the average person.

Affirmative Action and Educational Equity

Affirmative action generally refers to requirements for taking positive steps to ensure that disadvantaged individuals receive equal opportunity in employment and education. In general, affirmative action requirements are associated with the Fourteenth Amendment to the U.S. Constitution, Titles VI and VII of the Civil Rights Act of 1964, and subsequent legislation involving minority groups, women, and the handicapped.

Legislation outlaws discrimination

The Fourteenth Amendment guarantees all citizens equal protection of the law. Title VI of the Civil Rights Act prohibits discrimination in federally assisted educational programs on the basis of race, color, religion, and national origin. Title VII prohibits discrimination in employment on the basis of any of these criteria or on the basis of sex. Title IX of the Education Amendments of 1972 contained similar language regarding discrimination against women in federally assisted education programs, and section 504 of the Rehabilitation Act of 1973 extended similar protection to the handicapped (see Chapter 12).

Obligations for affirmative action

Much subsequent litigation involved definitions of discrimination and of the meaning of obligations to overcome past discrimination. In 1976 the U.S. Supreme Court ruled in *Washington* v. *Davis* that disproportionate impact alone does not prove the existence of unconstitutional discrimination.[68] For example, the fact that minority groups or women are underrepresented among employees in a school district or college is not by itself sufficient to prove an equal protection violation; plaintiffs also must offer proof of the defendants' deliberate intention to discriminate. However, the Court also ruled that disproportionate impact is enough to shift the burden of proof to the defendant. For example, if a school district uses a test for teacher hiring that disproportionately eliminates minority candidates, the district must prove that the test has some valid relationship to performance on the job.

Quotas not constitutional

During the 1970s federal regulations required that educational institutions receiving federal funds set and meet specific targets for hiring minority applicants and women by a definite deadline (in other words, quotas). Similar policies were being developed and encouraged regarding admission of minority students to higher education programs. This approach was prohibited when the U.S. Supreme Court ruled in 1978 in *Regents of the University of California* v. *Alan Bakke* that setting aside a specific number of places for minority admission to a medical school was unconstitutional.[69] However, this Supreme Court decision also provided support for approaches to affirmative action that do not set firm quotas for admitting or hiring minority applicants and women. The Court encouraged publicly supported institutions to devise policies that give some legitimate preference to applicants whose background (for example, minority group membership, economically disadvantaged history, rural origins) the institution might want to have represented more adequately among its employees or clients. In addition, the Court subsequently upheld the right of private employers to develop affirmative action plans giving minorities preferential treatment in employment.[70]

Affirmative action encouraged

Reduction-in-force and seniority

Another affirmative action issue that affects schools and teachers involves seniority rules for **reduction-in-force (RIF)**—that is, termination of teachers because of declining enrollment or financial problems in a school district. Negotiated agreements in most districts designate termination of employment according to seniority: the most recently hired are the first fired. However, a number of governmental units, including some school districts, initiated affirmative action plans that exempt minority employees from this seniority provision as long as the unit is below its target for minority employment. In June 1984, the Supreme Court ruled that this policy violated Title VII of the Civil Rights Act of 1964 unless the nonminority employees

68 *Washington* v. *Davis,* 426 U.S. 229 (1976).

69 *Regents of the University of California* v. *Alan Bakke,* 438 U.S. 265 (1978).

70 *Steelworkers* v. *Weber,* 443 U.S. 193 (1979).

who are released have only temporary status or it can be demonstrated that minority employees benefiting from the suspension of seniority rules have personally experienced overt discrimination.[71]

Aspects of educational equity involving minority, non-English-speaking, and handicapped students are discussed in Chapter 12 of this book. Efforts to equalize educational opportunities for females generally center on the reduction or removal of barriers to achievement and attainment in the schools. In the next chapter we point out that opportunities for women have been limited in part by socialization practices in the home and the larger society. Some of these limitations can be reduced through appropriate policies and actions within the educational system.

Sex barriers

Efforts to make the educational system more equitable for females have been stimulated by the Women's Educational Equity Act (WEEA) of 1974. Among the most important activities conducted under the WEEA have been the following:[72]

Efforts to improve educational opportunity for girls and women

- Programs to open math, science, and technology courses and careers to women and girls
- Programs to reduce sex stereotyping in occupational selection as well as curriculum materials
- Removal of admission restraints and encouragement of females to enroll in "nontraditional" vocational education courses, as well as reduction of barriers to female entry into apprenticeship training
- Programs to increase the representation of women in educational administration
- Special efforts to improve educational and career opportunities for minority, disabled, and rural women
- Programs to help school district officials and teachers work out comprehensive approaches for improving the educational opportunities for and career aspirations of girls and women
- Encouragement of greater participation by females in athletics

Athletic participation improved

Federal regulations require that more opportunities for athletic participation be provided to women in secondary schools and postsecondary institutions. The activities fostered by WEEA and the federal regulations have effectively raised women's athletic participation rates. According to the National Federation of State High School Associations, 1.85 million young women took part in secondary school athletics in 1980–81, compared with only 240,000 in 1970–71.

71 *Firefighters* v. *Stotts,* 52 U.S.L.W. 4757 (1984).

72 Joy R. Simonson and Jeffrey A. Menzer, *Catching Up: A Review of the Women's Educational Equity Act Program* (Washington, D.C.: Citizens Council on Women's Education, 1984).

The WEEA has been a small program funded at a peak of $10 million in 1980 and at only about $6 million a year since that time. However, this act, together with the efforts of many other agencies and private citizens, has improved educational opportunities for women.

Summing Up

1. Education-related court cases have significantly increased in the last twenty years. Such cases can be heard in both federal and state courts depending on the issues involved. Only opinions of the U.S. Supreme Court apply nationally.
2. Tenure protects teachers from dismissal except on specified grounds. These grounds include incompetency, immorality, insubordination, and unprofessional conduct. Teachers accused of such conduct are entitled to due process protections.
3. Teachers have the right to form and belong to unions and other professional organizations, but most states prohibit teachers from striking.
4. Teachers' rights involving freedom of expression, academic freedom, and censorship depend on a balance between individual and governmental interests. Teachers have rights guaranteed to individuals under the Constitution, but school boards have obligations to ensure the "proper" and "regular" operation of the schools, taking into account the rights of parents, teachers, and students.
5. Restraints on teachers' behavior outside school and on their grooming are not as stringent as they once were, but teachers still are expected to serve as role models and to behave in an exemplary manner. Definite standards must be upheld to avoid legal suits charging negligence when students are injured. In addition, teachers must obey copyright laws.
6. Students' rights have been clarified and expanded by the courts and include freedom of expression, due process in the case of suspension or expulsion, prohibition against bodily searches in the absence of specific grounds, limitations on the use of corporal punishment, and privacy of records.
7. Organized and mandated prayer and bible reading are not allowed in public schools.
8. The situation with respect to government support for nonpublic schools is mixed. For example, government may provide textbooks, tests, and psychological services for students at nonpublic schools, but it may not provide funds for field trips, projectors, science kits, or maps. Providing the latter is thought to entangle church and state.
9. Federal laws prohibit discrimination in educational employment and programming on the grounds of race, color, religion, national origin, and sex. School districts have an obligation to act affirmatively in providing equal opportunity for minorities and women. Teachers have an obligation to help ensure that equal opportunities are available to minority group members and females.

Discussion Questions

1. Should teachers be required to meet higher or different standards of personal morality than other citizens? Why or why not?
2. What are signs of child abuse? What reporting procedures do districts in your area follow?
3. Discuss the wisdom or lack of wisdom of the educational malpractice decisions. What types of malpractice suits might be successful in the future?
4. Debate the pros and cons of prayer, Bible reading, and religious observances in public schools.
5. What does your state constitution say about support to nonpublic schools? How much support and what type of support is given? What policies and practices are followed in adjacent states?

Suggested Readings

Education Week.

This weekly newspaper focuses on issues in elementary and secondary education; court cases and decisions are often reported.

LaMorte, Michael W. *School Law: Cases and Concepts.* Englewood Cliffs, N.J.: Prentice-Hall, 1982.

In this comprehensive text for the study of school law, the author uses excerpts from judicial opinions to convey important legal principles.

McCarthy, Martha M., and Nelda H. Cambron. *Public School Law: Teachers' and Students' Rights.* Boston: Allyn and Bacon, 1981.

Detailed explanations of teachers' and students' rights are illustrated through the use of applicable court cases.

Phi Delta Kappan.

Thomas Flygare writes an in-depth column on one legal topic each month, often focusing on current cases or issues before the courts.

West's Education Law Reporter.

This bimonthly compilation of current cases heard in federal and state courts includes summaries of judicial opinions. It is usually found in law libraries.

NO
PARKING

Part 4 Social Foundations

Educational systems are established to serve specific purposes in the societies in which they operate. For this reason, it is not possible to understand the way schools and other components of an educational system function without knowing something about the larger society and the ways in which it influences and is reflected by the educational system.

Chapter 10 asks how students are prepared to participate in our schools and our society and describes the major forces that mold student behavior. After discussing the relationship between culture and education, attention is given to several of the central socializing agents in contemporary society—the family, the peer group, the school, and television. The next section deals with sex roles in school and in the larger society, and with sex differences in educational achievement. The final section of the chapter is devoted to adolescent and youth culture.

In Chapter 11 we examine relationships between social class, race, and school achievement. After reviewing recent data indicating that working-class students tend to be much lower in achievement than are middle-class students, the chapter points out that there is little relationship between minority status and school performance after taking account of the low social class of disadvantaged minority groups. The problem of low school achievement is most severe among underclass students in concentrated poverty neighborhoods.

Chapter 11 also discusses possible reasons for the low achievement of working-class students, including home environment characteristics that do not provide good preparation for success in the traditional school, possible hereditary handicaps, and ineffective school instruction. We report that the influence of heredity does not appear to be well established in any precise way, but in any case most of the achievement problems among working-class students involves home environment considerations and ineffective instruction. Chapter 11 also describes recent research indicating that schools can teach low-achieving students much more effectively than they have done in the past.

Chapter 12 deals with specific issues involving educational opportunity. The first section, on desegregation, concludes that although much progress has been made in providing desegregated schooling to minority students in smaller towns and cities, particularly in the South, most minority students attend segregated schools in central-city locations within metropolitan areas. The next section discusses compensatory education to overcome the educational deficits of economically disadvantaged students. Recent research indicates that compensatory education may be having some positive but limited impact on the achievement of disadvantaged students.

Chapter 12 also discusses multicultural education, putting particular emphasis on cultural pluralism and on multicultural instruction that recognizes and responds to students' diverse learning styles and language backgrounds. The chapter concludes with a discussion of educational opportunities for handicapped students, particularly with reference to classification and labeling of students, mainstreaming, and the disproportionate placement of minority students in programs for the mentally retarded. One of the major conclusions of Chapter 12 is that schools must be made more effective for *all* students if equal educational opportunity is to become a reality in our society.

10

Culture, Socialization, and Education

Focusing Questions

What are the functions of education in transmitting cultural patterns?

What part is played by the schools in modern society?

How do sex roles and sex differences influence learning and achievement?

How does the culture of the schools socialize the young?

How have television and other mass media affected students?

What problems in youth culture affect the schools?

CULTURE IS THE MEANS OF ENSURING THE UNITY AND SURVIVAL of a society. The attitudes, behaviors, and understandings that individuals learn in groups—the culture of a large group or society and the subcultures of smaller groups—are what enable people to communicate with each other and to function within a set of common rules. To provide for transmission of culture and to allow society to function satisfactorily, young people must be **acculturated** (learn the concepts, values, and behavior patterns of individuals sharing a common culture) and **socialized** (prepared to function first as a young person and then as an adult) so that they can participate effectively in groups and in the larger society.

Many individuals and institutions play a part in helping to acculturate and socialize children and youth in our society. The family, of course, is most important for young children, but modern societies include formal institutions that help determine what a child learns and how well he or she is prepared to function in society. The school has been created for just this purpose, but other institutions also mold the attitudes, behaviors, and understandings of children and youth.

Chapter 10 provides an overview of some of the most important developments and problems involving acculturation and socialization of children and youth in our complex, technological society. Emphasis throughout the chapter will be on how the culture of socializing institutions affects young people's development and achievement—and on implications for the schools of conditions in and problems created by other institutions.

Culture and Education

In a widely used definition, **culture** has been characterized as continually changing patterns of "learned behavior" transmitted among members of society.[1] Anthropologist Ruth Benedict provided us with another definition when she said, "Culture is that which binds men together."[2] Culture not only provides the lens through which individuals perceive the world, it also guides people in responding to what they perceive. Language is perhaps the clearest illustration of communicating shared meanings. Cultural meanings are also infused into nonverbal behavior and physical objects. For example, materials found in ancient ruins help us learn about the people who once lived in that time and place. Culture is a way of thinking and behaving; it is a group's knowledge and customs, its memories, written records, and objects for present and future use.

Aspects of culture

1 John Cuber, *Sociology: A Synopsis of Principles,* 4th ed. (New York: Appleton-Century-Crofts, 1959), p. 60.

2 Ruth Benedict, *Patterns of Culture* (Boston: Houghton Mifflin, 1983), p. 14.

Neither a single individual, nor a group, nor an entire society can be understood without reference to culture. As anthropologist Clyde Kluckhohn points out, even those of us who pride ourselves on our individualistic behavior follow the customs of our culture most of the time.[3] The fact that we brush our teeth, eat three meals a day (rather than two or four), and sleep in a bed (not on the floor or on a sheep's pelt) reflects our culture.

If we lived in a different place and time, we would live in a different culture and we would think and behave differently than we do. So it is difficult for us objectively to evaluate cultures other than our own. Different cultures achieve specific benefits for their members relative to their place and time. Because we are bound up in our own culture, we tend to overlook different perspectives and alternative strategies in dealing with the world around us.

Acculturation and socialization in the schools

In modern societies, the school serves as perhaps the major institution devised by the adult generation for maintaining and perpetuating the culture; it imparts the tools necessary for survival and ensures the transmission of knowledge and values to future generations. In effect, the school provides us with a sense of the continuity and experience of our culture; it is a highly formal system for educating the young, an institution children are required to attend in order to be acculturated and socialized. The values, beliefs, and **norms** (rules of behavior) of a society are maintained and passed to the next generation, not merely by teaching about them, but also by embodying these elements of culture in the very operation of the educational system.

Most Americans tend to regard education as synonymous with schooling. Actually, a culture may have no schools, but it still educates its young through the family or special ritual and training. Schooling plays a major role in education in modern industrial cultures; it becomes increasingly important as cultures become more complex and the frontiers of knowledge expand. In simple, nontechnological societies, almost everyone becomes proficient over the whole range of knowledge necessary for survival. In complex societies people acquire different proficiencies and abilities; no individual can range over the entire body of complex knowledge or expect to be proficient in all areas of learning.

The techniques of education used by nonliterate peoples include overt training by elders, emulation of older children, attendance at ceremonies, observation of parents and elders doing daily tasks, and inculcation of proper values and conduct by codes of punishments and rewards. In technological societies education begins at home, and school takes on greater importance as the child becomes older. The schools become a crucial institution for helping the young acquire systematic knowledge, inculcating them with the ideas of the culture, and bridging the gap between generations. In contemporary life the mass media also serve an educational function by redefining values and ideas.

3 Clyde Kluckhohn, *Mirror for Man* (New York: McGraw-Hill, 1949).

Agents of Socialization

Societies include a number of important institutions for transmitting their culture to children and youth. Historically, the most important of these institutions in many societies have been the church, the peer group, the school, and, of course, the family. Some institutions such as the church have become less influential in socialization for modern society than they were in the past, but others such as the mass media have emerged to play a major part in socialization.

Decline of church influence

The Family

Though family organization varies from one society to another, the family is the major early socializing agent in each one; as such, it is the first medium for transmitting the culture to the child. Because the family is the whole world to the very young child, its members teach children what matters in life, often without realizing the impact they are having. The desire to achieve popularity, the belief that a girl should be docile, the motivation to excel in school, and other beliefs and values are passed from parent to child. The behaviors adults encourage and discourage and the ways in which they discipline the child also affect his or her basic orientation toward the world.

Home environment and social class

Many children do well in school because their home and family environment has provided them with good preparation for succeeding in the classroom; others do poorly because they are disadvantaged in this regard, and the schools generally have not been very successful in overcoming this disadvantage. Because differences in home and family environment are significantly associated with social class, we will discuss some of the major home environment influences on educational achievement in the next chapter. These influences include the use of language in the home, the effects of differing child-raising practices, and other aspects of the family environment that help (or fail to) prepare children to succeed in the traditional school. Changes and trends in the structure and characteristics of the contemporary family also are thought to have important implications for the child's educational development and for his or her success in school. In the remainder of this section, we will discuss some of these trends.

Increase in Working Mothers The percentage of working mothers with children under eighteen has been increasing steadily since 1950. In that year, 18 percent of these mothers were working; by 1983 57 percent were working, and the trend toward greater female participation in the labor force is expected to continue.[4] Reasons for the increase in working mothers include better opportunities for women, rising divorce rates, family financial pres-

4 Alex Kucherov, "10 Forces Reshaping America," *U.S. News and World Report,* March 19, 1984, p. 47; Bryant Robey, "Caution: Women at Work," *American Demographics* (April 1984), p. 11.

sures that require the mother to work, and changes in older cultural attitudes and patterns that dictated that mothers stay home.

Child-care arrangements

As mothers have gone to work, there has been a major change in child-care arrangements. By 1977 only 29 percent of the children of working mothers were cared for in their homes, as compared with 57 percent in 1958. No good data exist to portray the average quality of day-care arrangements for preschool children, but it is certain that such arrangements are less than satisfactory for many children.

Latchkey children

The increase in working mothers also has been associated with the phenomenon of so-called *latchkey children,* who return to empty homes "after school either to sit by the television or to roam the streets."[5] National data indicate that there are approximately 6 million latchkey children between the ages of six and thirteen.[6] Proponents of expanding government service for latchkey children argue that valuable services could be provided for them through the schools and other institutions and that many children are "losing their childhood" because they have to fend for themselves and/or take care of siblings while parents work. Opponents argue that research does not establish the value of such services, that we do not know how to construct and implement effective programs, and, in some cases, that absence of a parent or other adult helps children develop independence.[7] Meanwhile, government officials in New York City, as in some other locations, are considering using school buildings to provide after-school care for hundreds of thousands of primary-grade children.

After-school care

Effects of maternal employment

Relationships between maternal employment and children's school performance are not well established or understood. A task force of the National Academy of Sciences reviewed the research on this topic and found little evidence to indicate that the preponderant effects of maternal employment on achievement are either positive or negative.[8] However, Lois Hoffman reviewed this same research and found some indications that daughters of working mothers tend to have higher achievement scores than daughters of nonworking mothers (after adjusting for social class), but sons of working middle-class mothers tended to score low on measures of intellectual functioning.[9]

Single-Parent Families Related to the increase in working mothers has been a very rapid rise in the percentage of single-parent households, mostly headed by a never-married, divorced, or separated woman. Much of this in-

5 Bickley Townsend, "How We Live," *American Demographics* (January 1984), p. 6; also see Victor R. Fuchs, *How We Live: An Economic Perspective on Americans from Birth to Death* (Cambridge, Mass.: Harvard University Press, 1983).

6 Tom Mirga, "Dispute Delays House Action on American Defense Education Act," *Education Week* (May 9, 1984), p. 13.

7 Anne Bridgman, "Schools Urged to Seek Solutions to Troubles of Latchkey Children," *Education Week* (May 30, 1984), p. 10.

8 National Academy of Sciences, *Families That Work: Children in a Changing World* (Washington, D.C.: National Academy Press, 1982).

9 Lois W. Hoffman, "Maternal Employment," *American Psychologist* (October 1979), pp. 859–865.

There is little free time in a working mother's day, but most are very concerned about their children's education and schooling.
(David S. Strickler/Atoz Images, Inc.)

crease has been due to growth in the rates of divorce. Only 15 percent of persons sixty-five to seventy-four years of age in 1980 had ended their first marriage in divorce, as compared with 49 percent of those between twenty-five and thirty-four years of age who already had divorced or will do so in the future (based on current divorce rates).[10] Examining these data, some observers view modern marriage as something of a "roulette game," which likely as not will leave children at one point or another in "disrupted" families. In addition, the 1970s showed a sharp decline in the remarriage rate, so that fewer children of divorced parents subsequently live in two-parent families.

These trends were clearly spelled out in a study showing that the percentage of children growing up in families disrupted by divorce, separation,

10 Paul C. Glick, "How American Families Are Changing," *American Demographics* (January 1984), p. 24.

Disrupted families

or death of a parent rose rapidly among both white and black families between 1960 and 1975. Among five-year-old whites, for example, 14 percent of youngsters born in the 1968–1970 period had experienced disruption, as compared with 9 percent of those born in the 1956–1958 period. Comparable figures for black children were 42 percent for youngsters born in the 1968–1970 period as compared with 22 percent for the earlier period.[11] By 1981, only 76 percent of young people under eighteen years of age were living with both parents, and only 59 percent of children born in the 1980s will live with both parents until they are eighteen.[12] This trend is expected to continue. By 1990, 31 percent of children and youth under eighteen will probably be living in single-parent families. Seventy-eight percent of this group will be in families with no father present.

Conflicting research

Conflicting results have been reported in research on the impact of marital disruption and/or family structure on children's development and achievement. Much of this research has concentrated on the possible influence of growing up in a father-absent home. Some studies conclude that there is little measurable impact on children,[13] but others find a variety of negative impacts, including a greater likelihood of falling into poverty and severe emotional problems among many children.[14]

Educators have been primarily concerned that the absence of a father may lead to psychological and behavior problems in the school and may detract from students' achievement. Their concern became a matter of national controversy after publication of Daniel Moynihan's 1965 pamphlet in which he pointed out that a large and growing percentage of black children lived in female-headed families and concluded that this trend represented a form of "social pathology" that seriously harmed the children involved.[15] A 1980 study conducted by the National Association of Secondary School Principals indicated that students from one-parent families demonstrate lower achievement and more frequently are tardy, truant, and suspended from school than are students from two-parent families, even after taking into account differences in family income.[16]

Difficulties in research

The major reason why research dealing with effects of father absence on children has not been very conclusive is that it is so difficult to control for the effects of social class. A large percentage of families that "lost" a father declined in social class, and this change in status makes it difficult for re-

11 Larry Bumpass and Ronald R. Rindfuss, "Children's Experience of Marital Disruption," *American Journal of Sociology* (July 1979), pp. 49–65.

12 Glick, "How American Families are Changing," p. 25.

13 Jessie Bernard, *Remarriage* (New York: Russell & Russell, 1971); Diane Scott Jones, "Family Influences on Cognitive Development and School Achievement," in Edmund W. Gordon, ed., *Review of Research in Education 11* (Washington, D.C.: American Education Research Association, 1984).

14 Lee Rainwater and William L. Yancey, *The Moynihan Report and the Politics of Controversy* (Cambridge, Mass.: M.I.T. Press, 1967).

15 Daniel P. Moynihan, *The Negro Family: The Case for National Action* (Washington, D.C.: Government Printing Office, 1965).

16 B. Frank Brown, "A Study of the School Needs of Children from One-Parent Families," *Phi Delta Kappan* (April 1980), pp. 537–540.

searchers to identify the separate effects of each factor.[17] Even controlling for income does not necessarily allow for accurate assignment of social class effects that may be falsely attributed to father absence. Thus it may be clear, for example, that a very high proportion of low-achieving students at schools in poverty neighborhoods live in female-headed households, but so does a high proportion of better-achieving students who live there, and single-parent families may be as much or more a result of rather than a cause of problems in these neighborhoods.

Recent research on students from single-parent families

Nevertheless, educators are rightly worried about effects of the trend toward single-parent families, particularly since this phenomenon no longer centers as it once did on the poor and disadvantaged. It has spread to the middle class and can no longer be easily viewed as a problem only for social workers and welfare offices. In this context, a recent study by researchers at the U.S. Department of Education concluded that absence of a parent is associated with lowered reading and math achievement, particularly among elementary students and black students. The study also found that effects were greatest among single-parent families below or barely above the poverty level, and that students in two-parent homes achieve better when their mothers work.[18]

Comparison of children in divorced and intact families

A second recent study also provided strong evidence that divorce has negative effects on the development of school-age children. Conducted for the National Association of School Psychologists, this study compared a carefully selected national sample of second, third, and fifth graders from intact and divorced families. Even after taking account of differences in parents' occupation and education, the children from intact families scored higher than those in divorced families on a large number of measures of social behavior and adjustment as well as on academic and intellectual performance and development. Effects of divorce were particularly strong and consistent for boys. After reviewing the data, one member of the research team discussed the larger implications of these findings.

Children of divorce vulnerable

> It should be clear . . . that divorced-family children in our society are currently vulnerable to behavioral and academic difficulties. . . . a return to more stable child-rearing environments seems unlikely. Consequently, a more tenable approach may be to examine more assiduously, the post-divorce environments that facilitate child adjustment and emotional security. This task requires no less than the full commitment of educators, social service personnel, and all psychology disciplines.[19]

17 E. A. Blechman, "Are Children with One Parent at Psychological Risk? A Methodological Review," *Journal of Marriage and the Family* (February 1982), pp. 179–195.

18 Ann M. Milne, David E. Myers, Fran M. Ellman, and Alan Ginsburg. "Single Parents, Working Mothers and the Education of Elementary School Age Children" (Paper presented at the annual meeting of the American Educational Research Association, New York, March 1982); *idem.,* "Single Parents, Working Mothers and the Educational Achievement of Secondary School Age Children" (Paper presented at the annual meeting of the American Educational Research Association, Montreal, April 1983).

19 John Guidubaldi, "Adjusting to Divorce" (Paper presented at the annual meeting of the American Educational Research Association, New Orleans, April 1984), p. 5.

In an attempt to help educators respond to the trend toward single-parent families, the National Committee for Citizens in Education has made the following recommendations:[20]

Recommendations for schools

Send copies of report cards and other communications to the noncustody parent.

Include representation of single-parent families in curriculum materials.

Add library materials that show varied lifestyles and help children deal with death and divorce.

Cooperate with other agencies in improving child-care arrangements before and after school.

Conduct workshops to help teachers recognize and overcome negative expectations they may have developed for children from single-parent families.

Decline in Fertility Rates The birthrate in the United States and other Western societies substantially declined during the past two centuries. The total fertility rate (the number of children under five years old per 1,000 women) fell from 704 in 1800 to 248 in 1970 and 170 in 1980, but since that time has remained stable. This figure is below the population replacement level of 211. The markedly lower average number of children per family has made it easier for families to devote more resources to the education of girls and for mothers to seek employment outside the home.

Positive effects

Decline in the fertility rate probably has an overall positive effect on the educational system. It is true that the decrease in enrollment associated with this trend produced many problems for educators, which are discussed elsewhere in this book. On the other hand, the declining birthrate also has meant smaller families, a decrease in the size of the youth **cohort** (a generational group of individuals having the same age classification), and some "liberation" of mothers from the home. Many social scientists believe that children in small families—and particularly first- and second-born children—benefit in intellectual growth compared with children in large families, because on the average they may receive more attention and other resources from their parents.[21] Some research also indicates that youth in a small cohort have more opportunities than those in a larger cohort, other things being equal, particularly when they enter the labor market.[22] Freeing the mother from the responsibilities of many children in the home also may benefit children through gains in family income and education.[23]

20 P. A. Clay, *Single Parents and the Public Schools* (Columbia, Md.: National Committee for Citizens in Education, 1981).

21 Robert B. Zazonc and Gregory B. Markus, "Birth Order and Intellectual Development," *Psychological Review* (January 1975), pp. 74–88.

22 Richard Easterlin, *Birth and Fortune: The Impact of Numbers on Personal Welfare* (New York: Basic Books, 1980).

23 Fuchs, *How We Live*.

Diverse effects of family change

Educators' concerns appear justified

Decline in the nuclear family

Assessment of Trends Related to the Family The interrelated trends described thus far have been changing the structure and functioning of families in the United States. Many more mothers with children are working, the percentage of single-parent households—usually headed by females—has been increasing, and there has been a decline in the fertility rate. These trends are associated on the one hand with overall improvements in women's educational and occupational attainment, which we will describe later in this chapter; on the other hand, they are associated with an increase in teenage pregnancy and with a decline in social class among many families headed by a low-paid, female head-of-household. Research does not conclusively establish that the overall results are permanently damaging to children; in some respects, at least for some families, there probably are gains for children associated with maternal employment and with smaller family size. However, some research indicates that maternal employment and living in a single-parent or divorced family do indeed have detrimental effects for many children.

From a historical point of view, there probably are reasonable grounds for worrying about the overall effects of family change on the socialization and achievement of children and youth in the schools. Many historians believe that our system of universal education drew considerable support from the development of the **nuclear family** (two parents living alone with their children) that grew to prominence in Western societies during a 300- to 400-year period that ended when the divorce rate began to sky-rocket after the Second World War. The traditional nuclear family had many disadvantages, including the relatively limited roles it offered for women, but as historian Edward Shorter has described its evolution, the nuclear or "modern" family had many advantages in socializing children for success in modern society.[24]

Shorter and other historians describe the nuclear family as highly child-centered and as devoting many of its resources to protecting children from the dangers of hostile environments and preparing them for success in the traditional school and subsequent middle-class occupations. Decline in the nuclear family whose resources—particularly the mother's—were highly focused on the development of children means that the schools may have a more difficult time socializing students because a higher percentage of children may experience problems related to the increase in single-parent households and working mothers.

The Peer Group

While the family is the first and the most basic of the primary groups with which a child is associated, peer-group interactions soon become frequent—the play group for the small child and the teenage clique for the adolescent. The peer group provides significant learning experience in how to interact

24 Edward Shorter, *The Making of the Modern Family* (New York: Basic Books, 1975).

with others, how to be accepted by others, and how to achieve status in a circle of friends.

Functions of the peer group

Peers are relatively equal, as contrasted with the relationship between parents and their children or between teachers and their students. Parents and teachers sometimes can force young children to obey rules they neither understand nor like, but peers do not have formal authority to do this, and thus the true meaning of exchange, cooperation, and equity can be learned more easily in the peer setting. Peer groups increase in importance as the child grows up, reaching maximum influence in adolescence, by which time they sometimes dictate much of the students' behavior both in and out of school.[25]

Increasing influence of the peer group

Several sources of information indicate that the peer group has become increasingly important in the socialization of children and youth. For example, Suzanne Boocock collected data on the daily activities of children in several communities and found that children spend much of their time with friends, "fooling around," or watching television. She concluded that in comparison with earlier historical periods, "relatively few children of the 1970s seem to have strong linkages with the larger society."[26] Other studies indicate a decline in the influence of family and church relative to the peer group. A Syracuse study by Condry and Siman even found that some children were turning to their friends because they had little close contact with their parents.[27]

Research also indicates that influence of peers as compared with parents depends on the topic or problem under investigation. For example, one study of twelve- to sixteen-year-olds in a large urban area found that parental influence was less important than peer influence in predicting students' preference for and use of alcohol, but parental norms were more important in predicting attitudes toward achievement in school.[28]

Importance of friends

Peer Culture and the School Educators are particularly concerned with the workings and influence of the peer group and associated student culture characteristics within the school and classroom. A landmark 1961 study by James Coleman examined the functioning of adolescent society in high schools and found that there is a strong student culture in the schools, one that is different from adult culture.[29] Coleman and his team visited ten schools and examined the students' frame of reference and informal social system. They found that favored activities among students included dating, talking on the telephone, being in the same class, eating together with friends

25 H. D. Thornburg, "Can the Middle School Adapt to the Needs of Its Students?" *Colorado Journal of Educational Research* (January 1979), pp. 26–29.

26 Suzanne S. Boocock, *Students, Schools, and Educational Policy: A Sociological View* (Cambridge, Mass.: Aspen Institute, 1976), p. 10.

27 J. C. Condry and M. A. Siman, "Characteristics of Adult and Peer-oriented Children," *Journal of Marriage and the Family* (August 1974), pp. 543–554.

28 B. J. Biddle, B. J. Bank, and M. M. Martin, "Parental and Peer Influence on Adolescents," *Social Forces* (June 1980), pp. 1057–1079.

29 James S. Coleman, *The Adolescent Society* (New York: Free Press, 1961).

in school, "hanging around together," or just "being with the group" outside of school. Esteem was gained by a combination of friendliness and popularity, an attractive appearance and personality, and possession of skills and objects (cars, clothes, records) valued by the culture. The image of the athletic star for boys and the image of the activities leader for girls were most esteemed, and the brilliant student per se was one of the less esteemed images. Parallel data revealed that the brilliant student, especially the brilliant girl, fared poorly as a dating choice from the outset, and declined even further from the freshman to senior year.

Sources of popularity

No matter what the unique climate of the school or the parents' socio-economic status, the most popular male student was oriented to the athletic image. (However, the male student who was high in scholarship but was not an athlete had higher status than the student who was neither a scholar nor an athlete.) For girls good grades were relatively unimportant, and in most schools were even considered a detracting factor; it was important for girls not to appear smarter than boys. In general, the highly esteemed students were less favorable to the scholarly student than were the less esteemed students, although at the same time the highly esteemed students tended to have higher grades than the student body as a whole. The students with the highest status were also less adult-oriented (less concerned about parental or teacher approval) than the rest of the students.

Prestige groups in the high school

A more recent in-depth study of a single "representative" high school in the Midwest, with a population of lower- to middle-class students from small towns and suburban areas, found similar values in the student culture.[30] The three prestige groups were the boys who are athletes (or "jocks"), the "good-looking, personable" girls who dominated the extracurricular activities (especially the cheerleaders), and members of the music-drama group (who participated in the school band, planned school parties, decorated the halls prior to a big game or dance, and were in charge of the senior prom). The three major groups, consisting of a core of about 25 out of 400 seniors, made up the "power clique" and represented the most highly esteemed boys and girls; they were elected to almost all school offices, were actively engaged in all the major student activities, and generally earned high grades. However, compared to these top 25, the "brains" of the school had little power and esteem. They joined the Math Club, Science Club, Latin Club, and Chess Club. These groups met infrequently and often were discontinued by midyear.

Although considerable resentment toward those who ran the school did exist among the less esteemed and noninvolved students, these feelings were suppressed in class and only made known to their own friends. For example, "No student ever challenged the right of the central fifteen . . . students or the football players to run whatever activities there were."[31] All the students, regardless of their status, had their own group of friends and in truth each

30 Philip A. Cusick, *Inside High School* (New York: Holt, 1973).

31 Ibid., p. 74.

Peer group influence can promote or inhibit learning. This breakdancing student has clearly won the admiration of his peers, but would they be equally as admiring of his making their school's honor roll? *(Alan Carey/The Image Works)*

group paid little attention to others. It was extremely important to have friends; in fact, this "may have been the single most important thing in the school."[32] Not to have friends meant having no one to be with in the hallways or classrooms, no one to walk with to class, no one to talk to, no one to eat with. As one student said, "When I didn't have any friends, I hated this place," and another stated, "You can't go to high school without friends."[33]

Bounded friendship patterns

Friendship patterns were rigidly bounded. One did not "hang around" with just anyone. The student walked, talked, ate with, and spent most of his or her time with a few friends; this was particularly noticeable in the cafeteria. It was more important to sit with friends than to satisfy one's hunger. It was more important to have friends and be accepted by at least one group than to have good grades. When given a choice between failing a test or sitting alone in the cafeteria, most students indicated a preference for flunking the examination. The worst thing that could happen, according to one student, was to "walk around the halls alone."[34]

Recent research continues to support the conclusion that peer culture constitutes a major aspect of the socialization experience of students in the school. Thus John Goodlad and his colleagues inquired about student culture

32 Ibid.

33 Ibid., p. 66.

34 Ibid., p. 67.

Table 10.1
Secondary Students' Responses to the Question, "What Is the *One* Best Thing About This School?"

	My Friends	Sports	Good Student Attitudes	Nothing	Classes I'm Taking	Teachers	Other
Junior high respondents	37	15	10	8	7	5	18
Senior high respondents	34	12	12	8	7	3	14

Source: Compiled from data in John I. Goodlad, *A Place Called School* (New York: McGraw-Hill, 1984), pp. 76–77.

in the 1970s and early 1980s. The research team collected data from 17,163 students and 1,350 teachers and made detailed observations in more than 1,000 classrooms in thirty-eight representative public schools (almost equally divided between elementary, junior highs, and senior highs). Junior and senior high students were asked to respond to the questions, "What is the *one* best thing about this school?" As shown in Table 10.1, "My Friends" accounted for by far the largest number of responses at each level. Students also were asked to identify the types of students they perceived to be most popular. Only 14 percent of junior high respondents and 7 percent of senior high respondents selected "smart students"; instead, 60 percent of the junior high students and 79 percent of the senior high students selected either "good looking students" or "athletes."[35]

Friends very important to students

Pondering these data, Goodlad concludes that "physical appearance, peer relationships, and games and sports" are not just concerns carried into the school; these phenomena "appear to prevail" there: "One wonders how much the academic side intrudes into the personal and social—at least for some students."[36] Noting that Coleman and others reported similar findings in earlier decades, he further wonders "why we have taken so little practical account of them in schools."[37]

Recognizing the importance of the peer group

The implications of these studies on student culture in the schools are very important: peer relationships play an important part in determining what happens in the school and the classroom. David and Roger Johnson have identified a variety of actions such as the following that teachers should take:[38]

Conduct activities that encourage students to work and learn cooperatively. Stress joint rather than individual work whenever possible.

35 John I. Goodlad, *A Place Called School* (New York: McGraw-Hill, 1984), pp. 76–77.

36 Ibid., pp. 77–78.

37 Ibid., p. 75.

38 David W. Johnson and Roger T. Johnson, "Peers: The Key to Healthy Development and Socialization," *Character 2* (November 1981), pp. 1–8.

Teach interpersonal and small-group skills.

Assign children responsibility for the welfare of their peers.

Encourage students to support and accept other students.

Provide experience with success in cooperative work.

Structure opportunities for prosocial activities.

Counteract peer pressure for antisocial behavior.

Encourage older children to interact with and supervise younger children.

Encourage students to exchange information with peers.

Clearly, the centrality of peer concerns and culture for many students suggests a host of other questions and implications for educators, beyond those suggested by the Johnsons. We will return to this issue later in this chapter and in subsequent parts of this book.

Participation in Extracurricular Activities One of the major aspects of peer culture in the school involves participation in extracurricular activities. Polls continually show that students consider their involvement with others in extracurricular activities to be a highlight of their school experience. Many educators believe that this participation is a positive force in the lives of a large proportion of students.

However, investigators have had difficulty determining whether participation in extracurricular activities really does benefit students in other aspects of their personal and academic development. The basic reason for this difficulty is the problem of determining whether participation is a cause or an effect. It is known, for example, that students who have a high level of participation generally have higher grades, other things being equal, than those who do not participate. It may also be true, however, that students who have higher grades are more likely to participate for various reasons in school-sponsored extracurricular activities than those with low grades. Thus it is necessary to account for the possibility that high grades and participation go together initially if one wants to determine whether participation has a positive effect on grades. In addition, it also is desirable to know *how* participation results in higher grades, if it does. Do students who begin to participate come under the influence of highly motivated peers who provide a good academic model, or are the effects of participation transmitted in some other way?

Correlation between school participation and grades

Research on the effects of participation in extracurricular activities was limited until the 1970s, when scholars began to give more adequate attention to this topic. Much of the research concentrates on the effects of participation in athletics, probably because interscholastic athletics has been of particular concern to parents and educators. Major conclusions from the research are as follows: (1) there is very little solid evidence that participation in athletics improves academic performance; (2) there is considerable evidence that participation in extracurricular activities affects a number of so-

Effects of participation

cial and behavioral outcomes; and (3) in particular, participation in extracurricular activity—especially athletics, service and leadership activities, and music—contributes to the development of higher levels of educational and occupational aspiration and attainment (for example, more years of school completed later).[39] Higher educational and occupational aspirations in turn contribute to higher levels of income as an adult. The research also suggests that these effects probably are transmitted through peer associations, contacts with teachers, and encouragement from parents.[40]

Participation relatively alterable

These conclusions regarding the effects of extracurricular activities may have great significance for educators. Participation outside the curriculum probably is more "manipulable" (i.e. alterable by the school) than most other factors that are related to educational outcomes.[41] For example, the home environment of students is related to their aspirations, but it is difficult for educators to change the home environments of students who have low or unrealistic aspirations. Encouraging or facilitating appropriate student participation in extracurricular activities may be one of the most effective actions teachers and administrators can take to help improve students' aspirations and attainments.

The Culture of the School

Aspects of school culture

Each school has its own **subculture**—the set of values and behaviors that it reinforces and rewards. Education in school, compared with that in the family or peer group, is carried on in relatively formal ways. Groupings are formed not by voluntary choice but according to age, aptitudes, and sometimes sex. Students are tested and evaluated; they are told when to sit, when to stand, how to walk through hallways, and so on. There are many rules, regulations, and rituals that enhance group conformity. These include student codes, detailed time schedules, disciplinary procedures, and awards for attendance, achievement, conduct, or service to the school. In addition, school assemblies, athletic events, and graduation ceremonies—as well as the school insignia, songs, and cheers—all enhance the culture of the school and socialize the students.[42]

What are the typical behavior patterns exhibited by students and teachers in U.S. elementary and secondary schools? What student role behaviors are generally expected and demanded by teachers? A number of scholars have addressed these kinds of questions. In general, they have reached simi-

39 Duane F. Alvin and David L. Morgan, "Extracurricular Activities: Review and Discussion of the Research on Educational Practices" (Paper prepared for the State of Georgia Department of Education, 1979).

40 Luther B. Otto, "Extracurricular Activities," in H. Walberg, ed., *Improving Educational Standards and Productivity* (Berkeley, Calif.: McCutchan, 1982), pp. 217–227.

41 Luther B. Otto, "Extracurricular Activities and Aspirations in the Status Attainment Process," *Rural Sociology* (Summer 1976), pp. 217–233; Luther B. Otto and Duane F. Alvin, "Athletics, Aspirations, and Attainments," *Sociology of Education* (April 1977), pp. 102–113.

42 Edgar Z. Friedenberg, *Coming of Age in America* (New York: Random House, 1965); Jules Henry, *Culture Against Man* (New York: Random House, 1963); Edward Wynne, *Growing Up Suburban* (Austin: University of Texas Press, 1977).

lar conclusions concerning the cultural patterns that have prevailed in our schools over at least the past four or five decades.

Student Roles Gita Kedar-Voivodas of Fordham University has examined the research dealing with teacher expectations for student roles (that is, desired student behaviors and characteristics) within the social system of the elementary classroom. Despite what she found to be a "rather voluminous literature" on this topic, Kedar-Voivodas was able to identify three main types of student roles: the *pupil* role; the *receptive learner* role, and the *active learner* role.

Three major student roles

The *pupil role* and its expectations require that the students be "patient, docile, passive, orderly, conforming, obedient and acquiescent to rules and regulations, receptive to and respectful to authority, easily controllable, and socially adept."[43]

The *receptive learner role* requires students to be "motivated, task-oriented, ... good achievers, and as such, receptive to the institutional demands of the academic curriculum."[44] This role also requires that students work independently and efficiently despite distractions and perform homework and class assignments punctually and adequately.

Proactive learning

In the *active learner role,* according to Kedar-Voivodas, the student is proactive in going "beyond the established academic curriculum both in terms of the content to be mastered and in the processes" of learning; traits of the active learner include "curiosity, active probing and exploring, challenging authority, an independent and questioning mind, an insistence on explanations.[45] She notes that many educational philosophers, John Dewey and Maria Montessori among them, have said that the active learner role is a desired outcome of the educational enterprise.

Hidden curriculum

Kedar-Voivodas found, however, that students exemplifying the active learner role sometimes are rejected by teachers, despite the presumed desirability and importance of traits and behaviors such as curiosity, exploration, and independent questioning, in advancing student learning. Citing several studies, she concluded that many teachers apparently are "significantly more negative about children described as active, nonconforming, independent, and assertive, essentially active learner role attributes."[46] Kedar-Voivodas also analyzed the implications of these findings in terms of the difference between the school's "academic" curriculum, which demands successful mastery of cognitive material, and its "hidden" curriculum, which demands "institutional conformity."[47] (The **hidden curriculum** is what students learn, other than academic content, from what they do or are expected to do in school.)

43 Gita Kedar-Voivodas, "The Impact of Elementary Children's School Roles and Sex Roles on Teacher Attitudes: An Interactional Analysis," *Review of Educational Research* (Fall 1983), p. 417.

44 Ibid.

45 Ibid., p. 418.

46 Ibid., p. 428.

47 Ibid., 418.

Culture of the Classroom Philip Jackson examined previous research and observed classroom processes in elementary schools. He reported that there is a "constancy" in elementary schools, which he proceeded to describe as follows:

Classroom routines

> The daily schedule ... is commonly divided into definite periods during which specific subjects are to be studied or specific activities engaged in. ... Despite the diversity of subject matter content, the identifiable forms of classroom activity are not great in number. The labels: "seatwork," "group discussion," "teacher demonstration," and "question-and-answer period" ... are sufficient to categorize most of the things that happen. ... Each of these major activities are performed according to rather well-defined rules ... [such as] no loud talking during seatwork ... [and] raise your hand if you have a question. ... [Throughout the day the teacher serves as a] combination traffic cop, judge, supply sergeant, and time-keeper ... [in] a place where things often happen not because students want them to, but because it is time for them to occur.[48]

Emphasis on orderliness

Jackson's portrayal of elementary classrooms provides a detailed picture of the development and nature of the rules and regulations that help make up the culture of the school. The "rules of order that characterize most elementary school classrooms," he concluded, share the major goal of "prevention of 'disturbances.'" By the time students reach the upper grades, a multitude of rules are employed to avoid the disruption of on-going activities, and this "hidden curriculum," in his terminology, has developed the "habits of obedience and docility."[49] Thus the prevailing socialization pattern in the culture of the school and classroom is one that places greatest emphasis on what Kedar-Voivodas described as the obedient pupil role.

Typical patterns

A recent study has reached essentially the same conclusion as Jackson did regarding the culture of the elementary school. "A Study of Schooling," conducted by John Goodlad and his colleagues, provides comprehensive data and analysis on more than 1,000 elementary and secondary classrooms and describes the following general patterns, which appeared so widespread that Goodlad referred to them as characterizing an "extraordinary sameness of instructional patterns" typical of the varied schools and grade levels in the study.[50]

1. The "dominant pattern of classroom organization is a group" that the teacher treats as a whole. This pattern seems to arise from the need to "maintain orderly relationships among from 20 to 30 or more persons in relatively small space." Socialization into this pattern is "rather thoroughly achieved" by the end of the primary grades.

Teacher-centered

2. The teacher is the "external figure in determining the activities, as well as the tone ... and is virtually autonomous" in making decisions about matters such as selection of materials and instructional methods.

48 Philip W. Jackson, *Life in Classrooms* (New York: Holt, 1968), pp. 8–9, 13.

49 Ibid., pp. 104, 33.

50 Goodlad, *A Place Called School,* pp. 123–124, 236, 246.

3. There is not much praise or correction of students' performance or "teacher guidance in how to do better next time."
4. "Enthusiasm and joy and anger are kept under control." As a result, the general emotional tone is "flat" or "neutral."
5. Most student work involves "listening to teachers, writing answers to questions, and taking tests and quizzes," in all subjects at all grade levels. Students rarely learn from one another or initiate interaction with the teacher. Little use is made of audiovisual equipment, guest lecturers, or field trips. Except in physical education, vocational education, and the arts, there is little "hands-on activity." Textbooks and workbooks are the "media of instruction" in academic classes.
6. These patterns become increasingly rigid and predominant as students proceed through the grades.
7. Even in the early grades, many students do not complete their lessons or understand what they are supposed to do. Many said they were not getting much help from the teacher in overcoming errors and difficulties.

Emphasis on information

8. Instruction seldom goes beyond "mere possession of information" to emphasize "the ability to think rationally, the ability to use, evaluate, and accumulate knowledge. . . . [or arousal] of students' curiosity." This is true even in science and the social studies, subjects that should, in many people's opinion, emphasize such themes.

Passive learning

Summarizing the overall results of "A Study of Schooling," Goodlad wrote: "Students listened; they responded when called on to do so; they read short sections of textbooks or chose from among alternative responses in quizzes. . . . [but] they rarely planned or initiated anything, read or wrote anything of some length, or created their own products. And they scarcely ever speculated on meanings.[51]

Regularities of schooling

As we saw in earlier chapters of this book, such systematic emphasis on passive learning by rote is in opposition to much research on productive learning, to contemporary ideas on what education should accomplish, and to educational goals stressed in preservice and in-service teacher education. Why then, do so many classrooms function so much of the time in a way that is diametrically opposed to or, at the least, incompatible with many educators' views of desirable practice? This exceedingly important question needs careful consideration if change is to be brought about on a widespread basis in elementary and secondary schools. Goodlad gives it considerable stress in trying to determine why teaching generally proceeds the way it does even though teachers "might prefer simply to act on their beliefs about good pedagogy."[52] Philip Jackson and other observers of classroom life also have tried to explain why the "regularities" of schooling, as Goodlad and Jackson have described them, persist despite myriads of proposals and recommenda-

51 John I. Goodlad, "A Study of Schooling: Some Findings and Hypotheses," *Phi Delta Kappan* (March 1983), p. 468.

52 Goodlad, *A Place Called School,* p. 175.

tions for encouraging more active learning in the classroom. Some of the major reasons for the persistence of these classroom patterns are described below.

1. *Institutional requirements to maintain order.* As Philip Jackson emphasizes, a multitude of routines are devised and implemented to govern the interactions between twenty or thirty students and a teacher. Goodlad, Jackson, and other observers use terms like "institutional realities" to describe the forces that result in an emphasis on passive learning in accordance with detailed rules and regulations. Goodlad also uses the phrase "the circumstances of teaching" to describe the tension between active learning goals and the goals of order and control in the typical classroom.[53]

Institutional realities

2. *Student preferences for passive learning.* The degree to which many students resist efforts to engage them in active learning involving difficult cognitive tasks should not be underestimated. Some of the dynamics behind this type of reaction among students have been summarized by Walter Doyle in a paper analyzing the "intrinsic character" of academic work in elementary and secondary schools:

Restricting output

> Students restrict the amount of output they give to a teacher to minimize the risk of exposing a mistake. In addition, restricted output can elicit assistance from others in a classroom . . . [as in a] case in which first-grade pupils hesitated in giving answers until either the teacher or another student answered for them. . . . [As one older student said] "Yeah, I hardly do nothing. All you gotta do is act dumb and Mr. Y will tell you the right answer. You just gotta wait, you know, and he'll tell you."
>
> There is also evidence that students manage ambiguity and risk more directly by attempting to increase the explicitness of a teacher's instructions. . . . [For example, two researchers] met with strong resistance . . . when they attempted to shift information-processing demands in a mathematics class from routine or procedural tasks to understanding tasks. The students refused to cooperate and argued that they had a right to be told what to do. . . . [After their experience, the researchers] commented that "it is no longer a mystery why so many teachers and so many textbooks present ninth-grade algebra as a rote algorithmic subject."[54]

3. *Teachers' allocation of attention.* Related both to institutional realities of the classroom and students' reluctance to engage in independent learning, many teachers feel compelled to give the largest share of their time and attention to a limited number of students. In some cases these will be the slowest students—whom the teacher perceives as most in need of his or her help. In many cases, however, attention goes primarily to the brightest

53 Goodlad, "A Study of Schooling," pp. 469–470.

54 Walter Doyle, "Academic Work," *Review of Educational Research* (Summer 1983), pp. 184–185. Extended description of individual examples of these phenomena can be found in John Holt, *How Children Fail* (New York: Pitman, 1964).

and most successful students, who frequently are perceived as benefiting the most from extra attention. This attitude is particularly prevalent if there are so many "slow" students that the task of helping all of them seems virtually impossible. Helen Gouldner and her colleagues found these latter dynamics to be widespread in their study of an inner-city elementary school enrolling a large proportion of poverty students whose home environment did not prepare them to function well in the classroom.[55]

Difficulties in helping students

The few students who were well prepared to enter school and who tended to be from relatively high-status families in the all-black, predominantly working-class school studied, were the "pets"—teachers helped them throughout their school careers. The largest group (the "nobodies") consisted of students who received relatively little teacher attention and generally were neither disruptive nor particularly well motivated or successful. The remaining students were a small group of "troublemakers," who were unable or unwilling to conform to the routine demands of the classroom. With reference to the student roles delineated by Kedar-Voivodas, one can say that the troublemakers were those who could not or did not conform to the expected role of *pupil,* the nobodies fulfilled this role but were not receptive learners, and the teachers' pets were successful in discharging the role of receptive learner.

Pets, nobodies, and troublemakers

This type of reaction by the teachers and by the school as a whole was well in line with the school's "sorting and selecting" function, because the teachers—most of whom were black—could feel they were promoting success for at least some black students who were able to take advantage of opportunities in the classroom.[56] Such reactions undoubtedly are relatively more characteristic of inner-city schools than others, but it appears they also can be found elsewhere, particularly in schools that have a significant proportion of low-achieving, working-class students.

Sorting and selecting function

4. *Lack of practical knowledge on how to improve instruction.* Until recently, relatively little was known about how to change instruction so as to ensure more active, independent learning. Educators also knew relatively little about how to carry on the process of change in the schools. It is true that many thousands of studies have been conducted in the twentieth century on such varied topics as homogeneous grouping (designed in part to meet individual differences), methods of teaching subject matter, and use of television, teaching machines, and other technology. Unfortunately, the research more often than not pointed to the conclusions that no particular approach was better than any other, that a suggested approach failed as often or more often than it worked, and that—as found in the Equality of Educational Opportunity Study described in the next chapter—innovations proposed to improve learning did not seem to make much difference.

Innovative methods made no difference

55 Helen Gouldner, *Teachers' Pets, Troublemakers, and Nobodies* (Westport, Conn.: Greenwood, 1978), pp. 133–134.

56 This self-fulfilling prophecy and the way it operated at the school studied by Gouldner and her colleagues are described at greater length in Ray C. Rist, *The Urban School: A Factory for Failure* (Cambridge, Mass.: M.I.T. Press, 1973).

In this situation, it has been difficult for educators to move successfully away from traditional practices that appear to be antithetical to productive learning of higher-order skills. About all that a critic of traditional practice could do was describe and bewail negative learning environments found in the schools and plead with teachers to individualize instruction, provide for more active learning, and concentrate on improving students' thinking skills. Limited largely to this kind of rhetorical pep talk, criticisms frequently were perceived as personal attacks from people who do not "know" what teaching is like.

Realities in society

5. *Requirements that students learn to conform.* Nested within the institutional forces that impel teachers to emphasize passive learning are the realities that require children and youth to learn to function within institutions outside the school. Most people in contemporary society must function within large institutions that have been organized to carry out economic, political, and social functions, and children must be socialized to follow routines and regulations that make organized activity possible. Philip Jackson has summarized this part of the school's socialization mission as follows:

Preparation for later life

> it is expected that children will adapt to the teacher's authority by becoming "good workers" and "model students." ... Most students learn to look and listen when told to and to keep their private fantasies in check. ... Moreover, this skill ... is doubly important because the student will be called upon [to use it later]. ... The transition from classroom to factory or office is made easily by those who have developed "good work habits" in their early years.[57]

Institutional constraints

Many other reasons could be elaborated to explain why instructional patterns in the classroom have been relatively unaffected by contemporary learning theory, but most of them in one way or another involve institutional constraints that favor passive, rote learning and the difficulties inherent in implementing different approaches in the face of these constraints.[58] To provide students with sufficient assistance to ensure continuous and active mastery of progressively more difficult skills, for example, requires profound change in both the institutional realities and the fundamental cultural patterns of the traditional school. Changes of this magnitude require not just stressful changes in the behavior of teachers and students but organizational and pedagogical innovations that can make them possible. Recent efforts undertaken to introduce such innovations—sometimes with considerable success—will be described in Chapter 15.

Before concluding this discussion of cultural patterns in the school, we should mention research indicating that passive, rote learning is more likely to receive systematic emphasis in schools with low-achieving, working-class

57 Jackson, *Life in Classrooms,* p. 32.

58 Other reasons cited by Goodlad include lack of much external pressure for change, the tendency for teachers to teach the way they were taught, lack of adequate preservice and in-service training, and the relative freedom allowed to teachers to do as they please. See *A Place Called School,* pp. 298–299.

students than in those with high-achieving, middle-class students. Studies on this topic have been conducted by Jean Anyon, who examined elementary schools that differed markedly in social class.[59] She found that instruction in the predominantly working-class schools in her sample emphasized mostly mechanical skills such as punctuation and capitalization. In contrast, instruction in the middle-class school emphasized following directions to figure out the right answers, instruction in the "affluent professional" school emphasized working independently to "express and apply ideas and concepts," and instruction in the "executive elite" school emphasized development of analytical and conceptual skills. These findings indicate that passive, rote learning is most pervasive in schools with a large proportion of students from working-class families.

Positive aspects

Since much of this section has focused on negative aspects of school culture, we should emphasize that many positive statements can be made about elementary and secondary schools in the United States. Most schools provide an orderly learning environment, and most students learn to read and compute at a level required to function in our society. The large majority of students receive a high school diploma, and a high percentage proceed to some form of postsecondary education. Successful aspects of the U.S. system of education are pointed out in Chapter 11 and elsewhere in this book.

Television and Other Media

Other formal agencies share in socializing the child, but their influence today generally is much less than that of family, peer group, and school. Among these are the church, scouting groups, and similar character-building organizations. However, the mass media, especially television, are extremely influential in shaping the attitudes and behaviors of children as well as those of adults.

"A second school system"

Recent evidence makes it clear that television has become "a second school system." Children under five years old watch TV for an average of 24 hours a week, or about one-fifth of their waking hours. By the time a child graduates from high school, he or she will have spent 15,000 to 20,000 hours watching television as compared with 11,000 to 12,000 hours in school. Before children reach eighteen, they will "have seen 350,000 commercials urging them to want, want, want."[60] Clearly, television is an important influence in the lives of children and youth.

A "first curriculum"

Rather than viewing television as a second school system, Neil Postman views it and the other mass media (for example, radio, comic books, movies) as the "first curriculum" because it appears to be affecting the way children develop learning skills and orient themselves toward the acquisition of

59 Jean Anyon, "Social Class and the Hidden Curriculum of Work," *Journal of Education* (Winter 1980), pp. 67–92; reprinted in Henry Giroux and David Purpel, eds., *The Hidden Curriculum and Moral Education* (Berkeley, Calif.: McCutchan, 1983).

60 Evelyn Kaye, *The Family Guide to Children's Television: What to Watch, What to Miss, What to Change, and How to Do It* (New York: Pantheon, 1974), p. 7.

knowledge and understanding.[61] According to Postman and some other observers, television's curriculum is designed largely to maintain interest; the school's curriculum must accomplish other purposes, such as moral development and mastery of abstract thinking skills that may not be very interesting to children. In addition, watching television requires little in the way of effort and skills of the viewer.[62] Children develop the bad habit of not having to think or solve problems; rather, they are entertained and become accustomed to instant stimuli and responses. Teachers and parents have trouble competing with the media to gain children's attention. Educators face a formidable challenge in attempting to develop and maintain interest and motivation in schoolwork.[63]

TV and aggressive behavior

Educators and others who work with children are also concerned with media effects on the development of children's values and behaviors. For example, many adults are particularly worried that television and other media may encourage aggressive or violent behavior. A review of research on this issue concluded that effects of television on children's aggression are largely dependent on situational factors like the child's degree of frustration or anger, similarities between the available target and the target in the television portrayal, potential consequences such as pain or punishment, and opportunity to perform an act of violence.[64] A committee of behavioral scientists has reviewed research through 1981 and concluded that "television violence is as strongly correlated with aggressive behavior as any other behavioral variable that has been measured." This committee also pointed out that the number of violent acts per television program has been increasing and that children "learn to behave aggressively from the violence they see on television in the same way that they learn cognitive and social skills" from watching parents, teachers, siblings, and peers.[65]

Positive aspects

It also is true, however, that television can be an important force for positive socialization. This conclusion has been supported by research indicating that the "Sesame Street" program has helped both middle-class and lower-status youth,[66] and that children can become more cooperative and nurturant after viewing programs emphasizing these behaviors.[67] Recognizing both the

61 Neil Postman, *Teaching as a Conserving Activity* (New York: Delacorte, 1979).

62 Neal J. Gordon, "Television and Learning," in H. J. Walberg, ed., *Educational Environment and Effects* (Berkeley, Calif.: McCutchan, 1979), pp. 57–76.

63 Neil Postman, "The Day Our Children Disappear: Predictions of a Media Ecologist," *Phi Delta Kappan* (January 1981), pp. 381–385.

64 George A. Comstock, "Types of Portrayal and Aggressive Behavior," *Journal of Communication* (Summer 1977), pp. 189–198; L. Rowell Huesmann and Leonard D. Eron, "Factors Influencing the Effect of Television Violence on Children," in Michael J. A. Howe, ed., *Learning from Television* (New York: Academic Press, 1983).

65 U.S. Department of Health and Human Services, *Television and Human Behavior: Ten Years of Scientific Progress and Implications for the Eighties*. Vol. 1. Summary Report (Washington, D.C.: Government Printing Office, 1982), pp. 6, 38–39.

66 Aimee D. Leifer, Neal J. Gordon, and Sherryl B. Graves, "Children's Television: More Than Mere Entertainment," *Harvard Educational Review* (May 1974), pp. 213–245.

67 Rita W. Poulos, Eli A. Rubenstein, and Robert M. Leibert, "Positive Social Learning," *Journal of Communication* (Autumn 1975), pp. 90–97; David A. England, *Television and Children* (Bloomington, Ind.: Phi Delta Kappa, 1984).

good and the damaging effects that the media can have on children and youth, many individuals and groups have been working to bring about improvements. The Parent Teachers Association has made reform in television—particularly reduction in sex and violence during prime time—one of its major national goals, and organizations such as the National Citizens Committee for Broadcasting and Action for Children's Television have been established to collect information and lobby for change.

Research on school achievement related to television viewing indicates that there is a relationship, but the nature of the relationship is not entirely clear. The studies have been limited primarily to reading achievement. Some studies suggest that viewing television may reduce students' reading activities, but this conclusion is not well documented.[68] In addition, it is difficult to separate cases in which television "causes" reduced attention to reading activities from those in which low-performing students turn to television or other nonacademic activities for escape.

Television and school achievement

Relationships between viewing of television, achievement, age of the student, family environment, and other variables are multidimensional and complex. Thus a study of television viewing among more than 12,000 sixth graders in California found that watching television more than five to six hours a day was associated with low achievement in reading, mathematics, and writing across all social-class groups, but television viewing was positively associated with achievement for students low in social class, as long as they spent less than three or four hours a day in this manner.[69] Despite the absence of conclusive data, many educators are very concerned that watching television may lower achievement for large numbers of students.

General mass media effects

Apart from relatively direct effects on school achievement, television and other mass media such as the movies and the music industry have a major influence on acculturation and socialization of children and youth. The mass media obviously stimulate and reflect fundamental changes in attitudes and behaviors involving recreation, career aspirations, sexual relationships, drugs, and other matters. Unfortunately, there are no conclusive data to determine just how much the media affect children and youth or whether overall affects are positive or negative (depending, of course, on what one values as positive or negative). For example, the recent initiation of twenty-four-hour rock-music programming on cable television has been viewed both as a means to keep young people off the streets and as the beginning of the end of Western civilization. Although most observers would agree on the vast influence of the mass media, data to assess their effects more precisely are almost completely lacking.

In recent years there has been a growing concern that video and computer games may have a negative influence on the development of children and youth. The video game industry has become a multi-billion-dollar-a-year

68 R. Hornik, "Out-of-School Television and Schooling: Hypotheses and Methods," *Review of Educational Research* (Summer 1981), pp. 193–214.

69 California Assessment Program, *Survey of Sixth Grade School Achievement and Television Viewing Habits* (Sacramento, Calif.: State Department of Education, 1982).

business, much of it supported by young people who spend large amounts of time and money in video arcades. In addition to worries about possibly unproductive time expenditures, many educators and lay persons are concerned that video games may encourage the violent and aggressive attitudes that seem to be built into many of the games; reinforce habits and expectations involving "instant gratification" and "escapist" fantasies; encourage gambling as well as vandalism, theft, diversion of lunch money, and panhandling to obtain funds for the arcades; and magnify girls' disadvantages in learning about modern technology (boys make up a large majority of serious video game players). For reasons such as these, the NEA Representative Assembly passed a 1982 resolution opposing the commercial use of video games in schools and favoring local laws that will "minimize the economic exploitation of youth."[70]

Possible negative effects of video games

We also should emphasize that not all observers perceive the effects of video games as being primarily negative. For example, several psychologists have suggested that the games promote a new kind of spatial and geometric understanding.[71] Some of the arguments on this side of the issue have been summarized by Elizabeth Loftus as follows:

Possible positive effects

> They [video games] can provide young people with a taste for computers. Youngsters can interact with the games, not watch passively as they do with television. That makes games potentially a much more powerful educational device.
>
> I'm optimistic about the educational potential being realized because people today want to give their children every possible advantage. . . . Moreover, there are some games now that focus on rescue rather than destruction. Many of these games are designed by women and appeal more to girls than to boys.[72]

Sex Roles and Sex Differences in Achievement

Not only does society demand conformity to its fundamental values and norms, it also assigns specific roles to each of its members, expecting them to conform to certain established behavioral patterns. A good example of this type of socialization is found in **sex roles** (that is, the ways boys and girls and men and women are "supposed" to act). Sex roles vary from culture to culture, but within a given culture they are rather well defined, and they are developed through an elaborate schedule of selective reinforcement. For example, the preschool boy is ridiculed for playing with dolls, and girls are sup-

Sex roles vary with culture

70 Nancy R. Needham, "Thirty Billion Quarters Can't Be Wrong—Or Can They?" *Today's Education* (1982–83 Annual), p. 55.

71 Needham, "Thirty Billion Quarters Can't Be Wrong," p. 54.

72 "Being Hooked on Videogames Can Be Good for Your Kids," *U.S. News and World Report* (February 20, 1984), p. 72; also see Elizabeth Loftus, *Mind at Play: The Psychology of Video Games* (New York: Basic Books, 1983).

posed to be "feminine." Robert Havighurst has summarized early development of sex roles as follows:

> By age 3, there is a noticeable difference in behavior between boys and girls. Males show more initiative and are more active. Females are more dependent and are more nurturant. . . . [Research on toy preferences indicates] that five and six-year old children use [even] more sex-role stereotypes in explaining toy preferences. Thus, there is an increase of sex-stereotypes used by children as they grow older.[73]

Problems Reflected in the Schools

When children come of school age, they find that the elementary schools are largely staffed by females. The schools are dominated by traditionally "feminine" norms of politeness, cleanliness, and obedience. The school frowns on vulgar language and fighting; it suppresses aggressiveness and action-oriented behavior. This is a particular problem for boys because research indicates that on the average boys are more active than girls almost from the time they are born, and that this difference is related in turn to hormone differences.[74] Recent studies have clarified other ways in which boys may be at a particular disadvantage in the elementary school. According to some researchers in neuropsychology, boys (relative to girls) tend to learn through active manipulation of their environment, whereas girls tend to learn through verbal communication. One researcher has summarized several studies analyzing this difference as follows:

Disadvantages for boys

Different methods of learning

> By the time they are five or six, [all] children in . . . classrooms are expected to behave like girls. The system requires children to remain attentive to one task and stay seated in one place for a considerable period of time. . . . They must use fine motor systems in writing and drawing, and they must persevere at tasks that are largely linguistic or symbolic in nature. . . . Boys [usually] cannot sit still; they are distractible; they test the properties of objects. Such behavior interferes with the concentration they need to learn to read and write.[75]

Effects on boys

Reviewing research indicating that teachers tend to reward passive behavior and discourage active learning, Kedar-Voivodas concluded that this emphasis probably helps account for the relatively high rate of failure and infractions of school rules found among boys—boys receive many more reprimands from teachers than do girls, and by the time students enter the sec-

73 Robert J. Havighurst, "Sex Role Development," *Journal of Research and Development in Education* (Winter 1983), p. 61.

74 Ray H. Bixler, "Nature Versus Nurture: The Timeless Anachronism," *Merrill-Palmer Quarterly* (April 1980), pp. 153–159.

75 Diane McGuiness, "How Schools Discriminate Against Boys," *Human Nature* (February 1979), pp. 87–88.

ondary grades, boys outnumber girls thirteen to one in remedial classes and more than seven to one in classes for the emotionally impaired.[76]

By way of contrast, the problems that girls experience in the educational system generally reflect their socialization for dependency rather than aggressiveness. Until recently, most girls were not encouraged to prepare for or enter high-status occupations such as law or medicine or high-paying occupations requiring technical skills and training beyond high school. Instead they were expected to prepare for roles as wives and homemakers.[77] Except for a few occupations such as elementary teacher, social worker, and nurse, girls traditionally were not expected to enter fields that require college preparation. Because women were channeled into a few professions, those occupations tended to have relatively low pay and low status. Because women were available to fill jobs as teachers, for example, and because women were thought to require or demand less status and pay than men, a cycle was created wherein prestigious jobs were defined as "masculine" and less prestigious jobs were defined as "feminine." This type of socialization arrangement in schools and society did not motivate girls to achieve much beyond high school or to acquire skills that might contribute to later success in the economy. Furthermore, verbal communication of the kind in which girls tend to excel historically did not provide them with skills that lead to success in mathematics and science. As girls enter the secondary school, this tendency has had the effect of excluding girls from many educational opportunities.[78]

Disadvantages for girls

In addition, the emphasis placed on dependency in socializing females meant that girls were expected to be cooperative and even docile. In contrast, boys were taught to be competitive and to exercise leadership in overcoming obstacles.[79] As mentioned, socialization in the elementary school frequently tried to make boys obedient and cooperative, but in high school athletics were stressed and boys received more opportunities to learn leadership and competitive skills that would be important in later life. Until recently, girls had little encouragement or opportunity to learn these skills, and those who did were perceived as violating "proper" norms for female behavior in American society.

Cooperative girls and competitive boys

Sex Differences in Achievement and Ability

Recent studies in the United States indicate that sex differences in achievement have been getting smaller. For example, reading data on three age

76 Jayne E. Stake and Jonathan F. Katz, "Teacher-Pupil Relationships in the Elementary School Classroom: Teacher-Gender and Pupil-Gender Differences, *American Educational Research Journal* (Fall 1982), pp. 465–471; Anne K. Soderman, "Schooling All 4-Year-Olds: An Idea Full of Promise, Fraught with Pitfalls," *Education Week* (March 14, 1984), p. 19.

77 Leslie Aldridge Westoff, *Women in Search of Equality* (Princeton, N.J.: Educational Testing Service, 1979).

78 Aaron M. Pallas and Karl L. Alexander, "Sex Differences in Quantitative SAT Performance: New Evidence on the Differential Coursework Hypothesis," *American Educational Research Journal* (Summer 1983), pp. 165–182.

79 Frank L. Mott et al., *Women, Work, and Family* (Lexington, Mass.: D.C. Heath, 1978).

Reading and mathematics

groups (nine, thirteen, and seventeen year olds) collected by the National Assessment of Educational Progress indicate that although females scored about 5 percent higher than males in 1980, this gap was significantly smaller than in 1971. Conversely, in 1978 males in the seventeen-year-old group scored nearly 10 percent higher than females in higher-order mathematics achievement, but this difference was smaller than it had been in 1973, and there was no difference in scores among nine and thirteen year olds.[80] Research also indicates that female gains in mathematics probably are due in part to greater participation in math courses during the past few decades.[81]

Mathematics ability

Controversies concerning possible sex differences in ability frequently focus on the issue of whether a larger proportion of males than females have high innate ability with reference to higher-order mathematics skills, or in abstract cognitive ability in general. Research on this topic indicates that there is more variability among males than females: males are more likely to be either very high or very low in ability.[82] The relatively high proportion of males low in ability appears to be due to the fact that young boys are more vulnerable to childhood maladies than are girls.[83] Much of the support for the argument that a higher percentage of boys than girls are very high in ability has been provided by the Study of Mathematically Precocious Youth (SMPY) conducted by Camilla Benbow and Julian Stanley at Johns Hopkins University. Data from the study indicate that among more than 10,000 seventh and eighth graders scoring high on math in the Scholastic Aptitude Test, there are fourteen boys to every girl.[84] However, other researchers disagree with Benbow and Stanley's conclusion that this differential reflects a large innate ability component, instead pointing to sex-role limitations and stereotypes that they believe hamper the development of girls' higher-order abilities.[85]

Those who believe that learning differences between the sexes are present at birth point to differences that have been found in the brain functioning of boys and girls.[86] Research indicates that for most people, the left hemisphere (half) of the brain specializes in verbal tasks, while the right hemisphere specializes in nonverbal functions. Research also indicates, however,

80 Educational Commission of the States, *Changes in Mathematical Achievement 3* (Washington, D.C.: Government Printing Office, 1979); ibid., *Three National Assessments of Reading* (Washington, D.C.: Government Printing Office, 1981).

81 S. S. Peng, W. B. Fetters, and A. J. Kolstad, *High School and Beyond* (Washington, D.C.: Government Printing Office, 1981).

82 E. E. Maccoby and C. N. Jacklin, *Psychology of Sex Differences* (Palo Alto, Calif.: Stanford University Press, 1974).

83 Arnold Gessell, Frances L. Ilg, and Louise Bates Ames, *Infant and Child Care in the Culture of Today* (New York: Harper & Row, 1974), pp. 39–40.

84 Camilla P. Benbow and Julian C. Stanley, "Differential Course-taking Hypothesis Revisited," *American Educational Research Journal* (Winter 1983), pp. 469–473.

85 Karl L. Alexander and Aaron M. Pallas, "Reply to Benbow and Stanley," *American Educational Research Journal* (Winter 1983), pp. 475–477; Elizabeth Fennema, "Overview of Sex-related Differences in Mathematics" (Paper presented at the annual meeting of the American Educational Research Association, New York, March 1982); Daniel U. Levine and Allan C. Ornstein, "Sex Differences in Ability and Achievement," *Journal of Research and Development in Education* (Winter 1983), pp. 66–72.

86 Richard M. Restak, "The Other Difference Between Boys and Girls," *Educational Leadership* (December 1979), pp. 232–235.

Possible differences in brain functioning

that among right-handed persons, females appear to handle spatial functions more with the left hemisphere (relative to males), whereas males have less hemispheric specialization in spatial functions. Females also have more right hemispheric processing in verbal functions, compared to males.[87] Related studies indicate that the right hemisphere of the female brain has more verbal capacity than that of the male.[88] Laboratory research also suggests that sex hormones play a direct part in influencing the growth and development of the brain.[89]

Socialization aspects

Other observers, however, emphasize differences in socialization from the first day of life (boys are placed in a blue blanket, girls in pink) and argue that differences in experience and expectations account for most of the learning differences between boys and girls. While not necessarily arguing that brain or other physiological differences affecting learning do not exist or are of no importance, these observers argue that socialization differences are the major reason that boys and girls diverge in learning patterns and performance.[90] For example, one observer has reviewed evidence on sex differences in learning and concluded that, "When one examines the limited amount of the cognitive differences between the sexes, one is struck by their inconsequential nature, at least in terms of any kind of evidence that would warrant advising boys and girls to pursue different courses or careers on the basis of sex differentials in ability."[91]

Particular attention has been given in recent years to the possibility that women tend to perform poorly in math (and therefore in science and other fields dependent on math) because of socialization practices that make them anxious and fearful about mathematical analysis.[92] A related line of argument is that women fear success in traditionally male activities and occupations because succeeding would violate sex stereotypes and thereby invite ridicule and create identity problems.[93] One review of research concluded that while such considerations still depress achievement among females, the situation is complex, and few overall generalizations can be made concerning the degree to which various factors operate and interact in causing sex differences in ability and achievement.[94]

87 Julia Sherman, "Effects of Biological Factors on Sex-related Differences in Mathematics Achievement," in L. H. Fox and E. Fennema, eds., *Women in Mathematics: Research Perspectives for Change* (Washington, D.C.: National Institute of Education, 1977).

88 "The Split Brain: Studies in Laterality and Asymmetry," *The University of Chicago Division of the Social Sciences Report* (Autumn 1979), pp. 5–8.

89 C. Sue Carter and William T. Greenough, "Sending the Right Sex Messages," *Psychology Today* (September 1979), p. 112.

90 Gloria C. Fauth and Judith E. Jacobs, "Equity in Mathematics Education: The Educational Leader's Role," *Educational Leadership* (March 1980), pp. 485–489.

91 Julia A. Sherman, "Sex-Related Cognitive Differences: A Summary of Theory and Evidence," *Integrateducation* (January–February 1978), p. 40.

92 Shelia Tobias and Carol S. Weissbrod, "Anxiety and Mathematics: An Update," *Harvard Educational Review* (February 1980), pp. 63–70.

93 Georgia Sassen, "Success Anxiety in Women," *Harvard Educational Review* (February 1980), pp. 13–24.

94 Elizabeth Fennema, "Overview of Sex-related Differences in Mathematics" (Paper presented at the annual meeting of the American Educational Research Association, New York, March 1982).

Educational and Occupational Attainment of Women

Changing attitudes

Attitudes regarding sex roles changed substantially in the 1960s and 1970s. In particular, women's attitudes became much less traditional, as they developed more favorable views toward equal home and work roles for men and women.[95] This trend is likely to continue: American society, including males, will increasingly realize that women are one of the nation's greatest untapped natural resources. The social revolution involving the role of women is still in its early stages.

Educational gains

Until recently, women completed fewer years of schooling than did men. This difference has been diminishing, however, and by 1977 the average years of education completed for both men and women was 12.6. In 1979 females outnumbered males among college freshmen for the first time. By 1982, slightly more than half of all bachelor's and master's degrees were awarded to women—up from less than 40 percent in 1962; and 32 percent of all doctoral degrees were earned by women, compared with 11 percent in 1962. Since women with more education are more likely to seek paid employment than women with less education, this trend will increase the number of working women.

Occupational gains

Related gains were registered in the occupational status of women. For example, the percentage of accountants who were female increased from 15 in 1950 to 36 in 1980, the percentage of women among college faculty increased from 23 percent to 34 percent, and the comparable percentages among bank officials were 12 percent in 1950 and 42 percent in 1980. In addition, very large gains were made in the percentage of female students in law, medicine, business administration, and other professional studies; this will increase female employment in high-status employment in the future.

Much progress thus has been made in equalizing educational, economic, and social opportunities for females. Affirmative action in employment and education (see Chapter 9), encouraging girls to attend college and prepare for the professions, efforts to eliminate sexism from school curricula, and other actions to equalize opportunity are having an impact in the schools and the wider society.

Mixed indicators

Nevertheless much remains to be achieved, and implications for the educational system may not be entirely unidimensional. Despite recent gains, women still tend to be concentrated in low-pay, low-status occupations, and a higher proportion of female workers are in clerical and service jobs now than in 1910. Although the number of female scientists and engineers with doctoral degrees doubled between 1973 and 1983, in the latter year they still constituted only 12 percent of the total. In 1983, the average female worker earned only 61 percent of the annual income of the average male. The increase in the educational and occupational attainment of women is associated with growth in the percentage of working mothers and single-parent families; as we saw earlier, these trends may have a negative impact on chil-

95 "Fifteen-Year Study Documents Tremendous Changes in Women's Sex-Role Attitudes," *Institute for Social Research Newsletter* (Winter 1980), p. 3.

Mixed implications for the schools

dren and the schools. On the whole, however, female gains in education and employment not only signify some equalization of opportunity but also serve to strengthen the family, since this trend improves the social class and income of many families.

Adolescent and Youth Culture

Separate stage of life

In one sense the existence of a distinct youth culture can be viewed as a result of disjuncture in the process of socialization within the larger culture. The problem of "youth" is one that to some extent has been generated by defining youth as a separate stage in life. Adolescents have been excluded from many responsible activities within the community. Youth are thrown back into their own peer group, which has formed what we commonly call a "youth culture."

Separation of Youth

Postponing adulthood

In primitive and traditional cultures, the young are usually initiated into adult life after puberty. This initiation sometimes takes place through special rites and rituals designed to test and prove the young person's worthiness to assume adult roles. In such societies one is either a child or an adult; there is only a brief gap between the two—if there is any gap at all. In modern societies the young are forced to postpone their adulthood, and the period is labeled adolescence or youth.

A major reason for this postponement is that modern society, particularly in the United States, no longer has an economic need or a viable social role for this age group. Our common message to adolescents is grow up, leave us alone, play with friends, and finish school.

Distinctive youth stage

An extensive study of youth groups in different cultures is reported in S. N. Eisenstadt's comparison of anthropological and sociological data from primitive to modern societies.[96] In all societies, there is some grouping of *children* apart from adults—with various types of cooperative behavior and acceptable norms. However, it is mainly in Western civilizations that *youth* are distinctly separated from adults. In such cases, the adolescent group becomes an important bridge between the home and adult society. At the same time, the adolescent group becomes more and more isolated from the rest of society. This isolation, according to Eisenstadt, explains the strong emotional interdependence and intensive mutual identification of the adolescent group. For this reason, too, youth groups are susceptible to becoming the nuclei of various deviant movements that tend to resist adult authority.

In the same vein, Kingsley Davis contends that adolescence is the time when the individual is attaining physical maturity without attaining equal so-

96 S. N. Eisenstadt, *From Generation to Generation* (New York: Free Press, 1956).

cial maturity.[97] Full growth, strength, and mental capacity are reached shortly after puberty, but the adolescent still has a long way to go, in most societies, before full social status is reached.

Subordinate position

While earlier physical than social maturity is most pronounced in modern societies, it is a condition inherent in all human societies. In most cultures, Davis points out, power and advantage depend on social position, experience, and reputation rather than on brute strength or physical prowess. Insofar as these attributes have anything to do with age, they are more likely to come with middle age, or—in some societies—even old age. Thus, adolescents find themselves in a socially subordinate position despite their physical equality or superiority to older persons. To some degree, then, adult society has created a socially disadvantaged group of adolescents who have a secondary status in society.[98] This phenomenon is more obvious (and perhaps necessary) in modern societies; as society becomes more complex the lag between physical and social development becomes greater, and adolescence, as socially defined, extends farther into adulthood.

Drugs and Drinking

Declines in drug use

General usage of drugs and alcohol among youth has grown tremendously over the past few decades. However, use of some drugs has declined significantly in the past eight or ten years. Recent surveys on substance use and abuse among high school seniors can be summarized as follows:[99]

Cigarette smoking. The percentage of high school seniors who smoke half a pack or more every day declined from 19 percent in 1977 to 14 percent in 1981. This decline probably was due to increased concern about health and reduced peer pressure to smoke.

Daily or near daily marijuana use. The use of marijuana at least twenty times a month declined sharply from 11 percent in 1978 to 6 percent in 1983.

Annual marijuana use. The percentage of high school seniors who had used marijuana during the previous year declined from 51 percent in 1979 to 42 percent in 1983.

PCP ("Angel Dust"). Annual usage declined from 7 percent in 1979 to 2 percent in 1982.

"Poppers" and "snappers" (amyl and butyl nitrites). Annual use declined from 7 percent in 1979 to 4 percent in 1982.

97 Kingsley Davis, "The Child and the Social Structure," *Journal of Educational Sociology* (December 1940), pp. 217–229; idem., *Human Society* (New York: Macmillan, 1949).

98 Edgar Z. Friedenberg, *The Vanishing Adolescent* (Boston: Beacon Press, 1959); Margaret Mead, *Coming of Age in Samoa* (New York: Morrow, 1928).

99 Data are summarized largely from Lloyd D. Johnston, Gerald I. Bachman, and Phillip M. O'Malley, *Highlights from Student Drug Abuse in America 1975–1981* (Washington, D.C.: Government Printing Office, 1981); Bianca Cody, "Alcohol and Other Drug Abuse Among Adolescents," *Statistical Bulletin of Metropolitan Insurance Companies* (January–March 1984), pp. 4–13; and 1984 newspaper reports.

Tranquilizers. Annual use on a nonmedical basis declined from 11 percent in 1978 to 7 percent in 1982.

Heroin, barbiturates, LSD, and opiates other than cocaine. Half of 1 percent of 1982 seniors had used heroin the previous year, and about 10 percent had used barbiturates, LSD, and other opiates.

Cocaine. Annual use of cocaine remained stable at 12 percent from 1979 to 1982, after increasing from 6 percent in 1976.

Amphetamines. Sixteen percent of seniors had used amphetamines without medical supervision in 1982.

Stable alcohol pattern

Alcohol. Regular use of alcohol has remained fairly stable, with about 6 percent of seniors reporting daily use in 1983, and about 40 percent reporting "occasional binge drinking" (five or more drinks in a row at least once in the previous two weeks). However, the percentage of seniors who reported any use of alcohol the previous month dropped from 37 percent in 1979 to 27 percent in 1982.

Drug use implications

Concern about young people's use of alcohol, marijuana, and other relatively mild drugs arises in part because they may reinforce or stimulate alienation from social institutions or otherwise impede the transition to adulthood. Thus, although there is reason to believe that drugs more often follow from than cause negative outcomes such as low academic performance, rebelliousness, and criminal activity and a high proportion of heavy drug users among youth eventually "mellow out," some young people may be using drugs and alcohol to "escape from the demands of preparing for life."[100] And contrary to earlier opinions, some authorities now believe that mild drugs such as marijuana frequently are a steppingstone to stronger drugs such as cocaine and heroin.[101] Young people themselves believe that drugs and alcohol are a negative influence in their lives: the results of a national survey in 1984 showed that 58 percent of high school students cited either drugs or alcohol as the "single worst influence" in their lives.[102]

Suicide

Educators recently have become more concerned with suicide among young people. The data indicate that the suicide rate among persons fifteen to twenty-six years of age nearly tripled between 1950 and 1980, and some surveys suggest that as many as one in ten school-age youth may attempt suicide.[103] Reasons for this increase appear to include growth in unemployment

100 National Institute on Drug Abuse, *Marijuana and Health* (Washington, D.C.: Government Printing Office, 1977); M. Ramos, "The Hippies: Where Are They Now?" in F. R. Scarpitti and S. K. Datesman, eds., *Drugs and the Youth Culture* (Beverly Hills, Calif.: Sage, 1980), pp.243–247.

101 C. Clusen, "Marijuana Use Linked to Mediocre School Work, Said to Damage Teenage Health and Development," *Education Times,* 2, No. 39 (1981), p. 6; Carol J. Mills and Harvey L. Noyes, "Patterns and Correlates of Initial and Subsequent Drug Use Among Adolescents," *Journal of Consulting and Clinical Psychology* (April 1984), pp. 231–243.

102 "Today's Youth Edge Back to Tradition," *U.S. News and World Report,* April 9, 1984, p. 16.

103 Judy Folkenberg, "To Be or Not to Be: Preventive Legislation," *Psychology Today* (April 1984), p. 9.

For some teenagers, drinking may be an attempt to escape from the demands of school, parents, and peers and the pressures of impending adulthood. (Susan Lapides)

among youth, decline in religious values that inhibited suicide, and pressures or despondency associated with family divorce. In addition, sociologist Ronald Maris has cited the general situation of youth in trying to account for rising suicide rates.

Increase in suicide rate

> As social life gets more tense and stressful, the anger and dissatisfaction that people feel are greater. Usually there is no one to take it out on but themselves. This is the case with many young people. They are trying to kill something or someone they can't kill, so they kill themselves by default.[104]

104 "Why 30,000 Americans Will Commit Suicide This Year," *U.S. News and World Report,* April 2, 1984, p. 48.

Delinquency

Long-term increase

Juvenile delinquency has increased in recent decades, along with parallel and related increases in the size of the youth group, the influence of peer culture, use of drugs and alcohol, and the growth of poverty neighborhoods in big cities. By 1976, young people aged twelve to twenty accounted for 55 percent of all arrests for robbery although they made up only 24 percent of the population.[105]

Research on delinquency among youth has provided support for a number of generalizations. The most important are the following:[106]

Violent delinquency

Significant delinquency rates are found among youth of all social classes. However, violent delinquency is much more frequent among working-class than middle-class youth.

Although a large proportion of crimes are committed by persons under twenty-five, most delinquents settle down to a productive adult life.

Violent delinquency is in part a reflection of participation in a violent subculture.

Delinquency and unemployment

Delinquency is associated with unemployment. Daniel Glaser writes: "To combat youth crime is largely futile unless an effort is also made to assure legitimate employment for youths."[107] From this point of view, delinquency is a partial response to the restricted opportunity available to young people in modern society.

Family characteristics related to delinquency include lax discipline, especially by the father; lack of effective supervision; and lack of cohesiveness in the family.[108]

Delinquency is related to learning disabilities and associated low levels of school performance among teenage boys. Specific personality characteristics such as lack of impulse control make learning disabled youth more susceptible to delinquency.[109]

Problems Reflected in the Schools

Like other topics reviewed in this chapter, the situation of youth and the youth culture has enormous consequences for the educational system. In ad-

105 M. J. Hindelgang, "Variations in Sex-Race-Age-Specific Incidence Rates of Offending," *American Sociological Review* (June 1981), pp. 461–474; William J. Wilson, "Urban Poverty, Social Dislocations, and Public Policy" (Paper presented at the Future of Our City Conference, University of Chicago, 1982).

106 Paul A. Strasburg, *Violent Delinquents, A Report to the Ford Foundation from the Vera Institute of Justice* (New York: Monarch, 1978); R. L. Austin, "Adolescent Subcultures of Violence," *The Sociological Quarterly* (Autumn 1980), pp. 545–561.

107 Daniel Glaser, "Economic and Sociocultural Variables Affecting Rates of Youth Unemployment," *Youth and Society,* No. 1 (September 1979), p. 79.

108 James Q. Wilson, *Thinking About Crime* (New York: Basic Books, 1983).

109 M. Dunivant, "The Relationship Between Learning Disabilities and Juvenile Delinquency" (Paper prepared for the National Center for State Courts, Williamsburg, Va., 1982).

dition to obvious implications involving the motivation to learn of students who are part of a culture characterized by significant drug use, delinquency, and youth unemployment, the situation of youth has a direct influence on what happens in the schools, particularly secondary schools. It also raises fundamental questions about the nature and role of effective education for young people.

Schools reflect society

For educators the most direct problems are those that involve drugs and alcohol in the school, along with problems of violence and disorder on school grounds. Because young people do not simply leave larger cultural patterns behind when they enter the schoolhouse door, indicators of antisocial behavior in and around the schools have been a continuing topic of debate during the past twenty years. Thus, "discipline" in the schools was most frequently cited as the biggest problem in the public schools in fourteen of the last fifteen annual Gallup polls of public opinion on education, including 1983. "Drugs" was cited second most frequently in four out of five years between 1978 and 1983.[110] A related finding by Goodlad showed that among senior high students, "drug/alcohol use" was ranked as the most serious problem in their schools along with "student misbehavior," while junior high and middle school students ranked drug and alcohol use as the third most serious problem, behind "student misbehavior" and "lack of student interest."[111]

Violence and vandalism

Data on violence and vandalism in the schools indicate that these problems became much more serious in the 1960s and 1970s and reached alarming proportions by about 1975. Thus a major study conducted for the National Institute of Education (*Violent Schools—Safe Schools*, 1978) concluded that in 1976 and 1977 there were nearly three million students and teachers victimized by crime in U.S. secondary schools every month. The study also found, however, that only about 11,000 of these incidents resulted in injuries requiring medical attention (the vast majority involved petty theft or verbal abuse), and that 75 percent of principals reported that their schools did not have a serious crime problem.[112] More recent data indicate that school violence and crime have declined substantially since 1977, in part because improvements in security and instruction have been emphasized at difficult schools. For example, the percentage of teachers indicating that discipline problems impaired their ability to teach declined from 75 percent in 1979 to 45 percent in 1983, and data on some big-city school districts showed vast declines in the incidence of robberies and assaults.[113]

Recent reductions in problems

Despite recent improvements, crime, drugs, and violence in the schools are still matters of serious concern. "Disorder in Our Public Schools," a well-publicized report, was issued by several federal agencies in 1984. President

110 Stanley M. Elam, "The Gallup Education Surveys: Impressions of a Poll Watcher," *Phi Delta Kappan* (September 1983), pp. 26–32.

111 Goodlad, *A Place Called School*, pp. 72–73.

112 National Institute of Education, *Violent Schools—Safe Schools* (Washington, D.C.: Government Printing Office, 1978).

113 Ellie McGrath, "Preparing to Wield the Rod," *Time*, January 23, 1984, p. 57; Cindy Currence, "President's Approach to School Discipline Draws Criticism," *Education Week*, January 25, 1984, pp. 1, 16.

Ronald Reagan told a large national conference that the report indicated the need for "good old fashioned discipline" to solve problems of disorder in the schools.[114] Many educators and other observers took issue with the statistics in the report and the interpretations drawn from them, pointing out that the data were mainly from the 1976–1977 National Institute of Education study and did not recognize either subsequent reductions in disorder or the relatively limited proportion of violent crime.[115]

Underlying causes

Nevertheless, critics of the president's handling of this issue did not argue that the problem of disorder is unimportant, and U.S. Secretary of Education Terrell Bell himself declared that "brute force and enforcement" will not solve the problem of disorder in the schools. "What we need," he said, "is a more attractive school environment, more motivation," as well as a reduction of poverty in U.S. society. "Until we're able to help minorities make it in our society," he concluded, "we're going to continue to see this."[116] The need for improved instruction and equal opportunity in education are discussed in several subsequent chapters.

Summing Up

1. Changes in the family may be having a detrimental influence on children's behavior and performance in school. Although the situation is complicated and research has not been conclusive, increases in single-parent families and in the number of mothers who work appear to be having a negative effect for many students, while the decline in the fertility rate and in size of the family may be having a positive effect.
2. The peer culture becomes more important as children proceed through school, but it has an important influence on education at all levels of schooling. Educators should be aware of the importance of peer culture in the school and classroom, including the potentially positive effects of participation in extracurricular activities.
3. The culture of the school (that is, "regularities" in school practice) appears to stress passive, rote learning in many elementary and secondary schools, particularly in working-class schools and mixed-class schools with relatively large numbers of low-achieving students. This happens in part because schools are institutions that must maintain orderly environments, because many students prefer passive learning, because teachers generally cannot attend to the learning needs of all students very adequately, because little practical knowledge has been available on how to change this situation, and because students must learn to function within the rules and regulations of organizations and groups.
4. Television probably increases aggressiveness and violent behavior among some children and youth, and it may detract from achievement—particu-

114 Currence, "President's Approach to School Discipline," p. 1.

115 Joseph Scherer and Jim Stinson, "Is School Violence a Serious Concern?", *The School Administrator* (March 1984), pp. 19–20, 54.

116 Ibid.

larly in reading—among some children. The effects of video games, movies, and other mass media and the larger cultural effects of mass media are not well understood.

5. Girls traditionally have been disadvantaged in terms of preparation for full participation in the larger society, and both girls and boys have experienced important sex-role-related problems and difficulties in the school. However, educational and occupational opportunities for women have been improving rapidly. Although differences in school achievement by sex have been declining, there may be some sex differences in ability patterns regarding verbal skills (favoring females) and abilities related to advanced mathematics (favoring males).
6. In some ways, youth has become a separate stage of life marked by discernible subcultures involving adolescents and young adults. Problems involving drugs and drinking, suicide, delinquency, and related behaviors raise serious concerns involving the development of adolescents and youth both inside and outside the school.

Discussion Questions

1. Compare and contrast the socialization experience of the average urban adolescent in the United States with that of youth living in a rural or non-Western culture.
2. How do changes in social values affect the role and functioning of the schools?
3. Compare the youth generation of the 1960s with that of the 1970s. Which group will the youth of the 1980s more closely resemble? Why?
4. How does schooling differ from education? How should one define each term? What are the implications of this type of analysis?
5. How do adolescents gain high status within their peer group? What types of students are most popular? Why? How does the social composition of the school affect the status positions of peer groups?

Suggested Readings

Best, Raphaela. *We've All Got Scars: What Boys and Girls Learn in Elementary School.* Bloomington: Indiana University Press, 1984.

Detailed observations regarding gender-related interactions and behaviors in the elementary grades, including analysis of why relatively more boys than girls are poor readers and of differences in boys' and girls' participation in the academic curriculum and the hidden curriculum.

Fennema, Elizabeth, and M. Jane Ayer, eds. *Women and Education.* Berkeley, Calif.: McCutchan, 1984.

Chapters deal with women in the history of American education, sex differences in educational experience, women and mathematics, women's careers, and related topics.

Fuchs, Victor. *How We Live: An Economic Pespective on Americans from Birth to Death.* Cambridge, Mass.: Harvard University Press, 1983.

Nonhysterical analysis of the meaning and implications of recent changes in the family.

Goodlad, John I. *A Place Called School.* New York: McGraw-Hill, 1984.

Detailed descriptions and analysis of "regularities" in the schools' culture that encourage passive, rote learning.

Gordon, Edmund W., ed. *Review of Research in Education 11.* Washington, D.C.: American Educational Research Association, 1984.

Chapters by Diane Scott-Jones and Ann M. Clarke provide comprehensive reviews of research on family environment related to socialization, social class, and child development.

11

Social Class, Race, and School Achievement

Focusing Questions

What is the relationship between social class and success in the educational system?

After accounting for social class, are race and ethnicity associated with school achievement?

What are the major reasons for low achievement among working-class students?

What is the role of home and family environment in encouraging or discouraging high achievement?

Do environment and heredity interact to cause low achievement?

What does research say about possibilities of improving the achievement of working-class students?

What are the implications of social class–achievement relationships regarding our traditional goal of providing equal educational opportunities for all students?

AFTER PROVIDING A BRIEF EXPLANATION OF SOCIAL CLASS AND examining relationships among students' social class, racial/ethnic background, and performance in the educational system, this chapter discusses why working-class students in general and disadvantaged minority students in particular have shown patterns of low educational achievement and attainment. The chapter concludes with a discussion of the meaning and implications of these relationships, within the context of our nation's historic commitment to equal educational opportunity.

Evidence cited throughout the chapter indicates that elementary and secondary schools have not been very effective in overcoming the educational disadvantages of working-class students, though recent data also show that the schools could be much more effective than they generally are. From this point of view, implementing reforms to improve the performance of low-achieving, working-class students, particularly those in poverty schools in big cities, must be considered a major national goal of education in the United States.

Social Class and School Achievement

The American social-class system is now generally understood to consist of three broad classes—working, middle, and upper. It is well known that there is a high relationship between social class and educational achievement in America. Traditionally, working-class students have not performed as well as middle- and upper-class students. As you read the analysis in this section, you should ask yourself why it has been so difficult to improve the achievement of working-class students and what can be done to improve their achievement in the future.

Social-Class Categories

Most social scientists believe that populations can be classified within a number of social-class groups, which differ in their economic, social, and political interests and characteristics. One of the most commonly used classifications for social-class groups in the United States was developed in the 1940s by W. Lloyd Warner and his associates at the University of Chicago.[1] Warner and his colleagues frequently used four variables (occupation, education, income, and housing value) to classify individuals and families in five groups: upper class; upper middle class; lower middle class; upper lower class; and lower lower class. Individuals very high in occupational prestige, amount of education, income, and housing value are high in **socioeconomic status (SES);** they are viewed by others as upper-class persons and are influential and powerful in their communities. Conversely, persons low in socioeconomic status

Social-class groups

1 W. Lloyd Warner, Marcia Meeker, and Kenneth Eells, *Social Class in America* (Chicago: Science Research Associates, 1949).

are viewed as lower class. They do not generally exert much power or influence.

Today, the term *working class* is more widely used than *lower class*, but social scientists still generally use measures of occupation, education, and income to describe three to six levels of SES, ranging from upper class at the top to lower working class at the bottom. The **upper class** is usually defined as including wealthy persons having substantial property and investment, whereas the **middle class** includes nonmanual workers—distinguishing between small business owners and professionals (upper middle) and sales or clerical workers (lower middle). The **working class** is generally divided into upper working class (skilled manual workers, such as craftspersons and construction workers) and lower working class (unskilled manual workers).

The underclass

In recent years a number of observers also have identified an underclass group within the working class. The **underclass** generally resembles the lower working class, but as the term implies, many of its members are the third or fourth generation of a family to live in poverty and are dependent on public assistance to sustain a relatively meager existence. Usually concentrated in the inner core slums of cities or in deteriorated rural poverty areas, members of the underclass frequently have little or no hope that their economic and social situation will ever improve.[2]

Studies on Social Class and School Attainment

Middletown studies

One of the first systematic studies investigating relations between social class and achievement in the educational system was Robert and Helen Lynd's study of "Middletown" (a small midwestern city) in the 1920s. The Lynds concluded that parents, regardless of social-class level, recognize the importance of education for their children; however, working-class children do not come to school academically equipped to deal with the verbal symbols and behavioral traits required for success in the classroom.[3]

Sorting out the working class

The Lynds' observations of social class and the schools were repeated by W. Lloyd Warner and his associates in a series of studies of communities in New England, the Deep South, and the Midwest. The main function of school seemed to be sorting out students according to their potential for upward mobility, a process that tended to doom working-class students to remain in the working class. The schools served the middle and upper classes, particularly the latter, by teaching those skills that are essential for college preparation and high-status occupations. Because the working-class child is not prepared to conform to the school's middle-class standards and expectations, she or he is handicapped in the school system. "One group" [the lower class], they reported, "is almost immediately brushed off into a bin labeled 'nonreaders,' 'first-grade repeaters,' or 'opportunity class,' where they stay for

2 Ken Auletta, *The Underclass* (New York: Random House, 1982).

3 Robert S. Lynd and Helen M. Lynd, *Middletown: A Study in American Culture* (New York: Harcourt, Brace & World, 1929).

Table 11.1
Reading Scores and Socioeconomic Status, 1979

	Average Reading Score of Students (% Correct Answers)
Parental Education	
Not graduated high school	53
Graduated high school	60
Attended college	65
Type of Community	
Rural disadvantaged	59
Urban disadvantaged	53
Urban advantaged	68

Source: National Assessment of Educational Progress, *Three National Assessments of Reading: Changes in Performance, 1970–80* (Denver: Education Commission of the States, 1981).

eight or ten years and are then released through a chute to the outside world to become 'hewers of wood and drawers of water.' "[4]

Hundreds of studies have since documented the close relationship between social class and achievement in the educational system. For example, a clear picture of this relationship has been provided by the National Assessment of Educational Progress (NAEP), which periodically collects achievement information from nationally representative samples of students. As shown in Table 11.1, reading scores of thirteen-year-old students in 1979 varied directly with their social class. Students whose parents had not graduated from high school (that is, low SES students) had an average score of 53 percent correct on the NAEP reading test, whereas high SES students (that is, those with college-educated parents) had an average score of 65, nearly one-fourth higher than the low SES group. Similarly, students in disadvantaged urban and rural communities (neighborhoods with a high percentage of poverty residents) scored much lower than students in wealthier communities.

Social class and college attendance

Social class is associated with many educational outcomes in addition to reading achievement. On the average, working-class students have lower ability scores, are less likely to complete high school, and are less likely to enroll in and complete college than are middle-class students. Data showing the interrelations between several of these variables are given in Table 11.2, which indicates the percentages of 1972 high school graduates who attended college, by social-class background and ability level. As one might expect, students in the highest ability group (those ranked in the top 25 percent nationally) are much more likely to attend college than are students in the lowest ability group, and this is true at each socioeconomic level. Similarly, *at each ability level* students in the highest social-class group (the top 25 percent

4 W. Lloyd Warner, Robert J. Havighurst, and Martin B. Loeb, *Who Shall Be Educated?* (New York: Harper & Row, 1944), p. 38.

Table 11.2
Percentages of 1972 High School Graduates Who Entered and Graduated from College, by Social-Class (SES) Background and Ability Level

	Percent Entered College Ability Level				**Percent Graduated from College Ability Level**			
Social-Class (SES) Level	*Lowest 25%*	*Middle 50%*	*Highest 25%*	*Total*	*Lowest 25%*	*Middle 50%*	*Highest 25%*	*Total*
Lowest 25%	21	33	63	30	02	05	20	05
Middle 50%	23	47	73	47	02	10	27	12
Highest 25%	46	76	93	82	03	18	47	31
Total	24	50	81	51	02	10	35	15
Percentage of lowest social-class group in highest ability level					11			
Percentage of middle social-class group in highest ability level					25			
Percentage of highest social-class group in highest ability level					50			

Note: College attendance refers to entry in an academic program in 1972. College graduation refers to acquisition of a bachelor's degree four years later. Academic ability is measured by a composite reading and mathematics score. Social-class scores are a composite of father's and mother's education, father's occupation, parental income, and types of items in the home. Data were collected as part of the National Longitudinal Study of the High School Class of 1972.

Source: Computed and adapted from Bruce E. Eckland, Louis B. Henderson, and Andrew J. Kolstad, *College Attainment Four Years After High School* (Washington, D.C.: National Center for Education Statistics, 1981).

nationally) are much more likely to attend college than students in the bottom 25 percent. Overall, only 30 percent of low SES students attended college, as compared with 82 percent of high SES students.

Table 11.2 also shows the college graduation rates for the 1972 high school graduates. Because high SES, high-ability students who enter college are much more likely to remain and acquire a degree than are other students, graduation from college is even more limited to high SES students than attendance at college: 31 percent of the high SES group, as compared to only 5 percent of the low SES group, eventually obtained B.A. degrees. It also is noteworthy that 38 percent of all the bachelor's degrees awarded to 1972 high school graduates were earned by high-ability, high SES students, even though this group constitutes only 11 percent of the population (not shown in the table).

College graduation

Finally, Table 11.2 illustrates another relationship between social class and academic ability. It indicates that 50 percent of the students in the highest social class were also among the students with the highest academic ability. In contrast, only 11 percent of students in the lowest social class were in the high ability group.

Further evidence of the relationship between social class and school achievement can be found in studies of poverty neighborhoods in our very large cities. Data on the performance of students in such neighborhoods have provided an almost unremittingly bleak picture of ineffective schooling for the past three decades. For example, Levine and his colleagues examined sixth-grade achievement patterns at more than a thousand predominantly poverty schools (called "concentrated poverty schools") in seven big cities and reported that all but a handful had average reading scores more than a year below the national average. They also pointed out that at least one-fourth of the students at these schools cannot read well enough to be considered functionally literate. This pattern can be found at concentrated poverty schools in big cities throughout the United States.[5] Reasons for this discouraging national pattern are discussed in subsequent sections of this chapter.

Poverty neighborhoods

Race/Ethnicity and School Achievement

Patterns involving social class and educational achievement in the United States are further complicated by interrelationships among these variables and those of race and ethnicity. (The term **ethnicity** refers to shared culture and background. Members of an **ethnic group** usually have common ancestry and generally are similar in language, religion, and other cultural patterns. The term **race** generally is used to refer to groups of people with common ancestry and physical characteristics. Since there are no "pure" races, some scholars prefer to avoid reference to race and instead discuss group differences only or largely under the heading of ethnicity.[6]) As a result of centuries of oppressive treatment, the nation's largest racial minority group—black Americans—is much lower in social class than is the white majority. Several other major ethnic groups—Mexican Americans and Puerto Ricans, among them—are also disproportionately working class. In line with their low social-class standing, these racial and ethnic minority groups are also low in academic achievement, high school and college graduation rates, and other measures of educational attainment.

Race and ethnicity

The close association between social class, racial/ethnic minority status, and school achievement is shown in Table 11.3, which presents average reading scores obtained by a nationally representative sample of high school sophomores in 1980. As shown in the table, black students have the lowest SES scores and also the lowest language and math scores; non-Hispanic whites are highest on all three measures. Except for math scores among Asian-Pacific Americans, achievement scores parallel scores on socioeconomic status: the higher the SES score, the higher the reading and math scores. Black students, Hispanic students, and Native American students are

5 Daniel U. Levine et. al., "Concentrated Poverty and Reading Achievement in Seven Big Cities," *The Urban Review* (Summer 1979), pp. 63–80.

6 Howard M. Bahr, Bruce A. Chadwick, and Joseph H. Strauss, *American Ethnicity* (Lexington, Mass.: D. C. Heath, 1979).

Table 11.3
Language and Math Scores and Social-Class (SES) Scores of High School Sophomores, by Racial and Ethnic Group, 1980

Racial/Ethnic Group	Average Language Skills Score	Average Math Score	Percent in Lowest 25% SES	Percent in College-Bound Program
Black	14.5	6.5	45	29
Hispanic	15.6	7.7	43	23
Native American	18.5	7.8	36	23
Asian-Pacific American	25.2	16.6	22	47
White (Non-Hispanic)	27.8	15.5	18	37

Note: Language scores are a combination of scores in vocabulary, reading, and writing. The maximum scores for language and math skills were 57 and 38, respectively. Social class is a composite measure of father's and mother's education, father's occupation, parental income, and types of items in the home.

Source: Data available from National Center for Education Statistics, *High School and Beyond Study* (Washington, D.C.: National Center for Education Statistics, 1980).

much lower in SES than are non-Hispanic white and Asian-Pacific students, and have much lower academic achievement scores.[7] Table 11.3 also shows that, as one might expect based on academic achievement scores, non-Hispanic whites and Asian-Pacific students are much more likely to be in college-bound "academic" programs.

Relationships between social class, race/ethnicity, and achievement

Because social class, race/ethnicity, and school achievement are so closely interrelated, researchers frequently ask whether race and ethnicity are associated with performance in the educational system even after one takes into account the low socioeconomic status of blacks and other disadvantaged minority groups. In general, the answer has been that social class accounts for most of the variation in educational achievement by race and ethnicity. That is, if one knows the social class of a group of students, one can predict whether their achievement, ability scores, and college attendance rates are high or low; information about their racial or ethnic group does little to improve such a prediction. This generalization also means that working-class white students as a group are low in achievement and college attainment, whereas middle-class minority students rank relatively high on these variables. Such a pattern is evident in Table 11.4, which shows the probability of graduating from college in the United States when students are categorized by SES, race, and sex. The data in Table 11.4, which are taken from a 1979 follow-up study of 1972 high school graduates, clearly show that

7 Further analysis of these and other data also indicates that there is considerable variation within broad racial/ethnic classifications. For example, within the Hispanic group, Cuban Americans have much higher SES and achievement scores than do Mexican American and Puerto Rican students, though this pattern may be changing with the 1980's influx of low SES Cubans into Florida and other states.

Table 11.4
Percentages of 1972 High School Graduates Who Graduated from College, by Social-class Background, Sex, and Race

	Percent Graduated from College			
	Male		*Female*	
Social Class	*White*	*Black*	*White*	*Black*
Low	14	11	10	18
Medium	21	24	20	23
High	42	30	36	32

Note: College graduation refers to acquisition of a bachelor's degree between 1972 and 1979. Social-class scores are a composite of father's and mother's education, father's occupation, parental income, and types of items in the home. *Low social class* refers to respondents more than one standard deviation below the sample mean, *high social class* refers to persons more than one standard deviation above the mean, and *medium social class* refers to persons within one standard deviation of the mean. Data were collected as part of the National Longitudinal Study of the High School Class of 1972.

Source: Adapted from Karl L. Alexander, Cornelius Riordan, James Fennessey, and Aaron M. Pallas, "Social Background, Academic Resources, and College Graduation: Recent Evidence from the National Longitudinal Survey," *American Journal of Education* (August 1982), pp. 315–333, published by The University of Chicago Press. © 1982 by The University of Chicago.

at the low and middle SES levels, black high school graduates actually are more likely to graduate from college than whites.

Analyses like those we have presented support the conclusion that one of the central problems faced by disadvantaged minorities in the United States is that minority persons are still disproportionately working class and underclass, and their children are much less successful in the educational system than are the children of the middle class. Since education, particularly higher education, has become an important channel for gaining access to rewarding opportunities in the economic system,[8] working-class students in the disadvantaged minority groups are much less likely to obtain middle-class employment than are students from middle-class homes. From this point of view, the relative ineffectiveness of the schools in educating students from working-class homes—whether minority or nonminority—helps to perpetuate the current class system in the United States. The burden of poverty and low achievement falls disproportionately on the nation's racial and ethnic minority groups.

8 A. H. Halsey, "Toward Meritocracy? The Case of Britain," in J. Karabel and A. H. Halsey, eds., *Power and Ideology in Education* (New York: Oxford University Press, 1976); David L. Featherman and Robert M. Hauser, *Opportunity and Change* (New York: Academic Press, 1978); idem., *The Process of Stratification* (New York: Academic Press, 1977).

Reasons for Low Achievement Among Working-Class Students

Increasing importance of education

Educators and lay leaders became much more aware of and concerned about the low achievement of working-class students during the 1950s and 1960s, when expectations for high scholastic performance were rising. U.S. economic development made it increasingly important for students to acquire advanced skills in literacy, mathematics, and other educational areas. Much research aimed at understanding and overcoming the problems of low-achieving students was conducted during the 1950s and thereafter, and a variety of explanations have been advanced to explain the academic deficiencies of low-achieving students in general and low-achieving, working-class students in particular. While explanations of differing researchers are not necessarily mutually exclusive, we will group several of the major explanations under the following headings: home environment; the heredity versus environment debate; and ineffective instruction.

Home Environment

Chapter 10 pointed out that the family and home environment is the most important agent shaping the early socialization and education of the child. We also noted that the home environment is closely related to the family's social class. Thus, social-class differences in family and home environment are associated with the relatively low educational performance and attainment of working-class students.

Social-class differences in home environment

One way to categorize school–class-related home environment differences in socialization for success in school is to view these differences as involving *knowledge and understandings, cognitive and verbal skills,* and *values and attitudes.*[9] Regarding *knowledge and understandings,* Daniel Levine and Robert Havighurst have examined the data on social-class differences and concluded that middle-class children are more likely than working-class children to "acquire more knowledge of the world outside the home and immediate neighborhood"[10] through greater access to books and cultural institutions (for example, museums), parental teaching, and exploration of diverse environments. Knowledge and understandings acquired through exposure to the wider world are helpful to children when they enter school.

Cognitive and verbal skills

Differences in *cognitive and verbal skills* in particular reflect social-class differences in family language environments. The relatively wide and diverse experience of the middle-class child is important in developing cognitive and verbal skills, but advantages centering on the language used in the home are

9 For extensive discussion and illustration of these differences, see Daniel U. Levine and Robert J. Havighurst, *Society and Education.* 6th ed. (Boston, Mass.: Allyn and Bacon, 1984).

10 Ibid., p. 123.

probably even more important. Basil Bernstein has found that although both middle- and working-class children develop adequate skills with respect to "ordinary" or "restricted" language, middle-class children are superior in the use of "formal" or "elaborated" language. Ordinary, restricted language is grammatically simple and relies on gestures and further explanations to clarify meaning. The elaborated, or formal, language of the middle class is grammatically complex and provides greater potential for organizing experience within an abstract meaning system.[11] Similarly, Janet Holland has reported that the elaborated language of the middle-class child is more independent of the context (that is, more abstract) than "ordinary" language.[12] Bernstein, Holland, and many other scholars believe that facility in using elaborated language helps middle-class children excel in cognitive development, which is essential for school success.

Language in the home

Recent research has thrown additional light on how working-class children are hampered by their home language environment. For example, Catherine Snow and her associates have reported that working-class mothers are less likely than middle-class mothers to establish productive conversational *routines* and to provide *responsive talk* that helps children improve in abstract language. The authors believe that this difference may be due both to differential resources and different philosophies among families. "It is not yet clear," they conclude, "to what extent these different components of social class may interact; whether, for example, a particular style of interaction with children is caused by financial insecurity or by the parents' ideology."[13]

Working-class stress on obedience

Regarding *values and attitudes* associated with social-class differences in child-raising, working-class children are at a disadvantage because their socialization appears to emphasize obedience and conformity to a greater degree than the independence and self-directed thinking emphasized in middle-class families. Victor Gerkas reviewed fifty years of research on social-class differences in socialization and concluded that working-class parents are more likely to (1) emphasize physical punishment rather than reasoning, shame, and guilt; and (2) stress didactic teaching-learning, rather than self-regulated, independent learning.[14] Differences along these lines undoubtedly are related to the fact that working-class environments are relatively dangerous for children, as well as to differences in parents' education, resources, and knowledge of what child-raising practices help children develop intellectually. While working-class child-raising methods probably are becoming

11 Basil Bernstein, *Class, Codes, and Control* (London and Boston: Routledge & Kegan Paul, 1975); Basil Bernstein, "Codes, Modalities, and the Process of Cultural Reproduction: A Model," *Language and Society* (December 1981).

12 Janet Holland, "Social Class and Changes in Orientation to Meaning," *Sociology* (February 1984), pp. 1–18.

13 Catherine E. Snow, Clara Dubber, and Akke De Blauw, "Routines in Mother-Child Interaction," in Lynne Feagans and Dale Clark Farran, eds., *The Language of Children Reared in Poverty* (New York: Academic Press, 1982), p. 70.

14 Victor Gerkas, "The Influence of Social Class on Socialization," in Wesley R. Burr et. al., eds., *Contemporary Theories About the Family* (New York: Free Press, 1979).

more like those of middle-class families,[15] and while they may be superior in terms of preparing children to function in a hostile environment, socialization practices in working-class homes do not help children to function independently in the school and classroom. Based on intensive study of 700 families in Nottingham, England, John and Elizabeth Newson have summarized the origins of these patterns as follows:

> Parents at the upper end of the social scale are more inclined *on principle* to use democratically based, highly verbal means of control, and this kind of discipline is likely to produce personalities who can both identify successfully with the system and use it for their own ends later on. At the bottom end of the scale . . . parents choose *on principle* to use a highly authoritarian, mainly non-verbal means of control, in which words are used more to threaten and bamboozle the child into obedience than to make him understand the rationale behind social behavior . . . . Thus the child born into the lowest social bracket has everything stacked against him *including his parents' principles of child upbringing.*[16]

Social-class patterns not universal

It is important to emphasize that socialization differentials such as those described above reflect average differences across social-class groups, not universal patterns that distinguish all middle-class families from all working-class families. Thus, many working-class families do provide a home environment that is conducive to achievement, and the great majority of low-income parents try to provide their children with a positive learning environment. Nevertheless, differences in home environment and the difficulties that go along with poverty hamper the intellectual development of many working-class children.

The importance of the home and family environment for intellectual development also has been emphasized in studies by J. McVicker Hunt, Martin Deutsch, Benjamin Bloom, and other researchers. These studies generally indicate that environmental stimulation in working-class families is less conducive to intellectual development, on the average, than is the environment typical of middle-class families.

Hunt has summarized thousands of studies related to intellectual growth.[17] He outlines various schools of thought and beliefs relating to intelligence and concludes that while heredity sets the limits on individual potential, the role of environment is extremely important in shaping intellectual performance. Educators need to devise experiences that counteract depriva-

15 James D. Wright and Sonia R. Wright, "Social Class and Parental Values for Children: A Partial Replication and Extension of the Kohn Thesis," *American Sociological Review* (June 1976), pp. 527–537.

16 John Newson and Elizabeth Newson, *Seven Years Old in the Home Environment* (London: Allen & Unwin, 1976), p. 406. Chapter 6 in *Society and Education* by Levine and Havighurst describes in detail the advantages of emphasizing obedience in a working-class environment, particularly in the inner city.

17 J. McVicker Hunt, *Intelligence and Experience* (New York: Ronald Press, 1961); idem., "Psychological Development: Early Experience," *Annual Review of Psychology* (1979), pp. 103–143.

The socioeconomic environment in which children are raised is an important determinant of a child's academic achievement.
(Frank Siteman/Stock, Boston, left; Daniel S. Brody/Stock, Boston, right)

Preschool experience

tion and improve intellectual potential and achievement levels in schools. Preschool enrichment programs were strongly recommended as antidotes to educational disadvantage. Hunt, along with Deutsch, was instrumental in the trend toward **compensatory education**. According to the theory, education to compensate—or make up—for environmental disadvantages can do the most good at an early age, since the cognitive abilities of the child are developing at a rapid rate.

Stimulation in the home

Martin Deutsch also has outlined the main factors that affect the disadvantaged child's readiness to learn.[18] One factor he cites is the lack of variety of visual, tactile, and auditory stimulation in the working-class home. He explores the interrelations between social class, race, grade in school, and language skills. The language variables of abstraction, verbalization, and vocabulary are found to be correlated significantly with social class, race, and grade level. In other words, language ability is associated with class factors; when social class is taken account of statistically, however, black children are more handicapped than white; with increasing age, language deficiencies tend to increase. This coincides with the well-known fact that working-class students

18 Martin Deutsch, "The Role of Social Class in Language Development and Cognition," in A. H. Passow, M. L. Goldberg, and A. J. Tannenbaum, eds., *Education of the Disadvantaged* (New York: Holt, 1967), pp. 214–224.

fall further behind the national average in achievement as they proceed through the grades.

In a companion study, Deutsch and others developed a Deprivation Index that has a closer relationship to IQ score, language skills, and concept formation than does social class.[19] The Deprivation Index included items dealing with family activities, parent-child interaction, and learning experiences in the home. Data from a similar home environmental index developed by another group of researchers indicate that scores on this type of index provide a more accurate prediction of school success than do the social-class indicators.[20]

Deprivation Index

The environmental deprivation theory also holds that early years of development are more important than later years. Although not all human characteristics reveal the same patterns of development, the most rapid development of human characteristics, including cognitive skills, occurs during the preschool years. For example, Benjamin Bloom presented longitudinal data

19 Martin Whiteman and Martin Deutsch, "Social Disadvantage as Related to Intellectual and Language Development," Research Grant No. MH1098-3 (Paper presented at the Conference of Cultural Deprivation and Enrichment Programs, New York; Yeshiva University, April 1965). Later published in M. Deutsch et al., eds., *The Disadvantaged Child* (New York: Basic Books, 1967), pp. 337–356.

20 R. H. Dave, "The Identification and Measurement of Environmental Process Variables That Are Related to Educational Achievement" (Ph.D. dissertation, University of Chicago, 1963).

(data extending over a period of several years) that suggest that from birth to four years of age an individual develops 50 percent of his or her potential intelligence; from ages four to eight another 30 percent develops; and between ages eight and seventeen the remaining 20 percent develops.[21]

Early cognitive development

Based on the above estimates for intelligence and learning, home environment is crucial, according to Bloom, because of the large amount of cognitive development that has already taken place before the child enters the first grade.[22] Furthermore, the child's intellectual development is affected even during the prenatal stages, by the mother's general health, her diet, her alcohol intake and smoking habits, and biochemical changes related to stress and other emotional factors. In this regard, substantially more working-class mothers than middle- and upper-class mothers, and more black mothers than white mothers, suffer from poor physical and mental health as well as from poor diet.

Overcoming learning deficits

This does not mean that once a learning deficit occurs, remediation is impossible. But it does clearly imply that it is more difficult to effect changes for older children, and that a more powerful environment is needed to effect these changes.[23] Bloom's later work indicates that learning differences can be greatly reduced with appropriate environmental and learning conditions.[24]

Social class and home environment not synonymous

Since the relationships among social class, home environment, and intellectual development exhibit group patterns, there is room for individual differences among children in both deprived and enriched environments. It cannot be emphasized too strongly, for example, that a working-class child may have an enriched home environment and the child's middle-class counterpart may have a deprived home environment. Similarly, all children from deprived environments do not necessarily have limited school abilities, and all children from enriched environments do not have academic success; rather, social class and home environment frequently handicap or assist children in developing their mental capabilities.

The Heredity Versus Environment Debate

Role of heredity

During the past century there has been heated controversy concerning whether intelligence is determined primarily by heredity or environment. When IQ tests were undergoing rapid development early in the twentieth century, many psychologists believed that intelligence was determined primarily by heredity. They thought they were learning to assess innate differences in people's capacity through IQ tests and other measures of cognitive

21 Benjamin S. Bloom, *Stability and Change in Human Characteristics* (New York: Wiley, 1964), p. 88. See also Moshe Smilansky, *Priorities in Education: Pre-School; Evidence and Conclusions* (Washington, D.C.: World Bank, 1979).

22 Bloom, *Stability and Change in Human Characteristics,* p. 110.

23 Benjamin S. Bloom, *Human Characteristics and School Learning* (New York: McGraw-Hill, 1976).

24 Benjamin S. Bloom, *All Our Children Learning* (New York: McGraw-Hill, 1981).

development. Since economically disadvantaged populations and some minority groups such as blacks scored considerably below middle-income populations and nonminority groups, these *hereditarians* believed that working-class populations and minority groups were innately inferior in intellectual capacity.

Environmentalist View By the 1950s, most social scientists took the *environmentalist* position that environment is more important than heredity in determining intelligence. The preceding section discussed the views of some noted environmentalists—J. McVicker Hunt, Martin Deutsch, and Benjamin Bloom. Environmentalists stress the great importance of environment as it impinges on growth and development and the need for compensatory programs on a continuous basis beginning in infancy. They also criticize the use of IQ tests because these tests are seen as culturally biased. The differences in IQ scores between controlled groups of blacks and whites are attributed by the environmentalists to social-class differences and to racial prejudice in our society.

Environmental factors

Environmentalists continue to conduct research and report data they believe indicate that environment is much more important than heredity in determining intelligence. Sandra Scarr and Richard Weinberg, for example, have been studying differences between black children growing up in biological families and children growing up in adopted families. They have concluded that the effects of environment outweigh the effects of heredity.[25] Thomas Sowell has been studying IQ scores collected for various ethnic groups between 1920 and 1970. He has found that the scores of some groups such as Italian Americans and Polish Americans have substantially improved. He also has found that neither the patterns nor the levels of black mental test scores have been unique and that these scores "have risen by larger increments than have scores in the general population in response to such environmental improvements as better teaching or better test familiarity and test environment."[26]

Hereditarian View The hereditarian point of view underwent a major revival in the 1960s and 1970s, based on the writings of Arthur Jensen, William Shockley, and Richard Herrnstein. All three of these authors rekindled the emotional issues surrounding the relationship among race, social class, heredity, and intelligence. Basing their data on a review and reanalysis of previous research, as well as on their own studies, they each concluded independently that heredity is the major factor in determining intelligence—accounting for up to 80 percent of the variance.

25 Sandra Scarr and Richard A. Weinberg, "I.Q. Test Performance of Black Children Adopted by White Families," *American Psychologist* (July 1976), pp. 726–739; Sandra Scarr, *I.Q.: Race, Social Class, and Individual Differences* (Hillsdale, N.J.: Erlbaum, 1981).

26 Thomas Sowell, "Race and IQ Reconsidered," in T. Sowell, ed., *American Ethnic Groups* (Washington, D.C.: Urban Institute, 1978), p. 229; idem., *Ethnic America* (New York: Basic Books, 1981).

Arthur R. Jensen, one of the nation's leading educational psychologists, published a lengthy article in the Winter 1969 issue of the *Harvard Educational Review,* which presented the following conclusions:[27]

Jensen's conclusions

1. Blacks average about 15 points below the white average on IQ tests; this is due to the genetic difference between the two races in learning abilities and patterns.
2. Blacks as a group and "disadvantaged" children have more difficulty than do others in abstract reasoning—the basis for IQ measurements and for higher mental skills; unfortunately, the schools have assumed that all children can master higher cognitive skills.
3. Conversely, blacks and "disadvantaged" children tend to do well in tasks involving rote learning—memorizing mainly through repetition; these aptitudes can be used to help raise their scholastic achievement up to a point.
4. Compensatory education, which is costing taxpayers hundreds of millions of dollars a year (actually billions), has failed and will continue to fail because it is trying to compensate children of limited intellectual talents with learning processes and concepts that are really geared to students of average or above average talent.

Jensen made it clear that his data provide no basis for judging the intellectual capacity of any given individual but are based on group averages. He pointed out that the nature of the differences in intellectual skills between blacks and whites as groups and the role of genetics in these differences have not been fully explored. He strongly attacked those who argued that, with very few exceptions, children have the same potential for developing the same mental abilities and who also claimed that most differences in IQ scores are the result of social, psychological, and economic deprivation. Alluding to the overwhelming failures in compensatory education, he pointed out that in other fields when things go wrong, when machines fail or when treatments do not cure, people question their assumptions and theories. A fresh look at classroom and school failure is in order, and it should start, he declared, with a re-examination of the nature of intelligence.

Criticism of Jensen

The most comprehensive critical analysis of Jensen's conclusions appeared as a response in the next issue of the *Review.* The authors were fellow psychologists who support the view that environment plays the major role in IQ scores. Their main points are summarized below:[28]

1. Jensen's research is based on relatively small samples.
2. The environment-heredity interaction is impossible to separate and measure.

27 Arthur R. Jensen, "How Much Can We Boost IQ and Scholastic Achievement?" *Harvard Educational Review* (Winter 1969), pp. 1–123.

28 "How Much Can We Boost IQ and Scholastic Achievement: A Discussion," *Harvard Educational Review* (Spring 1969), pp. 273–356. Contributors were Jerome S. Kagan, J. McV. Hunt, James F. Crow, Carl Bereiter, David Elkind, Lee J. Cronbach, and William F. Brazziel.

3. IQ outcomes are affected by a host of environmental variables, such as malnutrition and prenatal care, which are difficult to measure.
4. Racial prejudice could account for any differences in IQ that might exist between blacks and whites.
5. IQ tests are biased and the scores do not necessarily measure intelligence.
6. Granted, billions of dollars have been spent on compensatory education and the results have not been impressive, but it is possible that we have not reached the threshold where the amount of money per child makes an impact.

After publication of his 1969 article, Jensen was under severe criticism in the professional literature; his classes were disrupted and his colleagues at the University of California at Berkeley made an unsuccessful effort to censure him. He and his family were threatened, he was denied the opportunity to address many professional audiences, and on some occasions he was prevented from finishing his lectures.[29] Attacks on Jensen continued after publication of his book, *Bias in Mental Testing,* in which he rejected the conclusion that differences in teacher expectations, test administration, cultural fairness of tests, and coaching are responsible for the average difference of 15 points in black and white IQ scores. He attributed at least 50 percent and perhaps as much as 75 percent of this difference to heredity.[30]

Jensen updates his position

Two years after Jensen's 1969 study, Richard Herrnstein delved into the history and implications of IQ scores and intelligence.[31] Herrnstein's article touched only lightly on the racial issue. "Although there are some scraps of evidence for a genetic component in the black-white difference," he wrote, "the overwhelming case is for believing that American blacks have been at an environmental disadvantage."[32] He contended that there is probably insufficient evidence to support either an environmental or a genetic hypothesis for racial differences in intelligence.

Herrnstein's position

Instead, Herrnstein charged boldly into another part of the heredity versus environment battlefield. His argument took the following form: "(1) If differences in mental abilities are inherited, and (2) if success requires these abilities, and (3) if earnings and prestige depend on success, then (4) social standing will be based to some extent on the inherited differences among people."[33]

The implication of his premise, further developed in a more recent work, is that as society comes closer to the ideal of equality of opportunity it also

29 Part of the criticism of Jensen focused on his use of data on twins, which had been collected by a distinguished British psychologist (Sir Cyril Burt). Many scholars now believe that these data were fabricated to support hereditarian conclusions. See Leon J. Kamin, *The Science and Politics of IQ* (Potomac, Md.: Erlbaum, 1974).

30 Arthur R. Jensen, *Bias in Mental Testing* (New York: Free Press, 1979).

31 Richard J. Herrnstein, "IQ," *The Atlantic* (September 1971), pp. 43–64.

32 Ibid., p. 57.

33 Ibid., p. 58.

"Meritocracy"

comes closer to "meritocracy," a system in which the ablest rise to the top.[34] The syllogism implies that social classes are genetically distinct, since the criteria for class membership tend to correlate with intelligence. It follows that equality of opportunity—while unquestionably desirable on both moral and practical grounds—can lead to a growing genetic gap between the classes. If intelligence is inherited and social inequalities are removed, then genetics will determine who achieves the more prestigious roles in society. The less intelligent will be able to compete only if they are given more than an equal opportunity. Note that the corollary of the syllogism is concerned with schooling. Educational success is highly dependent on mental abilities measured by IQ scores. Intelligence influences school success, and success in school correlates with social class. If 80 percent of intelligence is related to heredity, then this helps explain why compensatory programs have had limited educational value. Herrnstein's thesis runs counter to the traditional liberal and equalitarian stance that poverty, school failure, and intelligence result from the conditions of society—not from the individual's genetic background.

Threatening the equalitarian interpretation

Synthesizer's View The debate over the extent to which intelligence is inborn (hereditary) or acquired (environmental) continues. Although thousands of studies have addressed this issue, scientists still disagree vigorously on their interpretation. Some have concluded that intelligence is 80 percent or more inherited, while others have concluded that it is 80 percent or more acquired.[35]

A number of social scientists have taken a middle or "synthesizing" position in the controversy. The synthesizers point out that both heredity and environment contribute to differences in measured intelligence. For example, Christopher Jencks and his colleagues reviewed a large amount of data on the issue and divided the IQ variance into .45 due to heredity, .35 due to environment, and .20 due to interaction between the two (particular abilities thrive or wither in specific environments).[36] Robert Nichols reviewed all these and other data and concluded that the true value may be anywhere between .40 and .80 but that the exact value has little importance for policy.[37] Nichols and other synthesizers maintain that the best way to conceptualize the contribution of heredity to a trait such as intelligence is to think of heredity as determining the fixed limits of a range. It is the interaction effect (of both components) that yields the individual's measured intelligence. Educators want to identify the educational environments that will

Jencks's estimates

Interaction effects are crucial

34 Richard J. Herrnstein, *IQ in the Meritocracy* (Boston: Little, Brown, 1973); idem. "IQ Testing and the Media," *The Atlantic* (February 1982), pp. 68–74.

35 N. Bloch and Gerald Dworkin, eds., *The IQ Controversy: Critical Readings* (New York: Pantheon, 1976); Robert Cancro, ed., *Intelligence: Genetic and Environmental Influences* (New York: Grune & Stratton, 1971); Robert C. Nichols, "Policy Implications of the IQ Controversy," in L. S. Shulman, ed., *Review of Research in Education, VI* (Itasca, Ill.: Peacock, 1978).

36 Christopher Jencks et al., *Inequality: A Reassessment of the Effect of Family and Schooling in America* (New York: Basic Books, 1972).

37 Nichols, "Policy Implications of the IQ Controversy."

help each student live up to his or her innate potential and how much it may cost to supply this environment. Even if we cannot specify how much of the child's intelligence is the result of environmental factors, teachers (and parents) need to provide each child with a psychologically productive environment in which to realize her or his maximum potential.

IQ tests and academic content

Educators also need to recognize that some students who score low on IQ tests manage to perform well in school, and vice versa. Because intelligence tests generally require verbal skills and a middle-class background, improvements in environment *can* produce changes in IQ scores. Group scores differ on IQ tests, as well as in academic subjects; the reasons are open to debate. Note, however, that the cognitive domain is only one area of learning, and students with low IQ scores and/or low school grades can be quite successful in other domains of learning and in job performance. Perhaps educators themselves fuss too much about low IQ scores or low school grades, although it must be said in their defense that their job requires them to deal with and interpret such data. In general, educators committed to improving the performance of low-achieving students should be encouraged by recent studies indicating that the intellectual ability of disadvantaged students can be significantly improved. In this regard, Stephen Gould has reviewed evidence documenting an increase in IQ scores of the U.S. population during the past half-century and has reached the following general conclusion.:

> This general gain can hardly be ascribed to genetic causes; it reflects whatever improved literacy, earlier access to information through radio and television, better nutrition, and so forth have wrought in just thirty-five years. When we recognize that the average black-white difference is 15 points, and that gains of up to two thirds this amount have occurred in certain age groups as a result of general changes in environment not specifically directed toward this end, then why should we be ready to conclude that group differences are ineluctable?[38]

Ineffective Instruction

Certain school and classroom dynamics result in very low achievement among working-class students in the United States and, indeed, in other parts of the world. We have already noted that the home and family environment of many working-class students is lacking in the kind of educational stimulation that adequately prepares students for success in the classroom. The following list highlights some of the most important classroom-related obstacles to overcoming the educational disadvantages of students from working-class backgrounds.[39]

1. *Inappropriate curriculum and instruction.* Curriculum materials and instructional approaches in the primary grades frequently assume that

38 Stephen Jay Gould, "Jensen's Last Stand," *The New York Review of Books,* May 1, 1980, p. 43.

39 The discussion in this section is based in part on material in Levine and Havighurst, *Society and Education,* chapter 8.

students are familiar with vocabulary and concepts to which working-class students have had little or no exposure. As students proceed through school, terminology and concepts become increasingly abstract, and many working-class students fall further behind because their level of mastery is too rudimentary to allow for fluent learning. After grade three, much of the curriculum requires a degree of reading skill that many working-class students have not yet attained; hence they fall further behind in other subject areas. Judith Green has pointed out that much of this handicap involves general "linguistic patterns" that detract from students' "acquisition of strategies for participating in school activities and learning how to learn."[40]

Curriculum becomes increasingly abstract

2. *Differences between parental and school reinforcement of learning experiences and norms.* Working-class parents typically use physical punishment when their children actively misbehave or do not follow instructions; schools, on the other hand, tend to stress the middle-class approach, which emphasizes internalization of norms through feelings of shame and guilt. While the latter approach may be more productive—and even necessary—in helping children internalize rules and expectations, differences between the home and the school make it difficult for many working-class students to follow rules and procedures when sanctions are not consistent with those imposed at home. Many schools now attempt to make discipline policies clearer and more consistent, in order to alleviate this problem (see Chapter 15).

Schools stress internal discipline

3. *Lack of previous success in school.* Lack of academic success in the early grades, not only detracts from learning more difficult material later, but also damages a student's perception that he or she is a capable learner who has a chance to succeed in school and later life. Once students believe that they are inadequate as learners and lack control over their future (two characteristics of low-achieving, working-class students),[41] they are less likely to work vigorously at overcoming learning deficiencies.

4. *Difficulty of teaching conditions in working-class schools.* As working-class students fall further behind academically and as both teachers and students experience frustration and discouragement, behavior problems increase in the classroom and teachers find it still more difficult to provide a productive learning environment. This problem is compounded by the fact that teacher training programs generally have not provided teachers with much knowledge or skill in dealing with severe behavior problems in the classroom. One frequent result is that some teachers eventually give up trying to teach low achievers or seek less frustrating employment elsewhere.

Some teachers give up

40 Judith L. Green, "Research on Teaching as a Linguistic Process: A State of the Art," in E. W. Gordon, ed., *Review of Research in Education 10* (Washington, D.C.: American Educational Research Association, 1983), p. 207.

41 P. C. Broderick and T. E. Sewell, "Learned Helplessness and Attributions for Success and Failure in Children of Different Social Class" (Paper presented at the annual meeting of the American Educational Research Association, Montreal, April 1983).

Students viewed as inferior

5. *Teacher perceptions of student inadequacy.* Based on the low levels of achievement in their classrooms, many teachers in working-class schools reach the conclusion that large numbers of their students are incapable of learning. This view easily becomes a self-fulfilling prophecy because teachers who question their students' learning potential are less likely to work hard to improve academic performance,[42] particularly since improvement requires an intense effort that quickly consumes virtually all of a teacher's energy. And since students are influenced by their teachers' perceptions and behaviors, low teacher expectations generate further declines in students' motivation and performance.

Problems in homogeneous grouping

6. *Ineffective homogeneous grouping.* Educators faced with large groups of low achievers frequently address the problem by setting them apart in separate classes or subgroups in which instruction can proceed at a slower pace without detracting from the performance of high achievers. Unfortunately, both teachers and the students themselves tend to view concentrations of low achievers as "slow" groups for whom learning expectations are low or nonexistent. Ray Rist studied this type of arrangement at a working-class school in St. Louis and offered the following description of its effects on instruction:

> The class was divided into groups: those expected to succeed ("fast learners") and those expected to fail ("slow learners") .... this categorization had the following results:
>
> (1) Differential treatment was accorded the two groups in the classroom, the group designated as "fast" learners receiving the most teaching time, rewards, and attention from the teacher. Those designated as "slow learners" were taught infrequently, subjected to more control, and received little if any support from the teacher.
>
> (2) The interactional patterns between the teacher and the various groups in her class became increasingly rigidified, taking on caste-like characteristics, during the course of the school year. ....
>
> (3) The consequence of the differential experiences of the children within the same kindergarten classroom was that they were differentially prepared for the first grade. The first grade teacher grouped the children according to the amount of "readiness" material they had completed in kindergarten.[43]

Implications of the hazards of homogeneous grouping of low achievers are not entirely clear. On the one hand, individualized instruction in heterogeneous classes might make it possible for each student to make continuous progress at his or her own rate, but individualization is extremely difficult to implement effectively and probably requires such costly and systematic change in school practices as to constitute a virtual "economic impossibil-

42 Thomas Good, "How Teachers' Expectations Affect Results," *American Education* (December 1982), pp. 25–32.

43 Ray C. Rist, *The Urban School: A Factory for Failure* (Cambridge, Mass.: MIT Press, 1973), p. 91.

ity."[44] Thus teachers confronted with heterogeneous classes in working-class schools generally have not been able to work effectively with the large numbers of low achievers in their classrooms. One possible solution is to go ahead and group low achievers homogeneously for large blocks of reading and language arts instruction, but to make sure that the groups are small and are taught by highly skilled teachers who are enthusiastic about working with such students. This possibility is well in line with recent research indicating that "restrictive" school settings (that is, separate arrangements for low achievers) may have either positive or negative outcomes, depending on what one does to make instruction effective.[45] Issues involving homogeneous grouping are discussed further in Chapter 15.

7. *Delivery of service problems.* The problems we have described suggest that it is very difficult to deliver educational services effectively in classes or schools with a high percentage of low achievers. If, for example, a teacher in a working-class school has ten or twelve very low achieving students in a class of twenty-five, the task of providing effective instruction is many times more difficult than that of a teacher who has only four or five low achievers in a middle-class school. Not only do teachers in the former situation need to spend virtually all their time remediating low achievers' learning problems, but the negative dynamics that result from students' frustration and misbehavior make the task that much more difficult.

Difficult for the teacher

Basically the same observation can be offered regarding the work of administrators, counselors, and other specialized personnel in working-class schools: so much time is spent dealing with the relatively frequent occurrence of learning and behavior problems in the school or classroom that little or none may be left for working on delivery of improved services for all students. One recent study of working-class schools concluded: "Too obvious to miss in such settings is the large amount of time that some administrators are required to spend on discipline and serious family problems, the two of which are commonly related."[46] From this point of view, the working-class school can be called an *overloaded* institution in which a high incidence of serious problems makes it very difficult for educators to do anything at all effectively.

Working-class schools are overloaded

8. *Low standards of performance.* The end result of this series of problems is that by the time low-achieving, working-class students reach the upper elementary grades or the high school, they are required to accomplish very little—low performance has become acceptable to their teachers. Whether in a working-class or a mixed-status school, many working-class students make little or no effort to meet demanding academic requirements by

Low expectations and requirements

44 Michael Scriven, "Problems and Prospects for Individualization," in Harriet Talmage, ed., *Systems of Individualized Education* (Berkeley, Calif.: McCutchan, 1975), pp. 199–210.

45 Gaea Leinhardt and Allan Pallay, "Restrictive Educational Settings: Exile or Haven?" *Review of Educational Research* (December 1982), pp. 557–578.

46 Delores Durkin, "A Study of Poor Black Children Who Are Successful Readers" (University of Illinois at Urbana-Champaign Center for the Study of Reading, April 1982), p. 44.

the time they reach the secondary level. Julia Wrigley has summarized the way in which student-teacher interactions reinforce low performance requirements as follows:

> [Low-track students] dislike teachers who do not trouble to maintain educational illusions . . . . it is difficult to give up the idea of success through schooling; the student may well have given it up in a practical, day-to-day sense . . . but it is far more devastating to have teachers who . . . have already given up.
>
> . . . As academic work requires steady application in the absence of much immediate return . . . it is hard for many ghetto youth to muster this application in the face of the unemployment and low earnings that are pervasive in their milieu. Educational ambivalence is essential to the functioning of many ghetto schools; if the students lose faith entirely, they become impossible to control, yet the teachers do not want to foster hopeless illusions about their students' possible success. Thus, students are praised for work that might actually be below par, even while a climate of failure and misdirected application hangs over the entire school.[47]

Do Schools Make a Difference?

Research described to this point in this chapter demonstrates that most elementary schools, as they have been organized and operated, have not generally been effective in educating large proportions of students from working-class families. This pattern has raised the question, in the United States and elsewhere, of whether schools have any real impact on overcoming the social and educational handicaps of economically disadvantaged youth. The question was raised in a prominent fashion in 1966 when James Coleman and his colleagues reported on the results of a large national study commissioned by the federal government to help determine whether disadvantaged minority students were receiving equal opportunity in the U.S. system of public schools. The result, *Equality of Educational Opportunity,*[48] was the most massive educational research enterprise ever conducted.

Coleman and Jencks Studies

Coleman's equal opportunity study

When the data were in from 600,000 children and 4,000 schools, Coleman found that the effects of home environment far outweighed any effects the school program had on achievement. The report analyzed the results of testing at the beginning of grades one, three, six, nine, and twelve. Achievement of the average Mexican American, Puerto Rican, Native American, and black

47 Julia Wrigley, "A Message of Marginality: Black Youth, Alienation, and Unemployment," in Harry F. Silberman, ed., *Education and Work.* Eighty-first Yearbook of the National Society for the Study of Education, Part II (Chicago: University of Chicago Press, 1982), pp. 242–245.

48 James S. Coleman et al., *Equality of Educational Opportunity* (Washington, D.C.: Government Printing Office, 1966).

was much lower than that of the average Asian American or white at all grade levels. Moreover, the differences widened at higher grades. Teachers and school characteristics could not fully explain why blacks, who started only six months behind in reading at the first grade, ended up three-and-a-half years behind whites in reading at the twelfth grade.[49]

Having established the substantive and consistent test score differences among various ethnic and racial groups, Coleman and his colleagues turned to the task of accounting for these differences. Coleman found that the most important variable in or out of school remains the educational and social-class background of the child's family. The second most important factor is the educational and social-class background of the other children in the school. Both of these elements far outweigh such school characteristics as expenditure per student, number of library books, laboratories, and class size. The most logical method for improving the education of the disadvantaged, according to Coleman, was to integrate the schools and classrooms on a social-class basis so as to change the peer group influences. In effect, this also would require racial integration of lower-class blacks into largely middle-class white student bodies.

The Office of Education realized how startling the data were. The Coleman Report was asserting that schools, in general, have little impact on overcoming the disadvantages of low-achieving students. Little wonder that the Office of Education allowed the Coleman Report to go out of print.

Re-analysis confirms conclusions

Subsequent analyses of the Coleman data and additional large-scale statistical studies of the determinants of student achievement have shown the same results.[50] A large fraction of the variation in student performance levels is accounted for by out-of-school variables, such as characteristics of the students' homes. Another large fraction is attributable to the so-called peer group effect, that is, the characteristics of the students' classmates. Of the variation that is explained by school factors (about 30 percent), only part can be attributed to teachers.

In a four-year study reanalyzing the U.S. census figures, the Coleman Report, and a national longitudinal study of more than one hundred high schools (Project Talent), plus many smaller studies, Christopher Jencks and his associates, using highly sophisticated statistical procedures, concluded that:

1. The schools do very little to close the gap between the rich and the poor, the disadvantaged and the advantaged learner.
2. The quality of education has little effect on what happens to students' future income after they graduate.

49 Ibid., p. 21.

50 George W. Mayeske et al., *A Study of Our Nation's Schools* (Washington, D.C.: Government Printing Office, 1966); Frederick Mosteller and Daniel P. Moynihan, *On Equality of Educational Opportunity* (New York: Random House, 1972); Harvey Averch et al., *How Effective Is Schooling? A Critical Review and Synthesis of Research Findings* (Santa Monica, Calif.: Rand Corporation, 1972); Raymond Boudon, *Education, Opportunity, and Social Inequality* (New York: Wiley, 1973); Herbert J. Kiesling, *The Relationship of School Inputs to Public School Performance in New York State* (Washington, D.C. and Santa Monica: Rand Corporation, 1969).

3. School achievement depends largely on a single input, that is, the family characteristics of the students—and all other variables are either secondary or irrelevant.
4. There is little evidence that school reform (such as compensatory spending or racial or social-class integration) can substantially reduce cognitive inequality among students.
5. Hence, the achievement of complete economic equality regardless of ability would require actual redistribution of income.[51]

Jencks's conclusions

Jencks and his colleagues continued to study these issues and devoted several more years to analysis of the best available data on the relationships among family background, education, and later occupational status and income. To do this they utilized information from eleven major research studies that collected data on U.S. males aged twenty-five to sixty-four. The results of this analysis did little to change Jenck's previous conclusions: he and his colleagues reported that family background accounted for about 48 percent of the variation in occupational status and from 15 to 35 percent of the variation in income. They also found that educational attainment accounted for about 55 percent of the variation in occupational status and about 20 percent of the variance in income. Since family background is highly correlated with educational attainment, amount of education is not much related to occupational status and income after taking account of family background.[52] Jencks's overall conclusion in 1979 was essentially the same as it had been in 1973: past compensatory education efforts at equalizing personal characteristics such as educational attainment have been "relatively ineffective. . . . Thus, if we want to equalize income, the most effective strategy is probably still to redistribute income."[53]

International Studies

Cross-cultural research

Studies in other countries support the conclusion that schools have had relatively little success in overcoming the learning problems of economically disadvantaged students. In the 1950s researchers from a dozen countries of the International Association for the Evaluation of Educational Achievement (IEA) decided to assess children's achievement on a cross-national basis. The first major survey was in the area of mathematics, involving 133,000 elementary and secondary students, 13,500 teachers, and 5,450 schools in twelve technologically advanced countries, including the United States. After the mathematics survey the research institutions embarked on a six-subject survey: science, literature, reading comprehension, English and French as for-

51 Jencks et al, *Inequality: A Reassessment of the Effect of Family and Schooling in America.* In response to criticism of the study, see Christopher Jencks et al., "Inequality in Retrospect," *Harvard Educational Review* (February 1973), pp. 102–128.

52 Jencks et al., *Who Gets Ahead? The Determinants of Economic Success in America* (New York: Basic Books, 1979).

53 Ibid., p. 311.

eign languages, and civic education. Together with mathematics, these subjects cover practically all the principal subjects in the secondary curriculum. In this latter study, 258,000 secondary students and 50,000 teachers from 9,700 schools in nineteen countries (four of them underdeveloped countries) were involved. The task was administratively and technically complex. The first phase took place between 1966 and 1969. The second phase, comprising the field testing and analysis of data, took place between 1970 and 1973.

Poor showing of U.S. students in math

In the mathematics study, especially noticeable were the overall good showings of Japan and Israel and the poor showing of the United States.[54] But the range of difference between high- or low-performance countries decreased when the most able students were compared; this tends to support the proposition that the "cream" of mathematical talent is distributed equally over various countries. The data analysis, although complicated, tended to show that teacher and school characteristics are relatively unimportant in determining math achievement. Student characteristics correlated highly with achievement, and the child's social class accounted for the greatest share of variation in learning.

Americans scored low in reading

The six-subject survey was reported in nine volumes beginning in 1973. The reading survey is of most interest, at least to Americans. The relatively low scores of the Americans, compared to the Europeans, support the general view that many of our students are disadvantaged and have basic reading problems.[55] The data from the subject areas also tend to confirm the importance of the student's culture, particularly the home, in differences in achievement. The total effect of home background is considerably greater than the direct effect of school variables.[56] The data are also sufficiently detailed to conclude, as the science report does, that "learning is a continuous and cumulative process over generations."[57] Human beings learn during all their waking hours, most of which are spent at home and not in school; moreover, each generation provides the intellectual capital for the next to rise to higher and higher educational achievements. Significantly, the impact of schooling within a particular culture is shown to be generally more important for science and foreign language than for other areas.[58] Since the Coleman and Jencks data are based on reading and mathematical scores in the United States, the suggestion that certain subjects might be more ame-

School impact on selected subject areas

54 Torsten Husen, *International Study of Achievement in Mathematics: A Comparison of Twelve Countries,* I and II (New York: Wiley, 1967).

55 Robert L. Thorndike, *Reading Comprehension Education in Fifteen Countries* (New York: Wiley, 1973).

56 James S. Coleman, "Methods and Results in the IEA Studies of Effects of School on Learning," *Review of Educational Research* (Summer 1975), pp. 335–386; Torsten Husen, "An International Research Venture in Retrospect: The IEA Surveys," *Comparative Education Review* (October 1979), pp. 371–385.

57 L. C. Comber and J. P. Keeves, *Science Education in Nineteen Countries* (New York: Wiley, 1973), p. 298.

58 William E. Coffman, and Lai-min P. Lee, "Cross-National Assessment of Educational Achievement: A Review," *Educational Researcher* (June 1974), pp. 13–16.

nable to school influences is encouraging to those who feel that schools do have a significant effect on learning.

Of course, there are many limitations to such a large-scale study. There is the question of common content across countries; of age differences at school levels across countries (that is, not all thirteen-year-olds have had or are supposed to have had the same amount of schooling cross-nationally); of translation of content; and of the sheer magnitude of the data. Also, because of the size of the population, numerous variables, possibly not accounted for, may have affected the scores. The investigators are well aware of these problems; they merely claim that their statistical models provide a method for obtaining comparative information in selected subject areas and countries. The studies constitute the best models in existence for cross-national research on student achievement and schooling.[59]

Recent Studies

School effects

A number of recent studies regarding school effects on students tend to contradict the Coleman and Jencks conclusions in the continuing debate about the impact of schooling.[60] For example, one researcher who analyzed 178 school districts in Colorado found that the following characteristics do have an effect on student performance: (1) district student-teacher ratios, (2) administrative ratios, and (3) staff qualifications.[61]

Another group of researchers who believe that schools have an effect on pupil performance argue that most of the analysis on student achievement has been done at a given grade level. Their study emphasizes that the number of years of schooling is related to the acquisition and quality of one's knowledge.[62] They base their conclusions on secondary analysis of fifty-four surveys of the national adult population between ages twenty-five and seventy-two in the years between 1948 and 1971; the sample totaled over 76,000. After controlling for background variables such as age, sex, religion, place of residence, and occupation, the study concludes that with increased education (divided into three levels: elementary graduation, secondary graduation, and college graduation), there is increased awareness of domestic issues, foreign events, and popular culture. People with more formal education read more newspapers, magazines, and books; in effect, they have learned

59 Torsten Husen, "Are Standards in U.S. Schools Really Lagging Behind Those in Other Countries?" *Phi Delta Kappan* (March 1983), pp. 455–461.

60 Coleman and Jencks frequently have been misinterpreted as concluding that students do not learn in school. Instead, what they argued is that the schools do little to change students' initial disadvantages and advantages. Nor did they conclude that schools cannot make a difference, but only that few schools have been very successful in overcoming the effects of disadvantaged background in the past.

61 Charles E. Bidwell, "Nations, School Districts and the Schools: Are There Schooling Effects Anywhere?" *Journal of Research and Development in Education* (Fall 1975), pp. 57–69; Charles E. Bidwell and John D. Kasarda, "School District Organization and Student Achievement," *American Sociological Review* (February 1975), pp. 55–70.

62 Herbert H. Hyman and Charles R. Wright, *Education's Lasting Influence on Values* (Chicago: University of Chicago Press, 1979).

Learning how to learn

how to learn. The differential effects of education continue to be large even with the older groups; they begin to diminish only after age 60.

Well-organized schools and leadership count

Still other researchers have found that a careful search for unusually successful schools shows that a few schools have a much greater impact on student performance than most others with a similar student body, even in the case of inner-city schools. Thus one study of inner-city schools in London found that those that were well run and organized had a much more positive impact than those that were not.[63] Similarly, a review of the research on successful urban elementary schools in the United States concluded that those with outstanding leadership and focused goals had achievement levels superior to otherwise similar schools.[64] Researchers in Ireland have reported that some schools are much more effective than others, after taking into account students' social class. This latter study was particularly important because it showed that school effects are much more apparent when student achievement is measured with criterion-referenced tests related to the curriculum rather than with general standardized tests. That is, differences show up when one uses tests that are based on what is actually taught in the school rather than on general examinations produced by testing agencies.[65] Taken together, these and other studies indicate that outstanding schools can make a difference in terms of improving the achievement of disadvantaged students. Research dealing with school effectiveness and with the school improvement process is discussed in much greater depth in Chapter 15.

Traditional Versus Revisionist Interpretations

Growing recognition during the past few decades of the strong relationship between social class and school achievement has led to a fundamental disagreement between those who support the *traditional* view of the role and function of schools in our society and those who accept one or another variation of what is frequently called the *revisionist* view. The traditional view perceives the educational system as established and, to a substantial degree, functioning successfully to provide economically disadvantaged students with meaningful opportunities for social and economic advancement. Revisionists, by way of contrast, believe that the schools fail to provide most disadvantaged students with a meaningful chance to succeed in society. Most revisionists also believe that schools are not even designed to accomplish this purpose, but instead are actually established and operated to perpetuate the disadvantages of working-class students from one generation to the next.

63 Michael Rutter et al., *Fifteen Thousand Hours: Secondary Schools and Their Effects on Children* (Cambridge, Mass.: Harvard University Press, 1979).

64 David L. Clark, Linda S. Lotto, and Martha M. McCarthy, "Factors Associated with Success in Urban Elementary Schools," *Phi Delta Kappan* (March 1980), pp. 467–470.

65 George A. Madaus, "The Sensitivity of Measures of School Effectiveness," *Harvard Educational Review* (May 1979), pp. 207–230.

Schools with outstanding leadership and clearly defined goals can significantly improve the educational achievement of disadvantaged students.
(James H. Karales/Peter Arnold)

Revisionist View

This group of observers contends that the upper middle class has successfully conspired to enhance its own proper and prestige relative to lower-class and minority groups, both immigrants and native-born Americans.[66] By controlling the schools, the elite groups admitted few poor and minority youth into high school academic programs and institutions of higher learning; they channeled this "underclass" into second-rate secondary schools, third-rate community colleges, and fourth-rate jobs. In support of their thesis, the revisionists argue that working-class students in general, and minority disadvantaged students in particular, have always had a tough time in school. The curriculum discriminates against them, the IQ tests discriminate against them, their teachers discriminate against them, and so do their vocational guidance

66 Some of the revisionists frequently are referred to as "Neo-Marxists" because they believe that the capitalist system must be changed if schools are to provide truly equal opportunity for working-class students.

Discrimination built into the social-class system

counselors.[67] Many of the revisionists also believe that the educational system has been set up specifically to produce disciplined workers at the bottom of the class structure. This is accomplished in part by having the school emphasize discipline in working-class schools or classrooms, just as the working-class family and the factory labor system also emphasize external discipline. According to this point of view, the schools are based on a *correspondence principle,* which replicates the social relations of the factory in the socialization and education of working-class children and youth. Samuel Bowles has summarized this argument as follows:

> [The] division of labor . . . gives rise to distinct class subcultures. The values, personality traits, and expectations characteristic of each subculture are transmitted from generation to generation through class differences in family socialization and complementary differences in the type and amount of schooling ordinarily attained by children of various class positions.[68]

Traditional View

The traditional point of view, while it acknowledges the relationships between social class, educational achievement, and success in the economic system, emphasizes the opportunities that exist for working-class students to improve their status and the data indicating that many working-class youth do experience social mobility through the schools and other social institutions. Most traditionalists believe that our educational and economic institutions provide opportunity for working-class students to advance within a larger system that balances stress on excellence with provision of opportunity to succeed for those who start out disadvantaged.

Educational opportunity available

From this point of view, each individual is afforded the opportunity to succeed in elementary and secondary schools and go to college; the educational system in the United States is designed to allow the individual more chances to attend college than do the educational systems of most other countries. Students are not confronted with an examination that at age eleven or twelve shunts them into one of several tracks from which a shift is virtually impossible. Even if American students do poorly in high school, they can go to a community college and subsequently transfer to a university. Furthermore, relaxed admission standards at many four-year colleges permit open enrollment of any high school graduate. Ours is a flexible system that focuses on individual achievement.

67 Major writings of the revisionist scholars include the following: Martin Carnoy, ed., *Schooling in a Corporate Society* (New York: McKay, 1975); Paul C. Violas, *The Training of the Urban Working Class* (Chicago: Rand McNally, 1978); Richard H. deLone, *Small Futures* (New York: Harcourt Brace Jovanovich, 1979); Samuel Bowles and Herbert Gintis, *Schooling in Capitalist America* (New York: Basic Books, 1976); Michael W. Apple, *Ideology and Curriculum* (Boston: Routledge & Kegan Paul, 1979); Michael W. Apple and Lois Weis, eds., *Ideology and Practice in Schooling* (Philadelphia: Temple University, 1983); and Henry Giroux and David Purpel, eds., *The Hidden Curriculum and Moral Education* (Berkeley, Calif.: McCutchan, 1983).

68 Samuel Bowles, "Unequal Education and the Reproduction of the Social Division of Labor," in Carnoy, *Schooling in a Corporate Society,* p. 58.

The traditional view admits that schools serve as a screening device to sort different individuals into different jobs. But this screening process is not fundamentally based on race, ethnic origin, or income, as the revisionists contend. Along with recognizing marked differences in individual abilities, the traditional view recognizes that certain qualities lead to success in school and asserts that these are related to qualities that make the individual more productive on the job. Although these correlations may be imperfect, competitive firms can use this information and offer the better jobs to individuals who complete more schooling and do well in school. Put another way, the better educated get the better jobs because they have been made more productive by the schools. Additional years of schooling constitute an indication of this greater productivity. So long as jobs are based on competition and merit, those with greater abilities and better schooling will get the better jobs. The employer has to use some criteria to decide whom to hire; in a democratic society in which there is unimpeded mobility and equal opportunity, it is largely the amount and quality of education that counts—not the applicant's family connections, race, ethnic origin, or social class.

Merit plays a part

An Intermediate Viewpoint

This chapter began by providing data indicating that working-class students as a group perform more poorly in the educational system than do middle-class students. After examining some of the reasons that have been offered to account for this difference, we summarized several decades of research concluding that elementary and secondary schools generally fail to overcome the disadvantages that working-class students bring to school. Although several recent studies indicate that a few schools have succeeded in this regard, the overall pattern suggests that there is significant research support for some of the revisionists' conclusions.

On the other hand, it clearly is not true that all working-class students or all minority students fail in the schools and society, or that all middle-class students succeed. Thus an accurate portrayal of the relationships between social class and achievement in our educational and economic systems lies somewhere between the revisionist and the traditional viewpoints. Schools and other institutions in our society do not totally perpetuate the existing social class structure into the next generation, nor do they provide sufficient opportunity to break the general pattern wherein a great many working-class students perform at a predictably low level in the schools. Levine and Havighurst have reviewed the research on each side of the issue and offer an intermediate viewpoint that stresses the following:[69]

Schools neither fully replicate nor destroy the social-class system

1. Although no data allow us to pinpoint the exact percentage of working-class students who succeed in the schools or who utilize their education

69 Levine and Havighurst, *Society and Education.*

to advance in social status, the schools do serve as an important route to mobility for many economically disadvantaged children and youth.

2. Although many working-class students attend predominantly working-class schools in which their initial disadvantages are sometimes reinforced through ineffective delivery of instruction, many others attend mixed-status schools in which teaching and learning conditions are somewhat more conducive to high performance.

Mobility is least present at the top and the bottom

3. Research on social mobility in the United States indicates that it is mainly at the top and bottom levels that people tend to be "frozen" into the social-class position of their parents. That is, there is considerable intergenerational movement up and down between various levels of socioeconomic status from upper working class to upper middle class, but upper-class parents usually transmit their very high status to their children and lower working-class and/or underclass Americans generally do not improve their status.[70]

4. Social and demographic trends have concentrated the lowest status children in urban and rural poverty neighborhoods whose schools are very low on achievement measures. In addition, a disproportionately high percentage of students in these schools are from racial or ethnic minority groups—in particular, black, Hispanic, and Native American. For a large proportion of children in poverty neighborhoods, schools play an important part in the transmission of low status and disadvantage across generations.

Implications for equal opportunity

If one reviews the data cited in this chapter—which tend to be compatible with either a revisionist or an intermediate interpretation—the traditional public school function of providing equal educational opportunity takes on a more specific meaning. Historically, educational leaders such as Horace Mann worked to establish and expand the public school system partly because they felt this would help provide children and youth with an equal chance to succeed in life, regardless of the circumstances of their birth. Providing an equal educational opportunity is still viewed by most educators as one of the foremost goals of the public schools, but to a significant degree its attainment now depends on the provision of more effective educational opportunity for children—particularly minority children—who attend predominantly poverty schools. Issues involving the provision of educational opportunity will be discussed further in succeeding chapters of this book.

Summing Up

1. Social class is related to achievement in elementary and secondary schools as well as to entry into and graduation from college. Working-class students tend to be low in educational attainment; middle-class stu-

70 Featherman and Hauser, *Opportunity and Change.*

dents tend to be high. Low achievement is particularly a problem in poverty areas of large cities.

2. Working-class minority groups generally are low in educational achievement, but there is little or no independent relationship between race or ethnicity and achievement after taking account of social class.
3. Major reasons for working-class students' low achievement include the following: (a) their home and family environment does not prepare them well for success in the traditional school; (b) genetic considerations (that is, heredity) may interact with environment to further hamper achievement; and (c) traditionally organized and operated schools have not provided effective education for low-achieving, working-class students.
4. Problems and conditions in the schools that have limited the achievement of many working-class students include inappropriate curriculum and instruction; differences between parental and school learning experiences and norms; lack of previous success in school; difficult working conditions in working-class schools; teacher perceptions of student inadequacy; ineffective homogeneous grouping; delivery of service problems; and low standards and expectations for students.
5. Until recently, research in the United States and elsewhere indicated that schools seldom succeeded in overcoming the disadvantages of working-class students. However, research during the past ten years indicates that schools can be much more successful in this regard than most have been in the past, provided they have outstanding leadership and take appropriate steps to improve instruction.
6. To some extent, research on social class and education has provided support for the revisionist position that schools help perpetuate the existing social-class system, as contrasted with the traditional view that U.S. society and its educational system provide children and youth with equal opportunity to succeed regardless of their social-class background.
7. Recent research indicates that the schools can be much more effective, which means that the ideal of equal opportunity may be attained more fully in the future.

Discussion Questions

1. How does social class influence school performance? Discuss several different kinds of school performance.
2. What are the functions of social class in American society? What are the functions of social mobility in American society?
3. What can teachers and schools do to overcome each of the school-related problems that contribute to low achievement among working-class students?
4. Why is the principal's leadership so important in determining the effectiveness of a school?
5. Which revisionist arguments are the most persuasive? Which are most vulnerable to criticism?

Suggested Readings

Fussell, Paul. *Class.* New York: Summit, 1983.

Illustrates and examines social-class patterns involving housing, dress, recreation, and other behaviors.

Giroux, Henry, and David Purpel, eds. *The Hidden Curriculum and Moral Education.* Berkeley, Calif.: McCutchan, 1983.

Authors represented in the twenty chapters provide a comprehensive view of the revisionist position and related writings.

Gould, Stephen Jay. *The Mismeasure of Man.* New York: Norton, 1981.

Relatively nontechnical discussion of material on the hereditarian-environmentalist controversy.

Herndon, James. *The Way It Spozed to Be.* New York: Bantam, 1968.

A classic account of the way education works, or doesn't work, in inner-city schools.

Levine, Daniel U., and Robert J. Havighurst. *Society and Education,* 6th ed. Boston, Mass.: Allyn and Bacon, 1984.

A text on the sociology of education that pays special attention to issues involving social class, race/ethnicity, and school achievement.

Ogbu, John U. *Minority Education and Caste.* New York: Academic Press, 1978.

A detailed description and analysis of how minority racial status interacts with social class to affect opportunities in education and society.

Ravitch, Diane. *The Revisionists Revised. Studies in the Historiography of American Education.* Proceedings of the National Academy of Education (Palo Alto, Calif.: NAE, 1977).

One of the most extensive critiques of the work of the revisionists.

12

Providing Equal Educational Opportunity

Focusing Questions

What are the rationales for desegregation, compensatory education, multicultural education, and education of all handicapped children?

What is the situation regarding desegregation of schools? What have been the major obstacles and approaches in desegregating the schools?

What are the major approaches to compensatory education? What does research say about their effectiveness?

What is multicultural education? What forms does it take in elementary and secondary schools? What are its major benefits and dangers?

What does the law say about providing education for handicapped students? What are the major issues involving their education?

PROVISION OF EQUAL EDUCATIONAL OPPORTUNITY HAS BEEN A central theme of the educational system of the United States. Particularly since the middle of the nineteenth century, when Horace Mann and other reformers fought for the extension of the common school system, U.S. schools have had the stated purpose of helping children from low-status families succeed in our society. Stimulated in part by this goal, our public school system became the first in the world to aim at providing all students with educational opportunity through high school and postsecondary levels.

Chapter 11 indicated that in all too many cases, effective education is not being provided for economically disadvantaged and minority students. Stimulated by the civil rights movement of the 1960s, many people have recognized that educational opportunity should be improved not just for disadvantaged students, but for handicapped students as well. In addition, there has been widespread recognition that providing all citizens with equal opportunity, in education as in other areas, is a moral and political imperative for our society. Efforts to attain the goals of desegregation, compensatory education, multicultural education, and education for all handicapped students have thus become important components in our nation's quest to build a productive, multiethnic society.

In this chapter we examine desegregation, compensatory education for economically disadvantaged students, multicultural education (including bilingual education), and education for all handicapped students—four significant movements that have attempted to enlarge and equalize educational opportunities for students in U.S. schools. With the exception of compensatory education, these movements are intended to improve education for all students, but to some extent each focuses on providing more equal and more effective educational opportunities for low-achieving or underachieving disadvantaged students. Thus they are part of a larger reform effort to attain our historic national goal of providing all children with equal opportunity to succeed in schools and later life.

Desegregation

Desegregation and integration

Desegregation of schools refers to enrollment patterns wherein students of different racial groups attend the same schools, and students are not separated in racially isolated schools or classrooms. **Integration** refers to situations in which students of different racial groups not only attend schools together, but effective steps have been taken to accomplish two of the underlying purposes of desegregation: (1) to overcome the achievement deficit and other disadvantages of minority students and (2) to develop positive interracial contacts and relationships. Attention has shifted during the past three decades from simply placing students in desegregated schools to bringing about productive integration that provides equal and effective educational opportunity for students of all backgrounds. Much remains to be done, however, to fully achieve both desegregation and integration.

Segregation Before 1963

Slaves not full persons

The Declaration of Independence was first published in the July 10, 1776, issue of the *Pennsylvania Gazette.* That same issue carried an advertisement offering a black slave for sale. The United States Constitution itself provided for representation of the free population but allowed only three-fifths representation for "all other persons," generally meaning black slaves. Thus discrimination and oppression by race were deeply embedded in our national institutions from the very beginning. In most of the South, before the Civil War, it was a crime to teach a black slave to read and write.

After the Civil War, the Thirteenth, Fourteenth, and Fifteenth Amendments to the Constitution attempted to extend rights of citizenship irrespective of race. During Reconstruction, some gains were made by black Americans, most of whom lived, until 1945, in the South. After 1877, however, this progress generally ceased, and blacks throughout the South and in some other parts of the country were separated by legislative action in segregated institutions. Black Americans were required to attend separate schools; could not use public facilities set aside for whites;[1] were in certain places barred by law from competing for good employment, and were denied, through various electoral practices, the right to vote. In 1896, legislation that mandated segregation according to race was upheld in *Plessy* v. *Ferguson.* The U.S. Supreme Court said that requiring blacks to use separate public facilities (in this case, railroad services) was constitutional if the facilities were "separate but equal." This meant that where dictated by local law, blacks had to use separate publicly supported services and facilities (for example, transportation, recreation, restrooms, drinking fountains, and schools) and frequently had no access at all to private facilities (that is, hotels, restaurants, entertainment, and the like).

Segregated facilities

Much evidence collected during the first half of this century indicated that schools provided for black Americans were seldom equal to white schools on *any* measure of equality. For example, school officials in Russell County, Alabama, in the early 1930s spent $45.74 annually per student in white schools but only $2.55 per student in black schools.[2] Apart from issues involving equal resources and political equity (black taxpayers were helping provide superior resources for white schools), black parents and their supporters questioned whether equal educational opportunity was available when black students could not attend nearby schools on the same basis as white students. In many cases black students had to travel long distances at

Separate and unequal

1 In this chapter the term *whites* is used to refer to non-Hispanic whites, that is, citizens who are not classified as members of a racial or ethnic minority group for purposes of school desegregation.

2 United States Commission on Civil Rights, *Fulfilling the Letter and Spirit of the Law. Desegregation of the Nation's Public Schools* (Washington, D.C.: Government Printing Office, 1976), p. 2.

their own expense to attend the nearest black school, and in some cases there was no black senior high school within a hundred miles or more.

Segregated educational arrangements in higher education were challenged in the courts during the 1930s and 1940s. In *McLaurin* v. *Oklahoma State Regents* (1950), the Supreme Court required acceptance of a black graduate student at Oklahoma State University, although it did allow the university to seat him in a section of the classroom designated as "Reserved for Colored" and to separate him from other students in the library and cafeteria.

A number of suits challenging segregation in elementary and secondary schools were filed in the early 1950s. The first to reach the U.S. Supreme Court was a case in which lawyers for Linda Brown asked that she be allowed to attend white schools in Topeka, Kansas. Plaintiffs argued that segregated schools were inherently inferior for black students even if they provided equal expenditures, because forced attendance at a separate school automatically informed black students that they were second-class citizens. One result, according to such scholars as Kenneth Clark and John Ogbu,[3] is to destroy students' motivation to succeed in school and society.

Separate is unequal

In a unanimous decision that overturned *Plessy* v. *Ferguson* and forever changed U.S. history, the Supreme Court ruled as follows in May 1954, in *Brown* v. *Board of Education:*

> In the field of public education the doctrine of "separate but equal" has no place.... We hold that the plaintiffs and others similarly situated ... are, by reason of the segregation complained of, deprived of the equal protection of the laws guaranteed by the Fourteenth Amendment.

Effects of the *Brown* decision soon were apparent in many areas of U.S. society, including employment, voting, and all publicly supported services. After Mrs. Rosa Parks refused in December 1955 to sit at the back of a bus in Montgomery, Alabama, protests against segregation were launched in many parts of the country. Dr. Martin Luther King, Jr., along with other civil rights leaders emerged to challenge deep-seated patterns of racial discrimination. Fierce opposition to civil rights demonstrations made the headlines in the late 1950s and early 1960s, as dogs and fire hoses were sometimes used to disperse peaceful demonstrators. After three civil rights workers were murdered in Mississippi, the U.S. Congress passed the 1964 Civil Rights Act and other legislation that attempted to guarantee equal protection of the laws for minority citizens.

Emergence of civil rights movement

Initial reaction among local government officials to the *Brown* decision outlawing government-supported segregation was generally negative. Although the Supreme Court ruled in 1955 (*Brown II*) that school desegregation should proceed with "all deliberate speed" and that constitutional guarantees could not be withheld on the grounds that white citizens resisted change, massive resistance occurred, using such means as delaying reassign-

All deliberate speed?

3 John U. Ogbu, *Minority Education and Caste. The American System in Cross-Cultural Perspective* (New York: Academic Press, 1978).

ment of black students to nearby white schools, opening private schools with tuition paid by public funds, gerrymandering school boundary lines to increase segregation, paying transportation for whites who transferred out of desegregated schools, suspending or repealing compulsory attendance laws, and closing desegregated schools. National attention to the problem of actually attaining desegregation in education was increased after 1957, when Arkansas Governor Orval Faubus refused to allow school officials at Central High in Little Rock to admit five black students and President Eisenhower called out the National Guard. In 1963 only 2 percent of black students in the South were attending school with whites.

Desegregation Gains Since 1963

Since 1963, considerable progress has been made in desegregating public schools in medium-sized cities and towns and in rural sections of the United States. The South, in particular, has made significant progress and is now the most integrated region of the United States (see Table 12.1).

A series of Supreme Court decisions (see below) made it clear that school officials must take rigorous action to reassign and even transport students in order to reduce or eliminate racial segregation.

Responding to court orders and utilizing federal and other sources of assistance, school officials have been able to reduce the percentage of black

Table 12.1
Percentage of Black Students in Racially Segregated Public Schools, 1968 to 1980

	Percentage of Black Students in Schools 50 Percent or More Minority				**Percentage of Black Students in Schools 90 Percent or More Minority**			
	1968	*1972*	*1976*	*1980*	*1968*	*1972*	*1976*	*1980*
National	77	64	62	63	64	39	36	33
9 northeastern states	67	70	73	80	43	47	51	49
11 midwestern states	77	75	70	70	58	57	51	44
11 western states	72	68	67	67	51	43	36	34
6 border states and D.C.	72	67	60	59	60	55	43	37
11 southern states	81	55	55	57	78	25	22	23

Note: National figures are for the continental United States excluding Alaska and Hawaii.

Source: Gary Orfield, *Desegregation of Black and Hispanic Students from 1968 to 1980* (Washington, D.C.: Joint Center for Political Studies, 1982).

Desegregation required

students who attend racially isolated minority schools (usually defined as 90 percent or more minority) in the United States. As shown in Table 12.1, the percentage of black students attending such schools decreased from 64 percent in 1968 to 33 percent in 1980. Progress has been greatest in the South, where the percentage of black students in racially isolated schools decreased from 78 percent to 23 percent.

However, in 1980 one-third of all black students in the public schools still attended schools 90 percent or more minority, and segregation of minority students has continued or increased in many communities, particularly in larger cities and metropolitan areas where school segregation is associated with housing patterns that separate large groups of minority and nonminority citizens in relatively distant neighborhoods. Because students traditionally have attended the closest public school, communities in which blacks and whites live in separate neighborhoods have had predominantly one-race schools. Thus progress seems to have occurred in small and medium-sized communities in combating both **de jure segregation** (segregation resulting from laws, government actions, or school policies specifically designed to bring about separation) and **de facto segregation** (segregation resulting from circumstances associated with housing patterns rather than from laws or school policies). Nevertheless, segregation in large metropolitanized regions (such as the nine northeastern states in Table 12.1) has increased as housing segregation has become more pronounced. Today, the large majority of students in many big cities such as Atlanta, Chicago, Detroit, New York, and Philadelphia are minority students, and most attend predominantly minority schools.

Persistence of segregation

It should be noted that the percentage of Hispanic students attending predominantly minority schools has actually increased in all parts of the United States since 1972. In that year, 57 percent of Hispanics were in schools more than 50 percent minority; by 1980, 68 percent of Hispanic students (compared with 63 of black students) were in schools with enrollment more than 50 percent minority.[4] This trend toward greater segregation among Hispanic students reflects the movement of Hispanic population into inner-city communities in large urban areas, particularly the migration of Mexicans into cities in California and Texas and of Puerto Ricans into New York, Chicago, and other eastern and midwestern cities. By 1980, 57 percent of the Hispanic students in New York State and 40 percent of those in Texas were in schools 90 percent or more minority.[5]

Hispanic segregation

Evolving Desegregation Law

Actions taken to reduce segregation in local school districts have reflected decisions and mandates of the U.S. Supreme Court. The evolution of desegregation law has involved an increasing effort to provide district-wide solu-

4 Gary Orfield, *Desegregation of Black and Hispanic Students from 1968 to 1980* (Washington, D.C.: Joint Center for Political Studies, 1982).

5 Ibid.

tions to racial-isolation problems as well as a growing concern with metropolitan or regional solutions that cross school district boundary lines.

Removing vestiges of segregation

Desegregation after 1963 was greatly accelerated by the Supreme Court's 1968 *Green* v. *County School Board of New Kent County* decision, in which the Court required segregated districts to devise a desegregation plan that "promises realistically to work now," and by its 1971 *Swann* v. *Charlotte-Mecklenberg* decision supporting busing of students, revision of attendance zones, or other actions to remove the "vestiges" of state-imposed segregation, as long as the desegregation plan components were workable and feasible.

Keyes *decision*

Desegregation was further stimulated by the Court's 1974 *Keyes* decision involving the Denver schools, which concluded that if a portion of a school district is segregated as a result of official government action, the entire district may have to be desegregated. This decision laid the basis for court orders aimed at district-wide desegregation in Boston, Dallas, Cleveland, San Francisco, and several other large cities. The Supreme Court upheld the major elements of its *Keyes* ruling in 1979 in decisions involving public schools in Columbus and Dayton, Ohio, though it also said that the existence of predominantly minority and nonminority schools is not unconstitutional unless segregation has been caused by "intentionally segregative official acts."

Regional desegregation

A series of important Supreme Court decisions also provided a basis for some movement toward metropolitan or regional desegregation. In 1974 the Court rejected metropolitan desegregation for Detroit in *Bradley* v. *Milliken*, stating that the autonomy of existing school districts cannot be violated for desegregation purposes unless it can be shown that a constitutional violation in one district had a significant segregative effect in another district. However, the Court later upheld decisions that merged city and suburban districts in Louisville (1975) and in Wilmington, Delaware (1975). In both these cases, one major reason given for metropolitan desegregation was that prior to 1954 suburban black students were required to cross school district boundaries to attend segregated city schools.

Metropolitan desegregation arrangements also have been initiated as a result of the *Liddell* case in St. Louis. Twice upheld on appeals to the Supreme Court, federal judges hearing the *Liddell* case stimulated development of a 1983 voluntary plan that encourages and helps suburban districts to accept black students transferring from city schools and which also includes provisions for magnet schools and for improvement of segregated city schools.

Obstacles to Desegregation

Given the fact that residential patterns in most metropolitan areas are so highly segregated, a major stumbling block to desegregation of schools has been the desire of the majority of whites—and of many minority parents—to maintain neighborhood schools. Added to this resistance is the preference of some minority spokespersons for local control of their schools rather than for desegregation. In addition, opposition to desegregation has increased in school districts where a high percentage of minority students are from low-income families. Middle-class parents, whether nonminority or minority, are reluctant to send their children to schools with a high proportion of low-income students. They generally are quick to withdraw their children from schools in which desegregation has substantially increased the proportion of such students.

Middle-class withdrawal

In addition to the attitudinal resistance to desegregation, there are practical obstacles. Typically, the increasing concentrations of minority students in large cities have resegregated the neighborhoods to a greater extent than in previous generations. Under these conditions, attempts to integrate a decreasing number of white students with a stable or increasing number of minority students have increased the movement of white families to the suburbs. Middle-class minority families also have been withdrawing their children from low-status schools in the cities and enrolling them in private or suburban schools. The net result is that city school districts have become increasingly low income and minority in their student composition, with a high proportion of minority students attending predominantly minority, poverty schools.

Increasing black suburban student population

Another result is that some suburban public schools in metropolitan areas also are beginning to be resegregated as middle-class minority families move to suburbs next to the central city and then find that white enrollment falls as the white population declines and withdraws. Growing segregation of minority students in the suburbs is illustrated in the Cleveland Metropolitan Area, where the East Cleveland suburban school district has become nearly all black; in the Chicago Metropolitan Area, where the Harvey and Evanston Elementary Township school districts have become more than 50 percent black; and in the St. Louis Metropolitan Area, where the University City public schools have become more than 75 percent black. In the Los Angeles Metropolitan Area, a number of suburban school districts, including Baldwin Park, Duarte, Pasadena, and Pomona, have enrollments more than half minority.

Resistance to desegregation became more apparent in the 1970s as big-city school districts became increasingly low status and minority while the courts as well as state and federal executive agencies moved to desegregate public schools in the North and West. By the end of the decade, most big-city school districts had a large proportion of minority students, and widespread desegregation within their boundaries seemed attainable only by reassigning white students to sometimes distant minority schools that many were not willing to attend. In this context, public opinion indicated that less than one-fifth of white Americans and one-half of black Americans favored busing for purposes of school desegregation, and a substantial majority of the public favored a constitutional amendment to prohibit it.[6]

6 "Opposition to Busing Reaches Peak in Congress and Nation," *Phi Delta Kappan* (January 1976), p. 356.

Desegregation Plans

The trends described above make it clear that school desegregation problems are most serious in the nation's large metropolitan areas in which the central-city school population has become predominantly minority and low income. Desegregation is now an accomplished fact in much of the South and in many small towns and cities, but larger cities tend to have a substantial proportion of minority students attending racially isolated poverty schools, and suburban school districts tend to be predominantly white and middle or mixed in social class. Some suburbs have a desegregated student population, but many of these suburbs adjoin the central-city minority ghetto and are becoming resegregated as white families move farther out and are replaced by minority students from the city.

Desegregation nationally

Faced with this situation, educators and the courts have tried to find ways to reduce school segregation and otherwise to improve educational and social opportunities for students in the big cities. Solutions involving these goals have taken a variety of forms, such as the following:

Desegregation plan components

1. Alter attendance areas to include a more desegregated population.
2. Establish **magnet schools**—schools that incorporate specialized programs and personnel and tend to attract students from various parts of the city's school system (See Chapter 15 for further discussion of magnet schools.)
3. Permit students to attend school outside their neighborhood and pay for their transportation.
4. Bus students involuntarily to desegregated schools.
5. Pair schools, bringing two schools in adjacent areas together in one larger zone. For example, School A may enroll all students from grades one through four; School B enrolls all students from grades five through eight (Princeton plan).
6. Bring together three or more neighborhood schools to make one attendance zone, thereby increasing the pool of students and achieving better racial balance than with two schools (cluster plan).

Big-city segregation

Large central-city school districts with 60 percent or higher minority enrollment have not been able to provide desegregated schooling for most of the minority students within their existing boundaries. For example, a big-city district with 80 percent minority students can try to reassign and transport students to eliminate all predominantly one-race schools, but this frequently requires the school district to transport minority students from one predominantly minority school to another. Many of the middle-class students and/or nonminority students may leave in the process. In some cases, residential patterns in such districts require very long bus rides—as much as an hour one way. In addition, districts with a high percentage of poverty students often end up transporting students from one poverty school to another;

Forced busing of students has been one of the most publicized methods of desegregating schools—and one of the most painful.
(Ken Love/Atoz Images)

as indicated in Chapter 11, such schools generally are not functioning effectively. Many educators do not believe that this type of desegregation is very helpful.

For these and similar reasons, desegregation plans in some big cities include little, if any, student reassignment and leave most minority students in predominantly minority schools. Instead of desegregation, such plans generally concentrate on trying to improve the quality of instruction, especially in predominantly minority schools. The U.S. Supreme Court approved this type of plan in Detroit, where Judge Robert DeMascio issued a 1975 decision ordering that "The Detroit Board of Education and the General Superintendent . . . shall design, develop and institute a comprehensive instructional program for teaching reading and communication skills. Such educational program

Improving instruction

shall be characterized by excellence and shall be instituted in every school in the system." Judge DeMascio further ordered that the state government pay half the cost of the educational improvements. The Supreme Court affirmed this ruling on the grounds that such improvements can help to overcome the effects of past segregation and are needed even when students are in desegregated schools and classrooms.

Chicago example

A good example of a desegregation plan emphasizing instructional improvement is provided by the Chicago Public Schools. By 1983 the Chicago schools were only 15 percent white, and Judge Milton Shadur accepted the Board of Education's desegregation plan even though it left more than 400 schools predominantly minority (defined in Chicago as more than 70 percent minority). The most important components in the plan included the following: (1) desegregate all schools more than 70 percent white, mainly by bringing in minority students; (2) spend approximately $25 million per year to improve instruction at predominantly minority schools; (3) spend an additional $72,000 per school to improve education at schools that have a high percentage of minority enrollment combined with low achievement; and (4) continue to create magnet schools and programs.

Milwaukee example

In contrast to many very large big-city districts, many smaller city districts have been able to provide a substantial amount of desegregation for minority students, generally through voluntary arrangements such as magnet schools or through reassignment and transportation of students, or some combination of the two. For the most part, such districts have been able to accomplish this because they have a smaller percentage of minority students. Perhaps the best example is Milwaukee. At a time when its percentage of black students was approximately 40 percent, it increased the number of desegregated schools (defined as 25–50 percent black) from 14 in 1976 to 101 in 1978.[7] Most of this increase was achieved through (1) establishment of magnet schools; (2) a voluntary city-suburban transfer plan; and (3) redrawing of school boundaries.

In 1979 a federal judge accepted a five-year settlement in which the school board and the plantiffs agreed to withdraw litigation if the board would place at least 75 percent of the district's black students in desegregated schools. The board also agreed to improve instruction at schools that remained segregated. It was easy for the board to accept the desegregation target since it had very nearly reached that goal the year before. This settlement illustrates what can be accomplished through voluntary desegregation in all but the largest, most segregated cities.

Nonblack Minorities

Another aspect of desegregation that deserves special attention involves the status of nonblack minority groups. Depending on regional and local circumstances and court precedents, some racial minority groups may or may not

7 David A. Bennett, "The Impact of Court Ordered Desegregation" (Paper presented at an ERIC Conference on Impact of Courts on Schools, 1979).

be counted as minority for purposes of school desegregation in a particular city.[8] For example, Mexican-American students have been classified as unconstitutionally segregated in the Southwest and some other locations. The courts determined in the 1970s that they were victims of the same kinds of discrimination as were black students. In some northern cities such as Cleveland and Milwaukee, however, Mexican-American and other Hispanic students have not been explicitly designated by the courts to participate as minorities in a desegregation plan, even though many or most attend predominantly minority schools.

Mexican-American students as minorities in the Southwest

The situation is further complicated by the relatively large and growing number of Asian minority groups in many big cities. With rapid increases occurring in the numbers of Filipino, Korean, and Vietnamese students and the already substantial numbers of Chinese and Japanese students, many school districts face considerable uncertainty in trying to devise multiethnic desegregation plans. The court order for San Francisco, for example, has required multiethnic enrollment and busing of four groups (Asian-American, black, Hispanic, and non-Hispanic white), but Los Angeles is still considering whether or how Asian students should participate in desegregation plans in the future.

Asian students

Questions involving the desegregation of nonblack minority groups obviously will become more important in the future as the Hispanic population grows in Houston, Los Angeles, and other cities. Resolution of these issues will be difficult because bilingual services that tend to require some concentration of many of these students will conflict with desegregation goals emphasizing dispersal and multiethnic enrollment. In addition, parents of nonblack minority students tend to be more divided among themselves regarding the necessity for desegregation than are black parents; thus demand and support for desegregation of nonblack minority students vary greatly in accordance with local political circumstances. Many educators and lay leaders also are very uncertain concerning the question of whether or how to include middle-class Asian and Hispanic students in desegregation plans. Most of these students perform well academically, and many seem to be very well integrated into U.S. schools and society. Some concerned observers, such as Thomas Pettigrew, suggest that middle-class minority students should attend schools with low-income minority students in order to reduce economic isolation of the latter group in districts that have few nonminority students.[9]

Bilingual considerations

Effects on Student Performance and Attitudes

Independent of the legal issues and lack of public support for busing, the question ultimately remains: To what extent do students benefit from inte-

8 However, federal data collection activities are standardized and have required that student enrollments be reported separately for the following groups: "Black," "American Indian," "Spanish-Surnamed American," "Portuguese," "Oriental," "Alaskan Natives," "Hawaiian Natives," and "Non-Minority."

9 *Report of Dr. Thomas Pettigrew to the Superior Court of the State of California for the County of Los Angeles.* Case No. 822, 854, November 14, 1978.

grated schools? Although there is voluminous research on this subject, it is inconsistent and contradictory. There is a body of data that shows a positive relationship between desegregation and academic achievement (although most of the differences in achievement have been attributed to socioeconomic integration), but there is also evidence that shows no relationship, or even a negative relationship.[10]

Inconsistent and contradictory data

Similarly, there are data showing that desegregation has positive effects on interracial attitudes, but some studies indicate no effect or a negative effect. The data on minority students' aspirations are somewhat more consistent in indicating that desegregation frequently improves the educational aspirations and college enrollment of minority students by making these aspirations more realistic and better informed. Several studies also indicate that desegregated schooling helps minority students enter the mainstream "network" of social and cultural aspirations and contacts needed for success in later life.[11]

In addition, there are a few studies that focus on schools in which desegregation seems to have been carried out successfully and effectively. Studies focusing on this type of school avoid the problem typical in educational research of mixing well-implemented examples of an innovation with poorly implemented ones and then concluding that the innovation is universally unsuccessful. One of the most comprehensive studies of successful desegregated schools is a report evaluating the Emergency School Aid Act (ESAA), which provided hundreds of millions of dollars between 1972 and 1982 to facilitate desegregation. This study indicated that desegregation had a favorable impact on black achievement in schools with the following characteristics: resources are focused on attaining goals, administrative leadership is stronger, classroom lessons are more highly structured, parents are more heavily involved in the classroom, and staff make greater efforts to promote positive interracial attitudes.[12]

Successfully desegregated schools

In general, the research on the effects of desegregation and integration is complicated by statistical and sampling problems: (1) the difficulty of setting up control and experimental groups; (2) the varying definitions of social

10 Widely cited studies showing a positive relationship are the 1966 Coleman Report and the U.S. Commission on Civil Rights Report entitled *Racial Isolation in the Public Schools*. Widely cited to prove the opposite point are David J. Armor, "The Evidence on Bussing," *The Public Interest* (Summer 1972), pp. 90–126; Harold B. Gerard and Norman Miller, *School Desegregation* (New York: Plenum, 1975). For important reviews of the research that cite both positive and negative findings, see Nancy St. John, *School Desegregation: Outcomes for Children* (New York: Wiley, 1975); L. A. Bradley and G. W. Bradley, "The Academic Achievement of Black Students in Desegregated Schools: A Critical Review," *Review of Educational Research (Summer 1977), pp. 399–449; Ronald A. Krol, "A Meta Analysis of the Effects of Desegregation on Academic Achievement," Urban Review* (December 1980), pp. 211–224; Daniel U. Levine, "Desegregation," in *International Encyclopedia of Educational Research* Oxford: Pergamon, 1984).

11 Robert L. Crain and Rita E. Mahard, *The Influence of High School Racial Composition on Black College Attendance and Test Performance* (Washington, D.C.: National Center for Education Statistics Sponsored Reports Series NCES 78-212, January 1978); G. Forehand, M. Ragosta, and D. Rock, *Conditions and Processes of Effective School Desegregation* (Princeton, N.J.: Educational Testing Service, 1976); and Richard R. Scott and James M. McPartland, "Desegregation as National Policy: Correlates of Racial Attitudes," *American Educational Research Journal* (Winter 1982), pp. 397–414.

12 J.E. Coulson, *National Evaluation of the Emergency School Aid Act (ESAA): Survey of the Second-Year Studies* Washington, D.C.: System Development Corporation, 1976).

class and income; (3) the differing percentages of blacks and whites used in defining desegregation; (4) the fact that data are reported on a district- or schoolwide basis, which often fails to reflect the classroom racial mix; (5) the strong possibility that blacks who attend desegregated schools tend to come from relatively more stable homes than those living in the core of the inner city, as well as the possibility that whites who remain in desegregated and changing schools come from relatively less stable, low-income homes with less pressure for educational achievement; (6) the degree of disruption that may exist in schools that are in the process of desegregating or changing from predominantly white to black; and (7) the lack of longitudinal data to show cumulative efforts of desegregation at various grade levels.

Political and moral reasons for desegregation

Despite the mixed evidence regarding academic achievement, aspirations, and interracial attitudes, perhaps the most compelling reasons for integration are political and moral. Politically, two separate societies cannot continue to exist in America without serious harm to the body politic. Morally, our national policy must reflect a commitment to American ideals of equality.

Implementing Desegregation

Recognizing that many desegregation plans have been poorly implemented and have failed to raise minority students' achievement, researchers in recent years have concentrated on identifying actions that appear to be associated with successful implementation. Much of the research on this topic has been carefully examined by a team of researchers at Vanderbilt University and has been summarized in the following list of recommendations regarding *pupil reassignment*:[13]

Considerations involving effective implementation

Begin desegregation in the early grades.

Devise a mandatory plan, but provide students with options through magnet schools and programs.

Improve instruction at all participating schools.

Address special needs, such as bilingual education, multiethnic curriculum, and education of the handicapped.

Ensure a safe school environment.

Provide a "critical mass" (15 to 20 percent) of students of each racial or ethnic group at each participating school.

Vary the percentage of minority students in accordance with residential patterns and other factors.

13 Willis D. Hawley, "Effective Educational Strategies for Desegregated Schools," *Peabody Journal of Education* (July 1982), pp. 209–233; Willis D. Hawley et al., *Strategies for Effective Desegregation: Lessons from Research* (Lexington, Mass.: Lexington, 1982).

Recommendations for *improving achievement and race relations* as part of desegregation included the following:

Improving achievement and race relations

Limit the size of schools and instructional groups so that teachers can work with students on a personal basis.

Develop multiethnic curricula.

Make good human relations a fundamental goal in all aspects of school operation.

Provide for direct parent involvement.

Utilize cooperative student learning techniques.

Ensure that there are clear student behavior rules that are fairly and consistently enforced.

Encourage participation in extracurricular programs that enhance interracial interaction.[14]

Compensatory Education

Another aspect of our nation's commitment to equal educational opportunity is the compensatory education movement, which has sought to improve education for economically disadvantaged students. Proponents of **compensatory education**—an improved school environment with remedial programs and special activities—believe that it can compensate for many of the disadvantages experienced by these students and can result in more effective learning and greater educational achievement. Stimulated in part by the civil rights movement of the 1960s, compensatory education was expanded and institutionalized as part of President Lyndon Johnson's War on Poverty. Compensatory education has been funded largely by the federal government, although some states and local school districts also have set aside funds for this purpose.

Part of the War on Poverty

The Elementary and Secondary Education Act (ESEA) was passed in 1965 and immediately provided $1 billion in Title I funds to supplement and improve the education of economically disadvantaged children. (A disadvantaged child was defined as a child from a family below the government's official poverty level.) By 1981, Title I expenditures were nearly $3.5 billion per year, and other federal compensatory expenditures added over $2 billion more. In 1981, Title I of ESEA was revised and is now known as Chapter 1 of ECIA (Educational Consolidation and Improvement Act). Chapter 1 provides assistance to nearly 5 million students per year. Due to attempts to hold down the federal budget, Chapter 1 has not kept up with inflation since 1981.

14 Support for these and other recommendations also can be found in William J. Genova and Herbert J. Walberg, *A Practitioner's Guide for Achieving Student Integration in City High Schools* (Washington, D.C.: Government Printing Office, 1981); Robert L. Crain, Rita E. Mahard, and Rita E. Narot, *Making Desegregation Work* (Cambridge, Mass.: Ballinger, 1982); Levine, "Desegregation." The conclusions of recent research reviews are well in line with earlier national studies, such as Forehand, Ragosta, and Rock, *Conditions and Processes of Effective School Desegregation*.

Programs and Practices

Although most programs for school-age children usually have been funded with ESEA and ECIA money, other federal funds have been provided through the Manpower Development and Training Act of 1962, the Vocational Education Act of 1963, the Civil Rights Act of 1964, the Economic Opportunity Act of 1964, the Higher Education Act of 1965, the Bilingual Education Act of 1968, and the Emergency School Aid Act of 1972. A variety of programs from preschool to higher education have been authorized, with emphasis on reducing class size and providing remedial programs, special personnel, and enrichment experiences. An overview of these programs includes the following:

Funds for compensatory education

1. *Infant education and intervention in family life.* Programs of infant education and parental involvement range from helping the mother become a teacher of her child to improving family stability.

2. *Early childhood education.* Head Start and Follow-Through are the most common programs under this category. Whereas Head Start attempts to help disadvantaged children achieve "readiness" for the first grade, Follow-Through concentrates on sustaining readiness and supplementing in the early grades whatever gains are made by the children who have had a year's experience in Head Start. In 1984 Head Start served more than 400,000 students—approximately 20 percent of poverty children in the appropriate age bracket.

Preschool education

3. *Reading, language, and basic skills development.* More than half of the Chapter 1 projects deal directly with the improvement of reading and language through various materials, machines, and personnel.

4. *Bilingual education.* Emphasis and content of these programs vary, but they commonly focus on children whose mother tongue is not English. Hispanic children are the major target groups in these programs, but nationwide, bilingual programs are provided in more than sixty languages.

5. *Instructional materials.* A flood of new materials has been prepared for teaching disadvantaged and minority children. These range from textbooks to sophisticated language laboratories and computers.

6. *Guidance and counseling programs.* Various social, psychological, and vocational services have been provided for the disadvantaged. Social workers and community aides have been involved to help bridge the gap between school and home.

7. *Tutoring programs.* Individual and small-group tutoring programs have been greatly augmented. These have involved both volunteer and paid student tutors, as well as volunteer and paid community people. The programs at the public school level usually aim at also providing a positive older student or adult model.

Tutoring

Programs such as Head Start seek to help disadvantaged young children become better prepared for school by providing them with extra enrichment experiences.

(Michael D. Sullivan/ TexaStock©)

8. *School organization.* Many schools serving the disadvantaged have received funds for purposes of offering a variety of organizational plans ranging from extended school days and extended school years to open classrooms and flexible schedules.

9. *Dropout prevention programs.* Along with vocational and career education, a number of programs have aimed at preventing students from dropping out of school. Numerous work-study programs, on-the-job training programs, and financial incentives have been offered. Some of these programs have been incorporated into the regular school program; others have been offered in special centers. Some are in the daytime, others are in the evening or summer.

Teacher training

10. *Personnel training.* A great many preservice and in-service training programs have been funded to help teachers and administrators gain insight into teaching the disadvantaged.

11. *Additional school personnel.* The recruitment and training of teacher aides and paraprofessionals, along with nonpaid volunteers, have increased. Emphasis is on employing low-income workers from the local community for purposes of reducing the student-adult classroom ratio, enhancing school-community relations, and providing jobs to enhance the economy in low-income neighborhoods.

12. *School desegregation.* Money has been provided to aid schools and school personnel in dealing with desegregation problems.

13. *Higher education.* Special programs in this area include the following: (a) identifying students of college potential early in the secondary schools and enriching their learning experience; (b) accepting special provisions and lower academic requirements for college admission; (c) using admission criteria that allow open enrollment, whereby every high school graduate has the opportunity to attend a two-year or four-year college; (d) transition programs to increase the probability of success for disadvantaged youth once admitted into college; and (e) special scholarships, loans, and jobs.

Higher education

14. *Adult education.* Education has been provided for adults who are illiterate and those who need training in basic job skills.

Evaluation of Programs, 1965–1975

Programs not demonstrated successful

The overwhelming majority of compensatory efforts during the first decade of compensatory education were not shown to be effective in raising cognitive levels of target students. Despite the expenditure of billions of dollars per year, research indicated that students in compensatory education generally were not making long-range academic gains. For example, according to Richard Fairley, the former director of the Division of Compensatory Education of the U.S. Office of Education, of more than 1,200 educational projects evaluated between 1970 and 1972, only 10 had solid data that unambiguously demonstrated their success.[15] Even Head Start, the best known and most heavily funded compensatory program, turned out to be ineffective according to the Westinghouse–Ohio University evaluation of 104 centers. The evaluation report indicated that there was no significant difference in learning between Head Start children and a matched control group, and that the program failed to help disadvantaged learners catch up to their middle-class counterparts or to alleviate any of their cognitive deficiencies.[16]

"Fadeout"

A number of reasons have been suggested for the disappointing results documented in research on compensatory education before 1975. One is that as the programs were extended to larger numbers of children, the impact was watered down: efforts were not intensive, teachers were not well-trained, classes were too large. However, there was little evidence that even intensive programs managed to maintain more than moderate gains over a long period. Longitudinal studies of several compensatory programs also revealed a "fadeout" process; that is, the early gains made by these children

15 Richard L. Fairley, "Accountability's New Test," *American Education* (June 1972), pp. 33–35. Also see *Compensatory Education and Other Alternatives in Urban Schools* (Washington, D.C.: Government Printing Office, 1972).

16 Westinghouse Learning Corporation and Ohio University, *The Impact of Head Start* (Washington, D.C.: Government Printing Office, 1969); also see Harvey A. Averch et al., *How Effective Is Schooling? A Critical Review and Synthesis of Research Findings* (Santa Monica, Calif.: Rand Corporation, 1972).

eventually leveled off and were equivalent to gains made by children without such training after a few years of schooling.[17]

Evaluation After 1975

Data on compensatory education have justified a somewhat more positive view concerning its potential and actual impact than was prevalent before 1975. In part, recent positive results can be traced to correction of some of the most serious mistakes of the first decade. In addition, data on some particularly outstanding efforts did not become available until the latter half of the 1970s. Important changes in the organization, operation, and evaluation of compensatory education leading to a more positive assessment of its effectiveness included the following: (1) the federal and state governments improved monitoring procedures and required local school districts to spend a "comparable" amount of funds on disadvantaged and nondisadvantaged students *before* the addition of compensatory funds; (2) some states such as California and Michigan began to provide additional money as part of a systematic plan to reduce scattershot spending; and (3) the federal government required more adequate evaluation arrangements, provided technical assistance to make this possible, and initiated national studies designed to assess and improve compensatory education. By 1980, studies and data supported the conclusion that compensatory education can and sometimes does have relatively successful outcomes.

Improved monitoring procedures

1. Several big cities reported that student achievement in some low-income schools equaled or exceeded the national average through the second or third grades, indicating that preschool programs, Head Start, Follow-Through, and other early childhood compensatory education efforts were beginning to succeed.

Outstanding early childhood programs

2. Several studies of particularly outstanding early childhood education programs have shown that such efforts can have a long-lasting effect if they are well conceived and effectively implemented.[18] For example, Francis Palmer's longitudinal study of working-class black children who participated in a special preschool program in New York City showed that these children scored no higher than control group children in the first grade. When retested in the fifth grade, however, they scored nine points higher on IQ tests and three months higher in reading than did the control children.[19]

17 David J. Fox, *Expansion of the More Effective School Program* (New York: Center for Urban Education, 1967); Harry L. Miller and Roger R. Woock, *Social Foundations of Urban Education,* 2nd ed. (Hinsdale, Ill.: Dryden, 1974).

18 Irving Lazar et al., "Preliminary Findings of the Developmental Continuity Longitudinal Study" (Paper presented at the Office of Child Development Conference on Parents, Children and Continuity, El Paso, May 1977); *Lasting Effects After Preschool* (Washington, D.C.: Government Printing Office, 1979); The Consortium for Longitudinal Studies, *As the Twig is Bent: Lasting Effects of Preschool Programs* (Hillsdale, N.J.: Erlbaum, 1983).

19 Francis H. Palmer, "The Effects of Minimal Early Intervention on Subsequent IQ Scores and Reading Achievement" (Paper presented at the annual meeting of the American Psychological Association, Washington, D.C., September 1976).

Early intervention and basic skill emphasis

3. Reviews of many Follow-Through evaluation studies indicated that instructional approaches based on a well-defined curriculum with emphasis on the development of basic skills generally produce meaningful gains over a variety of cognitive and affective outcome measures.[20] A national evaluation of Follow-Through also provided some indication that "models that emphasize basic skills succeeded better than other models in helping children gain these skills."[21] (The term *basic skills* in this research referred particularly to relatively "mechanical" skills, such as spelling, decoding of words, and simple arithmetic computation.) This finding has been widely publicized and has been interpreted as supporting the conclusion that **direct instruction** — highly structured, whole-group instruction organized on a step-by-step basis—is the most effective way to teach basic skills to disadvantaged students in the primary grades.

As is evident from the preceding summary of research on compensatory education, the data can be interpreted in a variety of ways. Reviewing two decades of studies, for example, Stephen Mullin and Anita Summers have stated the following:

> After an extensive analysis of the compensatory education literature, we conclude (1) that participants have some slight edge over nonparticipants, (2) that the effects are probably not sustained, (3) that within the range of expenditures covered more dollars are not necessarily effective or cost-effective, and (4) that methodological problems alone do not account for the absence of robust results. We know what doesn't work, but we don't know what will work. . . .[22]

Contrasting interpretations

By way of contrast, Benjamin Stickney and Virginia Plunkett reviewed essentially the same literature and, emphasizing positive reports since 1975, reached the following conclusions:

> In light of the disappointing findings of earlier studies . . . , we view the recent Title I research and the reports from the preschool . . . [studies] as encouraging findings. Not only are researchers now finding compensatory education generally effective, but they have also indentified components of basic skills instruction that may be responsible for that success. For example, greater time on task, more frequent monitoring, and more parental involvement are rather consistently related to greater learning.
>
> It is somewhat ironic that cuts in compensatory education funding have been suggested just as these programs are beginning to demonstrate long-term, if modest, success. Born in an era of unrestrained optimism about the ability of society to solve its problems, compensatory education and early intervention

20 Eugene Tucker, "The Follow Through Planned Variation Experiment: What is the Payoff?" (Paper presented at the annual meeting of the American Educational Research Association, New York, April 1977).

21 Linda B. Stebbins et al., *Education as Experimentation: A Planned Variation Model, Volume IV-A, An Evaluation of Follow-Through* (Cambridge, Mass.: Abt Associates, 1977).

22 Stephen P. Mullin and Anita A. Summers, "Is More Better? The Effectiveness of Spending on Compensatory Education," *Phi Delta Kappan* (January 1983), p. 342.

programs passed through a time of reproach and pessimism about the persistence of the program effects. Today, both expectations and evaluations have become more realistic.[23]

Questions About Compensatory Education

Data since 1975 indicating that compensatory education can be successful does *not* prove that compensatory programs are now equalizing or can equalize educational opportunity for disadvantaged students. These data have been encouraging, but there still are many questions and problems concerning the status and effectiveness of compensatory education. The following are among the most central:

1. *Can compensatory education result in permanent meaningful gains for most disadvantaged students?* Students who make large gains frequently are dropped from Chapter 1 to make room for other students. In addition, the evidence indicates that the performance of many disadvantaged students entering secondary schools is still unacceptably low regardless of whether they have been in Chapter 1 or other compensatory programs. In big cities, for example, the average reading score of ninth graders at inner-city schools generally still is about the sixth-grade level. This means in turn that 50 percent or more of these students are unable to read well enough to succeed in schools or rewarding jobs later in life.

Achievement of poverty students still low

Despite some encouraging reports on the results of compensatory education, overall the situation regarding achievement of economically disadvantaged students remains bleak. For example, the average reading score of thirteen-year olds at Chapter 1 schools in big cities increased only slightly between 1970 and 1979 (from 52.3 to 53.8), and was almost as far below the national average at non-Chapter 1 schools in 1980 as it was in 1970.[24] Furthermore, the final report of the national Chapter 1 evaluation found that although participating students gained in reading scores in grades one through three, scores beyond this point did not improve.[25] These kinds of data support the general conclusion that the "modest influence of schools and the dependence of later achievement on background directly and on earlier abilities, which are highly correlated with background at the start of schooling, tend to result in a perpetuation" of the strong relationship between social-class background and achievement in the educational system.[26]

National situation still bleak

23 Benjamin D. Stickney and Virginia R. T. Plunkett, "Closing the Gap: A Historical Perspective on the Effectiveness of Compensatory Education," *Phi Delta Kappan* (December 1983), p. 290.

24 National Assessment of Educational Progress, "Has Title I Improved Education for Disadvantaged Students? Evidence from Three National Assessments of Reading." No. SY-DS-SO. ED 201 995 (Denver, Colo., Educational Commission of the States, April 27, 1981).

25 R. M. Stonehill and J. I. Anderson, *An Evaluation of ESEA Title I—Program Operations and Educational Effects.* Washington, D.C.: Government Printing Office, 1982.

26 E. Y. T. Won, "A Reexamination of School and Background Influences on Academic Achievement" (Paper presented at the annual meeting of the American Education Research Association, Los Angeles, April 1981), p. 6.

What instructional methods are best?

2. *What type of early instruction should be provided?* Much of the uncertainty regarding instruction for early compensatory education involves the issue of whether programs should utilize a behavioristic direct-instruction approach or should emphasize conceptual development and abstract thinking skills. Some direct instruction programs have had excellent results through the third grade, but performance levels fall when participating children enter the middle grades. Results in cognitive-oriented programs stressing independent learning and development of thinking skills generally have not been as good in terms of mastery of "mechanical" skills in the primary grades, but some of the best cognitive approaches have resulted in gains that show up later in basic and conceptual skills.[27] The frequent fall-off in scores as children enter the middle grades is probably due in part to inadequate conceptual development in the primary grades.

Compensatory education at the secondary level

3. *What should be done at the secondary school level?* Although most sizable programs of compensatory education have been carried out at the elementary level, some efforts have been initiated in secondary schools and a few secondary programs have reported promising results. Some success has been achieved in individual classrooms, in "schools-within-a-school," and in "street academies" or store-front schools.[28]

Are the programs financially feasible?

4. *Is it financially feasible to include most economically disadvantaged students in effective compensatory education programs?* Research on early compensatory education has demonstrated that important gains can be made in improving the performance of disadvantaged students, but effective programs for the most disadvantaged poverty students tend to be expensive because they require prolonged intervention in the home and family environment. At present no one can say exactly what proportion of economically disadvantaged children requires this type of intervention, but the true percentage is likely to be fairly high and per pupil costs are likely to run several thousand dollars per year. It is clear that effective compensatory education on a national scale will cost significantly more than is now available for this purpose, despite the fact that expenditures for compensatory education already constitute 70 to 80 percent of U.S. Department of Education funds and 20 to 25 percent of the funds the federal government spends on a variety of education activities.[29] All this leads to a real question concerning the public's willingness and ability to spend additional money on compensatory education, as well as the cost-effectiveness ratio for success.

27 David P. Weikart, James T. Bond, and James McNeil, "Ypsilanti Perry Preschool Project: Preschool Years and Longitudinal Results Through Fourth Grade," *Monographs of the High/Scope Educational Research Foundation* (Series No. 3, 1977).

28 Daniel U. Levine, "Educating Alienated Inner City Youth: Lessons from the Street Academies," *Journal of Negro Education* (Spring 1975), pp. 139–149.

29 Estimates in this section depend on how one defines and classifies federal expenditures for education.

A National Issue

Can schools succeed in poverty neighborhoods?

A fundamental question concerning compensatory education and other educational reform efforts is whether they really can provide, particularly for minority students in concentrated poverty neighborhoods, a chance to succeed in the schools and later in life. There is great uncertainty concerning the possibility or likelihood that desegregation and/or compensatory education will provide meaningful opportunities for students in concentrated poverty neighborhoods in big cities. As mentioned in Chapter 11, several revisionist critics of U.S. schools and society argue that public schools have failed and will fail in the future to provide equal opportunity for the poor in the absence of fundamental reforms in U.S. society as a whole. For example, Richard deLone's *Small Futures,* published for the Carnegie Council on Children, argues that economically disadvantaged children do not have much opportunity to develop or demonstrate "meritocratic" abilities that would enable them to succeed later in the schools and society.[30] He argues in part that neighborhood, school, and other environmental conditions are such that children in poverty families develop or are taught feelings of futility and powerlessness that ensure their failure in the classroom; for this reason, reform programs "such as Head Start or parent education may succeed briefly in making apparent changes ... [but] usually lack the historical scope to sustain the changes they induce.[31] Only major social and economic changes in basic policies dealing with full employment, affirmative action, and income redistribution, he concluded, can give the poor a meaningful opportunity to improve their lot in U.S. society.

Similarly, Kenneth Keniston's *All Our Children: The American Family Under Pressure*[32] and John Ogbu's *Minority Education and Caste: The American System in Cross-Cultural Perspective,*[33] both published for the Carnegie Council on Children, also conclude that compensatory education is unlikely to prove effective in the absence of more fundamental changes in U.S. society. Keniston and the Council point out that parents have surrendered or lost much of their supervision over children to other institutions and conclude that tax policies to significantly redistribute income are required so that low-status parents can provide environmental conditions conducive to their children's success in school and society. Based on his studies of low-status black communities, Ogbu argues that black children in poverty communities are not likely to demonstrate adequate motivation and performance in school unless caste-type barriers to minority advancement are systematically eliminated in all aspects of U.S. society. Thus he attacks the assumption that "im-

30 Richard H. deLone, *Small Futures: Children, Inequality, and the Limits of Liberal Reform* (New York: Harcourt Brace Jovanovich, 1979).

31 Ibid., p. 168.

32 Kenneth Keniston et al., *All Our Children: The American Family Under Pressure* (New York: Harcourt Brace Jovanovich, 1977).

33 Ogbu, *Minority Education and Caste.*

Changing society before changing schools

proving black school performance and educational attainment is a prerequisite to increasing effectively their opportunities in society." Instead, he concludes, "The present study suggests that the reverse may be the case, so that there is a need to plan the policies and programs dealing with social and occupational barriers in terms of their possible effects on black school performance."[34]

National reforms

To a degree, the conclusions of many revisionists reflect the widespread pessimism concerning educational reform that was prevalent in the 1970s. It remains to be seen whether further efforts to improve education for disadvantaged students will become sufficiently effective on a national scale—expensive though this may prove—to belie the assertions of those who believe that basic changes in economic policy amounting to or approaching a social revolution are necessary if disadvantaged youngsters are to have a real chance to succeed in U.S. society. In recent years the effective schools movement has attempted to bring about improvements in both "regular" and compensatory educational services provided to disadvantaged students. Effective schools research, along with related reform efforts, is discussed at length in Chapter 15.

Multicultural Education

A multiethnic population

Concern with multicultural education has grown throughout the 1970s and 1980s. More than most other countries, the United States consists of a large number of ethnic and racial groups with a diversity of distinctive cultural patterns and histories. For example, the 1980 census enumerated the population of some of the ethnic groups within the Asian-Pacific category as follows: Cambodian—16,044; Chinese—806,027; Filipino—774,640; Guamanian—32,123; Hawaiian—167,253; Indian—361,544; Japanese—700,747; Korean—354,529; Samoan—42,050; Taiwanese—16,390; Thai—45,290; and Vietnamese—261,714. The Hispanic category included the following ethnic populations: Central and South American origin—840,000; Cuban—794,000; Mexican—7,326,000; Puerto Rican—1,748,000; and "Other Spanish" descent—1,370,000.

Multicultural education includes all students

Some aspects of multicultural education focus on providing more equal educational opportunity for students whose cultural and/or language patterns make it difficult to succeed in traditional school programs. However, educators also are concerned with the larger aspects of multicultural education that make it important and valuable for *all* students. Thus some of the broad thrusts within multicultural education deal with the goals of ensuring positive intergroup and interracial attitudes and contacts, enabling all students to function in a multiethnic society, and adapting instruction to students' group-related learning styles. From this point of view, the movements toward de-

34 Ibid., p. 6.

segregation and compensatory education also can be considered as aspects of multicultural education.

From Melting Pot to Cultural Pluralism

Although the United States always has been pluralistic in its population composition, emphasis through much of our history has been on assimilation of subcultures into the national mainstream rather than on maintenance of group subcultures. Some groups—particularly blacks, Hispanics, and Native Americans—were systematically segregated from the national culture, but most had substantial opportunity to acquire the cultural patterns required for success in the larger society. Of course, it should not be necessary to give up one's group identity completely in order to participate in the mainstream, but for much of our history emphasis was placed on assimilation into the national culture, perhaps because this may have seemed necessary in building a new nation of so many diverse groups.

Historic emphasis on assimilation

Whatever the reasons, the emphasis was on assimilation, and as early as 1782 St. John de Crevecoeur commented that the colonists were being "melted" into a "new race" of men. Israel Zangwill's 1908 play "The Melting Pot" popularized this term and called attention to the challenge of "Americanizing" the large streams of immigrants who were entering the United States. Zangwill and others believed that each group should be able to participate fully in American society and contribute to a melded culture without having to become uniform in all cultural patterns, but many other "established" citizens advocated a type of "Americanism" that insisted on conformity with prevailing "Anglo" influences in language, religion, attire, and other cultural patterns.

Creating Americans

Throughout our history, the public school system has stressed the development of an American identity, particularly in the late nineteenth and twentieth centuries, when vast numbers of immigrants passed through the admitting gates at Ellis Island in New York. Students in the common system of public schools learned how "Americans" were supposed to talk, look, and behave, sometimes in classes of fifty or sixty pupils representing the first or second generation of immigrants from ten or fifteen countries. Beyond the stress on learning English, the school stressed habits of cleanliness and punctuality as well as civic spirit and patriotism.[35]

Extremes in educational melting

From our vantage point today, the schools sometimes went too far in emphasizing a particular set of behaviors and standards. For example, Mexican-American students in the Southwest were frequently prohibited from speaking Spanish even on the playground, insistence on observance of Protestant religious customs in the schools helped stimulate the establishment of Catholic school systems in many big cities, and black students in many parts of

35 David B. Tyack, ed., *Turning Points in American Educational History* (Waltham, Mass.: Blaisdell, 1967); David B. Tyack and Elisabeth Hansot, *Managers of Virtue: Public School Leaders in America, 1820–1980* (New York: Basic Books, 1982).

the country were confined to separate schools.[36] In general, however, the public schools played a major part in acculturating and socializing the children of generations of immigrants into our larger national society.

Mobility among ethnics

Except for the most segregated minorities, non-Anglo ethnic groups were able to achieve substantial mobility.[37] An expanding economy, cheap land on the frontier, free public schools, availability of jobs in government and politics, and other opportunities made it possible for them to enter the mainstream of society, in the process acquiring many of the attitudes and behaviors of the typical American while also enriching the national culture with their contributions in language, the arts, food, sports, entertainment, scholarship, and other aspects of culture.[38]

Melting pot questioned

Nevertheless, in the 1950s and 1960s scholars and laypeople began to realize that the melting pot had not melted its ingredients: ethnic identity not only was not being completely eliminated, it seemed to be undergoing a resurgence. Andrew Greeley, for example, described how the Irish in the United States maintained themes and practices from their traditional culture[39] and Glazer and Moynihan's study of major ethnic groups in New York City found that ethnic identification was increasing as a result of the downgrading of working-class occupational statuses, international events that stimulated an affirmation of ethnicity, and the decline in traditional forms of patriotism.[40] Other observers pointed out that blacks, Hispanics, Native Americans, and some European ethnic groups had been systematically discriminated against in a manner that revealed the shortcomings of the melting pot concept.[41]

Shift to cultural pluralism

In the 1960s, the civil rights movement emerged and fought to reduce the exclusion of minority groups. Emphasis shifted (in some interpretations) from the melting pot's stress on uniformity to a stress on diversity and cultural pluralism. In place of the metaphor of the melting pot, the concept of cultural pluralism introduced new metaphors such as a "tossed salad" or a "mosaic" that allow or require maintenance of distinctive group characteristics within a larger whole. The American Association of Colleges of Teacher Education (AACTE) has defined **cultural pluralism** as follows:

> To endorse cultural pluralism is to endorse the principle that there is no one model American .... [and] is to understand and appreciate the differences that exist among the nation's citizens. It is to see these differences as a positive

36 James W. Sanders, *The Education of an Urban Minority* (New York: Oxford University Press, 1977).

37 Historical mobility data for a number of ethnic and racial groups in the United States are reviewed in Alice Kessler-Harris and Virginia Yans-McLaughlin, "European Immigrant Groups," in Thomas Sowell, ed., *American Ethnic Groups* (Washington, D.C.: Urban Institute, 1978), pp. 107–137.

38 Richard Pratte, *Pluralism in Education* (Springfield, Ill.: Thomas, 1979); Stephen Steinberg, *The Ethnic Myth* (New York: Atheneum, 1981).

39 Andrew Greeley, *That Most Distressful Nation* (Chicago: Quadrangle, 1973).

40 Nathan Glazer and Daniel P. Moynihan, *Beyond the Melting Pot,* 2nd ed. (Cambridge, Mass.: MIT Press and Harvard University Press, 1970).

41 Howard Bahr, Bruce A. Chadwick, and Joseph H. Strauss, *American Ethnicity* (Lexington, Mass.: D. C. Heath, 1979); Michael Novak, *The Rise of the Unmeltable Ethnics* (New York: Macmillan, 1971); Gene Ruffini, "Employment Equity and Euro-Ethnics," *Perspectives* (Summer 1983), pp. 40–44.

> force. . . . Cultural pluralism is more than a temporary accommodation to placate racial and ethnic minorities. It is a concept that aims toward a heightened sense of being and of wholeness of the entire society based on the unique strengths of each of its parts.[42]

Balance between assimilation and separation of groups

It should be emphasized that acceptance of or stress on cultural pluralism does not mean that one supports a philosophy aiming at cultural, social, or economic separation. Depending on how cultural pluralism is defined, it may or may not stress integration in cultural, social, or economic matters, but generally it lies somewhere between total assimilation of ethnic or racial groups into a uniform mass on the one hand and strict separation of groups from each other at the opposite pole.

Cultural Pluralism and Multicultural Education

Multicultural education as a school responsibility

Recognizing and responding to social trends emphasizing the desirability of cultural pluralism, educators have been examining and developing ways to build the goals of a constructive pluralism into the educational system of the United States. The AACTE views this goal as a major educational responsibility because of the fact that schools "play a major role in shaping the attitudes and beliefs of the nation's youth . . . [and in] preparing each generation to assume the rights and responsibilities of adult life." The AACTE statement describes multicultural education as education that "values" cultural pluralism and urges that it be made an "integral part" of education at all levels.[43] The Association's most recent statement on multicultural education says that it should be emphasized in all teacher education programs.[44]

Translating goals into practice

School officials at every level of the educational system in the United States have been developing specific approaches for translating the goals of multicultural education into practice in the classroom. In particular, state departments of education, national professional organizations, local school district curriculum developers and supervisors, and colleges of teacher education have been introducing guidelines for providing constructive multicultural education for all students. Many observers view various aspects of multicultural education as being particularly important not just for improving the educational opportunities of disadvantaged minority groups in the United States, but also for enriching the lives of all students and ensuring positive intergroup relationships in our multiethnic society.[45]

42 "No One Model American. A Statement of Multicultural Education" (Washington, D.C.: American Association of Colleges of Teacher Education, 1972), p. 9.

43 Ibid., p. 14.

44 National Council for the Accreditation of Teacher Education, *Standards For the Accreditation of Teacher Education* (Washington, D.C.: The Council, 1982).

45 James A. Banks, "Educating Minority Youths: An Inventory of Current Theory," *Education and Urban Society* (November 1982), pp. 88–103; Edith W. King, "Aspects of Ethnicity and Multicultural Teaching," *Multicultural Teaching* (Spring 1984), pp. 33–35.

Multicultural Instruction

Different instructional approaches with different ethnic groups

One of the key areas in which educators are attempting to develop effective approaches for multicultural education involves the use of differential instructional approaches in teaching students with differing ethnic and racial backgrounds. Some of the most important and frequently discussed approaches have concerned student learning styles, dialect differences among ethnic and racial groups, and bilingual education.

Emphasis on personal relationships

Student Learning Styles A good example of a serious attempt to explore the possibility of differentiating instruction according to learning styles associated with students' background is the bicognitive education described and advocated by Manuel Ramirez and Carlos Castañeda. After conducting preliminary research with Hispanic students, Ramirez and Castañeda concluded that Chicano children tend to be more "field sensitive" than nonminority children. Field-sensitive children are described as being more influenced by personal relationships and by praise or disapproval from authority figures than are "field-independent" students. Ramirez and Castañeda reviewed the implications of these findings for instruction and concluded that a "field-sensitive curriculum" should be "humanized through use of narration, humor, drama, and fantasy" and should emphasize "description of wholes and generalities" and be "structured in such a way that children work cooperatively with peers or with the teacher in a variety of activities.[46] Ramirez and his colleagues have since worked out more concrete materials and methods for emphasizing bicognitive development in the primary grades.[47]

Although bicognitive instruction and similar approaches may improve instruction for many minority students in the future, little research has yet been reported to indicate that these approaches are of proven value in improving the performance of disadvantaged students.[48] It also should be noted that the learning styles of field-sensitive minority students may be associated as much or more with low socioeconomic status as with ethnicity or race per se.

Another example of an effort to identify instructional approaches uniquely suited to students' ethnic or racial background has been provided by Vera John-Steiner and Larry Smith, who have worked with Pueblo Indian children in the Southwest.[49] They concluded that schooling for these children would be more successful if it took better account of their "primary learning" patterns (learning outside the school) and organized classroom in-

46 Manuel Ramirez and Carlos Castañeda, *Cultural Democracy, Bicognitive Development, and Education* (New York: Academic Press, 1974), p. 142. Also see James A. Vasquez, "Bilingual Education's Needed Third Dimension," *Educational Leadership* (November 1979), pp. 166–169.

47 Barbara Cox, Janet Macaulay, and Manuel Ramirez, *Young Children Learning* (New York: Pergamon, 1982).

48 Leigh Chiarelott and Leonard Davidman, "Learning Style Inventories: Implications for Curriculum and Instruction" (Paper presented at the annual meeting of the American Educational Research Association, Montreal, April 1983).

49 Vera John-Steiner and Larry Smith, "The Educational Promise of Cultural Pluralism" (Paper prepared for the National Conference on Urban Education, St. Louis, Missouri, 1978).

struction in a manner more compatible with these patterns. These investigators point out that primary learning tends to take place in *personal* communication with emotionally significant individuals, in *tutorial* situations (face-to-face) in which learning is *pervasive* (not limited to a single setting) and highly *adaptive* (closely linked to the concerns and needs of the community).

Adaptive learning

In the case of Pueblo children, the researchers found that primary learning also emphasized verbal instruction and exploratory play. The researchers concluded that teachers should do more to "match their techniques with the previous learning of the child"—particularly in the middle and upper grades. It should be noted, however, that the value of this approach is not well documented and its specific implications for classroom instruction have not been worked out in much detail.

Matching teaching activities with children's experiences

Another promising approach that adjusts instruction to fit students' cultural learning styles is the Kamehameha Early Education Program (KEEP) in Hawaii. The KEEP approach combines whole-group direct instruction with individualized work in learning centers. The program format addresses the cultural background of students by emphasizing mutual student-teacher participation, narration of student-produced stories in language arts, instant feedback, no penalization for "wrong" answers, and discussion of students' responsibilities as group members. Roland Tharp has reported that this attempt to "capitalize on the teaching-learning interaction characteristic of the Hawaiian sibling-care-taking society" has had positive effects on student achievement.[50]

Nonstandard dialects

Recognition of Dialect Differences Many educators have become concerned with the problems of teaching students who speak nonstandard dialects that may hamper their progress in the traditional classroom. Historically, U.S. public schools have attempted to teach "proper" or standard English to students who speak nonstandard dialects, but simplistic insistence on proper English sometimes has caused students either to reject their own cultural background or to view teachers' efforts in this direction as demeaning and hostile.

In recent years educators have been particularly concerned with learning problems encountered by students who speak black English. A number of scholars have been studying the black English dialect and have succeeded in identifying its underlying grammatical forms and differences from standard English.[51] This research shows that black English is not simply a form of "slang," rather, it systematically differs from standard English in grammar and syntax. Because black English seems to be the basic form of speech of many low-income black students who are not succeeding academically, some educators have proposed that the school teach such students in black English until they learn to read. Other proposals and experiments have advocated teaching English as a foreign language to students who speak black English

50 Roland Tharp, *The Direct Instruction of Comprehension: Results and Description of the Kamehameha Early Education Program* (Honolulu: The Kamehameha Early Education Program, 1981).

51 J. L. Dillard, *Black English* (New York: Random House, 1972).

or other nonstandard dialects, emphasizing students' personal experience in teaching language, and using a variety of other transitional techniques.

Research on teaching in black English or other dialects has not provided much support for the conclusion that students will gain academically if initially taught in their own dialect. Thus one review of the research dealing with black English has concluded that "there is, as yet, no conclusive empirical evidence in the literature supporting the belief that using any of the methods which purport to minimize the interference of black English on reading performance ... is more successful than the traditional standard instructional materials."[52] In addition, there usually is considerable disagreement among members of dialect communities concerning the way in which the school should teach English. In working-class black communities, for example, many or most parents believe or insist that their children should be taught only in "proper" English so that they will acquire the language skills required for success in the larger society. Research also indicates that many students who use black English in spontaneous speech are able to use standard English in reading and language tests.[53]

Black dialect vs. "proper" English

Despite lack of research indicating the superiority of any particular method for teaching students with nonstandard dialects, educators still should seek constructive ways to overcome the learning problems many of these students encounter in standard English classrooms. This task became particularly important when a federal judge ruled in 1979 that the Ann Arbor, Michigan, school district must recognize that students who speak black English may need special help in learning standard English.[54] The court ordered the school district to submit a plan defining the steps it will take to identify children who speak black English and then to take their dialect into consideration in teaching them to read. Although the decision is not binding on anyone outside the Ann Arbor schools, it may exert an important influence in many school districts struggling to provide effective multicultural education for students who speak nonstandard dialects.

Bilingual Education **Bilingual education,** which provides instruction in their native language for non-English-speaking students, has been expanding in U.S. public schools. In 1968 Congress passed the Bilingual Education Act and in 1974 the Supreme Court ruled in *Lau* v. *Nichols* that the schools must take steps to help students who "are certain to find their classroom experiences wholly incomprehensible" because they do not understand English. Congressional appropriations for bilingual education increased from $7.5 million in 1969 to $139.4 million in 1984. Although the federal and state governments fund bilingual projects for more than sixty language

52 J. R. Harber and D. N. Bryan, "Black English and the Teaching of Reading," *Review of Educational Research* (Summer 1976), pp. 397–398.

53 Jane W. Torrey, "Black Children's Knowledge of Standard English," *American Educational Research Journal* (Winter 1983), pp. 627–643.

54 "Schools Must Help Break Down the 'Black English' Barrier," *Phi Delta Kappan* (October 1979), p. 144.

Increasing numbers of public schools in the United States are offering bilingual education programs. *(Paul Conklin)*

Focus on Hispanic bilingual projects

groups speaking various Asian, Indo-European, and Native American languages, the large majority of children in these projects are Hispanic.

Bilingual education has been expanding partly because the federal Office of Civil Rights (OCR) has been insisting that educational opportunities be improved for limited-English-speaking (LES) and non-English-speaking (NES) students. The Supreme Court's unanimous decision in the *Lau* case involving Chinese children in San Francisco did not focus on bilingual education as the only remedy for teaching non-English-speaking students. Instead, the Court said "Teaching English to the students of Chinese ancestry is one choice. Giving instruction to this group in Chinese is another. There may be others."

However, in practice, federal regulations for implementing the *Lau* decision have tended to focus on bilingual education as the most common solution for helping LES and NES students, generally suggesting that school districts initiate bilingual programs if they enroll more than twenty students of a given language group at a particular grade level. Bilingual programs have proliferated accordingly, but there is considerable disagreement concerning the kinds of programs that can or should be offered. Since 1983 the federal government has indicated some willingness to accept English as a second language (ESL) or other nonbilingual approaches for providing help to LES and NES students.

Controversies over bilingual education have become somewhat embittered as federal and state actions have led to the establishment of additional programs. As in the case of teaching through dialect, there are arguments between those who would "immerse" children in an English-language environment and those who believe initial instruction will be more effective in the native language. Divided on this issue, residents in some ethnic neighborhoods have engaged in bitter internal struggles over establishing bilingual programs in the public schools.

Maintenance vs. transitional programs

Educators and laypeople concerned with LES and NES students also argue over whether emphasis should be placed on teaching in the native language over a long period (maintenance) or proceeding to teach in English as soon as possible (transitional). The latter approach, frequently referred to simply as TBE (transitional bilingual education), has been supported by federal guidelines and legislation in some states, partly on the grounds that public schools should teach basic skills in languages other than English only until students can learn in English. On the one side are those who favor maintenance because they believe that this will help build or maintain a constructive sense of identity among ethnic or racial minorities.[55] On the other side are those who believe that cultural maintenance programs are harmful because they separate groups from one another or discourage students from mastering English well enough to function successfully in the larger society.[56]

Bilingual staff

Adherents and opponents of bilingual education also differ on the related issues of whether bilingual programs sometimes or frequently are designed to provide teaching jobs for native language speakers and whether individuals who fill these jobs are competent in English. Observers who favor bilingual/bicultural maintenance tend to believe that the schools need many adults who can teach LES or NES students in their own language, while many observers who favor transitional programs feel that very few native language or bilingual speakers are required to staff a legitimate program.

Educators are particularly concerned with the question of whether bilingual education is effective in improving the performance of low-achieving students. Some scholars who have examined the research believe that bilin-

55 Leonard C. Pacheco, "Educational Renewal: A Bilingual/Bicultural Imperative," *Educational Horizons* (Summer 1977), pp. 168–176.

56 Noel Epstein, *Language, Ethnicity, and the Schools: Policy Alternatives for Bilingual-Bicultural Education* (Washington, D.C.: George Washington University Institute for Educational Leadership, 1977).

gual education has brought about little if any improvement in the achievement of participating students. For example, Keith Baker and Adriana de Kanter reviewed twenty-eight studies that met their standards for methodological adequacy. They concluded that bilingual programs were not consistently successful and that "structured immersion" (placement in regular classes with special assistance provided outside of class) sometimes was more successful than TBE.[57] Other scholars disagree, arguing that well-implemented bilingual programs do improve achievement. For example, Heidi Dulay and Marina Burt reviewed twelve technically acceptable studies and reported: "Despite the recentness of this complex innovation, more than half of the findings show that bilingual education worked significantly better than monolingual programs.[58] Iris Rotberg examined both the "favorable" and "unfavorable" studies and reached the following conclusion: "initial learning in the native language might be more desirable, both academically and psychologically, for children who come from low-income families and also are not proficient in their native language."[59]

Conflicting research on bilingual education

Despite disagreements on the effects of existing programs, most researchers on bilingual education agree that much more than bilingual education is needed to improve the performance of economically disadvantaged LES and NES students. In this regard, Joshua Fishman has summarized the research literature by stating that "on the whole," bilingual education is "too frail a device in and of itself, to significantly alter the learning experiences of the minority-mother-tongue in general or their majority-language-learning success in particular ... precisely because there are so many other pervasive reasons why such children achieve poorly; ... removing the extra burden does not usually do the trick."[60]

Disadvantaged students need more than bilingual education

It should be noted that many scholars believe that bilingual education ideally should be provided for all students, regardless of their ethnic group.[61] In this regard a group of civic leaders and government officials has recommended the following emphases and actions to make bilingual education a positive force for cultural pluralism in the future:[62]

Overall emphasis on building a "language-competent" society

A "no-holds-barred insistence on full mastery of English"

Emphasis on multilingual competence, rather than just on English remediation

57 Keith A. Baker and Adriana de Kanter, "Effectiveness of Bilingual Education: A Review of the Literature" (Paper prepared for the U.S. Office of Education, Office of Planning, Budget, and Evaluation, 1981).

58 Heidi Dulay and Marina Burt, "Bilingual Education: A Close Look at Its Effects," *Focus of the National Clearinghouse for Bilingual Education* (January 1982), pp. 1–4.

59 Iris C. Rotberg, "Some Legal and Research Considerations in Establishing Federal Policy in Bilingual Education," *Harvard Educational Review* (May 1982), p. 35.

60 Joshua A. Fishman, "Bilingual Education—A Perspective," *IRCD Bulletin* (Spring 1977), p. 5.

61 Ibid.

62 Academy for Educational Development, "A New Direction for Bilingual Education in the 1980s," *Focus of the National Clearinghouse for Bilingual Education* (March 1982), pp. 1–4.

Bilingual education for everyone

Expanded bilingual programs that include English-speaking children, so that non-English speakers and English speakers can help each other learn

Increased attention to the international political and economic advantages of multilingual competence

Dangers in Multicultural Education

Multicultural education can be indispensable for achieving constructive cultural pluralism in a nation composed of diverse ethnic groups. At the same time, however, multicultural education potentially can be harmful or damaging. In general, the potential dangers of multicultural education are the same as those associated with the larger concept of cultural pluralism. Major dangers include the following:

Too much emphasis on differences

1. *Multicultural education can emphasize separatism in a way that is divisive and disunifying.* If too much emphasis in multicultural education is placed on differences and separation, educators may neglect unifying themes and similarities that are desirable in a society in which groups are interdependent. Emphasis on differences may lead to neglect of the need to develop citizens who understand and act on national and universal responsibilities of citizenship.

In addition, educational arrangements for some aspects of multicultural education such as bilingualism may conflict with constitutional requirements for ethnic and racial desegregation. For example, bringing students from a particular ethnic group together in a bilingual program may increase their segregation within a school district or school.

Dangers of separation and isolation

2. *Multicultural education may be used to justify second-rate education for economically disadvantaged students or minority students.* Encouraging the separation of disadvantaged students in "remedial" education programs or of minority students in "ethnic studies" programs under the guise of cultural pluralism can result in the establishment or maintenance of programs that are widely viewed as second rate. Unless great efforts are made to maintain the quality and reputation of such programs, students who participate in them may find that the diplomas or degrees they receive are viewed as worthless or second class.

3. *Multicultural education may lead to fragmentation of the school curriculum.* For example, to the extent that attempts are made to broaden the curriculum to achieve all the possible goals of cultural pluralism, attention may be diverted from other equally or more important topics. Attempts to incorporate a large amount of material on ethnic diversity, according to one observer, may "trivialize rather than enrich the curriculum."[63]

Equal opportunity is the underlying goal

Despite these potential dangers, there is little doubt that concern with multicultural education reflects a healthy recognition that systematic steps must be taken to ensure positive intergroup relationships and provide more

63 Harry S. Broudy, "Educational Unity in a Pluralistic Society," *School Review* (November 1977), p. 75.

Table 12.2
Number of Students Receiving Public Educational Services by Type of Handicap, 1977 and 1983

Type of Handicap	1977	1983
Speech impaired	1,302,666	1,134,197
Mentally retarded	969,547	780,831
Learning disabled	797,213	1,745,871
Emotionally disturbed	283,072	353,431
Crippled and other health impaired	141,417	52,026
Hard of hearing and deaf	89,743	75,337
Orthopedically impaired	87,008	57,506
Visually handicapped	38,247	31,096
Deaf-blind and other multihandicapped	NA[a]	68,032
Total	3,708,913	4,298,327

NA[a] = Not an applicable category in 1977.
Source: U.S. Department of Education.

effective educational opportunities for all groups of students in a multiethnic society. As in the case of desegregation and compensatory education, educators will disagree among themselves on just what steps should be taken to provide all students with more effective education. However, concern for attaining the goal of equal opportunity will continue as a prominent theme in U.S. education.

Education for All Handicapped Children

Growth of special education

One of the major developments in education in the 1970s and 1980s has involved schooling for handicapped children. Large gains have been made in providing and improving education for handicapped students. The numbers of handicapped students served in or through public education in 1977 and 1983 are shown in Table 12.2. As indicated in the table, the total number served increased from 3,708,913 in 1977 to 4,298,327 in 1983. Analysis conducted by the U.S. Department of Education indicates that approximately 68 percent of handicapped students receive most of their education in regular classes, about 25 percent are in self-contained classes, and the remaining 7 percent are in special schools.[64]

The growth of special education has been associated with the civil rights movement and its concern with making equal educational opportunity available for all students. This concern was highlighted by the U.S. Supreme Court in *Brown* v. *Board of Education:*

> In these days, it is doubtful that any child may reasonably be expected to succeed in life if he is denied the opportunity of an education. Such an opportu-

64 Susan G. Foster, "Rise in Learning-Disabled Pupils Fuels Concern in States, Districts," *Education Week* (April 25, 1984), pp. 1, 18.

> nity, where the state has undertaken to provide it, is a right which must be made available to all on equal terms.

Although the *Brown* decision addressed the segregation of black children in separate schools, it also served as a precedent in establishing the rights of handicapped students to be provided with equal educational opportunity.[65] This right was officially affirmed in 1974 when a United States District Court ruled in *Pennsylvania Association for Retarded Children, Nancy Beth Bowman et al.* v. *Commonwealth of Pennsylvania, David H. Kurtzman:*

> the Commonwealth of Pennsylvania has undertaken to provide a free public education for all its children between the ages of six and twenty-one years. It is the Commonwealth's obligation to place each mentally retarded child in a free, public program of education and training appropriate to the child's capacity.

Legal mandates

The Kurtzman case and other judicial decisions have reflected federal laws that extended a right to treatment and access to educational services to handicapped students under the Fifth and Fourteenth Amendments to the Constitution. These amendments state that no person can be deprived of liberty and of equal protection of the laws without due process. Federal legislation focusing on the rights of the handicapped and governing much of the subsequent activity and improvement in the education of handicapped students was spelled out in three major laws: the Rehabilitation Act of 1973; Public Law 93-380 in 1974; and Public Law 94-142 (The Education for All Handicapped Children Act) in 1975. The Rehabilitation Act provided that no "program" or "activity" receiving federal assistance could exclude or discriminate against persons solely because of their handicaps. PL 93-380 authorized increased levels of aid to states for the implementation of special education services and set forth due process requirements to protect the rights of handicapped students and their families. PL 94-142 set forth as national policy the goal that "free appropriate public education . . . must be extended to handicapped persons as their fundamental right."

The basic requirements spelled out in these laws and subsequent judicial interpretations are as follows:

Requirements for special education students

1. Handicapped persons, however severe their disability, must be provided with free, appropriate public education.
2. Testing and assessment services must be fair and comprehensive (testing cannot be based on a single criterion such as an IQ score).
3. Parents or guardians have access to information on diagnosis and may protest decisions made by school officials.
4. Individual education plans (IEPs) that include both long-range and short-range educational goals must be provided. These plans must include periodic review of the instructional goals and methods elected.

65 Wayne Sailor and Doug Guess, *Severely Handicapped Students* (Boston: Houghton Mifflin, 1983).

5. Educational services will be provided in the "least restrictive" environment; exceptional children may be placed in special or separate classes only for the amount of time judged necessary to provide appropriate services. If a recipient of federal assistance demonstrates that placement in a regular educational setting cannot be achieved satisfactorily, the student must be provided adequate and free alternative service. Thus a school district receiving federal funds must either place handicapped students in the regular program and give special assistance or provide appropriate placement elsewhere at public expense.[66]

Special education expenditures

Largely as a result of these federal mandates, special education expenditures rose steadily in the 1970s and 1980s. There are now more than four million handicapped students who constitute almost 10 percent of public school enrollment. The average annual cost of educating handicapped students is roughly twice the national average of approximately $2,500. However, although the federal government requires local school districts to provide free appropriate education for all students aged three to twenty-one, it provides only a few hundred dollars per child extra to help make this possible. Federal expenditures for special education increased from $75 million in 1969 to $1.2 billion in 1980; almost 75 percent of the nation's handicapped children now are receiving special services as compared with less than half in 1974; and nearly 40 percent of handicapped children previously confined to institutions now receive part of their education in public schools.[67]

Further progress needed

Nevertheless, much progress still needs to be made in many school districts that tend to have high percentages of mentally retarded, learning disabled, and emotionally disturbed students. For example, a 1980 report presented data indicating that thousands of handicapped children in many big cities are on waiting lists for placement in special education programs. The report further charged that the federal Bureau of Education for the Handicapped (BEH) has failed to monitor and enforce PL 94-142 effectively. According to this report, the BEH has the power to delay or withhold federal funds and to issue cease and desist orders to states that do not comply with the law, but it generally has failed to take these steps to ensure compliance.[68]

Classification and Labeling of Students

Many of the problems associated with improving education for handicapped children are related to difficulties in identifying and classifying students who require special education. It is very difficult to be certain, for example, whether a slow child is mentally retarded and could benefit from special educational services or is simply a slow learner who requires more time and guidance to learn. Similarly, it is difficult to determine whether a child who

66 B. Marian Swanson and Diane J. Willis, *Understanding Exceptional Children and Youth* (Chicago: Rand McNally, 1979); Sailor and Guess, *Severely Handicapped Students.*

67 "Update on Special Ed Successes by the Feds," *Phi Delta Kappan* (April 1980), p. 158.

68 "BEH Fails to Enforce, Monitor Handicapped Law, Group Says," *Education Daily* (n.d.), pp. 7–8.

is working below capacity has brain damage or some other learning disability, or is performing poorly because he or she is poorly motivated or poorly taught. (Of course, all three reasons may be operative for the same child.)

Difficulty in classifying students

Specialists in special education disagree among themselves on what constitutes a "learning disability" that requires special education services and on what services should be provided for a particular disability. Similar problems are encountered in distinguishing between children who are severely versus mildly emotionally disturbed, partially deaf versus nonhearing, or close to some borderline (which may be very fuzzy and ill defined) on other aspects of handicapped status. Maynard Reynolds, an authority on classification of handicapped students has described the overall problem as follows:

> The procedures used to categorize children for special placements are left over in part from practices in the 19th century asylums of Europe. Some adjustments have been made by extending or enlarging the notion of mental retardation to include the educable retarded and the concept of mental illness to include emotionally disturbed and behaviorally disturbed (and disturbing?) children. A poorly defined category, learning disabilities, has been added to fill in the gaps between other categories; the label is applied to children who do not respond to ordinary instruction in the schools and yet do not fit any traditional category.[69]

Reynolds also points out that the vagueness of the learning disabilities (LD) category has encouraged school districts to use this classification because they can obtain some federal funds to improve educational services for designated students. Since most LD students spend much or most of their time in regular classes (least restrictive environment) but receive extra assistance or are in some special classes, LD services are frequently a form of compensatory education for disadvantaged students and low-achieving students who otherwise might not have special assistance. This helps to explain why the number of students in the LD category has grown so large. Research indicates that half or more of the LD students in the schools do not meet criteria commonly accepted by experts in special education.[70]

Does anybody know what "learning disabilities" are?

Uncertainty in accurately classifying students is connected with fundamental questions regarding appropriate treatment for a given child. As indicated above, placement in the LD or other special education categories may make appropriate assistance available to students in a relatively nonrestrictive setting, but at the same time the child is labeled as having a "learning problem" or as "handicapped" in learning. Educators are concerned about this type of labeling. As state government requirements to provide special services for handicapped students increased during the 1950s, a higher percentage of students than in earlier decades was being labeled as handicapped and placed in separate programs to improve their learning. During the 1960s, however, many educators and parents began to question the special-class ap-

Dangers in labeling

69 Maynard C. Reynolds, "Classification of Students with Handicaps," in Edmund W. Gordon, ed., *Review of Research in Education 11* (Washington, D.C.: American Educational Research Association, 1984), p. 89.

70 Foster, "Rise in Learning-Disabled Pupils."

proach, primarily on the grounds that it isolates mildly handicapped children from other students. In so doing, critics argue, it fails to prepare them to function in the larger society, and it generates feelings of inadequacy and inferiority among students who are shunted aside in classes organized for the "emotionally disturbed" or "retarded" and taught at a slow pace. Critics also are concerned with the possibility that handicapped classification may generate a self-fulfilling prophecy: students labeled as disturbed, for example, may be more inclined to act in a disturbed manner because the label makes this behavior acceptable and expected.[71]

Problems in evaluation

Researchers concerned with the effects of labeling have tried to determine whether classification and placement in a special class or program really do have a detrimental effect on students. Among the variables they have considered are effects on self-concept, peer acceptance, and postschool outcomes. This type of research is very difficult to conduct because of problems involving definition of terms, the measurement of program effects, and the fact that differing students have different reactions to a given program or placement. Moreover, the likelihood that labeling may have a negative effect does not mean that placement in a regular class or setting necessarily will be more beneficial.

Overcoming problems in restrictive settings

Two researchers who reviewed studies on labeling thus were forced to conclude that the allegedly overall negative effects of special or separate classes or programs for the handicapped were not well established. However, neither has it been proved that separate classes or programs for the handicapped are more beneficial, on the average, than is placement in regular or normal classes.[72] A recent review of research on this topic concluded that for students with mild learning problems, restrictive educational settings need not detract from achievement provided that effective practices are used to overcome problems such as stigmatization and slow pacing of instruction. The authors also concluded, however, that less restrictive settings generally are preferable on ethical grounds.[73]

Mainstreaming

Mandate for mainstreaming

Despite the lack of conclusive data showing detrimental effects of labeling and special classes for the handicapped, some courts have weighed the evidence and concluded that special placement probably does have detrimental effects for many students, particularly for those who are or might be classified as only mildly handicapped. In addition, PL 94-142 now requires that handicapped students be placed in the **least restrictive environment** —the handicapped child should participate in regular or "normal" educational programming to the fullest extent possible. Efforts to place handicapped chil-

71 Donald L. Macmillan and C. Edward Meyers, "Educational Labeling of Handicapped Learners," in D. C. Berliner, ed., *Review of Research in Education* 7 (Washington, D.C.: American Educational Research Association, 1979), pp. 121–194.

72 Ibid.

73 Gaea Leinhardt and Allan Pallay, "Restrictive Educational Settings: Exile or Haven?" *Review of Educational Research* (Winter 1982), pp. 557–578.

dren in regular class settings generally are referred to as "mainstreaming" and have been encouraged and carried out in school districts throughout the country since the passage of PL 94-142.

Fundamentally, **mainstreaming** is the movement toward integrating handicapped children into regular schools and classrooms, providing maximum opportunities not only to join in usual school activities but also to be "counted in" among their nonhandicapped peers. It is not intended to be a wholesale elimination of special services, programs, or classes for children with exceptional needs. Extra professional support may include a wide range of services, including interpretation by specialists skilled in working with a particular handicap and provision of special equipment needed to help a child with a serious disability. But even if a disability is severe and a child needs to spend a relatively great amount of time away from the regular classroom, he or she can still be encouraged to take part in activities such as art, music, or shop that are open to other children.

Extra support from specialists

Research on mainstreaming has led to conclusions as ambiguous as the results of studies of labeling and special class placement. Three researchers who examined the literature on mainstreaming concluded that the data regarding effects on self-esteem are inconclusive. They did report, however, that mainstreaming can improve the social acceptance of handicapped students, provided that direct interventions are made to achieve this goal.[74] Their overall conclusion was as follows: "First and foremost, there is little evidence that mainstreaming practices result in superior performance among handicapped students." They went on to speculate that this general finding probably is related to difficulties in defining and measuring various mainstreaming approaches, as well as to the special placement settings with which they then are compared. Available evidence indicates that amount of time in regular classes, without considering the quality of instruction or the criteria employed to determine who gets mainstreamed and for how long, has little impact on social or academic outcomes.[75]

Research on mainstreaming

Researchers who have reviewed the data on special class placement and mainstreaming thus seem to agree that research has not provided conclusive support for either approach. In part, this can be attributed to the probability that neither approach is carried out very well in a large number of settings; in this case one would expect to find that both are ineffective and neither is superior to the other. The research indicates that regular classroom teachers have not been well prepared to work with handicapped students in their classes.[76]

Researchers agree

74 Melvyn I. Semmel, Jay Gottlieb, and Nancy M. Robinson, "Mainstreaming: Perspectives on Educating Handicapped Children in Public Schools," in Berliner, *Review of Research in Education* pp. 223–279.

75 Semmel, Gottlieb, and Robinson, "Mainstreaming"; R. Bruce Baum, "Educating the Exceptional Child in the Regular Classroom," *Journal of Teacher Education* (November–December 1979), pp. 20–22.

76 Thomas E. Linton and Kristen D. Juul, "Mainstreaming: Time for Reassessment," *Educational Leadership* (February 1980), pp. 433–435.

Educators are increasingly advocating the placement and instruction of handicapped students in regular classroom settings.
(Bob Daemmrich/TexaStock©)

Improving mainstreaming efforts

However, these pessimistic observations should not be viewed as justifying despair concerning the future of mainstreaming or other efforts to improve education for handicapped students. Mainstreaming may prove to be a positive answer to the long tradition of isolating handicapped students, but in itself it is not a panacea. To be effective, mainstreaming requires a variety of special resources and educators who are skilled in and dedicated to creating an effective learning environment and acceptance for handicapped students. Thus one important educational goal is to make the mainstreaming approach now mandated by the federal government more successful than it has been. This overall goal has been supported by a recent review of research on mainstreaming, which reached the following general conclusion.

> There is no support in the research for a retreat from mainstreaming toward self-contained special education classes, except perhaps for very low IQ students in cases where individualized instruction or other supports cannot be used in regular classes.... Training programs for regular teachers to help them meet the instructional and socio-emotional needs of academically handicapped students must continue, and teachers should receive training in methods (such as cooperative learning, individualized instruction, or combinations of these) that enable them to meet diverse needs in the same classroom.[77]

77 Nancy A. Madden and Robert E. Slavin, "Mainstreaming Students with Mild Handicaps: Academic and Social Outcomes," *Review of Educational Research* (Winter 1983), p. 560.

Disproportionate Mental Retardation Placement of Minority Students

Data on special education placement show that students from some racial minority groups are much more likely to be designated for mental retardation programs than are non-Hispanic white students. In 1982, for example, 3.46 percent of black students and 1.73 of Native American students were in classes for the educable mentally retarded, as compared with 1.07 percent of non-Hispanic whites. Some observers believe that placement in classes for the retarded has been too dependent on intelligence tests, which have been constructed for use with middle-class whites.[78] Some also believe that disproportionate numbers of minority students are shunted into classes for the emotionally disturbed or the retarded mainly to alleviate teachers' problems in dealing with culturally different children and youth. Many educators and parents worry that such placements may constitute a new version of segregation and discrimination by sentencing minority students to special classes with low or nonexistent educational expectations.

Overuse of IQ tests

Several courts have been sympathetic to this criticism and have issued rulings to make it less likely that students will be misassigned to special education classes. In a 1970 case (*Diana* v. *Board of Education*), for example, a California court examined the claim of nine Mexican-American children who felt they had been improperly classified as mentally retarded on the basis of an IQ test on which their scores ranged from 52 to 68. When tested by a bilingual psychologist and allowed to respond in Spanish or English, their IQs increased by an average of 15 points. The court ruled that: (1) all children whose primary language is not English must be tested in both their primary language and English; (2) the tests cannot depend solely on vocabulary, general information, or other experience-based items; and (3) districts that have a disparity between the percentage of Mexican-American students in regular classes and in classes for the retarded must be able to show that this disparity is due to valid classification methods. In another case (*Larry P.* v. *Riles*) in 1972, after hearing evidence that the dialect and family environment of many black students caused invalid low scores on IQ tests, a California court ruled that black students could not be placed in EMR classes (classes for the educable mentally retarded) on the basis of IQ tests "as currently administered."

Courts intervene

An Optimal Learning Environment?

Requirements of PL 94-142 and related legislation specify that school officials must prepare an individualized educational plan for handicapped students, including special services to help achieve educational goals specified in the plan. These requirements have frequently been interpreted as implying that an "appropriate" free education for the handicapped requires whatever ser-

78 R. A. Quantz, "Mild Mental Retardation and Race," *Educational Studies* (Winter 1981–82), pp. 387–393.

vices are necessary to help them derive as much benefit from education as do other students—perhaps an optimal learning environment for the handicapped.

Optimal learning environment is expensive

However, providing an optimal learning environment for handicapped—particularly severely handicapped—students (and perhaps for *any* student) can be very expensive. Thus, arguments arose between school officials, who claimed they could not afford to provide maximally effective education for some handicapped students, and parents or other advocates who believe that handicapped students have a constitutional right to whatever services are needed to ensure maximum educational gains.

Definition of "benefit"

The issue went to the U.S. Supreme Court in 1982, when the parents of a deaf first-grader named Amy Rowley demanded that she be provided with a sign-language interpreter in academic classes. Local educators argued that they had provided an FM hearing aid, a tutor of the deaf, and a speech therapist, but could not provide an interpreter. In *Board of Education of Hudson Central School District* v. *Rowley,* the Court ruled that though the law requires the provision of such "supportive services" as "may be required to assist a handicapped child *to benefit* from public education," it does not require a particular level of benefit above the "basic floor of opportunity ... [which] consists of access to specialized instruction and related services individually designed" for a child.[79]

Constitutional scholar Mark Yudof reviewed the *Rowley* decision and assessed its major impact as follows:

School district prerogatives

> The Court in effect said that school officials will decide whether the additional costs are worth it in terms of the educational payoff for the child. Furthermore, local and state officials are to decide whether to prefer enhanced learning for gifted or normal children or for handicapped children .... the school district decides, as a matter of public policy, on whom the benefits should be bestowed. Obviously, different school districts and states may decide such questions differently .... There is uniformity only as to the basic floor and as to the procedures, but not as to the general educational content of special education.[80]

Directions for the Future

Legislation to provide equal educational opportunity for handicapped students has led to expansion of special education services, much of it in the form of mainstreaming with special assistance or some separate classes for designated students. We have seen, however, that research does not provide strong evidence that mainstreaming has been any more successful on a wide-

79 However, in 1984 the Supreme Court reaffirmed that certain supportive services might be required to make basic educational opportunities truly available for a handicapped child. In deciding the case of Amber Tatro, an eight-year-old with spinal bifida, the Court ruled that school officials must provide intermittent catheterization.

80 Mark Yudof, "Education for Handicapped: Rowley in Perspective," *American Journal of Education* (February 1984), p. 172.

spread basis than have separate programs that label and isolate the handicapped child.

What should be done, then, to improve education for handicapped students? In addition to calls for improving methods used to classify handicapped students, experts in special education have been trying to develop more accurate and effective ways to diagnose and treat learning problems. Many observers have suggested that less energy should be given to classifying and treating special education students in distinct groups; instead, efforts should concentrate on providing more effective schooling—a more optimal learning environment—for all low- or underachieving students. This approach would involve combining and probably increasing funding for compensatory education and special education in one category to improve education, using knowledge of effective teaching and schooling, for all students who need special assistance.[81]

More effective education for all students

Summing Up

1. Much desegregation has been accomplished in smaller school districts, especially since 1963, but the concentration of minority students and economically disadvantaged students in big-city districts has made it difficult to bring about stable desegregation.
2. Compensatory education seemed to be unsuccessful until evidence accumulating in the latter half of the 1970s began to justify a more positive conclusion. However, many serious questions remain concerning the degree to which compensatory education can have substantial and lasting results on a large scale.
3. Efforts to contribute to constructive cultural pluralism through education include multicultural instruction approaches that take account of student learning styles, recognize differences in dialect, and provide for bilingual education. While multicultural instruction has not been shown to have consistent effects on achievement, some promising results have been reported. In particular, bilingual education and methods responsive to student learning style differences may help improve the performance of economically disadvantaged minority students.
4. Legislative and court mandates have led to a large expansion in education for handicapped students. As part of this process, educators are trying to mainstream handicapped students as much as possible in order to avoid the damaging effects of labeling and separation. Although research is not clear concerning the overall gains and losses associated with mainstreaming and special placement, many observers believe that the underlying problem centers on provision of more effective instruction to all low-achieving or underachieving students.
5. Questions and actions involving desegregation, compensatory education, multicultural education, and education for all handicapped students cen-

81 Reynolds, "Classification of Students with Handicaps"; Daniel J. Reschly, "Beyond IQ Test Bias: The National Academy Panel's Analysis of Minority EMR Overrepresentation," *Educational Researcher* (March 1984), pp. 15–19.

ter on the goal of providing equal educational opportunity for all students. For this reason, all four of these topics also relate to the broader goal of making schools more effective.

Discussion Questions

1. What are the pros and cons of desegregation and integration? (Be sure to include in the discussion academic learning, psychological factors, political factors, and moral factors.)
2. What is the difference between de jure and de facto segregation? What implications do these two types of segregation have for the North and South?
3. Why is compensatory education an important national issue? What larger conclusions follow from one's viewpoint concerning its success or failure?
4. What are some of the major goals and components of multicultural education? What can teachers in predominantly white, middle-class schools do to advance its goals?
5. What can regular teachers do to help special education students who are mainstreamed in their classes?

Suggested Readings

Consortium for Longitudinal Studies. *As the Twig is Bent: Lasting Effects of Preschool Programs.* Hillsdale, N.J.: Erlbaum, 1983.

Describes the long-lasting effects of unusually well-planned and successful preschool programs for disadvantaged students.

Hechinger, Fred M., and Grace Hechinger. *Growing Up in America.* New York: McGraw-Hill, 1975.

Desegregation, compensatory education, and multicultural education figure prominently in this nontechnical history.

Levine, Daniel U., and Robert J. Havighurst. *Society and Education.* 6th ed. Boston: Allyn and Bacon, 1984.

This text on the sociology of education provides detailed analysis on all the topics discussed in this chapter.

Sims, William E., and Bernice Bass de Martinez, eds. *Perspectives in Multicultural Education.* Washington, D.C.: University Press, 1981.

Useful ideas and suggestions for planning and delivering instruction to achieve the goals of our multiethnic society.

Stephan, Walter G., and Joel R. Feagin, eds. *School Desegregation: Past, Present, and Future.* New York: Plenum, 1980.

Excellent chapters deal with, among other topics, the status of desegregation, effects of desegregation, "white flight" from desegregated schools, and improvement of instruction in desegregated classrooms.

Strain, Phillip S., and Mary Margaret Keer. *Mainstreaming of Children in Schools.* New York: Academic Press, 1981.

Discussion of research on mainstreaming and analysis of mainstreaming issues important for classroom teachers.

Tyack, David B., and Elisabeth Hansot. *Managers of Virtue: Public School Leaders in America, 1820–1980.* New York: Basic Books, 1982.

Includes historical materials and perspective on the growth of common schools in our multiethnic society.

BUNTE KINDERWELT 1972
BOOKS
BOOKS

Part 5 Schools in a Changing Society

This final section of the text deals with the aims of education, curriculum in the schools, and recent efforts to make schools more effective. All three topics reflect changes taking place in society. As society changes, the aims of education tend to be modified—some goals receive greater emphasis, some receive less, and new goals become evident. The content of the curriculum also changes in response to demands placed on the schools and the development of new knowledge and techniques. In recent years, much of the emphasis in elementary and secondary education has been on improving the effectiveness of instruction.

Chapter 13, on the aims of education, begins with a discussion of how goals for the schools are formulated and the differences between broad aims and specific objectives. After providing an historical perspective on the aims of education in the United States, the chapter describes several recent national reports that are influencing the formulation of goals for the future. The concluding section provides a broad overview of past, current, and probable future goals.

In Chapter 14 we begin by describing historical influences on curriculum and instruction and then examine the fundamental differences between subject-centered and student-centered approaches. We next describe some of the most important recent innovations in curriculum and instruction: team teaching; teacher aides; flexible scheduling; individualized instruction; instructional television; programmed instruction; and computer-assisted instruction. The chapter concludes by outlining a possible agenda for the future.

Chapter 15 first summarizes research on school effectiveness and on the school improvement process and then highlights several promising instructional approaches. After describing the recommendations of prominent authors who have offered proposals for making schools more effective, the chapter ends with a discussion of a number of other major issues involving school effectiveness.

13

Aims of Education

Focusing Questions

What should the schools teach?

How are aims formulated? How are objectives formulated?

What are the major differences between aims and objectives?

In what way does the social order affect educational priorities?

What groups of students have been targeted for special treatment in the 1950s, 1960s, 1970s, and 1980s? What emphasis has there been on the academically talented and on the economically disadvantaged?

What are the major themes of recent policy reports on education? What aims will be most important in the future?

CONTEMPORARY SOCIETY CHANGES FUNDAMENTALLY AND RAPIDLY. As it changes, we must fit ourselves into the present and project ourselves into the future. We look to the schools to help us cope with the climate of change. As a society, we react to change and social pressures by revising the aims of education, and, in turn, the schools respond by changing their programs. Few educators would dare talk about changing school programs without some mention of the aims they have in mind. All that is to be done in schools, it is usually asserted, is to be done with the aims of schooling in mind. Schooling, the argument goes, is a rational process directed at achieving some end.

The word *aims* is often used interchangeably with the terms *goals, purposes, ultimate objectives,* and *broad objectives.* **Aims** are important guides in education, although they cannot be directly observed or evaluated; they are statements that connote a desired and valued competency, a theme or concern that applies to education in general. Aims are usually formulated on a national or state level by prestigious commissions or professional groups; they are intended to guide schools in defining the nature of their subject matter and student activities. Examples of aims might be: "Preparing students for democratic citizenship," or "Preparing students for a vocation."

Establishing Aims

It would be nice to maintain that educators appraise the tendencies of the times and develop aims to help shape social forces. This approach conceives of schools as an instrument for change, but it has rarely been the case. Educators usually react to the times and change the aims to meet the new social pressures and forces. This approach conceives of the school as a mirror of society.

Schools as a mirror of society

When we examine the aims of society, we must take into account not only the forces of change and social pressures but also existing philosophies. People react differently to the same events: they appraise, reflect, and react to the tendencies of the times according to their biases and values. In short, the aims we advocate are based not only on social forces impinging on society but also on our philosophy of education. American educational philosophy, according to R. Freeman Butts and Lawrence Cremin, has been rooted in the democratic way of life and in the search for freedom.[1]

Without philosophy we lack a framework for developing aims. What is the point of seeking answers if one has not asked the right questions—if one has no framework or philosophy to guide the inquiry? The crux of the issue today is whether, given current trends and forces, educators can develop aims to fit the problems that confront society; each generation must find its own way.

Aims reflect a philosophy

1 R. Freeman Butts and Lawrence A. Cremin, *A History of Education in American Culture* (New York: Holt, 1953); R. Freeman Butts, *Public Education in the United States: From Revolution to Reform* (New York: Holt, 1978).

Current trends and forces are political and social in nature—and they put public pressure on the schools to develop timely and relevant aims. Indeed, we live in an age of tension and conflict, whereby trends and forces in society impact on schools—resulting in the need for schools to experiment and change. School priorities are established in response to national and community pressures. For example, the Cold War with the Soviet Union and economic competition with Japan affect national pride and the economy. Faced with a seeming crisis, people turn to the schools for the key to the achievement of our national goals. Many problems related to youth have surfaced at the community level, and schools are forced to respond and establish priorities that are related to serving youth.

National and community pressures

In analyzing and responding to national and community problems, we must ask what are the responsibilities of the school in contrast to those that properly belong to the family, church, industry, and various social or youth agencies? What responsibilities should the school share with other institutions or agencies? As we attempt to answer these questions, our aims of education evolve. They provide direction for developing a program and organizing schools and classrooms to make the most effective use of the time and abilities of students and teachers.[2]

Assigning responsibilities to schools and other institutions

It also seems that in many cases when we speak of aims, the language is so general that we cannot agree on the intent. For example, what does the phrase "Preparing students for democratic citizenship" mean? What do people have in mind when they claim that the schools should stress citizenship preparation? We simply do not know what the phrase means descriptively, in spite of its common use; hence, to say that people agree on or share an educational aim is often misleading. We must recognize that aims only suggest a direction for people to follow. They are too vague to tell parents what the schools are attempting to accomplish and teachers what they are expected to teach or what their students are expected to learn. In communicating aims, the schools need to translate them into statements that will clearly describe what is intended.[3] These translations correspond to **objectives**. Without this translation of aims into objectives, it is difficult to make accurate judgments about planning curriculum and instruction strategies or to evaluate what has been planned.

Clarifying our intentions

Moving from Aims to Objectives

Aims are too broad to be specifically applied to a particular curriculum or instructional procedure. Objectives are formulated at the classroom level to achieve the aims of the school. Objectives make it possible to organize learning experiences in terms of the school's objectives as well as to specify cri-

2 Ernest L. Boyer, "Clarifying the Mission of the American High School," *Educational Leadership* (March 1984), pp. 20–23; Glenys G. Unruh, "Curriculum Politics," in F. W. English, ed., *Fundamental Curriculum Decisions,* 1983 ASCD Yearbook (Alexandria, Va.: Association for Supervision and Curriculum Development, 1983), pp. 99–111.

3 Jack R. Frymier, *A School For Tomorrow* (Berkeley, Calif.: McCutchan, 1973); Jon Wiles and Joseph Bondi, *Curriculum Development: A Guide to Practice* (Columbus, Ohio: Merrill, 1979).

teria for evaluating performance against objectives. For each aim, many objectives can be formulated.

Ralph Tyler's outline has become a model for curriculum planners. Tyler identified four fundamental questions in developing aims:

Tyler's four questions

1. What educational purposes should the school seek to attain?
2. What educational experiences can be provided to help attain these purposes?
3. How can these educational experiences be effectively organized?
4. How can we determine whether the purposes have been attained? [And to what extent?][4]

Information sources in developing aims

Based on these questions, Tyler listed and discussed the information sources needed to move from aims toward objectives. Five information sources were examined: (1) studies of learners themselves; (2) studies of contemporary society outside of school; (3) suggestions from subject specialists, teachers, administrators, and parents; (4) the use of a philosophy in selecting objectives; and (5) the use of psychology of learning in selecting objectives.

While other models for planning aims and objectives are available, Tyler's concepts can serve as a starting point. When translating aims into objectives, many educators first formulate intermediate objectives and then formulate specific or instructional objectives. **Intermediate objectives** are usually nonbehavioral objectives written in terms of grade levels or subjects; for example, "The development of reading skills" or "The appreciation of art." These objectives are usually incorporated into state and local school guidelines. They describe what the schools intend to accomplish and provide general direction, but they are still too vague for teachers and students to know exactly what is intended. The need, then, is to be more precise in wording objectives or to state them as instructional objectives. The ultimate goal is for curriculum specialists or groups of teachers to establish objectives at the classroom level.

Instructional Objectives

Behavioral terms

Instructional objectives (specific descriptions of what is to take place in the classroom or of learning outcomes) are stated in behavioral terms, that is, terms that can be observed or measured. They are formulated to help teachers and students know if they are achieving the intermediate objectives, that is, the objectives of the grade level or subject. They are intended to direct student activity toward acquiring specific skills. An intermediate objective might be formulated as follows:

4 Ralph W. Tyler, *Basic Principles of Curriculum and Instruction* (Chicago: University of Chicago Press, 1950), p. 1.

1. The students will understand mathematical computations.
   Making it specific, we might state:
2. The students will be able to add two-digit numbers.
   Making it more specific, we might then state:
3. The students will be able to add 10 + 15 + 36.
   Making it still more specific, we might state:
4. The students are to add 10 + 15 + 36 in 30 seconds.
   And making it perhaps as specific as possible, we might state:
5. The students will be able to add 10 + 15 + 36 without the use of any book, slide rule, or mechanical device. They will use paper and pencil, show all the work on the spaces provided, and finish within 30 seconds.

Some educators, such as Robert Mager, advocate a very specific approach, similar to step 5 of our example.[5] They contend that an instructional objective must describe (1) the *behavior* of the learner when demonstrating his or her achievement of the objective, (2) the *conditions* imposed upon the learner when demonstrating the mastery of the objective, and (3) the *minimum proficiency* level that will be acceptable. To write a behavioral objective in American history using the Magerian approach, we might state:

> The student is to read the biography of Benjamin Franklin. He or she is then to prepare a one-thousand-word oral statement combining three or more important facets of the man's life in a five-minute presentation to the class to be judged successful by at least three out of five students who have also read the biography.

One more example should suffice, this time in science:

> After studying the unit, the student must be able to complete a 100-item multiple-choice examination on the subject of pollution. Acceptable performance will be 80 items answered correctly within an examination period of 60 minutes.

Direction vs. trivia

Some educators strongly advocate this specific approach, claiming that it helps us define exactly what we mean; provides a method for arranging sequences of content; promotes direction for teachers and students; provides a guide for determining teaching methods, materials, and activities; and provides a guide for constructing tests and other measurements.[6] Other educators advocate a less specific approach, but one that is still behavioral and measurable.[7] They contend that the Magerian method for stating instruc-

5 Robert F. Mager, *Preparing Instructional Objectives,* 2nd ed. (Belmont, Calif.: Fearon, 1975).

6 Robert Kibler, Larry L. Baker, and David T. Miles, *Behavioral Objectives and Instruction,* 2nd ed. (Boston: Allyn and Bacon, 1981); W. James Popham, *Criterion-Referenced Measurement* (Englewood Cliffs, N.J.: Prentice-Hall, 1978).

7 Robert L. Ebel, "Some Comments about Educational Objectives," *School Review* (Autumn 1967), pp. 261–266; Norman E. Gronlund, *Stating Behavioral Objectives for Classroom Instruction,* 2nd ed. (New York: Macmillan, 1978); Bruce J. Tuckman, *Evaluating Instructional Programs,* rev. ed. (Boston: Allyn and Bacon, 1979).

tional objectives produces an unmanageable number of objectives, leads to trivia, and wastes a lot of time; they also contend that it is difficult to know or prescribe all of our objectives in advance. The entire procedure becomes too mechanistic and rigid. This difference in opinion is intensified to some extent because specifying classroom goals in terms of precise objectives "goes against tradition, which usually states goals in [broader or] loftier terms of attitudes, analytical skills, understanding, and appreciation of subject matter."[8] The use of taxonomies (discussed in the next section) is considered more acceptable by some critics of the Magerian approach.

Taxonomy

Another way of translating aims into instructional objectives is to categorize the desired outcomes into a classification system analogous to classifying books in a library, chemical elements in a periodic table, or the divisions of the animal kingdom. Through this system, known as a **taxonomy,** standards for classifying our aims and objectives have been established and educators are now better able to communicate and add precision to their language.

Three domains of learning

The educational taxonomy calls for the classification of three domains of learning—cognitive, affective, and psychomotor. It is rooted in Tyler's ideas that (1) all words in a scientific system should be defined in terms of observable events and (2) educational objectives should be operationally defined in terms of performances or outcomes. The *Taxonomy of Educational Objectives, Handbook I: Cognitive Domain* was developed by a committee of thirty-six AERA members headed by Benjamin Bloom. The cognitive domain includes objectives that are related to recall or recognition of knowledge and the development of higher intellectual skills and abilities.[9] The *Taxonomy of Educational Objectives, Handbook II: Affective Domain* by David Krathwohl and his associates is concerned with aims and objectives related to interests, attitudes, and feelings.[10] The psychomotor domain, dealing with manipulative and motor skills, was never completed by the original group of educators. A classification of psychomotor objectives by Anita Harlow closely resembles the intent of the original group and also is based on hierarchical levels.[11]

Below is a brief listing, along with illustrative examples, of the types of objectives of the three domains of learning.

8 Gordon H. Bower and Ernest R. Hilgard, *Theories of Learning*, 5th ed. (Englewood Cliffs, N.J.: Prentice-Hall, 1981), p. 538. Also see R. Douglas Greer, "Contingencies of the Science and Technology of Teaching and Prebehavioristic Research Practices in Education," *Educational Researcher* (January 1983), pp. 3–9; Jere E. Brophy, "If Only It Were True," *Educational Researcher* (January 1983), pp. 10–12.

9 Benjamin S. Bloom et al., *Taxonomy of Educational Objectives, Handbook I: Cognitive Domain* (New York: McKay, 1956).

10 David R. Krathwohl, Benjamin S. Bloom, and Bertram Masia, *Taxonomy of Educational Objectives, Handbook II: Affective Domain* (New York: McKay, 1964).

11 Anita J. Harlow, *Taxonomy of the Psychomotor Domain: A Guide for Developing Behavioral Objectives* (New York: McKay, 1972).

The Cognitive Domain

Cognitive objectives

1. *Knowledge.* Included at this level are objectives related to (1) knowledge of specifics such as terminology and facts; (2) knowledge of ways and means of dealing with specifics such as conventions, trends and sequences, classifications and categories, criteria, and methodologies; and (3) knowledge of universals and abstractions such as principles, generations, theories, and structures. Example: To identify the capital of France.

2. *Comprehension.* Objectives at this level include (1) translation, (2) interpretation, and (3) extrapolation of materials. Example: To interpret a table showing the population density of the world.

3. *Application.* Objectives at this level are related to the use of abstractions in particular situations. Example: To predict the probable effect of a change in temperature on a chemical.

4. *Analysis.* This includes objectives related to breaking a whole into parts and distinguishing (1) elements, (2) relationships, and (3) organizational principles. Example: To deduce facts from a hypothesis.

5. *Synthesis.* This includes objectives related to putting parts together in a new form such as (1) a unique communication, (2) a plan of operation, and (3) a set of abstract relations. Example: To produce an original piece of art.

6. *Evaluation.* This is the highest level of complexity and includes objectives related to judging in terms of (1) internal evidence or logical consistency and (2) external evidence or consistency with facts developed elsewhere. Example: To appraise fallacies in an argument.

The Affective Domain

Affective objectives

1. *Receiving.* This objective is indicative of the learner's sensitivity to the existence of stimuli and includes (1) awareness, (2) willingness to receive, and (3) selected attention. Example: To recognize musical instruments played on a record.

2. *Responding.* This includes active attention to stimuli such as (1) acquiescence, (2) willing responses, and (3) feelings of satisfaction. Example: To contribute to group discussions by asking questions.

3. *Valuing.* Included in this objective are beliefs and attitudes of worth in the form of (1) acceptance, (2) preference, and (3) commitment. Example: To argue over an issue involving health care.

4. *Organization.* This level of internalization involves (1) conceptualization of values and (2) organization of a value system. Example: To organize a meeting concerning a neighborhood's housing integration plan.

5. *Characterization.* This is the highest level of internalization and includes behavior related to (1) a generalized set of values and (2) a characterization or philosophy of life. Example: To wage war in order to preserve a way of life.

The Psychomotor Domain

Psychomotor objectives

1. *Reflex movements.* These objectives include (1) segmental reflexes (involving one spinal segment) and (2) intersegmental reflexes (involving more than one spinal segment). Example: To contract a muscle.

2. *Fundamental movements.* Included in these objectives are behaviors related to (1) walking, (2) running, (3) jumping, (4) pushing, (5) pulling, and (6) manipulating. Example: To run a 100-yard dash.

3. *Perceptual abilities.* These objectives include (1) kinesthetic, (2) visual, (3) auditory, (4) tactile, and (5) coordination abilities. Example: To distinguish distant and close sounds.

4. *Physical abilities.* Included at this level are objectives related to (1) endurance, (2) strength, (3) flexibility, (4) agility, (5) reaction-response time, and (6) dexterity. Example: To do five sit-ups.

5. *Skilled movements.* This includes objectives concerning (1) games, (2) sports, (3) dances, and (4) the arts. Example: To dance the basic steps of the waltz.

6. *Nondiscursive communication.* This level includes objectives related to expressive movement through (1) posture, (2) gestures, (3) facial expressions, and (4) creative movements. Example: To act a part in a play.

Assumes knowledge of previous skills

The categories of the three taxonomies describe levels of complexity from the simple to the more advanced. Each level is built upon and assumes acquisition of the previous skill. One must have knowledge of facts, for example, before he or she can comprehend material. The taxonomy as a whole is a useful source for developing educational objectives and for categorizing and grouping existing sets of objectives. Perhaps the greatest difficulty is deciding between adjacent categories, particularly if the objectives have not been clearly stated. To avoid becoming frustrated while categorizing objectives into appropriate categories, classroom teachers are advised to work in groups and share opinions. By studying and using the taxonomy, you may eventually appreciate it as a valuable tool for implementing objectives and formulating test items.

Basic Guidelines

Some basic guidelines can be set for formulating your instructional objectives regardless of which approach you use.

1. Objectives should be related to aims.
2. Objectives should be appropriate to the subject and the academic level of your students.
3. Objectives should describe behaviors that you actually intend to bring about in class.
4. Objectives should be stated in the form of expected learning outcomes. (We must know precisely what is expected of students.)
5. Objectives should be stated in behavioral terms, that is, they should be observable and/or measurable.
6. Objectives should be stated through action verbs (such as, *to identify* or *to compare*) so as to note finitely observable, measurable behavior.
7. Objectives should be brief and trimmed of excessive wordiness.
8. Objectives should be grouped logically so as to make sense in determining units of instruction and evaluation.
9. Objectives should be periodically revised.
10. In developing objectives, you should feel free to consult other sources for help.[12]

While these approaches sound very logical and appealing, several questions come to mind. For example, whose values should be embodied in formulating the aims of the schools? Should the federal government be involved? Should state officials? Should teacher organizations or teacher representatives? And how should these groups be involved? When we move to objectives, how can both teacher and local community prerogatives be preserved and enhanced? How can communication between educators and parents be improved in the process of formulating objectives?

Questioned relationship between aims and objectives

Other problems also arise. It is a great leap from general aims to behaviorally stated objectives. What evidence is there that those behaviors that are measured bear a reasonably close relationship to these aims? According to one observer, "The enthusiast, sometimes quite unwittingly, still confuses the technical process of stating objectives with the empirical one of establishing real rather than merely assumed relationships between a specific performance measured and a [general aim] desired."[13] The absence of adequate evidence does not destroy the validity of the above approach, but it does raise serious questions about the wisdom of forcing this approach on teachers, as some educators advocate.

Whether the performances we stress and reward in school add up to our expressed aims is a difficult question to answer; in fact, many experienced educators avoid the issue. Admittedly, we lack an educational science that can derive properly inferred objectives from our stated aims even though we have the techniques for stating the objectives rather precisely. But there is

12 Gronlund, *Stating Objectives for Classroom Instruction;* Robert F. Mager, *Troubleshooting* (Belmont, Calif.: Pitman, 1983); and W. James Popham, *Modern Educational Measurement* (Englewood Cliffs, N.J.: Prentice-Hall, 1981).

13 John I. Goodlad, "A Perspective on Accountability," *Phi Delta Kappan* (October 1975), p. 109.

no need for disillusionment—only caution. We can now move on to an examination of some of the major aims of American education.

Historical Perspective

The Mental Discipline Approach

Prior to the twentieth century, subject matter was organized and presented as a mere accounting of information. Improvements were made largely within the broad framework of existing subjects to improve reasoning and mental faculties. Proponents of the **mental discipline approach** believed that the mind is strengthened through mental exercises, just as the body is strengthened by exercising. Social and psychological concerns of the learner were largely ignored. Traditional subjects, such as Latin and geometry, were valued for their cultivation of the intellect; the more difficult the subject and the more the student had to exercise the mind, the greater the value of the subject.

Value of the mental discipline approach

Three major committees of the era (the Committee of Fifteen on Elementary Education, the Committee of Ten on Secondary School Studies, and the Committee on College Entrance Requirements), organized by the NEA between 1893 and 1895, strengthened this educational mold for years to come. As Ellwood Cubberley pointed out, "The committees were dominated by subject-matter specialists, possessed of a profound faith in mental discipline. No study of pupil abilities, social needs, interest, capabilities or differential training found a place in their [committee members] deliberations."[14]

The Committee of Ten's recommendations best illustrate this tough-minded, mental discipline approach. The committee, headed by one of the most influential figures of the time, Harvard University President Charles Eliot, selected nine academic subjects around which to organize the high school curriculum: (1) Latin, (2) Greek, (3) English, (4) other modern languages, (5) mathematics, (6) physics, astronomy, and chemistry, (7) natural history (biology, botany, zoology, and physiology), (8) history, civil government, and political economy, and (9) geography, geology, and meteorology.[15] The committee's refusal to recognize the value of art, music, physical education, and vocational courses was based on the theory that these subjects had little mental or disciplinary value.

Nine academic subjects

In analyzing the effects of the committee's actions, Daniel and Laurel Tanner recently wrote, "The choice of these subjects and the omission of others from consideration was enough to set the course for secondary education" for many years and indirectly set the tone at the elementary school level, too. As "might be expected," the committee suggested that "the nine

Setting the course for many years

14 Ellwood P. Cubberley, *Public Education in the United States,* rev. ed. (Boston: Houghton Mifflin, 1947), p. 543.

15 *Report of the Committee of Ten on Secondary School Studies* (Washington, D.C.: National Education Association, 1894).

subjects be taught sooner" and that all subjects except Latin and Greek be taught at the elementary school level.[16] Even though less than 5 percent of all students at that time went to college, this college preparatory program established a curriculum hierarchy, from elementary school to college, that promoted academics and ignored the majority of students who were noncollege bound.

Progressive education as a new pedagogy

Gradually, however, demands were made for various changes in the school to meet the needs of a changing social order. The pace of immigration and industrial development led a growing number of educators to question the classical curriculum and the constant emphasis on mental discipline and to oppose the methods of incessant drill. The adherents of the new pedagogy represented the growing and influential progressive voice in education. They emphasized schoolwork and school subjects designed to meet the needs of everyday life for *all* children. By the turn of the twentieth century, the effort to reform the schools along more progressive lines was moving into full swing. Out of this movement came a number of committees and organized groups whose new educational aims are still influential.

Cardinal Principles

Perhaps the most widely accepted list of educational aims in the twentieth century was compiled by the Commission on the Reorganization of Secondary Education in 1918. Its influential bulletin was entitled *Cardinal Principles of Secondary Education.* The seven areas of life, or aims of secondary education, designated by the commission are discussed below.

Broadened aims of education

1. *Health.* The secondary school should ... provide health instruction, inculcate health habits, organize an effective program of physical activities, regard health needs in planning work and play, and co-operate with home and community in safeguarding and promoting health interests ....
2. *Command of fundamental processes.* The facility that a child of twelve or fourteen years may acquire ... is not sufficient for the needs of modern life. [Further instruction in the fundamentals is urged.]
3. *Worthy home membership.* Worthy home membership as an objective calls for the development of those qualities that make the individual a worthy member of a family, both contributing to and deriving benefit from that membership ....
4. *Vocation.* Vocational education should equip the individual to secure a livelihood for himself and those dependent on him, to serve society well through his vocation, to maintain the right relationships toward his fellow workers and society, and, as far as possible, to find in that vocation his own best development ....
5. *Civic education.* Civic education should develop in the individual those qualities whereby he will act well his part as a member of neighborhood,

16 Daniel Tanner and Laurel N. Tanner, *Curriculum Development: Theory into Practice,* 2nd ed. (New York: Macmillan, 1980), p. 233.

The whole-child concept emphasizes the encouragement not only of intellectual growth but of social, psychological, and moral growth as well—such as the qualities of caring and concern for a friend's feelings shown by the young girl in this photo. *(Elizabeth Crews)*

town or city, state, and nation, and give him a basis for understanding international problems ....

6. *Worthy use of leisure.* Education should equip the individual to secure from his leisure the recreation of body, mind, and spirit, and the enrichment and enlargement of his personality ....
7. *Ethical character.* In a democratic society ethical character becomes paramount among the objectives of the secondary school. Among the means for

> developing ethical character may be mentioned the wise selection of content and methods of instruction in all subjects of study and the social contacts of pupils with one another and with their teachers.[17]

Educate all youth for "complete living"

The goals cited in 1918 are still found in one form or another in statements of major goals of contemporary education, as may be seen from the discussion to follow. The most important aspect of the document is that it emphasizes the aim of secondary schools to educate *all* youth for "complete living," not just college-bound youth for mental vigor. The commission noted that more than two-thirds of entering high school students dropped out prior to graduation. It endorsed the concept of meeting the various and diverse needs of students, while providing a common ground for teaching and enhancing American ideals and educating all citizens to function in a democratic society.

Purposes of Education in American Democracy

Twenty years later the Educational Policies Commission of the NEA, which included the presidents of Harvard and Cornell, the U.S. commissioner of education, and a number of progressive pedagogical specialists, issued a report entitled *The Purposes of Education in American Democracy.*[18]

Aims in the 1930s

Concerned with the problems of out-of-school youth and unemployment resulting from the Great Depression and with the general need to adjust to daily life patterns, these educators put forth a comprehensive set of four equally important aims (which they called objectives): (1) self-realization, (2) human relations, (3) economic efficiency, and (4) civic responsibility. The objectives of *self-realization* pertained to the inquiring mind, speech, reading, writing, numbers, sight and hearing, health knowledge, health habits, public health, recreation, intellectual interests, aesthetic interests, and character formation. The objectives of *human relationships* concerned respect for humanity, friendship, cooperation with others, courtesy, appreciation of the home, conservation of the home, homemaking, and democracy in the home. The objectives of *economic efficiency* encompassed work, occupational information, occupational choice, occupational efficiency, occupational appreciation, personal economics, consumer judgment, efficiency in buying, and consumer protection. The objectives of *civic responsibility* related to social justice, social activity, social understanding, critical judgment, tolerance, conservation of resources, social applications of science, world citizenship, law observance, economic literacy, political citizenship, and devotion to democracy.

17 Commission on the Reorganization of Secondary Education, *Cardinal Principles of Secondary Education,* Bulletin no. 35 (Washington D.C.: Government Printing Office, 1918), pp. 11–15.

18 Educational Policies Commission, *The Purposes of Education in American Democracy* (Washington, D.C.: National Education Association, 1938).

Education for All American Youth

Aims in the 1940s

During the mid-1940s the Educational Policies Commission continued to modify and formulate the aims of education. Influenced by World War II, it stressed aims related to democracy and world citizenship, as well as those related to the general needs of children and youth. Its most influential report, *Education for All American Youth,* listed "Ten Imperative Needs of Youth." All youth need to develop skills and/or attitudes that enhance the following: (1) productive work experiences and occupational success, (2) good health and physical fitness, (3) rights and duties of a democratic citizenry, (4) conditions for successful family life, (5) wise consumer behavior, (6) understanding of science and the nature of man, (7) appreciation of arts, music, and literature, (8) wise use of leisure time, (9) respect for ethical values, and (10) the ability to think rationally and communicate thoughts clearly.[19]

The whole child

Prior to World War I, the aims of education represented a perennialist philosophy of education and a mental discipline approach to learning. During the period from the 1918 Seven Cardinal Principles to the 1944 Ten Imperative Needs, the aims were dominated by the philosophy of progressivism and by the offshoot science of child psychology. During this period, emphasis was placed on the "whole child" and life adjustment; hence, educational aims stressed social, psychological, vocational, moral, and civic responsibilities. Aims related to cognitive or mental growth were not preeminent at this time; they were simply on a par with other important aims of education. The whole-child concept and the corresponding growth of child psychology had a tremendous impact on the schools. Underlying this movement was the view that schools had to be concerned with the growth and development of the entire child, not just with certain selected mental aspects of the child's growth.

Focus on the Academically Talented

During the era of the Cold War and the Soviet Sputnik flight (1957), international events gave major impetus to the movement to re-examine subject matter. The country was appalled at the notion of losing technological superiority to the Soviets; national pride was challenged; national goals were threatened; physical survival seemed to be at stake.

Return to academic essentials

The critics claimed that there was too much stress on the whole child and on general education at the expense of intellectual rigor. They called for a return to academic essentials and mental discipline. "Concern with the personal problems of adolescents [had] grown so excessive as to push into the background what should be the school's central concern, the intellectual development of its students," stated noted historian Arthur Bestor.[20] Admiral Hyman Rickover wondered why Johnny could not read while Ivan could and

19 Educational Policies Commission, *Education for All American Youth* (Washington, D.C.: National Education Association, 1944).

20 Arthur Bestor, *The Restoration of Learning* (New York: Knopf, 1956), p. 120.

did. He demanded that in the national interest, there be a return to the basics, a beefing up of our science and mathematics courses, and a "de-emphasis of life-adjustment schools and progressive educationalists."[21]

Hard on the heels of Sputnik came national legislation to support training, equipment, and programs in fields deemed vital to defense. The major legislation was the National Defense Education Act, which singled out science, mathematics, modern languages, and guidance (often thought of as a way to steer youth into the three former fields and into college if they had the ability). The focus on certain subjects and academically talented youth was often couched in terms of a free people surviving in a world threatened by the spread of communism. Writing during the aftermath of Sputnik, William Van Til wrote, "The end result was that both national interest and available funds [in education] coincided. The scholars had a genuine opportunity to reconstruct the content of their separate subjects," particularly on the high school level.[22] To many leaders of this period, it was clear that the way to reconstruct subject matter was to call together the scientific community and university scholars who most intimately knew the particular subject, along with some curriculum specialists who might help with regard to methodology. Funds were readily available from government and foundation sources.

National legislation to support our aims

John Gardner, the president of the Carnegie Corporation, expressed the crucial need of the day in his 1956 annual report:

Shift in emphasis to the gifted

> It is not just technologists and scientists that we need, though they rank high in priority. We desperately need our gifted teachers, our professional men, our scholars, our critics, and our seers .... As the cradle of our national leadership, their vitality and excellence become a matter of critical importance.
>
> Concern for the full use of human capacities will produce intensive efforts to salvage the able youngsters who are now lost to higher education.[23]

In 1952, as chairman of the Educational Policies Commission, James Conant had endorsed a progressive policy document that urged a student-centered, whole-child approach to schooling. By 1959 Conant's vision was still to "provide a good general education for *all* the pupils," but there was also an emphasis now on "educating adequately those with a talent for handling advanced subjects."[24] After visiting fifty-five high schools across the country, he concluded:

> If the fifty-five schools I have visited, all of which have a good reputation, are at all representative of American public high schools, I think one general criticism

21 Hyman G. Rickover, *Education and Freedom* (New York: Dutton, 1959), p. 190.

22 William Van Til, "In a Climate of Change," in E. F. Carlson, ed., *Role of Supervisor and Curriculum Director in a Climate of Change,* 1965 ASCD Yearbook (Washington, D.C.: Association for Supervision and Curriculum Development, 1965), p. 21.

23 John W. Gardner, "The Great Talent Hunt," in the *Annual Report for the Fiscal Year Ended September 30, 1956* (New York: Carnegie Corporation, 1956), pp. 12, 20.

24 James B. Conant, *The American High School Today* (New York: McGraw-Hill, 1959), p. 15.

> would be in order: The academically talented student, as a rule, is not being sufficiently challenged, does not work hard enough, and his program of academic subjects is not of sufficient range.[25]

In the midst of intense criticism of schools and school people, Conant came to the defense of the educational establishment and saw little need for radically changing schools. Conant's influential book, *The American High School Today,* was a blueprint for moderate reform—that is, for upgrading the curriculum in general, especially mathematics, science, and foreign language; requiring more academic subjects; tightening standards and grades; pushing students to their maximum cognitive potential; and grouping students according to their abilities. Although he gave some consideration to slow and average learners, his major emphasis for reform still pertained to serving the needs of the highly gifted (the intellectually highest 3 percent of the student population on a national basis) and the academically talented (the top 20 percent in terms of scholastic aptitude).

Moderate reform

Many of the policy statements during this period focused on the academically bright student, although each expressed concern for every child, whatever his or her capabilities. Various aims were listed, but great emphasis was placed on identifying and developing the abilities of the talented, as well as on the three Rs and on academic subjects such as English, foreign languages, science, and mathematics, as well as on ability grouping and testing.

Ability grouping and testing

Focus on Disadvantaged Students

During the 1960s the social conscience of America burst forth—coinciding with concern over poverty, racial discrimination, and equal educational opportunity. Hence, new aims and educational priorities surfaced. The majority of students at that time did not go on to college and a large percentage of students dropped out of school or graduated as functional illiterates. Under those circumstances serious problems could be anticipated if our aims and priorities continued to be narrowly directed at our most able students. The shift to the problems of disadvantaged students gradually accelerated until this population became the number-one concern in education. The swing was exemplified by the changes in the writings of the same educators—John Gardner and James Conant—who previously had stressed the need to challenge the gifted student.

Number-one concern in education

At first the shift was gradual, and this can be illustrated by John Gardner's concern for both the talented and underachieving child, for both excellence and equality. Questioning whether we can be equal and excellent too, he concluded that

> No democracy can give itself over to extreme emphasis on individual performance and still remain a democracy—or to extreme equalitarianism and retain its vitality . . . .

25 Ibid., p. 40

> A society such as ours has no choice but to seek the development of human potentialities at all levels. It takes more than an educated elite to run a complex, technological society. Every modern, industrialized society is learning that hard lesson.[26]

Gardner noted that extreme forms of equalitarianism and proportional representation of groups in school or jobs tend to eliminate both excellence and merit, but that, on the other hand, extreme forms of elitism based on excellence and merit could create a permanent underclass among the less able. He tried to draw a middle position, sounding a note of urgency that other educators would soon echo.

A middle position

In 1961, the same year that John Gardner's book was published, James Conant wrote *Slums and Suburbs.* Only two years before, Conant had advocated academic rigor and upgraded academic subjects, as well as greater attention to the top 20 percent of the high school graduates. Now he urged educators and policy makers to pay closer attention to the inner-city and disadvantaged child. He urged that slum schools be upgraded and greater attention be given to the less able student. Conant wrote:

Closer attention to the disadvantaged child

> I am concerned we are allowing social dynamite to accumulate in our large cities. I am not nearly so concerned about the plight of the suburban parents [and their children] who have difficulty finding places in prestige colleges as I am about the plight of parents in the slums whose children either drop out or graduate from school without prospects of either future education or employment .... Leaving aside human tragedies, I submit that a continuation of this situation [youth out of school and out of work] is a menace to the social and political health of the large cities.
>
> The improvement of slum conditions is only in part a question of improving education. But the role of the schools is of utmost importance .... Added responsibility, however, requires additional funds. Indeed, the whole question of financing public education in the large cities is a major national concern.[27]

Conant's new position was a sign of the times—a shift in educational aims to focus on the disadvantaged. Historically a strong advocate of academic excellence, and a former scientist, he was expressing a new viewpoint: one that would correct the educational discrepancies among students by placing greater emphasis on less able students, especially inner-city students.

Social upheaval of the 1960s

Given the student unrest and urban riots of the 1960s, it was easy to accept the arguments of an impacted crisis in schools and society. The government reports that were published in the 1960s strongly suggested an impending social upheaval. The needs of disadvantaged groups were stressed, both in schools and society; and these needs were reflected in reports of the National Advisory Commission on Civil Disorders in 1967 and the National Advisory Council on the Education of Disadvantaged Children in 1969. A

26 John W. Gardner, *Excellence: Can We Be Equal and Excellent Too?* (New York: Harper & Row, 1961), pp. 74, 77.

27 James B. Conant, *Slums and Suburbs* (New York: McGraw-Hill, 1961), p. 2.

new political bias seemed to evolve; in education it overlooked the average and above-average student, and in social and economic arenas it overlooked what was later to be called "middle America."

Expanded Priorities

Multicultural, bilingual, and handicapped students

The focus on the disadvantaged extended into the 1970s, but the definition of the disadvantaged was expanded to include multicultural, bilingual, and handicapped students—and to a lesser extent women. Our multicultural and bilingual efforts were characterized by increased federal funding for Hispanic, Asian American, and Native American students; by the Bilingual Education Act in 1968, which expanded bilingual programs in American schools; and by the 1974 U.S. Supreme Court ruling in *Lau* v. *Nicholas,* which stated that schools must take steps to help students who "are certain to find their classroom experiences wholly incomprehensible" because they do not understand English. The courts, as well as policy makers and educators, took an active role in providing educational opportunities for limited-English-speaking (LES) and non-English-speaking (NES) students. Despite controversies concerning specific approaches and programs and recruitment of personnel that have surfaced (see Chapter 12), multicultural and bilingual education are growing in importance and will continue to impact on our schools in the 1980s.

New certification requirements

During the 1970s, much activity and concern surfaced for special education, especially for handicapped and learning disabled students. New pressure groups, new courses, advanced degrees, new certification requirements, and new teachers and new faculty at colleges and universities stimulated recognition of special education, as have new policies and programs. The cornerstone of these policies and programs can be traced to passage of the Education for All Handicapped Children Act (PL 94-142) in 1975.

Handicapped students are defined by the act as those who are mentally retarded, hard of hearing, deaf, orthopedically impaired, other health impaired, speech impaired, visually handicapped, emotionally disturbed, and children with specific learning disabilities who by reason thereof require special education and related services. The legislation mandates a free and appropriate public education for all handicapped children and youth. Handicapped students must be provided with special education and related services at public expense under public supervision and direction. Schools must adopt policies that serve all handicapped students and conduct searches to locate such students.

Searching for handicapped students

Today concern for the handicapped is very much alive, and the courts continue to take an active role in protecting the rights of and improving educational opportunities for the handicapped. Monies earmarked for the handicapped continue to increase in real dollars and in proportion to spending on nonhandicapped students; moreover, an increasing number of students are being identified as handicapped. Approximately 10 to 12 percent of the pub-

Serving more handicapped students

lic school enrollment are considered handicapped, and we are presently spending twice the national average of $2,000 annually to educate these students.[28] This increase indicates that educators and policy makers recognize that many students who did not receive help in the past in fact need special help—not that contemporary students have more problems than students of earlier generations.

Concern for the gifted and talented student reached a low point during the 1960s and 1970s. The commitment to educating the gifted and talented child was slight compared to efforts directed at the disadvantaged and at other special populations, such as the bilingual, handicapped, or learning disabled student. As two authorities stated in the mid-1970s, only "a very small percentage of the gifted and talented population [was] being serviced by existing programs, [about] 4 percent of the 1.5 to 2.5 million children."[29] A low funding priority and lack of trained personnel, coupled with few pressure groups for the gifted and talented, resulted in a scarcity of programs for these children—who in terms of numbers represent a real minority.

Minimal funding for gifted and talented students

National priorities in the 1970s (like those in the 1960s) for the most part did not focus on the average, ordinary student who was nonrich, nonpoor, nonminority, nongifted, and non-newsworthy. There was (and still is) very little in the educational literature on the cultural, social, and educational diversity of students in "middle" America—what it is like to grow up or to go to school in Astoria, New York; Lombard, Illinois; or Whittier, California. Because they were rarely defined as a special group with special characteristics and needs, remedial or special programs for these students were minimal. In the late 1970s and early 1980s, some attention was unwittingly devoted to them as a result of other trends, such as the national testing program, minimum competency testing, basic skills programs, and the theme of national excellence in schools, but special programs and services for the average child remain minimal.

Needs of average students

Educational Aims of the 1980s

In the 1980s national attention turned to the need for educational excellence and higher academic standards for all students. The educational dimensions of this problem were amply documented in a number of policy reports released in 1983, all calling for reforms to improve the quality of education in the United States.

Policy reports call for reform

28 *Digest of Educational Statistics, 1982* (Washington, D.C.: National Center for Education Statistics, 1982), table 33, p. 42; Daniel U. Levine and Allan C. Ornstein, "Some Trends in Educating Handicapped Students," *Journal of Curriculum Studies* (July 1981), pp. 261–265.

29 A. Harry Passow and Abraham J. Tannenbaum, "Education of the Gifted and Talented," *Bulletin of National Association of Secondary School Principals* (March 1976), pp. 4–5. Also see Abraham J. Tannenbaum, *Gifted Children: Their Psychology and Education* (New York: Macmillan, 1983).

Overview of Policy Reports

Documenting the decline in American education

To support their alarming statements about the decline of American education, and the need for academic reform, the policy reports detailed a host of devastating trends and statistics:

1. Schools and colleges had shifted away from requiring students to take what had twenty years ago been the standard academic core curriculum for graduation: foreign language, mathematics, science, English, and history; elective courses and remedial courses have replaced standard academic courses.
2. Requirements for graduation had been lowered; fewer students were enrolled in rigorous or even academic courses. (According to a recent National Science Foundation report, only 9 percent of high school graduates take one year of physics; 16 percent take one year of chemistry; less than 5 percent of American students study a foreign language beyond the first year, and only 15 percent study a language at all).
3. Grade inflation was on the rise, and students were required to complete less homework (75 percent of high school students complete less than one hour of homework a night).
4. Average achievement scores on the Scholastic Aptitude Tests (SAT) demonstrate a virtually unbroken decline from 1963 to 1980. Average verbal scores fell over 50 points and mathematics scores dropped nearly 40 points.
5. International comparisons of student achievement, completed a decade ago, reveal that on nineteen academic tests American students were never first or second and, in comparison with other industrialized nations, were last seven times.
6. Some 23 to 25 million American adults are functionally illiterate by the simplest tests of everyday reading and writing.
7. About 13 percent of all seventeen year olds in the United States are considered functionally illiterate, and this illiteracy rate jumps to 40 percent among minority youth.
8. ***Complaints of business and military*** Business and military leaders complain that they are required to spend millions of dollars annually on costly remedial education and training programs in the basic skills or three Rs. Between 1975 and 1980, remedial mathematics courses in four-year colleges increased by 72 percent and now constitute one-fourth of all mathematics courses taught in these institutions. As many as 25 percent of the recruits in the Armed Forces cannot read at the ninth-grade level.[30]

These deficiencies come at a time when the demand for highly skilled military personnel and workers in labor and industry is accelerating rapidly and

30 The above figures are found in the five policy reports discussed in this section.

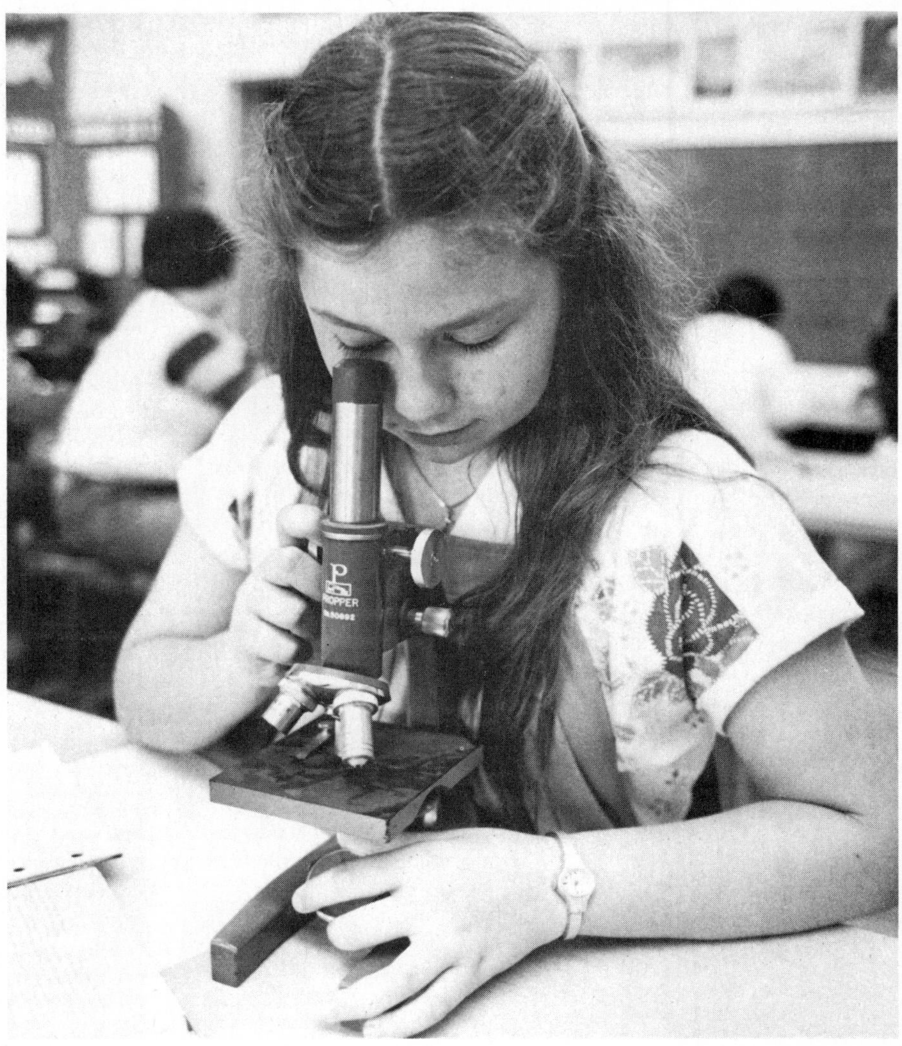

A key educational aim of the 1980s is the need for academic excellence and higher standards for all students.
(Jim Anderson/Woodfin Camp and Associates)

amidst growing concern that the United States is being overtaken by other nations in commerce, industry, science, and technology.

Emphasis on academic and gifted students

The five major reports released in 1983 are summarized in Overview 13.1. All of the reports emphasize the need to strengthen the curriculum in the core subjects of English, math, science, foreign language, and social studies. Technology and computer courses are often mentioned, either as a component of science or math or as a separate subject area. High-level cognitive and thinking skills are also stressed. While many of the reports are concerned with all students, they stress academic, college-bound, and even gifted students.

Overview 13.1

Selected Recommendations of Five National Reports on Education Published in 1983

Theme	***Academic Preparation for College*** **(The College Board)**	***Making the Grade*** **(Twentieth Century Fund)**
Curriculum objectives	Improve preparation in English, math, science, computers, foreign languages, the arts. Improve student competencies in reading, writing, speaking, listening, reasoning, math, study skills. Raise college entrance requirements.	Improve English language and advanced learning in math and science. Initiate alternative programs for students with learning problems and a voucher program for disadvantaged students.
School practices	Emphasize improvement of study and independent learning skills.	No comparable provision.
Federal role	Develop a national standard for academic achievement in secondary education.	Emphasis on the federal government providing special education programs for poor, minority, immigrant, and handicapped students. Similar emphasis on the federal government providing programs to develop scientific literacy among all citizens and advanced math and science training for secondary students.

All the reports emphasize tougher curricula standards and courses. With the exception of *Making the Grade,* all five reports mention the need for colleges to raise their admissions requirements. Because the reports for the most part center on curriculum requirements involving academic subject matter and college requirements, the reports as a group seem much more oriented to secondary than elementary education.

Overview 13.1 (cont.)

Selected Recommendations of Five National Reports on Education Published in 1983

***Educating Americans for the 21st Century* (National Science Foundation)**	***Action for Excellence* (Education Commission of the States)**	***A Nation at Risk* (The National Commission on Excellence in Education)**
Require one hour daily of math and thirty minutes of science in grades K–6. Devote more time to math and science in the secondary grades and provide more advanced courses. Raise college entrance requirements.	Establish and improve minimum competencies in reading, writing, speaking, listening, reasoning, economics. Strengthen programs for gifted students. Raise college entrance requirements.	Strengthen graduation requirements in the five "new basics": English, math, science, social studies, and computer science. Increase foreign languages for the college-bound. Provide rigorous courses in vocational education and arts. Raise college entrance requirements.
Consider longer school day, week, and/or year.	Consider longer school day. Emphasize order and discipline and more rigorous grading with periodic testing. Assign more homework. Revitalize the curriculum to encourage independent learning and reduce dropout rates.	Consider 7-hour school day and 200-day school year. Tighten attendance and discipline. Provide periodic testing and more rigorous grading. Place and group students by performance rather than age. Assign more homework. Improve textbooks and other instructional materials.
Federal government should maintain a national mechanism for measuring student performance; it should have input in establishing national goals for education.	Create policies that foster partnerships between the private sector and education. Federal government has an essential supporting role in financing education.	Federal government, in cooperation with the states and localities, should help meet the needs of special populations such as the disadvantaged, minority, and bilingual students; the handicapped, gifted, and talented. Advocates national standardized tests, and the identification of the national interest in education.

With regard to school practices, three of the reports—*Educating Americans for the 21st Century, Action for Excellence,* and *A Nation at Risk*—recommend increasing homework, time for learning, and time in school. Authors of *A Nation at Risk* and *Action for Excellence* strongly encourage more rigorous grading, testing, homework, and discipline. The College Board's *Academic Preparation for College* and *Action for Excellence* also stress improvement of student competencies in skill areas such as reading, writing, and reasoning, rather than in subject areas.

Educational improvement in the national interest

As for the federal role in education, many of the reports use such terms as "emergency," "urgency," "crucial to national survival," "global competition," and the like—reminding us of the post-Sputnik era. The implications of many reports, especially *Making the Grade, Educating Americans for the 21st Century,* and *A Nation at Risk,* are likely to enhance the federal role in education.

All of the reports are concerned that the schools are pressed to play too many social roles, that the schools cannot meet all these expectations, and that they are in danger of losing sight of their key role of teaching the basic skills and the core academic subjects (math, science, English, foreign language, and history or civics), new skills for computer use, and high-level skills for the world of work and technology. The reports consider the restoration of academic excellence to be the overriding national aim. It is basic and imperative for effective educational reform. The individual reports are discussed in the following pages.

Academic Preparation for College The Educational Equality Project of the College Board combines the judgments of hundreds of school and college educators in an attempt to strengthen the academic quality of secondary education.[31] Although the project members take the position that we can have both excellence and equality of opportunity, they focus on academic preparation as the essential recommendation for reform; in fact, the project grew out of concern over the drop in academic standards, cited as a major cause of the decline in SAT scores, and a softening of college admission requirements.

Six basic academic competencies

The report, *Academic Preparation for College,* outlines what college entrants need to know and what they should be able to do. Reading, writing, speaking, computation skills, reasoning, and studying are considered to be the six basic academic competencies; computer skills appears as an afterthought and is described as an emerging need. The six areas of competencies (not including computer skills) cut across the disciplines; they are considered to be interrelated and interdependent as well as being prerequisites for learning the basic academic subjects (listed below) and for learning how to learn. "Without such competencies . . ., knowledge of academic subjects is unattainable."[32] At the same time, learning the basic academic subjects strengthens these competencies.

The basic academic competencies may appear to be a rehash of old favorites. Although not new, these skills have not previously been identified as explicitly as they are in the project report, which defines them in measurable terms. Each academic competency contains a corresponding list of abilities,

31 Educational Equality Project, *Academic Preparation for College* (New York: The College Board, 1983).

32 Ibid., p. 7.

so that students and teachers know what is expected of them and so that outcomes can be achieved.

The second element of the report is the specification and rationale for studying the six basic academic subjects. The report asks and answers the question, Why do students need to study English, the arts, mathematics, science, social studies, and foreign language? The explanations are significant in an era of academic decline because they establish new expectations, actually national standards for academic achievement, for those who set educational policy and plan curriculum.

Counteracting academic decline

In general, the report emphasizes doing well, not just doing time; it focuses on results and learning outcomes. Most important, it presents the teaching and learning of academic competencies in conjunction with academic subjects. This represents a broad based, comprehensive, behavioral, back-to-basics, discipline-based approach to learning.

Making the Grade The report of the Twentieth Century Fund Task Force also asserts that the schools are involved in too many social causes, drifting from one to another, and that they are in danger of losing sight of their fundamental purpose; that is teaching basic and complex thinking skills.[33]

Losing sight of fundamental purpose

Although the task force supports the common commitment to local and state control of schools, it advocates more federal monies for and commitment to improving education and helping state and local governments meet their school responsibilities. It goes so far as to suggest a common curriculum, with federal input, to guarantee the teaching of basic skills at the elementary level and complex skills at the secondary level. The report focuses on upgrading science and mathematics education and links this to a crucial national need. Task force members believe the federal government must provide financial incentives to increase our supply of teachers in science, mathematics, and foreign language. The report is also concerned that many students are not literate in formal English and communication skills. Its authors believe the federal government must support and increase programs for students with limited command of the English language, and it must insure that all students have the opportunity to learn a foreign language.

Science, math, and national needs

As for equality, the task force applauds past and current federal efforts to insure that the needs of special students—the disadvantaged, handicapped, non-English speaking—are met, despite the inability of many states or local governments to do so. It asks the federal government to intensify its efforts to provide financial assistance for compensatory and special education programs. It suggests, however, that the federal government monitor activities to insure that its support is not misdirected.

Increasing the federal role in education

Finally, the task force reminds us that the schools have the preeminent responsibility for educating our children and youth—and for shaping the fu-

33 Twentieth Century Fund Task Force, *Making The Grade: Report on Federal Elementary and Secondary Education Policy* (New York: The Twentieth Century Fund, 1983).

Human resources capital

ture character and minds of our people. No government can afford to ignore its most precious resources, particularly when there is ample evidence those resources are not being developed to their fullest potential.

Educating Americans for the 21st Century The National Science Board Commission, appointed by the National Science Foundation, issued its report under the lengthy title *Educating Americans for the 21st Century: A Plan for Action for Improving Mathematics, Science, and Technology for All American Elementary and Secondary Students So That Their Achievement Is the Best in the World by 1995.*[34] "The nation that led the world into the age of technology is failing to provide its own children with the intellectual tools needed for the 21st century,"[35] begins the report. The report compares Americans' international achievement scores in science and math with the scores of students from other technological nations and warns that "we must return to basics, but the basics of the 21st century are not only reading, writing, and arithmetic,"—[they also include] communication and higher problem-solving skills, and scientific and technological literacy—the thinking tools that allow us to understand the technological world around us."[36]

Scientific and technological literacy

In addition to raising requirements in math, science, and technology in elementary and secondary schools, the commission calls for minimum state-mandated requirements for high school graduation. These requirements would include three years of mathematics and three years of science and technology, including one semester of computer science. The report calls for increased federal involvement to produce essential talent, such as trained doctors and scientists; to provide leadership to improve the quality of the school's program in math, science, and technology; and to establish national goals for education. The commission would establish national goals for education, ensure the assessment of student achievement on the national level, and monitor progress annually.

Vital talent

Action for Excellence The report of the Task Force on Education for Economic Growth, sponsored by the Education Commission of the States, is titled *Action for Excellence.*[37] The task force included thirteen governors, fourteen chief executives of major corporations, six educators, four leaders of educational organizations, and one head of a labor union. The report talks about international industrial competition, the obsolescence of skills, and the need for schools to change their concepts of literacy and basic skills. It calls for emphasizing "basic skills" and "high-order skills" to meet the demand for "highly skilled human capital" in the "new era of global competition." In general, the skills identified are geared to industrial-business productivity. In ad-

Skilled human capital

34 The National Science Board Commission, *Educating Americans for the 21st Century* (Washington, D.C.: National Science Foundation, 1983).

35 Ibid., p. v.

36 Ibid., p. 10.

37 Task Force on Education for Economic Growth, *Action for Excellence: A Comprehensive Plan to Improve Our Nation's Schools* (Denver, Colo.: Education Commission of the States, 1983).

dition, the report advocates that industrial leaders participate with school managers in school planning, budgeting, and management and that they conduct realistic courses about the world of work in the factories and offices of American industry.

A Nation at Risk The report by the National Commission on Excellence in Education, compiled by a panel appointed by the Department of Education, indicates that the well-being of the nation is presently being eroded by a rising tide of mediocrity.[38] This mediocrity is linked to the foundations of our educational institutions and is spilling over into the workplace and other sectors of society. What was unimaginable a generation ago has begun to occur—other nations are surpassing our educational attainments and industrial output.

Rising tide of mediocrity

"If an unfriendly foreign power had attempted to impose on America the mediocre educational performance that exists today, we might well have viewed it as an act of war." We have in effect, "been committing an act of unthinkable, unilateral educational disarmament." Given present educational trends, for the first time in our history, "the educational skills of one generation will not surpass, will not equal, will not even approach, those of their parents."[39]

Educational disarmament

The report lists several aspects of educational decline—lower achievement scores, lower testing requirements, lower graduation requirements, lower teacher expectations, fewer academic or solid courses, more remedial courses, and higher illiteracy rates. The report states that the United States has compromised its commitment to educational quality as a result of conflicting demands placed on the nation's schools and concludes that the schools have attempted to tackle too many social problems that the home and other agencies of society either will not or cannot resolve.

The report calls for, among other things, tougher standards for graduation, including more courses in science, mathematics, foreign language, and the "new basics" such as computer skills; a longer school day and school year; far more homework; improved and updated textbooks; more rigorous, measurable, and higher expectations for student achievement; higher teacher salaries, based on performance, and career ladders that distinguish among the beginning, experienced, and master teacher; demonstrated entry competencies and more rigorous certification standards for teachers; accountability from educators and policy makers; and greater fiscal support from citizens.

Longer school day and year

Assessment of the Reports

Some Criticisms Although nearly all educators have welcomed the increased public attention that followed publication of the national reports and

38 National Commission on Excellence in Education, *A Nation at Risk: The Imperative for Educational Reform* (Washington, D.C.: U.S. Department of Education, 1983).

39 Ibid., p. 14.

studies, many have offered severe criticisms of and serious reservations about one or more of the findings and recommendations. Some of the most frequently expressed concerns and criticisms—particularly regarding *A Nation at Risk*—are summarized in the following list.

Idealistic and unrealistic

1. The reports are too idealistic and unrealistic. Many schools are so far behind in teaching even "minimum competencies" that in no way can they bring students up to standards represented by these reports.
2. Most of the reports focus too much attention on course requirements, standards, and time considerations rather than on the cognitive skills to be mastered, the extent of mastery to be attained by students, and the fact that many noncognitive skills are important, too.
3. The recommendations may be considered merely a rehash of the past. Writes one observer, "the 'new' recommendations are actually old recommendations. . . . I don't know what they will accomplish that they didn't accomplish in the past."[40]
4. The reports largely ignore what is known about school change and improvement, that the process is complex and involves teachers, school administrators, and community members. The reports gloss over the resistance to and realities of change. State and local officials should, therefore, examine these reports carefully before adopting their recommendations.

Glossing over reality

5. The reports support elitist solutions to educational reform—emphasizing requirements for advanced courses, special programs for the gifted and talented, and higher graduation and college admission standards. There is little doubt that the reports leave themselves vulnerable to such charges by largely ignoring the particular problems of low-achieving students.

Limited resources and competing priorities

6. Changes called for in the reports will be enormously expensive to implement effectively, and come at a time when the federal government has been reducing support for education. Many educators are concerned because the national reports do not clearly inform the public of the high cost of carrying out their proposals. While it is true that school districts and governments easily can "accomplish" such changes as more rigorous graduation requirements merely by mandating them, the history of school improvement efforts shows that substantial funding is required to initiate and support effective change on a school-by-school basis. In addition, many of the recommendations have high direct costs. For example, the American Association of School Administrators estimates that implementation of just two proposals from *A Nation at Risk*—raising salaries of beginning teachers to a "market-sensitive" level and lengthening the time spent in school to seven hours a day for 200 days a year—will require a 27 percent increase in existing school budgets.[41]

40 William G. Spady, "The Illusion of Reform," *Educational Leadership* (October 1983), pp. 31–32.

41 *The Cost of Reform* (Arlington, Va.: American Association of School Administrators, 1984).

Impact and Implementation Despite the criticisms by some members of the educational establishment, the reports have created national excitement, captured national attention, and spotlighted nationwide concern for the quality of education. Publication and discussion of these and other national reports and studies have reinforced and accelerated many federal, state, and local activities designed to improve education. (Many observers variously refer to the reports and subsequent actions as a "flood," an "avalanche," or an "explosion.")

Major reaction

By late 1983, the U.S. Department of Education compiled a list of actions that had been taken, largely at the state level, to improve the quality of education. Titled *Meeting the Challenge: Recent Efforts to Improve Education Across the Nation,* the report provided a state-by-state summary of new developments in educational legislation and policy. The department's compilation indicated that forty-two states had undertaken curriculum reform, forty-four had increased high school graduation requirements, twenty-nine had increased college entrance standards, many had moved toward a longer school day or school year, forty-two had introduced initiatives regarding teacher certification or preparation, and twenty had raised teacher salaries.[42]

The reports are intended to act as a starting point—not a blueprint—for reform. Although a good deal of goal setting remains at the local and state levels, a framework at the national level has been established. There exists now the climate for and the criteria against which to measure national educational reform, which can and should filter down to schools throughout the nation.

Swings of the Pendulum

In examining the aims of education from the turn of the twentieth century until today, we see considerable reiteration, but we also note considerable evolution: from education for mental discipline to the whole-child concept, from the emphasis on academically oriented students to nonacademic students and again to academically oriented students. These aims appear to be linked to the sweep of social change. For example, the early twentieth-century adherents of mental discipline advocated rigorous intellectual training, as did the essentialist critics and conservative thinkers of the 1950s and 1980s. At the turn of the century public schools stressed an academic curriculum, and this priority reasserted itself during the era of the Cold War and the space race; it is reappearing in the 1980s as a result of concern over economic competition with foreign countries. In the early 1900s progressive educators sought to broaden the aims of school to serve all children and youth, especially nonacademic and vocationally oriented students; beginning in the

Social change

42 U.S. Department of Education, *Meeting the Challenge: Recent Efforts to Improve Education Across the Nation* (Washington, D.C.: U.S. Department of Education, November 1983).

early 1960s and continuing into the 1970s this priority reappeared with emphasis on poor and minority students, and later handicapped students. While concern for disadvantaged groups remains, the pendulum has now moved to the center—even past it; our priorities are more diffuse, and there is concern for various other students—including average, academic, and talented groups.

Moving to the center

In looking at the broad sweep of American educational aims you may ask yourself the question: Are the schools expected to do more than is feasible? Increasingly, the schools are being burdened by the rest of society with roles and responsibilities that other agencies and institutions no longer do very well, or, for that matter, want to do. The schools are seen as ideal agencies to solve the nation's problems. Many people refuse to admit to their own responsibilities in helping children develop their capabilities and adjust to society. More and more, the schools are being told that they must educate *all* children, regardless of the initial input.

Demands of interest groups

The importance of social pressure and various interest groups also needs to be stressed. As society changes, and as different groups seek to further their interests and promote their causes, the aims of education must change. Thus, rarely will there be complete agreement on the aims of education, much less on what the schools should teach. Popular rhetoric and slogans of the day, as well as the demands of interest groups, must be balanced by a consideration for the good of the general public.

So long as society is dynamic and composed of a conglomeration of cultural and social groups, the debate over the means and ends of education will stir up controversy. Perhaps this is good; perhaps this is what makes a society viable and able to resist decay. Indeed, this controversy is as old as Western civilization itself. More than 2,000 years ago Aristotle wrote:

> As things are . . . mankind [is] by no means agreed about the existing things to be taught. The existing practice is perplexing, no one knowing on what principle we should proceed. . . . About the means there is no agreement; for different persons, starting with different ideas about the nature of virtue, naturally disagree about the practice of it.[43]

Education must be relevant

Unquestionably, aims of education must be relevant or meaningful to the times. If the schools are not adaptable to changing conditions and social forces, how can they expect to produce people who are? This issue is pointedly illustrated in a satire on education entitled *The Saber-Tooth Curriculum.*[44] It describes a society in which the major tasks for survival were catching fish to eat, clubbing horses, and frightening away saber-tooth tigers. The school in this society set up a curriculum to meet its needs: namely, teaching courses in these three areas of survival. Eventually conditions changed: the

43 *The Works of Aristotle, Politics,* Book VIII, trans. B. Jowett (Oxford: Clarendon Press, 1921), p. 1338.

44 Harold Benjamin, *The Saber-Tooth Curriculum* (New York: McGraw-Hill, 1939).

streams dried up, and the horses and tigers disappeared. Social change necessitated learning new tasks for survival, but the school curriculum continued to feature catching fish, clubbing horses and frightening saber-toothed tigers. Today we live in a highly technical, automated, and bureaucratic society; we are faced with pressing social and economic problems—aging cities, the effects of centuries of racial and sexual discrimination, an aging population, unemployment and a displaced workforce, exhaustion of our natural resources, the pollution of the physical environment, and the threat of nuclear devastation. These forces and trends are highly interrelated, mutually reinforce each other, and are accelerating. In an era of space technology, telecommunication, computers, and robots, schools cannot continue to teach the skills that were appropriate for the Industrial Revolution. Whether we allow the times to engulf us, or whether we can cope with our new environment will depend to a large extent on what kinds of skills are taught to our present-day students—and on the development of appropriate national aims of education.

Coping with change

Summing Up

1. We must learn to live with some disagreement about what the schools are all about and what the aims of education should be.
2. Aims are usually translated into objectives at the classroom level. Two popular methods for writing objectives are based on the Magerian approach and the use of taxonomies. The educational taxonomy entails three domains of learning: cognitive, affective, and psychomotor.
3. As society changes, so do the aims of education. Since the turn of the century, American aims of education have gone through at least five periods, each with a different focus of attention: academic rigor and mental discipline; the whole child; academically talented students; disadvantaged, minority, and handicapped students; and, in the 1980s, tougher academic standards for all students.
4. Five major reports released in 1983 emphasized the need for educational excellence and higher academic standards in our schools.
5. As we approach the end of the 1980s, one of the chief aims of society seems to be that the schools became a key instrument for solving our technological problems and preparing our workforce for the future. The years ahead will severely test this aim.

Discussion Questions

1. In terms of aims and objectives, why is the question "What are schools for?" so complex?
2. Why is the bulletin *Cardinal Principles of Secondary Education* such an important milestone in American education? How did it differ from later approaches or reports? Do the seven principles seem valid today?
3. Are the proposed objectives of the Educational Policies Commission, set forth in *The Purpose of Education in American Democracy* and *Education for All American Youth,* desirable objectives for education today? How might you modify them?

4. Who should have educational priority: underachievers, average students, or above-average students?
5. Why is it important for the aims of education to change as society changes?

Suggested Readings

Bloom, Benjamin S., et al. *Taxonomy of Educational Objectives, Handbook I: Cognitive Domain.* New York: McKay, 1956.

A classic text on how to write behavioral objectives in the cognitive domain of learning.

Conant, James B. *The American High School Today.* New York: McGraw-Hill, 1959.

Written during the Sputnik era, the book focuses on many recommendations for upgrading the high school curriculum.

Cremin, Lawrence A. *Traditions of American Education.* New York: Basic Books, 1977.

A historical treatment of schooling and the social structure of American education.

Gardner, John W. *Excellence: Can We Be Equal and Excellent Too?* New York: Harper & Row, 1961.

Written about twenty-five years ago, the theme remains relevant today; the questions and issues raised still elicit concern in American schools and society.

Mager, Robert F. *Troubleshooting.* Belmont, Calif.: Pitman, 1983.

A book on how to write behavioral objectives.

National Commission on Excellence in Education. *A Nation at Risk: The Imperative for Educational Reform.* Washington, D.C.: U.S. Department of Education, 1983.

Among the recent reports on American education, this one has had the most political impact.

Walberg, Herbert J., ed. *Improving Educational Standards and Productivity.* Berkeley, Calif.: McCutchan, 1982.

A series of essays on how to improve the schools and improve educational productivity.

14

Curriculum and Instruction

Focusing Questions

How does curriculum content reflect changes in society?

What forces affect curriculum change?

What are some of the ways in which curriculum may be organized?

How might your work as a teacher be different in a school that utilizes team teaching? flexible scheduling? computerized instruction?

What are some of the instructional innovations that characterize the era of school reform?

What are some trends that seem likely to affect curriculum and instruction?

AMERICANS—PERHAPS MORE THAN CITIZENS OF ANY OTHER country—have demanded the utmost from their schools. We ask the schools to teach children to think, to socialize them, to alleviate poverty and inequality, to reduce crime, to perpetuate our cultural heritage, and to produce intelligent, patriotic citizens. Inevitably, American schools have been unable to meet all of these obligations. Nonetheless, the American public continues to demand much from its schools, and it is the **curriculum**—the planned experiences provided through instruction—that is the focal point of these demands. Consequently, the curriculum is continuously modified as the goals and objectives of the schools are revised, as student populations change, as issues are debated, as interest groups are activated, and as society changes. Keep these concepts in mind as this chapter sweeps through time to note the shifts in curriculum and to put our curricular heritage in perspective.

As we examine curriculum, we will also examine instructional activities that relate to curriculum. To some extent they are intertwined. Teaching a curriculum involves instruction, which is the process of a curriculum—its methods and materials. Although some educators argue for a separation, based on theoretical and traditional grounds, other educators recognize that in reality the two realms of knowledge need to be synthesized. As a result, some schools of education offer separate courses in curriculum and instruction, while others combine some of them.

Curriculum involves instruction

Historical Influences

Part 2 examined the historical development of the American schools. Here we will briefly summarize the historical factors that shaped curriculum. A changing society demands changes in education, which, in turn, require changes in the curriculum. That is to say, as the role of schools changes, the aims and objectives are modified and so is the curriculum. By analyzing the historical trends in curriculum, we may better understand the themes that pervade curriculum today.

A changing society requires curriculum changes

As noted in Chapter 5, three different regional attitudes toward the functions of education arose during colonial times. In the New England colonies education was considered to be the responsibility of the commonwealth. The middle Atlantic colonies saw education as a function of the local community, or more precisely, the local religious denominational group. In the southern colonies, responsibility for education was left to the family. With the exception of the rich, who could afford private education, parental neglect of children's education was evident in the South. In general, the major purpose of education during the colonial years was to meet the needs of religion; learning the catechism and various prayers was a part of the reading program. As the schools evolved, the three Rs were stressed, and the practical values of reading, writing, and doing simple mathematical sums were associated with the new occupations and apprenticeship programs.

Early emphasis on religion and the three Rs

Instruction was usually inadequate; it consisted mostly of rote recitations and oral readings. Attitudes toward children were steeped in Calvinist traditions. Children were born in sin, and it was the function of the teacher (and other adults) to beat the sin out of them.[1] The famous *New England Primer* was the most widely used book in colonial schools for more than a hundred years; all the editions contained the alphabet, some sounds, and syllables. The content was of a religious nature. It has been estimated that more than 3 million copies of the *Primer* were sold.[2] In 1740 Thomas Dilworth published *A New Guide to the English Tongue*, which contained a mixture of grammar, spelling, and religious material. It was followed a few years later by the *Schoolmaster's Assistant*, a widely used mathematics text. Noah Webster's spellers first appeared in 1783; they were continuously revised and set the standard for spelling until midway through the nineteenth century.[3]

Only a small percentage of colonial youth took advantage of secondary schooling. The Latin grammar school continued to be the main instrument of schooling for the privileged class in the early colonial period, while the academy was designed to offer a more practical curriculum for future tradesmen and workers. The academy eventually became a dual-purpose institution, preparing students both for the world of work and for college; since academies offered the classical curriculum, they drove the old Latin school out of existence. The new academies, however, did offer a larger variety of courses and the result was great variation in secondary school curricula.

Academy replaces the Latin grammar school

From the time of the American Revolution until approximately 1850, great uniformity prevailed and very little change in the elementary school curriculum occurred. Reading, spelling, writing, and arithmetic continued to be stressed in the elementary schools, along with good manners and morals. The *McGuffey Readers*, first published in 1836, were used in most elementary school districts throughout the nineteenth century. But as curricula changed, more and more subjects were included. Between 1850 and 1875 penmanship, advanced mathematics and science, music, art, and physical education were added.

Common schools and free public high schools

In the meantime the common schools, which evolved in Boston in the 1820s, became popular, particularly on the frontier; and in 1874 the concept of free public schooling was extended to the high school level. Thereafter the academy dwindled in importance. Although many of the new high school students had no intention of going to college, the high school curriculum concentrated on academic and college preparatory subjects, thus illustrating the pervasive influence of the ideals of mental discipline.[4]

As the scientific and industrial revolution shaped the United States from the second half of the nineteenth century to the present, a companion move-

1 Ellwood P. Cubberly, *Public Education in the United States* (Boston: Houghton Mifflin, 1934).

2 John A. Nietz, *Old Textbooks* (Pittsburgh: University of Pittsburgh Press, 1961).

3 R. Freeman Butts, *Public Education in the United States* (New York: Holt, 1978).

4 Merle Curti, *The Growth of American Thought*, 2nd ed. (New York: Harper & Row, 1951); David Nasaw, *Schooled to Order: A Social History of Public Schooling in the United States* (New York: Oxford University Press, 1979).

ment for social reform of schools evolved. Much of the impetus for change came from the **progressive movement** in education; it was part of a larger political reform movement, which focused on many sectors of society—labor, housing, health, social-welfare, as well as education. There was increased recognition of the relationship between schools and society—and of the need to reform both. The purposes of schools gradually were broadened to meet the new demands. Social problems relating to unemployment, poverty, urbanization, and the Americanization of immigrants who did not speak English came to be responsibilities of the schools. The curriculum was broadened to meet the diverse needs of all children and youth. Courses in citizenship, family living, home economics and health education, and a number of vocational courses were offered.[5] School curriculum and teaching methods shifted from a complete disregard for the learner, accompanied by respect for the subject matter only, to a strong regard for the child's interests, motives, and abilities.

Progressivism in schools and society

On a general level there was gradual movement away from traditional subjects and teaching techniques toward utility in subject matter and toward student interests and self-expression, but changes were gradual and peripheral. Robert and Helen Lynd's description of Middletown schools illustrates the normal, regimented world of schooling in the mid-1920s.

Regimented classrooms

> Immovable seats in orderly rows fix the sphere of activity of each child. For all, from the timid six-year-old entering for the first time to the most assured high school senior, the general routine is much the same. Bells divide the day into periods. For the six-year-olds the periods are short (fifteen to twenty-five minutes) and varied; in some they leave their seats, play games, and act out make-believe stories, although in "recitation periods" all movement is prohibited. As they grow older the taboo upon physical activity becomes stricter, until by the third or fourth year practically all movement is forbidden except the marching from one set of seats to another between periods, a brief interval of prescribed exercise daily, and periods of manual training or home economics once or twice a week. There are "study periods" in which children learn "lessons" from "textbooks" prescribed by the state and "recitation periods" in which they tell an adult teacher what the book has said. With high school come some differences; more "vocational" and "laboratory" work varies the periods. But here again the lesson-textbook-recitation method is the chief characteristic of education.[6]

In many ways the description of the Middletown schools indicates that progressive education did not carry over in mass scale beyond the universities and their campus laboratory schools. The same sort of mechanical bureaucracy that infected Middletown characterized most of the schools in Boston, Chicago, and New York. While there were shining examples like the

5 R. Freeman Butts, *The Revival of Civic Learning* (Bloomington, Ind.: Phi Delta Kappa, 1980); Lawrence A. Cremin, *American Education: The National Experience* (New York: Harper & Row, 1980).

6 Robert S. Lynd and Helen M. Lynd, *Middletown* (New York: Harcourt, Brace, 1929), p. 188.

Progressivism left its mark

Dalton, Massachusetts, and Winnetka, Illinois, schools, some school systems still used *McGuffey* into the 1930s. Yet, this progressivism did leave its mark, helping to increase educational opportunity for all students in a number of ways: (1) school organization shifted from eight-year elementary schools and four-year high schools to three-year junior high and senior high schools to give greater attention to the requirements of pubescent children; (2) the curriculum was reorganized and extended to areas such as vocational education, agriculture, home economics, physical education, and the arts; (3) extracurricular activities expanded; (4) students were grouped with greater flexibility to meet varying needs; (5) students and teachers tended to be more active and more informal in their relationships with one another; (6) innumerable materials and media were introduced into the classroom; and (7) certification of teachers required more education.[7]

New science, new math

The Cold War and Sputnik in the 1950s curtailed the progressive movement in education and produced a demand for academic rigor—a concentration on the three Rs, accompanied by drill and seatwork, at the elementary level, and the essential, core subjects of science, math, English, modern languages, and history at the secondary level. New science, new math, and the early introduction of foreign language were products of the fifties. Concepts and courses previously postponed until the upper elementary grades or junior high school were introduced at the primary grade level. These were serious and competitive times in schools and society. The opinions of researchers, scientists, and academic specialists prevailed in the area of curriculum; there was little time for play or frills or for meeting the social and psychological needs of the child; it was a return to the mental discipline approach and to testing and tracking students. The smartest survived and were pushed forward.

Social reformers

This academic, subject-centered approach to education produced a reaction in the mid-1960s, and for the next fifteen years, educational psychologists and social reformers introduced several new courses, including elective and remedial courses, as well as new approaches to learning. This was the era of "radical reform," "relevancy," and "humanistic education"; cognitive learning was put on the back burner—affective learning and attempts to meet the needs of the whole child came to the fore.

Curriculum is maturing

As the 1980s unfold, international competition has resurfaced—as has the cry for tougher standards and educational productivity. The academic curriculum is being expanded. The field of curriculum is maturing—moving beyond schools and including programs in business, industry, the military, government, and health. Curriculum today incorporates many disciplines, among them philosophy, psychology, sociology, and politics. Curriculum is developing an international character and is moving into the area of computers and instructional technology.

Looking back at the schools since the colonial period, curriculum change can be viewed as an evolutionary process of offering courses in more and

7 Lawrence A. Cremin, *The Transformation of the School* (New York: Random House, 1964).

Curriculum change as an evolutionary process

more subjects, followed by an attempt to develop scientific and conceptual principles. In brief, the seventeenth- and eighteenth-century schools emphasized the three Rs at the elementary school level and Greek, Latin, and higher mathematics at the secondary school level. The nineteenth century witnessed additional course offerings, especially in history, science, and mathematics. The twentieth century saw the development of a general and diversified curriculum to fit the needs of a diversified student population, as well as the development of curriculum as a field of study.

Curriculum Organization

The shifts and changes in curriculum organization that resulted from the increased complexity of the American schools over the past one hundred years can be viewed from the perspectives of two basic schools of thought. One emphasizes the subject, the other emphasizes the learner. In the first case, the curriculum is viewed as a body of content—or subject matter—leading to certain achievement outcomes or products. The second case views curriculum in terms of the needs and attitudes of the student; the concern is with process—in other words, with the climate of the classroom or school.

Extremes on a continuum

Actually, both views represent the two extremes of a continuum, and most practitioners (and researchers) rely on some curriculum blend within this continuum. While most teachers tend to emphasize one school of thought over the other, they still incorporate both choices in the classroom. Very few of us employ pure cognitive (subject-matter) or pure psychological (student needs and interests) approaches in the teaching-learning process.

Subject-Centered Curriculum

Subject matter is both the oldest and the most recent framework for curriculum organization. It is also the most common—primarily because it is convenient. In fact, the departmental structure of secondary schools and colleges tends to prevent us from thinking about the curriculum in any other way. Curricular changes usually occur at the departmental level. Courses are added, omitted, or modified, but faculty members rarely engage in comprehensive, systematic curriculum development and evaluation. Even in the elementary schools, where self-contained classrooms force the teachers to be generalists, curricula are usually organized by subjects.

Proponents defend the subject-centered curriculum on four grounds:

1. Subjects are a logical way to organize and interpret learning.
2. Such organization makes it easier for people to remember information for future use.
3. Teachers (in secondary schools, at least) are trained as subject-matter specialists.
4. Textbooks and other teaching materials are usually organized by subject.

Pros and cons of subject matter

Critics, however, claim that the subject-centered curriculum is fragmented, a mass of facts and concepts learned in isolation. They see this kind of curriculum as deemphasizing life experiences and failing to consider adequately the needs and interests of students. The emphasis, such critics argue, is on the teaching of knowledge, the recall of facts. Thus the teacher dominates the lesson, allowing little student input. Let us look at six variations on the subject-centered curriculum.

Subject-Area Curriculum The subject area is the oldest and most widely used form of curriculum organization. It has its roots in the seven liberal arts of classical Greece and Rome: grammar, rhetoric, dialectic, arithmetic, geometry, astronomy, and music. Modern subject-area curricula trace their origins to the work of William Harris, superintendent of the St. Louis school system in the 1870s. Steeped in the classical tradition, Harris established a subject orientation that has virtually dominated U.S. curricula from his day to the present.

Common, special, and elective content

The modern **subject-area curriculum** treats each subject as a specialized and largely autonomous body of verified knowledge. These subjects can be organized into three content categories, however. *Common content* refers to subjects considered essential for all students; these subjects usually include the three Rs at the elementary level and English, history, science, and mathematics at the secondary level. *Special content* refers to subjects that develop knowledge and skills for particular vocations or professions, for example, business mathematics and physics. Finally, *elective content* affords the student optional offerings. Some electives are restricted to certain students, say, advanced auto mechanics for vocational students or fourth-year French for students enrolled in a college-preparatory program. Other electives, such as photography and human relations, are open to all students.

Perennialist Curriculum Two conservative philosophies of education are basically subject-centered: **perennialism** and **essentialism**.[8] Perennialists believe that a curriculum should consist primarily of the three Rs, Latin, and logic at the elementary level, to which is added the study of the classics at the secondary level. The assumption, according to Robert Hutchins, is that the best of the past—the so-called permanent studies, or classics—is equally valid for the present.[9]

Latin, logic, and the classics

Perennialists believe that the main purpose of education is the cultivation of the intellect, along with emphasis on certain timeless values about work, morality, and family living. They believe that only certain studies have this power. They reject consideration of students' personal needs and interests or the treatment of contemporary problems in the curriculum on the

8 These two terms were coined by Theodore Brameld in *Patterns of Educational Philosophy* (New York: Holt, 1950).

9 Robert M. Hutchins, *The Higher Learning in America* (New Haven: Yale University Press, 1936).

ground that such concerns detract from the school's mission of cultivating the mind.

Essentialist Curriculum Essentialists believe that the curriculum must consist of the three Rs at the elementary level and at the high school level of five major disciplines: English (grammar, literature, and writing), mathematics, the sciences, history, and foreign languages.[10] They believe these subject areas constitute the best way of systematizing and keeping up with the explosion of knowledge.

Five major disciplines

Essentialism shares with perennialism the notion that the curriculum should focus on rigorous intellectual training, a training possible only through the study of certain subjects. Although the perennialist sees no need for nonacademic subjects, the essentialist is often willing to add such studies to the curriculum provided they receive low priority. Modern-day essentialists are willing to provide minimal play and puzzle activities at the primary grade level, so long as these activities are cognitively oriented, but workbook and drill-like activities still prevail—along with the three Rs. For the perennialists, there is no time to play.[11]

Both perennialists and essentialists advocate educational meritocracy. They favor high academic standards and a rigorous system of grading and testing to help schools sort students by ability. The goal is to educate each person to the limits of his or her potential. Today, many parochial schools and academically oriented public schools stress various aspects of the perennialist and essentialist curricula.

Subject Structure Curriculum During the 1950s and 1960s, the National Science Foundation and the federal government devoted sizable sums to the improvement of science and mathematics curricula at the elementary and secondary levels. New curriculum models were formulated according to the structure of each subject or discipline. The subject structure curriculum rejects memorization, factual information, and rote learning—characteristic of most subject-centered curricula—and stresses those unifying concepts, rules, and principles that define and limit a subject and control the methods of research and inquiry. Structure brings together and organizes a body of knowledge, while it dictates appropriate ways of thinking about the subject and of generating new data. Other subjects quickly followed the lead of mathematics and the sciences.

Unifying concepts and principles

Those who advocated this kind of focus on structure nonetheless rejected the idea that knowledge is fixed or permanent. They regarded teaching and learning as continuing inquiry, but they confined such inquiry within the established boundaries of subjects, ignoring or rejecting the fact that

10 Arthur Bestor, *The Restoration of Learning* (New York: Knopf, 1956).

11 See Herbert J. Klausmeier, *Learning and Teaching Concepts* (New York: Academic Press, 1980); B. Othaniel Smith, "Curriculum Content," in F. W. English, ed., *Fundamental Curriculum Decisions*, 1983 ASCD Yearbook (Alexandria, Va.: Association for Supervision and Curriculum Development, 1983), pp. 30–39.

many problems cut across disciplines. Instead, they emphasized the students' cognitive abilities. They taught students the structure of a subject and its methods of inquiry so that students would learn how to learn. They tended, however, to dismiss learners' social and psychological needs. As Philip Phenix wrote: "There is no place in the curriculum for ideas which are regarded as suitable for teaching because of the supposed nature, needs, and interests of the learner, but which do not belong within the regular structure of the discipline."[12]

New methods of inquiry

The emphasis on structure led each discipline to develop its own unifying concepts, principles, and methods of inquiry. Learning by the inquiry method in chemistry differed from learning by the inquiry method in physics, for example. Moreover, curriculum planners could not agree on how to teach the structure of the social sciences and the fine arts. Science and mathematics programs continue even today to provide the best examples of teaching according to the structure of a subject.

Back-to-Basics Curriculum A strong back-to-basics movement has surfaced today among parents and educators, called forth by the general relaxation of academic standards in the 1960s and 1970s and by declining student standardized test scores in reading, writing, and computation. Automatic promotion of marginal students, the dizzy array of elective courses, and textbooks designed more to entertain than to educate are frequently cited as reasons behind the decline in basic skills. Even the mass media have attacked the "soft-sell approach" to education. The concerns voiced today parallel those voiced after Sputnik. The call today is less for academic excellence and rigor, however, than for a return to basics or minimum standards. Annual Gallup polls have asked the public to suggest ways for improving education; since 1976 "devoting more attention to teaching the basics" and "improving curriculum standards" have ranked no lower than fifth in the list of responses.[13]

Settling for the basics

By 1983, all of the states had implemented statewide testing programs for various grade levels, and in twenty-seven states the tests were mandated. In ten states (Alabama, California, Florida, Hawaii, Louisiana, Nevada, New York, North Carolina, Tennessee, and Virginia) the test was required for high school graduation.[14]

Demand for solid subjects

Although the back-to-basics movement means different things to different people, it usually connotes an essentialist curriculum with heavy emphasis on reading, writing, and mathematics. So-called solid subjects—English, history, science, and mathematics—are taught in all grades. History means

12 Philip H. Phenix, "The Disciplines as Curriculum Content," in A. H. Passow, ed., *Curriculum Crossroads* (New York: Teachers College Press, 1962), p. 64.

13 See the annual Gallup polls published in the September or October issues of *Phi Delta Kappan*, 1976 to 1984. Also see Stanley M. Elam, "The Gallup Education Surveys," *Phi Delta Kappan* (September 1983), pp. 26–32.

14 *Educational Governance in the States, A Status Report on State Boards of Education, Chief State School Officers, and State Education Agencies* (Washington, D.C.: U.S. Department of Education, 1983).

A back-to-basics curriculum places heavy emphasis on cognitive learning and especially on the basic skills of reading, writing, and mathematics computation.
(Laimute Druskis/ Jeroboam)

U.S. and European history and perhaps Asian and African history but does not include Afro-American history or ethnic studies. English means traditional grammar, not linguistics or nonstandard English; it means Shakespeare and Wordsworth, not *Catcher in the Rye* or *Lolita*. Creative writing is frowned upon. Science means biology, chemistry, and physics—not ecology. Mathematics means old math, not new math. Furthermore, these subjects are required. Proponents of the basics consider elective courses in such areas as scuba diving, transcendental meditation, and hiking to be nonsense. Some even consider humanities or integrated social science courses too "soft." They may grudgingly admit music and art into the program—but only for half credit.

Devaluation of diplomas

Proponents of the movement believe that too many illiterate students pass from grade to grade and eventually graduate, that high school and college diplomas are meaningless as measures of graduates' abilities, that minimum standards must be set, that the basics (reading, writing, math) are essential for employment, and that students must learn survival skills to function effectively in society. Some of these advocates are college educators who would do away with open admissions or related entrance requirements and grade inflation; they would simply insist that their institutions require students to meet reasonable standards in the academic disciplines—that students be able to understand their homework assignments, write acceptable essays, and perform numerical computations accurately.[15]

Criticism of back-to-basics

Critics point out that the decline in standardized test scores—a grave concern of the back-to-basics enthusiasts—may be linked less to curriculum than to higher student/teacher ratios, a decrease in the number of low-achieving students who drop out of school, the competing influence of television, and the more permissive attitudes of society. They worry that a focus on basics will suppress the students' creativity and shortchange other domains of learning, encouraging instead conformity and dependence on authority. Others expect the back-to-basics movement to fail because teaching and learning cannot be defined and limited precisely and because testing has too many inherent problems.[16]

While the debate is raging, the movement is spreading quickly in response to public pressure. State legislators and state boards of education seem convinced of the merit of minimum standards. But there remain unanswered questions. If we are to adopt a back-to-basics approach to education, what standards should be considered minimum? Who determines these standards? What do we do with students who fail to meet these standards? Are we simply punishing the victims for the schools' inability to educate them? How will the courts deal with the fact that proportionally more minority than white students fail the competency tests in nearly every case? What is the issue—minimum competency or equal educational opportunity? And, when all is said and done, are we not educationally speaking, reinventing the wheel?

15 Ben Brodinsky, "Back to Basics: The Movement and Its Meaning," *Phi Delta Kappan* (March 1977), pp. 522–527; Chester Finn, "The New Basics for Everyone," *Educational Leadership* (October 1983), pp. 28–29; and Melvin E. Levison, "The Basics—The Etymology of Reading, Writing and Arithmetic," *National Association of Secondary School Principals* (September 1983), pp. 219–253.

16 Gene Glass, "Minimum Competence and Incompetence in Florida," *Phi Delta Kappan* (May 1979), pp. 602–605; Arthur E. Wise, "Minimum Competency Testing: Another Case of Hyper Rationalization," *Phi Delta Kappan* (May 1979), 596–598; and Arthur E. Wise, "On Standards and Public Policy," *Educational Leadership* (October 1983), pp. 42–44.

Higher Standards Curriculum There is a demand today for tougher academics. The demand for higher achievement (not just minimum competency) for all children (not just college-bound students) focuses on the cognitive and academic areas. The ability to think, reason, and solve problems, to take serious subjects such as calculus, physics, and advanced foreign language are stressed. Proponents believe that we must upgrade our definition of minimum competencies to include advanced skills and knowledge, including computer and communication competencies, that will be required for tomorrow's technological world. They believe we must increase the time and quality of instruction, and reestablish the prestige of our teachers and schools.[17] The health and vitality of our economy and international position are linked to the strength of our educational institutions.

Upgrading the curriculum

It is easy to argue for greater emphasis and tougher standards in mathematics, science, and foreign language—even for computer literacy. But if students take more courses in these subject areas, observers point out, they will have fewer opportunities to study such areas as culture and the arts, thus raising the question of curriculum balance. It is possible that students not going to college will be overlooked or pushed into poorly equipped classrooms and second-rate programs.[18] Appropriate mathematics, science, and other classes for vocational and non-college bound students should be developed. Although students should be required to speak fluently at least one foreign language, we must not forget our immigrant and limited-English-speaking students who must learn formal English.

Increasing requirements and offering additional courses in the subject areas we have mentioned will have an impact on the supply of teachers, too. New teachers of math, science, and foreign language will be needed—exacerbating the existing shortage of qualified teachers in these subject areas. Moreover, math and science teachers are increasingly seeking employment outside of education.

Raising standards costs money

Raising standards will cost money. Teacher salaries, for example, will have to be raised to attract—and retain—teachers in math, science, and foreign language. We will have to improve, and in some cases build, science laboratory facilities. Schools will need to introduce new instructional materials, including updated textbooks, computers, and language laboratories. In addition, research suggests that it is effective to begin instruction in these subject areas in the elementary grades. Given an era of federal retrenchment in education, state and local deficits, and school cutbacks, the agenda for excellence in curriculum policy may have to sit on the back burner—while educators and society settle for the basics.

17 Albert Shanker, "The Real Crisis in Public Schools," *Educational Digest* (March 1983), pp. 10–11; Herbert J. Walberg, "Can We Raise Standards," *Educational Leadership* (October 1983), pp. 4–6.

18 Elliot W. Eisner, "The Kind of Schools We Need," *Educational Leadership* (October 1983), pp. 48–55; B. Othaniel Smith et al., "The Impact of Increasing Requirements in Math and Science," *Educational Leadership* (October 1983), pp. 36–41.

Student-Centered Curriculum

If the subject-centered curriculum focuses on cognitive aspects of learning, the **student-centered curriculum** emphasizes students' interests and needs—the affective aspects of learning. The student-centered approach, at its extreme, is rooted in the philosophy of Jean Jacques Rousseau, who encouraged childhood self-expression. Implicit in Rousseau's philosophy is the necessity of leaving the child to his or her own devices; he considered creativity and freedom essential for children's growth. Moreover, he thought children would be happier if they were free of teacher domination, the demands of subject matter, and adult-imposed curriculum goals.

Progressivism and student interests

Progressive education gave impetus to the student-centered curriculum. Progressive educators believed that, when the interests and needs of learners were incorporated into the curriculum, intrinsic motivation resulted. This does not mean to imply that the student-oriented curriculum is dictated by the whims of the learner. Rather, advocates believe that learning is more successful if the interests and needs of the learner are taken into account. One flaw of student-centered curriculum, however, is that it sometimes overlooks important cognitive content.

A balanced curriculum

John Dewey, one of the chief advocates of the student-centered curriculum, attempted to establish a curriculum that balances subject matter with students' interests and needs. As early as 1902, he pointed out the fallacies of either extreme. The learner was neither "a docile recipient of facts" nor "the starting point, the center, and the end" of school activity.[19] More than thirty years later, Dewey was still criticizing over-permissive educators who provided little education for students under the guise of meeting those students' expressive and impulsive needs.[20] Dewey sought instead to use youngsters' developing interests to enhance the cognitive learning process. (In the 1980s, one hears the call for nearly the same synthesis; some advocates of educational excellence are asking educational psychologists and student-centered educators to combine students' interests with academic rigor, cognitive concepts with concepts of the learner.)

There are at least six variations of the student-centered curriculum.

Child-Centered Curriculum The movement from the traditional subject-dominated curriculum toward a program emphasizing student interests and needs began in 1762 with the publication of Rousseau's *Émile*, in which Rousseau maintained that the purpose of education is to teach people to live. Early in the next century the Swiss educator, Johann Pestalozzi, began to stress human emotions and kindness in teaching young children. Friedrich

19 John Dewey, *The Child and the Curriculum* (Chicago: University of Chicago Press, 1902), pp. 8–9.

20 John Dewey, *Art and Experience* (New York: Capricorn Books, 1934) and *Experience and Education* (New York: Macmillan, 1938).

Permissive atmosphere in kindergartens

Froebel introduced the kindergarten in Germany in 1837. He emphasized a permissive atmosphere and the use of songs, stories, and games as instructional materials. Early in the twentieth century Maria Montessori, working with the slum children of Rome, developed a set of didactic materials and learning exercises that successfully combined work with play. Many of her principles became popular in the United States during the 1960s as part of the compensatory preschool movement.

Experimental schools

Early progressive educators in the United States adopted the notion of child-centered schools, starting with Dewey's organic school (which he described in *Schools of Tomorrow*) and including many private and experimental schools—the best known of which were Columbia University's Lincoln School, Ohio State's Laboratory School, the University of Missouri Elementary School, the Pratt Play School in New York City, the Parker School in Chicago, and the Fairhope School in Alabama.[21] These schools had a common feature: their curricula stressed the needs and interests of the students. Some stressed individualization; others grouped students by ability or interests.

Child-centered education is represented today by programs for such special groups as the academically talented, the disadvantaged, dropouts (actual and potential), the handicapped, and minority and ethnic groups. Many of these programs are carried on in **free schools** or **alternative schools** organized by parents and teachers who are dissatisfied with the public schools. These schools are typified by a great deal of freedom for students and noisy classrooms that sometimes appear untidy and disorganized. The teaching-learning process is unstructured. Most of these new schools are considered radical and anti-establishment, even though many of their ideas are rooted in the child-centered doctrines of progressivism.

Summerhill, a school founded in 1921 by A. S. Neill and still in existence today, is perhaps the best-known free school. Neill's philosophy was to replace authority with freedom.[22] He was not concerned with formal learning; he did not believe in textbooks or examinations. He did believe that those who want to study *will* study and those who prefer not to study will *not*, regardless of how teachers teach. Neill's dual criteria for success were the ability to work joyfully and the ability to live a happy life.

Recent radicals

Although Neill, Edgar Friedenberg, Paul Goodman, and John Holt[23] all belong to an earlier generation of school reformers, younger radicals have emerged. They include George Dennison, James Herndon, Ivan Illich, Herbert Kohl, and Jonathan Kozol. These educators stress the need for, and in

21 A number of these early experimental schools are discussed in detail by John Dewey and his daughter Evelyn in *Schools of Tomorrow*, published in 1915. Another good source is the 1926 yearbook of the National Society for the Study of Education, a two-volume work titled *The Foundations of Curriculum* and *Techniques of Curriculum Construction*. Lawrence Cremin's *The Transformation of the School*, published in 1961, is still another good source. Finally, Ohio State's Laboratory School is best summarized in a 1938 book titled *Were We Guinea Pigs?*, written by the senior class.

22 A. S. Neill, *Summerhill: A Radical Approach to Child Rearing* (New York: Hart, 1960).

23 See Edgar Z. Friedenberg, *The Vanishing Adolescent* (Boston: Beacon Press, 1959); Paul Goodman, *Growing Up Absurd* (New York: Random House, 1960) and *Compulsory Mis-Education* (New York: Horizon Press, 1964); and John Holt, *How Children Fail* (New York: Pitman, 1964) and *How Children Learn* (New York: Delta, 1972).

many cases have established, child-centered free schools or alternative schools.[24]

Critics condemn these schools as places where little cognitive learning takes place. They decry a lack of discipline and order. They feel that the reformers' attacks on establishment teachers and schools are overgeneralized and unfair. They do not find the radicals' idea of schooling to be feasible for mass education. Proponents counter that children do learn in these schools, which—instead of stressing conformity—are made to fit the child.

Activity-Centered Curriculum This movement, which grew out of the private child-centered schools, has strongly affected the public elementary school curriculum. William Kilpatrick, one of Dewey's students, was its leader. Kilpatrick differed with Dewey's child-centered view; he believed that the interests and needs of children could not be anticipated, making a preplanned curriculum impossible. He attacked the school curriculum as unrelated to the problems of real life and advocated purposeful activities that were as lifelike as possible and that were tied to a child's needs and interests.[25]

Purposeful activities

During the 1920s and 1930s, many elementary schools adopted some of the ideas of the activity movement, perhaps best summarized and first put into practice by Ellsworth Collings, a doctoral student of Kilpatrick's.[26] From this movement a host of teaching strategies emerged, including lessons based on life experiences, group games, dramatizations, story projects, field trips, social enterprises, and interest centers. All of these activities involved problem solving and active student participation; they emphasized socialization and the formation of stronger school-community ties.

Recent curriculum reformers have translated ideas from this movement into community and career-based activities intended to prepare students for adult citizenship and work and into courses emphasizing social problems. They have also urged college credit for life experiences. Secondary and college students often earn credit today by working in welfare agencies, early childhood programs, government, institutions, hospitals, and homes for the aged.[27]

Relevant Curriculum Unquestionably, the curriculum must reflect social change. This point is well illustrated in *The Saber-Tooth Curriculum*, a satiric

24 See George Dennison, *The Lives of Children: The Story of the First School* (New York: Random House, 1969); James Herndon, *The Way It Spozed to Be* (New York: Simon & Schuster, 1969); Ivan Illich, *Deschooling Society* (New York: Harper & Row, 1971); Herbert R. Kohl, *The Open Classroom* (New York: Random House, 1969) and *On Teaching* (New York: Schocken, 1976); Jonathan Kozol, *Free Schools* (Boston: Houghton Mifflin, 1972).

25 William H. Kilpatrick, "The Project Method," *Teachers College Record* (September 1918), pp. 319–335.

26 Ellsworth Collings, ed., *An Experiment with a Project Curriculum* (New York: Macmillan, 1923). Another description of the activity-centered program was provided by Harold Rugg and Ann Shumaker, *The Child-Centered School: An Appraisal of the New Education* (Yonkers, N.Y.: World Book, 1928).

27 James S. Coleman et al. *Youth: Transition to Adulthood, Report of the Panel on Youth of the President's Science Advisory Committee* (Chicago: University of Chicago Press, 1974); Mario D. Fantini, *The Reform of Urban Schools* (Washington, D.C.: National Education Association, 1970).

book on education, written in 1939 by Harold Benjamin under the pseudonym Abner J. Peddiwell.[28] He describes a society in which the schools continued to teach fish-catching (because it would develop agility), horse-clubbing (to develop strength), and tiger-scaring (to develop courage) long after the streams had dried up and the horses and tigers had disappeared. The wise men of the society argued that "the essence of true education is timeless . . . something that endures through changing conditions like a solid rock standing squarely and firmly in the middle of a raging torrent."[29] Benjamin's message was simple: the curriculum was no longer relevant.

Fish-catching, horse-clubbing, and tiger-scaring

The 1960s and 1970s saw a renewed concern for a relevant curriculum, but with a somewhat different emphasis. There was less concern that the curriculum reflect changing social conditions and more concern that the curriculum be relevant to students. This shift was part of the Dewey legacy: learners must be motivated and interested in the learning task, and the classroom should build on their real-life experiences.

Relevant to students

The demand for relevance came from both students and educators. In fact, the student disruptions of the last two decades were related to this demand. Proponents who advocate this approach today see as needs: (1) the individualization of instruction through such teaching methods as independent inquiry and special projects; (2) the revision of existing courses and development of new ones on such topics of student concern as environmental protection, drug addiction, urban problems, and cultural pluralism; (3) the provision of educational alternatives (such as electives, minicourses, open classrooms) that allow more freedom of choice; and (4) the extension of the curriculum beyond the school's walls through such innovations as work-study programs, credit for life experiences, and external degree programs.[30]

Credit for life experiences

Efforts to relate subject matter to student interests have been largely ad hoc, and many were fragmented and temporary, a source of concern to advocates of relevance. In other cases, changes made in the name of relevance have in fact watered down the curriculum.

Hidden Curriculum The notion of a **hidden curriculum** implies that values of the student peer group are often ignored when formal school curricula are planned. Some educators have focused on the hidden curriculum—the informal, covert, obscure dynamics of the classroom and school—that affects what is learned.[31] Along with other factors (such as social class, family, home life, intelligence, and personality), students' achievement and behavior

28 Harold Benjamin, *The Saber-Tooth Curriculum* (New York: McGraw-Hill, 1939).

29 Ibid., pp. 43–44.

30 Michael W. Apple, *Education and Power* (Boston: Routledge & Kegan Paul, 1982); Arno A. Bellack and Herbert M. Kliebard, *Curriculum and Evaluation*, A Research Series by the American Educational Research Association (Berkeley, Calif.: McCutchan, 1977); and Anthony N. Penna, Henry A. Giroux, and William F. Pinar, eds., *Curriculum and Instruction: Alternatives in Education* (Berkeley, Calif.: McCutchan, 1981).

31 Philip A. Cusick, *Inside High School* (New York: Holt, 1973); Joyce L. Epstein and Nancey L. Karweit, eds., *Friendships in School* (New York: Academic Press, 1983); and Giroux and Purpel, *The Hidden Curriculum and Moral Education*.

seem to be related to their status and roles in school; it is suggested that peer association, friendship selection, and student cliques control much of adolescent performance both inside and outside of school. These social interactions are related to students' personal characteristics, abilities, interests, and age—and correlate with achievement scores, extracurricular activities, student-teacher interactions, and even career choices. Sometimes these hidden, informal social interactions conflict with the formal curriculum and with classroom and school rules.

Students as cunning strategists

The hidden curriculum includes the strategies adopted by students to outwit and outguess their teachers. According to John Holt and other educators, "successful" students become cunning strategists in a game of beating the system.[32] Experience has taught them that trickery and even occasional dishonesty pay off. The implication is that teachers must become more sensitive to students' needs and feelings in order to minimize counterproductive behavior. A school that encourages personal freedom and cooperative group learning—instead of competitive individualization, lesson recitation, "right" answers, and textbook/teacher authority—is more conducive to learning because the atmosphere is free of trickery and dishonesty. Or so the argument goes.

Rituals, rules, and regularities

There is another type of hidden curriculum, the culture of the school—its rituals, rules, and regularities. Since the classic work of Willard Waller, who explored normal school procedures—promptness, neatness, docility, adult authority and control, and so on—the hidden social and psychological dynamics of the school have been examined with a good deal of exactitude and zeal.[33] Philip Jackson, in *Life in Classrooms*, examines how elementary students sit, listen, wait, and raise their hands; how they sharpen their pencils, stand in line, and file out of school.[34] Bel Kaufman, in a best-selling fictionalized account of a high school, *Up the Down Staircase*, describes how the system imposes a stillness and silence on teachers and students who prefer lively and active classrooms; how bells, schedules, and interruptions over the loudspeaker, and petty rules and administrative memos, hinder the teaching and learning process.[35] More recently, Philip Cusick and Sara Lightfoot have analyzed how some students are lost in the "cracks," getting by with grades of C, and how there is a quiet indifference and a sense of conformity in many working-class schools.[36] In all of these studies, there are the common themes of praise and criticism, rewards and punishment for purposes of modifying student behavior—for control and conformity—a hidden agenda.

Students lost in the "cracks"

Another interpretation of the hidden curriculum suggests that some intentional school behavior is not formally recognized in the curriculum or dis-

32 John Holt, *How Children Fail*; Jere Brophy and Carol M. Evertson, *Student Characteristics and Teaching* (New York: Longman, 1981).

33 Willard Waller, *The Sociology of Teaching* (New York: Wiley, 1932).

34 Philip W. Jackson, *Life In Classrooms* (New York: Holt, 1968).

35 Bel Kaufman, *Up the Down Staircase* (Englewood Cliffs, N.J.: Prentice-Hall, 1964).

36 Philip A. Cusick, *The Equalitarian Ideal and the American High School* (New York: Longman, 1983); Sara L. Lightfoot, *The Good High School* (New York: Basic Books, 1983).

cussed in the classroom because of its sensitivity or because teachers do not consider it important. At the same time, students sometimes see what is taught as phony, antiseptic, or unrelated to the real world. For example, some ethnic or minority groups are discussed in a derogatory manner in some homes. This raises several questions. Should curriculum specialists or teachers try to suppress the hidden curriculum in order to further the purposes of the school? Or should they try to incorporate it into school life? At what age is the student mature enough to discuss such sensitive topics as racial and ethnic stereotypes? A student-oriented school, some educators contend, would try to reduce the disparity between the student's world outside of school and that within.[37]

Phony, antiseptic curriculum

Humanistic Curriculum Like many other modern curriculum developments, humanistic education began as a reaction to what was viewed as an overemphasis on cognitive learning in the late fifties and early sixties. Terry Borton, a Philadelphia schoolteacher, was one of the first to write about this movement. He contended that education had only two major purposes: subject mastery and personal growth.[38] Nearly every school's statement of objectives includes both purposes, but Borton, and later others, asserted that objectives related to personal growth, feelings, and the happy life were included only for show.[39] Almost everyone knows, the argument went, how little schools have done to promote learning related to personal insights and the affective domain. Some educators believe the time has come for schools to put into practice their goals for children's social and personal growth.

Subject matter and personal growth

In his best-selling book, *Crisis in the Classroom*, Charles Silberman also advocates the humanizing of U.S. schools.[40] He charges that schools are repressive, teaching students docility and conformity. He believes that schools must be reformed, even at the price of deemphasizing cognitive learning. He suggests that elementary schools adopt the methods of the British infant schools. At the secondary level, he favors independent study, peer tutoring, and community and work experiences.

Docility and conformity

The humanistic model of education grew out of the human potential movement in psychology. Within education it is rooted in the work of Arthur Jersild, who linked good teaching with knowledge of self and students, and in the work of Arthur Combs and Donald Snygg, who explored the impact of

37 Martin Carnoy and Derek Shearer, *Economic Democracy* (White Plains, N.Y.: Sharpe, 1980); Mario D. Fantini and Gerald D. Weinstein, *The Disadvantaged Child* (New York: Harper & Row, 1968); and William Pinar, *Curriculum Theorizing: The Reconceptualists* (Berkeley, Calif.: McCutchan, 1974).

38 Terry Borton, *Reach, Touch, and Teach* (New York: McGraw-Hill, 1970).

39 Michael W. Apple, "Curriculum in the Year 2000: Tensions and Possibilities," *Phi Delta Kappan* (January 1983), pp. 321–326; Louise M. Berman and Jessie A. Roderick, eds., *Feelings, Values, and the Art of Growing*, 1977 ASCD Yearbook (Washington, D.C.: Association for Supervision and Curriculum Development, 1977); Elliot W. Eisner, "The Art and Craft of Teaching," *Educational Leadership* (January 1983), pp. 4–13; and Gene I. Maeroff, *Don't Blame the Kids: The Trouble with America's Pubic Schools* (New York: McGraw-Hill, 1983).

40 Charles A. Silberman, *Crisis in the Classroom* (New York: Random House, 1971).

self-concept and motivation on achievement.[41] Combs and Snygg considered self-concept to be the most important determinant of behavior.

A humanistic curriculum emphasizes affective rather than cognitive outcomes. Such a curriculum draws heavily on the work of Abraham Maslow and of Carl Rogers.[42] Its goal is to produce "self-actualizing people," in Maslow's words, or "total human beings" as Rogers puts it. The works of both psychologists are larded with such terms as *choosing, striving, enhancing*, and *experiencing*—as well as *independence, self-determination, integration*, and *personal relationships*.

"Self-actualizing people"

Advocates of humanistic education contend that the present school curriculum has failed miserably by humanistic standards, that teachers and schools are determined to stress cognitive behaviors and to control students *not* for students' good but for the good of adults. Humanists emphasize more than affective processes; they seek higher domains of consciousness, aesthetics, and morality.[43] But they believe today's schools are unconcerned with higher planes of understanding, enhancement of the mind, or self-knowledge, which leads students, they believe, to turn to such out-of-school activities as drugs, yoga, transcendental meditation, group encounters, T-groups, and psychotherapy.

Higher domains of consciousness

Humanists would attempt to form more meaningful relationships between students and teachers; they would foster student independence and self-direction and promote greater acceptance of self and others. The teacher's role would be to help learners cope with their psychological needs and problems, to facilitate self-understanding among students, and to help students develop fully.

Values-Centered Curriculum A curriculum that stresses values is related to affective learning and personal growth. The affective domain, discussed in the previous chapter, has as its most advanced level of feelings and emotions the values area in which the act of valuing, organizing values, and behaving according to value commitments are emphasized. It is this system of values, according to which people behave individually and in common, that educators today have attempted to clarify.

System of values

Conflicts in values are inevitable in a society as diverse and complex as ours. As social and economic conditions change, and they do very rapidly in our modern society, so do people and ideas they value. The values a person

41 Arthur T. Jersild, *In Search of Self* (New York: Teachers College Press, 1952) and *When Teachers Face Themselves* (New York: Teachers College Press, 1955); Arthur Combs and Donald Snygg, *Individual Behavior*, 2nd ed. (New York: Harper & Row, 1959). Also see Arthur Combs, ed., *Perceiving Behavior, Becoming*, 1962 ASCD Yearbook (Washington, D.C.: Association for Supervision and Curriculum Development, 1962).

42 Abraham H. Maslow, *Toward a Psychology of Being* (New York: Van Nostrand Reinhold, 1962) and *Motivation and Personality*, 2nd ed. (New York: Harper & Row, 1970); Carl R. Rogers, *On Becoming a Person* (Boston: Houghton Mifflin, 1961) and *Freedom to Learn* (Columbus, Ohio: Merrill, 1982).

43 Apple, *Education and Power*; Elliot Eisner, *The Educational Imagination* (New York: Macmillan, 1979); and Maxine Greene, *Landscapes of Learning* (New York: Teachers College Press, 1978).

A student-centered curriculum focuses on the interests, needs, and experiences of the individual student—the affective aspects of education.
(Dailo Nardi/Freelance Photographers Guild)

Value confusion

holds depend on many factors, including environment, education, and personality. People often suffer from value confusion—the symptoms of which are apathy, uncertainty, inconsistency, overconforming, or overdissenting.[44] Value clarification is designed to overcome value confusion and to help persons become positive and purposeful.

According to Louis Raths and his associates, who have developed one of the most popular books on the subject, the process of valuing follows seven requirements: "choosing freely, choosing from alternatives, choosing after thoughtful consideration, prizing and cherishing, affirming, acting upon choices, and repeating . . . as a pattern in life."[45]

Teaching valuing

There are five distinct ways to teach valuing. The first is *inculcation*, in which accepted values are taught with the support of common law. Next is

44 Arthur M. Combs, *A Personal Approach to Teaching* (Boston: Allyn and Bacon, 1982).

45 Louis E. Raths, Merrill Harmin, and Sidney B. Simon, *Values and Teaching*, 2nd ed. (Columbus, Ohio: Merrill, 1978), pp. 27–28.

moral development, highlighting moral and ethical principles and their application. Third is *analysis* of issues and situations involving values. Fourth is *clarification*, the method Raths emphasizes. The fifth is *action learning*, by which values are tried and tested in real-life situations.[46] In addition, the humanistic approaches used by Abraham Maslow and Carl Rogers may be described as *evocation*, a calling forth from the individual of personal values and the ability to make choices and think creatively.

Lack of attention to cognitive learning

A drawback to humanistic and value-clarification theories is the lack of attention to cognitive learning. When asked to judge the effectiveness of their curriculum, both humanists and value educators generally rely on testimonials and subjective assessments. They may also present students' paintings, poems, interviews, and reports or talk about improvement in student behavior and attitudes. They present very little empirical evidence or student achievement scores, however, to support their stance. Moreover, the humanists disagree on how they should teach self-actualization, self-determination, human striving, and the like; value educators do not concur on the values they teach or how to teach them. Until these issues are resolved, we shall continue to flounder in the areas of affective learning.

Curriculum Contrasts: An Overview

Subject matter and student needs

Recapping the subject-centered and student-centered curricula, each represents an extreme on a continuum that is rooted in the past and present practices of curriculum organization. Most schooling in the United States falls somewhere between the two—effecting a tenuous balance between subject matter and student needs, between cognitive outcomes and psychological factors.

Regardless of a teacher's personal bias or approach, decisions on what is taught and how curriculum is organized are usually influenced by the philosophical orientation of the school at which he or she is teaching. More traditional schools that subscribe to a perennialist or essentialist philosophy generally advocate a subject-centered curriculum. Schools that are oriented more toward progressive or reconstructionist education tend to use a student-centered curriculum. (Overview 14.1 summarizes the various subject-centered and student-centered curricula and their corresponding philosophies, content emphases, and instructional emphases.) Regardless of one's views or one's aims or objectives, one need not take an extreme position on the subject matter—student interests continuum. We would expect some type of blend, although many educators would emphasize one organizational approach (subject or student emphasis) over another.

Actually, the relative emphasis on subject matter or student interests is essentially a question of philosophical orientation, and to a lesser extent,

46 Ronald C. Doll, *Curriculum Improvement: Decision Making and Process*, 4th ed. (Boston: Allyn and Bacon, 1978); Alexander Frazier, *Values, Curriculum, and the Elementary School* (Boston: Houghton Mifflin, 1980).

Overview 14.1

Curriculum Organization Approaches

Curriculum Approach	Corresponding Philosophy	Content Emphasis	Instructional Emphasis
Subject-Centered			
Subject-area curriculum	Perennialism, essentialism	Three Rs; academic, vocational, and elective subjects	Knowledge, concepts, and principles; specialized knowledge
Perennialist curriculum	Perennialism	Three Rs; liberal arts; classics; timeless values; academic rigor	Rote memorization; specialized knowledge; mental discipline
Essentialist curriculum	Essentialism	Three Rs; liberal arts and science; academic disciplines; academic excellence	Concepts and principles; problem solving; essential skills
Subject structure curriculum	Essentialism	Science, math, and foreign language; academic disciplines; academic excellence	Concepts and principles; problem solving; intuitive thinking; learning how to learn
Back-to-basics curriculum	Essentialism	Three Rs; academic subjects	Specific knowledge and skills; drill; attainment of measurable ends or competencies
Higher standards curriculum	Perennialism, essentialism, reconstructionism	Academic subjects; computer literacy; academic excellence and educational productivity	Knowledge; concepts and principles; learning how to learn; attainment of measurable ends or competencies

learning theory. From these philosophical and theoretical concerns, we must eventually move to the area of curriculum development; this is a technical concern and involves systematic reflection and planning.

Curriculum Development

Curriculum at the national level

Techniques for curriculum development include a wide range of activities, among them assessing the needs of learners, developing objectives, and selecting or creating instructional materials and activities. At the national level, curriculum-making is minimal and indirect. It is limited to federally financed

Overview 14.1 (cont.)

Curriculum Organization Approaches

Curriculum Approach	Corresponding Philosophy	Content Emphasis	Instructional Emphasis
Student-Centered			
Child-centered curriculum	Progressivism	Student needs and interests; student experiences	Play oriented; creative expression; free learning environment
Activity-centered curriculum	Progressivism	Student needs and interests; student activities; school-community activities	Active, experimental environment; project methods; effective living
Relevant curriculum	Progressivism, reconstructionism	Student experiences and activities; felt needs	Social and personal problems; reflective thinking
Hidden curriculum	Progressivism, reconstructionism	Implicit processes; social norms	Hard to recognize, unaccounted for factors; cultural assimilation; conformity and control
Humanistic curriculum	Progressivism, reconstructionism	Introspection; choice	Individual and group learning; flexible, artistic, psychological methods; self-realization
Values-centered curriculum	Reconstructionism	Democratic values; crosscultural and universal values; choice and freedom	Feelings, attitudes, and emotions; existentialist thinking; decision making

curriculum projects at universities and a few educational regional laboratories, the curriculum influence of private foundations and nonprofit organizations, and the school materials and textbooks produced by publishing companies in cooperation with professional educators.

In this connection, specialized personnel—subject specialists or curriculum specialists, learning theorists, and editors—make most of the decisions on what should be taught and—to a lesser extent—on how. These specialists are influenced by professional opinion as well as by the popular media. They seek the advice of and listen to other professionals in the field of education, to textbook sales people, and to marketing surveys. In their attempt to plan and develop curriculum, they are particularly sensitive to the views of teachers, school administrators, and schoolboard members.

Curriculum at the state level

Curriculum development at the state level is mainly limited to curriculum guides and booklets. These materials are prepared by a professional staff in state departments of education assisted by curriculum consultants and college professors. The purposes and goals set forth in these materials are usually formulated in committees composed of these professional educators and selected lay persons.[47] State guides and booklets tend to focus on aims and objectives according to subjects and grade levels; they correspond with state laws and change when priorities and trends change. For example, today there is concern for developing curriculum in the area of multicultural education, sex education, international education, and handicapped education, and this is reflected in new state-produced curriculum materials.

Curriculum at the district level

The most common arena for curriculum development is the local school district, although curriculum making at individual schools is increasing. School districts often employ personnel who specialize in curriculum development at the central office level; these specialists include among others subject-matter specialists, test consultants, representative teachers and administrators, and sometimes lay persons. They should and usually do consider local and regional history and culture in developing the curriculum, as well as current economic and social trends in focusing on goals, content, and instructional activities.

At the school level, the teacher or a group of teachers organized by subject or grade level often develop a curriculum that is appropriate for the students. In some cases, they may work with parents and administrators. At the high school level student representatives may be on the committee or team involved in curriculum development. Committee members are encouraged to keep in mind state and local district goals and laws pertaining to subject matter. Although many teachers at the classroom level rely on such outside sources as textbooks and courses of studies to determine the content and scope of the curriculum, they should modify it to satisfy the needs and interests of their students.

Textbook adoption

Here it should be noted that textbook adoption has become an important issue confronting school districts and schools, and in a few cases (for example, Texas) it involves an entire state. To the extent that textbook publishers try to satisfy potential customers, it may be said that certain content and even pictures are omitted, added, or treated in a manner so as to attract the largest audiences. A sales adoption in Texas or in the Detroit school district has tremendous monetary implications, much more than an adoption in a school district enrolling only 1,000 students.

Relying on textbooks

To the extent that curriculum committees or teachers rely on textbooks as the major source of content in the classroom, curriculum-making decisions are made by those who write, publish, and select textbooks. In those cases, curriculum content is reflected

47 George A. Beachamp, "Curriculum Design," in F. W. English, ed., *Fundamental Curriculum Decisions*, 1983 ASCD Yearbook (Alexandria, Va.: Association for Supervision and Curriculum Development, 1983), pp. 90–98; John D. McNeil, *Curriculum: A Comprehensive Introduction*, 2nd ed. (Boston: Little, Brown, 1981).

by what is in the textbook. There is danger in this approach. When the textbook becomes the basis of curriculum making and curriculum content, revisions in curriculum (and instruction) usually occur only when the textbook is revised or when one textbook replaces another textbook.

Instructional Innovations

Although many educators differ in their definition of curriculum, the majority recognize that curriculum and instruction are interrelated. To carry out the curriculum one must rely on instruction—programs, materials, and methods. The search for new programs and methods of instruction is continuous. The era of the 1950s and 1960s, in particular, saw a major effort to reform curriculum and instruction. It was regarded by many educators as an era that would transform the schools. As the New York State commissioner of education wrote in 1960:

High hopes for reform

> Never before have so many new approaches developed in such a relatively short period . . . we are learning that many of the old ways of operating our schools are not necessarily the best ways. New methods of organization, the use of new technological devices and new concepts of the role of the teacher provide answers that numbers alone cannot provide.[48]

The era of reform has carried over to the present. This section describes a number of instructional practices or innovations that have been popular during the last twenty-five years.

Team Teaching

The team teaching approach is rooted in the early organizational plans of the twentieth century, particularly the Gary Plan and the Batavia Plan. It was reintroduced and modernized in 1957 at the Franklin School in Lexington, Massachusetts, under the directorship of Robert Anderson with the assistance of the Harvard Graduate School of Education. From this experiment the team teaching approach became one of the most widely discussed and frequently adopted organizational programs.

Teachers combine their abilities and interests

Team teaching is an arrangement whereby two or more teachers combine their abilities and interests to complement each other and assume joint responsibility in teaching students.[49] The original experiment by Robert Anderson involved both large teams, composed of five or six teachers, and small teams, composed of three teachers. The titles *team leader* and *senior teacher* were used to designate teachers who had responsibility for leadership in the

48 James E. Allen, "Forward," in Arthur D. Morse, ed., *Schools of Tomorrow—Today* (Garden City, N.Y.: Doubleday, 1960), p. 6.

49 Robert H. Anderson, Ellis A. Hagstrom, and Wade M. Robinson, "Team Teaching in an Elementary School," *School Review* (Spring 1960), pp. 71–84.

teams. Each team was assigned a part-time clerical aide, and the two large teams also were assigned a quarter-time teaching assistant.

As various schools across the country adopted the team concept, the team patterns varied. Most of the present plans provide for a learning situation where the master teacher or teacher with the most knowledge of the subject instructs a large group and where students have the opportunity to work in small groups with other teachers and to do individual work as well. An experienced or master teacher is usually teamed with less experienced teachers, student teachers, and a teacher aide.

Remuneration for increased responsibilities

The teacher designated as a team leader is sometimes paid an additional remuneration for his or her increased responsibilities. This stipend is supposed to serve as a means of holding able teachers in the classroom, rather than losing them to administration. In most cases, however, the schools using the team approach do not distinguish either the role or salary of various team teaching members. Rarely does the team have an aide or clerical assistant. Cooperative planning of curriculum and instruction is essential; however, in some instances there is conflict over the inadequate performance of team members and there is little time for planning. Charles Silberman's description of team planning seems to be characteristic of most schools.

Little time for planning

> An elementary school in one of the wealthiest suburbs in the United States claims to be using team teaching in its fifth grade. What this means is that some teachers are handling math and science, others English and social studies. It is called team teaching because the teachers allegedly "get together and discuss all the children." "Isn't that kind of conference difficult to fit into a full teaching schedule?" a visitor asks with feigned innocence. "Well, you know how it is," comes the reply. "We fit it in during lunch hour, or we stay around after three for a few minutes."[50]

The team approach has been successfully adopted in some form by many school systems, but it seems to have failed to achieve its intended purpose in many other places. Educators are still in the process of learning how to make team teaching work effectively in the classroom.[51]

Teacher Aides

Teacher aides, sometimes called paraprofessionals or auxiliary personnel, often are required to perform the tasks assigned to the educational assistant under differential staffing. However, the case for teacher aides can be considered independently of any particular model of faculty utilization.

Teacher aides were originally used to offset the shortage of classroom teachers in the early 1950s. The idea of using teacher aides on a systemwide basis was first tried in the Bay City, Michigan, schools in 1953. From there it

50 Silberman, *Crisis in the Classroom*, p. 162.

51 Mary Saily, "Teachers Team to Cope With Complex Materials," *Educational R & D Report* (Winter 1979), pp. 1–5.

quickly spread across the country. In 1967 a nationwide NEA survey showed that almost one in five schoolteachers, or 19 percent, had assistants of some kind.[52] About 14 percent shared the services of one or more aides with other teachers, and 5 percent had one or more aides of their own. Twice as many elementary school teachers as high school teachers reported having aides. The typical aide at that time earned about $2 per hour. Job qualifications varied among school systems. Most of them required at least a high school diploma.

Jobs for minorities

A massive program to train several hundred thousand auxiliary personnel was funded by the federal government in the late 1960s. Impetus for the program stemmed from a desire to train minority teachers, to provide jobs in ghetto areas, and to fight the War on Poverty, coupled with the advent of Headstart and Follow-Through programs. Thus the ranks of teacher aides had swelled to 200,000 by 1970, and it was estimated that by 1975 the number was 400,000.[53] This trend came to a halt, however, as federal spending decreased in the Nixon-Ford administration and as the demand for teachers waned in the 1970s.

Trend has now diminished

Across the country, state departments of education have been slow to develop and apply certification requirements for teacher aides—partially because of the past oversupply of teachers and the extra costs involved for instruction. Many wealthy school districts have a healthy number of aides in relation to their student enrollments, especially at the elementary level, while many large school districts employ them sparingly.

At present New York City is one of the few school systems that is still committed to teacher aides, who are referred to as paraprofessionals. The school system employs twice as many paraprofessionals as any other school system—about 10,000. They have permanent status and are unionized with the teachers. They have full medical and hospital coverage, obtain free schooling at the colleges, and in 1984 generally earned between $6.00 and $8.65 per hour depending on their education and experience.[54] Most important, a career ladder program has been developed for them; they may improve their education and job opportunities and move up the ladder to become regular teachers.

Flexible Scheduling

Although there are literally hundreds of different methods for grouping students and teachers, one of the most widely discussed proposals, which was introduced in the 1950s, is the concept of *modular scheduling*—a popular example of flexible scheduling. The idea, proposed by J. Lloyd Trump, is to organize the school around large-group instruction, small-group discussion,

52 "How Paraprofessionals Feel About Teacher Aides," *NEA Journal* (November 1967), pp. 16–17.

53 Allan C. Ornstein, Harriet Talmadge, and Anne W. Juhasz, *The Paraprofessional's Handbook* (Belmont, Calif.: Fearon, 1975); Stanley S. Robin and Martin O. Wagenfeld, *Paraprofessionals in the Human Services* (New York: Human Sciences Press, 1980).

54 Telephone conversation with Hanna Neuhaus, Director of Inservice Training for Paraprofessionals, United Federation of Teachers, New York City, May 4, 1984.

and independent study.[55] About 15- to 20-minute units of time replace the regular bell schedule and permit greater flexibility and variations in scheduling.

Organizing large, small, and independent groups

Large-group instruction includes activities carried out in groups of 100 or more students and occupies about 40 percent of the time. Instruction is carried out by a particularly competent teacher, and he or she is provided with additional time for preparation. Small-group instruction consists of ten to fifteen students and occupies about 20 percent of the students' time. Most of this activity is related to the large-group instruction, with the teacher serving as a consultant or counselor. Independent study consists of students in small groups of two or three, or as individuals, engaging in independent work on projects and research in laboratories, resource centers, libraries, and outside school. This occupies 40 percent of the students' time. Teachers and other personnel serve as consultants, and greater responsibility is afforded to the students.

Periodically the students are regrouped in order to cope with differences in student abilities and interests. Flexibility of grouping is a key concept. Students tend to enjoy the subject matter more, because of increased student interaction, independence in work and special projects, and flexibility in the delivery system. Teachers work ten to twenty hours and have more time for professional preparation and professional conferences. More time also is devoted to student conferences. The plan relies on a team teaching approach where high salaries are sometimes paid to team leaders and commensurately higher salaries to master teachers. A few schools have introduced some sort of flexible scheduling. Most schools, however, still maintain the older daily schedule.[56]

Individualized Instruction

The 1950s and 1960s saw a renewed stress on individualized learning, with new content and materials designed for individual learning, new instructional activities to provide a one-to-one teacher-student relationship, new machines to aid in this process, and a new philosophy that students should proceed at their own rate of comprehension. Thus a supporter of the individualized approach noted: "For half a century we have been committed to individualized instruction. . . . Yet only now have (we) been able . . . to act on our conviction with the prospect of success."[57] With the advent of team teaching, teacher

55 J. Lloyd Trump, *Images of the Future* (Washington, D.C.: National Association of Secondary School Principals, 1959); J. Lloyd Trump and Dorsey Baynham, *Focus on Change* (Chicago: Rand McNally, 1961).

56 Gary D. Fenstermacher and John I. Goodlad, eds., *Individual Differences and the Common Curriculum*, Eighty-second Yearbook of the National Society for the Study of Education Part I (Chicago: University of Chicago Press, 1983); Dan C. Lortie, *School-teacher* (Chicago: University of Chicago Press, 1975).

57 Alexander Frazier, "Individualized Instructions" (Paper presented at the Annual Meeting of the Association for Supervision of Curriculum Development, Los Angeles, November 1968) p. 1. Also see Alexander Frazier, "Individualized Instruction," *Educational Leadership* (April 1968), p. 616.

aides, flexible scheduling, and independent study, he concluded that education was ready to assume responsibility for preplanned individualized learning programs.

Principles of programmed and behavioral instruction

One of the best known individualized programs of the late 1950s and early 1960s was the Project on Individually Prescribed Instruction (IPI), which was developed at the University of Pittsburgh and later became known as Adaptable Environments for Learning (AEL). IPI applied the principles of programmed instruction and behavioral instruction. The curriculum was stated in behavioral objectives with proficiency levels; each student was diagnosed, and an individual plan was developed for each subject; several materials were introduced to provide a variety of paths for mastery of any given objective; learning tasks were individualized for each student; and there was continuous evaluation.

Individualized objectives and rates of learning

Other systems for delivering individualized instruction in elementary and secondary schools that appeared in the late 1960s are the University of Wisconsin's Individually Guided Education (IGE) and the Program for Learning in Accordance with Needs (PLAN). IGE is a total educational system for formulating and carrying out instructional programs for individual students in which planned variations are made in what each student learns, in how he or she goes about learning, and in how rapidly he or she learns. Instructional objectives are developed for each student; the student participates in a one-to-one relation with the teacher, teacher aide, or another student; and the program includes independent study, small-group instruction, large-group instruction, and various classroom activities. The actual mix of these activities for each student depends on the abilities of the student, the objectives to be attained, and the costs involved.[58] IGE was developed as an alternative to age-graded education and to unstructured open education, but it can be implemented in either age-graded or ungraded schools and in either self-contained or departmentalized classrooms.

The five components of the PLAN system are as follows: (1) a set of educational objectives, (2) related teaching-learning units, (3) a set of tests, (4) guidance activities to enhance self-understanding, and (5) an evaluation system. Individualization is essentially accomplished by (a) ungraded materials appropriate to the student level of achievement, (b) alternative sets of materials for each unit of instruction, and (c) two-week modules, arranged according to each student's level of achievement.[59]

All three systems—IPI, IGE, and PLAN—have been field tested and are used today to a limited extent. There have been various reports of success and significant gains in student achievement and comparative skills. The plans have not been implemented on a mass scale because of their cost and

58 Herbert J. Klausmeier, "The Wisconsin Research and Development Center for Cognitive Learning," in H. J. Klausmeier and G. T. O'Hearn, eds., *Research and Development Toward the Improvement of Education* (Madison, Wis.: Dembar Educational Research Services, 1968), pp. 146–156; Herbert J. Klausmeier and Richard E. Ripple, *Learning and Human Abilities*, 3rd ed. (New York: Harper & Row, 1971). Also see Klausmeier, *Learning and Teaching Concepts* (New York: Academic Press, 1980).

59 John C. Flanagan, "Program for Learning in Accordance with Needs" (Paper presented at the Annual Conference of the American Educational Research Association, Chicago, February 1968).

administrative obstacles. In many respects, these individualized approaches are the forerunner of today's diagnostic learning approaches, such as mastery learning, continuous progress, and direct instruction. Nevertheless, the majority of schools today are still geared to group instruction, group norms, and group expectations, rather than individual student differences.[60]

Group instruction prevails

Instructional Television

In the late 1950s a great many educators saw the new medium as a panacea for many educational ills. Instructional television (ITV) was expected to solve the teacher shortage, enable master teachers to reach more students, and make it possible to substantially increase class size. In addition, television was expected to reduce some of the inequalities of educational resources, enable students in rural and small schools to receive high quality instruction, and make available instruction in specialized subjects. It also was supposed to provide a library of tapes and kinescopes that would be reused like library books.

Both the Ford Foundation and the federal government poured tens of millions of dollars into a variety of ITV experiments. In Hagerstown, Maryland more than one hundred live programs were transmitted each week from five studios to 37 elementary and secondary schools containing 90 percent of the 18,000 students of Washington County schools. In Southwest Indiana, lessons were transmitted to more than 23,000 students in 108 schools. These experiments served as models to guide other school systems in adopting educational television.[61]

Criticisms of ITV

The experiments were initially perceived to be making a real contribution to education, and they became a vital part of many school systems; eventually, however, educational television was criticized for fragmenting learning, impersonalizing it, and standardizing it into mere information acquisition. Television failed to consider individual interests and learning rates; the costs were high; there were technical difficulties—and the effort was not considered worthwhile, since ITV mainly served as low-level occasional enrichment.

After a decade of intensive effort and expenditures, its most ardent advocates had to admit that ITV had not made a decisive impact on the schools.[62] Recent reviews of the research on instructional television indicate that although children can learn from TV in the classroom, few people can agree on how to use it most effectively.[63] The question that needs to be explored today, however, is why the medium proved so disappointing. Even

60 Benjamin S. Bloom, *Human Characteristics and School Learning* (New York: McGraw-Hill, 1976); John I. Goodlad et al., *A Study of Schooling* (Los Angeles: University of California Press, 1979).

61 Morse, *Schools of Tomorrow—Today*; Alexander J. Stoddard, *Schools for Tomorrow* (New York: Fund for the Advancement of Education, 1957).

62 Alvin C. Eurich, *Reforming American Education* (New York: Harper & Row, 1969).

63 Gretchen S. Barbatsis, "The Nature of Inquiry and Analysis of Theoretical Progress in Instructional Television from 1950–1970," *Review of Educational Research* (Summer 1978), pp. 399–434; Mary F. Compton, "Television Viewing Habits of Early Adolescents," *Clearing House* (October 1983), pp. 59–62.

"Sesame Street" and the "Electric Company," each of which reaches between 15 and 20 million children regularly and was originally intended to help disadvantaged children catch up with other students, had to be reassessed. "Sesame Street" and "The Electric Company" did improve the learning of disadvantaged children, but they helped more affluent youngsters at the same time and thus did little or nothing to close the gap between the two groups. There is some indication that students react positively to the use of ITV in the elementary schools, but the history of ITV in high schools has been one of many unproductive experiments and unfulfilled promises.[64]

Cable television and telecommunications

The most recent potential for instructional television involves cable television, telecommunication systems, and video disc players—hooked up to either home or school TV screens. Certainly school districts can telecast programs to various schools and classrooms for minimal or reasonable cost with their own district-wide system or via cable companies that must provide some educational programming for a nominal fee in most communities. It is possible, also, for students to share some instruction and to interact on the TV screen among themselves or with special tutors, teachers, or resource instructors, through special cable connections.[65] At present, however, few school systems utilize these instructional methods.

Programmed Instruction

Although a number of auto-instructional devices were developed during the 1920s, their impact was inconsequential. Except for sporadic use mainly during World War II, such devices were virtually forgotten until B. F. Skinner stimulated a new surge of interest in 1954.[66]

The principles of programmed instruction were derived from Skinner's principles of operant conditioning, which were based on his laboratory work with animals. A relatively small unit of information called a frame is presented to the learner as a *stimulus*. The learner is required to make a *response* by completing the statement or answering a statement. By a feedback system, the learner is informed if the response is correct or wrong. If wrong, he or she is told why. If correct, the response is *reinforced*. The learner is then presented with another frame, and the stimulus-response-reinforcement cycle is repeated until a series of hundreds or thousands of frames is presented and the program is completed in a logical sequence of information.

Stimulus-response-reinforcement cycle

64 Gerald S. Lesser, *Children and Television: Lessons from Sesame Street* (New York: Random House, 1974); Thomas Miller, "Identification Process and Sensory Impact of Children's Television Programming on the Preschool Child," *Child Study Journal* (September 1983), pp. 203–207; and Charles F. Schuller, "Using Instructional Resources and Technology," in D. E. Orlosky, ed., *Introduction to Education* (Columbus, Ohio: Merrill, 1982), pp. 400–429.

65 Nancy Henderson, "The Cable Connection Channels Kids' and Teachers' Creativity," *American School Board Journal* (January 1984), pp. 30–32, 40; William Hanks, "Using Cable Access Channel Increases Student Motivation," *Journalism Education* (August 1983), pp. 33–34.

66 B. F. Skinner, "The Science of Learning and the Art of Teaching" (Paper presented at a Conference on Current Trends in Psychology, University of Pittsburgh, March 1954.) For a current description of his approach to programmed instruction, see B. F. Skinner, "The Steep and Thorny Way to a Science of Behavior," *American Psychologist* (January 1975), pp. 42–49.

The instructional sequences are simplified to such a degree that if the percentage of errors of the average learner is more than 10 percent, the program usually is considered to be in need of revision.

Skinner called the device a "teaching machine." Since more attention was focused on the machine than on the instructional program, more machines than programs were produced during the first years of the movement, and many commercial companies produced them in ranges of $20 to $2,000. The concept caught on but as criticism of programmed instruction snowballed, the "boom" turned into a "bust." Even Sidney Pressey, the leading researcher who had worked with programmed instruction in the 1920s, attacked the procedures of the fifties as based on "a false premise that the important features of human learning are to be found in animals." He maintained that programmed learning procedures "fragmented learning, ... [reinforced] rote learning" and dehumanized education.[67]

Video materials

Despite these criticisms, the principles of programmed instruction are in use today, at home, in school, and in various computer-assisted programs and video disc materials, which provide immediate feedback and instant access to information. In stark contrast to the old printed methods and workbook materials, programmed instruction can be individualized, so that students interact with new video materials on the TV screen. The instruction depends on the student's entry level and is designed to accommodate many styles and rates of learning. Writing the software is crucial. With computer systems, programs can be quite sophisticated and can provide individualized programmed materials and methods to suit almost any student.[68]

Computer-Assisted Instruction

Three different types of instruction

The application of computer technology has increased steadily since the first commerical computer began operation in 1951. In education the computer is capable, first of all, of presenting individualized lesson material almost simultaneously with feedback and correction. The tutorial system offers a second approach, in which a computer takes over the responsibility for presenting inquiry learning. As soon as the student manifests a clear understanding of a concept or problem, he or she moves to the next exercise. The third and most sophisticated level of student-computer interaction is the dialogue system, which permits the student to conduct a genuine dialogue with and ask questions of the computer.

There are several advantages to using the computer for instruction: the current emphasis on individualized instruction, the increasing amount of new knowledge to be learned, the growing need for periodic upgrading of

67 Sidney L. Pressey, "Teaching Machine and Learning Theory Crisis," *Journal of Applied Psychology* (February 1963), p. 5.

68 Vicki B. Cohen, "The Interactive Features in the Design of Videodisc Materials," *Educational Technology* (January 1984), pp. 16–20; David H. Jonassen, "The Generic Disc: Realizing the Potential of Adaptive, Interactive Videodiscs," *Educational Technology* (January 1984), pp. 21–24.

one's education, and the unlimited diversity it presents for curriculum and teaching. Critics point out that the use of the computer limits human interaction in teaching and learning, that it leaves the role of the teacher unspecified, and that it provides little insight into student purposes, motives, or feelings. Most important, some educators believe that the values of individuality and human freedom are threatened by the widespread use of technology in education. Most of these same fears have been raised over the years with the introduction of other types of education machines—a perceived conflict between humanism and technology—but they remain important factors to consider.

Criticisms of computerized instruction

Because of their lowered costs and their pervasiveness in the home, in the workplace, and in government, computers will be widely used in the classroom. Although computerized instruction did not have a widespread impact on education from the 1950s to 1970s, schools tend to mirror society. Computers are beginning to have a significant effect on the classroom of the 1980s. The trouble is, according to one observer, that no one really knows how to use computers well for educational purposes.[69] Nevertheless, the potential is great and will occasion changes in the day-to-day operation of the classroom.

Computers enter the classroom

Although microcomputers are easily adapted to school instructional settings, appropriate software is needed before the schools can expand their commitment to computer-assisted instruction. (Most present computer software was initially developed for nonschool use.) Other problems include the need to train teachers who will be versed in computer instructional design and programming. Concern also has been raised about the nature of computer systems and languages, that they are somewhat complex and turn off many students who become frustrated or lose patience.[70] None of these problems are insoluble, but they are reasons for the slow school adoption of computers despite the widespread use of them in other sectors of society.

Computer systems and languages

Additional Innovations

More innovations between 1950s and 1980s

In addition to the aforementioned major innovations, many other innovations have been adopted only on a piecemeal basis. The following are representative innovations of the period between the 1950s and the 1980s:[71]

1. *Resource center.* A specialized center with learning materials specially selected to meet the needs of the students and staffed with teachers, teacher aides, and other special personnel.

69 Decker F. Walker, "Reflections on the Educational Potential and Limitations of Microcomputers," *Phi Delta Kappan* (October 1983), pp. 103–107.

70 David E. Tanner and David G. Armstrong, "Computer-Oriented Programs: Demonstrated Sex Appeal, but Embrace with Care," *High School Journal* (April–May, 1983), pp. 235–239; Walker, "Reflections on the Educational Potential and Limitations of Microcomputers."

71 Allan C. Ornstein, "Change and Innovation in Curriculum," *Journal of Research and Development in Education* (Winter 1982), pp. 27–33.

2. *School-within-a-school.* A large school organized into smaller units for administrative and/or instructional purposes.
3. *Open space facilities.* Classrooms and/or schools organized to permit students and teachers to move about and share space in various ways, ranging in size and purpose, but suggesting flexibility.
4. *Language laboratories.* Equipment used to present recorded voices as part of the audiolingual approach to learning a language.
5. *Telephone amplification.* Long-distance discussions held by students and/or the teacher with persons from outside the school, with amplification for the entire classroom to hear.
6. *Simulation or gaming.* An experience used to create a problematic situation, usually logical or reality-oriented, involving students in role playing and/or decision making.
7. *Pass-fail.* The option for students to take a specified number of courses, usually elective courses and no more than one course per term, on a pass-fail basis instead of for traditional grades.
8. *Nongraded programs.* A series of programs open to students without regard to grade level and/or sequence of courses. The students usually work at their own pace.
9. *Criterion-referenced tests.* Tests devised to measure specific learning changes, usually involving stated behavioral objectives and expected competencies.
10. *Independent study.* Work conducted by the student on a topic of interest, using school or nonschool resources with the teacher serving as a resource agent or guide.
11. *Community study.* Work done by students in the community, preferably with some health, social, or business institution, in conjunction with their school program and under the supervision of a teacher and another person or group of people outside the school; the focus is practical, not academic.
12. *Instructional materials center.* A center that houses a variety of printed and audiovisual materials for student use.

The 1980s has witnessed renewed interest in developing new curriculum and instructional techniques to meet the current and future needs of our students and society. A genuine reassessment is underway that may lead to major changes in our schools. In the discussion that follows, we will look at some of the possible directions that curriculum and instruction may take in the future.

Curriculum Trends: An Agenda for the Future

Opinions differ on the directions education will take, and library shelves are filled with volumes describing current and anticipated changes in society and education. Despite disagreements, however, considerable consensus exists on several broad trends that are likely to have a major impact on curriculum planning in the educational system. Some of the most important of these trends are listed below. The emerging curriculum responds to the urge to break away from traditional disciplines, to develop more interdisciplinary approaches. In the curriculum of the future, subject matter most likely will be less compartmentalized and more integrated and holistic. Although traditional subject boundaries will remain, there will be increased cross-subject material; knowledge will no longer be considered fragmented or linear, but multidisciplinary and multidimensional.

Less compartmentalized, more integrated curriculum

1. *Communications.* Technology will make it possible to revolutionize the communication of information and understanding in the classroom. The technological revolution in communications has been proceeding for many years, but most observers agree that there is no real end in sight. Substantial improvements in communications capacity will continue at an accelerating rate for the next few decades. Predictable and envisioned improvements in technology lead to such scenarios as the following:

Each student will have at his or her disposal a television receiver, either in his or her home or in a publicly supported learning center. Closed circuit and cable telecourses will be commonplace, and video discs and video-taped "telelessons" will replace textbooks and written materials. Students will have available a dial-access facility that permits access, via laser or a telephone, to a central learning center equipped with high-speed computers that can communicate with computers in any learning resource center anywhere in the world.[72]

2. *Computers.* We are in the midst of a technological and information revolution spawned by new networks and combinations of computer data bases—combined with telephones, satellite and cable transmission systems, and robots. Like the Industrial Revolution, this new revolution will ultimately affect how we work, where we live, and the quality of our lives. Terms such as *postindustrial society* and *third wave* connote the transformation that is now taking shape.[73] Miniaturization is certainly a key part of this revolution. Silicon chips the size of a child's fingernail have been developed with enormous memory capacity and ability to calculate. Hence, some knowledge of computers is fast becoming essential; in the future, many high-paying jobs will require this knowledge. People without it may very well be relegated to lower-paying jobs or find themselves unable to move beyond a certain point in the workforce or management team.

Silicon chips

The fourth R

Computer literacy will stand beside the three Rs as a fundamental skill. Knowing how to retrieve information, as opposed to having access to infor-

72 Glen E. Eye, "Instructional Technology Reshapes the School," in R. W. Hostrop, ed., *Education Beyond Tomorrow* (Homewood, Ill.: ETC Publications, 1975), pp. 23–33; Robert Gaynor, "Telecommunications Technology Review," *Educom* (Winter 1981), pp. 22–24.

73 Daniel Bell, *The Coming of Post-Industrial Society* (New York: Basic Books, 1976) and *The Third Technological Revolution* (New York: Basic Books, 1984); Alvin Toffler, *The Third Wave* (New York: Morrow, 1980).

mation, will mark the difference between an educated person and a semieducated person. If we are to take advantage of the ever-increasing quantity of information, commonly referred to as the *knowledge explosion,* we will have to rely on computer-based tools. We will need to distinguish between three levels of computer knowledge: (1) computer literacy, suggesting knowledge of how computers work and what they are used for; (2) computer competency, being able to use it as a tool in a particular field; and (3) computer expertise, suggesting the person whose profession is computing.[74]

750,000 to 1,000,000 computers in schools

Teachers are waking up to the fact that computers are here to stay and can be effective tools of instruction. In 1980, some 50,000 microcomputers were used in the nation's schools; by 1990, the number should reach 750,000 to 1 million; in other words, there will be several computers to a school. It is also envisioned that most secondary schools will be offering students an average of 30 minutes per day at a computer terminal, not to mention that many elementary schools already have students learning on computers, and some 50,000 or more teachers will be teaching computers as their main subject.[75]

What actually happens will depend to a large extent on the money available for the purchase of computers, the software available for student use, and the way computers are adopted into the curriculum.

What should be the objectives of using computers in schools?

Should they be restricted to students who have mathematical abilities? to certain grade levels? to particular subjects?

Should they be used to teach other subjects (that is, to provide drill or tutoring) or be used to teach about computing and programming?

Should students be charged user fees for using computers?

Training teachers for computer use

Who will train teachers in computer use?

Do we reorganize the classroom and have computers at every desk, say, as in an office, or do we limit our expectations to a computer laboratory?

How we resolve these questions will determine to some extent the trends that take effect by 1990.

Second or third careers

3. *Lifelong learning.* The trend toward lifelong learning is occurring in all modern societies as a result of the knowledge explosion and rapid social, technological, and economic changes that persuade or force people to prepare for second or third careers and to keep themselves updated on new developments that affect their personal and social goals. Education will continue to become more of a "lifelong" enterprise and increasingly will take

74 Judith A. Turner, "Ohio State Eyes 'Computer Literacy,' " *Chronicle of Higher Education* (January 11, 1984), pp. 1, 14.

75 Gary L. Donhardt, "Microcomputers in Education: Elements of a Computer-Based Curriculum," *Educational Technology* (April 1984), pp. 30–32; Arthur S. Melmed, "Information Technology for U.S. Schools," *Phi Delta Kappan* (January 1982), pp. 308–311.

place outside the confines of the traditional school. Taking note of these trends, the Carnegie Commission has developed the concept of a "step-in, step-out" educational system for lifelong learning. This means that people could move in and out of educational programs throughout their lives.

Some observers believe that much of the learning that has been provided by elementary, secondary, and postsecondary schools may be provided by business and industry in the future.[76] Still other scenarios envision educating adolescents and adults through a network of community resources and individually appropriate learning opportunities.[77]

4. *International cooperation.* Although historically the United States has taken a relatively isolationist position, interdependence among nations no longer allows Americans to ignore what happens elsewhere or to remain ignorant of developments in far-distant countries. Educators will feel the need to place a greater emphasis on understanding other nations and cultures than they have in the past.

A global village

In an era of rapid change and ever-increasing global interdependence, we are forced to appraise the tendencies of the times and recognize that the oceans no longer protect us from the problems or realities of the rest of the world. For instance, more than 50 percent of our oil is imported from the Middle East, a most unstable part of the world where tribal and religious conflicts can and already have interrupted the flow of energy imports, with the potential of causing major disruptions in the United States. About 15 million Third World children died of hunger last year, and another 800 million or more (about 20 percent of humanity) go to bed hungry or malnourished.[78] On a "small planet" like ours, other people's problems or strengths, sooner or later, affect us. We do indeed inhabit a global village; there is no escaping it.

Peace education

Both the United States and Soviet Union possess enough nuclear warheads to destroy the world. If a computer malfunctions or an unforeseen contingency develops, we are 30 minutes from nuclear destruction. Indeed, the effects of nuclear war have been vividly portrayed from the 1950s (*On the Beach* and *A Canticle for Leibowitz*) to the 1980s (*The Fate of the Earth* and *The Day After*, two television scenarios). The nuclear freeze and disarmament movements have swept across the United States, Western Europe, and Japan; they are filtering down into the schools and curriculum under the umbrella of peace education and the teaching of peacemaking strategies.[79]

76 Michael W. Apple, "Curriculum in the Year 2000," *Phi Delta Kappan* (January 1983), pp. 321–326; Russell C. Doll, "Speculations on the Meaning of the Trend Toward Corporate Education," *Phi Delta Kappan* (January 1980), pp. 333–337.

77 Mario Fantini, "From School System to Educational System," in P. Wagschal, ed., *Learning Tomorrows: Commentaries on the Future of Education* (New York: Praeger, 1979), pp. 109–117; Ivan Illich, *Deschooling Society*, 2nd ed. (New York: World, 1983).

78 Robert Heilbroner, *An Inquiry into the Human Prospect* (New York: Norton, 1980); Alvin Toffler, *Previews and Premises* (New York: Morrow, 1983).

79 See Stanley E. Elam, "Educators and the Nuclear Threat," *Phi Delta Kappan* (April 1983), pp. 533–537; Fred Rose, "Students Call for Nuclear Age Education," *Educational Leadership* (May 1983), pp. 42–43.

Innovative learning in today's schools must be widely international if a country is to participate effectively in the world. Educators need to raise the right issues and ask the right questions. The schools must revive dying foreign language programs. They might expand travel exchange programs and perhaps make study in another culture a requirement for graduation. For the near future, schools and colleges may be restricted by budget problems, but the need will become more evident and money may loosen up in this area of curriculum.

5. *Environmental education.* Mounting concern over such problems as pollution, overpopulation, and depletion of food and natural resources has created demands for more knowledge and new programs in ecology and environmental education. Much of the relevant content has long been included in traditional earth sciences, biology, and geography courses and in conservation programs. The new demand calls for a more meaningful and better coordinated program that raises the theme of crisis. Many people—including educators—believe that the worldwide ecosystem is in jeopardy and can no longer support the growing world population.[80]

The parade of grim environmental realities makes a long list, with extinction of large portions of vegetation, topsoil, natural resources, and animal life (*Homo sapiens* included) a real possibility sometime in the twenty-first century. If these threats are acknowledged as real, no educational system hoping to prepare students for the world tomorrow could fail to treat the environment as an important subject.

Rather than terrifying students about ecological disaster, the school system should help students understand that the environment is globally connected with humankind, which is a globally dominant species that has the potential wisdom to keep the environment safe from ruin. That is a more hopeful, less paralyzing view of the world, and a challenge for curriculum specialists.

6. *Energy education.* Between 1973 and 1980, the total heating bill more than doubled for American consumers, despite reduced fuel consumption. The cost of heating is expected to double again by 1986, partially as a result of deregulation and partially as a result of increased foreign costs and profit-taking at home.[81] Our entire society is faced with spiraling costs for all forms of fuel, electricity, and water. The need for an energy-wise policy, one that reduces consumption and waste and makes efficient and safe use of synthetic fuels, solar energy, waste products, and even coal is paramount if we are to maintain our economic health and standard of living.

Spiraling energy costs

We need to educate children for their roles as energy consumers and voters and as potential energy-related workers or technicians. Although there

80 Paul Ehrlich and Anne Ehrlich, *Extinction: The Causes and Consequences of the Disappearance of Species* (New York: Random House, 1981); *The Limits of Growth, A Report to the Club of Rome's Projection of the Predicament of Mankind*, 2nd ed. (New York: New American Library, 1974).

81 Allan C. Ornstein, "Frostbelt/Sunbelt Energy Policies: Social and Economic Implications," *High School Journal* (December–January 1984), pp. 92–103.

are many different opinions concerning the future direction of policies, consensus exists that it is essential to educate the public about energy; such an education starts at home and continues in the schools.

7. *Ethnic education and cultural pluralism.* That a rapid growth of curriculum offerings in various ethnic studies followed on the heels of black studies is not surprising. The sense of neglect and the need for identity and recognition are by no means limited to blacks. There are several ways to look at the rise of ethnic consciousness. On the positive side is the hope that these programs will lead to greater understanding of various groups and will enhance the concepts of cultural richness and diversity and of ethnic self-esteem. On the negative side is the possible divisive effect of these programs on the body politic, loosening the ties that bind our society together.

Cultural richness and diversity

The focus varies from state to state, ranging from little interest in ethnic studies to considerable legislation instituting various programs. In some cases, even though no laws or defined policy have been established on the state level, there is considerable local activity. Nearly forty states have published materials and media on the subject of ethnicity, nearly thirty states have formulated policy statements on ethnic studies, and nearly twenty states have mandated ethnic studies in school curriculum.[82] This trend should spread, since immigration has recently increased as more Third World people are entering this country.

8. *Nonsexist curriculum.* Curriculum and instruction are also influenced by Title IX of the Education Amendments of 1972 and by other laws and forces that aim to reduce sexism in education. Curriculum efforts in elementary, secondary, and postsecondary schools include a requirement that institutions develop programs to meet the athletic needs and interests of both sexes. There is recognition that women need to be trained, placed, and advanced in leadership positions in schools and colleges as teachers, coaches, officials, directors, administrators, and members of governing boards.

Educators are also working to reduce sexual stereotyping and other forms of sexism in textbooks and instructional materials. A comprehensive body of research indicates six forms of sex bias in textbooks—invisibility, stereotyping, imbalance, unreality, fragmentation, and language—which need to be corrected.[83] Sex bias tends also to operate in teacher expectations, teacher interaction patterns, vocational counseling, career education, and employment practices. Many people feel the need to bring sex equity from the periphery of conferences and meeting to the core and mainstream of school life, particularly as it relates to curriculum and instructional practices.

Sex bias in textbooks

9. *Dieting and exercise.* With the exception of a few health-conscious individuals, we have become a nation of junk eaters and flabby people. Amer-

82 See James A. Banks, *Multiethnic Education: Theory and Practice* (Boston: Allyn and Bacon, 1981); Thomas Sowell, ed., *American Ethnic Groups* (Washington, D.C.: Urban Institute, 1978).

83 Vincent Rogers et al., "Sex Education—Curriculum Issues," *Journal of Research and Development in Education* (Winter 1983), pp. 45–52; David Sadker and Myra Sadker, "The Development and Field Trial of a Non-Sexist Teacher Education Curriculum," *High School Journal* (May 1981), pp. 331–333.

Multicultural and ethnic education can help students become more aware of the cultural richness and diversity of our society.
(Nancy Hays/ Monkmeyer Photo Service)

icans are literally addicted to a diet of excessive sugar, salt, fats, refined starches, and caffeine. The cumulative effect of American eating habits, coupled with lack of exercise, is directly related to a shortened life span. Schools ought to provide guidance about diet and exercise, eliminate junk food from lunches and vending machines, develop adult programs that encourage healthy growth and development, and encourage parents to supervise their children's food consumption and exercise program. Recent research linking good nutrition and exercise for children to good health, proper growth and development, positive social behavior, and healthier adult years should lead schools to incorporate increased nutrition and exercise into the curriculum.[84]

Proper nutrition and exercise

10. *Sex education.* Despite objections from some community groups and sporadic controversy, sex education is filtering down to the elementary school curriculum. Because of mounting divorce rates, illegitimacy, and venereal disease among our youth, many educators and citizen groups have deemed sex education essential. Traditional instruction units in hygiene, home economics, and family living have been supplemented with comprehensive explanations and prescriptions about dating, marriage, parenthood, and health problems.

84 Judith Herr and Winifred Morse, "Food for Thought: Nutrition Education for Young Children," *Young Children* (November 1982), pp. 3–11.

As sex education programs in school increase, controversy among home, church, and school will probably grow, as well. Course content, discussion, and pictures could be controversial issues in some communities, as could the school's appropriate role and whether alternative modes of sex education are more appropriate. To be sure, sex education can be viewed as a health issue; a matter of moral values or religious beliefs; a family concern; a social, psychological, or physical matter; or an educational issue.[85] In our changing and pluralistic society, all of these views have merit. Curriculum specialists and teachers will have to wrestle with them.

Alternative approaches to sex education

11. *Aging education.* Not only are we an aging society, but all of us are on the same conveyor belt—the only difference is that we got on at different times. Some people feel that the schools should teach students to understand the problems and prospects of aging—how to cope with it on an individual basis (even though it may seem distant when we are young) and how to help loved ones (parents and grandparents) deal successfully with this developmental stage of life. There is something to be learned from traditional societies that center around large kinship groups; postindustrial society should be educated about the worth of the aged—perhaps one of the greatest untapped resources.

The conveyor belt is moving for us all

Eventually, the curriculum should treat many of the problems of aging as a form of discrimination, as another "ism." This emphasis parallels changes in curriculum concerning racism, ethnicism, and sexism.

Reform of vocational education

12. *Career education.* There is a widespread reform of vocational education. The long-standing discontent with vocational education has finally led to the development of work motivation programs for *all* youth. Characteristic of these career programs is the extension of career guidance activities, the involvement of community groups and business groups, and the increased provision of career information and occupational training at the high school level.

We can expect to see greater emphasis on teaching job-related skills and on disciplining students according to the norms that guide the workplace. As the nation moves increasingly into a postindustrial and information society, the potential for job unemployment and underemployment is great. Increased use of computers and robots are expected to replace 15 to 25 million manufacturing jobs (and another 5 million service jobs) by 1990; the decline in American manufacturing jobs will roughly coincide in magnitude with the agricultural revolution and will represent about 5 to 10 percent of the workforce.[86]

Postindustrial and information society

85 Mario D. Fantini, "Sex Education: Alternative Modes of Delivery," *Journal of Research and Development in Education* (Winter 1983), pp. 1–7.

86 "Jobs of the 1990s," *Fortune*, May 16, 1983, pp. 116–123; "Machines That Think," *U.S. News and World Report*, December 5, 1983, pp. 59–61; and "Unemployment," *Fortune*, May 16, 1983, pp. 107–115.

The workers who accept technology and are willing to retrain are far more likely to be employed than the workers who resist such innovation. Students who are counseled and educated properly will not emerge from school with obsolete knowledge and skills and will be better equipped for today's—and tomorrow's—job market. The situation in many of our educational (and employment) institutions is dismal now; we are unprepared to help American children and adults make the massive adjustments that lie ahead. There is no nationwide plan—educational, industrial, or governmental—that assesses the future occupational needs of society and focuses schooling and the nation's workforce on such needs; we are instead permitting the free market system and supply-and-demand swings of the workforce to dictate the future.

Viable and obsolete occupations

Society must prepare a future workforce, consisting of technicians, engineers, and managers, in the following areas: weapons and space; energy and nuclear systems; housing rehabilitation; hazardous pollution and industrial wastes; genetics; agricultural and processed food products; holographics and optics; tool and die, machine, and foundry systems; lasers and robots; allied health and geriatric services; and communication, mass media, computer, and information systems.[87] In short, the schools must identify (in cooperation with industry and government, one would hope) obsolete occupations, assess the new technologies and services, and prepare students for viable careers.

13. *Values education.* The greatest danger in planning future curriculum is the subordination of human values to technological advances. Worthwhile human goals ought not be replaced by computerized and mechanized techniques that may do more harm than good. For example, it may be undesirable to teach more facts about history if students are unable to use these facts to better understand the people they interact with and world in which they live. Similarly, drug education programs may only stimulate drug abuse unless students also understand how dangerous drugs are abused in everyday life. In short, when we plan curriculum, we need to be aware of the byproducts—both intended and unintended—and to weigh our immediate gains against their consequences. Apparent success could turn into disaster if the technological experts of tomorrow rush pell-mell into curriculum planning without knowing the effects of the new learning on the social and psychological development of the child, as well as on the attitudes and behaviors of teachers, parents, and community groups. The questions that we must always keep in mind as we move into the future are: "What kinds of people do we wish to produce?" and "What kinds of human behavior do we wish to encourage?"

What kinds of people we wish to produce

87 Allan C. Ornstein, "What Are We Teaching in the 1980s?" *Young Children* (November 1982), pp. 12–17; Harold G. Shane, "The Silicon Age II: Living and Learning in an Information Epoch," *Phi Delta Kappan* (October 1983), pp. 126–129.

Summing Up

1. Curriculum revision in the past was uniform and slow to change because the society was slow to change. Today the social changes are swift and curriculum modification must keep pace.
2. In organizing the curriculum, most educators hold to the traditional concept of curriculum as the body of subjects, or subject matter. Nevertheless, a number of contemporary educators are more concerned with the experiences of the learner, and in this respect regard the student as the focus of the curriculum.
3. In developing the curriculum, educators engage in a process of planning and selecting the elements and procedures of curriculum. Curriculum development takes place at several levels: national, state, school district, and local school.
4. The 1950s and 1960s produced several instructional innovations. Many of these reforms are in use in today's classrooms and schools.
5. As we move into the mid-1980s, we must rely on new courses and new concepts to help us cope with change. Although many sensitive and frightening questions must be resolved in the future—the possibility of nuclear warfare, pollution of the atmosphere, fuel scarcity, racial polarization, poverty—the basic curriculum questions remain the same. We ask ourselves: How can the schools meet the new challenges? How can schools best serve both the individual and society? What should be taught and how? And, is the curriculum relevant now and in the future?

Discussion Questions

1. Define curriculum and support your definition with at least three examples.
2. Describe a team-teaching program you would adopt for an elementary or secondary school. What problems might you encounter?
3. Summarize the rationale for flexible scheduling as it pertains to the learner and teacher.
4. How can the schools best adopt computers for instruction?
5. Discuss the problems and prospects of the curriculum trends discussed in the chapter. What other trends can you foresee?

Suggested Readings

Doll, Ronald C., *Curriculum Improvement: Decision Making and Process*, 4th ed. Boston: Allyn and Bacon, 1978.

An excellent overview on curriculum improvement, with emphasis on practical principles, problems, and solutions.

English, Fenwick W., ed. *Fundamental Curriculum Decisions*. 1983 ASCD Yearbook. Alexandria, Va.: Association for Supervision and Curriculum Development, 1983.

Twelve chapters by authorities in the field, who examine various aspects of curriculum; emphasis is on contemporary issues.

Joyce, Bruce, Richard H. Hersh, and Michael McKibbin. *The Structure of School Improvement*. New York: Longman, 1983.

The authors discuss the pattern of relationships among individual components of school change and innovation, including teachers, administrators, curriculum specialists, and community members.

Tanner, Daniel, and Laurel N. Tanner. *Curriculum Development: Theory into Practice, 2nd ed.* New York: Macmillan, 1980.

A historical overview of curriculum coupled with a synthesis of research, theory, and practice.

Tyler, Ralph W., *Basic Principles of Curriculum and Instruction*. Chicago: University of Chicago Press, 1950.

A classic text on how to develop a curriculum.

15

School Effectiveness and Reform

Focusing Questions

What are the characteristics of effective schools?

What does research say about the school improvement and reform process?

What types of instructional approaches can improve achievement?

What proposals are being made to reform high schools?

How can schools cooperate with other institutions?

What is the role of magnet and alternative schools?

Are nonpublic schools more effective than public schools?

How can rural schools be made more effective?

Should the United States emulate Japan?

THERE HAS ALWAYS BEEN CONSIDERABLE VARIATION IN INSTRUCtional patterns and effectiveness among the many thousands of elementary and secondary schools in the United States. Research in the 1970s and 1980s has now enabled educators to identify unusually effective schools and to describe some of the characteristics associated with their success. In addition, many potential reforms and improvements are currently being proposed to increase the effectiveness of U.S. schools. The purpose of this chapter is to summarize some of the major developments and issues involving the improvement of instruction in elementary and secondary schools. We will examine findings about the nature of effective schools, the school reform process, promising approaches for improving instruction, and a number of other important themes frequently discussed under the heading of school effectiveness.

Characteristics of Effective Schools

The push for greater school effectiveness has become a national growth industry in the 1980s, generating hundreds of research studies as well as thousands of discussion papers and school- and district-level improvement plans. This section describes some of the most important findings from this vast flood of materials.

Effective Teaching

One conclusion supported by recent research on effective schools is that teachers in these schools make use of effective instructional practices. Studies that focus on this idea are referred to as *effective teaching* or *effective instruction* research. This section summarizes what this research has to say about classroom management, effective instruction, and grouping of students.

Classroom Management Research on classroom management indicates that effective teachers utilize a variety of techniques to develop productive discipline and to motivate students. Effective teachers do the following:[1]

Successful classroom management techniques

1. They make sure that students know what the teacher will not tolerate.
2. They make certain that students know what to do if they need help or if they complete assignments early.
3. They follow through with reminders and rewards to enforce the rules.
4. They provide a smooth transition between activities.
5. They give students assignments of sufficient variety to maintain interest.
6. They monitor the class for signs of confusion or inattention.

1 Jere Brophy, "Classroom Organization and Management," *Elementary School Journal* (March 1982), pp. 265–285; Edmund T. Emmer, Carolyn M. Evertson, and Linda M. Anderson, "Effective Classroom Management at the Beginning of the School Year," *Elementary School Journal* (May 1980), pp. 219–231.

7. They use variations in eye contact, voice, movement, and academic activities to focus attention during lessons.
8. They do not respond to discipline problems emotionally.
9. They arrange the physical environment to complement their instructional objectives and methods.

Effective classroom management relies on a systematic strategy that starts with advanced preparation and planning before the school term and is reinforced throughout the year.

Delivery of instruction

Effective Instruction During the past decade, research has identified what appear to be the most important considerations in delivering instruction effectively in elementary and secondary schools, particularly with reference to improvement of students' comprehension skills. Some of the considerations emphasized in recent research are as follows:[2]

1. Effective teachers provide an overview of what is to be learned.
2. Readiness activities emphasize the linking of new information to prior knowledge and the preteaching of difficult vocabulary.
3. Emphasis is placed on examples and applications of concepts, principles, and vocabulary terms.
4. Explanations are provided of examples utilized in instruction.
5. Teachers monitor students' comprehension.
6. Learning cues, including cautions concerning probable errors, are provided.
7. Strategies for vocabulary learning and/or metacognitive learning (understanding and monitoring one's own learning) are taught.
8. Students engage first in guided practice and then in independent practice.
9. Stress is placed on continuous feedback to correct learning errors and provide positive reinforcement.

Homogeneous vs. heterogeneous grouping

Grouping of Students Research on grouping of students for effective instruction is complex and controversial. As we noted in Chapter 11, research indicates that homogeneous grouping by ability—a common strategy in the past—has failed to improve the performance of low achievers. On the other hand, heterogeneous grouping generally has not been successful unless it has utilized effective individualized and small-group methods that allow students to proceed at their own pace (continuous-progress instruction). Unfortunately, individualized, continuous-progress instruction has seldom succeeded, because it requires an enormous amount of planning, effort, and instructional resources to be effective.[3] When teachers have neither adequate

2 Beau Fly Jones, Laurence B. Friedman, Margaret Tinzmann, and Beverly E. Cox, "Enriched Mastery Learning: A Model of Comprehension Instruction Within a Mastery Learning Framework," in Daniel U. Levine, ed., *Implementation and Impact of Mastery Learning* (San Francisco: Jossey-Bass, 1984).

3 Michael Scriven, "Problems and Prospects for Individualization," in Harriet Talmage, ed., *Systems of Individualized Education* (Berkeley, Calif.: McCutchan, 1975).

assistance nor resources for providing students with continuous individual guidance, students tend to spend a good deal of time in unproductive seatwork.

A comprehensive discussion of the problems involved in grouping students for more effective instruction is beyond the scope of this text. However, the most important considerations can be summarized as follows:

Key considerations

1. Homogeneous grouping of low achievers can be successful if adequate steps are taken to eliminate low expectations, stigmatization (students' feelings that they can't learn because they are in a "dummy" class), and related problems.[4]
2. The number of low-achieving students must be kept small enough for the teacher to instruct them effectively.[5]
3. Either homogeneous or heterogeneous grouping can be effective, provided there are appropriate arrangements for scheduling of students, preparation of teachers, provision of supplies, and related matters.

Elementary Education

Most of the recent research on effective schools has focused on elementary education. Authors of various studies generally have identified specific characteristics of effective elementary schools and have usually defined effectiveness at least partly in terms of outstanding student achievement.

Edmonds's research

Studies of School Effectiveness One of the best-known studies is that of Ronald Edmonds and his colleagues, who define an effective school as one in which working-class students score as high as middle-class students on basic skills tests. Based on analysis of such schools, Edmonds identified an effective school as one in which there is (1) strong leadership, (2) an orderly, humane climate, (3) frequent monitoring of student progress, (4) high expectations and requirements for all students, and (5) focus on teaching important skills to all students.[6]

Other observers and groups frequently extend this type of list to include one or more additional characteristics. A good example is the analysis utilized by the Connecticut School Effectiveness Project, which describes an effective school as having the following characteristics:[7]

1. A *safe and orderly environment* that is not oppressive and is conducive to teaching and learning

4 Gaea Leinhardt and Allan Pallay, "Restrictive Educational Settings: Exile or Haven?" *Review of Educational Research* (Winter 1982), pp. 557–578.

5 Daniel U. Levine, "Some Key Themes and Considerations in Implementing Mastery Learning", in Levine, *Implementation and Impact of Mastery Learning;* Rebecca Barr and Robert Dreeben, *How Schools Work* (Chicago: University of Chicago Press, 1983).

6 Ronald R. Edmonds, "Programs of School Improvement: An Overview," *Educational Leadership* (December 1982), pp. 4–11.

7 Joan Shoemaker, "Effective Schools: Putting the Research to the Ultimate Test," *Pre-Post Press* (1982), p. 241.

Characteristics of effective elementary schools

2. A *clear school mission* through which the staff shares a commitment to instructional goals, priorities, assessment procedures, and accountability
3. *Instructional leadership* by a principal who understands and applies the characteristics of instructional effectiveness
4. A climate of *high expectations* in which the staff demonstrates that all students can attain mastery of basic skills
5. High *time on task* brought about when a high percentage of students' time is spent "engaged" in planned activities to master basic skills
6. Frequent *monitoring of student progress* using the results to improve individual performance and also improve the instructional program
7. Positive *home-school relations* in which parents support the school's basic mission and play an important part in helping to achieve it

Instructional and organizational arrangements

Additional insight has been provided by a 1982 report by Levine and Stark[8] on instructional and organizational arrangements at high-achieving inner-city schools in Chicago, Los Angeles, and New York. Community District 19 schools, in Brooklyn, New York, introduced a comprehensive reading approach that emphasized the Chicago Mastery Learning Reading Program (CMLRP), which is specifically designed to teach higher-order comprehension skills. After implementing the new reading program, the percentage of students in grades 2–8 reading more than a year below grade level fell from 45 percent in 1979 to 26 percent in 1983. The Los Angeles schools in the study had participated in the Curriculum Alignment Project,[9] in which the staff attended workshops that helped them coordinate instructional methods and materials with tests on specific skills emphasized in each grade and classroom. When such training is successful, teachers are less likely to rely solely on textbooks regardless of whether they are too simple or too advanced for students; instead, they are more likely to select from texts and other available materials or create new materials that are most appropriate for teaching a specific skill to a particular group of students. Drawing on the CMLRP, Curriculum Alignment training, and similar approaches, the unusually effective schools in this study exemplified the following characteristics:

Alignment of objectives, materials, and testing

1. Teaching objectives, materials, and testing were painstakingly aligned with each other. Teachers were selecting and emphasizing the most important learning objectives, looking for the best instructional materials to teach them, reducing duplication in instruction across grades, and moving away from page-by-page teaching of the textbook. Thus they were overcoming some of the instructional problems we described in Chapters 10 and 11.
2. Substitutes for the "pullout" approach had been introduced to provide compensatory education for low-achieving students. Rather than pulling students out of class for additional instruction that was not coordinated

8 Daniel U. Levine and Joyce Stark, "Instructional and Organizational Arrangements That Improve Achievement in Inner-city Schools," *Educational Leadership* (December 1982), pp. 41–48.

9 Fred Niedermeyer and Steve Yelon, "Los Angeles Aligns Instruction with Essential Skills," *Educational Leadership* (May 1982), pp. 618–620.

with the regular classroom, arrangements were made to fully coordinate compensatory and regular instruction.

3. Relatively great emphasis was placed on teaching higher-order cognitive skills.
4. Steps had been taken to ensure that appropriate instructional materials were easily and immediately available to teachers.
5. Systematic efforts had been made to minimize teachers' record-keeping work.
6. Emphasis was placed on improving the quality of students' homework and on increasing parent involvement in student learning.

Minimized record-keeping

Several individuals and agencies have gone further in "mining" the research to identify characteristics thought to be present at unusually effective schools. A good example of a thoughtful document of this type is the list of effective practices prepared for the Alaska Effective Schooling Program in cooperation with the Northwest Regional Educational Laboratory. After defining *practices* as "procedures, approaches, and attitudes" that focus the entire school on helping children learn, the authors described 129 specific practices under 33 headings.[10]

Many additional characteristics

Evaluation of Effective Schools Research A number of points should be kept in mind. First, one should recognize that there is widespread confusion concerning the definition of an effective school. Reports and plans are being discussed all over the United States, but there are nearly as many definitions of effective schools as there are people discussing them. Some people have in mind a school with unusually high academic achievement (taking account of social class), but others are thinking about a "self-renewing" school that can identify and solve internal problems, a school that promotes students' personal growth, a school that has shown improvement in academic achievement, or a school that concentrates on developing independent study skills and love for learning. And some people apparently have in mind no specific definition at all when they write or talk about making schools more effective.

Definitions differ

Second, most of the more rigorous studies have been concerned entirely or largely with inner-city schools. Those schools identified as unusually effective in such studies generally have been poverty schools in which academic achievement is higher than that at most other schools with similarly disadvantaged students. It is more difficult to identify unusually effective schools outside the inner city, where high achievement is more common. In addition, the key components of effectiveness outside the inner city may differ somewhat from those at poverty schools.

Research emphasizes inner-city schools

10 Alaska Effective Schooling Program, *Effective Schooling Practices* (Portland, Or.: Northwest Regional Educational Laboratory, n.d.). Another list of 50 selected characteristics was used to construct a school-diagnosis questionnaire is described in David A. Squires, William G. Huitt, and John K. Segars, *Effective Schools and Classrooms: A Research-Based Perspective* (Washington, D.C.: Association for Supervision and Curriculum Development, 1983).

Little experimental research

Third, nearly all the research on effective schools is correlational. That is, researchers have identified characteristics (correlates) of unusually effective schools, but few studies have manipulated a particular variable, such as leadership qualities of the principal or expectations for students, to determine the effect on achievement gains. This failure makes it difficult to be sure that work to improve a given characteristic will make any real difference.

Methodological problems

Fourth, other methodological problems have left much of the research vulnerable to criticism.[11] For example, schools identified as effective in a given subject (say, reading) during a given year may not be effective on other measures or the next year. In addition, controls for students' social class and family environment frequently are not adequate to attribute high achievement to school characteristics. This can happen, for example, when magnet schools enrolling inner-city students are judged as unusually effective, but further research would show that their students came from highly motivated poverty families dissatisfied with their neighborhood schools.

More specificity needed

Fifth, the general level of most characteristics cited in the literature is such that they tend to "beg the question" of what teachers and principals should do in the schools. For example, saying that a school requires good leadership and a productive climate does not provide much direct guidance on how to accomplish these objectives. It is probably necessary to state many characteristics at a general level because more specific recommendations would not fit all schools. Nevertheless, many educators believe that much of the school effectiveness literature is still too vague to offer real assistance in the schools. (On the other hand, it should be recognized that some of the effective school characteristics, such as Levine and Stark's findings on the negative effects of "pullout," have relatively specific, practical implications based on considerable support from research.)

Importance of school-level emphasis

Sixth, the emphasis in effective schools research clearly is on school-level or schoolwide practice, rather than on teaching in individual classrooms. The research says that teachers in effective schools use effective instructional practices (as described above), but it is the school-level emphasis that makes the movement potentially potent in overcoming the obstacles to improvement (that is, the "regularities" of traditional schooling) described in Chapter 10. The effective schools movement views the school as an institution in which consistent and coordinated change can yield large gains in student performance. For example, one of the frequent problems in schools is that many students—particularly low achievers—are reluctant to engage in difficult learning tasks oriented toward higher-order skills, and many teachers accommodate them by emphasizing rote learning, which at least contributes to an orderly environment. This type of situation is unlikely to change significantly unless all or most of the teachers in a school work together to raise expectations and requirements for better performance on meaningful learning dimensions.

Consistency throughout the school

11 See John H. Ralph and James Fennessey, "Science or Reform: Some Questions About the Effective Schools Model," *Phi Delta Kappan* (June 1983), pp. 689–694.

Secondary Education

Little research available

Few studies have focused on identifying the characteristics of effective secondary schools. One reason for the shortage of research is the small number of inner-city secondary schools that stand out as having high achievement. Hard as it has been to find unusually successful inner-city elementary schools (in terms of academic achievement), finding successful secondary schools has been almost impossible.

Intermediate Schools In the past few years, a few inner-city secondary schools have demonstrated that their students' achievement can be raised to relatively high levels. After searching to find high-achieving inner-city **intermediate schools** (defined as junior high schools including grades 7, 8, and 9 or middle schools including grades 7 and 8), Levine and his colleagues identified five such schools in four big cities.[12] In addition to finding that these schools had the same general characteristics that researchers had identified for effective elementary schools, the investigators concluded that effective inner-city intermediate schools in their sample strongly emphasized the following commonalities:

Characteristics of effective intermediate schools

1. Organizational arrangements facilitated improved reading performance among low-achieving students.
2. Teachers emphasized achievement of higher-order cognitive skills.
3. Guidance and personal development of students were emphasized.
4. Expectations and requirements for student performance were high throughout the school.

One interesting and important fact about the successful intermediate schools was that each had somewhat different approaches and mixtures of approaches for attaining the goals implicit in the four characteristics described above. Some of the approaches used by these schools included the following:

Arrangements for low achievers

1. Effective arrangements for low achievers
   a. Small classes of low achievers taught by highly skilled teachers
   b. More time devoted to reading, language, and math
   c. Individual and small group tutoring
   d. School-within-a-school units for low achievers
2. Emphasis on higher-order skills
   a. Availability of elective courses emphasizing these skills
   b. Instructional materials designed to teach higher-order skills
   c. Improved coordination between electives and regular courses
   d. Instructional strategies designed to develop thinking and comprehension skills

12 Daniel U. Levine, Rayna F. Levine, and Eugene E. Eubanks, "Instructional and Organizational Characteristics of Unusually Effective Inner City Intermediate Schools" (Paper prepared for the School of Education, University of Missouri-Kansas City, 1983); idem., "Characteristics of Effective Inner City Intermediate Schools, *Phi Delta Kappan* (June 1984), pp. 707–711.

Effective schools emphasize higher-order cognitive skills and high academic expectations. *(Frank Siteman/Jeroboam)*

3. Emphasis on guidance and personal development
   a. Large numbers of counselors and guidance personnel
   b. Elective courses emphasizing personal development
   c. Utilization of community agencies
   d. Group counseling
4. High institutional expectations
   a. Contracts with students and parents
   b. Required summer school for failure in any subject
   c. Schoolwide point systems for students
   d. Weekly or biweekly report cards

Institutional expectations

Structural changes

All five schools made *structural* changes to improve the performance of their students, particularly their low achievers. By **structural change,** we mean major modifications in the school schedule as well as in the way students and teachers are assigned to classes. For example, one of the schools had changed the typical pattern so that classes of low achievers were much smaller than average classes; another had assigned seventh and eighth graders to only two teachers each for English, social studies, science, and math; and several had reduced the time devoted to science and social studies in order to increase the allocation for reading and math. Such changes appear to be prerequisite to school effectiveness at the secondary level.[13]

13 See, for example, William A. Firestone and Robert E. Herriott, "Prescriptions for Effective Elementary Schools Don't Fit Secondary Schools," *Educational Leadership* (December 1982), pp. 51–53; Theodore R. Sizer, "High School Reform: The Need for Engineering," *Phi Delta Kappan* (June 1983), pp. 679–683.

Conforms with middle school philosophy

Most characteristics of effective inner-city intermediate schools probably are important in effective nonurban schools, although the importance of a given characteristic may vary somewhat from one type of school to another. The emphasis on students' higher-order thinking skills and personal development is a standard component of middle school philosophy; from this point of view the successful inner-city schools identified by Levine and his colleagues had not done much more than make major structural changes needed to implement goals frequently recommended by experts on the education of adolescents.

Senior highs are complex

Existing literature is questionable

Senior High Schools Unusually effective senior high schools have been even harder to identify than effective intermediate schools. Because the goals and programs of most senior high schools are so diverse and complex, it is difficult to conclude that one school is generally more effective than another, even when the social class of the student body is taken into account. In addition, hardly any senior high schools serving a representative poverty population stand out as being relatively high in achievement. Thus the most frequent definition of effectiveness at the elementary and intermediate levels is not applicable. Several authors have attempted to draw conclusions from descriptions of inner-city senior high schools that they identified as unusually successful.[14] Close examination of their writings, however, generally indicates that these schools either constituted high-dropout environments where only a relatively small and selective group of students advanced beyond the ninth grade or they utilized extremely rigorous discipline policies that led many students to transfer (or drop out) and thus provided a better learning environment for those who remained. The latter strategy may be defensible on several grounds, particularly if a school district establishes small alternative schools for students eliminated from regular high schools. However, schools employing this strategy offer little guidance for identifying the characteristics of senior high schools that successfully serve a comprehensive population with a high proportion of alienated or low-achieving students.

Developments at South Boston High School

One of the few senior high schools for which concrete data indicate unusual effectiveness is South Boston High School. Reform of South Boston occurred over several years during a time of continuing turmoil in the Boston school system, but by 1980 impressive data were available on improvement in the performance of students.

Between 1979 and 1980, for example, average reading scores went from the 16th percentile to the 40th percentile in the ninth grade and from the 18th to the 32nd percentile in the tenth grade. In addition, the percentage of graduates attending postsecondary education institutions increased from less than 8 percent in 1976 to 40 percent in 1980. Changes that appear to

14 For an example, see Thomas Sowell, "Black Excellence: The Case of Dunbar High School," *The Public Interest* (Spring 1974), pp. 5–12.

have been most important in accounting for these and other improvements at South Boston included the following:[15]

Changes at South Boston

1. A new principal and administrative team made major changes in traditional organizational patterns and insisted that staff re-examine their instructional methods.
2. More than two-thirds of the faculty were replaced by teachers willing to discard ineffective traditional methods.
3. Nearly all ninth and tenth graders were placed in reading and writing courses rather than in traditional English classes.
4. Students were placed in mathematics courses rather than in "business mathematics," which for the most part repeated beginning arithmetic.
5. A number of in-school and out-of-school alternatives were established. These alternatives include a self-contained school-within-a-school that emphasized academic learning and a mini-school that emphasized experiential learning and individualized instruction.
6. Work-study programs based on learning opportunities in the community were made available to many students after the ninth grade.
7. Discipline, including strict attendance and tardiness policies, was very firm but also fair.
8. An effective in-school suspension program was introduced. This approach differs from many in that participating students are fully isolated from the remainder of the school during their period of suspension.
9. Guidance in personal development was emphasized for students in the ninth and tenth grades.
10. School pride and spirit were systematically emphasized.

General characteristics supported in previous research

Since no two schools share exactly the same problems and possibilities, one cannot say that a successful senior high school should implement the identical changes as were introduced at South Boston. However, some of the South Boston characteristics, such as systematic emphasis on school spirit, firm but fair discipline, and emphasis on development of reading and math skills, have received considerable support in research on effective high school approaches for improving student performance, particularly among low achievers.[16] In addition, South Boston illustrates the importance of structural change.

Examples of structural changes

After studying the literature on high schools (both junior and senior) that are trying to improve the performance of low achievers in reading and

15 This portrayal of South Boston is drawn from the authors' personal observations and from Geraldine Kozberg and Jerome Winegar, "The South Boston Story: Implications for Secondary Schools," *Phi Delta Kappan* (April 1981), pp. 565–569.

16 National Institute of Education, *Violent Schools—Safe Schools* (Washington, D.C.: Government Printing Office, 1978).

other subjects, Levine and Sherk identified some of the most viable and promising structural changes.[17]

School-within-a-school

1. *School-within-a-school for low achievers.* Students who can read but are more than two or three years below grade level are assigned to a school-within-a-school serving 80–120 students and staffed by four or five teachers (English, reading, math, science, and social studies) and a coordinator. If teachers in this type of program are specially selected for their ability and willingness to work with low achievers, participating students can make very large gains in reading and other basic skills. This approach is illustrated in a 1983 booklet by Wehlage.[18]

Grouping by previous reading achievement

2. *Intragrade grouping by previous achievement.* An alternate approach to providing effective reading instruction for low achievers is to group across grade levels for English. Grouping should not involve a large number of levels, in order to avoid potential disadvantages of homogeneous grouping. High schools in Detroit, Kansas City, and elsewhere are developing promising approaches, which generally involve three levels: (1) nonreaders; (2) poor readers—often the majority of students in the inner city; and (3) students at or above grade level. Nonreaders are taught in very small groups, and a major effort is made to provide appropriate instruction for poor readers.

Dewey High School

3. *A longer and different school day.* Possibilities for changing the school day to facilitate student achievement in various subjects are exemplified by the John Dewey High School in Brooklyn, New York.[19] Dewey appears to have successfully provided effective educational opportunities for its diverse student body through such interrelated changes as a lengthened school day, establishment of independent learning centers in every major subject, and provision of smaller classes and extra assistance for low-achieving students.

Cleveland Heights High School

4. *Achievement centers.* The achievement center is a promising approach under development at Cleveland Heights (Ohio) High School. After specific learning objectives are identified for a given grade and subject area (for example, tenth-grade English), an achievement center is established for both remedial and developmental purposes. A student who does not have skills prerequisite for a particular unit or who needs special assistance in developing his or her full potential will attend the achievement center instead of or in addition to the regular class. Achievement center placement gener-

17 Daniel U. Levine and John K. Sherk, Jr., "Organizational Arrangements to Increase Productive Time for Reading in High Schools" (Statement prepared for International Reading Association response to *A Nation at Risk*, November 1983).

18 Gary G. Wehlage, *Effective Programs for the Marginal High School Student* (Bloomington, Ind.: Phi Delta Kappa, 1983).

19 Sol Levine, "The John Dewey High School Adventure," *Phi Delta Kappan* (October 1971), pp. 108–110.

ally replaces the regular class for about two weeks, and close coordination is maintained between achievement center staff and the regular teacher.

Five-school project

5. *Instructional teams.* The potential value of instructional teams as a basis for secondary school organization is suggested in a recent study of five diverse schools. The study attempted to identify and assess approaches for implementing flexible instructional programming, individual goal setting for students, multiple learning options, and other arrangements designed to ensure productive learning.[20] Organizational arrangements included the establishment of instructional and advisory units consisting of four academic teachers and about 120 students.

Some Conclusions About Projects to Improve School Effectiveness

Effective schools projects are widespread

Improvement at Milwaukee elementary schools

Attempts to improve instruction in elementary and secondary schools, both in the inner city and elsewhere, are being based on effective schools research. For example, educators in Chicago, Detroit, Milwaukee, Memphis, New York, and St. Louis are trying to create successful inner-city schools by introducing the practices identified in previous research. Departments of education in California, Connecticut, Florida, New Jersey, Ohio, and other states are providing services to help low-performing schools become more effective. Among eighteen Milwaukee elementary schools that have been participating in a project to raise achievement in the inner city, the percentage of fifth-grade students reading in the lowest performance category decreased from 55 percent in 1979 to 37 percent in 1983, and the comparable decline in math was from 42 percent to 21 percent. In the past, successful inner-city elementary schools were "mavericks," whose success was attributed mainly to the efforts of an atypical principal. It now appears to be possible to create such schools through careful planning and implementation of improved arrangements for curriculum and instruction.[21] Further information on the Milwaukee project has been provided by Maureen Larkin, who has analyzed differences between the schools that improved a great deal and those that improved least. She described the following characteristics and practices of the high-improvement group.

Articulation of objectives and standards

> *The more effective schools had clearly articulated their grade level objectives and minimum standards in each subject area.*
>
> The staff ... participated in the development of the grade level objectives and standards and communicated to students and parents that mastery of these objectives was prerequisite for success at the next grade level.

20 Herbert J. Klausmeier, Ronald C. Serlin, and Monica C. Zindler, *Improvement of Secondary Education Through Research: Five Longitudinal Case Studies,* Progress Report No. 83-12 (Madison, Wis.: Center for Education Research, 1983); Herbert Klausmeier, James Lipham, and John Danesh, *The Renewal and Improvement of Secondary Education* (Lanham, Md.: University Press of America, 1984).

21 Daniel U. Levine and Eugene E. Eubanks, "A First Look at Effective School Projects in Milwaukee and New York," *Phi Delta Kappan* (June 1983), pp.697–702.

Emphasis on homework

> *The more effective schools developed a schoolwide homework policy that expected all students to complete daily homework assignments.*
>
> . . . The principals and teachers enforced the policy by monitoring the doors at dismissal and sending empty-handed students back to their rooms.
>
> *Teachers in these schools planned to teach the entire grade level curriculum content to all of the students.*
>
> Teachers used content coverage schedules to plan on a yearly, weekly, and daily basis.[22]

Other encouraging reports

Although hundreds of projects designed to make public schools more effective are underway in the United States, very few have collected the long-term data on student performance needed to determine whether most are likely to be ultimately successful. On the other hand, encouraging preliminary reports are coming in from a number of locations. Initial assessment of the Maryland School Improvement Through Instructional Process Program indicates that two-thirds of the teachers participating in the active teaching component (which incorporates principles of effective teaching) or the mastery learning component believe that the project has improved their performance.[23] Provided that effective schools projects make good utilization of what is known about the school improvement process, they may well lead to widespread gains in student performance.

The School Improvement and Reform Process

Promulgating, legislating, and even packaging change is not the same as actually changing. Analysis of past efforts to improve schools has resulted in a much better understanding of the steps that must be taken to ensure that reform efforts have a significant and lasting impact. Among the lessons that can be deduced from past innovative efforts are the following:

Failure to implement

Improper implementation

1. *Adaptive problem solving.* Implementation of an innovation frequently either is not carried out successfully (that is, the innovation is never truly implemented) or has little or no effect on students because a host of problems arise to stifle practical application. For example, experts may devise a wonderful new science curriculum for fourth graders and school districts may purchase large quantities of the new curriculum materials, but teachers may choose not to use the materials, may use them improperly because they do not fit the existing curriculum or schedule, or may not know how to use them. Innovations are not likely to be implemented successfully

22 Maureen McCormack Larkin, "Insights into the School Effectiveness Process," *The Effective School Report from Research and Practice* (March 1984), p. 4.

23 Sheppard Ranbom, "Maryland Reports Achievement Gains Follow Use of New Teaching Methods," *Education Week*, April 25, 1984, p. 9.

unless the organization introducing them is *adaptive* in the sense that it can identify and solve day-to-day implementation problems.[24]

2. *School-level focus.* Because the innovating organization must identify and solve day-to-day problems, the focus in bringing about change must be at the level of the individual school building where many of the problems occur.[25]

3. *Leadership and shared agreements.* Implementation of a significant innovation requires change in many institutional arrangements, including scheduling of staff and student time, selection and utilization of instructional methods and materials, development of new behaviors and attitudes on the part of teachers and students, and mechanisms for making decisions. The building principal, who is responsible for arrangements throughout the institution, usually is the key person in successfully implementing change. In addition, the faculty must have a "shared culture," or shared vision of the kinds of changes that are possible and necessary to improve their instructional program; otherwise, the staff is unlikely to seriously consider proposals that require significant change in existing behaviors and arrangements.

Shared vision

Some sites require much more time and effort to develop shared agreements than do others. At some schools there is considerable agreement that achievement must be improved and that this requires change in many current arrangements; here the problems of change management are largely technical. At other schools, lip-service given to the need for improvement does not denote any real willingness to change existing practices. If this is the case, the first emphasis must be on organizational development designed to help faculty better evaluate what they are doing and make informed decisions on how to improve their program.[26]

Some schools need organizational development

4. *Teacher involvement.* Because people who are expected to alter their working patterns will not cooperate fully unless they have a voice in designing and implementing change, teachers who are to use innovative methods and materials in the classroom must have an opportunity to help select and evaluate them.[27]

5. *Multiple obstacles.* Major changes require not only a good deal of time and many resources but also a systematic examination of all their implications and a plan for overcoming the many obstacles that will arise; otherwise they will be swallowed up by forces that tend to maintain stability. As

24 Willis D. Hawley, "Horses Before Carts: Developing Adaptive Schools and the Limits of Innovation" in Dale Mann, ed., *Making Change Happen?*, (New York: Teachers College Press, Columbia University, 1978), pp. 224–253; Michael Fullan, *The Meaning of Educational Change* (New York: Teachers College Press, Columbia University, 1982).

25 John I. Goodlad, *A Place Called School* (New York: McGraw-Hill, 1984).

26 Gordon L. Lippitt, *Organization Renewal* (Englewood Cliffs, N.J.: Prentice-Hall, 1982).

27 Stuart C. Rankin, "A View from the Schools," in Gary A. Griffin, ed., *Staff Development*. Eighty-second Yearbook of the National Society for the Study of Education (Chicago: University of Chicago Press, 1983), pp. 251–259.

A principal's leadership and ability to create among the faculty a sense of shared vision about needed changes are essential elements of the school improvement process.
(James H. Karales/Peter Arnold, Inc.)

Tendency toward equilibrium

one observer has noted, "Organizations legitimately seek a state of equilibrium in order to sustain themselves. . . . Schools can tolerate only so much change and still attend to the business of 'keeping school,' and planned change programs should be sensitive to that need."[28]

Ownership important

Insistence on change

6. *Combination top-down and bottom-up approach.* Because years of research underlined the importance of teacher participation in decisions, researchers in the 1960s and 1970s tended to emphasize a "bottom-up" approach in the change process in order to encourage a sense of "ownership" among teachers asked to devote much time and energy to implementing improvements in curriculum and instruction. However, research in the 1980s has tended to underline the importance of "top-down" components in initiating change succesfully. Insistence on and support for change by administrators, school board members, and others at the school, district, and state levels frequently are required to initiate meaningful action at the classroom level. Two major, independent studies of innovation efforts have concluded that top-down initiation and support of the change process frequently is required to institutionalize long-term improvements.[29] Organizational development specialist Matthew Miles has delineated the stance of top-level administrators who communicate to principals and teachers an understanding that

28 Wayne J. Doyle, "A Solution in Search of a Problem. Comprehensive Change and the Jefferson Experimental Schools" in Mann, *Making Change Happen?,* p. 97.

29 A. Michael Huberman and Matthew B. Miles, *Motivation Up Close: A Field Study in 12 School Settings,* vol. 4, *People, Policies and Practices: Examining the Chain of School Improvement* (Andover, Mass.: The Network, 1982); David D. Marsh and Paul Berman, "Conceptualizing the Problem of Increasing the Capacity of Schools to Implement Reform Efforts" (Paper delivered at the annual meeting of the American Educational Research Association, New Orleans, April 1984).

"we are going to try a new approach, you are going to implement it, and we are going to help you."[30] Miles believes that administrative *pressure* and *support* frequently lead teachers to develop *mastery* of an innovation. Mastery helps develop the *commitment* to implement the change effectively.[31]

Of course, the support provided to improve instruction at the school level must be extensive and well-planned, with considerable emphasis on local adaptation and decision making. From this point of view, successful change seems to require a mixture of top-down initiation and bottom-up decision making. This mixture will vary with the situation in particular schools and districts, the nature and stage of the change, and other considerations. For example, large urban districts typically function in a relatively turbulent and difficult environment that requires relatively more initial top-down initiative; implementing a change—such as individualized instruction—that involves fundamental reform of all arrangements throughout a school requires relatively more emphasis on bottom-up adaptation.

Top-down and bottom-up mixtures

7. *Data collection.* One particularly important component in carrying out the change process is the collection of data identifying possible deficiencies in a school's arrangements and outputs. Other things being equal, faculty will be more likely to change their behavior and arrangements if data clearly indicate a need for such change. For this reason, leading efforts at organizational improvement generally have emphasized the collection of appropriate data to identify needs and directions for institutional improvement.[32] Many effective school projects utilize questionnaires, interviews, and document analysis to prepare comprehensive school profiles, which attempt to pinpoint problems in a school and specify the issues that need to be addressed in designing change.

Projects depend on problem identification

8. *Training of staff.* Staff development (formerly called in-service education) is a core activity in the school improvement process. Staff development to support improvement should be centered on the school as the basic unit, *not* on the individual teacher. In the case of an elementary school, the entire staff should participate; in secondary schools, departments may be the appropriate unit for some activities. Staff development should be an interactive process in which teachers and administrators work together at every stage. Collaborative planning develops collegial responsibility for improvement.[33] Staff development generally is most successful when it takes place during the regular school day.

Collegial staff development

30 Matthew B. Miles, personal communication, March 27, 1984.

31 Matthew B. Miles, "Unraveling the Mystery of Institutionalization," *Educational Leadership* (December 1983), pp. 14–19.

32 Data collection components of an organizational development or improvement effort frequently are referred to as "survey feedback." See Fullan, *The Meaning of Educational Change,* and Richard A. Schmuck et al., *The Second Handbook of Organizational Development in Schools* (Palo Alto, Calif.: Mayfield, 1977).

33 Lawrence Lezotte, "Building Collegiality," *The Effective School Report from Research and Practice* (April 1984), p. 4; Bruce Joyce and Renee Clift, "The Phoenix Agenda: Essential Reform in Teacher Education," *Educational Researcher* (April 1984), pp. 5–18.

Promising Instructional Approaches

Many new approaches

Many instructional approaches developed during the past decade show great promise for improving the quality of education in elementary and secondary schools. We already have mentioned several such approaches, including bi-cognitive instruction and the Kamehameha Early Education Program described in Chapter 12. We do not have space to describe or even list all of the instructional approaches that educators are now developing and implementing in elementary and secondary classrooms. Instead, we will illustrate some of these exciting possibilities by describing three evolving instructional approaches that appear to be successful when they are implemented effectively

Student Team Learning

Learning teams

Student Team Learning (STL), along with other forms of cooperative student learning, constitutes one of the most powerful instructional approaches developed in recent years. The STL approach incorporates a set of techniques in which students work in four- to five-member learning teams and receive recognition based on the degree to which all team members have individually mastered a common body of information or skills. The class follows a regular sequence of activities: a period of lecture-discussion; another period of team study, in which team members use worksheets to practice the materials and to assess one another; and a third period in which students are either individually quizzed or compete against members of other teams in an academic game.

Student scores are based on improvement over their own past performance or on their game scores in competition with equals; both of these systems make it possible for all students to do well if they work hard. Team scores are the average of members' individual scores, and the most successful teams are recognized in class newsletters or on bulletin boards. Student Team Learning methods thus constitute a relatively comprehensive program, based on psychological theories of group performance and group rewards, but also containing many separable elements, such as rewards for improvement, a regular schedule of teaching-study-quiz, and public recognition for successful performance.[34]

Positive research results

Research on Student Team Learning has shown positive results over a range of student outcomes in such areas as reading, math, science, and social studies. Properly implemented, STL results in significant gains in academic achievement as well as improvement in attitudes toward school, self-concept, and other noncognitive objectives of cooperative learning. Research indicates that low achievers can benefit academically from team learning and that cooperation in the classroom may "fit" the learning style of many minority

34 Robert E. Slavin, "Cooperative Learning," *Review of Educational Research* (Summer 1980), pp. 315–342; idem., *Cooperative Learning* (New York: Longman, 1983).

Cooperative student learning is one of the most promising instructional approaches that has been developed in recent years.
(Victoria Arlak)

students. In addition, team learning can contribute to positive interracial attitudes while avoiding the disadvantages of homogeneous grouping.[35]

Team Assisted Individualization

Robert Slavin and other developers of STL have been preparing and testing a modified version called Team Assisted Individualization (TAI), which combines the advantages of team learning, mastery learning (described below), and individualized instruction. Early research on TAI in teaching mathematics in grades three through six indicates that it can bring about large gains in student achievement and student attitudes.[36]

Teacher Expectations and Student Achievement

Another promising and increasingly popular approach for improving teaching and learning, particularly among low-achieving students, is Teacher Expecta-

35 Bruce R. Hare and Daniel U. Levine, "A Critical Overview of Issues Involving Effective Desegregated Schools" (Paper prepared for the National Institute of Education, June 1984).

36 Robert E. Slavin, N. A. Madden, and M. Leavey, "Combining Cooperative Learning and Individualized Instruction: Effects on Student Mathematics, Attitudes, and Behavior," *Elementary School Journal* (May 1984), pp. 409–422.

tions and Student Achievement (TESA) training, which was developed under the auspices of the Los Angeles County Superintendent of Schools.[37]

Improved interaction needed

Extensive research has shown that teacher interaction with students perceived as low achievers is less motivating and less supportive than interaction with students perceived as high achievers. In addition, high achievers get more opportunities—and more time—to respond to questions.[38] When high achievers do have difficulty, teachers tend to give clues or rephrase the question more frequently than they do for low achievers. Training in TESA is designed to help teachers overcome this type of classroom pattern. It consists initially of five workshops scheduled about one month apart, emphasizing fifteen important teaching skills, such as equitable distribution of instructional time, individual help for students, higher-order questioning, and acceptance of appropriate student responses.

Teachers help each other

Following each workshop, participants observe each other four times. While being observed, teachers consciously attempt to practice the interactions addressed in the workshop with all students. The observation data are provided to the teacher, who can utilize them to re-examine his or her teaching practices. TESA thus reflects research indicating that staff development is most effective when it allows teachers to observe and assist one another in real classroom settings.[39] Workshops in the TESA approach are offered regularly as part of school improvement projects in many school districts.

Mastery Learning

Steps in mastery learning

The major steps of the instructional sequence used in mastery learning are (1) to *define* a specific objective, (2) to *teach* the skill or understanding in the objective, (3) to administer a criterion-referenced *test* to assess mastery of the objective,[40] (4) to *provide corrective instruction* for students who have not mastered the objective and enrichment, acceleration, or other alternatives for those who demonstrated mastery, and (5) to *re-test* the group that needed additional work. Benjamin Bloom and his colleagues have emphasized whole-group instruction during the first teaching component.[41] Some other advocates and developers have emphasized small group and individualized teaching.[42]

Many approaches other than mastery learning (as defined above) emphasize mastery teaching and testing of specific learning objectives. Such ap-

37 Sam Kerman, "Teacher Expectations and Student Achievement," *Phi Delta Kappan* (June 1979), pp. 716–718.

38 Thomas L. Good, "How Teachers' Expectations Affect Results," *American Education* (December 1982), pp. 25–32.

39 Lezotte, "Building Collegiality."

40 A criterion-referenced test is one that assesses mastery of a specific skill (criterion) or set of skills. Thus a student's score represents mastery or nonmastery of a skill, rather than his or her achievement compared with other students.

41 James H. Block and Lorin W. Anderson, *Mastery Learning in Classroom Instruction* (New York: Macmillan, 1975).

42 Joan S. Hyman and S. Alan Cohen, "Learning for Mastery: Ten Conclusions After 15 Years and 3,000 Schools," *Educational Leadership* (November 1979), pp. 104–109.

Mastery-type learning

proaches, which are almost synonymous with curriculum alignment (coordinating objectives, methods, materials, and testing) can be viewed as mastery-type learning. They are often referred to as outcomes-based education.[43] As described earlier in this chapter, curriculum alignment, an outcomes-based emphasis, and mastery learning are characteristic of effective schools.

Research on mastery learning (as defined by Bloom) indicates that it can be a very powerful force in improving student achievement, particularly among low achievers. Mastery learning can bring about achievement gains, in many subjects and at many grade levels, comparable to the 2 standard deviation gains attainable through tutoring students as individuals or in very small groups. This means that mastery learning can raise the student now at the 50th percentile to the 90th percentile or above, and the low achiever now at the 10th or 15th percentile can improve to the 50th percentile or above. Mastery learning itself can give gains of 1 standard deviation. Gains of 2 standard deviations are possible when mastery learning is combined with enhancement of students' entry skills on concepts prerequisite to the instruction, emphasis on appropriate cues and feedback-reinforcement and on students' active participation, and/or work with parents to improve the home learning environment. Bloom concludes, moreover, that these gains can be attained for higher mental-process skills, not just low-level mechanical learning.[44]

Very large achievement gains

Bloom's research has been conducted mostly with individual classes using teacher-made tests, but recent research indicates that comparable results can be attained using standardized tests in entire schools and school districts. Jones and Spady have examined mastery learning in Johnson City, New York; Red Bank, New Jersey; and several other school districts.[45] According to their findings, enormous gains in academic achievement are being registered when mastery learning is implemented effectively. Jones and Spady agree with Bloom's conclusion that effective implementation depends on paying adequate attention to students' entry skills (in other words, it is imperative to teach prerequisite skills if necessary), careful scope and sequencing of objectives and instruction, and utilization of some of the principles of effective instruction (for example, clarifying major goals, reinforcing correct responses, encouraging student participation). Mastery learning implemented on a schoolwide or districtwide basis, they further conclude, yields gains when combined with emphasis on quality of instruction that approach the 2 standard deviation level obtainable from tutoring.

School and district gains

Like direct instruction, however, mastery learning seems to be particularly susceptible to ineffective implementation caused by overemphasis on

43 Stephen E. Rubin and William G. Spady, "Achieving Excellence Through Outcome-Based Instructional Delivery," *Educational Leadership* (May 1984), pp. 37–44.

44 Benjamin Bloom, "The Search for Methods of Group Instruction as Effective as One-to-One Tutoring," *Educational Research* (May 1984), pp. 4–18.

45 Beau Fly Jones and William G. Spady, "Enhanced Mastery Learning as a Solution to the Two Sigma Problem," in Daniel U. Levine, ed., *Implementation and Impact of Mastery Learning* (San Francisco: Jossey-Bass, 1985).

narrow, low-order skills that are relatively easy to teach and test. Teachers implementing mastery learning frequently bog down in keeping records of student performance on a multitude of separate skills. Perhaps because mastery learning is so susceptible to these and other pitfalls,[46] it sometimes fails to bring about substantial gains in student achievement. Like any other instructional approach, it will not be successful if it ignores findings on the school improvement process discussed elsewhere in this chapter.

Pitfalls in mastery learning

It is important to emphasize that the instructional approaches described above are not mutually exclusive. They all tend to draw on a larger knowledge base that delineates characteristics of effective instruction, and they generally can be combined with each other or with related approaches to constitute a larger program of instructional improvement. Thus, for example, STL can be incorporated as a learning approach in mastery learning, and the teacher-student interactions emphasized in TESA can inform the implementation of mastery learning or STL. Indeed, many schools are emphasizing several approaches in their school effectiveness improvement projects.

Combined approaches

Given the very large gains in student achievement, particularly among low achievers, that have been registered in some schools implementing recently developed instructional approaches, it now is possible to conceive of a national pattern in which nearly all students are high achievers. Most students can achieve at a level currently attained by only the top 15 or 20 percent. Of course, being able to conceive of such a pattern does not mean it is going to happen, and most observers would say that such a prediction is unrealistic. To a significant extent, substantial improvement in our schools will depend on the degree to which change efforts reflect what is known about the school improvement process.

Visions of future achievement gains

High School Reform Proposals

In addition to the proposals for high school improvement in the national reports discussed in previous chapters, proposals for comprehensive reform of high schools have been offered by several prominent educators. Two of the most highly publicized proposals for reform of this kind have been offered by Ernest Boyer and by Theodore Sizer.

Boyer's High School

High School, written by Ernest Boyer, is a report prepared for the Carnegie Foundation for the Advancement of Teaching.[47] Published in 1983, *High School* is based in part on a three-year study in which twenty-five educators

46 Lorin W. Anderson and Beau Fly Jones, "Designing Instructional Strategies Which Facilitate Learning for Mastery," *Educational Psychologist* (Fall 1981), pp. 122–123.

47 Ernest L. Boyer, *High School* (New York: Harper & Row, 1983).

collected data at fifteen diverse senior high schools. Eighteen pages of proposals for improvement and reform are offered with reference to twelve major themes:

Twelve themes emphasized

1. Goals must be stated more clearly, focusing on mastery of language, a core of common learning, preparation for work and further education, and community service.
2. Emphasis on language development should stress writing, speaking, and listening.
3. The core curriculum should expand from about half the units required for graduation (as at present) to about two-thirds.
4. More should be done to help students make the transition to work and further education.
5. Students should participate and learn in the community.
6. Working conditions of teachers must be improved.
7. Improvements must be made in teaching methods and materials.
8. Technology should be used to enrich curriculum.
9. More flexibility is needed in school size, the use of time, and other organizational arrangements.
10. Principals should have a greater leadership role that includes selecting and rewarding teachers.
11. More "connections" are needed with other institutions.
12. There must be a public commitment to excellence.

Smaller load for teachers

Among Boyer's most important recommendations were those dealing with teachers' working conditions. These recommendations included proposals that high school teachers should have a daily load of only four regular classes and one small seminar, should have an hour a day for class preparation, and should be exempt from monitoring halls, lunchrooms, and recreation areas.

Sizer's Horace's Compromise

Horace's Compromise: The Dilemma of the American High School, based partly on Theodore Sizer's visits to eighty high schools, is the first of three reports in a study sponsored by the National Association of Secondary School Principals and the National Association of Independent Schools.[48] In this book, a teacher named Horace must choose between "covering" the prescribed curriculum and in-depth teaching of important concepts and understandings.

Similarity to Adler's Paideia proposal

Somewhat similar to Mortimer Adler's Paideia proposal discussed in Chapter 6, Sizer's book recommends that high schools concentrate on using didactic instruction, coaching, and Socratic instruction to develop knowl-

48 Theodore R. Sizer, *Horace's Compromise: The Dilemma of the American High School* (Boston: Houghton Mifflin, 1984).

edge, skills, and understandings, respectively. The curriculum should be divided into four major areas: inquiry and expression; mathematics and science; literature and the arts; and philosophy and history. Sizer advocates a system of mastery learning in all subjects. He also emphasizes more active learning, and reduced emphasis on "coverage" and on what he views as mindless approaches to minimal competency testing. He particularly wants to eliminate the tacit understanding between students who say "I will be orderly . . . if you don't push me very hard" and teachers who respond "You play along with my minimal requirements and I will keep them minimal."[49]

Unproductive tacit understanding

Perhaps the greatest virtue of Sizer's proposals is that they explicitly recognize the difficulties of high school teaching. He states flatly that special arrangements such as a school-within-a-school should be provided for high school students who cannot read, write, or do math, and he also emphasizes structural changes that will be needed to improve students' higher-order cognitive skills. Regarding the latter objective, he has pointed out that teachers cannot provide appropriate coaching in skill development for 150 to 180 students a day; accordingly, he advocates that teams of seven or eight teachers should work with groups of about 100 students in teaching the four curriculum areas specified above. At a minimum, he says, high school teachers should have no more than 80 students a day. Sizer would make these teacher-pupil ratios possible by eliminating the separate functions of teachers now assigned to counseling, the arts, physical education, and other specialized areas.[50] Regarding the change process, he implicitly criticizes many of the 1983 national reports.

Teams of teachers and students

Contrast with national reports

The proposals by Boyer and Sizer pay much more attention to the realities of schooling and research on the school change process than do the national reports cited in Chapter 13. Focusing change effort on the building level is one of their central themes, as is the difficulty of improving education when teachers are overburdened with too many students. Thus these proposals are, from some points of view, much more "radical" than those of the national reports. As one might have expected, the bulk of reform activity taking place nationally seems to center on relatively "easy" changes involving such national report recommendations as increasing graduation requirements and modifying teacher certification regulations. It will be interesting to see whether future reform efforts reflect proposals for fundamental change such as those offered by Boyer and Sizer.

Other Themes Involving School Effectiveness

Practically everyone who wants to change education says that the reason is to make schools more "effective." We do not have space (or the inclination)

49 Theodore Sizer, "The Teacher as Coach: Fewer Facts, More Learning," *Education Week* (November 16, 1983), p. 12.

50 Also see Theodore Sizer, "High School Reform: The Need for Engineering," *Phi Delta Kappan* (June 1983), pp. 679–683; idem., "Compromises," *Educational Leadership* (March 1984), pp. 34–37.

to describe all the themes that are under discussion nationally as part of the effort to improve the effectiveness of the schools. The most important such themes that have not been adequately described elsewhere in this book will be discussed briefly in the following pages.

Cooperation with Other Institutions

Many schools and school districts are attempting to improve the quality of education in elementary and secondary schools by cooperating with other institutions, particularly business and industry. Some of the most promising efforts along these lines include the following:

Adopt-a-school programs

"Partnership" or "adopt-a-school" programs in which a business, a church, a university, or some other community institution works closely with an individual school in providing assistance such as tutors or lecturers, funds or equipment for vocational studies, computer education, or other subjects, help in curriculum development, and provision of community learning opportunities.

Boston compact

Cooperation in preparing young people for productive lives in a modern society. One of the best current examples is in Boston, where a "compact" has been made through which the schools are trying to improve basic skills and attendance of secondary students, and businesses are providing part-time jobs for students and full-time employment opportunities after graduation.

Joint conduct of activities such as health education, drug education, and counseling of high school students.

Joint conduct of school improvement projects in which the emphasis is on helping faculty utilize research to improve curriculum and instruction.[51]

Coordination with community institutions

In addition to providing specific assistance to the schools, community institutions in many locations are coordinating their efforts with the schools so as to improve the delivery of educational services and reduce duplication and waste in expenditure of government money. Mario Fantini has argued forcefully that the schools may have taken on so many responsibilities (such as development of athletes, vaccination of children, and driver education) that their attempts to improve academic achievement are frequently diffuse and half-hearted. Fantini concluded that much progress in instruction might be made by reassigning nonacademic responsibilities to other agencies. For example, education in the use of modern technology might best be provided by conducting classes at leading businesses, and driver education might be shifted to insurance companies.[52]

51 Examples are described in Leslie L. Huling, Judith A. Richardson, and Shirley M. Hord, "Three Projects Show How University/School Partnerships Can Improve Effectiveness," *NASSP Bulletin* (October 1983), pp. 54–59.

52 Mario D. Fantini, "Toward a National Public Policy for Urban Education," *Phi Delta Kappan* (April 1982), pp. 544–546.

Teachers College Dean Michael Timpane has reviewed recent increases in support of and cooperation with the schools. He has called it a "rediscovery" of the public schools by business.[53] One 1983–84 survey of public school–private sector interaction in twenty-two big cities identified many examples of productive cooperation, including cases where businesses had helped obtain millions of dollars of additional funding for education. The author tentatively concluded, however, that large "pay-offs" are "much rarer than the mythology that sustains prospectors." More needs to be done to coordinate school efforts with those of other institutions.[54]

Not many large pay-offs yet

Magnet and Alternative Schools

Another major effort to improve and reform the public schools has involved the establishment of magnet and alternative schools. **Magnet schools** attract enrollment on a voluntary basis by offering special instructional programs or curricula designed to appeal to students in more than one neighborhood attendance area. Most magnet schools attract students by providing either a special field of study (for example foreign languages, preparation in a career field such as health care) or a distinctive approach to instruction (for example, either "open" education or "traditional" education). Some magnet schools, such as the Bronx High School of Science in New York City, have existed for many years. Such schools usually were not referred to as magnets until the 1970s, when many big-city districts established magnet schools to increase voluntary desegregation. Rather than serving only an academic elite, magnet schools today generally are designed to provide students of all ability levels with an opportunity to participate in a specialized or alternative instructional program not available in their local schools. This approach has been a major thrust of activity in many cities.[55] For example, since 1977 Milwaukee has established magnet schools in visual and performing arts; applied technology; marketing and business; college preparation; finance and commerce; communications and media; health sciences; and other areas.

Growth of magnet schools

Growth of magnet schools was greatly accelerated by passage of the 1976 amendment to the Emergency School Aid Act (ESAA) providing for the funding of desegregated magnet schools. By 1980, hundreds of school districts had established one or more magnet schools. However, support for establishment of magnet schools declined considerably in the 1980s when the amount of federal money targeted for voluntary desegregation was drastically reduced.

Recent decline in funding

53 Michael Timpane, "Business Has Rediscovered the Public Schools," *Phi Delta Kappan* (February 1984), pp. 389–392.

54 Dale Mann, "All That Glitters: Public/Private Sector Interaction in Twenty-Two U.S. Cities" (Report prepared for the Exxon Education Foundation, February 10, 1984) (draft), p. 1.

55 Cheryl Stanley, "A National Survey of Magnet Schools Utilized for Voluntary Desegregation" (Paper presented at the annual meeting of the American Educational Research Association, San Francisco, April 1979); James Lowry Associates, *Survey of Magnet Schools* (Washington, D.C.: National Institute of Education, 1984).

Many types of alternative schools

Alternative schools provide alternatives to learning opportunities available in the average public school. From this point of view magnet schools are a type of alternative school. So, too, are many parochial and other nonpublic schools; schools for special-needs students, such as the physically handicapped or the emotionally disturbed; institutions such as street academies, storefront schools, high school "outposts" designed to make education more relevant for inner-city students; and schools without walls, which draw heavily on community resources for learning.[56]

Characteristics of alternative schools

A national survey of alternative schools has indicated that, compared with more traditional schools, they tend to have the following characteristics: enrollment of students who have not succeeded in traditional schools or want a different kind of education, greater individualization, more independent study, more openness to the outside community, small size, high staff morale, high attendance, satisfied students, freedom from external control, and high concern for noncognitive goals of education.[57]

Alternative schools provide choice

Advocates of the alternative school movement point out that generally only one model of education is available to parents in any given public school neighborhood. Some advocates argue for creating alternative schools within the system; others argue for greater alternatives outside the system, contending that the only true alternatives *are* outside the system. Inside *or* outside the existing establishment, alternatives would permit parents and students to choose the school that best suits them.[58]

Criticism of alternative schools

Arguments against alternatives center on the fact that there is little empirical evidence that alternative schools make a difference in achievement and other goals. Moreover, many of these alternative schools have the reputation of de-emphasizing cognitive skills while focusing mainly on affective education. Critics also worry that the proliferation of alternatives outside the system may increase divisiveness and polarization, including the encouragement of private all-white or all-black schools. Proliferation of alternatives within the public system, on the other hand, may "drain off" the most motivated students from "regular" schools and divert attention of parents and educators from the task of improving the system as a whole.

Effectiveness of Nonpublic Schools

The question of whether nonpublic schools are more effective than public schools in bringing about high academic achievement and accomplishing other goals has emerged as an important issue in education. As we mentioned in Chapter 8, proposals have been made to provide families with

56 Daniel U. Levine, "Educating Alienated Inner City Youth: Lessons from the Street Academies," *Journal of Negro Education* (Spring 1975), pp. 139–148.

57 Mary Anne Raywid, "Synthesis of Research on Schools of Choice," *Educational Leadership* (April 1984), pp. 70–78; idem., "Schools of Choice: Their Current Nature and Prospects," *Phi Delta Kappan* (June 1983), pp. 684–694.

58 Mario D. Fantini, *Public Schools of Choice: A Plan for the Reform of American Education* (New York: Simon & Schuster, 1973); Jonathan Kozol, *Free Schools* (Boston: Houghton Mifflin, 1972).

vouchers and tax credits to support attendance at nonpublic schools, and some movement is occurring in these directions. To some extent, the desirability of such proposals as public policy hinges on the argument that nonpublic schools tend to be more effective than public schools.

Study by Coleman

Debate regarding the effectiveness of nonpublic schools has been spurred by publication of an important study by James Coleman and his colleagues comparing nonpublic and public schools.[59] Among the major conclusions of this study were the following: (1) when family background factors are taken account of, students in nonpublic schools have higher achievement than students in public schools; (2) nonpublic schools provide a safer and more orderly environment; (3) except for Catholic schools, nonpublic schools are smaller, have smaller class size, and encourage more student participation than do public schools; (4) nonpublic schools require more homework and have better attendance; and (5) superiority in school climate and discipline (for example homework, attendance) account for the higher achievement of nonpublic students.

Coleman study conclusions

Most of the subsequent analysis and scrutiny of this study's conclusions have been critical of the authors' major findings.[60] Other researchers have concluded that taking better account of family background variables eliminates the achievement superiority of nonpublic students, that taking account of achievement level upon entry to high school also eliminates the achievement difference between public and nonpublic students, and that higher scores of students in nonpublic schools are associated primarily with relatively high proportions of enrollment in college-track programs.

Criticism of Coleman conclusions

Coleman and his colleagues have defended the study's methods and conclusions.[61] In particular, they have argued that nonpublic schools enhance achievement by placing a relatively high percentage of students in college-bound programs. Since public and nonpublic schools differ greatly on this factor, and since it is difficult to isolate student motivation differences even after one has taken account of family background and social class, researchers will probably continue to argue over the relative effectiveness of public and nonpublic schools.

Coleman defense

Meanwhile, several researchers have published other studies concluding that nonpublic schools are superior in effectiveness. For example, Andrew Greeley analyzed data on Catholic schools and reached essentially the same

59 James Coleman, Thomas Hoffer, and Sally Kilgore, *Public and Private Schools* (Washington, D.C.: National Center for Education Statistics, 1981); idem., *High School Achievement: Public, Catholic, and Private Schools Compared* (New York: Basic Books, 1982).

60 Ellis B. Page and Timothy Z. Keith, "Effects of U.S. Private Schools: A Technical Analysis of Two Recent Claims," *Educational Researcher* (August–September 1981), pp. 7–22; Herbert J. Walberg and Timothy Shanahan, "High School Effects on Individual Students," *Educational Researcher* (August–September 1983), pp. 4–9; Arthur Goldberger and Glen Cain, "The Causal Analysis of Cognitive Outcomes in the Coleman, Hoffer, and Kilgore Report," *Sociology of Education* (April 1982), pp. 103–122; Doug Willms, "Is There Any Private School Advantage?" *IFG Policy Perspectives* (Winter 1982), pp. 1–2.

61 James S. Coleman and Thomas Hoffer, "Response to Taeuber—James Cain—Goldberger and Morgan," *Sociology of Education* (October 1983), pp. 218–234.

conclusions as did Coleman,[62] moreover, a recent in-depth study of Catholic schools concluded that their rigorous academic core curriculum has been beneficial to their students, regardless of background.[63] Issues involving the effectiveness of nonpublic versus public schools, and policy implications drawn from research on these issues, are likely to remain important.

Rural Education

Little research and attention

The particular problems of rural schools have received little attention during the past fifty years. This neglect has recently been rectified to some extent by a small group of scholars who have been trying to determine what should be done to provide high quality education in a rural setting.

Thoughtful analysis in thirteen rural communities has helped clarify the characteristics and problems of rural schools as well as innovations that might make rural schools more effective. Paul Nachtigal and his colleagues who carried out the study reached a number of conclusions.[64]

1. Typical rural schools are closely linked and interdependent with their communities.
2. The critical elements for rural school improvement are very much community dependent in terms of both what is done and how it is carried out. For this reason, staff development arrangements that are effective in urban areas tend not to work well in rural areas.

Rural schools diverse

3. Because there is tremendous diversity in rural America, school improvement efforts also should be diverse.
4. Improvement efforts in rural areas should emphasize helping local school and community persons define and redefine their particular problems.

Advantages of smallness

5. The small scale of rural schools offers potential advantages. Teachers can know students personally and individualize instruction, teachers and principals can work closely with community groups, and schools can draw on community resources to improve learning.
6. Technology such as television and microcomputers can improve instruction in rural schools.

Other authors have also attempted to determine how to make rural schools more effective. One analysis of appropriate training for persons who

62 Andrew M. Greeley, *Catholic High Schools and Minority Students* (New Brunswick, N.J.: Transaction, 1982).

63 Anthony Bryk et al., *Effective Catholic Schools: An Exploration* (Washington, D.C.: National Catholic Educational Association, 1984).

64 Paul W. Nachtigal, ed., *Rural Education. In Search of a Better Way* (Boulder, Colo.: Westview, 1982).

hope to teach in rural areas indicated that such training should prepare teachers in a larger number of content areas for a broader age range of students than do conventional programs.[65] Other educators have analyzed ways in which rural schools can assist in community development or redevelopment.[66] In general educators are carefully reassessing the desirability of consolidating schools to gain efficiency versus the advantages that can be present for teachers and students in very small schools.[67]

Reassessing benefits of consolidation

Should the United States Emulate Japan?

As Japan's economy has challenged the United States in both international and domestic markets, educators as well as lay leaders have begun to assess the role of Japanese education in that nation's economic gains. They wonder whether the United States should emulate some aspects of the Japanese educational system.

That the Japanese system has many admirable outcomes is supported by several sources of data. The International Studies of Educational Achievement mentioned in Chapter 12 show that Japanese students score consistently high across subject areas, particularly science and math. One study of mathematics achievement concluded that U.S. students fall further behind the Japanese for every year in school; by fifth grade, the lowest Japanese classes score higher than the highest U.S. classes.[68] Preliminary analysis of international data has also indicated that Japanese students have half as many absences for reasons other than illness as U.S. students and that the typical Japanese student spends much more time on homework than the typical American student.[69] Only about 1 percent of the Japanese population is functionally illiterate, even though Japanese is much harder to read and write than English.[70]

Japanese students high in achievement

On the other hand, Japanese students feel less control over their future, are less likely to feel they are worthy persons, and are less likely to plan for and enroll in college than are U.S. students.[71] In addition, violence and suicide have become serious problems among Japanese adolescents who are unable to meet high standards in the classroom. Many Japanese educators believe that their system overemphasizes rote learning and multiple-choice

Problems in Japanese education

65 Sara Massey and Jeanie Crosby, "Special Problems, Special Opportunities: Preparing Teachers for Rural Schools," *Phi Delta Kappan* (December 1983) pp. 265–269.

66 Stuart Rosenfeld, "Something Old, Something New: The Wedding of Rural Education and Rural Development," *Phi Delta Kappan* (December 1983) pp. 270–273.

67 Jonathan P. Sher, ed., *Education in Rural America* (Boulder, Colo.: Westview, 1977).

68 Herbert J. Walberg, "Scientific Literacy and Economic Productivity in Economic Perspective," *Daedalus* (Spring 1983), pp. 1–28.

69 William B. Fetters et al., "Schooling Experiences in Japan and the U.S.: A Cross-National Comparison of High School Students" (Paper presented at the annual meeting of the American Educational Research Association, Montreal, April 1983).

70 Robert C. Christopher, *The Japanese Mind* (New York: Simon & Schuster, 1983).

71 Fetters et al., "School Experiences in Japan and the U.S."

examinations to such an extent that it stifles creativity and higher-order learning.[72]

Drawing on the work of several scholars, John Cogan has identified the following major features of the Japanese system of education:[73]

Characteristics of Japanese education

1. Public interest in and support for education are high.
2. Schools have demanding requirements and standards, but they also emphasize art, music, and physical education to develop the "whole person."
3. Students spend about 240 days per year in school, as compared to 180 days in the United States.
4. Teachers have public respect and professional security.
5. Children are taught to be responsible for their schools and for one another.
6. Schools have orderly climates.
7. Parents and teachers emphasize the importance of education for long-range success.

Cogan thus points out that the Japanese educational system has many strengths, but he also concludes that rigid emphasis on national examinations distorts the curriculum toward low-order skills, generates violence and widespread alienation among adolescents, and fundamentally constitutes an enormous selection-and-sorting process that disenfranchises a high percentage of children and youth.[74] Some educators and lay leaders in the United States have singled out Japan's longer school year, rigorous examination standards, and high level of classroom discipline. They have argued for similar goals in U.S. schools.

Hard to transplant

Cogan agrees that we may be able to adopt some of these policies, but he points out that it is dangerous to take practices that are thought to work in one culture and transplant them to another. He concludes that "Americans would be wise to fully investigate the nature of education in Japan before jumping on a 'let's go Japanese' band wagon."[75]

It should be noted that some other industrial countries also seem to be making great strides in some aspects of elementary and secondary education.

Improvement efforts elsewhere

For example, Germany has long had outstanding arrangements for vocational education through a school-business apprenticeship system, France and Venezuela are initiating national efforts to encourage the intellectual development of preschool children, and England is attempting to modify its national examination system to stimulate mastery learning in the schools. It is impor-

72 John Woronoff, *Japan: The Coming Social Crisis* (Tokyo: Lotus, 1982).

73 John J. Cogan, "Should the U.S. Mimic Japanese Education? Let's Look Before We Leap," *Phi Delta Kappan* (March 1984), pp. 463–468.

74 Ibid.

75 Ibid., p. 463.

tant that U.S. educators learn more about such efforts and adopt those international practices that can improve our own system of education.

Summing Up

1. Research indicates that schools that are unusually effective in improving student achievement have initiated effective instructional practices. They exemplify other characteristics on a schoolwide basis—among them outstanding leadership, high expectations for students, focus on important learning skills, and an orderly, humane climate. Research also has identified somewhat more specific characteristics such as alignment between teaching and testing, emphasis on higher-order skills, and high time on task.
2. Effective secondary schools possess the characteristics identified as being important in research on elementary schools, but they also have introduced fundamental structural changes, particularly as regards more successful delivery of instruction for low-achieving students.
3. It now seems possible to create effective schools, provided one recognizes and utilizes what has been learned about the school improvement and reform process.
4. Student Team Learning (STL), Teacher Expectations and Student Achievement (TESA) training, mastery learning, and other recently developed approaches for improving instruction, when successfully implemented, can bring about very large gains in student achievement.
5. Greater cooperation with other institutions and establishment of magnet and other alternative schools may help to improve the effectiveness of our educational system.
6. Some recent research indicates that nonpublic schools are more effective than public schools, but many researchers question the validity of this conclusion.
7. The United States can learn much from educational developments in Japan and other nations, but caution should be exercised in borrowing from other societies.

Discussion Questions

1. How can schools and school districts become more effective than they are now? What kinds of resources are needed to make this possible?
2. How do instructional innovations such as mastery learning, TESA, and STL address problems of school effectiveness? Which effective school characteristics do they focus on?
3. What does the research say about the relative effectiveness of public and nonpublic schools?
4. Why should educators be somewhat cautious in reading and interpreting the effective schools research? What mistakes are most likely to be made in interpreting this research?
5. What might be done to raise the average student to the 90th percentile or

above in academic achievement? Do you think this is likely to happen at many schools? Why or why not?

Suggested Readings

Brookover, Wilbur, et al. *Creating Effective Schools.* Holmes Beach, Fla.: Learning Publications, 1982.

Chapters are devoted to improvement of school climate, high expectations for learning, and other aspects of effective schools.

Dianda, Marcella R. *The Superintendents' Can-Do Guide to School Improvement.* Washington, D.C.: Council for Educational Development and Research, 1984.

Step-by-step analysis and description of what can be done to make schools more effective.

Fullan, Michael. *The Meaning of Educational Change.* New York: Teachers College Press, Columbia University, 1982.

Combines excellent analysis of both the theoretical basis and the practical implications of research on the school change process.

Goodlad, John I. *A Place Called School.* New York: McGraw-Hill, 1984.

A thoughtful analysis of the problems and possibilities for reform in elementary and secondary schools, beginning with a chapter entitled "Can We Have Effective Schools?" and concluding with two excellent chapters, "Improving the Schools We Have" and "Beyond the Schools We Have."

Joyce, Bruce R., Richard H. Hersh, and Michael McKibbin. *The Structure of School Improvement.* New York: Longman, 1983.

Detailed analysis and recommendations regarding possibilities for improving education in accordance with recent research on effective schools and the school improvement process.

Nachtigal, Paul M. *Rural Education.* Boulder, Colo.: Westview, 1982.

Thoughtful analysis of the special problems of rural education and promising avenues for possible improvement.

Epilogue: Social Trends and the Future of American Education

Some "predictions" are not so much predictions of what is likely to happen as descriptions of the certain results of current and recent trends. We will begin this epilogue by reviewing several such trends, which have major implications for the educational system. We will conclude with a brief review of possibilities for improving schools to meet the challenges of the future.

The Movement Toward Service Jobs and a Postindustrial Society

The percentage of the population working in manufacturing and agriculture fell from 68 percent in 1900 to 31 percent in 1980. It is expected to fall to 27 percent in 1995. Conversely, the percentage of workers in white-collar, service-related jobs increased from 31 percent to 69 percent and is predicted to reach 73 percent in 1995.[1] The workforce in the United States has become much more white-collar and middle class, and an increasing percentage of the population provides services. Much of the growth in service jobs has involved information processing of one sort or another.[2] Many economists and sociologists view these trends as change from an "industrial" to a "postindustrial" economy.

Movement toward a postindustrial, information-processing society may further polarize the upper-class and upper-middle class segment of the population on the one hand and the working-class and underclass segment on the other. For example, government statistics indicate that both the very-high-income and the very-low-income segments of the population grew be-

1 George T. Silvestri, Johon M. Lukasiewicz, and Marcus E. Einstein, "Occupational Employment Projections Through 1995," *Monthly Labor Review* (November 1983).

2 John Naisbitt, *Megatrends* (New York: Warner Books, 1982).

tween 1970 and 1982, reducing the middle-income segment by 7.4 percent.[3] This trend was particularly pronounced during the period from 1978 to 1983, when the low-income segment increased by 13 percent and the high-income segment increased by 3 percent.[4]

The consequences of these trends will be wide-ranging. Two of the most important implications for education are described below.

1. Students will have to master increasingly complex skills in order to obtain rewarding employment. Landing a highly paid job in the future will depend more and more on possession of relatively abstract skills involving problem-solving and flexible thinking.[5]

In this regard, it is important to note that although the performance of elementary and junior high students has been improving in reading and math, performance of senior high students—particularly those with high ability scores—has been declining with respect to higher-level thinking skills.[6] This achievement trend led the National Commission on Excellence to assert that the quality of U.S. education signaled a nation "at risk."

2. Rapid technological change together with an aging labor force will make "recurrent" or "life-long" education more important (see Chapter 13).[7] Recurrent education opportunities will be particularly important in retraining workers displaced by the decline of manufacturing industries and the rise in information-processing jobs.

Growth of Minority Population and a Minority Underclass

Partly because the current minority population is relatively young and partly because of the high level of immigration, the minority population (primarily black, Hispanic, and Asian) in the United States is expected to increase from 20 percent in 1980 to 28 percent in 2000 to 35 percent in 2020.[8] Minority students already constitute the majority of the student population in twenty three of our twenty five largest cities; nearly all of the sixty largest big-city

3 "Is There a Middle Class?" *American Demographics* (May 1984), p. 13.

4 "Trickle Down," *Harper's* (April 1984), p. 27. Some of the recent polarization may be due to the prolonged period of inflation and recession in the late 1970s and early 1980s, which may be slowed or reversed by economic recovery in the mid-1980s.

5 Lynn L. Gisi and Ray H. Forbes, *The Information Society: Are High School Graduates Ready?* (Denver: Education Commission of the States, 1982); Office of Technology Assessment, *Computerized Manufacturing Automation: Employment, Education, and the Workplace* (Washington, D.C.: Government Printing Office, 1984).

6 Archie LaPointe, "The Good News About American Education," *Phi Delta Kappan* (June 1984), pp. 663–668.

7 Susan J. Peters, "Recurrent Education," *Institute for Research on Educational Finance and Governance Policy Perspectives* (Summer 1983), pp. 1–4.

8 Leon F. Bouvier and Cary B. Davis, *The Future Racial Composition of the United States* (Washington, D.C.: Population Reference Bureau, 1982).

What kind of world will these school children live in when they grow up—and will their years of schooling have prepared them adequately for it? (David S. Strickler/Atoz Images, Inc.)

school districts will have a large majority of minority students by the year 2000.[9] Minority population will also increase in many suburban school districts.

As we noted in Chapter 11, much of the minority population lives in concentrated poverty neighborhoods in big cities. Much of this underclass population is black and Hispanic–from Puerto Rico and Central America on the East Coast and Mexican-American in the West and Southwest. Data on the status of black Americans in general and on the school performance of black students in particular indicate that the underclass has become an increasingly prominent element in U.S. schools and society.

The percentage of black families headed by women increased from 21 percent of all black families in 1960 to 42 percent in 1983. Because female-headed families constituted an increasing percentage of the poverty population over the past twenty years, some observers refer to this phenomenon as the "feminization of poverty."

At the same time, the percentage of unemployed black males has increased substantially. In 1960, 75 percent of adult black males were employed, compared with only 54 percent in 1982—the remaining 46 percent

9 Ian McNett, *Demographic Imperatives: Implications for Educational Policy* (Washington, D.C.: American Council on Education, Forum of Educational Organization Leaders, and Institute for Educational Leadership, 1984).

were out of work or no longer in the workforce. Unemployment among black males has been a major reason for the growth of female-headed families in the inner city.[10] It is difficult to overestimate the extent to which unemployment and crime in the surrounding community adversely affect the school performance of youth in the inner city. Between 1969 and 1982, the employment rate among black high school graduates who did not attend college fell from 53 percent to 32 percent.[11] This pattern makes it exceedingly difficult to motivate black inner-city youth to stay in high school and improve their academic performance.

Partly because social disorganization—indicated by family breakdown, crime and delinquency, unemployment, drug addiction, and very low school achievement—has become more widespread and acute among inner-city minority groups, expensive efforts to provide compensatory education have had relatively few positive results (see Chapter 12). Unless the school effectiveness movement succeeds in raising achievement at inner-city schools (Chapter 15), employment opportunities for inner-city youth are greatly improved, and gains are made in deconcentrating the poverty population through desegregation of schools and housing (Chapter 12), the prospects for substantially improving achievement and reducing social disorganization in the inner city will be bleak.

The Challenge for Education

To meet these challenges, education will have to become more effective than it has been. This is true with respect both to the development of higher-order cognitive skills and to the pressing educational problems of disadvantaged students. How can the schools change to meet these challenges?

Schools alone will not be able to solve all of our major national problems. Alleviation of the problems associated with poverty in general and the urban underclass in particular will require large-scale, coordinated, national action involving employment, housing, transportation, reduction of discrimination, family policy, and other social support systems. Provision of opportunity enabling young people to participate productively on an equitable basis in a postindustrial society increasingly built on information processing will require effective national policies with respect to foreign economic competition, federal fiscal and monetary policy, articulation between industry and postsecondary education, internal and external migration, pollution, and other social, economic, and political issues. Nevertheless, education is clearly an important component in our efforts to meet these challenges and maintain a high quality of life in the United States.

10 Tom Joe and Peter Yu, *The Flip Side of Black Families Headed by Women* (Washington, D.C.: Center for the Study of Social Policy, 1984).

11 Morton H. Sklar, "Job Training Partnership Act and Dropout Youth," *Jobs Watch Alert* (August 13, 1984), p. 2.

Glossary

Academic freedom A protection permitting teachers to teach and freely discuss with students subject matter relevant to the course without restriction from administrators or other outside influences and pressures.

Academy A private or semipublic secondary school that was dominant in the United States from 1830 through 1870.

Accountability Holding teachers, administrators, and/or school board members responsible for student performance, or relating expenditures to outcomes.

Activity-centered curriculum A curriculum that emphasizes purposeful and lifelike experiences and, more recently, student participation in school and community activities; an example of a student-centered curriculum.

Affective domain Objectives or test items related to interests, attitudes, and feelings; part of the taxonomy of education.

Affirmative action A method of redressing the wrongs of past discrimination against minorities in employment and education, usually through a negotiated plan; sex, race, ethnic background, and national origin are classifications that may be included in affirmative action programs.

Aims Broad statements that provide guidelines or direction for what schools should teach; value-laden statements, usually developed by national, state, or local commissions or professional groups.

Alternative schools A school, public or nonpublic, that provides learning opportunities different from those in local public schools.

Axiology The area of philosophy that examines value issues, especially in ethics and aesthetics.

Back to basics curriculum Emphasis on the three Rs at the elementary level and academic subjects at the secondary level; also included is a defined minimum level of academic standards; an example of a subject-centered curriculum.

Behavioral objectives *See* Instructional objectives.

Bilingual education Special arrangements for teaching students who are not fluent in the national language.

Board of education A group of people, elected or appointed, with the powers and duties given by the state to operate the schools within a defined school district or location.

Certification State government review and approval providing a teaching candidate with permission to teach.

Chief state school officer A person serving as chief executive of the state school board of education; sometimes called the state superintendent or commissioner of education.

Child-centered curriculum A curriculum rooted in the early works of Rousseau, Pestalozzi, Froebel, and Montessori, emphasizing materials that combine play with academic work at the primary grade level and freedom and academic work at the elementary and secondary levels; an example of a student-centered curriculum.

Cognitive domain Objectives or test items related to knowledge and higher intellectual skills and abilities; part of the taxonomy of education.

Collective bargaining A procedure for resolving disagreements between employers and employees through negotiation; for teachers, involves many aspects of their work and salary, as well as their relationship with students, supervisors, and community.

Common school A publicly supported and locally controlled elementary school.

Compensatory education Educational experiences and opportunities designed to overcome or compensate for deficits or obstacles associated with a student's disadvantaged background.

Competency-based teacher education A teacher education approach that requires students to demonstrate minimum competence levels on specific teaching tasks.

Comprehensive high school A public secondary school that offers a variety of curricula, including a common core, to a diverse student population.

Compulsory attendance The requirement according to state law that children and adolescents attend school until reaching a specific age.

Computer-assisted instruction The application of computers for instructional purposes; individualized lesson material is presented almost simultaneously with feedback and correction.

Concentrated poverty schools Schools with a high proportion of disadvantaged students; usually located in the inner-core poverty sections of big cities.

Consolidation The trend toward combining small or rural school districts into larger ones.

Continuing teacher contract Contract that is automatically renewed from year to year without requiring the teacher's signature.

Cultural pluralism Acceptance and encouragement of cultural diversity within a larger society.

Curriculum Planned experiences provided through instruction, which enable the school to meet its aims.

Curriculum alignment Coordinating instructional planning, materials, and testing so that materials can accomplish a given learning objective and what is taught coincides with what is tested.

Curriculum development The processes and techniques involved in assessing the needs of learners, formulating aims and objectives, and selecting or creating instructional materials, media, and activities.

Decentralization The trend toward dividing large school districts into smaller units.

De facto segregation Segregation associated with and resulting from housing patterns.

De jure segregation Segregation resulting from laws or government action.

Department of education (DOE) One of twelve U.S. cabinet-level departments that operate at the executive level of the federal government; now in charge of federal educational policy and the promotion of programs to carry out policies.

Desegregation Attendance of students of different racial backgrounds in the same school and classroom.

Dual-track system The European school pattern of separate primary schools for the masses of population and preparatory and secondary schools for the upper socioeconomic classes.

Due process A formalized legal procedure with specific and detailed rules and principles designed to protect the rights of individuals.

Educational vouchers A flat grant or payment representing a child's estimated school cost or portion of the cost; in effect, the parent or child may choose a school, public or private, and payment is made to the school for accepting the child.

Elementary school An educational institution for children in grades 1 to 6 or 1 to 8, often including kindergarten as well.

Enculturation The process whereby an individual takes on or acquires the culture; as used in education, it refers to the child's acquisition of the cultural heritage by both formal and informal educational means.

Epistemology The area of philosophy that examines knowing and theories of knowledge.

Essentialism The educational theory that emphasizes basic skills of reading, writing, and arithmetic and subject matter disciplines such as mathematics, science, history, geography, and language.

Essentialist curriculum A curriculum based on essentialist philosophy and consisting of the three Rs at the elementary level and five major disciplines (English, math, science, history, and foreign language) at the secondary level; emphasis is on academic competition and excellence; an example of a subject-centered curriculum.

Ethics The branch of axiology that examines questions of right and wrong and good and bad.

Ethnic group A group of people with a distinctive culture and history.

Existentialism The philosophy that examines human self-definition by choice-making of a personal nature.

Expulsion Dismissal of a student from school for a lengthy period, ranging from one semester to permanently.

Flexible scheduling The organization of the school day around condensed units of time, say, 15 to 20 minutes, to enhance greater flexibility and variation in scheduling of courses.

Head Start A government program that provides preschool education for disadvantaged students.

Hidden curriculum What students learn, other than academic content, from what they do or are expected to do in school.

Hornbook A single sheet of parchment, containing the Lord's Prayer, letters of the alphabet, and vowels, covered by the flattened horn of a cow and fastened to a flat wooden board; it was used during the colonial era in primary schools.

Humanistic curriculum A curriculum that stresses the personal and social aspects of the student's growth and development; stress is on self-actualizing, moral, esthetic, and higher domains of thinking; an example of a student-centered curriculum.

Idealism The philosophy that conjectures that reality is spiritual or nonmaterial in essence.

Individualized instruction Curriculum content and instructional materials, media, and activities designed for individual learning; the pace, interests, and abilities of the learner are taken into consideration.

In loco parentis Latin term meaning in the place of the parents; a concept whereby a teacher or school administrator assumes the rights, duties, and responsibilities of the parents during the hours the child attends school.

Instruction The processes of a curriculum; the methods and materials of the teacher.

Instructional objectives Narrowly defined statements written in behavioral terms and in terms that can be measured and observed; in education, they are written at the classroom level for and sometimes by the teachers.

Integration The situation in which students of different racial backgrounds are desegregated, and effective action is taken to develop positive interracial contacts and to improve the performance of low-achieving minority students.

Intermediate objectives Objectives formulated to achieve the aims of a school, school district, or state department of education; they are written at the grade or subject level and by the professional staff of the school district or state department of education.

Intermediate unit An educational unit or agency in the middle position between the state department of education and the local school district, usually created by the state to provide supplementary services and support staff to local school districts.

Junior high school A two-to-three-year school which is intermediate between elementary and high school and is designed to meet the educational needs of students in their early adolescent years, commonly grades 7 to 9.

Kindergarten A preschool, early childhood educational environment, first designed by Froebel in the mid-nineteenth century.

Laboratory school An experimental school designed to apply research to educational practice.

Land grant college A state college or university, offering agricultural and mechanical curricula, funded originally by the Morrill Act of 1862.

Latin grammar school A college preparatory school of the colonial era that emphasized Latin and Greek studies.

Least restrictive environment An educational setting for handicapped students that is as normal or regular as possible.

Magnet schools A type of alternative school that attracts voluntary enrollment owing to special instructional programs or curricula, frequently in part for purposes of desegregation.

Mainstreaming Placing handicapped students in regular classes for much or all of the school day, while also providing additional special services, programs, and classes as needed.

Mastery learning An instructional approach in which students are tested after formative (initial) instruction, and corrective instruction and retesting are provided for those who did not master the objectives initially.

Merit pay A plan that rewards workers, for example, teachers, partially or primarily on the basis of performance or objective standards.

Metaphysics The area of philosophy that examines issues of a speculative nature dealing with ultimate reality.

Middle school A two-to-four-year school which is intermediate between elementary and high school and is designed to meet the educational needs of students in the middle grades, commonly grades 5 to 8.

National assessment of educational progress Periodic assessment of achievement, using nationally representative samples of elementary and secondary students.

National Institute for Education (NIE) An agency of the U.S. Department of Education whose major purpose is to carry out research and development in education.

Normal school A two-year teacher educational institution that was popular in the nineteenth century.

Perennialism The educational theory that emphasizes rationality as the major purpose of education; it asserts that the essential truths are recurring and universally true.

Perennialist curriculum A curriculum based on perennialist philosophy and consisting of the three Rs, Latin, and logic at the elementary level and the classics at the secondary level; also carries a religious or moral overtone; an example of a subject-centered curriculum.

Pragmatism The philosophy that judges the validity of ideas by their consequences in action.

Profession An occupation rated high in prestige and salary, requiring extensive formal education and a defined body of knowledge beyond the grasp of laypersons, whereby those in the profession control licensing standards and have autonomy in their work environment.

Professional practice commission A state commission or committee that permits educators to set professional standards and minimal requirements of competency.

Psychomotor domain Objectives or test items related to reflex, motor, and skilled physical movements; part of the taxonomy of education.

Realism The philosophy that construes reality to be dualistic in nature; that is, it contains a material and a conceptual component.

Relevant curriculum A curriculum that considers the interests and experiences of the student; consists of numerous course electives, extension courses, minicourses, and alternative courses; an example of a student-centered curriculum.

Scholasticism The intellectual and educational approach used by educators in medieval universities; it involved the study of theological and philosophical authorities.

School infrastructure The basic facilities and structure that underpin the school plant, such as plumbing, sewerage, heat, electricity, roof, masonry, carpentry.

Secondary school A post-elementary school, such as a junior or senior high school or middle school, which is designed to meet the educational needs of students in their adolescent years, usually grades 7 to 12.

Social reconstructionism The theory of education that advocates that schools and teachers act as agents of deliberate social change.

Socioeconomic status (SES) Relative ranking of individuals according to economic and social prestige and power; usually measured in terms of occupation, education, and income, and generally viewed in terms of social class categories ranging from working class to upper class.

Socratic method An educational method attributed to the Greek philosopher Socrates by which the teacher encourages the student's discovery of truth by asking leading and stimulating questions.

State board of education An influential and powerful state education agency that serves in an advisory function for the state legislature and regulates policies necessary to implement legislative acts related to education.

State department of education An agency that operates under the direction of the state board of education, accrediting schools, certifying teachers, appropriating state school funds, conducting research, and issuing reports among other duties.

State school code A collection of laws that establish ways and means of operating schools and conducting education in a state.

Student-centered curriculum A curriculum viewed in terms of the needs and attitudes of the student or learner; emphasis is on the process or climate of the classroom or school.

Student team learning A form of cooperative learning in which students work in heterogeneous groups.

Subject-centered curriculum A curriculum viewed in terms of a body of content or subject matter; achievement is based on defined outcomes such as test scores, correct answers, or responses judged to be appropriate.

Subject structure curriculum A curriculum that focuses on the concepts, rules, and principles of a subject; the structure of a subject delineates and organizes a body of knowledge into a discipline; an example of a subject-centered curriculum.

Superintendent of schools The executive officer of the local school district, whose policies are subject to school board approval.

Taxonomy A classification system of organizing information; in education, it serves as a method for translating aims into instructional objectives.

Teacher aides People assigned tasks by the school to assist the classroom teacher or to help in audiovisual presentations, yard or hallway patrol, or clerical work; sometimes called paraprofessionals or auxiliary personnel.

Teacher center A place to conduct in-service training of teachers on site or within or near the school district; teachers have input and decision-making power concerning services provided.

Teacher expectations and staff development training A staff development approach in which teachers work with and observe one another to improve their interactions and effectiveness of students, particularly low achievers.

Team teaching An arrangement between two or more teachers who combine their efforts, abilities, and interests and assume joint responsibility in teaching students.

Tenure Permanence of position granted to educators after a probationary period, which prevents their dismissal except for legally specified causes and through formalized legal procedures.

Town school The eighteenth- and early nineteenth-century elementary school of New England that educated children living in a designated area.

Transitional bilingual education Teaching students in their own language until they can learn in the national language.

Tuition tax credits Tax reductions for parents or guardians of children attending public or private schools.

Values "Should" or "ought" imperatives that relate to ethical behavior or aesthetic appreciation.

Values-centered curriculum A curriculum that emphasizes affective learning and personal growth, dealing with morality, personal biases, personal choice, value clarification, and the social world in general; an example of a student-centered curriculum.

Author Index

Subject Index

Reader Response Form

We would like to find out what your reactions are to *An Introduction to the Foundations of Education,* Third Edition. Your evaluation of the book will help us respond to the interests and needs of the readers of future editions. Please complete the form and mail it to College Marketing, Houghton Mifflin Company, One Beacon Street, Boston, MA 02108.

1. We would like to know how you rate our textbook in each of the following areas:

	Excellent	Good	Adequate	Poor
a. Selection of topics	___	___	___	___
b. Detail of coverage	___	___	___	___
c. Order of topics	___	___	___	___
d. Writing style/readability	___	___	___	___
e. Explanation of concepts	___	___	___	___
f. Study aids (e.g., marginal notes, focusing questions, overview charts, glossary, summing up)	___	___	___	___
g. Attractiveness of design	___	___	___	___

2. Please cite specific examples that illustrate any of the above ratings.

____

____

____

3. Describe the strongest feature(s) of the book.

____

____

____

4. Describe the weakest feature(s) of the book.

____

____

____

5. What other topics should be included in this text?

____

____

____

6. What recommendations can you make for improving this book?

____

____

____